SHAKESPEARE SURVEY

68

Shakespeare, Origins and Originality

ADVISORY BOARD

SHAKESPEARE SURVEY

68

Shakespeare, Origins and Originality

EDITED BY

PETER HOLLAND

CAMBRIDGE
UNIVERSITY PRESS

CAMBRIDGE
UNIVERSITY PRESS

University Printing House, Cambridge CB2 8BS, United Kingdom

One Liberty Plaza, 20th Floor, New York, NY 10006, USA

477 Williamstown Road, Port Melbourne, VIC 3207, Australia

314-321, 3rd Floor, Plot 3, Splendor Forum, Jasola District Centre, New Delhi - 110025, India

79 Anson Road, #06-04/06, Singapore 079906

Cambridge University Press is part of the University of Cambridge.

It furthers the University's mission by disseminating knowledge in the pursuit of education, learning and research at the highest international levels of excellence.

www.cambridge.org
Information on this title: www.cambridge.org/9781107519770

First published 2015
First paperback edition 2021

A catalogue record for this publication is available from the British Library

Library of Congress Cataloging in Publication data
Shakespeare survey 68: volume 68 : Shakespeare, origins and originality / edited by Peter Holland.
pages   cm. – (Shakespeare survey ; 68)
Includes bibliographical references and index.
ISBN 978-1-107-10884-4 (hardback)
1. Shakespeare, William, 1564–1616 – Criticism and interpretation.
1. Holland, Peter, 1951– editor. II. Holland, Peter. III. Title: Shakespeare, origins and originality.
PR2976.S33843   2015
822.3′3 – dc23   2015012665

ISBN 978-1-107-10884-4 Hardback
ISBN 978-1-107-51977-0 Paperback

EDITOR'S NOTE

Volume 69, on 'Shakespeare and Rome' will be at press by the time this volume appears. The theme of Volume 70 will be 'Creating and Re-creating Shakespeare' and will consist only of papers given at the World Shakespeare Congress in 2016; the theme of Volume 71 will be 'Shakespeare and London'.

Submissions should be addressed to the Editor to arrive at the latest by 1 September 2017 for 71. Pressures on space are heavy and priority is given to articles related to the theme of a particular volume. Submissions may be made either as hard copy sent to the Editor at The Shakespeare Institute, Church Street, Stratford-upon-Avon CV37 6HP, or as an e-attachment to pholland@nd.edu. All articles submitted are read by the Editor and at least one member of the Advisory Board, whose indispensable assistance the Editor gratefully acknowledges.

Unless otherwise indicated, Shakespeare quotations and references are keyed to *The Complete Works*, ed. Stanley Wells, Gary Taylor, John Jowett and William Montgomery, 2nd edition (Oxford, 2005).

Review copies should be addressed to the Editor as above. In attempting to survey the ever-increasing bulk of Shakespeare publications our reviewers inevitably have to exercise some selection. We are pleased to receive offprints of articles which help to draw our reviewers' attention to relevant material.

P.D.H.

CONTRIBUTORS

ABDULHAMIT ARVAS, *Michigan State University*
CATHERINE BELSEY, *Swansea University*
BETTINA BOECKER, *University of Munich*
TOM CHEESMAN, *Swansea University*
JANET CLARE, *University of Hull*
NICHOLAS CRAWFORD, *University of Montevallo*
PÉTER DÁVIDHÁZI, *Institute of Literary Studies, Hungary*
MICHAEL DOBSON, *University of Birmingham*
MARGRETA DE GRAZIA, *University of Pennsylvania*
EWAN FERNIE, *University of Birmingham*
KATE FLAHERTY, *Australian National University*
LYNN FOREST-HILL, *University of Southampton*
ANDREW JAMES HARTLEY, *University of North Carolina, Charlotte*
JAMES HIRSH, *Georgia State University*
PETER HOLLAND, *University of Notre Dame*
RUSSELL JACKSON, *University of Birmingham*
FARAH KARIM-COOPER, *Shakespeare's Globe*
DAVID KATHMAN, *Independent Scholar*
PETER KIRWAN, *University of Nottingham*
BI-QI BEATRICE LEI, *National Taiwan University*
LAURIE MAGUIRE, *Magdalen College, Oxford*
JELENA MARELJ, *Queen's University, Kingston*
JEAN-CHRISTOPHE MAYER, *French National Centre for Scientific Research*
ALFREDO MICHEL MODENESSI, *Universidad Nacional Autónoma de México*
RUTH MORSE, *Université-Paris-Diderot*
ANDY MURPHY, *St Andrew's University*
JOHN V. NANCE, *Florida State University*
CAROL CHILLINGTON RUTTER, *University of Warwick*
CHARLOTTE SCOTT, *Goldsmiths, University of London*
ROBERT SHAUGHNESSY, *University of Kent*
JAMES SHAW, *Bodleian Libraries, University of Oxford*
JYOTSNA G. SINGH, *Michigan State University*
EMMA SMITH, *Hertford College, Oxford*
GARY TAYLOR, *Florida State University*
STANLEY WELLS, *Shakespeare Birthplace Trust*

CONTENTS

CONTENTS

ILLUSTRATIONS

SHAKESPEARE'S ANECDOTAL CHARACTER

MARGRETA DE GRAZIA

The Character of the Man is best seen in his Writing.

(Nicholas Rowe)

Why is the Shakespeare of the anecdotes at such variance with the Shakespeare of the biographies? The biographical narrative gives us a Shakespeare of increasing worldly success: more property, more literary acclaim, a coat of arms and a posthumous monument in stone as well as in print. The anecdotal Shakespeare, however, is quite notorious: he violates decorum, breaks laws and even commits sacrilege. Stephen Greenblatt has noted that the biographical Shakespeare left a clean record behind, especially for a man of the theatre: 'The fact that there are no police reports, no privy council orders, indictments, or post-mortem inquests'.[1] This, he maintains, 'tells us something significant about Shakespeare's life – he possessed a gift for staying out of trouble'. But anecdotal Shakespeare repeatedly, almost consistently, *is* in trouble, one might even say *asks* for trouble. Why do these two forms of life-writing deliver such antithetical Shakespeares: the one delinquent and the other respectable?

* * *

The first biography of Shakespeare is generally considered to be *Some Account of the Life &c.* by Nicholas Rowe, prefixed to his 1709 edition, *The Works of Mr. William Shakespear*.[2] The edition ushered Shakespeare into the eighteenth century in a brand new format. It divided into six volumes the monolithic folio volume in which the works

had been reproduced four times in the course of the seventeenth century (1623, 1632, 1663–64, 1685). But it also broke from the folio tradition by replacing its elegiac front matter with a forty-page biography. The folio dedication, address and verses responding to Shakespeare's death were discarded and replaced in 1709 with an account of his life, from his birth in Stratford to his grave and monument there. That life performed the same unifying function as had the folio's elegiac preliminaries.[3] Prefacing the works of a modern author with a life was something of a novelty. Its value was not self-evident as were those of 'the great Men of Antiquity' – 'their Families, the common Accidents of their Lives, and even their Shape, Make and Features' (i). And indeed the idea of featuring a life was not Rowe's but that of his publisher. It was Jacob Tonson's intent to publish Shakespeare in a bibliographic and typographic format modelled on that accorded to translations of the ancients. As

---

[1] Stephen Greenblatt, 'The Traces of Shakespeare's Life', in *The New Cambridge Companion to Shakespeare*, ed. Margreta de Grazia and Stanley Wells (Cambridge, 2010), p. 4.

[2] *The Works of Mr. William Shakespear*, 6 vols., ed. Nicholas Rowe (London, 1709) I, pp. i–xl. Subsequent citations to Rowe's *Some Account* will appear parenthetically hereafter. For Alexander Pope's substantial revision of Rowe's *Some Account*, published in his 1725 edition and reprinted throughout the eighteenth century, see S. Schoenbaum, *Shakespeare's Lives* (Oxford, 1991), p. 91.

[3] On Shakespeare's decease as the unifying postulate of the First Folio, see Margreta de Grazia, 'Shakespeare's Timeline', *Shakespeare Quarterly*, 65 (2014), 379–98.

1. Gerard van der Gucht: Frontispiece to *The Works of Mr. William Shakspear*, ed. Nicholas Rowe (London, 1709).

the works of Homer and Virgil, for example, had appeared in multi-volumed format with a prefatory Life, so too would Shakespeare's.[4]

The classicizing intent of Rowe's edition is apparent in its frontispiece (Illustration 1).

Its subject is clear: Shakespeare is being crowned by Comedy and Tragedy, with winged Fame aloft, triumphantly trumpeting Shakespeare's glory, and dark Ignorance quelled under Comedy's foot. The engraved frame is studiously antiquated, with its voluminously draped figures, laurel wreaths and branches, thespian masks and instruments, raised pedestal, and arched recess of classicized pilasters. But the figure honoured by the classical trappings is altogether modern: in period doublet with loose shirt-ties. Even the medium of his likeness is modern: a painted portrait rather than a stone bust, taken from the early seventeenth-century Chandos portrait. The clashing temporalities of frame and enframed are intended to jar. In a witty inversion, the classical world is paying homage to the modern author, instead of the other way around.

Yet anyone who had read the earlier notices about Shakespeare (in Thomas Fuller, William Winstanley, Edward Phillips or Gerard Langbaine) or the critical commentaries on him (by Ben Jonson, John Dryden or Thomas Rymer) might have been surprised to see him so honoured. From the time of his death and throughout the seventeenth century, Shakespeare was known for his lack of learning, particularly his unfamiliarity with the ancients. Born and bred in Stratford, with no formal education beyond grammar school, how could it be otherwise? The engraving foregrounds a problem that dogged Shakespeare until well into the eighteenth century: how could a poet who had neglected the classics be himself a classic? Indeed what Rowe terms his 'Ignorance of the Ancients' (iii) might link him more to the sad figure underfoot than the one laureated by the classical genres. One might also question whether Shakespeare deserved the double crown from Comedy and Tragedy; as Rowe will point out, the majority of Shakespeare's plays were too generically mixed to qualify as either (xvii). And there is something else anomalous: a painting

does not belong on a stone pedestal. Precariously propped up against Comedy's elongated forearm, the portrait would topple, were she to move.

In fact, the frame was designed not for Shakespeare, but for Pierre Corneille. It was lifted for Rowe's edition from the engraving appearing on the frontispiece of several early collections of his works.[5] In the original engraving, a bust of Corneille sits securely on the stone plinth (Illustration 2). As Stuart Sillars points out in discussing the two engravings, the honorific statuary is perfectly appropriate to the author who is 'arguably the most complete adherent to Aristotelian principles as reinvented by French academic critics'.[6] But how could the poet indifferent to the classical authorities be elevated to the status of classic? If there were an English counterpart to Corneille, it would have been the poet who, as we shall see, influentially defined himself against Shakespeare – Ben Jonson. As John Dryden would conclude in comparing the two dramatists, it was Jonson who wrote correct plays and who also laid down in his *Timber or Discoveries*,

---

[4] On Jacob Tonson's deployment of features associated with translations of the classics (a prefatory life, octavo size, typefaces and print ornaments, quality of paper, and engraved portraits and illustrations) in Rowe's edition of Shakespeare, see Robert B. Hamm Jr., 'Rowe's Shakespeare (1709) and the Tonson House Style', *College Literature*, 31 (2004), 179–205. Paulina Kewes also discusses Tonson's commissioning of Rowe, 'Shakespeare's Lives in Print, 1662–1821', in Robin Myers, ed., *Lives in Print: Biography and the Book Trade from the Middle Ages to the 21st Century* (New Castle, DE, and London, 2002), 55–82.

[5] For details on the French original and English adaptation, see T. S. R. Boase, 'Illustrations of Shakespeare's Plays in the Seventeenth and Eighteenth Centuries', *Journal of the Warburg and Courtauld Institutes*, 10 (1947), p. 86. Though the signature beneath the engraving reads 'M: V dr. Gucht sculp' (Michael van der Gucht), a Flemish engraver employed by Tonson, Boase attributes the engraving to his son, Gerard van der Gucht.

[6] Stuart Sillars, *The Illustrated Shakespeare, 1709–1875* (Cambridge, 2008), 35. Sillars misidentifies the source of Shakespeare's portrait in the roundel as 'a replica of the Droeshout portrait'. On Corneille's classicism or *régulier*, see John D. Lyons, 'Regularity: Articulating the Aesthetic', in *Kingdom of Disorder: The Theory of Tragedy in Classical France* (West Lafayette, Ind., 1999), pp. 1–42, esp. pp. 1–9.

2. Guillaume Vallet, after Antoine Paillet: Frontispiece to *Oeuvres de Pierre Corneille* (Rouen, 1664).

'as many and profitable Rules for perfecting the Stage, as any wherewith the *French* can furnish us'.[7]

* * *

As Rowe maintains at the very start of his *Some Account*, Shakespeare's education was limited. He was educated in Stratford, 'for some time in a Free-school, where 'tis probable he acquir'd that little *Latin* he was Master of' (ii). Nor was his provincial grammar school education ever completed. According to Rowe, his father, Mr John Shakespear, a wool-dealer with ten children, under straitened circumstances, 'was forc'd to withdraw him from thence, and unhappily prevented his further Proficiency in that Language' (iii). Because he needed his eldest son to help with his own trade, the boy's schooling continued in his father's workshop: 'he could give him no better education than his own employment' (ii).

After the account of Shakespeare's aborted education, Rowe moves on to his forced departure from Stratford: 'an Extravagance that he was guilty of, forc'd him both out of his Country and that way of Living which he had taken up' (v). He poached deer from Sir Thomas Lucy's park, 'more than once', is prosecuted, and then protests so bitterly that Sir Thomas redoubles his prosecution, compelling Shakespeare to flee to London, an outlaw. Rowe has named his offence carefully: it is an 'extravagance', a word that maintained close connection to its Latin roots (*extra*, beyond + *vagari*, to wander) into the eighteenth century; in John Kersey's 1702 *A New English Dictionary*, 'extravagant' is defined as 'wandering beyond the due bounds', and is synonymous with 'disordinate', 'irregular', 'wild', 'savage', 'furious' and 'hair-brain'd'. By 'robbing a park', Shakespeare both trespasses on another man's land and seizes his property.[8] And he offends 'more than once'. When made accountable, he strikes back with another injury, this time against Lucy's reputation, with a libellous ballad. And his vindictiveness does not stop when he flees Stratford: in London, many years after the trespass, as Rowe relates, it is still rankling when he satirizes his old prosecutor in *The Merry Wives of Windsor* (xviii).

As his career began in Stratford with offence and injury, so too does it end there, 'some Years before his Death' (xxv), and in another instance of going too far. In retirement, by virtue of his 'pleasurable Wit, and good Nature', he spends time 'in pleasant conversation' with various of his neighbours; 'Amongst them . . . he had a particular Intimacy with Mr. *Combe*, an old Gentleman noted thereabouts for his Wealth and Usury' (xxxvi). On the assumption that Shakespeare would outlive him, Mr. Combe 'in a laughing manner' asks the poet to write his epitaph. Shakespeare 'immediately' obliges, but hardly in the jocular spirit of the request. His epitaph first reduces Combe's chances of salvation to ten per cent, the interest rate he has been charging, '*Ten in the Hundred lies here ingrav'd / 'Tis a Hundred to Ten, his Soul is not sav'd*', before envisioning his outright damnation: '*If any Man ask, Who lies in this Tomb? / Oh! ho! quoth the Devil, 'tis my John-a-Combe*'. Thus a genial request produces a hostile response, '[T]he Sharpness of the Satyr is said to have stung the Man so severely, that he never forgave it.' Rowe says no more, but this is the anecdote that later Shakespearians are most keen to repudiate, as repelled by Shakespeare's maleficence here as they are by Hamlet's desire to kill Claudius at his prayers.[9] Both forms of malice, by targeting the afterlife of the soul, overstep divine prerogative.

Thus upon both leaving Stratford and returning to it, in his first piece of writing as well as his last, Shakespeare acts in violation of laws and norms. He ends up exiled from his native town at the

---

7 *An Essay of Dramatick Poesie*, ed. Samuel Holt Monk (Berkeley, 1971), vol. 17, p. 58, in *The Works of John Dryden*, ed. Edward Niles Hooker, H. T. Swedenberg Jr. and Vinton A. Dearing, 20 vols. (Berkeley, 1956–2000).

8 See entry for 'extravagant', *Lexicons of Early Modern English*, leme.library.utoronto.ca/

9 On the unsettling possibility that this epitaph, rather than *The Tempest*, might be Shakespeare's last non-collaborative work, see Alfred Corn, 'Shakespeare's Epitaph', *Hudson Review*, 64:2 (2011), 295–303, p. 295.

start of his career and alienating his companions at its close. Two pieces of injurious writing frame his career: a libellous ballad and a scathing epitaph, both in excess of their respective occasions, the one felonious, the other bad-mannered. It could be said that extravagance characterizes his behaviour from start to finish.

And not only his behaviour. When Rowe remarks on the 'beautiful Extravagance, which we admire in *Shakespear*' (iii), it is not law or manners that Shakespeare has exceeded, but the rules of art. Shakespeare's abbreviated grammar school education accounts for an undisputed fact: 'It is without Controversie, that he had no knowledge of the Writings of the Antient Poets' (iii). This can be inferred 'from his Works themselves, where we find no traces of anything that looks like an Imitation of [the Ancients] . . . so that his not copying at least something from them, may be an Argument of his never having read 'em'. The plays do reveal some learning: 'Some *Latin* without question he did know, and one may see up and down in his Plays how far his Reading that way went.' Rowe supposes it went about as far as that of Chiron, 'one of the *Gothick* princes' in *Titus Andronicus* who recognizes '*a Verse in* Horace' from his schoolboy Latin, 'Which, I suppose, was the Author's Case' (iv). Rowe is puzzled by how Shakespeare could have based *The Comedy of Errors* on Plautus's *Menaechmi*, doubting he was 'Master of *Latin* enough to read it in the Original' (xv) and knowing of no contemporary translation. Yet while Shakespeare's unfamiliarity with the Ancients is blamed for his incorrect and irregular writing, it might also be credited with his explosive vitality: 'For tho' the knowledge of [the Ancients] might have made him more Correct, yet it is not improbable but that the Regularity and Deference for them . . . might have restrain'd some of that Fire, Impetuosity, and even beautiful Extravagance, which we admire in *Shakespear*' (iii).

The irregularity of Shakespeare's plots is so well known that Rowe hardly comments on it, except to complain that the plot in *The Merchant of Venice* turns on 'that extravagant and unusual kind of Bond' (xxi) in which a loan of 3000 ducats can be quit with a pound of flesh. *The Tempest* is the exception, singled out for its respect of the unities: 'the Unities are kept here with an Exactness uncommon to the Liberties of his Writing' (xxiii). In general, however, the 'Liberties of his Writing' prevail, without attention to generic decorum or the dramatic unities.

While irregularity mars plots (held primary by the Ancients), it makes for Shakespeare's most applauded characters. There is the 'extravagant Character of Caliban . . . a wonderful Invention in the Author, who could strike out such a particular wild image . . . one of the finest and most uncommon Grotesques that was ever seen' (xxiv). The melancholy of Jaques in *As You Like It* is 'as singular and odd as it is diverting' (xx). Petruchio is an 'uncommon piece of Humour' (xviii). Grinning and cross-gartered, 'the fantastical Steward *Malvolio*' is another favorite: 'there is something singularly Ridiculous and Pleasant' in him (xix). Also singled out for admiration is the 'irregular Greatness of mind in *M. Antony*', the Roman general who 'o'erflows the measure' (xxx).

By consensus, Shakespeare's greatest character is the fat knight who admits to living 'out of all order, out of all compass': '*Falstaff* is allow'd by every body to be a Master-piece' (xvii). His extravagances are multiple: 'theft, lying, cowardice, vain-glory: and in short, every kind of viciousness' (xviii). If there is any fault in his characterization, it is that Shakespeare 'has given him so much Wit as to make him almost too agreeable'; audiences, therefore, regret his banishment in *2 Henry IV.* Wit is the faculty Shakespeare also possesses in abundance; Rowe notes 'the advantages of his Wit' (viii), 'the Reputation of his Wit' (ix), 'the power of his Wit' (x). He and Falstaff have something else in common: 'Amongst other Extravagances, in *The Merry Wives of Windsor*, [Shakespeare] has made [Falstaff] a Dear-stealer', and made Falstaff's prosecutor a Warwickshire justice who possesses a coat of arms 'very near' that of Shakespeare's prosecutor, Sir Thomas Lucy. It is not Hamlet or Prospero who bears a special affinity to Shakespeare, but Falstaff. So, too, do his other singular characters: their excesses reflect his unruly anecdotal character as well as the irregularity of his style.

* * *

For the middle period of Shakespeare's life, Rowe has no records, other than the plays themselves. The reference to the vestal virgin in *A Midsummer Night's Dream* is 'plainly' a compliment to Queen Elizabeth (viii), who admired and encouraged Shakespeare: 'Queen Elizabeth had several of his Plays Acted before her, and without doubt gave him many gracious Marks of her Favour.' Yet she is not so pleased when in his history plays he provocatively named his fat rogue after the Protestant martyr Sir John Oldcastle. She commanded Shakespeare to change the name, and he does alter it, but not without offending the descendants of another Sir John, a Knight of the Garter and war hero: 'The [first] Offence was indeed avoided; but I don't know whether the Author may not have been somewhat to blame in his second Choice' (ix). (Anecdotal Shakespeare specializes in writing that offends the living and the dead: a libellous ballad, a scathing epitaph and a defamatory impersonation.) The Queen seems less concerned to protect noble reputations in her next command: she 'commanded [Shakespeare] to continue [him] for one Play more, and to shew him in Love' (viii–ix). The possibility of Falstaff's making a comeback may have come at the suggestion of the Epilogue at the end of *2 Henry IV* who allows for a sequel in which 'Falstaff shall die of a sweat', though not in the fashion of his original namesake, who was hanged and burned: 'For Oldcastle died a martyr, and this is not the man'. While the Epilogue's promise is never realized in *Henry V*, the Queen's command resulted in *The Merry Wives of Windsor*, and '[h]ow well she was obey'd, the Play it self is an admirable Proof'. The play, it must be said, admirably proves no such thing. Hiding in a dirty laundry basket and pilloried in the guise of 'the fat woman of Brentford', 'the greasy knight' comes closer to the Epilogue's dying of a sweat than Elizabeth's being 'in Love'. Rowe praises the '*Billet-doux*' Falstaff sends to Mistress Ford and Mistress Page, but with qualification: they are 'very good Expressions of Love

in their Way' (xix). 'In their Way' seems to imply the unusual status of Falstaff's love letters, mass-produced with mercenary intent. Shakespeare, it would seem, either neglected the royal command or indeed flouted it.

The same paragraph that describes Queen Elizabeth's patronage of Shakespeare tells of the Earl of Southampton's. Evidence for this relationship, too, is located in Shakespeare's works, in this instance, the dedication of *Venus and Adonis* to Southampton.[10] Rowe uses the same epithet to describe Southampton's patronage, as he had Elizabeth's – 'Marks of Favour' – but with suggestive additions: Shakespeare 'had the Honour to meet with many great and uncommon Marks of Favour and Friendship from the Earl of *Southampton*, famous in the Histories of that Time for his Friendship to the unfortunate Earl of *Essex*'. Shakespeare received not only 'Favour' but 'Friendship' from Southampton, who in turn was renowned for his 'Friendship' with the Earl of Essex, who was 'unfortunate' in having led a rebellion against the Queen in which Southampton colluded: both were tried for treason, the former executed, the latter incarcerated. Shakespeare, Rowe had earlier noted, had also been acquainted with Essex, as could be inferred from *Henry V*, which in its final act features 'a Compliment very handsomly turn'd to the Earl of Essex' (vii). Especially after notice of Shakespeare's lax obedience to the Queen's commands, his association with her two adversaries might hint at errant political leanings, another form of extravagance.

Startling to Rowe is the exceptional magnitude of Southampton's patronage, '[a] Bounty very great, and very rare at any time': £1000 (x). To enable his eighteenth-century readers to appreciate the sum's enormity, Rowe gives its current equivalent. £1000 in Shakespeare's day was 'almost equal to that profuse Generosity the present Age has shewn to French Dancers and Italian

---

[10] Rowe does not mention the dedication to Southampton in *Lucrece*, though he does name *Tarquin* and *Lucrece* among the works by Shakespeare not included in his edition, *Some Account*, p. xxxix.

Eunuchs' (x). Rowe's figures are quite accurate. In 1700, Thomas Betterton, the actor and manager of the Duke's Company whom Rowe credits with the gathering of materials for his *Some Account* (xxxiv), bemoaned the crushing expense of procuring French dancers.[11] In 1710, Senesino, a celebrated castrato from Sienna (for whom Handel wrote arias) was offered the vast sum of £2000 a year to perform in London.[12] This adds a peculiar cast to Southampton's generosity: the sum he has given Shakespeare in exchange for his services to literature approximates what theatre impresarios of Rowe's day were willing to pay out to French dancers, known for their sexual availability and technique, and to Italian castrati, whose sexual ambiguity piqued prurient curiosity.[13] What was there about Shakespeare that drew such outlandish munificence from Southampton? His *Venus and Adonis*? His politics?

* * *

In relating Shakespeare's London encounters, Rowe moves down the social ladder, from queen to earl to 'private' friends: first the courtly Edmund Spenser and then the urban Ben Jonson. While the episodes involving Elizabeth and Southampton derive from Shakespeare's works – the Falstaff plays and the dedication to *Venus and Adonis* respectively – the accounts of these two friendships issue from Spenser's and Jonson's. Rowe quotes three elegiac stanzas from *Tears of the Muses* (1591), 'lamenting [Willy's] Absence with the tenderness of a Friend' (xi). He is confident that Spenser's 'pleasant Willy' is Shakespeare, 'dead of late'. It needn't matter that Shakespeare outlived Spenser by over a decade, for the verses are not intended literally: 'Mr. Spencer does not mean that he was then really Dead'. His absence was the result of his having withdrawn from the stage, 'out of a disgust he had taken at the then ill taste of the Town, and the mean Condition of the Stage' (xii). The identification allows for another variation on Shakespeare's unlicensed behaviour: the crude and coarse state of culture in his time.

Shakespeare's friendship with Ben Jonson also has a textual source, Jonson's heavily Latinate commonplace book, *Timber or Discoveries* (1641).[14] *Some Account* tapers off by reproducing in full Jonson's entry on Shakespeare. It begins obliquely, as if targeting not Shakespeare, but his fellow players, Heminge and Condell, who in the preliminaries to the First Folio had praised the state of Shakespeare's manuscript papers:

I remember the Players have often mention'd it as an Honour to Shakespear, that in Writing (whatsoever he penn'd) he never blotted out a Line. My Answer hath been, Would he had blotted a thousand, which they thought a malevolent Speech. I had not told Posterity this, but for their Ignorance, who chose that Circumstance to commend their Friend by, wherein he most faulted. (xxxviii)

For Heminge and Condell, clean manuscript pages attest to a direct relation between what Shakespeare wrote and what the Folio printed. Transmission is unmediated, with no contaminating interference from players or printers, allowing for a direct transmission from Shakespeare's mind to his hand to his papers to the Folio printers: 'His mind and hand went together: And what he thought, he uttered with that easinesse, that wee have scarce received from him a blot in his papers.'[15] (The same claim appears on the Folio's title page: 'Published according to the True and Originall Copies'.) But Jonson misconstrues the claim, perhaps intentionally, taking it as not an advertisement of the Folio's proximity to the author, but rather of the author's breezy writing practice. The claim irks Jonson, not

---

[11] See David Roberts, *Thomas Betterton: The Greatest Actor of the Restoration Stage* (Cambridge, 2010), p. 168.

[12] On the *'prix exorbitant'* commanded by Senesino, see Jonathan Keates, *Handel: The Man & His Music* (1985, rev. ed. London, 2008), p. 167.

[13] On the sexually charged body of the castrato, see Roger Freitas, 'The Eroticism of Emasculation: Confronting the Baroque Body of the Castrato', *The Journal of Musicology*, 20 (2003), 196–249.

[14] *Discoveries*, ed. Lorna Hudson, in *The Cambridge Edition of the Works of Ben Jonson*, gen. ed. Ian Donaldson *et al.*, 7 vols. (Cambridge, 2012), vol. 7, pp. 521–2.

[15] A Folger copy of the First Folio on Early English Books Online; *Mr. William Shakespeares comedies, histories, & tragedies* (London, 1623), STC22273, sig. A2–A3.

because he doubts it, but because it applauds what should be censured: in their 'Ignorance', the players 'chose that Circumstance to commend their Friend by, wherein he most faulted'. Lest posterity be deceived, he counters their boast with a blast: 'Would he had blotted a thousand'.

To a printer, papers covered with blots would be a nightmare. To a classically minded stylist, however, they would signal skilled writing. For both Horace and Quintilian, multiple cancellations are the sign of careful and sustained revision.[16] Jonson translates Horace's *Art of Poetry* where he cites Quintilian on the necessity of reworking verses, by blotting or reforging: 'If to Quintillius you recited aught . . . He'd bid blot all, and to the anvil bring / Those ill-turned verses, to new hammering'.[17] Petrarch's manuscripts are exemplary in this respect. His working papers and successive drafts display his many erasures, insertions, transpositions and inversions, all signs of his craftsmanship, skill and rhetorical technique.[18] Blots indicate that verses have been worked and reworked. As in Latin, *opera* presupposes *operare*, so in its Old English cognate, a work implies work. Though Jonson deemed his own plays 'works' when he included them in his 1616 folio, *The Workes of Benjamin Jonson*, it is doubtful that he would have considered Shakespeare's plays 'works'. Shakespeare simply did not work hard enough. He dashed off his poems and plays with no regard to rules and models.

Lest readers think his critique 'Malevolent' (as the players had), Jonson declares parenthetically his affection and esteem for Shakespeare, 'And to justifie mine own Candor, (for I lov'd the Man, and do honour his Memory . . . .)'. Then follows a sentence of unusual grammatical and semantic complexity:

He was, indeed, Honest, and of an open and free Nature, had an Excellent Fancy, brave Notions, and gentle Expressions, wherein he flow'd with that Facility, that sometimes it was necessary he should be stopp'd: *Sufflaminandus erat*, as Augustus said of Haterius. His Wit was in his own Power, would the Rule of it had been so too.

(xxxviii)

The main clause commends Shakespeare's nature (as 'Honest', 'open' and 'free'); the first subordinate clause extends the praise to his writing ('flow'd with that Facility'); but the second subordinate clause brings the praise up short ('he should be stopp'd'). What begins in commendation ends in condemnation, and definitively, when backed by two quotations from Seneca, the first quoted in Latin, the second in Jonson's translation. In discussing proper style, Seneca gives the negative example of Haterius who spoke so rapidly and impulsively that Emperor Augustus commented that he be braked.[19] So rapid were his outpourings, according to Seneca, 'that he would muddle them, burst into tears, speak ex tempore and become so profuse in his language that he had to be stopped'. What began as praise of Shakespeare's expansive character turns into blame of his free-flowing style – writing that spills out in such facile fluency, that it must be stopped, as Jonson stops the course of his own sentence with ten punctuation marks, including a 'double prick' or colon after 'stopp'd:' before quoting Seneca, the arbiter of style, who is quoting Augustus, the emperor of Rome. As Augustus checked the orator Haterius, so Jonson would bridle Shakespeare. Liberality, in government as in writing, risks licentiousness, unless controlled by laws or rules, what Rowe terms, 'the Regularity of those written Precepts' of the Ancients (xxvi).

Rowe relates how the friendship between Shakespeare and Jonson began. The aspiring Jonson was about to have his work rudely rejected

---

[16] On the prime importance of revision in Quintilian, see *The Orator's Education*, ed. and trans. Donald A. Russell, 5 vols. (Cambridge, MA, 2001), vol 4, 10.4; for Horace, see *Satires* I.x. and *Ars Poetica*, lines 72–3.

[17] *Horace his Art of Poetry, Made English by Ben Jonson*, ed. Colin Burrow, in *The Cambridge Jonson*, vol. 7, lines 626–9. Burrow notes that these lines were underlined in Jonson's copy of the Latin, see n. p. 62.

[18] I am grateful to William Kennedy for drawing my attention to the significance of Petrarch's heavily revised working papers as a manifestation of his poetic craft or art.

[19] See Lewis A. Sussman, *The Elder Seneca* (Leyden, 1978), 108–9, 170–1.

by the players when Shakespeare interceded to recommend him: 'After this they were profess'd Friends, tho' I don't know whether the other ever made him an equal return of Gentleness and Sincerity' (xiii). But clearly the 'return' was not 'equal'. While Shakespeare promoted Jonson's career at its start, Jonson detracted from Shakespeare's after his death. Yet Jonson's antipathy was not personal but stylistic: indeed there is no separating the two. What Jonson couldn't abide about Shakespeare's style was its unruliness or irregularity. As Rowe astutely noted, even Jonson's praise for him was tinged with opprobrium: 'And if at times he has affected to commend him, it has always been with some Reserve' (xiii). Jonson was the correct poet, the one who respected the classical genres, translated Horace's *Arts Poetica*, and devised an English Grammar to regularize the vernacular; so dedicated was he to correctness that he proofed his own 1616 folio. Unlike extravagant Shakespeare, he knew when to stop.

* * *

Rowe is careful to distance himself from Jonson's outright critique. After commenting on Shakespeare's vigour, fire and imagination, he pulls back: 'I would not be thought by this to mean, that [Shakespeare's] Fancy was so loose and extravagant, as to be Independent of the Rule and Government of Judgment' (vii). After all, the success of his edition depended on securing Shakespeare's pre-eminence. Yet the examples he gives of Shakespeare's poetic heights might well have satisfied Jonson's literary standards. While he singled out Shakespeare's extravagant characters for admiration, as we have seen, when it comes to poetry, the passages he applauds and reproduces in full do not demonstrate the 'beautiful extravagance' in which Shakespeare 'gives his Imagination an entire Loose, and raises his Fancy to a flight above Mankind and the Limits of the visible world' (xxiii). They are instead enframed and balanced set-pieces, models of stylistic rule and measure, fully under control, in decorous iambs with mid-line caesuras. Jaques' Seven Ages of Man speech from *As You Like It* is quoted in its entirety (xxi–xxii). Beginning with

a universalization ('All the World's a Stage') and then breaking systematically into seven distinctive parts, the speech is admired because it accomplishes what Horace maintained was so difficult: to speak of the universal specifically, '*Difficile est proprie communia dicere*' (xx). Rowe also holds Shakespeare up to classical precedent when he praises 'The Image of Patience', in Viola's self-referential speech, as a 'Sketch of Statuary'; 'the greatest Masters of *Greece* and *Rome*' would have been hard pressed to equal it (xvii):

> She never told her love,
> But let concealment, like a worm i' the bud,
> Feed on her damask cheek: she pined in thought,
> And with a green and yellow melancholy
> She sat like patience on a monument,
> Smiling at grief.

As with Jaques' speech, syntactic parallels dominate: 'She never told her love . . . she pined in Thought . . . She sat like patience'. The compressed lines are nicely fitted to the emotion they suppress.

From the tragedies, Rowe selects a passage from *Hamlet* and, once again, measures it against ancient models, this time finding a close analogue. *Hamlet* and *Electra* are 'founded on much the same Tale' (xxxi). Each of the two princes must take revenge on his father's murderer who in each case has married his mother. Yet Rowe is offended by the 'Manners' Sophocles has given to Electra's two children.

Orestes embrues his Hands in the Blood of his own Mother; and that barbarous Action is perform'd, tho' not immediately upon the Stage, yet so near, that the Audience hear *Clytemnestra* crying out to *Æghystus* for Help, and to her Son for Mercy: While *Electra*, her Daughter, and a Princess . . . stands upon the Stage and encourages her Brother in the Parricide. (xxxii)

In a fine reversal of the contest between the Ancients and the moderns, it is the Ancient Sophocles who violates dramatic decorum, with both character (the high born Electra and Orestes 'ought to have appear'd with more Decency') and action (the shocking matricide carried out within hearing range of the audience). By contrast, modern Shakespeare restrains the action of his prince. Though his motives for abhorring his mother, 'heighten'd by Incest', are greater than those of Orestes, Shakespeare reins him in: 'the Poet restrains [Hamlet] from doing Violence to his Mother' and 'he makes [Hamlet's] Father's Ghost forbid that part of his Vengeance'. Rowe crowns his praise by quoting the Ghost's controlling and controlled injunction to Hamlet to leave Gertrude's punishment to heaven and her own conscience.

But Rowe's classical leanings are most apparent at the close of his essay when he credits Jonson's characterization of Shakespeare: 'As to the Character given of him by *Ben Johnson*, there is a good deal true in it' (xxxix). Character here references not his 'free and open' personality but its stylistic equivalent: his unregulated fluency. To support Jonson's position, Rowe introduces a passage from Jonson's own authority. Horace, in his letter to Augustus, describes the early rustic Roman poets who began to avail themselves of Greek models with some success, but they avoided erasure, thinking it would vitiate their writing.[20]

> —Naturâ sublimis & Acer
> Nam spirat Tragicum satis & fæliciter Audet,
> Sed turpem putat in Chartis metuitq; Lituram.

In this jaunty idiomatic translation of the passage, the final 'Lituram' is translated with the Folio's notorious monosyllable:

> Nay, [Rome] essayed a venture of her own,
> And liked to think she'd caught the tragic tone;
> And so she has:– the afflatus comes on hot;
> But out, alas! she deems it shame to blot.[21]

Like Heminge and Condell, the uncouth early Romans did not know that the shame was not in blotting but in not-blotting, the telltale sign of a poet who just let himself go. In the same Horatian and Quintilian tradition as Jonson, Alexander Pope accuses of insufficient blotting not only Shakespeare but John Dryden, England's first official poet-laureate:

> And fluent Shakespeare scarce effac'd a line.
> Ev'n copious Dryden, wanted, or forgot,
> *The last and greatest Art, the Art to blot.*[22]

Shakespeare never mastered 'The art to blot'.

Rowe allows that not all of Jonson's commentary was unfavourable to Shakespeare, 'at times [Jonson] has affected to commend him', but he adds 'it has always been with some Reserve, insinuating his *Uncorrectness*, a careless manner of Writing, and want of Judgment' (xiii). This could be said about Rowe as well: in his *Account*, he, too, as we have seen, has insinuated Shakespeare's '*Uncorrectness*', including in his final quote from Horace. It could also be said of the entire tradition of Shakespeare's reception from the 1623 Folio to well into the eighteenth century.

* * *

However much Shakespeare was praised, the Jonsonian charge that he lacked control is repeated, elaborated and debated for over a century after his death. In his rural ignorance of the Ancients, he was thought to violate all three of the unities; he also offended generic decorum by intermixing tragedy and comedy and concomitantly blurred social distinctions by intermingling high and low characters. Shakespeare's conceits are often deemed excessive, his lines overly enjambed, his figures strained, his puns symptomatic of incontinence. Dryden, in *The Grounds of Criticism in Tragedy* (1679), accuses him of doing violence to the language by exceeding the limits of judgement: 'I may venture to maintain, that the fury of his fancy often transported him beyond the bounds of Judgment, either in coyning of new words and phrases, or racking words which were in use, into the violence of a Catachresis.'[23] In the early notices on Shakespeare, the charge that

---

[20] In *De Oratore*, Cicero also notes that the Romans at first thought they could be eloquent on the basis of 'their own native ability and reflection', without 'the rules of art' of their Greek predecessors. *Cicero: On the Ideal Orator*, trans. James M. May and Jakob Wisse (New York and Oxford, 2001), p. 60.

[21] *The Satires, Epistles and the Art of Poetry of Horace*, trans. John Conington (London, 1904), *Epistles*, Bk. 2.1, lines 214–17.

[22] Alexander Pope, *The First Epistle of the Second Book of Horace Imitated: To Augustus*, lines 279–81.

[23] *The Works of John Dryden: Preface, Troilus and Cressida or, Truth Found too Late*, ed. George R. Guffey (Berkeley, Los Angeles, London, 1984), XIII, p. 244.

Shakespeare wanted art occurs repeatedly: Thomas Fuller in his *Worthies of Warwickshire* (1662) and William Winstanley who copied him in his *The Lives of the Most Famous English Poets* (1687) regard Shakespeare as 'an eminent instance of the truth of that Rule, *Poeta non fit, sed nascitur*, one is not made, but born a Poet. Indeed his Learning was very little . . . so nature it self was all the art which was used upon him.'[24] Shakespeare's natural wit was thought to substitute for the learning he lacked, but it never quite offset that lack. As Edward Phillips (1675) explained, 'where the polishments of art are wanting, as probably [Shakespeare's] learning was not extraordinary, he pleaseth with a certain wild and native elegance'.[25] He is paraphrasing his uncle, John Milton, who in his commendatory sonnet in the Second Folio (1632) ascribed to Shakespeare the facility of flowing 'easy numbers' in contrast to the strain of 'slow-endeavouring Art'.[26] In his *L'Allegro*, the contrast with Jonson is explicit: the studied drama of Jonson's 'learnèd sock' is pitted against the spontaneous outpouring of 'Shakespeare fancy's child, / Warble his native wood-notes wild'.[27] The notorious Thomas Rymer outdoes his critical cohort in hostility: 'In Tragedy he appears quite out of his Element; his Brains are turn'd, he raves and rambles, without any coherence, any spark of reason, or any rule to controul him, or set bounds to his phrenzy.'[28]

But even those who are in the business of promoting Shakespeare insinuate his incorrectness: Rowe's successors, all Tonson editors, however much they exalt Shakespeare, take occasion to comment on his defects. Alexander Pope concludes the Preface to his edition by admitting that Shakespeare, 'in comparison of those [authors] that are more finished and regular', has parts that are 'childish, ill-plac'd, and unequal'; in contrast to their stately neoclassical edifices, his are Gothic, with 'dark, odd, and uncouth passages'.[29] The editor Theobald maintains, 'We have scarce any Book in the English Tongue more fertile of Errors, than the Plays of SHAKESPEARE', and it was not only the blunders of compositors that accounted for the fact that no author was 'more various from himself'.[30] Samuel Johnson termed Shakespeare

'an author not systematick and consequential, but desultory and vagrant', and blamed his stylistic impetuosity on a tendency 'to oversupply his phrases . . . and to rush precipitously from one thought to another'.[31] Other poets displayed crafted cabinets of precious rarities – finished, wrought, and polished – whereas Shakespeare's mine of gold and diamonds is 'clouded by incrustations, debased by impurities, and mingled with a mass of meaner minerals'.[32] Even as late as Thomas Warton's monumental three-volume *History of English Poetry* (1781), considered England's first modern literary history, Shakespeare's extravagance remains salient: 'We behold him breaking the barriers of imaginary method.'[33]

And as a result of Shakespeare's defects, the skills of others – scholars, playwrights, critics – are needed to bring his work up to the neoclassical standards of what he was being raised to become: an English classic. The intellectual labours that emerge during this period presuppose his need of regulation. Editing goes about correcting, perfecting and rectifying his texts as well as evening out his meter, distinguishing prose from verse, ordering acts and scenes, elucidating obscure passages. Adaptations seek to better his drama by recasting it to observe the unities, generic decorum, smoother and more balanced syntax and meter. According to

---

24 Thomas Fuller, *The History of the Worthies of England*, ed. P. Austin Nuttall, 3 vols. (New York, 1965), III, pp. 284–5.

25 Edward Phillips, *Theatrum Poetarum* (1675), in Brian Vickers, ed., *William Shakespeare: The Critical Heritage 1623–1801*, 6 vols. (London, 1974–81), vol. 1, p. 13.

26 'On Shakespeare' (lines 9–10), in *John Milton*, ed. Stephen Orgel and Jonathan Goldberg (Oxford, 1991), p. 20.

27 *L'Allegro* (lines 132–3), in *John Milton*, ed. Orgel and Goldberg, p. 25.

28 Thomas Rymer, *A Short View of Tragedy* (1693), in Vickers, *The Critical Heritage*, vol. 2, p. 58.

29 Alexander Pope, Preface, *The Works of Shakespeare* (1725), in Vickers, *The Critical Heritage*, vol. 2, p. 415.

30 Lewis Theobald, *Shakespeare Restor'd* (London, 1726), I; Vickers, *The Critical Heritage*, vol. 2, p. 476.

31 Samuel Johnson, Preface, *The Plays of William Shakespeare* (1765), in Vickers, *The Critical Heritage*, vol. 5, p. 39.

32 Vickers, *The Critical Heritage*, vol. 2, p. 476.

33 Thomas Warton, *The History of the English Language*, 3 vols. (London, 1781), p. 499.

Brian Vickers, 'There is no comparable instance of the work of a major artist being altered in such a sweeping fashion.'[34] Even actors needed to set limits. Francis Gentleman notes an affinity between David Garrick's style of acting and Shakespeare's style of writing: 'they both appear regardless of rules and mechanism: The beautiful wildnesses of nature seem to have attracted both, and in different stiles they appear to have pursued the same track.'[35] And yet there is a difference: 'Mr. Garrick is never so entirely luxuriant, nor so trifling . . .' Critics attempted to cultivate taste and judgement by setting Shakespeare's stylistic faults or vices apart from his beauties or virtues. His works were fertile ground for criticism because they abounded in both, as Pope noted: 'as he has certainly written better, so he has perhaps written worse'.[36] It is because Shakespeare never blotted that there is need for editorial rectification, dramatic adaptation and literary criticism.

There is also a need for anecdotes, for they give life to the breaches of rule that all these practices attempt to eliminate by correcting, adapting, critiquing. Anecdotal Shakespeare's bad-mannered, uncouth and offensive behaviour is the fictive correlate of his critical standing as an irregular and unlearned poet. Other anecdotes are collected after Rowe, first by George Steevens in his 1778 edition, where Rowe's *Some Account* is followed by an appendix of 'Additional Anecdotes'.[37] In one of them, the stylistic opposition between Shakespeare and Jonson is put into narrative form. Shakespeare decides on a christening gift for his godson, Jonson's son: a dozen latten christening spoons with Latin inscriptions, which he must rely on Jonson to translate, rather pathetically since such mottos tended to be quite simple, at the level of *Fides* or *Deo Gratias*. Another anecdote marks the beginning of his writing career earlier than in the deer-poaching episode. As a boy in his father's butcher's shop, Shakespeare declaims in high tragic style while slaughtering a calf. The combination of carnage and oratory recalls Caesar's slaughter at the Capitol in *Julius Caesar*, which Brutus hopes will be seen as sacrifice, not butchery; 'It was a brute part of him to kill so capital a calf there' (3.2.101), quips Hamlet, likening Caesar and Polonius (who once played the part of Caesar) to that sacrificed or butchered calf.[38] Lofty oratory doesn't belong in the butcher's shop any more than, by classical rule, a bloodbath does on stage. Other anecdotes place him in the London theatre. Having pre-empted Richard Burbage's nighttime tryst with an infatuated admirer, Shakespeare when 'caught at his game' by Burbage justifies his usurpation by appealing to the order of regnal succession: 'William the Conqueror was before Rich. the 3'. Another illicit liaison is reported with the Oxford inn-keeper's wife en route to London, one that produces William Davenant, who was not only William Shakespeare's namesake, godchild and 'poetical child', but, as the anecdote intimates, his biological child as well, begotten by the stealth of nature rather than by law.

* * *

The anecdotes, both of Rowe's *Some Account* and those collected subsequently, register the same problem as the criticism, adaptation and editing: how to manage Shakespeare's stylistic licence while raising him to the status of an English classic. The anecdotes compress and fictionalize that licence into 'little personal stories' of Shakespeare's extravagance, featuring a character named Shakespeare who typically surpasses limits: stealing deer, ignoring the Queen, pre-empting his colleague's tryst, begetting children out of wedlock, pushing

---

[34] Vickers, *The Critical Heritage*, vol. 1, p. 6.

[35] Francis Gentleman, *Life of Shakespeare*, in *Bell's Edition of Shakespeare's Plays*, 8 vols. (London, 1774), p. 26.

[36] Pope, in Vickers, *The Critical Heritage*, vol. 2.

[37] *The Plays of William Shakespeare*, ed. George Steevens, 10 vols. (London, 1778), vol. 1, p. 203.

[38] Katherine Duncan-Jones conjectures that Shakespeare might have seen or perhaps participated in a mumming play or Whitsun 'pastime' in which the slaying of a calf was staged, and considers it early preparation for the 'high-style slaughter of innocents' in his own plays, of Prince Edward in *3 Henry VI* and of Macduff's children in *Macbeth*: see *Shakespeare: An Ungentle Life* (London, 2001), pp. 17–18. For Duncan-Jones and Shakespeare's biographers in general, the plays originate in Shakespeare's experience. But for anecdotal Shakespeare it is just the reverse: his experience originates in the plays.

a *jeu d'esprit* too far, and never blotting. But that character is not the man who lived from 1564 to 1616. It is another kind of character altogether, one that, like the word 'character', is akin to letters and therefore to writing itself. Rowe's pronouncement, this article's epigraph, is thus perfectly tautological: 'The Character of the Man is best seen in his Writing' (xxxvii).

The anecdotes are less a form of biography than of literary criticism: they record not the life Shakespeare lived between 1564 and 1616 but the impression his works made after his death. The anecdotes, then, have been misclassified as early biography, proto-biography, biography manqué, aspiring towards the accuracy of documentary facts and the coherence of linear narrative, but falling far short. It was his works that mattered: not how he lived but how he wrote – or how he was thought to have written at a time before he is elevated above all other writers, so that the poet who followed no models becomes himself the model.

To return to this article's opening question: why is the Shakespeare of the modern biographies at such variance with the Shakespeare of the seventeenth- and early eighteenth-century anecdotes: the one wayward, the other upright? Quite simply, the subject of the anecdotes is not the subject of biography. The anecdotes are not about the man but about the writing that goes by the same name. This will change, of course. Romanticism will take the previous generation's stylistic vagaries and recast them as genius. Shakespeare will then no longer exist beyond the critical pale.[39] Shakespeare, then, is no longer beyond the pale. Indeed he is at the very centre of the English canon, or, in Harold Bloom's oracular pronouncement, of the literary canon at large: 'Shakespeare is the Canon. He sets the standard and the limits of literature.'[40] And his character will shape up accordingly.

---

[39] Michael Dobson notes a shift in how Shakespeare's provincial origins are perceived in the nineteenth century: as the source not of his small learning in a provincial grammar school but of his sublime inspiration from idyllic nature, particularly the banks of the Avon. 'A Boy from Stratford', in Zachary Leader, ed., *On Life-Writing* (forthcoming).

[40] Harold Bloom, *The Western Canon: The Books and School of the Ages* (New York, 1994), p. 47.

WHAT IS A SOURCE? OR, HOW SHAKESPEARE READ HIS MARLOWE

LAURIE MAGUIRE AND EMMA SMITH

But peradventure some man will denie that this was done by imitation, seeing the thinges be not all one in both the writers. I answere that imitation is not in things that be all one, but in things that be like, and that which is like, must be, not the same, but another thing.

(Johannes Sturm, *A Rich Storehouse* (1570), sig.H1v)

At our feast wee had a play called Twelve Night, or What You Will, much like the Commedy of Errores, or Menaechmi in Plautus.

(John Manningham's Diary, 2 Feb 1601, p. 18)

I'll have these players / Play something like the murder of my father.

(*Hamlet*, 2.2.596–7)[1]

In their edition of *The Tempest*, Virginia and Alden Vaughan conclude that 'scholars will probably never be able to identify with much confidence the numerous narrative, psychological and thematic threads that Shakespeare wove into *The Tempest*' (pp. 148–9).[2] They are less optimistic than Kenneth Muir, identifying the play in 1957 as one where the 'Main Source' is 'Not known' with the expectant 'it is highly probable that there was a main source as yet unidentified'.[3] Finding the source (or a source) of *The Tempest* has become not only a holy grail but something of a scholarly niche of the Shakespeare industry. Journals regularly include essays with Darwinian titles that claim 'A Source for *The Tempest*', '*The Tempest*...: A New Source' or the more cautious and circumscribed 'A Possible Source of a Passage in *The Tempest*' (our emphasis).[4] In the last few years alone Austen Saunders has proffered Richard Cosin's *Conspiracie for Pretended*

Reformation (1592) as a source for the moment when Shakespeare's shipwrecked Italians exclaim over their miraculously dry clothes; Todd Borlik has proposed the life of the Anglo-Saxon hermit and fen-dweller St Guthlac, described in medieval saints' lives and dramatized in a lost Elizabethan play, as the source of both plot and character (Prospero and Caliban); and the Vaughans have revised their Arden 3 edition of the play to include a

---

[1] Johannes Sturm, *A Ritch Storehouse or Treasury for Nobilitye and Gentlemen* (London, 1570); *Diary of John Manningham*, ed. John Bruce, Camden Society (London, 1868); with the exception of *The Tempest*, all Shakespeare quotations are from the Oxford *Complete Works*, ed. Stanley Wells and Gary Taylor, 2nd edn (Oxford, 2005).

[2] William Shakespeare, *The Tempest*, ed. Virginia Mason Vaughan and Alden T. Vaughan (London, 1999, rev. 2011).

[3] Kenneth Muir, *Shakespeare's Sources* (London, 1957), pp. 255–7; p. 261. The other two sourceless plays are *A Midsummer Night's Dream* and *Love's Labour's Lost*.

[4] These titles come from: William W. E. Slights, 'A Source for *The Tempest* and the Context of the *Discorsi*', *Shakespeare Quarterly*, 36 (1985), 68–70; Gary Schmidgall, '*The Tempest* and *Primaleon*: A New Source', *Shakespeare Quarterly*, 37 (1986), 423–39; Paul F. Cranefield and Walter Federin, 'A Possible Source of a Passage in *The Tempest*', *Shakespeare Quarterly*, 14 (1963), 90–2. Other articles make their claim with interrogatives or variant vocabulary ('influence', 'genesis'). See Gail Kern Paster, 'Montaigne, Dido and *The Tempest*: "How Came that Widow Dido in?"', *Shakespeare Quarterly*, 35 (1984), 91–4; Richard Hillman, 'Chaucer's Franklin's Magician and *The Tempest*: An Influence Beyond Appearance', *Shakespeare Quarterly*, 34 (1983), 426–32; and W. Stacey Johnson, 'The Genesis of Ariel', *Shakespeare Quarterly*, 2 (1951), 205–10.

new section on 'Shakespeare's Sources Revisited' (pp. 139–49).[5]

Not all sources are created equal, however, and the above articles use the same noun to identify both the local (the origin of a line) and the large (the origin of plot and character). Further, we continue to look for sources even as methodology for assessing or admitting them remains undertheorized. Although post-structuralism has given us the giddy proposal that every text is and can only be a tissue of citations authored by the limited cultural resources of the literary language rather than by any particular individual authorial agent, this permissive textual interplay has had little impact on, for example, the kinds of sources cited in an appendix to a modern critical edition. David Scott Kastan's appendix to his 2002 Arden 3 edition of *1 Henry IV* identifies the problem: 'it is not so apparent what should be considered as a source', but he goes on, apparently pragmatically: 'the dependence upon an earlier text for plot or sometimes character, is what marks that text as source'.[6] Despite the methodological shrug, therefore, Kastan's sources for the play – Holinshed, Daniel, *The Famous Victories* – are precisely those listed by R. P. Cowl and A. E. Morgan in the first Arden edition of the play in 1914 and again in A. R. Humphreys' Arden 2 edition of 1960, and they do the same intellectual work.[7] Source study, unlike its Edwardian scholarly contemporaries, has not substantively revisited its intellectual foundations during the course of the twentieth century: whereas everything else about New Bibliography has been re-examined, source study has been remarkably resistant to reassessment. Geoffrey Bullough's still unchallenged *Narrative and Dramatic Sources of Shakespeare*, published between 1957 and 1975, has its feet firmly in the amateur criticism of the eighteenth and nineteenth centuries, decrying the modern 'cult of the PhD thesis' which has 'led to exaggerated claims for obscure and doubtful analogies'. Bullough offered only minimal explanation of his own scholarly procedures in the General Conclusion appended to his eighth volume: 'I have limited my scope to narrative and dramatic sources of some degree of probability and have also printed

analogues which may suggest how Shakespeare's contemporaries and predecessors approached similar topics, and also how individual or traditional his treatment was.'[8] Many of us accustomed to using Bullough may not have been fully conscious of what he intended by that distinction between 'source' and 'analogue', since that information is withheld until the final volume in the series.

A recent development is the qualification of the word 'source'. Thus, Thomas and Tydeman talk of 'major' sources – '"major" in the sense that they supplied Marlowe with the bulk of his material'.[9] Meredith Skura talks of a 'plot source', one that suggests 'a sequence of actions' and Jonathan Bate talks of a 'direct source' by which he means 'the sort that Arthur Brooke's translation of Bandello was for *Romeo and Juliet*'.[10] The editors of the Arden 3 *Tempest* distinguish between a 'principal source for [the play's] plot', a 'cluster of sources for its central themes', and 'general sources...for...minor themes, some of its characterizations and some of its language' (309). Clearly, the stand-alone word 'source' has outlived its usefulness.

An explosion of new terms, influenced by more theoretical ideas of intertextuality, has recently been added to the conventional vocabulary for textual relationships which now ranges

---

[5] Austen Saunders, 'A New Source for *The Tempest*? Richard Cosin's *Conspiracie for Pretended Reformation* (1592)', *Notes & Queries*, 59 (2012), 547–9; Todd Borlik, 'Caliban and the Fen Demons of Lincolnshire: The Englishness of Shakespeare's *Tempest*', *Shakespeare*, 9 (2013), 25–51.

[6] David Scott Kastan, ed., *1 Henry IV*, Arden Shakespeare (London, 2002), pp. 339–40.

[7] William Shakespeare, *The First Part of King Henry the Fourth*, ed. R. P. Cowl and A. E. Morgan (London, 1914), pp. xii–xxii; William Shakespeare, *The First Part of King Henry the Fourth*, ed. A. R. Humphreys (London, 1960), pp. xxi–xxxix.

[8] Geoffrey Bullough, *Narrative and Dramatic Sources of Shakespeare*, vol. 8 (London, 1975), pp. 342, 346.

[9] Vivien Thomas and William Tydeman, *Christopher Marlowe: The Plays and their Sources* (London, 1994), p. 4.

[10] Meredith Skura, 'What Shakespeare Did to Marlowe in Private: Dido, Faustus, and Bottom', in *Christopher Marlowe the Craftsman: Lives, Stage and Page*, ed. Sarah K. Scott and Michael Stapleton (Aldershot, 2010), pp. 79–90; p. 86; Jonathan Bate, *Shakespeare and Ovid* (Oxford, 1994), p. 240.

widely: 'origins', 'genesis', 'borrowings', 'sense-impressions', 'materials from which a writer has clearly derived stimulus and motivation' (Thomas and Tydeman), 'echoes', 'traditions', 'inherited sets of expectations, reflexes and conventions' (Miola), 'influence' (Vaughan and Vaughan), an 'originary event' (Dawson), 'line of descent', 'signature technique' (Tudeau-Clayton), 'echo chamber' (Dennett), 'model' (Charney), 'performance cita-tion' (Carlson), 'reaction' (Bradbrook), 'invitation' (Pitcher), 'verbal seepage' (Wiggins), 'discursive environment' (Siemon), 'provocative agent' (Brooke), 'indebtedness', 'indirect influence', 'stimulus' (Paster), 'genealogical link' (Hamilton), 'traffic', 'data' (Clare), 'meme' (Dawkins).[11] But source studies are still without the rethinking this lexis implies and the apparatus of the standard edition still reprints the same examples. Review-ing the plausibility of suggested new sources for *The Tempest*, the Vaughans revert to Bullough's *Narrative and Dramatic Sources of Shakespeare* as the ultimate authority: 'we concur with Bullough [that Jacob Ayrer's 1618 play] "throws little light upon Shakespeare's play"' (p. 56).

Accounts of Greenblatt's much-quoted 'ele-phant's graveyard' of source study seem to suggest, with the Vaughans, that this intellectual stasis is because we have not found many entirely convincing new sources for Shakespeare, whereas perhaps the blockage is in our limited practical understanding of what a source might be. Intro-ducing the *Aeneid* as 'a text to which we somehow *must* refer when talking about *The Tempest*', Donna Hamilton queries her own instinctive vocabulary: 'clearly, we would have all sorts of problems were we to claim . . . that the *Aeneid* is the source for *The Tempest*'. Part of the problem, she realizes, is that 'the story line of *The Tempest* does not match from beginning to end the story line of the *Aeneid*' and Jonathan Bate makes the same objection: 'it is extremely difficult to make the pattern fit'.[12] Furthermore, traditional source study does not have room for cognitive theory in which memories can be distorted or in which material one reads earlier in life remains with one longer. Petrarch reports that he 'swallowed as

a boy what I would ruminate upon as an older man. I have thoroughly absorbed these writings, implanting them not only in my memory but in my marrow, and they have so become one with my mind that were I never to read them for the remainder of my life, they would cling to me, having taken root in the innermost recesses of my mind.'[13] Colin Burrow is unusual in proposing a category of 'inspired misremembering', argu-ing that 'misremembering and mislearning . . . can be as much a response . . . as careful imitation and artful echoes'. His focus is Shakespeare's classical learning ('the subject of Shakespeare's classical learning cannot be approached simply by

---

[11] Thomas and Tydeman, *Christopher Marlowe*, pp. 1–2; Robert S. Miola, *Shakespeare's Reading* (Oxford, 2000), pp. 13, 14, 169; Vaughan and Vaughan, eds., *The Tempest*, p. 148; A. B. Dawson, '"The Arithmetic of Memory": Shakespeare's The-atre and the National Past', in *Shakespeare Survey 52* (Cam-bridge, 1999), pp. 54–67; p. 54; Margaret Tudeau-Clayton, 'Wearing "wonder-wounded hearers": Shakespeare's eman-cipatory poetics', paper delivered at SAA, Toronto, 2013; Daniel C. Dennett, *Kinds of Minds: Toward an Understanding of Consciousness* (New York, 1996), p. 155; Maurice Char-ney, 'The Voice of Tamburlaine in Early Shakespeare', *Com-parative Drama*, 31 (1997), 213–23; p. 213; Marvin Carl-son, *The Haunted Stage: Theatre as Memory Machine* (Ann Arbor, MI, 2003), p. 11; M. C. Bradbrook, 'Shakespeare's Recollections of Marlowe', in Philip Edwards, Inga-Stina Ewbank and G. K. Hunter, eds., *Shakespeare's Styles: Essays in Honour of Kenneth Muir* (Cambridge, 1980), pp. 191–204; p. 203; John Pitcher, 'A Theatre of the Future: *The Aeneid* and *The Tempest*', *Essays in Criticism*, 34 (1984), 193–215; p. 199; Martin Wiggins, *Shakespeare and the Drama of his Time* (Oxford, 2000), p. 2; James R. Siemon, ed., *Richard III* (London, 2009), p. 28; Nicholas Brooke, 'Marlowe as Provocative Agent in Shakespeare's Early Plays', in *Shake-speare Survey 14* (Cambridge, 1961), pp. 34–44; p. 34; Paster, pp. 91, 92; Donna B. Hamilton, *Virgil and 'The Tempest': The Politics of Imitation* (Columbus, Ohio, 1990), p. 4; Janet Clare, *Shakespeare's Stage Traffic* (Cambridge, 2014), p. 2; '"Art to Enchant": *The Tempest*, Sources and Sorcery', paper given at ISA, Stratford, August 2014 (see below, pp. 109–17); Richard Dawkins, *The Selfish Gene* (Oxford, 1989), p. 192.

[12] Donna B. Hamilton, 'Defiguring Virgil in *The Tempest*', in *Critical Essays on Shakespeare's 'The Tempest'*, ed. Virginia Mason Vaughan and Alden T. Vaughan (New York, 1998), pp. 17–38; p. 17; Bate, *Shakespeare and Ovid*, p. 244.

[13] Francesco Petrarch, *Letters on Familiar Matters: Rerum famil-iarium libri XVII–XXIV*, trans. Aldo S. Bernardo (Baltimore and London, 1985), pp. 212–13.

the tabulation of sources'[14]) but his concept (and caveat) is applicable to source study generally.

In most cases of source study, however, the strength of any claim to have identified a potential source – its proof of concept – is based on the evident continued legibility of that source in the text. This in itself causes problems, as R. S. Miola notes in his discussion of verbal echoes: 'one scholar's echo, signalling indebtedness, is another scholar's coincidence, signifying nothing' (pp. 13–14). The concept of equivalence or closeness (parallel passages must be demonstrably parallel) was an inevitable premise of twentieth-century source study, influenced as it was, first by the quantifying predilections of early New Bibliography and then by the pattern-recognition skills of Bullough's wartime scholarship.

The governing idea that the source text should remain visible in the target text diverges in significant ways from early modern understandings of the way the writer should deploy his reading. Jonson's injunction in *Discoveries* appropriately combines a number of commonplaces to instruct the poet how 'to convert the substances or riches of another poet to his own use'. Jonson envisages *imitatio* as paradoxically a copy of, and a transformation of, the original. On the one hand, the poet is 'to make choice of one excellent man above the rest, and so to follow him till he grow very he'; on the other, he is 'to draw forth out of the best and choicest flowers, with the bee, and turn all into honey'.[15] Petrarch described this as the difference between reading 'hastily and quickly' so that 'these really belong to others, and I have them in my possession with the awareness that they are not my own', and the 'leisurely' reading such that 'I may forget whose they are and whether they are mine or others'.[16]

The most extensive description of this humanist paradox is in Johannes Sturm's 1549 *Nobilitas Liberata*, published in an English translation in 1570.[17] Sturm explains to his readers that 'imitation is not in things that be all one, but in things that be like, and that which is like, must be, not the same, but another thing'. The writer's technical and artistic skill is in 'hid[ing] and cover[ing] lyke thinges by unlike using and handling'.[18] An author's greatest

dependence on a source may obscure the visibility of that source. Prospero's description of his usurping brother is a perfect description of this process of *imitatio*: he 'new created / The creatures that were mine' (1.2.81–2).

Stuart Gillespie's entry on Marlowe in his *Shakespeare's Books* at times comes close to this early modern idea: he moves from identifying traditional Marlowe 'echoes' in *Midsummer Night's Dream* through the more distant Marlovian 'manner' in *Titus Andronicus* to the *Jew of Malta* being the source 'for the atmosphere, though not the plot' of the Jessica–Shylock relationship in *Merchant of Venice*. He argues that by 1599 (the date of *As You Like It*), 'Marlowe's presence is so spectral that it is not clear whether Shakespeare's audience is meant to register it'.[19] He then offers the generally agreed exception to this argument: *Dido Queen of Carthage*, where Aeneas's tale of the fall of Troy is retold by the Player in *Hamlet* (1601–02). Gillespie juxtaposes indistinct haunting with apparently clear citation. We want to develop and unite these notions. For us, *Dido Queen of Carthage* is not a *Hamlet*-specific citation but a text which haunts Shakespeare throughout his career. And he continues to engage with it as late as (and perhaps most subtly in) *The Tempest*.

In proposing *Dido Queen of Carthage* as a more thoroughgoing and systemic source for *The Tempest* than has previously been identified, we are trying also to investigate some of the assumptions of source study. We are also proposing a more agonistic relationship between Marlowe and Shakespeare

---

[14] Colin Burrow, 'Shakespeare and Humanist Culture', in *Shakespeare and the Classics*, ed. Charles Martindale and Tony B. Taylor (Cambridge, 2004), pp. 9–27; pp. 14, 15, 22.

[15] Ben Jonson, *Discoveries*, ed. Lorna Hutson, in *The Cambridge Edition of the Works of Ben Jonson*, ed. David Bevington, Martin Butler and Ian Donaldson, vol. 7 (Cambridge, 2012), pp. 582–3.

[16] Petrarch, *Letters*, pp. 212–13.

[17] See chapter 1 of Hamilton's *Virgil and 'The Tempest'* for an excellent analysis of this text.

[18] Sturm, sig. H1v; sig. G4r.

[19] Stuart Gillespie, *Shakespeare's Books: A Dictionary of Shakespeare's Sources* (London, 2001), pp. 324–5, 327.

than is traditionally promoted. Shakespeare's poetic engagement with Marlowe's legacy is a narrative told in different ways – as a story about the development of blank verse as a dramatic medium, for example, or as a competition at the level of parallel individual dramas such as *Edward II* and *Richard II*, or even, as Harold Bloom allows but then dismisses in the preface to the second edition of *The Anxiety of Influence*, a strong precursor.[20] Bloom's language of Shakespeare's 'triumph', 'emancipation' and 'exorcism' sees Shakespeare's 'struggle with poetic influence fully resolved' in the reference to the 'dead shepherd' of *As You Like It*.[21] All critics who write on Marlowe's influence on Shakespeare identify a point at which Shakespeare decisively becomes his own man. That point is sometimes seen as 1599 (*As You Like It*), sometimes identified as late as *The Tempest*.[22] In substituting *Dido* for *Faustus* as the dominant Marlowe Ur-text of *The Tempest*, we identify Shakespeare's relation to his brilliant rival as distinctly unresolved even at the end of his career, and we also suggest a different model of memory at work in source studies. This, then, is an article not about what Shakespeare read (or saw) but about how he remembered (and what he could not forget).

DIDO QUEEN OF CARTHAGE AND THE TEMPEST

Washed up on the island beach and spitefully anatomizing their situation, Antonio and Sebastian query Gonzalo's use of the phrase, 'Widow Dido':

Antonio. Widow? A pox o' that. How came that 'widow' in? Widow Dido!
Sebastian. What if he had said 'widower Aeneas' too?
                                    (2.1.82–4)

We are not the first to pause over this dialogue. Tony Tanner calls it 'pointless banter', Deanne Williams says it is 'curiously aimless' and Frank Kermode finds it unparalleled for 'irrelevance' in the entire Shakespeare canon.[23] Some critics take the allusion in very general terms: the passage is simply an instruction to 'remember the *Aeneid*', says Jan Kott.[24] For others the dismissive

helplessness of historical distance is all that can be proffered: 'The whole passage may well have held a meaning for Shakespeare's contemporaries that is lost to us', although Kermode conceded the possibility that 'an understanding of this passage will modify our image of the whole play'.[25]

Adrian follows Antonio and Sebastian's derisory interrogatives with a more reflective line that cues further discussion: '"Widow Dido", said you? You make me study of that' (2.1.86–7). We will try to answer our larger question, 'What is a source?', by moving from Shakespeare to Marlowe/Virgil and then to larger considerations of memory and influence.

The Dido passage in the *Tempest* gets twenty-five lines of discussion. That the passage is not incidental or irrelevant can be seen in the way its material is reinforced by repetition. Dido is stressed six times, and Carthage three times:

---

[20] The play-for-play approach is seen most obviously in Marjorie Garber, 'Marlovian Vision/Shakespearean Revision', *Research Opportunities in Renaissance Drama*, 22 (1979), 3–9; Robert A. Logan, *Shakespeare's Marlowe: The Influence of Christopher Marlowe on Shakespeare's Artistry* (Aldershot, 2007) and Gillespie, *Shakespeare's Books*, pp. 324–7.

[21] Harold Bloom, *The Anxiety of Influence: A Theory of Poetry*, 2nd edn (Oxford, 1997), pp. xliv, xliii, xliv. For James Shapiro, this moment when Shakespeare 'explicitly acknowledg[es] and identif[ies] a literary rival for the first and only time in a play or poem' represents Shakespeare's relegation of Marlowe to the past, his digestion of Marlowe's lyric poetry now being 'virtually complete' (*Rival Playwrights; Marlowe, Jonson, Shakespeare* (New York, 1991), pp. 102, 117).

[22] 'Marlowe may well have been on Shakespeare's mind in subsequent comedies and romances; but the pressure of his lyric and comic worlds was past by 1600' (Shapiro, *Rival Playwrights*, p. 117); 'It was not until his very last sole-authored play that Shakespeare came to final grips with *Dr Faustus*' (Jonathan Bate, *The Genius of Shakespeare* (London, 1997), p. 129).

[23] Tony Tanner, *Prefaces to Shakespeare* (Cambridge, MA, 2010), p. 804; Deanne Williams, 'Dido, Queen of England', *ELH*, 73 (2006), 31–59; p. 51; Frank Kermode, ed., *The Tempest* (London, 1956), pp. 46–7.

[24] Jan Kott, 'The Aeneid and The Tempest', *Arion*, n.s., 3 (1978), 424–51.

[25] Anne Barton, ed., *The Tempest* (Harmondsworth, 1968), p. 153; Kermode, ed., *The Tempest*, p. 47.

Adrian. She was of Carthage, not of Tunis.
Gonzalo. This Tunis, sir, was Carthage.
Adrian. Carthage?
Gonzalo. I assure you, Carthage. (2.1.87–90)

Shakespeare knew his Virgil and certainly he used Virgil in *The Tempest* – the disappearing feast removed by harpies comes from Book 3 of the *Aeneid* and when Ferdinand encounters Miranda in Act 1 he quotes Aeneas ('o dea certe', *Aeneid* 1.328; 'most sure the goddess', *Tempest* 1.2.423).[26] But there is also a dramatic source close to hand – as it happens, a dramatic version of Virgil: Marlowe's *Dido*. *The Tempest* has long been seen as a play without a major source: we want to investigate those repeated references as signposts to Marlowe's *Dido, Queen of Carthage*.

The lexical parallels are many, as are the dramatic parallels in situation. We'll begin, traditionally, with parallel passages, moving on to situational and dramatic echoes, although the three are often interlinked:

1. Venus reassures the distressed Aeneas:

> And for thy ships which thou supposest lost,
> Not one of them hath perisht in the storm.
> (*DQC*, 1.1.235–6)[27]

Prospero reassures the distressed Miranda that:

> there is no soul –
> No, not so much perdition as an hair
> Betid to any creature in the vessel
> Which thou heard'st cry, which thou sawst sink
> (*Tempest*, 1.2.29–32)

And Prospero is later given similar reassurance by Ariel:

> *Prospero.* But are they, Ariel, safe?
> *Ariel.* Not a hair perished. (*Tempest*, 1.2.217)

2. When the shipwrecked Trojans first enter in 1.1, Achates tries to cheer Aeneas:

> Doe thou but smile and clowdie heaven will cleare
> Whose night and day descendeth from thy browes.
> (*DQC*, 1.1.155–6)

At the identical point in *The Tempest* Gonzalo tries to cheer the bereaved King Alonso:

> It is foul weather in us all, good sir,
> When you are cloudy. (*Tempest*, 2.1.147–8)[28]

3. Here is Marlowe's Dido offering herself to Aeneas and holding back from him. Aeneas has asked her what she 'may desire / And not obtaine' (3.4.7–8). She replies:

> The thing that I will dye before I aske
> And yet desire to have before I dye.
> (*DQC*, 3.4.9–10)

Here is Miranda in *The Tempest*, simultaneously offering herself to Ferdinand, and holding back from him, torn between desire and modesty. She weeps, she says,

> At mine unworthiness, that dare not offer
> What I desire to give, and much less take
> What I shall die to want. (*Tempest*, 3.1.77–9)

The similarity of situation makes this a dubious parallel by New Bibliographical textual rules. But the situation is *very* specific in its similarity: both Miranda and Dido think they have fallen freely in love when each is in fact a plaything of a higher power – the classical gods or a Milanese magician. And consider the rhythm and the rhetoric: the antithesis is striking – not one but *two* antitheses. Shakespeare is learning

---

26 For further parallels with the *Aeneid* see Pitcher, 'A Theatre of the Future', 193–215; Hamilton, *Virgil and 'The Tempest'*, pp. 22–6; Vaughan and Vaughan, eds., *The Tempest*, pp. 56–8; David Lindley, ed., *The Tempest* (Cambridge, revised edition, 2013), appendix 2.

27 All references to *Dido, Queen of Carthage* are from Roma Gill, ed., *The Complete Works of Christopher Marlowe*, vol. 1 (Oxford, 1986).

28 Conceptual blending in which facially expressed emotions are linked to weather is not uncommon, as in *King John*: 'A fearful eye thou hast . . . / So foul a sky clears not without a storm; / Pour down thy weather: how goes all in France?' (4.2.106, 108–9). What is unusual in the examples from *Dido* and *Tempest* is the symbiosis: Aeneas's and Alonso's emotions affect their companions' emotional weather.

an acoustic, a strategy and a rhetorical strategy is a kind of source.[29]

4. The dramaturgical set ups in *Dido* and *The Tempest* are also the same. A group of shipwrecked travellers is split in two, each ignorant of the other's survival. When one group of Trojans first meets Aeneas, they recognize him only by his voice – but then discount that recognition:

> I heare *Aeneas* voyce, but see him not,
> For none of these can be our Generall.
> (*DQC*, 2.1.45–6)

In *The Tempest*, Trinculo encounters his companion Stephano, recognizing him by his voice and then discounting this recognition:

> I should know that voice. It should be – but he is
> drowned.   (*Tempest*, 2.2.87–8)[30]

From linguistic parallels to situational parallels:

5. In *Dido*, Cupid performs his sleight of hand with the arrow on Dido's breast/heart under instruction from Venus. It is entirely his own mischief that makes him do the same with the Nurse. In *The Tempest*, Ariel acts under instruction from the supernaturally powerful Prospero; it is entirely his own mischief that makes him impersonate Trinculo in 3.2.

6. Achates' attempt to cheer up Aeneas by extolling the virtues of the shore on which they have been shipwrecked (pleasant air and fertile soil; 1.1.178–9) is paralleled in Adrian and Gonzalo's positive comments about the island's air and green grass, 'advantageous to life' (2.1.37, 49, 52).

7. Aeneas's long narrative to Dido is a tale of loss, of exile from the city. So too is Prospero's to Miranda.

8. J. B. Steane calls the world of *Dido* a 'lotosland where men are spellbound as children and all are enticed into forgetfulness'.[31] Tony Tanner notes the same of the *Tempest*: 'the island is full of sleep, could itself be asleep and dreaming. A "strange drowsiness", "wondrous heavy"' (2.1.202–3) is everywhere. Many scenes end in sleep or trance. ('They fell together all . . . they

dropped as by a thunderstroke', 2.1.207–8), and by the end you feel the difference between waking and dreaming is terminally blurred.[32]

Steane, who anticipated us in several of the parallel passages we have noted, concluded that 'Shakespeare had a copy of *Dido* or knew it well, that the memory remained with him as late as *The Tempest*, and that few contemporary plays moved him more than this'.[33] We will come back to this play's influence on Shakespeare throughout his canon, but now we want to turn to Marlowe. We need first to recap the relationship between Marlowe's play and its Virgilian source. In part our argument suggests that *Dido* is so resonant for Shakespeare because it is itself so conscious of its source: it is a source about sources.[34]

Aeneas

All *Dido* critics agree that Marlowe's Aeneas is not Virgil's. He is weak, vacillating, mendacious, a poor father, neglectful of women, lacking in

---

[29] As William Empson knew: commenting on a parallelism in Shakespeare's Sonnet 58 ('Be where you list' // 'Do what you will'), he noted the way these lines have the rhythm of a sonnet by Philip Sidney and concluded that Shakespeare structured them 'after his model' in Sidney (*Seven Types of Ambiguity* (London, 1984), p. 86).

[30] It might be thought that this parallel is merely the similarity of situation, and that therefore any shipwreck play might produce a similar effect. But sampling Anon's *The Thracian Wonder*, Greene and Lodge's *A Looking Glass for London*, and Heywood's *The Captives* suggests that the echo in *The Tempest* is distinctive.

[31] J. B. Steane, *Marlowe: A Critical Study* (Cambridge, 1964), p. 39.

[32] Tanner, *Prefaces*, p. 810.

[33] Steane, *Marlowe*, p. 55.

[34] Current textual expertise finds no evidence to believe the 1594 quarto's identification of Nashe as Marlowe's co-author although Gary Taylor notes that Marlowe and Nashe are very hard to tell apart ('Imitation or Collaboration? The Early Shakespeare Canon', paper delivered at ISA, Stratford, August 2014). Clare Harraway notes the irony of the title page's dual ascription: it 'multiplies points of origination in a process which only serves to accentuate critical anxieties about indebtedness': *Re-Citing Marlowe* (Aldershot, 2000), p. 114.

any confident sense of Trojan identity or destiny. When Virgil's Dido meets him, Aeneas declares, 'I am Aeneas of Troy' ('adsum, / Troïus Aeneas'). Marlowe's Aeneas says, 'Sometime I was a Troian, mightie Queene, / But *Troy* is not, what shall I say I am?' (2.1.75–6). Virgil's Aeneas, despite his shipwreck, is glorious: 'godlike in face and shoulders: for his mother herself had shed upon her son the beauty of flowing locks, with youth's ruddy bloom, and on his eyes a joyous lustre; even as the beauty which the hand gives to ivory'.[35] Marlowe's Aeneas is so bedraggled that Ilioneus does not recognize him. Dido comments on his 'base robes' (2.1.79) and has to dress him up. In speech, Aeneas constantly stresses his abjectness and, as Don Cameron Allen notes, rivals Uriah Heep in his 'umbleness.[36] Dido repeatedly corrects him:

> Remember who thou art; *speake like thy selfe*:
> Humilitie belongs to common groomes.
>
> (2.1.100–1; our emphasis)

But Aeneas has no self to speak like. He is emptied out: not 'pious' Aeneas, not 'golden-tongued' Aeneas, not 'warlike' Aeneas.[37] In Act 4, Marlowe's Aeneas resolves to sail away, citing destiny; but what in Virgil is filial obedience, Marlowe presents as a 'slippery abdication of responsibility'.[38] Aeneas offers four unconvincing justifications in twenty lines: destiny calls him; Jove wills it; his mother wills it; the Fates bid (4.3.1–21). Marlowe turns Virgilian destiny into bathos.

These differences from Marlowe's source in Virgil are concentrated in 2.1 when Aeneas narrates the downfall of Troy. In Virgil this tale of destruction is not one of finality but of loss leading to a new beginning, a secular *felix culpa*; Creusa appears to Aeneas and tells him to move forward. The details of the destruction are few, and mostly summary. Whereas in Virgil Aeneas's suffering stems from the 'displaced Trojans' wandering', in Marlowe it is about the 'violence of Troy's downfall'.[39] Marlowe adds brutality, piling up gory detail upon gory detail. The details are unflinching: 'Yong infants swimming in their parents bloud, / Headles carkasses piled up in heapes,/

Virgins halfe dead dragged by their golden haire' (2.1.193–5); Pyrrhus 'tooke his fathers flagge,/ And dipt it in the old Kings chill cold bloud, / And then in triumph ran into the streetes, / Through which he could not passe for slaughtred men' (2.1.259–62).

In Carthage, Marlowe's Aeneas knows that this will not be an easy story for him or for his auditors. Dido initially asks Aeneas to speak simply so that she may resolve two competing accounts:

> For many tales goe of that Cities fall,
> And scarcely doe agree upon one poynt.
>
> (DQC, 2.1.108–9)

Aeneas warns her that she has requested 'a woefull tale' – merely the 'memory' of Troy's destruction makes him faint. Dido's response is intriguing:

> What, faints *Aeneas* to remember *Troy*,
> In whose defence he fought so valiantly?
>
> (2.1.114, 117–18)

To paraphrase her lines: 'In Virgil you were triumphant. Remember that.' She is collating the man who speaks to her with his Virgilian source. She does this again at the end of Aeneas's speech, when she, Anna and Iarbas ask further factual questions. 'What became of aged Hecuba?' asks Anna.

---

35 Virgil, *The Aeneid* I–VI, trans. H. Rushton Fairclough, rev. G. P. Goold (Cambridge, MA, 1916, rev. 1999), 1.595–6, pp. 302–03.

36 Don Cameron Allen, 'Marlowe's Dido and the Tradition', in *Essays on Shakespeare and Elizabethan Drama in Honor of Hardin Craig*, ed. Richard Hosley (London, 1963), pp. 55–68; p. 166.

37 Asked who the stranger is, Ilioneus identifies him as 'warlike Aeneas' but Dido refutes this description: 'Warlike Aeneas and in these base robes!' (2.1.79). (Deanne Williams accepts Ilioneus' description; see Williams, 'Dido, Queen of England', p. 46.)

38 Williams, 'Dido, Queen of England', p. 47.

39 Timothy D. Crowley, 'Arms and the Boy: Marlowe's Aeneas and the Parody of Imitation in *Dido, Queen of Carthage*', *English Literary Renaissance*, 38 (2008), 408–38; p. 416. Marlowe was not yet eight years old when Huguenot refugees from the St Bartholomew's Day massacre flooded into Canterbury.

'How got Aeneas to the fleet again?' asks Iarbas. 'But how scapt *Helen*, she that causde this war?' asks Dido (2.1.290–2).[40]

Aeneas's omission of Helen is notable given the prominence accorded her in his account in Virgil. Aeneas catches sight of Helen, flattened against the wall inside the temple of Vesta. She is terrified. Aeneas wants revenge on Helen for the destruction of his city and, in a long internal dialogue, he debates whether there is glory in attacking a woman. He concludes that in this case, yes, there is, because it is punishment for her wickedness. Killing her will prevent her returning in triumph to Greece. He is not only angry with Helen but aware of his anger. Venus then appears to him to check his wrath. In another long passage she explains the need to control his fury, to focus on the future, and she says the gods are to blame not Helen. Helen is a lengthy focal point in Virgil.

The questions posed by Marlowe's Dido and Anna are logical – or perhaps illogical – given that Aeneas has not mentioned Helen or Hecuba. Once again, Dido is reminding Aeneas of his source: 'get back to Virgil; give us Book 2'. This, of course, has been Dido's expectation from the moment she saw Aeneas – that he would be Virgil's Aeneas, and that the narrative he will tell is the one we know from the *Aeneid*.

That this was never going to happen is obvious from Aeneas's arrival in Carthage. He is frozen: in grief, in retrospection, unable to move on emotionally from Troy. He compares himself with Niobe, not only a model of grief but a model of stasis: a statue. Without Troy and its king, Aeneas is nothing: 'when I know it is not [Priam], then I die'. Memory of Troy, triggered by the walls of Carthage, is 'not cathartic but traumatic'.[41] He fantasizes not about returning to Troy and avenging himself on the Greeks but about *Priam* doing this. Aeneas is washed up in more ways than one. When Achates reminds him that Priam is dead (and 'Troy is sackt' adds Aeneas), Aeneas responds with the classic statement of survivor guilt: 'And why should poore *Aeneas* be alive?' (2.1.33–4).

It is the moment of horror when his city is destroyed and its citizens butchered that he replays in his tale to Dido. This is not the narrative she has requested – a narrative of factual clarification; it is not the narrative Virgil gives us, in which destruction is the beginning of *translatio imperii*.

What is a source?

As we have seen, Dido's conscious recollection of the source and the play's self-conscious assessment of its divergences from its Virgilian model make it hard to avoid a discussion of how sources function in the play. Critics are divided about how closely Marlowe follows the *Aeneid*. Clifford Leech writes that Marlowe 'follows Virgil with at times schoolboy slavishness', while T. M. Pearce judges that one third of the lines are carried over from Virgil, and Roma Gill's Oxford edition includes the play in the volume on 'Translations'; in contrast, J. B. Steane says that 'not more than one-seventh or one-eighth of the play follows Virgil with any closeness'.[42] A similar dispute characterizes the identification of Marlowe's presence in the Player's speech in *Hamlet*, where critics populate a spectrum between 'Marlovian' and 'non-Marlovian'. Harold Jenkins says that the Player's speech 'seems to echo [*Dido*] at one or perhaps two points, though I think not more'. H. J. Oliver believes that 'Shakespeare is not only quoting Marlowe but half-affectionately pushing over the verge of absurdity what is only trembling on the brink of it'. James Shapiro thinks Shakespeare stylistically indebted to Marlowe throughout: he 'creates the

---

40 In Virgil Dido does not interject. Instead Aeneas anticipates the one question she might want to ask: 'Perhaps, too, you may inquire what was Priam's fate' ('Forsitan et, Priami fuerint quae fata, requiras' (2.505; pp. 350–1).

41 Efterpi Mitsi, '"What is this but stone?" Priam's statue in Marlowe's *Dido, Queen of Carthage*', *Word and Image*, 27 (2011), 443–9; p. 444.

42 Clifford Leech, 'Marlowe's Humor' in Richard Hosley, ed., *Essays on Shakespeare and Elizabethan Drama in Honor of Hardin Craig* (London, 1963), pp. 69–81; p. 72; T. M. Pearce, 'Evidence for Dating Marlowe's Tragedy of Dido', in J. W. Bennett, Oscar Cargill and Vernon Hall, eds., *Studies in the English Renaissance Drama* (New York, 1959), pp. 231–47, p. 232; J. B. Steane, *Marlowe*, p. 52.

"feel" of a Marlovian speech', exaggerating its stylistic features 'in order to recreate its effects'.[43]

None of the available models of source study seems quite to work. What we are proposing sees *Dido*'s relation to *The Tempest* in terms taken not from traditional source studies but from the discourses of trauma studies via Freud and Mary Jacobus on the one hand, and from hauntology, via Marvin Carlson and Derrida on the other. Both hauntology and trauma studies allow for the unconscious or unbidden irruption of past texts into the present.

Trauma

Trauma and the operations of memory are key to the construction of both plays. *Dido Queen of Carthage* is structured around the trauma of Aeneas's 'wofull tale', 'whose memorie like pale deaths stony mace / Beates forth my senses from this troubled soule' (2.1.114–16); a similarly lengthy recollection and reconstruction of the traumatic exile from Milan shapes the opening act of *The Tempest*. Both Marlowe's Aeneas and Shakespeare's Prospero experience trauma through forms of disrupted memory – flashback, narrative, haunting – and both their plays offer multiple narratives, parodies, echoes and inset art objects we might want to understand collectively as a post-traumatic aesthetic. It's tempting – and not unrewarding – to tick off Aeneas's or Prospero's characterization in their plays against the checklist in the American Psychiatric Association's *Diagnostic and Statistical Manual of Mental Disorders* for post-traumatic stress disorder – 'recurrent, involuntary, and intrusive distressing memories', 'feelings of detachment or estrangement from others', 'irritable behavior and angry outbursts', 'hypervigilance', 'problems with concentration', 'markedly diminished interest or participation in significant activities', and 'persistent, distorted cognitions about the cause or consequences of the traumatic events that lead the individual to blame him/herself or others'.[44]

Critics who have used modern psychological theories of trauma to think about the literature of this period have tended to focus on characters' psychology – such as, for example, Deborah Willis's important essay on *Titus Andronicus*.[45] But in bringing trauma towards source study, the concept is useful not as an attribute of characters but as one of plays: it is located textually, rather than psychologically. We want to understand the relationship between the plays as that between trauma and its later manifestations, and to propose this somatic and psychological model as a new kind of source study. Perhaps we can understand the imaginative hold of *Dido* across Shakespeare's writing career in terms of a trauma response – we can recast *Dido* as what trauma theory understands as a 'stressor' rather than a 'source', and then look for its transformed, repressed, unbidden traces in *The Tempest*. As Aeneas recalls and reconstructs the experience of Troy, or as Prospero fashions the narrative of his overthrow, so *The Tempest* refers to, is occupied by, and attempts to process, the trauma

---

[43] Harold Jenkins, ed., *Hamlet* (London, 1982), p. 479; H. J. Oliver, ed., *Dido, Queen of Carthage* and *The Massacre at Paris* (London, 1974), pp. 32–3; Shapiro, *Rival Playwrights*, pp. 129, 132.

[44] American Psychiatric Association, *Diagnostic and Statistical Manual of Mental Disorders: Fifth Edition DSM-5* (Arlington, VA, 2013), pp. 271–2.

[45] Deborah Willis, 'The Gnawing Vulture: Revenge, Trauma Theory, and *Titus Andronicus*', *Shakespeare Quarterly*, 53 (2002), 21–52. See also Matthew Martin, 'Translatio and Trauma: *Oedipus*, *Hamlet* and Marlowe's *Dido, Queen of Carthage*', *LIT: Literature Interpretation Theory*, 23 (2012), 305–25. Richard Martin identifies Aeneas's trauma without articulating it as such: 'Aeneas reacts with *uncharacteristic sensitivity* to his own imaginative recreation of the horrors of war', in 'Fate, Seneca and Marlowe's *Dido, Queen of Carthage*', *Renaissance Drama*, 11 (1980), 45–66; p. 59, our emphasis. Reviewers of the Globe production of *Dido* (2003) identified Aeneas as traumatized: '[Will] Keen's Aeneas...suggests repressed trauma in his riveting, hushed account of Greek atrocities' (Kate Bassett, *Independent*, 24 June 2003); 'a man traumatised by his memories of Carthage' (Charles Spencer, *Telegraph*, 24 June 2003); 'Aeneas...suffers a crisis of identity brought on by trauma, not love' (Michael Caines, *TLS*, 15 August 2003). The Arden 3 editors of *The Tempest* note that Prospero 'wrecks [his enemies'] ship (an ironic recompense for their sending him to sea in a leaky vessel), then traumatizes them' (p. 146). The editors' parenthesis underplays the quid pro quo trauma.

of Marlowe's doomed brilliance. We have thought a lot about survivor guilt as a possible psychological paradigm for the late plays, thinking of a Shakespeare in his late forties facing his own retirement and looking back as the last of the generation of writers who shaped his early career – Kyd (died 1594), Greene (died 1592), Peele (died 1596), Nashe (died c.1601), Chettle (dead by 1607) and, most of all, of his exact contemporary Marlowe: he is now surrounded by younger writers (Fletcher, born 1579; Middleton, born 1580; Jonson, born 1572).[46]

Thus the source for *The Tempest* is the alternately receding and intrusive memory of, or even the trauma of, Marlowe's *Dido* – rather than *Dido* itself. Memory here is less the photocopy function of having, say, North's translation of Plutarch's *Lives* open on the table while writing *Antony and Cleopatra*, or of Brooke being a 'direct source' for *Romeo and Juliet*. Instead it shares the qualities psychologists attach to traumatic memory: intrusive, detailed, multi-sensory recollections of the stressor; disturbed or partial recall, often unbidden; false or fictive associated memories with a similar affect. The consequence of that redefinition means that the conclusive evidence for the source is not its instant or accurate visibility within the text but rather its distorted and fragmentary emanation.

In fact, we might note, not entirely in passing, that Troy itself plays a significant role in Freudian theories of memory. Freud was fascinated both by the *Aeneid* and by Heinrich Schliemann's discovery of the ruins of Troy in 1870, and drew on his hero's achievement in his frequent adversion to archaeological metaphors for the unconscious. In a letter to Fliess, Freud likened the psychoanalytic process to 'the technique of excavating a buried city', and elsewhere he exulted in a successful analytic breakthrough recovering childhood memories in 'a persistent patient' with 'It is as if Schliemann had once more excavated Troy, which had hitherto been deemed a fable.'[47] A young acquaintance's inability to quote Dido's 'famous' line 'Exoriar(e) aliquis nostris ex ossibus ultor' is understood by Freud as a psychic disturbance due to the

anxiety that his girlfriend might be pregnant. The example helps Freud to the questions of forgetting, substitution and memory function that preoccupy him in *The Psychopathology of Everyday Life*.[48] Freud takes a quotation from the *Aeneid* as the epigraph to *The Interpretation of Dreams*, and in the essay 'Screen Memories' he isolates Aeneas's speech to his fellow Trojan exiles: 'Forsan et haec olim meminisse iuvabit' ('Perhaps even this distress it will some day be a joy to recall', 2.203, pp. 276–7) 'as an eloquent affirmation of what he hoped would be the eventual successes of the "talking cure".'[49]

For Elizabeth Jane Bellamy, Aeneas's recollection of Troy in the *Aeneid* is foundational in establishing epic as the 'literary genre most concerned with remembering'.[50] And certainly references to Troy in early modern England often collocate it with remembering: Sidney's *Apology* urges 'Only let Aeneas be worn in the tablet of your memory'; Anthony Munday's mayoral pageant *Triumphs of Re-United Britannia* (1605) has Brute building '*New Troy*, in memorie/ Of whence I came'; Thomas Heywood asks 'what pen of note, in one page or other hath not remembered Troy?'.[51] Hamlet prompts the Players to that Marlovian remembrance of 'Aeneas' tale to Dido' with 'if it live in your memory, begin at this line' (2.2.451–2). The long speeches in *Dido, Queen of Carthage* are

---

[46] Late Shakespeare seems preoccupied with some of those lost contemporaries: the return to Greene as the source for *The Winter's Tale*, for instance.

[47] J. Moussaieff Masson, ed., *The Complete Letters of Sigmund Freud to Wilhelm Fliess, 1887–1904* (Cambridge, MA, 1985), letter dated 21 December 1899, pp. 391–2.

[48] Sigmund Freud, *The Psychopathology of Everyday Life*, trans. Anthea Bell (London, 2002), pp. 12–16.

[49] Elizabeth Jane Bellamy, *Translations of Power: Narcissism and the Unconscious in Epic History* (Ithaca, NY, 1992), p. 55. See also Ellen Oliensis, 'Freud's *Aeneid*', *Vergilius*, 47 (2001), pp. 39–63.

[50] Bellamy, *Translations of Power*, p. 52.

[51] Katherine Duncan-Jones and Jan van Dorsten, eds., *Miscellaneous Prose of Sir Philip Sidney* (Oxford, 1973), p. 98; Anthony Munday, *The Triumphs of Re-United Britannia* (London, 1605), sig. B3; Thomas Heywood, *The Iron Age* (London, 1632), sig. A2r-v.

indeed a feat of memory for the Aeneas actor. But *The Tempest*, too, is preoccupied by memory – almost every character is enjoined to 'remember', as the island takes on an aspect of recollection in which geographic and historic distance – the dark backward and abysm of time – are conflated.[52] As Miranda half-remembers her own childhood: ''Tis far off / And rather like a dream than an assurance / That my remembrance warrants', 1.2.44–6). She, like the play's other characters, is being prompted to remember something that happened long before the play began. For the story of *The Tempest* that something is Prospero's exile from Milan. For the work *The Tempest*, that something is Marlowe's *Dido, Queen of Carthage*.

Hauntology

Although trauma describes Aeneas' state – and perhaps Prospero's too – the word may be too negative for the relationship between the plays and the dramatist-survivor. It is not meant this way. We employ the term in the way trauma theorists do to refer simply to memories of 'an originary event', where the 'something that has already happened acquires meaning after the fact'. As Freud writes, trauma simply describes 'any excitations from outside which are powerful enough to break through the protective shield'.[53] It is a commonplace to acknowledge that Marlowe's plays were, to the young Shakespeare at least, powerful 'excitations from outside'. The notion of breached boundaries is developed helpfully, in a different vein, by Derrida who explores memory through the trope of ghosts and haunting – what he names 'hauntology'. Colin Davis glosses Derrida's felicitous coinage in ways that are suggestive for our concern here with the absent presence of the source: 'Hauntology supplants its near-homonyn ontology, replacing the priority of being and presence with the figure of the ghost as that which is neither present nor absent, neither dead nor alive.'[54]

We have already noted the prominence of spectral imagery in critical works on *Dido* and *The Tempest*. Stuart Gillespie talks of Marlowe's spectral presence in Shakespeare; John Pitcher identifies Virgil as a spectral presence in *The Tempest*.[55] Derrida helps us see why this image is so relevant: 'A masterpiece always moves in the manner of a ghost.' It becomes a thing, 'that thing, the Thing that, like an elusive specter, engineers a habitation without proper inhabiting, call it a *haunting*, of both memory and translation'. Memories do not recognize borders, 'by definition, they pass though walls, these revenants, day and night, they trick consciousness and skip generations'.[56] Derrida could be paraphrasing Sturm on how hidden sources work in *imitatio*, and his words certainly characterize *The Tempest*'s relation to *Dido* and *Dido*'s relation to *The Tempest*. So too does Derrida's recurrent interrogative refrain: 'Hath this thing appeared again tonight?'

In thinking of memory as a ghost, we may note the insightful verb Shakespeare uses for Old Hamlet's spectre. It 'appears'; it is not summoned. Derrida's spectral concept of memory does not operate as it does for the speaker of Sonnet 30: 'When to the sessions of sweet silent thought / I *summon* up remembrance of things past' (our emphasis). Ghosts

---

52 Tony Tanner notes that the verb to 'remember' is used more often in *The Tempest* than in any other Shakespeare play (p. 809). Evelyn Tribble examines the play's tensions between different forms of memory ('"The Dark Backward and Abysm of Time": *The Tempest* and Memory', *College Literature*, 33 (2006), 151–68. In the Globe production of 2013 characters regularly forgot key details and had to be prompted (e.g. Ariel forgot where Sycorax was born).

53 Dawson, 'Arithmetic', p. 54; Mary Jacobus, *Border Crossings: Traumatic Reading and Holocaust Memory* (Oxford, 1999), pp. 124, 131. Critics describe the Reformation as causing a national trauma; see Patrick Collinson, *From Iconoclasm to Iconophobia: the Cultural Impact of the Second English Reformation*, Stenton Lecture (Reading, 1986); Anthony Dawson, '"Priamus is Dead": Memorial Repetition in Marlowe and Shakespeare', in Peter Holland, ed., *Shakespeare, Memory and Performance* (Cambridge, 2006), pp. 63–86.

54 Jacques Derrida, *Specters of Marx*, trans. Peggy Kamuf (New York, 1994), p. 10. Colin Davis, 'État Présent: Hauntology, Spectres and Phantoms', *French Studies*, 59 (2005), 373–9; p. 373.

55 Gillespie, *Shakespeare's Books*, p. 327; Pitcher, 'A Theatre of the Future', p. 197.

56 Derrida, *Specters of Marx*, pp. 18, 30.

do not respond to commands; the source-spectre *Dido* comes unbidden and unexpectedly.

When Hamlet decides to 'follow' the ghost, Derrida asks, 'What does it mean to follow a ghost? And what if this came down to being followed by it, always, persecuted perhaps by the very chase we are leading?' His question about circularity, about cause and effect, introduces a specular 'anachrony' as he explains that 'This Thing meanwhile looks at us and sees us not see it even when it is there.'[57] But in terms of source study it also introduces a temporal anachrony (something we are familiar with from post-structuralism). This anachrony, this 'spectral asymmetry' as Derrida calls it, is particularly relevant to the struggle that Marlowe's and Shakespeare's plays stage with their precursor texts.

Exploring *The Tempest*'s intertextual moments, Barbara Mowat introduces us to the idea of 'infracontext'. Texts and associations intrude on the audience's/reader's awareness, creating (in Claes Schaar's phrasing) a 'vertical context system': recognition is the moment when 'surface contexts, operating as a signal, trigger a memory of the infracontext'.[58] The beauty of this schema, as Mowat realizes, is its anachrony. It shifts the focus from the source-reading author (and from the source-hunting critic) to the source-recognizing reader. It also allows multiple and even contradictory infracontexts to coexist (thus obviating Hamilton's initial anxiety with a *Tempest* that 'does not match' its putative source in the *Aeneid* or Bate's difficulty in making 'the pattern fit'). Infracontexts do not require a pattern. Like ghosts, they come and go.[59] 'Enter the ghost, exit the ghost, re-enter the ghost.'[60]

For Marvin Carlson all drama is about ghosts (as the title of his book, *The Haunted Stage* indicates) because drama is about memory. Every aspect of theatre is about reappearance: known actors in new roles, new actors in known roles, the redeployment of props, the retelling of familiar stories, the recycling of audiences who carry in 'their collective memory the awareness that drives the theatre experience'. Carlson gives author, text, production, actor and audience equal weight in

the ghosting process, although his discussions of author and audience are of particular relevance to our argument. Ibsen gives Carlson his theme: 'all plays might be called *Ghosts*'; 'ghosting presents the identical thing they have encountered before, although now in a somewhat different context'.[61] An audience watching *The Tempest* in 1611 would have been very aware of this.

Although John Pitcher felt, pessimistically, in 1984 that Virgil's exclusion from Bullough meant that the *Aeneid* would never enter the mainstream as a source for *The Tempest*, that has not proved to be the case. Jonathan Bate says of Gonzalo's 'widow Dido' allusion that 'Shakespeare [is] vigorously waving a flag marked *Aeneid*' and Donna Hamilton's book-length study has waved the flag even more vigorously.[62] The *Aeneid* is the version of the Dido story with which modern readers are most familiar – Marlowe's play still tends to be dismissed as juvenilia, notwithstanding Martin Wiggins' compelling revisionist argument about dating[63] – and so the stress on rehabilitating Virgil as context is understandable. But as we will illustrate in the next section, *Dido* is omnipresent in the Shakespeare canon. Part of *The Tempest*'s complex infracontextual multiplicity is its haunting by not one but two classical predecessors.[64]

---

[57] Derrida, *Specters of Marx*, pp. 10, 6.

[58] Barbara A. Mowat, '"Knowing I loved my books": Reading *The Tempest* Intertextually', in Peter Hulme and William H. Sherman, eds., '*The Tempest' and its Travels* (London, 2000), pp. 27–36; p. 28.

[59] Deanne Williams notes that Prospero's arrival on the island makes him an Aeneas figure, but in giving fresh garments to shipwrecked sailors he is a Dido ('Dido, Queen of England', p. 53). Hamilton finds types of Aeneas in almost all the male characters in the play (p. 26).

[60] Derrida, *Specters of Marx*, p. xx.

[61] Carlson, *The Haunted Stage*, pp. 48, 1, 7.

[62] Pitcher, p. 199; Bate, p. 243. Even so, editors do not quite know what to do with *The Aeneid*. The Vaughans devote two pages to Virgil in a section on 'classical models' (pp. 56–8) whereas David Lindley's New Cambridge edition has an appendix of 'parallel passages from Virgil and Ovid' (Cambridge, revised edn, 2013), appendix 2.

[63] Martin Wiggins, 'When did Marlowe write *Dido Queen of Carthage*?', *Review of English Studies*, 59 (2008), 521–41.

[64] Mowat, '"Knowing I loved my books"', p. 30.

DIDO AND SHAKESPEARE

Let us explore *Dido, Queen of Carthage* across Shakespeare's career. *Dido*'s own self-conscious relation to its source makes it a particularly apt play to attach itself to Shakespeare's imagination. The ongoing influence of *Dido* is not simply a matter of occasional recall or deployment: this is the play Shakespeare could not forget. Its fingerprints are everywhere, and once we acknowledge that ubiquity, new direct allusions become visible and audible. It can be heard in *Julius Caesar* when Portia sends Lucius to the Forum with a message, telling him, '*Stay not to answer me, but get thee gone*' (2.4.2). Dido, similarly anxious, says the same to Anna when she sends her to the waterside at 4.4.3: '*Stay not to answer me*; run, Anna, run'. The half-line command that the plays have in common might seem innocuously formulaic; the fact is, it appears nowhere in early modern drama before 1611/1623 except in these two plays.[65] In *Richard III* Queen Margaret laments that she will die 'neither mother, wife, nor England's queen' (1.3.206). In *Dido*, King Priam laments that he dies 'neither father, lord, nor king' (2.1.237). In *As You Like It*, Phoebe conceals the onset of her love for Ganymede by telling Silvius that 'I love him not, nor hate him not' (3.5.128). In the early stages of love, Dido tells Aeneas cryptically, 'I love thee not – / And yet I hate thee not' (*DQC*, 3.1.171–2). In *Comedy of Errors*, when Adriana asks her inattentive husband if she has lost her beauty, contrasting his previous devotion with his current neglect, her lines parallel Dido's to Aeneas:

Dido.   The time hath been
When Dido's beauty chain'd thine eye to her.
Am I less fair than when thou sawest me first?
O then Aeneas 'tis for grief of thee!
                              (*DQC*, 5.1.113–16)

Adriana. The time was once when thou unurged
        wouldst vow
That never words were music to thine ear,
That never object pleasing in thine eye . . .
Unless I spake, or looked.
                    (*Comedy of Errors*, 2.2.116–18, 121)

And compare with

Hath homely age th'alluring beauty took
From my poor cheek? Then he hath wasted it.
                    (*Comedy of Errors*, 2.1.88–9)[66]

In *Antony and Cleopatra* Cleopatra vacillates, hesitates to speak her emotions, and forgets what she wanted to say:

Sir, you and I must part; but that's not it.
Sir, you and I have loved; but there's not it;
That you know well. Something it is I would –
O, my oblivion is a very Antony,
And I am all forgotten.
                    (*Antony and Cleopatra*, 1.3.88–92)

In *Dido*, Dido vacillates, hesitates to speak her emotions, and forgets what she wanted to say:

And yet Ile speake, and yet Ile hold my peace,
Doe shame her worst, I will disclose my griefe:
Aeneas, thou art he, what did I say?
Something it was that now I have forgot.
                    (*DQC*, 3.4.27–30)

Meredith Skura detects the influence of *Dido* on *A Midsummer Night's Dream*, finding it responsible for tone, plot and character: a 'mockery of love's dotage' with 'puppet-like' characters chasing each other in a chain. She also detects verbal parallels: between Titania's bower and Venus's and Dido's bowers, between Dido's and Hermia's serpents and between the two play's magical enchantments where Venus's plans for the sleeping Ascanius ('asleep', 'purple hyacinth', 'milk-white', 'dote') cue Oberon's 'milk-white', 'purple', 'sleeping', 'dote' (*Dream*, 2.1.167–71).[67]

(Non-)coincidences like these mean that when the Shakespeare canon refers to Dido, one has to suspect a source in Marlowe as much as a source

---

[65] *Dido* reuses the line (reversing it: 'Run *Anna*, run, stay not to answere me') at 5.1.210.

[66] See Dorothea Kehler, 'Shakespeare's Recollection of Marlowe's *Dido, Queen of Carthage*: Two Notes', *American Notes and Queries*, 14 (2010), 5–10.

[67] Skura, p. 82. For further parallels see Williams, 'Dido, Queen of England', pp. 49–50.

in Virgil. The *Dido* references begin at the start of Shakespeare's career. In *Titus Andronicus*, Lucius is invited to speak

> as erst our ancestor
> When with his solemn tongue he did discourse
> The lovesick Dido's sad-attending ear
> The story of that baleful-burning night
> When subtle Greeks surprised King Priam's Troy.
>
> (*Titus Andronicus*, 5.3.79–83)

Earlier in the play Tamora invites Aaron to après-hunt erotics:

> And after conflict such as was supposed
> The wand'ring prince and Dido once enjoyed
> When with a happy storm they were surprised,
> And curtained with a counsel-keeping cave,
> We may, each wreathèd in the other's arms,
> Our pastimes done, possess a golden slumber...
>
> (2.3.21–6)

In *2 Henry VI* Margaret similarly woos Suffolk with a *Dido* reference, one that fits more with the antics of Marlowe's Ascanius than with Virgil's:

> How often have I tempted Suffolk's tongue –
>
> . . .
>
> To sit and witch me, as Ascanius did,
> When he to madding Dido would unfold
> His father's act, commenced in burning Troy!
>
> (*2 Henry VI*, 3.2.114–18)

In *The Taming of the Shrew* Lucentio's servant and *confidant*, Tranio, is as dear to him 'As Anna to the Queen of Carthage was' (1.1.152). In *A Midsummer Night's Dream* Hermia swears by 'that fire which burned the Carthage queen / When the false Trojan under sail was seen' (1.1.173–4). All the above references are concentrated in a narrow window in the late 1580s/early 1590s, suggesting the immediate influence of *Dido*. But they continue less overtly.

When Henry V threatens the citizens of Harfleur, his envisaged atrocities include old men's heads dashed against walls, babies spitted on pikes, virgins desecrated (3.3.84–126). *Henry V* is usually seen as Shakespeare's attempt to write a *Tamburlaine* play. In fact, these violent details correspond to

Aeneas's memories of the fall of Troy. When the bloody captain struggles to capture Macbeth's cold savagery he too echoes the play. Aeneas's description of the murder of Priam – 'Then from the navell to the throat at once, / He ript old *Priam*' (2.1.255–6) – produces both Macbeth's rebel 'unseamed... from the nave to the chops' (1.2.22) and Macduff from his mother's womb 'untimely ripped' (5.10.16). When in Act 5 of *Coriolanus* the characters discuss Coriolanus's imminent revenge on Rome, they repeatedly envisage the city as burning: Coriolanus's eye is 'red as 'twould burn Rome' (5.2.64); this memorable image is supported by four more references to Rome on fire. The characters' obsession with the city burning is notable since there is no mention of it in Shakespeare's source in Plutarch – perhaps because Plutarch is not Shakespeare's source at this point, but *Dido, Queen of Carthage*. The references are not just a Shakespeare addition to the account in Plutarch but a *Marlowe–Shakespeare* addition: Aeneas's description of the sack of Troy makes seven references to the city on fire. When Shakespeare thought of the worst thing he could imagine, he remembered Marlowe's *Dido*.

We mentioned above Phoebe's riddling line to Silvius in *As You Like It* as echoing Dido's cryptic comment to Aeneas. Just before this moment, Phoebe quotes Marlowe directly when, having fallen in love with Ganymede, she apostrophizes Marlowe:

> Dead shepherd, now I find thy saw of might:
> 'Who ever loved that loved not at first sight?'
>
> (*As You Like It*, 3.5.82–3)

James Shapiro cites *As You Like It* in support of his argument that Shakespeare's response to Marlowe is defined by its belatedness, six years after Marlowe's death. In fact, as we have tried to show, Shakespeare's engagement with Marlowe begins early and runs late. And it is an engagement that specifically centres on *Dido*.

Richard Martin says that *Dido* 'is not a work of major literary significance. It did not spark the kind of popular imitations that *Tamburlaine* and *Edward II* did.'[68] It is not clear whether these two statements are causally connected – that imitations prove the significance of a work. Of course, as we noted at the start of this article, imitations can occlude their origins. But the constant, covert presence of *Dido* throughout the Shakespeare canon suggests that Shakespeare saw this play as having major literary significance.[69] James Shapiro is not being fanciful in supposing that Shakespeare, like Hamlet, singled out *Dido*: 'one speech in it I chiefly loved, 'twas Aeneas' tale to Dido' (*Hamlet*, 2.2.448–9).[70]

CONCLUSION

In *The Genius of Shakespeare*, Jonathan Bate writes that Marlowe is the only contemporary whom Shakespeare 'overtly alludes to rather than subliminally absorbs';[71] we think he does both. And when J. B. Steane compared Aeneas's Troy speech in Marlowe with its source in Virgil, he concluded that this 'is the work of a man who has made his Virgil so thoroughly and imaginatively his own that his version of the story is *virtually independent of its source*'.[72] That is exactly the relationship we are positing between *The Tempest* and *Dido*. Antony Dawson makes a similar point about *The Tempest* and the *Aeneid*: 'I don't see Shakespeare wrestling with Virgil but rather inhabiting him.'[73] We would substitute Marlowe for Virgil.

Steane and Dawson have stumbled upon Sturm's definition of source in which the most significant source may be the most thoroughly assimilated, most subliminally absorbed – and therefore the most invisible. But Shakespeare does not want this source to be invisible: invisibility defeats the point of *imitatio*. Sturm advises writers both to advertise and conceal their source – since the former enables the reader to admire the latter. Discussing Virgil's use of Theocritus, Sturm recommends his method: 'he woulde have it knowne whom he imitateth, although he would not have it spyed, how and after what sort he doth it'.[74] Donna Hamilton explains the pleasure this experience of cognitive *fort–da* affords: the reader has 'the pleasure . . . in discovering the artistry that the concealment itself promoted'.[75] Marvin Carlson

makes the same point when he discusses drama's recycling of material: 'it encourages audiences to compare varying versions of the same story, leading them to pay closer attention to how the story is told and less to the story itself'.[76] 'Widow Dido' brings the source explicitly into the play so that *The Tempest*, like Marlowe's *Dido, Queen of Carthage* can explore the thematic nexus between past and present, remembering and forgetting – between originary moments and their aftermath.

Coda

We might add, by way of coda, that locating Prospero's island prompts almost as much critical ink as identifying the play's source. The play teases us with New World references – the still-vexed Bermudas, Miranda's 'brave new world', Caliban's anagrammatic name and his Patagonian god, Setebos, Prospero's enslavement of the native,

---

[68] Martin, 'Fate, Seneca and Marlowe's *Dido*', p. 46.

[69] Recent stage history, including productions at the Globe (dir. Tim Carroll, 2003), the site-specific Angels in the Architecture production in St Barnaby's Soho and Kensington Palace (dir. Rebecca McCutcheon, 2007, 2008), the National Theatre (dir. James MacDonald, 2009), and Edward's Boys (dir. Perry Mills, 2014) also belies Martin's conclusion that Dido is a 'bookish play, better read than viewed' (p. 66). It is not clear whether Shakespeare saw or read the play (or both). On its title page the Quarto, published in 1594, assigns the play to the Children of her Majesty's Chapel, for whom there is no record of London performance between 1584 and 1600.

[70] Shapiro, *Rival Playwrights*, p. 131.

[71] Jonathan Bate, *The Genius of Shakespeare* (London, 2008), p. 104.

[72] Steane, *Marlowe*, p. 41 (our emphasis).

[73] Dawson, 'Priamus', p. 82.

[74] Sturm, sig.H1v. A modern work in a different medium – film – illustrates this point: *The Imaginarium of Dr Parnassus* (2009, dir. Terry Gilliam) is subtly indebted to *The Tempest*.

[75] Hamilton, *Virgil and The Tempest*, p. 16.

[76] Carlson, p. 27. Jackson Cope locates this phenomenon locally when he analyses *Dido*'s fondness for triple effects, for dramaturgical repetition with variation: it requires the audience to react to 'doubleness', to hold 'simultaneous consciousness of actor and role, story world and stage world' (Jackson I. Cope, 'Marlowe's *Dido* and the Titillating Children', *ELR*, 4 (1974), 315–25; p. 321).

Trinculo's plan to exploit him by exhibition.[77] But it is also markedly Mediterranean – Tunis, Carthage, Algerian Sycorax, Italians en route to Milan and Naples.

Several critics observe that the wedding from which the Italians are returning took place in North Africa. Claribel was married in Tunis, giving us (in a gendered reverse), the happy ending that Virgil and Marlowe decline to provide.[78] We want to develop these points: we think *The Tempest* takes place on the way back from *Dido,* *Queen of Carthage.* There has just been a romantic rendezvous in North Africa and the men are on their way to Italy. In other words, the play's geography is suspended between a source and a destination. *The Tempest* thus lives in a place 'full of noises' (3.2.138), the very space of Shakespeare's imitative and haunted invention.

---

[77] See Bate, *Genius of Shakespeare*, pp. 242–3).

[78] Dawson, 'Priamus', p. 72; Williams, 'Dido, Queen of England', p. 51.

IMITATION OR COLLABORATION? MARLOWE AND THE EARLY SHAKESPEARE CANON

GARY TAYLOR AND JOHN V. NANCE

Shakespeare imitated other playwrights. Shakespeare also collaborated with other playwrights. But how do we know which is which? Does Shakespeare imitating Marlowe differ, in demonstrable ways, from Shakespeare collaborating with Marlowe?

Shakespeare and Marlowe cohabited in an artistic culture dominated by *imitatio, translatio* and *aemulatio*.[1] Bart van Es therefore begins *Shakespeare in Company* with a chapter titled 'Imitation and Identity'. He concludes that 'Shakespeare's early drama is often spectacularly imitative, and as a result his personal voice is much less distinct'. In an early modern culture of 'normative imitation', van Es warns us, 'the voices of men such as Marlowe, Greene, Kyd, and Peele merge, almost imperceptibly, with [Shakespeare's] own style'. To make matters worse, 'Shakespeare's working conditions in the early 1590s were very similar, and in many cases identical, to those of his fellow dramatists.'[2] In the Elizabethan commercial theatre, imitation intertwined with collaborative authorship. There is now almost universal agreement, among respected specialists in attribution, that at least three of Shakespeare's early plays were collaborations: *Titus Andronicus, 1 Henry VI* and *Edward III*. And a growing body of evidence, of independent kinds, supports the historical consensus that Shakespeare also co-wrote *2 Henry VI* and *3 Henry VI* (and also *Arden of Faversham*).[3]

Although mainstream Shakespeare scholarship now accepts the evidence for his Jacobean collaborations, consensus about the early canon has been harder to achieve. Michael Hattaway's rejection of

the evidence for Nashe's presence in *1 Henry VI* is typical: 'I *do not believe* that stylistic analysis is sufficient to prove or disprove authorship, as *it is likely* that at an early stage in his career Shakespeare was moving freely between the various verse registers that were being deployed in the plays in which

---

We are grateful to Hugh Craig, Gabriel Egan, MacDonald P. Jackson, John Jowett, Rory Loughnane and the audience at the 2014 International Shakespeare Conference for their helpful criticisms of an earlier version of this essay.

[1] Thomas Greene's *The Light in Troy: Imitation and Discovery in Renaissance Poetry* (New Haven, 1982) remains the classic articulation of this aesthetic. For more recent treatment of these themes, see Janet Clare, *Shakespeare's Stage Traffic: Imitation, Borrowing and Competition in Renaissance Theatre* (Cambridge, 2014), pp. 1–28; A. E. B Coldiron, 'Cultural Amphibians', *Yearbook of Comparative and General Literature*, 51 (2003–4), 45–58, and *Printers without Borders: Translation and Textuality in the Renaissance* (Cambridge, 2015); Vernon Guy Dickson, *Emulation on the Shakespearean Stage* (Farnham, 2013).

[2] Bart van Es, *Shakespeare in Company* (Oxford, 2013), pp. 36, 37, 55.

[3] For overviews see Hugh Craig, 'Authorship', in *The Oxford Handbook of Shakespeare*, ed. Arthur F. Kinney (Oxford, 2012), pp. 23–30; Gary Taylor, 'Why Did Shakespeare Collaborate?', in *Shakespeare Survey 67* (Cambridge, 2014), pp. 1–17; MacDonald P. Jackson, *Determining the Shakespeare Canon* (Oxford, 2014); Marina Tarlinskaja, *Shakespeare and the Versification of English Drama, 1561–1642* (Farnham, 2014). Although not everyone agrees with all these conclusions, it would be unwise to base any argument about Shakespeare on writing that is now widely doubted; therefore, when we refer to the early Shakespeare canon we include from these six plays *only* the scenes most confidently and widely accepted as his. Moreover, although we accept that Shakespeare wrote six scenes in *Arden*, none of our conclusions depend on *Arden*.

he was *probably* acting' (our italics).[4] Hattaway here makes a statement of personal belief, supported by claims about probability, but he gives no empirical evidence for those alleged probabilities.[5] More generally, he asserts that an imitation cannot be distinguished from the original.

We may, or may not, be able, in particular cases, to separate identity from imitation empirically. But we can certainly distinguish them conceptually. Identity is cellular and systemic. Imitation is selective and semiotic.

Identity is cellular, because the physical mechanisms that create biological identity are located in small, cellular or sub-cellular structures. Obviously that is true of DNA, and we are sometimes told that forensic stylometry reveals 'the DNA of an author'. But that's not a particularly happy, or useful, metaphor. It makes authorship sound biologically predetermined. In fact, as John Frow reminds us, 'bodies are never just bodies' and personal identities emerge from a complex assemblage that include *habitus*, social networks and temporal experience.[6] Authorial identity in particular is a non-genetic option, constructed by creating new sentences in a local, historically specific language. Shakespeare's plays and poems were constructed by the higher-level cognitive functions of the neural network behind his famously domed forehead. No doubt Shakespeare's genius owes something to his inherited DNA, which bequeathed him that forehead and its large frontal lobe capacity. But our inherited genome gives human brains extraordinary plasticity, especially in the earliest years of development, a plasticity that makes it possible for us to construct new neural connections in response to our encounters with specific physical and social environments, to learn languages and to develop a personal style.[7]

Identity is systemic, because it depends not upon any single isolated cell, or any collection of identical cells, but upon the interaction of complex systems of differentiated cells. Languages, as Saussure taught us, are systemic; social identities, as Bourdieu taught us, depend upon mechanisms of distinction within systemic fields of potential action.[8] DNA is systemic; so is the human neural net.

Just as every species is composed of related but genetically distinct individuals, so every language is composed of related but distinct idiolects. And idiolects, as the founder of sociolinguistics William Labov taught us, belong to social groups shaped by shifting generational, geographical and educational frames.[9] For that reason, the British sociolinguist Jonathan Hope and the Australian computational stylistician Hugh Craig, using different methods, could each statistically distinguish rural Midlands Shakespeare, born in 1564, from urban college-educated Middleton, born in 1580.[10]

---

[4] Hattaway, ed., *The First Part of King Henry VI*, New Cambridge Shakespeare (Cambridge, 1990), pp. 42–3. For a more recent reiteration of such claims, see Warren Chernaik, 'Shakespeare as Co-Author: The Case of *1 Henry VI*', *Medieval and Renaissance Drama in England*, 27 (2014), 192–220.

[5] For the logical weakness of such loose appeals to probability, see Gary Taylor, 'Sleight of Mind: Cognitive Illusions and Shakespearian Desire', in *The Creation and Re-creation of Cardenio: Performing Shakespeare, Transforming Cervantes*, ed. Gary Taylor and Terri Bourus (New York, 2013), pp. 125–68.

[6] Frow, *Character and Person* (Oxford, 2014), p. 285.

[7] We are not neuroscientists, but these observations are uncontroversial. See *Journal of Neurolinguistics* (1985–); particularly relevant to the humanist grammar school is Jubin Abutalebi and David Green, 'Bilingual language production: the neurocognition of language representation and control', *Journal of Neurolinguistics*, 20 (May 2007), 242–75. For early foundations, see Christopher Shaw and Jill McEachern, eds., *Toward a Theory of Neuroplasticity* (London, 2001); more recently, relevant samples of the literature include Katherine Woollett and Eleanor A. Maguire, 'Acquiring "the Knowledge" of London's Layout Drives Structural Brain Changes', *Current Biology*, 21 (2011), 2109–14, and Daniel J. Miller *et al.*, 'Prolonged Myelination in Human Neocortical Evolution', *Proceedings of the National Academy of Sciences*, 109 (2012), 16480–5.

[8] Ferdinand de Saussure, *Course in General Linguistics*, trans. Roy Harris (La Salle, 1983); Pierre Bourdieu, *Distinction: A Social Critique of the Judgment of Taste*, trans. Richard Nice (Cambridge, MA, 1984), and *The Field of Cultural Production* (New York, 1993).

[9] William Labov, *The Social Stratification of English in New York City* (Washington, DC, 1966); *Sociolinguistic Patterns* (Philadelphia, 1972); *Principles of Linguistic Change*, 2 vols. (Oxford, 1994–2001).

[10] Hope, *The Authorship of Shakespeare's Plays* (Cambridge, 1994), and 'Middletonian Stylistics', in *The Oxford Handbook of Thomas Middleton*, ed. Gary Taylor and Trish Thomas

Unlike identity, imitation is selective and semi-otic. Imitation is selective because we cannot (and early moderns certainly could not) identify and replicate all the fine-grained cellular detail of the huge complex changing system of any individual linguistic identity. When Shakespeare wanted to imitate, on stage, the speech of an Irishman, Welsh-man or Scot, he represented it with just a few selec-tive deviations from normative English grammar and pronunciation.[11] Imitation is semiotic because it depends on pattern recognition: the writer must first recognize a pattern in another person's lexical or gestural language and then replicate that pattern to ensure that we also recognize those selected fea-tures as the sign of a particular identity.

The most famous imitation of Shakespeare is the engraved portrait on the title page of the 1623 edition of his *Comedies, Histories, & Tragedies*. Imi-tation is selective and semiotic, and 'This Figure that thou here seest put' is not Shakespeare, but instead a deficient substitute that stands (as Ben Jonson's caption-poem explicitly recognized) 'for' Shakespeare. Within the limits of a particular text technology and a particular artisan's talent, the Droeshout engraving figuratively represents what were presumably, in 1623, just a few recognizable and socially meaningful features of Shakespeare's physical identity at a particular moment in the fifty-two years of his life. Like innumerable other Shake-speare logos and trademarks, the minimalist David Hockney drawing reproduced on the cover of New Cambridge Shakespeare editions is another imita-tion, representing even fewer Shakespeare features, but recognizable because of the historical ubiquity of that 1623 imitation.

Imitation is an aesthetic, empathic activity that produces an aesthetic, affective object. By contrast, identity is an evolving assemblage best represented by an analytical object. (This binary can, of course, be deconstructed, but for two-handed, two-eyed, two-frontal-lobed organisms like ourselves it is a useful tool.) Like an Excel document, identity is cellular and systemic. Because there may be more potential synaptic connections between neurons in the average human brain than there are elementary particles in the universe, we cannot produce an Excel document large enough to represent Shake-speare's brain.[12] But we can offer a miniature illus-trative fragment (in Table 1).

This identity-profile consists of a system of cells; in this case, the cells record, vertically, a decision-tree, a sequence of overlapping linguis-tic choices: the first and second word of a pas-sage, then the second and third word, then the string of those first three words together. In the full Excel document, we continue this process through 173 successive words, recording every sequence and every close collocation.[13] (Why 173 words? We'll explain that shortly.) Each of those overlap-ping and interconnected verbal decisions is then mapped, horizontally, against a larger linguistic sys-tem, in this case the sociolect of 80 surviving play-texts written between the building of the Theatre in 1576 and the formation of the Chamberlain's Men in mid-1594.[14] These rows of data map the

---

Henley (Oxford, 2012), pp. 443–72; Craig, 'Authorial Attribution and Computation Stylistics: If You Can Tell Authors Apart, Have You Learned Anything about Them?', *Literary and Linguistic Computing*, 14 (1999), 103–13, and Hugh Craig and Arthur F. Kinney, *Shakespeare, Computers, and the Mystery of Authorship* (Cambridge, 2009).

[11] Jonathan Hope, *Shakespeare and Language: Reason, Eloquence and Artifice in the Renaissance* (London, 2010), pp. 98–137.

[12] V. S. Ramachandran *et al.*, *Phantoms in the Brain: Probing the Mysteries of the Human Mind* (New York, 1998), p. 8.

[13] For a fuller account of this procedure, see Gary Taylor, 'Empirical Middleton: Macbeth, Adaptation, and Micro-attribution', in *Shakespeare Quarterly*, 65 (2014), 239–72. Here, an 'x' in column 2 indicates that the collocation is unique, not appearing anywhere else in the set of early plays (and thus not providing any links that might help establish authorship); in column 3, 'x' indicates that the collocation is too common to provide reliable evidence of authorship. In all the remaining columns (and here we provide only a small sample) 'x' indicates that the collocation appears in that particular play.

[14] Our list of 80 texts is smaller than the list generated by the Literature Online (LION) database (accessed from 1 July to 7 November 2014). From its 113 plays for those years (inclusive), we eliminated fourteen. *Sir Thomas More, Two Lamentable Tragedies, Thracian Wonder, Alarum for Lon-don, Caesar and Pompey, Thorny Abbey, Edward IV Part One* and *Edward IV Part Two, Guy Earl of Warwick, Grim the Col-lier of Croydon* and Greville's *Mustapha* are given later dates by Martin Wiggins and Catherine Richardson in *British Drama 1533–1642: A Catalogue*, vols. 2–4 (Oxford, 2012–14).

Table 1 Cellular Shakespeare (sample fragment) 153 cells tracing collocations in ten successive words in *Titus Andronicus*

	None	>5	R3	TGV	Malta	Old Wives Tale	Selimus	Sapho	Cyrus
within the	o	x	o	o	o	o	o	o	o
within the compass	o	x	o	o	o	o	o	o	o
within the compass of my curse	o	o	x	o	o	o	o	o	o
the compass	o	x	o	o	o	o	o	o	o
the compass of	o	x	o	o	o	o	o	o	o
compass of	o	x	o	o	o	o	o	o	o
compass of my	o	o	o	o	o	o	o	x	x
of my	o	x	o	o	o	o	o	o	o
of my curse	x	o	o	o	o	o	o	o	o
my curse	o	o	o	o	o	o	x	o	o
my curse wherein	x	o	o	o	o	o	o	o	o
curse wherein	x	o	o	o	o	o	o	o	o
curse wherein I	x	o	o	o	o	o	o	o	o
the day . . . wherein I	o	o	o	x	o	x	o	o	o
the day . . . where I [verb] not	o	o	o	x	o	o	o	o	o
wherein I	o	x	o	o	o	o	o	o	o
wherein I [verb] not	o	o	o	o	x	o	o	o	o

frequency and distribution of all the verbal combinations recorded in the first column. The full Excel document for those 173 words contains 377 rows and 80 columns, or 30,160 individual cells. Compared to a full-length play, 173 words is a small sample of text; but by comparison to other scholarly data-sets for attributing plays, this Excel document is massive (far too large to reproduce here). A classic stylistic binary like 'feminine endings', for instance, would each produce only 42 cells for the 21 verse lines of this sample text.

Our conceptual distinction between identity and imitation has been verified in case studies using computational analysis of large data samples. John Burrows and Hugh Craig have shown that Romantic imitations of Renaissance drama are easily distinguished from their models, because they select and exaggerate a few features of the earlier plays, and imitations by one Romantic writer can also be distinguished from imitations by another Romantic writer.[15] Burrows has also shown that Fielding's *Shamela* can be statistically distinguished from Richardson's *Pamela*, even though Fielding selects and replicates various features of Richardson's style, in a way that distinguishes *Shamela* from the rest of Fielding's novels.[16] Even without such data, scholars recognize that *The Jew of Malta* is reflected in *The Merchant of Venice*, that *Edward II* inspired *Richard II*, that *Dido* haunted *The Tempest*;[17] but only conspiracy theorists imagine that Marlowe wrote or co-wrote those three plays in the Shakespeare folio.

In addition, we eliminated three academic translations of Euripides, Seneca and Plautus. Another nineteen of LION's texts were Shakespeare plays that we dated later than mid-1594 (*Comedy of Errors, Love's Labour's Lost, Romeo and Juliet, King John*), or were duplicates of Shakespeare plays, which either supply the same information, or are deeply disputed (the so-called 'bad' quartos).

15 J. F. Burrows and D. H. Craig, 'Lyrical Drama and the Turgid Mountebanks: Styles of Dialog in Romantic and Renaissance Tragedy', *Computers and the Humanities*, 28 (1994), 63–86.

16 Burrows, 'Who Wrote *Shamela*? Verifying the Authorship of a Parodic Text', *Literary and Linguistic Computing*, 20 (2005), 437–50.

17 See the article by Laurie Maguire and Emma Smith in this volume.

But methods that work for whole plays, or whole novels, will not necessarily help us with smaller samples.[18] Thomas Dekker testified in a lawsuit that he wrote 'one act' of a play, but also 'one speech' in another act.[19] Scenes were certainly discrete units of performance and of composition. So too were long speeches. Shakespeare wrote a twenty-one line soliloquy retrospectively inserted (Addition 3) at the beginning of Scene 8 of *Sir Thomas More*. Sometimes a scene, or French scene, consists of a single speech. Prologues, epilogues, songs and letters or poems read aloud on stage were often physically separated from the rest of the playbook, and sometimes written by a different author.[20] Our only early anecdote about Shakespeare 'when he was a boy' is John Aubrey's claim that 'when he kill'd a Calfe he would doe it in a high style, and make a Speech'.[21] Robert Y. Turner and W. C. Clemen both traced the evolution of different types of 'long speech' or 'oration' from *Gorboduc* to the early 1590s.[22] A long speech represents, on stage, a single voice, and for a poet a long verse speech is, in effect, its own poem. For the actor, too, long speeches represent a distinct acting problem, and Shakespeare's are still widely used as audition pieces.

TITUS ANDRONICUS, 5.1.124−44

To test whether we can distinguish actual Shakespeare from Shakespeare imitating someone else, in a single speech, it seems reasonable, perhaps inevitable, to begin with Marlowe. In an influential article in *Shakespeare Survey* in 1961, Nicholas Brooke began by declaring, 'There are a number of eruptions in Shakespeare's work of passages which are unmistakably Marlovian in tone and attitude, to a degree which would almost justify a disintegrator in identifying them as Marlowe's work.'[23] One of his examples is Aaron's defiant speech beginning 'Ay, that I had not done a thousand more' (5.1.124−44).[24]

Brooke described this as Shakespeare's 'full imitation of Barabas's catalogue of evil' in *The Jew of Malta*. That connection was first noticed in 1773 by Isaac Reed, and endorsed by many editors in the

intervening two centuries. In 1980 M. C. Bradbrook called Aaron's speech 'Shakespeare's most direct borrowing from *The Jew of Malta*'. In 1991 James Shapiro analysed it as a particularly striking example of Shakespeare's 'assimilative imitation' of Marlowe; in 1995 Jonathan Bate's influential Arden edition included Barabas's speech in an appendix as an important source for *Titus*. Bart van Es cited it again in 2013.[25] This speech (173 words long) should provide a perfect specimen − chosen by a long line of other critics, not us − to test

---

18 For attribution of smaller samples, see John V. Nance, 'Shakespeare, Theobald, and the Prose Problem in *Double Falsehood*', in *Creation and Re-Creation*, ed. Taylor and Bourus, pp. 109−24, and Gary Taylor, 'A History of *The History of Cardenio*', in *The Quest for Cardenio: Shakespeare, Fletcher, Cervantes and the Lost Play*, ed. Gary Taylor and David Carnegie (Oxford, 2012), pp. 11−61. However, Theobald's imitations of Shakespeare are separated from the originals by more than a century; it is not self-evident that a writer imitating his contemporaries would be so easy to distinguish from his model.

19 Charles Sisson, '*Keep the Widow Waking*: A Lost Play by Thomas Dekker', *Library*, 4 (1927), 39−57.

20 See Tiffany Stern, *Documents of Performance in Early Modern England* (Cambridge, 2009).

21 Aubrey, *Brief Lives*, ed. John Buchanan-Brown (London, 2000), p. 289.

22 Clemen, *English Tragedy Before Shakespeare: The Development of Dramatic Speech*, trans. T. S. Dorsch (London, 1961); Turner, *Shakespeare's Apprenticeship* (Chicago, 1974); Clemen, 'Some aspects of style in the Henry VI plays,' in *Shakespeare's Styles: Essays in Honour of Kenneth Muir*, ed. Philip Edwards, Inga-Stina Ewbank and G. K. Hunter (Cambridge, 1980), pp. 9−24.

23 Brooke, 'Marlowe as Provocative Agent in Shakespeare's Early Plays', *Shakespeare Survey 14* (Cambridge, 1961), pp. 34−44, p. 34.

24 Although we cite Shakespeare's *Complete Works* (Oxford, 2005), our data, for him and other playwrights, has all been checked against the original documents, using Literature Online and EEBO 'variant spelling' functions.

25 Leo Kirschbaum, 'Some Light on *The Jew of Malta*', *Modern Language Quarterly*, 7 (1946), 53−6; John Dover Wilson, ed., *Titus Andronicus* (Cambridge, 1948), p. lxii; Bradbrook, 'Shakespeare's recollections of Marlowe', in *Shakespeare's Styles*, p. 193; Shapiro, *Rival Playwrights: Marlowe, Jonson, Shakespeare* (New York, 1991), pp. 120−1; *Titus Andronicus*, ed. Jonathan Bate, New Arden Shakespeare (London, 1995), pp. 286−7; van Es, *Shakespeare in Company*, p. 34.

whether we can in fact distinguish imitation from identity.

There are a number of different ways to analyse the cellular lexical data provided by Aaron's speech.[26] First, using existing public databases – Literature Online and Early English Books Online Text Creation Partnership (EEBO-TCP) supplemented by Oxford Scholarly Editions Online – we checked every word sequence and collocation in the passage against all extant plays dated 1576–1594, and identified those that occur in only one other early play.[27] As we would expect, some of the results look like random scatter: of the eighty early playbooks in this set, twenty-two different plays, by at least ten named playwrights, contain at least one unique collocation.[28] Obviously, a single parallel is meaningless.[29] Four playwrights – Greene, Kyd, Lyly and Marlowe – can boast three unique dramatic parallels; obviously, all four men did not write this one speech, so we can deduce that two or three parallels are, here at least, no more significant than one.[30] By contrast, Shakespeare's early plays contain eight of the twenty-eight unique parallels to this passage (29%), more than double any other playwright.[31]

We then tried a second test on the same data: ignoring authorship completely, we simply identified the individual early plays with the most parallels. The anonymous *Troublesome Reign* has two, as do Greene's *Selimus*, Kyd's *Spanish Tragedy* and Shakespeare's *Two Gentlemen of Verona*. Again, this test confirms that two unique links are not enough. The only plays with more than two are Marlowe's *Jew of Malta* and Shakespeare's *Richard III*, each with three. Shakespeare here shares the top spot with the playwright (and the play) he was imitating. Shakespeare also wrote the only play in this list that is not a tragedy; genre cannot explain the strong connection with *Two Gentlemen*. Shakespeare is also the only playwright with more than one play in this list of works with more than one unique parallel. The greater spread of the Shakespeare parallels may be one useful way to distinguish identity from imitation. Imitation is selective; identity is systemic. Shakespeare here is selectively imitating one play, and one character, by Marlowe, but Shakespeare's own identity links the passage more comprehensively to his early verbal neural net: this single

[26] In this and subsequent tests, we exclude parallels between the speech under consideration (here, *Titus* 5.1) and the speech it is alleged to be imitating (here, *Jew of Malta* 2.3). That is, we are looking for evidence of authorship (identity) outside the two passages that literary critics have seen as proof of imitation.

[27] In order to improve accuracy, we did each search twice – once by Taylor, once by Nance (separately, without consulting Taylor's data) – and then checked one set of results against the other. Searches conducted June–November 2014.

[28] By 'unique' we mean that it appears only once elsewhere in the database. Our searches included variant grammatical forms, and we also did proximity searches for content words (nouns, verbs, adjectives, adverbs) near one another. If there was an exact match for a string of two or more words, we did not count near-matches (different grammatical forms, or different word order). In the absence of an exact match, we counted unique matches of variant forms: singular for plural (and vice versa), and different verb tenses. However, we discounted parallels that involved too many variations (different number plus different tense, combined with different word order, for instance).

[29] Single unique parallels come from: Anonymous, *Knack to Know a Knave* (barns and); Daniel, *Cleopatra* (did not some); Hughes *et al.*, *Misfortunes of Arthur* (a thousand . . . things); Lodge, *Wounds* (trees have); Peele, *Arraignment* (men's cattle). Nashe may also have one parallel, depending on his share of *Dido* (on the barks of trees). Robert Wilson has two: *3 Ladies* (in Roman letters) and *3 Lords* (day and yet). Two also appear in the anonymous *Troublesome Reign*, which some scholars attribute to Peele.

[30] GREENE: *Selimus* (as kill . . . man / would kill a), *Orlando* (trees . . . carved). KYD: *Spanish Tragedy* (quench them with / their dear friends), *Soliman* (between two friends). LYLY: *Bombie* (a maid or), *Campaspe* (skin as), *Endymion* (come within the compass of). MARLOWE: *Malta* (I curse the day / set . . . enmity . . . deadly enmity). If we knew who wrote which bits of *Dido*, Marlowe might have four parallels; but that would still leave him with only half as many as Shakespeare.

[31] *Richard III* (within the compass of my curse / dead . . . their graves / I have done a), *TGV* (a thousand more / the day . . . wherein I [verb] not), *2 Henry VI* 3.3 (set . . . upright), *3 Henry VI* 1.3 (I digged up . . . graves), *Edward III* sc. 2 (2.1) (ten thousand more). The eight wholly or partly Shakespearian plays we include – based on the chronology of the 2005 *Complete Works*, and also on the online chronology of the forthcoming third edition of the Norton Shakespeare (New York, 2015) – are the three *Henry VI* plays, *Richard III*, *Edward III*, *Titus Andronicus*, *Two Gentlemen* and *Taming of the Shrew*.

speech of 173 words contains unique parallels to six of his early plays.

The three serious contenders here are Shakespeare (who wrote most of *Titus Andronicus*), Marlowe (whose work this passage imitates) and Peele, who is now widely recognized as author of at least the first scene of *Titus*.[32] We therefore ran a third test: limiting ourselves to Shakespeare, Marlowe and Peele, we searched their poetry as well as their plays, still checking their uniqueness against the larger corpus of early plays.[33] Shakespeare's poetry here is confined to the early *Venus and Adonis* and *Rape of Lucrece*. By this reckoning, Peele remains with just one unique parallel; Marlowe has lost one in *Malta*, but gained one in his translation of *Lucan*, leaving him still with three (or four if we count *Dido*). But Shakespeare now has eleven unique parallels: having lost one in *Richard III*, he gains one in *Venus* and three in *Lucrece*.

Titus 5.1.124–44	Early Shakespeare	Marlowe
Unique Parallels (Plays): total	8	3
Highest # per play	3 (+2)	3
Plays & Poems: total	11	3

In all three tests, however we categorized or counted the data, the result was the same: the language of Marlowe does indeed haunt this speech, but Shakespeare consistently comes out on top. We can, here, empirically distinguish identity from imitation.

THE JEW OF MALTA, 2.3.176–99

But before we get too confident about these results, they should be checked against another control set. We ran the same three tests on the passage that Shakespeare was imitating in *Titus*: the speech by Barabas in *The Jew of Malta*, beginning 'As for myself, I walk abroad a-nights'.[34] The full Marlowe speech is longer, so we limit ourselves to its first 173 words, the same number as the Shakespeare/Aaron speech. By ensuring that the sample sizes are the same, we guarantee that the results can be easily and reliably compared.

The language of the *Malta* speech contains only eighteen unique parallels to the eighty extant playbooks written between 1576 and 1594. Some of these are the usual random scatter.[35] In our first test, three playwrights have more than two unique parallels: Lyly and Shakespeare (each with three), and Marlowe (with four).[36] Marlowe's is the smallest of those three dramatic canons, so his higher total is notable. In the second test, only one single-author play contains more than one unique parallel: Marlowe's *Jew of Malta*, with two.[37] The third test (expanding the database to include the poems of Marlowe, Peele and Shakespeare) added only one more link: to Marlowe's *Elegies*

---

32 For a useful summary of the evidence for Peele's authorship of the first scene, see Brian Vickers, *Shakespeare, Co-Author: A Historical Study of Five Collaborative Plays* (Oxford, 2002), pp. 148–243. But see also William W. Weber, 'Shakespeare After all? The Authorship of *Titus Andronicus* 4.1 Reconsidered', in *Shakespeare Survey 67* (Cambridge, 2014), pp. 69–84, which demonstrates that Vickers misleadingly combines good evidence for Peele in the first scene with bad evidence in 4.1. The first scene of the 1594 Quarto includes what the Folio, and most later editions, separate and label 2.1.

33 Adding the poetry from these three writers changes the totals for unique parallels, not only because it adds some new parallels that do not appear anywhere in the drama of 1576–1594, but also because some of the parallels that were unique in the plays are no longer unique when the poems are added to the searches.

34 Christopher Marlowe, *The Jew of Malta*, ed. N. W. Bawcutt, Revels Plays (Manchester, 1978). The earliest extant text, the 1633 quarto, may reflect late editing or adaptation by Dekker: see David Lake, 'Three Seventeenth-Century Revisions: *Thomas of Woodstock*, *The Jew of Malta*, and *Faustus B*', Notes and Queries, 228 (1983), 133–43.

35 In addition to those in the next note: Greene's *Orlando* (content to lose) and *James IV* (thieves I am), Greene and Lodge's *Looking Glass* (every moon), Wapull's *Tide* (and always kept), the anonymous *Arden* Sc. 1 (along . . . my door), *1 Henry VI* 2.3 (in my gallery) and *Troublesome Reign* (priests with).

36 MARLOWE: *Malta* (see 'em / and poison [verb]), *Faustus* (that I may walking), *2 Tamburlaine* (began to practice). LYLY: *Midas* (groaning under), *Endymion* (now and then to), *Sapho* (first upon). SHAKESPEARE: *2 Henry VI* 3.2 (sick . . . groaning), *Titus* 2.3 (and enemy), *Richard III* (my stratagems).

37 There are also two in *2 Henry VI*, but the second (with extorting) is in 4.7, apparently not by Shakespeare – and attributed to Marlowe by Craig and Kinney (*Mystery of Authorship*, pp. 68–77).

(being young, I studied). Marlowe thus has at least five unique parallels to these 173 words – and probably six (if Hugh Craig is correct in attributing to him the Cade scenes of *2 Henry VI*).

Malta 2.3.176–99	Early Shakespeare	Marlowe
Unique Parallels (Plays): total	3	4
Highest # per play	1	2
Plays & Poems: total	3	5

Just as all three tests identified Shakespeare as the author of Aaron's speech in 5.1 of *Titus*, so all three tests here identify Marlowe as the author of Barabas's speech in 2.3 of *The Jew of Malta*. In both cases, authorial imitation is distinct from authorial identity.

TITUS ANDRONICUS, 2.1.1–25

But this single binary comparison, of one Marlowe speech with one Shakespeare speech, is a small sample on which to base a larger theory about the contrast between identity and imitation in early English commercial plays. So we tried another example from the same character in the same Shakespeare play: Aaron's first speech, beginning 'Now climbeth Tamora Olympus' top'. Like Aaron's long speech in 5.1, his first speech has been cited and analysed by many critics as an example of Shakespeare imitating Marlowe: Brooke, Bradbrook, Shapiro and van Es, again, but also Maurice Charney and Robert A. Logan.[38] Everyone seems to agree that this speech contains traces of Marlowe's style. But, ironically, in another part of the critical forest, attribution scholarship has become increasingly confident that Shakespeare was *not* the author or imitator here. Dover Wilson, Hugh Craig, Arthur Kinney, MacDonald P. Jackson, Marina Tarlinskaya, Brian Vickers and Gary Taylor all agree that George Peele wrote the beginning of *Titus Andronicus*, including this speech and the entire scene in which it occurs.[39] Jonathan Bate's 1995 Arden edition insisted that Shakespeare wrote the whole play; but by 2007 even Bate had

accepted the overwhelming evidence for Peele's co-authorship.[40]

So both these speeches by Aaron contain recognizable traces or signs of Marlowe, but the two imitations were apparently written by two different playwrights. That consensus is supported by the lexical, cellular, systemic evidence. Once again, as always, there is a scatter of random data.[41] But only three playwrights have more than two parallels: Lyly (with three), Marlowe (with nine) and Peele (with eleven).[42] Even though Marlowe unquestionably haunts this speech, as he haunted Aaron's speech in Act 5, he is again not the dominant figure in the data. Only three plays contain more than two unique parallels: Marlowe's *Faustus* and Peele's

---

[38] Charney, 'The Voice of Marlowe's Tamburlaine in Early Shakespeare', *Comparative Drama*, 31 (1997), 214; Logan, *Shakespeare's Marlowe: The Influence of Christopher Marlowe on Shakespeare's Artistry* (Aldershot, 2007), pp. 37–8.

[39] Wilson, ed., *Titus Andronicus*, Cambridge Shakespeare (Cambridge, 1948), pp. xxv–xxxiv; Craig and Kinney, *Mystery of Authorship*, pp. 27–33; Jackson, 'Stage Directions and Speech Headings in Act 1 of *Titus Andronicus* Q (1594): Shakespeare or Peele?', *Studies in Bibliography*, 49 (1996), 134–48 and 'Shakespeare's Brothers and Peele's Brethren: *Titus Andronicus* Again', *Notes and Queries*, 242 (1997), 494–5; Tarlinskaya, *Shakespeare's Verse: Iambic Pentameter and the Poet's Idiosyncrasies* (New York, 1987), pp. 121–4; Taylor, 'Why Did Shakespeare Collaborate?'

[40] Jonathan Bate and Eric Rasmussen, eds., *The RSC Shakespeare: The Complete Works* (2007), pp. 1618–19.

[41] *A Shrew* (wait upon this); Daniel, *Cleopatra* (servile thoughts); Greene, *Orlando* (his . . . coach and); Greene and Lodge, *Looking* (in pearl and gold); Kyd, *Soliman* (sun . . . with his beams); Sidney, *Antonius* (charming eyes). The anonymous *Knack to Know an Honest Man* has two (when the golden sun / siren that).

[42] PEELE: *Edward I* (upon . . . honour wait / earthly honour / thy imperial / Prometheus tied to Caucasus / and servile), *Alcazar* (climbeth . . . aloft / advanced above / the golden sun . . . glistering), *David* (as when the . . . sun . . . glist'ring . . . beams), *Descensus Astrae* (gallops the zodiac), *Arraignment* (wit doth). MARLOWE: *Faustus* (Olympus top / mount aloft with / that will charm), *Edward II* (sit . . . secure / his shipwreck), *1 Tamburlaine* (crack . . . lightning flash / in triumph long), *2 Tamburlaine* (eyes than / and shine in). LYLY: *Endymion* (pale envy), *Gallathea* (reach as), *Love's Metamorphosis* (this siren). Attributing *Dido* entirely to Marlowe would give him a tenth unique parallel (his glistering).

Alcazar each have three, but Peele's *Edward I* has five. Thus, whether we look for the largest number of unique dramatic parallels by author or by play, Peele is the likeliest candidate. If we add the early poetry of Shakespeare, Marlowe and Peele, we add four more unique parallels: none for Marlowe, one for Shakespeare – but three for Peele.[43] In all three tests, again, we can distinguish the imitator from the imitated.

Titus 2.1.1–25	Peele	Marlowe
Unique Parallels (Plays): total	11	9
Highest # per play	5	3
Plays & Poems: total	14	9

Remarkably, not a single unique dramatic parallel for this speech comes from the early Shakespeare canon. The cellular lexical evidence from these two speeches thus strongly, and independently, supports the twenty-first-century consensus that Peele wrote Aaron's first speech. Although Aaron is chronologically the first blackamoor character in Shakespeare's canon, Peele had already brought silent black characters on stage in *Edward I* (in the stage direction '*Queene Elinor in her litter borne by four Negro Mores*'), written a long speech for an actor '*appareled like a Moore*' (and riding on a lynx) in London's Lord Mayor's pageant of 1585, and created the evil '*negro Moore*' Muly Hamet Seth ('*Blacke in his looke, and bloudie in his deeds*') in *The Battle of Alcazar*.[44] Peele introduced Aaron the Moor to audiences, and must certainly have contributed to the outline of the character in the initial scenario for *Titus Andronicus*. We can distinguish Peele from Shakespeare, even when both of them are imitating Marlowe.

THE MASSACRE AT PARIS, SC. 2.31–52

Again, we can compare this Marlovian imitation from *Titus* with its Marlovian source. Most critics believe that Aaron's first speech was inspired by the first soliloquy of the Guise in Marlowe's *Massacre*, beginning 'Now, Guise, begins those

deep-engendered thoughts'.[45] Again, the Marlowe speech is longer, so we limit this analysis to the first 173 words.

Twentieth-century editors believed that the only surviving text of Marlowe's *Massacre* is a 'bad quarto' produced by memorial reconstruction. That may be true, but claims about memorial reconstruction are often based on alleged echoes of other plays in the 'suspect text'. As we have already demonstrated, a systemic cellular analysis of any long speech in an early modern play is going to turn up lots of unique parallels to other plays. Such 'echoes' are therefore useless as evidence for memorial reconstruction; the pattern of random distribution of parallels with a single text or author in *Massacre* resembles what we have seen in *Titus* and *Malta* (and no one suspects those texts of memorial corruption).[46] If *Massacre at Paris* is a bad quarto, the known author of the Guise's

---

[43] Shakespeare, *Venus* ('to wanton' as a verb); Peele, *Garter* (out of . . . shot / envy's threatning reach), *Anglorum Feriae* (the . . . sun gallops the zodiac in his).

[44] *The Device of the Pageant* (London, 1585), sig. A2; *The Famous Chronicle of King Edward the first* (London, 1593), sig. E1; *The Battle of Alcazar*, ed. W. W. Greg, Malone Society (London, 1907), lines 310, 18.

[45] *Dido, Queen of Carthage* and *The Massacre at Paris*, ed. H. J. Oliver, Revels Plays (London, 1968), pp. 99–101.

[46] Seven plays have only a single unique link with this passage, and most of them are anonymous: *Common Conditions* (wait that), *King Leir* (this head, this heart, this hand and sword), *True Tragedy of Richard the Third* (kindred to the), *Wars of Cyrus* (the top with). Well-attributed plays in this category include: Hughes *et al.*, *Misfortunes of Arthur* (quenchles thirst); Peele, *Edward I* (mount the . . . wings). The anonymous *Locrine* has two links (peasant to / the high pyramides), and so does Daniel's *Cleopatra* (be extinguished / what glory). Two professional playwrights also have two links, each in a separate play: KYD, *Soliman* (at last have), *Spanish Tragedy* (downfall . . . the deepest hell); SHAKESPEARE, *Richard III* (kindred . . . the king), *3 Henry VI*, 2.4 (hand . . . executes). There may be another Shakespeare parallel if we accept the attribution to him of the quarrel scene (Sc. 8) in *Arden* (matters of import). Craig and Kinney (*Mystery of Authorship*, pp. 78–99) and Jackson (*Determining the Shakespeare Canon*, pp. 9–126) agree in assigning scenes 4–9 of *Arden* to Shakespeare; Tarlinskaya gives him scenes 4–8 (*Versification*, pp. 105–11, 264). But Brian Vickers believes the whole play is Kyd's, in which case this would be a third parallel for Kyd instead of Shakespeare.

soliloquy is nevertheless correctly identified by a systematic lexical search. The first test identifies only two early playwrights with more than two unique parallels to this speech. Greene has four (or five if he wrote the relevant passage in *John of Bordeaux*, where he seems to have collaborated with Chettle).[47] But Marlowe has five – and possibly six (if he wrote the relevant passage in *Dido*), or seven (if Craig is right to give him the Cade scenes in *2 Henry VI*), or even nine (if he wrote all the non-Shakespearian scenes in that play).[48] But these uncertainties about the scale of Marlowe's dominance should not obscure the fact that he is the strongest candidate if we limit ourselves to uncontested cases, and also the strongest if we accept the widest possible definitions of the Greene and Marlowe dramatic canons. The second test, of single plays with more than one parallel, confirms that conclusion: the anonymous *Locrine* and Greene's *James IV* have two each, but Marlowe's *Edward II* has three.[49] Finally, the third test leaves the results unchanged, with Marlowe dominant, because the poems of Marlowe, Shakespeare and Peele do not provide any additional unique links. In all three tests, the correct author (Marlowe) comes out on top.

Massacre 2.31–52	Early Shakespeare	Marlowe
Unique Parallels (Plays): total	2	4
Highest # per play	1	3
Plays & Poems: total	2	4

Most scholars assume that the speech in *Titus* imitates the speech in *Massacre*, but if Martin Wiggins is right about the dates of those two plays then *Massacre* is imitating *Titus*.[50] Our tests cannot determine the direction of imitation. Nevertheless, we can say that Peele's canon supplies only a single unique parallel with the Guise's lines (from *Edward I*). Peele is indistinguishable here from six other cases in which a single non-Marlowe play supplies one unique parallel; Peele is less likely than Daniel, Kyd, Shakespeare, Greene or Marlowe to

have written this speech. The results for the Guise speech (5 Marlowe, 1 Peele) are very similar to those for the Barabas speech (4 Marlowe, 0 Peele). Real Marlowe is easy to distinguish from Peele, even in so small a sample.

I HENRY VI, 5.3.1–24

In all these first four examples, a systemic cellular map of the lexical evidence correctly identifies the author of the speech, despite the potential static created by imitation. Consequently, we should be able to use the same tool to test a sample that attribution scholars have not yet been able to identify confidently or consensually. R. B. McKerrow, Dover Wilson, Gary Taylor, Hugh Craig, Paul Vincent, Macdonald P. Jackson and Brian Vickers all agree that Nashe wrote all (or most) of the first act of *1 Henry VI*, and there is also a consensus that Shakespeare did not write Joan of Arc's long speech beginning 'The Regent conquers and the Frenchmen fly'.[51] Six different playwrights have

---

47 *James IV* (beyond my reach / for this this), *Orlando* (and thereon set), *Alphonsus* (this heart, this hand); *John of Bordeaux* (deep . . . thoughts).

48 *Edward II* (leveled . . . is the chiefest / is there in a / wait . . . attendance), *Malta* (a common good), *Faustus* (top . . . aspiring). Marlowe(?): *2 Henry VI*, 4.7 (resolution honor's), 1.1 (wake when others . . . sleep), 1.2 (set the diadem). Marlowe and Nashe: *Dido* (I will either).

49 So does *2 Henry VI*, but all three of those parallels fall in parts of the play identified, by many criteria and a long line of editors, as un-Shakespearian. If Craig and others are right about Marlowe's share of that play, then those three parallels are further evidence for Marlowe. If the fundamentalist view that Shakespeare wrote the whole play were correct, then we would have to conclude that Shakespeare is as likely as Marlowe to have written (at least this part of) *Massacre at Paris*.

50 Wiggins, *Catalogue*, *Titus* (item 928; 3:180), *Massacre* (item 947; 3:211).

51 Wilson, ed., *The First Part of King Henry VI*, Cambridge Shakespeare (Cambridge, 1952), pp. xxi–xxxi, 194; Taylor, 'Shakespeare and Others: The Authorship of *Henry the Sixth, Part One*', *Medieval and Renaissance Drama in England*, 7 (1995), 145–205; Craig and Kinney, *Mystery of Authorship*, pp. 40–68; Vincent, *When 'harey' Met Shakespeare: The Genesis of 'The First Part of Henry the Sixth'* (Saarbrücken, 2008), pp. 301–2; Vickers, 'Incomplete Shakespeare; or, Denying

at various times been seriously proposed as the author of Joan's speech; the very number of candidates is enough to make most scholars simply throw up their hands and dismiss the whole business of attribution as farcical. But most early conjectures were based on nonsensical or dubious evidence, of a kind that no current scholar would respect. Nevertheless, we considered all six candidates (Greene, Kyd, Marlowe, Nashe, Peele and Shakespeare).

Again, we limited ourselves to the first 173 words of the speech ('The Regent . . . forsake me'). Again, as usual, there is a scattering of random parallels.[52] The dramatic canons of Peele and Kyd contain no unique parallels to this passage. Nashe has one; Greene's plays contain only two (or maybe one).[53] Shakespeare's plays also contain only two.[54] We have already seen, again and again, that just two unique parallels in 173 words is unreliable evidence of authorship. By the usual criteria of our first test, such results would rule out all five of those candidates. The complete absence of Peele parallels is radically incompatible with the results in *Titus*, 2.1.1–25; the results here closely resemble those for our three other control samples, not written by Peele (*Titus*, 5.1.124–44, *Malta*, *Massacre*). As for Greene, he is less likely to have written this speech than the Guise's speech in *Massacre* (four unique parallels) or Aaron's speech in *Titus* 2.1 (three). The two Shakespeare parallels are in marked contrast to the eight in *Titus*, 5.1.124–44. In fact, Shakespeare and Greene have fewer links to this speech than Lyly.[55]

Against the weakness of all the other conjectured authors of this passage, the strength of Marlowe's claim is evident: his nine unique parallels almost double the combined total for all five alternative candidates. Moreover, the Marlowe parallels come from six different plays (more plays than the other five candidates combined).[56] In our second test, only three plays have more than one link to this passage: Lyly's *Gallathea* and Daniel's *Cleopatra* (each with two) and *Faustus* (with four).

Nevertheless, it might be objected that these results are unfair to Nashe and Kyd, because few of

their plays survive or are securely identified. Since we now have six candidates, instead of three, our third test has to be modified, to take account of the non-dramatic canons of all the likeliest authors. But some modification seems necessary, because of the huge size of the non-dramatic canons of Greene and Nashe. These are our own word-counts of the canons of these six authors, as we have identified them for these experiments.[57]

Co-Authorship in *1 Henry VI*', *Shakespeare Quarterly*, 58 (2007), 311–52; Jackson, *Shakespeare Canon*, p. 21.

[52] Single hits are mostly in anonymous plays or parts of plays: *Famous Victories* (conquers and the), *Common Conditions* (now help ye), *Troublesome Reign* (that admonish), *Locrine* (and aid me in), *Clyomon and Clamydes* (your accustomed), *Edward III* anonymous Sc. 4 (of a further), *2 Henry VI* anonymous 1.3 (benefit so); Wilson, *3 Lords* (wont to feed); Daniel, *Cleopatra* (diligence to / soul and all).

[53] The Nashe parallel comes in the first act of *1 Henry VI* (the French the). Greene has *Alphonsus* (if you will grant) and *George a Greene* (give . . . the foil). For the latter, Wiggins acknowledges that contemporary sources are contradictory, but nevertheless accepts Greene's authorship, for confusing reasons (*British Drama*, vol. 3, p. 109).

[54] *3 Henry VI*, 1.4 (get the field), *Edward III* Sc.2 (2.2) (my soul my body).

[55] *Gallathea* (spirits that are / my body nor), *Midas* (I'll lop).

[56] *Edward II* (the lordly), *Faustus* (familiar spirit / cull out), *2 Tamburlaine* (regions under earth), *Massacre* (oh hold me), *1 Tamburlaine* (to your wonted). *Malta* (see . . . forsake me). A third *Faustus* parallel (see they) uniquely combines the imperative verb meaning 'look' with the pronoun 'they' referring to devils. The fourth *Faustus* parallel (aid me in this enterprise) is uniquely present, verbatim, in the 1616 text only; but the 1604 version has 'aid me in this attempt' (which is closer than anything but the 1616 text), and *Elegies* has the otherwise unique collocation 'aid . . . enterprise'. Because of the uncertainties about the text of *Faustus*, we have counted these three variants of the phrase as only a single unique parallel, rather than three.

[57] These counts do not include stage directions or speech prefixes; compounds are counted as two words unless hyphenated in the original text. The Nashe dramatic total includes Act 1 of *1 Henry VI*. Both Marlowe totals include the 1616 additions to *Faustus* (9384 words). There is no question that Marlowe wrote at least part of *Dido* but we do not know which parts (if any) are Nashe's; our treatment of the play is designed to prevent the uncertainties about it from undermining our results.

	Dramatic	Non-dramatic	Total
Greene	118,802	554,624	673,426
Marlowe (with *Dido*)	118,038	35,998	154,036
Early Shakespeare	110,381	24,356	134,587
Marlowe (w/o *Dido*)	104,448	35,998	140,446
Peele	98,828	15,155	113,983
Kyd	54,004	24,833	78,837
Early Nashe (with *Dido*)	34,850	286,97	322,767
Early Nashe (w/o *Dido*)	21,260	286,397	309,177

1 Henry VI 5.3.1–24	Early Shakespeare	Marlowe
Unique Parallels (Plays): total	2	9
Highest # per play	1	4
Plays & Poems: total	2	9

Greene's dramatic canon here is larger than Shakespeare's or Marlowe's (or anyone else's), so he should not be underrepresented in our tests of any of these speeches – even without taking any account of his huge non-dramatic canon.[58] The word-total gap between Peele and Marlowe is as great as the gap between Marlowe and Greene, but that did not prevent Peele from dominating the results in *Titus*, 2.1.1–25. Indeed, we could eliminate Peele's disadvantage by counting his dramatic and non-dramatic canon against the dramatic canons of Shakespeare and of Marlowe-without-*Dido*; his word total would then be slightly greater than theirs. This procedure would refine our preceding tests, but would not substantially change the results.

The smallest of these dramatic canons is Nashe's. If we add Nashe's non-dramatic work, it becomes, instead, the second-largest canon (though still less than half the size of Greene's). But Nashe's early poetry and prose add only five unique parallels to his total.[59] With a canon more than double the size of Marlowe's, he still has fewer unique parallels to this passage than Marlowe and he still has no single work with more than two parallels. Adding the non-dramatic works of Shakespeare, Kyd, Peele and Marlowe does not change the results at all. The third test thus does nothing to diminish Marlowe's dominance of the linguistic evidence in this passage.

Kyd, with the smallest of these six canons, has recently been proposed by Brian Vickers as the author of most of *1 Henry VI*, including this scene.

But the databases, methods and results that Vickers uses to make that claim have been discredited in independent studies by Hugh Craig, Arthur Kinney, John Burrows, Gabriel Egan, MacDonald P. Jackson and Gary Taylor.[60] That general critique of his methods and conclusions is here specifically confirmed by the cellular lexical data. Kyd's canon does not contain a single unique parallel to Joan's speech. Given that Kyd's canon contains three plays, and that twenty-one other plays of the period 1576–94 have at least one unique parallel here, Kyd is one of the most unlikely candidates for authorship of this speech. Marlowe, with eight unique parallels, has one for every 14,000 words of his dramatic canon; or, if we omit the collaborative *Dido*, one every 12,000 words. On that basis, Kyd would need five unique parallels to become more plausible than Marlowe here.

Marlowe is the only candidate, besides Kyd, to have been supported by twenty-first-century attribution scholars. Marlowe was specifically identified

---

58 Including Greene's huge non-dramatic canon would give him only two additional unique parallels: *Penelope's Web* (proofs of your) and *Euphues his Censure* (feed you with). With a canon almost six times that of Marlowe, he would have only half as many unique links to this passage.

59 *Unfortunate* (of your accustomed), *Penniless* (Spirits . . . under earth / England give), *Strange News* (may get the), *Christ's Tears* (my body shall). The example of 'to your wonted' in *Strange News* means that the parallel in *Tamburlaine* is no longer unique, removing one Marlowe parallel but not adding to Nashe's own total.

60 See Craig and Kinney, *Mystery of Authorship*, pp. 56–9; John Burrows, 'A Second Opinion on "Shakespeare and Authorship Studies in the Twenty-First Century"', *Shakespeare Quarterly*, 63 (2012), 355–92; Gabriel Egan, 'Shakespeare: Editions and Textual Studies', *The Year's Work in English Studies*, 91 (2012), 328–410, esp. pp. 390–2; Jackson, *Shakespeare Canon*; Taylor, 'Empirical Middleton'.

as the author of this speech by Thomas Merriam, and as the author of most of the Joan scenes by Hugh Craig.[61] Using entirely different methods, we have demonstrated that Marlowe is the dominant figure in this speech, in a pattern that cannot be attributed to imitation.

I HENRY VI, 4.2.15–38

Joan's speech does not look like Shakespeare. It does not even look like Shakespeare when he is most obviously imitating Marlowe. And it also does not look like Shakespeare when he was writing his share of *1 Henry VI*.[62] This is evident if we compare Joan's speech with one by another French character in this play. All modern attribution scholars agree that Shakespeare wrote the General's speech in 4.2, beginning 'Thou ominous and fearful owl of death'.[63] Again, we limit our analysis to the same sample size, the first 173 words (ending with 'Shall'). However you look at the systemic cellular data, the Shakespearian speech in 4.2 contrasts with the Marlovian speech in 5.3.

Again, there is the usual random scatter. Peele, Greene, Lyly and Wilson all have just one parallel; altogether there are fifteen plays with one, which here as elsewhere is meaningless.[64] Nashe certainly has one, but he may also have another (if he wrote the relevant part of *Dido*). Kyd has two – meaning he's more likely to have written this speech (which Vickers and all others give to Shakespeare) than the speech by Joan in 5.3 (which Vickers gives to Kyd).[65] But two parallels in a passage of this length are never enough to establish authorship. The only two plausible candidates for 4.2 are Marlowe and Shakespeare. But whereas the evidence in 5.3 strongly favoured Marlowe, the evidence in 4.2 strongly favours Shakespeare. Shakespearian scenes in his early plays contain at least eight unique links to this passage (and nine if he wrote *1 Henry VI*, 4.6).[66] Marlowe by contrast has only four (or five if we assign *Dido* to him, rather than Nashe).[67]

In our second test (identifying single plays with more than one parallel), *Arden* has two – and both occur in the few scenes that Jackson, Kinney and Tarlinskaya assign to Shakespeare. For those who

accept Shakespeare's presence in those scenes of *Arden*, this raises his total to ten or eleven unique parallels to this passage.[68] There are also two parallels in another collaborative play, *1 Henry VI*, but one of these occurs in a scene (3.3) that no recent investigator gives to Shakespeare and so the two parallels may belong to different authors. The same is true in *2 Henry VI*, where five parallels are split between Shakespeare scenes (two) and scenes probably not by Shakespeare (three).[69] All three of these plays are associated with Shakespeare, and all three include parallels in scenes attributed to him by scholars who accept that the play is collaborative. The only play of undisputed single authorship with more than one parallel is Shakespeare's *Richard III*, with five. It has as many as all Marlowe's plays combined (including *Dido*) – and as many as Peele's, Nashe's, Greene's and Kyd's plays combined. Shakespeare clearly dominates the results in test two.

[61] Merriam, 'Faustian Joan', *Notes and Queries*, 245 (2002), 218–20; Craig and Kinney, *Mystery of Authorship*, pp. 62–77.

[62] From Malone to the present, scholars have disputed whether Shakespeare's contribution to the play was written after the rest. Our analysis does not resolve that dispute nor depend on a particular answer to it.

[63] Brian Vickers makes his attribution of 4.2 to Shakespeare explicit in 'Shakespeare and Authorship Studies in the Twenty-first Century', *Shakespeare Quarterly*, 62 (2011), 106–40, esp. pp. 123–4.

[64] Peele, *Alcazar* (war . . . tangle); Greene, *Friar* (dew thee); Lyly, *Mother Bombie* (upon no); Wilson, *Cobbler* (that now begins to). Single parallels also occur in the following anonymous plays or scenes: *Cyrus* (out and fight), *Clyomon* (praise that I), *Edward III* Sc. 15/4.7 (retire the), *1 Henry VI*, 3.3 (but English).

[65] Nashe, *Summer* (of thy tyranny) and possibly *Dido* (turn thee); Kyd, *Spanish* (squadrons pitched), *Soliman* (the glass that).

[66] *Richard III* (owl . . . death / have ta'en the sacrament / sacrament to / Christian soul / there thou); *2 Henry VI*, 3.1 (the period of . . . tyranny), 5.1.116–17 (bloody scourge the); *Shrew* (lo there); *1 Henry VI*, 4.6 (of flight). Taylor and Craig give 4.6 to Shakespeare; Vincent and Vickers do not.

[67] *Faustus* 1616 (their bloody), *Malta* (well fortified and), *Edward II* (strong enough to), *1 Tamburlaine* (valiant man of).

[68] *Arden* Sc.4 (way . . . for redress), Sc.6 (pitched to).

[69] Non-Shakespearian scenes in *2 Henry VI*: 1.4 (of an invincible), 2.4 (tangle thee), 4.7 (no Christian).

Test three confirms this pattern. Including the non-dramatic works adds one more unique parallel for Shakespeare, but nothing to Marlowe's count (or Peele's or Kyd's).[70] Even Nashe's outsized non-dramatic canon does not challenge Shakespeare's superiority in the overall totals.[71]

1 Henry VI 4.2.15–38	Early Shakespeare	Marlowe
Unique Parallels (Plays): total	8	4
Highest # per play	5	1
Plays & Poems: total	9	4

Shakespeare tops the charts in all three tests here, just as Marlowe topped them all in 5.3. By these criteria, the General's speech in 4.2 looks like Shakespeare's in 5.1 of *Titus Andronicus*. But the very strength of this evidence for Shakespeare in 4.2 of *1 Henry VI*, or in 5.1 of *Titus*, shows how weak is the evidence for Shakespeare's authorship of Joan's speech. The results for Joan's speech resemble those in *The Jew of Malta* or *The Massacre at Paris*. Marlowe wrote Joan's speech, as clearly as Shakespeare wrote the French General's. Marlowe haunts Shakespeare in 4.2, as he did in *Titus* 5.3 (and as he haunted Peele in *Titus* 2.1). But the distinction between imitation and authorship is clear enough.

I HENRY VI, 5.3.24–5.4.15

The identification of Marlowe as the author of 173 words of Joan's long speech in 5.3 does not mean that he wrote all the play's unattributed scenes, or all the Joan scenes, or even all of what editors traditionally identify as '5.3'.[72] On the other hand, it seems unlikely that Marlowe would have contributed only 173 words to the play. We therefore decided to look at the remaining words that complete the action begun by Joan's entrance. If Marlowe wrote the beginning of Joan's speech before her capture, we might expect him to continue writing until her capture and exit, at the end of what the Oxford Shakespeare identifies as 5.4, and what other editors identify as 5.3.44. This is an

additional 166 words (or perhaps 169, depending on how we count compounds): not identical to the sample sizes we have used until now, but close enough.

As always there is insignificant scatter. In the first test, Peele has no unique parallels; Greene, Kyd and Wilson have one each, as do three anonymous plays and *Dido* (which may or may not be Nashe).[73] Both Shakespeare and Lyly have three parallels, which means Shakespeare is no more likely to have written this passage than Lyly – and Lyly never wrote for the outdoor amphitheatres, so far as we know.[74] That leaves only Marlowe, with eight unique parallels (or nine if the one in *Dido* is his).[75] Marlowe more than doubles the total for his nearest competitors; he also outscores the combined total for Peele, Greene, Kyd, Nashe and Shakespeare. In the second test, only five plays have more than a single parallel: Lyly's *Sapho and Phao*, and four plays by Marlowe (*1 Tamburlaine, Massacre, Faustus* and *Edward II*). In the third test, Marlowe's *Elegies* gives him another parallel, keeping him well ahead of

---

[70] *Lucrece* (and . . . owl . . . death).

[71] Nashe, 'To the Gentlemen Students' (from the liberty to), *Tears* (glory . . . praise), *Mirror for Martinists* (begins to run), *Terrors* (process of his), *Penniless* (eyes that see). Added to the maximum two from his plays, the pamphlets raise his total to only seven, against a minimum of nine for Shakespeare.

[72] The Oxford Shakespeare breaks the traditional '5.3' into three short scenes, separated by a cleared stage. Editors who disagree nevertheless accept that there are three 'French scenes' here, and such breaks coincide elsewhere with changes of authorship: compare *All Is True* 3.2 (divided between Shakespeare and Fletcher after an exit).

[73] Greene, *Alphonsus* (to buckle with); Kyd, *Soliman* (mischief light); Wilson, *3 Lords* (France I think); Anonymous, *Common conditions* (strong for me); *Locrine* (spirits now); *Arden*, Sc. 1 (can please your).

[74] Shakespeare, *Taming* (and may you), *3 Henry VI* 2.2 (I prithee give . . . tongue), *Richard III* (be suddenly); Lyly, *Love's Metamorphosis* (changed to a), *Sapho* (doth bend her brows / your beds).

[75] *1 Tamburlaine* (glory droopeth / your dainty), *Massacre* (droopeth to / curse . . . miscreant), *Faustus* (ugly . . . change . . . shape thou / and try if), *Edward II* (Circe . . . change my shape / suddenly surprise), *Dido* (fell . . . enchantress).

any other candidate.[76] Marlowe dominates all three tests, as he did for the earlier segment in 5.3.

1 Henry VI 5.3.24–5.4.15	Early Shakespeare	Marlowe
Unique Parallels (Plays): total	3	8
Highest # per play	1	2 (+2+2+2)
Plays & Poems: total	3	9

As we noted above, this second sample is not exactly the same size as the other six we have tested. We could make the comparison exact if, instead of arbitrarily beginning at the end of the preceding 173-word segment, we instead counted backward from the structural closure provided by her exit. This alternative divison would add seven words from the end of the previous section ('French the foil. See they forsake me'). That would subtract one unique parallel from the preceding segment, but add another unique parallel to Marlowe's total in this segment. Thus, whether we count 173 words forward from Joan's entrance or 173 words backward from her exit as a prisoner, Marlowe dominates the results.

So far, the evidence in this paper has been quantitative, but not statistical. We have shown a consistent pattern of numerical differences but we have not evaluated those differences by calculating probabilities. But the improbable scale of the contrast between the evidence from Shakespeare and Peele, in Aaron's two speeches, should be evident even to an untrained eye.

	Unique Shakespeare (drama)	Unique Peele (drama)
Titus 2.1	0	11
Titus 5.1	11	1

According to Fisher's Exact Probability Test, in a homogeneous set this degree of difference would happen only about one time in one hundred thousand.[77] It is that unlikely that these two speeches are both by Shakespeare, or both by

Peele.[78] The disparity becomes even greater if we add the results from the other speech undoubtedly by Shakespeare:

	Unique Shakespeare (drama)	Unique Peele (drama)
Titus 2.1	0	11
Titus 5.1 + 1 Henry VI 4.2	19	2

Now, the chances of random fluctuation are only six in ten million. These two authors are very far apart, stylistically. There is a similar contrast between Peele and the Joan segment we have analysed in 1 Henry VI:

	Unique Marlowe (drama)	Unique Peele (drama)
Titus 2.1	8	11
1 Henry VI 5.3–5.4	17	0

Here, Fisher's Test calculates a probability of only about one in five thousand. Peele is more like Marlowe than he is like Shakespeare (no surprise), but the statistical difference is still undeniably significant enough to distinguish the two writers. If we added the Malta and Massacre totals to those for 1 Henry VI 5.3–5.4 and contrasted that larger Marlowe set to the Peele set in Titus 2.1,

---

[76] Marlowe, Elegies (sleeping on ... bed). Shakespeare adds Venus (head ... crest) and Lucrece (too weak ... too strong); but an example of 'be surprised' in Lucrece makes that same phrase in Richard III no longer unique, giving Shakespeare a grand total of only four. Nashe adds parallels from Pasquil (head fall) and 'To the Gentlemen Students' (think I have you); his 'changed to a' (Tears) does not add to his total, but cancels out Lyly's unique parallel in Love's Metamorphosis.

[77] There are many online sites that will automatically calculate Fisher's Exact Test; we used the one at vassarstats.net. Adding The Troublesome Reign of John, King of England to the Peele results in 5.1 would still leave the chances at only one in ten thousand.

[78] For probabilities, populations and samples see 'Testing for Significance' in Anthony Kenny, The Computation of Style (Oxford, 1982), pp. 105–19.

the improbability would double (to one in ten thousand). There is a similar contrast between Shakespeare and Marlowe.

	Marlowe	Shakespeare
1 Henry VI 5.3–5.4	17	5
1 Henry VI 4.2.15–38 + *Titus* 5.1.124–44	7	16

Fisher's Test gives less than three chances in one thousand that these two sets belong to the same population or were created by the same agent. It gives virtually the same result if the *Malta* and *Massacre* speeches are added to the Marlowe set. The contrast here is statistically significant; we can distinguish Shakespeare from Marlowe, even when Shakespeare is imitating Marlowe. But the contrast between Shakespeare and Marlowe is not as great as the contrast between Shakespeare and Peele. No single authorial identity is equidistant from all others. The numbers here tell us something we already knew: that Shakespeare and Marlowe are closer together than either of them is like Peele. But, for all that, they are demonstrably and statistically distinguishable.

Our university colleagues in other departments almost always end their publications with the statement 'More research is needed.' More empirical research, using this kind of corpus linguistics, is indeed needed. The full pattern of collaboration in *1 Henry VI* will only become clear once our cellular lexical data has been integrated with other kinds of evidence produced by Craig, Vincent, Tarlinskaya and others. We need similarly detailed and comprehensive studies of all the plays from the 1580s and early 1590s. Only then will we be able to situate Shakespeare's early career, his imitations and collaborations in the context of the larger field of London playwriting before the formation of the Chamberlain's Men.

Nevertheless, some preliminary conclusions seem justified. Identity is cellular and systemic. Imitation is selective and semiotic. We can distinguish Shakespeare from Marlowe, even when Shakespeare is imitating Marlowe. We can distinguish Peele from Marlowe, even when one is imitating the other. We can distinguish Marlovian Peele from Marlovian Shakespeare. As Hugh Craig concluded, on the basis of an entirely different methodology, Shakespeare and Marlowe did collaborate with Nashe on *1 Henry VI*. Early Shakespeare is not so indistinguishable from his contemporaries after all. From the very beginning, Shakespeare was, in his own words, 'like himself'.

'O JEPHTHAH, JUDGE OF ISRAEL': FROM ORIGINAL TO ACCRETED MEANINGS IN HAMLET'S ALLUSION

PÉTER DÁVIDHÁZI

O Jephthah, judge of Israel, what a treasure hadst thou?

In Act 2 scene 2 the little dialogue between Hamlet and Polonius can be taken as a case study in how allusions work. An allusion is always a call to remember and a test of memory. To spot and identify the familiar phrase or motif within the text requires a semi-conscious act of recalling and sifting through similar phrases or motifs from the past; hence studying the workings of an allusion may reveal the functioning of the smallest examinable link in cultural memory. Whether an exclamation, as in the First Quarto of 1603, or a question, as in the Second Quarto of 1604–05 and the First Folio of 1623, Hamlet's sentence is baffling for Polonius because of its abruptness: there was no mention of Jephthah in their previous encounters and it is not clear what relevance, if any, the allusion can have at that moment. As usual, Hamlet wants to take Polonius off guard, so he gives him no clue, hence we, spectators or readers, likewise have to rely on our unaided memory alone. At this point neither Polonius nor the play's audience is enabled to realize that the phrase 'Jephthah, judge of Israel' figures at the beginning of a ballad based on the biblical story of Jephthah and his daughter: 'I have read that many years agoe, / When Jepha, judge of Israel, / Had one fair daughter and no more . . .'. But if not as a verbatim quotation, nevertheless the unique biblical name and the characteristic biblical status followed by the ominous hint in the second half of the sentence may well have evoked the story of Judges 11: 29–40, especially because in Shakespeare's time Hamlet's utterance could appeal to a widespread knowledge of the Bible and the fate of its emblematic figures.[1]

Hamlet is frugally apportioning the necessary bits of information to ensure a barely sufficient level of recognition and it remains doubtful whether the name, office and unspecified 'treasure' provide enough to remind Polonius of the entire story: 'What a treasure had he, my lord?' There is no way to tell whether Polonius truly does not remember it or just pretends that he does not. But whichever is the case, Hamlet was waiting for precisely this question so that he can aim the next shot closer to the old man's heart: 'Why, / One fair daughter and no more, / The which he loved passing well'. The last two lines are taken verbatim from the ballad, and this time the quotation is more discernible because its rhythm sets it apart, but, again, Polonius may or may not have heard the ballad before. All that his response indicates, if only 'aside', is that he recognizes the target of the hint: 'Still on my daughter'. (In the Quarto of 1603 his sentence was more explicit: 'Ah, still harping o'my daughter!', and here the weight of 'harping' is almost too light to suggest that he recognized the allusion and its serious threat.) Hamlet, once in the bullying mode, is not contented with this much; he wants to make sure that Polonius understands all the menacing implications: 'Am I not i'th' right, old Jephthah?' Now Polonius recognizes or, again, pretends to recognize for the first time that all the bits and pieces of information

[1] See Hannibal Hamlin, *The Bible in Shakespeare* (Oxford, 2013), pp. 2–3, 9–42.

fall into a pattern and suggest a coherent analogy of fathers and daughters: 'If you call me Jephthah, my lord, I have a daughter that I love passing well.' Yet for Hamlet the bare acknowledgement of the suggested parallel between Jephthah's daughter and Polonius's Ophelia would not suffice without a confirmed awareness of the mutually fatal outcome: 'Nay, that follows not'. Polonius is anxious, or pretends to be anxious, to know: 'What follows then, my lord?' Hamlet could quote the gruesome end of the story from the final stanzas of the ballad but he chooses to quote the ominously enigmatic lines from the first stanza:

> Why,
> > As by lot,
> > God wot,
> and then, you know,
> > It came to pass
> > As most like it was.
> The first row of the pious chanson will show you
> > more . . . .   (2.2.339–57)[2]

Hamlet's casual 'you know' may suggest that the ballad was popular (and not only in the fictive world of the play) and its quoted part could be expected to work as an effective reminder. Although the quoted lines do not reveal what exactly it was that God wot (knew), what was most likely, and what came to pass, by now the intended lesson is obvious enough even for those spectators who cannot recall what happened finally either in the ballad or in Judges 11: 29–40. They can infer that Jephthah somehow lost his daughter and Polonius must be careful, otherwise he, too, may lose Ophelia; they can probably realize that Hamlet's allusion, frightful and alarming as it is, was probably meant to warn Polonius and, possibly, to save Ophelia. The scene shifts quickly, and there is not much time in the theatre to ponder on covert meanings. Yet the processing of allusions to well-known elements of one's culture is proven to be easier and thus quicker than usually expected,[3] and even those slower to respond may feel that there is more to this brief exchange than meets the eye.

'WHAT FOLLOWS THEN, MY LORD?' HAMLET'S ALLUSION AS AN INTERPRETATIVE MODEL

The question is not only what Hamlet himself meant to say by this sudden allusion, but what function it serves in the play as a whole. His reference to Jephthah is a menacing intimation of what may or may not follow in the plot; hence his punning remark ('Nay, that follows not') refers not only to the logical inconsistency of Polonius's argument and to the proper sequence of lines quoted in the ballad but also to the likelihood that what follows in the plot may be just as devastating as Jephthah's predicament. Moreover, this indicates a further, ultimate function of Hamlet's allusion: to identify the ballad and Judges 11: 29–40 as the appropriate subtexts for comparison and contrast whereby to explore the complex problematics of the entire play. Though Polonius is understandably surprised by Hamlet's associative leap, Shakespeare's choice of this emblematic story from Judges need not surprise us any more than his other references to this book in his plays. Remembering that the main question at issue in Judges is that 'of right rule and fitting rulers, the sequence of judges devolving by stages toward the state of general anarchy and civil war', and that 'the writer in Judges, addressing himself to the origins of a murderous civil war, wanted to show his audience what could happen when an Israelite community casts away the fundamental bonds of civilized intercourse',[4] we can feel the general affinity (in addition to the diverse occasional reasons) that may have made Shakespeare allude to the book of Judges both in his history plays (*2 Henry IV, Henry V, 1 Henry VI, 3 Henry VI, Henry VIII*) and elsewhere (*Love's Labour's Lost, The Merchant of Venice, Hamlet, King Lear, Cymbeline,*

---

[2] *Hamlet*, ed. Ann Thompson and Neil Taylor, Arden Shakespeare, Third Series (London, 2006), pp. 263–4.

[3] Hamlin, *The Bible in Shakespeare*, pp. 41–2.

[4] Robert Alter, *The World of Biblical Literature* (London, 1992), pp. 62, 113.

The Tempest).[5] Though not one of Shakespeare's most frequently quoted books of the Bible, Judges is certainly one of the most Shakespearian books both in its thematics and latent concerns, and it reveals a great deal about the political fears and anxieties surfacing in *Hamlet*. Chapter 11, the story of Jephthah, epitomizes all these; moreover, it resembles *Hamlet* in its motif of revenge as well. Jephthah had been disowned and expelled by his half-brothers on the ground that he was born out of wedlock and by a prostitute. Subsequently he becomes an able military leader abroad but, when the Gileadites ask him to come back and lead their forces against the Ammonites, first he gives vent to his anger, reminding them of their share in his former banishment ('Did not ye hate me, and expel me out of my fathers house? how then come you unto me now in time of your tribulation?' 11: 7), and when he accepts their offer (having first upgraded it from 'captaine' of the Gileadite troops to 'head over all the inhabitants of Gileád' 11: 6–8), he offers God anything for winning the battle and thus becoming the ruler of the very people which had driven him away.[6] Thus his *ressentiment* fuels his obsessive ambition to win at all costs, makes him blind to collateral damage, prompts his vow and ultimately leads to his daughter's death. Implicitly hinting at such parallels, Hamlet's allusion is a call for us, spectators and readers, to remember the biblical story as a probable or at least possible model of the unfolding plot. As was rightly argued about *Titus Andronicus*, in that play the reference to the story of Virginius killing his own daughter served not only Titus himself by providing (in his own words) 'A reason mighty, strong, and effectual; / A pattern, precedent, and lively warrant / For me, most wretched, to perform the like' (5.3. 35–57), but may have given Shakespeare one of the main classical literary patterns and dramatic precedents for structuring his entire play.[7] Similarly, though not in terms of origin, I argue that Hamlet's allusion to Jephthah and his daughter serves not only Hamlet's purposes in Act 2, scene 2, but may also provide an interpretative model for the whole play, highlight the interpretative significance of the suggested correspondences (similarities and differences) between the two fathers and daughters and reveal the ensuing relevance of such terms as sacrifice, burnt offering, victim, obedience, virginity, providence and responsibility.

Yet to realize the diverse functionings of this interpretative model in different epochs one should note that this is an intricate allusion of multiple origins and resonances. Hamlet's allusion is direct and indirect at the same time: directly, indeed verbatim, quoting from a ballad, and indirectly referring to its biblical origin, not only to Judges 11: 29–40 but to a range of related or relatable texts, reaching far beyond the Geneva Bible Shakespeare read or the Bishops' Bible he heard in church. In Shakespeare's time the ballad must have reminded the play's spectators (or indeed readers of its earliest printed versions) of a biblical story closely intertwined with an age-old yet still persistent tradition of disapproving interpretations reaching far beyond the actual biblical text of Judges and ranging from marginal notes to sermons and literary or other artistic adaptations.[8] As was recently demonstrated, it is not only the main text of the Geneva Bible that inspired Shakespeare through his intensive mode of reading but its glosses and cross-references as well; moreover, the problems of inheritance (or lack of it) by primogeniture were well-known to Shakespeare and his audience and hence the contemporary legal practice must have accentuated the relevance of biblical stories about the rivalry between first-born and second-born sons.[9] The plot of

5 See Naseeb Shaheen, *Biblical References in Shakespeare's Plays* (Newark and London, 1999), pp. 776–7.

6 References are to the *The Geneva Bible: A Facsimile of the 1560 Edition*, introduction by Lloyd E. Berry (Peabody, MA, 2007).

7 Jonathan Bate, 'Introduction', in *Titus Andronicus*, ed. Jonathan Bate, Arden Shakespeare, Third Series (London, New Delhi, New York, Sidney, 2013), pp. 90, 92.

8 John L. Thompson, *Writing the Wrongs: Women of the Old Testament among Biblical Commentators from Philo through the Reformation* (Oxford, 2001), pp. 100–78; Wilbur Owen Sypherd, *Jephthah and his Daughter: A Study in Comparative Literature* (Newark, DE, 1948).

9 Barbara A. Mowat, 'Shakespeare Reads the Geneva Bible', in *Shakespeare, the Bible, and the Form of the Book: Contested Scriptures*, ed. Travis DeCook and Alan Galey (New York, 2012), pp. 25–39.

Judges 11 is triggered by a special variant of sibling rivalry, as here it is the younger half-brothers who disown Jephthah allegedly because of his illegitimate status ('Thou shalt not inherit in our fathers house: for thou art ye sonne of a strange woman', 11: 2), and the last phrase is glossed in the margin ('That is, of an harlot'), dovetailing with the ominous introduction of Jephthah in the first verse as 'a valiant man, but the sonne of an harlot' (11: 1). This ambivalence of status is theologically elaborated by the marginal note and cross-reference attached to Jephthah's vow in 11: 30–1; they were meant to reconcile Paul's tribute to Jephthah (in the Epistle to the Hebrews listing him among the great examples of all-conquering faith) and the traditional condemnation of his sinful vow: 'As the Apostle commēdeth Iphtáh for his worthy entreprise in deliuering the people, Ebr. 11, 32: so by his rashe vowe & wicked performance of the same, his victorie was defaced: and here we se [!] that the sinnes of the godly do not vtterly extinguish their faith.'[10] The subtle analytic distinction between *making* and *performing* the vow in order to condemn it on both accounts is characteristic of a long tradition of commentaries both Jewish and Christian,[11] and this lineage is accentuated by a further marginal note of the Geneva Bible at the fatal enounter between father and daughter, charging the father with rashness and a fatally inadequate awareness of the relevant legal requirements: 'Being ouercome wt blinde zeale, and not considering whether the vowe was lawful or no'.[12] This suggests, implicitly but unambiguously, that Jephthah's performance of the rash vow was not only 'wicked', as branded before, but also totally uncalled for, and he need not (and should not) have fulfilled it. Churchgoers of the time were regularly hearing sermons and homilies,[13] so Shakespeare could hear this charge elaborated or at least mentioned; in the first *Book of Homilies* (1547) the seventh homily, 'Against Swearyng and Periurie', deplored Jephthah's 'fonde and vnaduised' oath as a promise both 'moste folishly' *made* and 'most cruelly' *performed*, 'so commytting agaynst God, double offence'.[14] Shakespeare's awareness of this traditional division of Jephthah's offence into two or three different

impious acts is clearly indicated in *Henry VI Part 3*, where George, Duke of Clarence singles out one of them: 'Perhaps thou wilt object my holy oath. / To keep that oath were more impiety / Than Jephthah when he sacrificed his daughter' (5.1.92–4).[15]

In *Hamlet* several characters use the word 'rash' with various evaluative implications, and their statements add up to a more circumspect and sophisticated problematization of rashness, ranging from the Queen's strongly disapproving, 'O, what a rash and bloody deed is this!' (3.4.25), or Hamlet's 'Thou, wretched, rash, intruding fool' (3.4.29) to Hamlet's final reflection on the occasional advantages of impulsive, unpremeditated acts: 'Rashly – / And praised be rashness for it – let us know / Our indiscretion sometime serves us well / When our deep plots do fall . . .' (5.2.6–9).[16] Yet in Act 2 scene 2 Hamlet's allusion evokes the pejorative biblical meaning with all its controversial implications, like the one that surfaces in *Titus Andronicus*, in Titus's question about another father who had caused the death of his daughter, though for different reasons and not by chance: 'Was it well done of rash Virginius / To slay his daughter with his own right hand, / Because she was enforced, stained and deflowered?' (5.3.36–8).[17] The expectation to condemn the rash vow must have been clear for any reader of Anthony Munday's elaborate poem 'The Complaint of Jephthah' and of his concise acrostic verse on rashness, published together in his 1579 *The Mirror of Mutabilitie*. As it is unlikely that Munday changed his mind on this issue, the same condemnatory interpretation of Jephthah's rash vow must have been echoed by

[10] *The Geneva Bible: A Facsimile of the 1560 Edition*, 114v.

[11] See Thompson, *Writing the Wrongs*, pp. 100–78.

[12] *The Geneva Bible: A Facsimile of the 1560 Edition*, 114v.

[13] See Shaheen, *Biblical References in Shakespeare's Plays*, pp. 55–62.

[14] *Certayne sermons or homelies appoynted by the Kynges Maiestie to be declared and redde* (London, 1547), sig. h1v.

[15] *The Oxford Shakespeare: The Complete Works*, ed. Stanley Wells and Gary Taylor (Oxford, 1998), p. 119.

[16] See Ann Thompson and Neil Taylor's note in *Hamlet*, Arden Shakespeare, pp. 433–4.

[17] *Titus Andronicus*, Arden Shakespeare, p. 266.

his and Dekker's *Jeffa* or *Jepha Judge of Israel*, a play that was mentioned in Henslowe's *Diary* several times as rehearsed, and most probably was performed in 1602.[18] Philip Stubbes's *The Anatomie of Abuses*, published three times from 1583 to the end of the century, voicing a harsh moral critique of social customs, referred to Jephthah's daughter in the chapter on 'the horrible Vice of pestiferous Dauncing' [!] but parenthetically deplored the father for 'making a rashe vow'.[19] In a more erudite and sophisticated way a similar message was elaborated in George Buchanan's Latin play *Jephthes sive Votum*, published in Paris first in 1554. It was exceptional that a poetic rendering, such as Samuel Rowlands's *The Virgine-sacrifice of Duke Jepthahs daughter* (1605), narrated the story with equal compassion for father and daughter, not castigating him for either making or fulfilling his vow, though noting that 'the end of *Amons* slaughter / begins the tragedie of his owne daughter'.[20] In addition to the thriving biblical culture of Shakespeare's time, a literary world teeming with such references must have helped at least some parts of the audience or readership realize what Hamlet's allusion was about, although none of this could render the meaning of its suggested interpretative model obvious.

'TO BURN / FOR HIS OFFERING':
A CHAIN OF INDIRECT
ALLUSIONS

Hamlet's allusion is of multiple origins, it is indeed a chain of allusions referring to biblical and literary texts that exist in many variants, both in their respective original languages and as translations. To start with, Hamlet evokes the well-known story in at least two versions that are closely related to each other yet differ significantly, not the least in their ways of handling Jephthah's ominous vow. Although the title of the ballad (*Jepha Judge of Israel*) and the opening formula of its first line ('I have read that . . .') can be taken as references to the Bible, the vow itself is not quoted in the (allegedly) very words of Jephthah as in Judges 11: 30–1, but summed up in reported speech: 'To God the Lord

he made a vow, / If he might have a victory, / At his return to burn / For his offering the first quick thing, / Should meet with him then, / From his house when he came agen, agen.' The vow in the Geneva Bible features a direct quotation: 'And Iphtáh vowed a vow vnto the Lord, and said, If thou shalt deliuer the children of Ammón in to mine hands, Thē that thing that commeth out of the dores of mine house to mete me, when I come home in peace from the children of Ammón, shal be the Lords, and I wil offer it for a burnt offring' (Judges 11: 30–1).

Quoting from the ballad and indirectly recalling the biblical story, Hamlet is alluding to this fatal vow by Jephthah, but this vow, in turn, may well be taken as a verbal and topical allusion to similar former vows in the Bible. In Jephthah's vow both the conditional *if − then* structure and the reversal of the *do ut des* (I give so that you give) formula into an even more straightforward *da ut dem* (give so that I give) may recall Numbers 21: 2, where even the key phrases were the same: 'So Israél vowed a vowe vnto the Lord, and said, If thou wilt deliuer *and* giue this people into mine hand, then I will vtterly destroy their cities.' In both instances God seems to have accepted the terms or at least delivered the enemy into the vower's hands. If not the victorious return from a battle, in Genesis 28: 20–2 it is the similarly safe return from a journey that is spelled out as the condition of Jacob's vow: 'Then Iaakób vowed a vowe, saying, If God wil be with me in this iourney which I go, and will giue me bread to eat, and clothes to put on: So that I come againe vnto my fathers house in safety, then shal the Lord be my God. And this stone, w[c] I haue set vp *as* a piller, shalbe Gods house: and of all that y[u] shalt giue me, wil I giue the tenth vnto thee.' But probably more effectively than such

[18] See Sypherd, *Jephthah and his Daughter*, pp. 144–5.
[19] Philip Stubbes, *The Anatomie of Abuses*, London, 1584, fo. 102v.
[20] Samuel Rowlands, *A theater of delightfull recreation* (London, 1605), pp. 30–1. It was Bernard Sharratt who drew my attention to this neglected text; I thank him for his ever-helpful suggestions.

verbal (phraseological or syntactic) resemblances, it was the striking similarity with a dreadful archetypal situation, that is, with the facing of one's duty (allegedly divine) to sacrifice one's own child, that might have prompted *Hamlet*'s audience to associate Jephthah's vow with Genesis 22, where God commanded Abraham to sacrifice his son, Isaac, as the same type of burnt offering: 'And he said, Take now thine onely sonne Izhák whome thou louest, & get thee vnto the lande of Moriáh, and offre him there for burnt offring vpon one of the mountaines, which I will shewe thee' (22: 2). True, the comparison can only reveal the sharp contrast that any biblical-minded contemporary must have realized; when Abraham was just about to comply with the divine command, God mercifully replaced Isaac with a ram, thus preventing the same type of human sacrifice that Jephthah was allowed to perform. Yet remembering the divine rescue operation and Isaac's miraculous survival could only accentuate the troubling memory of how Jephthah's daughter, another young human being, was inexorably sacrificed, especially because Ophelia had so much in common with her that Hamlet's allusion must have sounded appropriate enough to warrant a similar death.

For Shakespeare and his biblical-minded contemporaries even the type of offering Jephthah promised in his vow (in the ballad: 'to burn / For his offering'; in the Geneva Bible: 'I wil offer it for a burnt offring') could evoke further (previous) biblical texts that specified the distinct rules of this particular ritual. First of all, once the animal was flayed and the skin given to the officiating priest, no part of the animal's body was allowed to be set apart for human consumption, because it was meant entirely for God, as clearly prescribed by Leviticus 1: 9 and 1: 13: 'the Priest shal burne all on the altar', 'the Priest shall offer the whole & burne it vpon the altar . . . for a swete sauoure vnto the Lord'. The two salient features of the burnt offering, its ascending smoke and the undiminished wholeness of the burned animal, are alternatively represented by the two terms that designate it in the Hebrew Bible: עולה ('that which ascends') or כליל ('entire(ly)', 'whole'). Though

the latter term seems to be historically earlier, they focus on different aspects of the same ritual process, their meanings complement each other and, as the two words sometimes (as in Psalm 51: 21) occur together, they were once considered a hendiadys, meaning 'entirely burnt offerings'.[21] The idea that the pleasant odour of the smoke will ascend to the Lord figured in other ancient religions as well, and it is part of the 'Roman rites' Lucius reports to have been 'performed' in *Titus Andronicus*: 'the sacrificing fire, / Whose smoke like incense doth perfume the sky' (1.1.146–8).[22] The Hebrew phrase in Leviticus 1: 9, ריח־ניחוח, means a tranquilizing fragrance and implies the hope of a soothing effect, just as the marginal note attached to Lev 1: 9 explains the 'swete sauour' in the Geneva Bible in terms of appeasement: 'a sauour of rest, which pacifieth the angre of the Lord'. The formidable question implied in the notion of ascent is whether the odour of the burnt offering will indeed be found pleasant by the Lord; if so, He will accept the offering; however, it can be rejected. The reassuring gesture of acceptance is assumed, albeit in a polytheistic frame, by Lear's remark: 'Upon such sacrificies, my Cordelia, / The gods themselves throw incense' (*King Lear*, 5.3.20–1). In the case of Jephthah's daughter the question is especially pertinent because the archetypal subtext of the scene, Genesis 22, recalls that the Lord once prevented a comparable human sacrifice even though in that case He had ordered it himself. What if Jephthah's assumptions are wrong and the Lord, though for some unfathomable reason He did not intervene this time, does not accept the daughter's killing and burning on the altar as a legitimate sacrifice? This would mean that her death had no transcendental approval, function, status and meaning, and maybe no meaning whatsoever, thus nothing to distinguish it from sheer murder. As Othello shuddered

---

[21] Jacob Milgrom, 'Comment: The Burnt Offering: Name, Antiquity, Function', in *Anchor Bible: Leviticus 1–16*, trans., introduction, commentary by Jacob Milgrom (New York, 1991), pp. 172–4. See M. Kamler, *Comments of R. David Kimhi (Radak) on the Torah* (Jerusalem, 1970).

[22] *Titus Andronicus*, Arden Shakespeare, p. 137.

at the thought of this possibility ('O perjured woman! Thou dost stone my heart, / And makes me call what I intend to do / A murder, which I thought a sacrifice', *Othello*, 5.2.68–70), and Brutus found it repellent ('Let us be sacrificers, but not butchers, Caius', *Julius Caesar*, 2.1.166), the question is no less daunting when the biblical logic of Hamlet's allusion applies it to Ophelia's death. Was it providential, a part of the divine scheme of things, like the fall of a sparrow in Hamlet's later allusion to Matthew 10: 29 (5.2.197–8), or did she die as a casualty of sheer human aberration?

The question is especially menacing because the death of Jephthah's daughter as a possible memento for Ophelia's future is too brutal to be remembered. Neither the ballad Hamlet is quoting, nor the biblical narration of Judges 11: 29–40 displays the horrifying details of what exactly happened to Jephthah's daughter in the end or how she was killed and burnt on the altar. The ballad only confirms that 'And when that time was come and gone, / That she should sacrificed be, / This virgin sacrificed was, / For to fulfill all promises'; and the Geneva Bible is even more cryptic: 'And after the end of the two monethes, she turned againe vnto her father, who did with her according to his vowe which he had vowed...' (Judges 11: 39). But we should not forget that for the biblical-minded to read or hear Jephthah's vow and its promise of burnt offering could function as an unmistakable reference to a well-defined priestly tradition of ritual sacrifices, especially to verses 1: 3–17 in Leviticus where this was described in painstaking detail as the very first of the main types of offering. As regards the rules of the ritual process, we are told here that whoever brought the animal to the door of the tabernacle, 'he shal put his hand vpon the head of the burnt offring', then kill the animal, flay it and cut it to pieces (Leviticus 1: 5–6), so that the priests, Aaron's sons, can do the rest, that is, sprinkle the blood on the altar, make the fire and put the gobbets of meat and bones on it to be burned. These details may have come to mind to fill the blank spaces of the reticent narration at the end of both the ballad and the biblical text, long before the advent of illustrations or paintings mercilessly, indeed indulgently, visualized the tactfully suppressed parts of the story.

These details, especially shocking when a human being is to be sacrificed, were but thinly veiled by Hamlet's allusion to the ballad and Judges 11: 29–40, and could be imagined by the biblically-minded because of the vow's implied reference to Leviticus 1: 1–17. Their implicitness is very far from the stark openness of *Titus Andronicus* describing a human sacrifice first by Lucius in his command ('Away with him, and make a fire straight, / And with our swords upon a pile of wood / Let's hew his limbs till they be clean consumed' (1.1.127–9)) and afterwards by Lucius whose words, addressed to Titus, appeal to the visual imagination: 'See, lord and father, how we have performed / Our Roman rites: Alarbus' limbs are lopped / And entrails feed the sacrificing fire...' (1.1.142–5). Although here the human sacrifice itself was performed off-stage, as (animal) sacrifices had been in ancient Greek tragedy,[23] it was so much foregrounded verbally, that the detailed ritual immediately horrified not only Tamora, the mother of the victim ('O cruel, irreligious piety!' (1.1.130)), and Chiron ('Was never Scythia half so barbarous!' (1.1.131)), but most probably some of Shakespeare's contemporary audience as well. Unlike any such verbal visualization, Hamlet quotes the enigmatically vague first stanza of the ballad, and the dialogue is interrupted before Polonius could respond to the last bit ('It came to pass / As most like it was'), so it takes time even for the most biblical-minded spectators, or even readers, to realize the awful event to which these lines refer. Although the difference in explicitness is mainly due to the different dramaturgical function of the two scenes in their respective plays, a further possible cause to be considered is that Hamlet's allusion, however indirectly biblical it is, could still be *expected* to recall the awesome ritual process, so there was much less need to spell out everything than in the

---

[23] Albert Henrichs, '"Let the Good Prevail": Perversions of the Ritual Process in Greek Tragedy', in *Greek Ritual Poetics*, ed. Dimitrios Yatromanolakis and Panagiotis Roilos (Cambridge, MA, 2004), pp. 191–3.

case of the 'Roman rites'. Without some recognizable clues the Elizabethan spectators could not have remembered, and hence could not have visualized, that Alarbus's limbs were to be hewed or lopped, because it was not part of their everyday routine to read or hear texts about ancient Roman ritual. The biblical story of Jephthah and his daughter, however, recalls the corresponding technical description of the sacrifice in Leviticus, including that the person who brings the animal to the altar has to do the slaughtering himself (1: 5), which gives an especially sinister connotation to Hamlet's warning to Polonius: if you are not careful you will not only unwittingly precipitate your daughter's death but your deed will be as grave as actually killing her.

'EUM HOLOCAUSTUM OFFERAM': THE EMERGENCE OF AN ACCRETIVE ALLUSION

If allusions were to be confined to those intended by the author, as has been suggested,[24] then we would be overwhelmed not only by the much-debated problems, both theoretical and practical, ensuing from the elusiveness of authorial intention,[25] but we would have to ignore the entire afterlife of the alluding text, and no allusion could be allowed to refer to any text later than the death of the author nor to any later interpretations of earlier texts. Yet I propose to accept, if only as a separate type, allusions that are created by later and unintended accretion of meaning. Used intransitively, the verb *to accrete* means to grow by being added to; hence an accretive allusion is created by some later and probably unforeseen (sometimes clearly unpredictable) addition of meaning. Although to some extent every utterance is prone to accrete new meanings, as our use of language does not cease to make connections between the new and the old, the accretive nature of allusions is especially challenging, because the intervention of new meaning leads us far beyond the old one without breaking away altogether, retaining some of its well-known salient features, and thus suggesting an intricate, embarrassing, often unwanted continuity that seems easier to discard than to face and explore.

Just as the editors of etymological dictionaries have often found it easier to set apart meanings as if they had nothing to do with each other except in their identical form (considered merely accidental), and hence the metaphorical logic or subconscious psychology of some etymological connections has rarely been explored.[26] In literary studies later accretions of meaning were often discarded without proper study, considering the new addition discontinuous, its effects irrelevant or even detrimental, and any interest in them not worthy of the serious scholar. Yet by studying the unintended later meanings of the biblical reference in the ballad that Hamlet quoted one can realize how an accretive allusion (or the accreted meanings of any allusion) can challenge our interpretation of a literary text and, indirectly, our implied standards of judgement.[27]

But first we have to accept that although Hamlet quoted an English ballad, and Shakespeare was most familiar with the Geneva Bible, we need not always confine the ballad's biblical allusion to the Geneva Bible. Regardless of Hamlet's purpose or Shakespeare's intention, the ballad refers to the biblical story by no specific biblical quotation; thus it is not committed either to one concrete translation or to the original Hebrew text and hence practically each and every variant of this intertextual and multi-lingual allusion could be fully legitimate for us to consider. If the Prince of *Denmark*, coming home from a *Latin*-speaking university in a *German*-speaking Wittenberg, can quote an *English* ballad when talking to a *Danish* courtier called *Polonius*, the language domain of this fictive

---

[24] William Irvin, 'What Is an Allusion?', *Journal of Aesthetics and Art Criticism*, 59 (2001), p. 290; Hannibal Hamlin, *The Bible in Shakespeare*, p. 80.

[25] *On Literary Intention*, ed. David Newton-de Molina (Edinburgh, 1976).

[26] For a notable exception see Theodore Thass-Thienemann, *The Interpretation of Language*, 2 vols. (New York, 1973). See Pesaresi, Massimo Mandolini, review of *Gabriele Costa: Le origini della lingua poetica indeuropea: voce coscienza e transizione neolitica*, *Annali di Italianistica*, 18 (2000), 480–1.

[27] On the surfacing of implied standards, see J. L. Austin, 'A Plea for Excuses', in *Philosophical Papers* (Oxford, 1979), pp. 194–5.

world is paradoxical enough to leave some room to manoeuvre; by the same token, if we can accept that the play's motifs are denominationally mixed, for example 'a young man from Wittenberg, with a distinctly Protestant temperament, is haunted by a distinctly Catholic ghost',[28] then our discussion need not always be limited to one or two Protestant Bibles of Shakespeare's time, and our interpretation of a play so much interspersed with Latin phrases need not exclude occasional references to the Vulgate. When the ballad refers to Jephthah's vow we may well think of its text in the Geneva Bible, 'that thing that commeth out of the dores of mine house to mete me, . . . shal be the Lords, and I wil offer it for a burnt offring' (Judges 11: 31), but, for once, we may just as well let the ballad allude to the Vulgate, where the same part of the vow reads like this: 'quicumque primus fuerit egressus de foribus domus meae mihique occurrerit . . . eum holocaustum offeram Domino' (Liber Iudicum 11:31). The word 'holocaustum' requires no explanation here, because it is a regular technical term much used in the Old Testament and well-defined in Leviticus. In Leviticus 1: 3 the Vulgate uses the same term as in Jephthah's vow and spells out its necessary and sufficient conditions: 'si holocaustum fuerit eius oblatio ac de armento masculum immaculatum offeret ad ostium tabernaculi testimonii ad placandum sibi Dominum'. (In the Geneva Bible, as quoted above, it is rendered like this: 'If his sacrifice be a burnt offring of the herde, he shal offer a male without blemish, presenting him of his owne voluntary wil at the dore of the Tabernacle of the Congregacion before the Lord' (1: 3).) A few verses later in the minute description of the ritual process the term is used again in 1: 9: 'adolebitque ea sacerdos super altare in holocaustum' ('and the Priest shal burne all on the altar: *for* it is a burnt offring'), then in 1: 10 and 1: 13, referring to the burnt offering of the flocks (sheep or goat), then in 1: 14 and 1: 17, applied to the burnt offering of the fowls (turtle doves or young pigeons), each time repeating the basic definition, making it the closing formula of the chapter: 'et adolebit super altare lignis igne subposito holocaustum est et oblatio suavissimi odoris Domino' ('and

the Priest shal burne it vpon the altar vpon the wood that is in ye fire: *for* it is a burnt offring, an oblatió made by fire for a swete sauour vnto the Lord.'). The English Bibles that were possibly read or heard by Shakespeare before writing *Hamlet* did not use the Anglicized word *holocaust* either in these verses or elsewhere in the text, but the Douay-Rheims Bible, published in two volumes in 1609–10, followed the Latin Vulgate closely and resolutely enough to adapt the word in Jephthah's vow in Judges 11: 31 ('Whosoever shall first come forth out of the doors of my house, . . . the same I will offer a holocaust to the Lord') and in all the relevant places in Leviticus (1: 3; 1: 9–10; 1: 13; 7: 2; 9: 16–17) and elsewhere in the Old Testament. Though the word was used by English authors earlier in Shakespeare's time (Philip Stubbes in his 'Epistle Dedicatorie' of *The Anatomie of Abuses*, first published in 1583, wrote that the Lord commanded Moses to build a tabernacle 'that therin his law might be read, his ceremonies practiced, Sacrifices, Victimats & Holocausts offred'[29]), it was in the first volume of the Douay Old Testament in 1609 that its use as a biblical word in English began, only a few years before the translators of the 1611 King James Bible cited it as one of the many examples of the 'obscuritie of the Papists' they decided to shun.[30] Although most of the other such terms have remained obscure ever since, and it was rightly observed that 'such words as *Pasche, Corbana, Parasceue,* and *Azymes* are as strange-sounding today as they were in 1582' (the publication date of the Rheims New Testament),[31] the word *holocaust* has moved in the opposite direction: it became familiar and transparent long before it reappeared in modern Catholic translations, such as the *New Revised Standard Version Bible: Catholic Anglicized Edition*, published in 1989, 1995 and 1999.

---

[28] Stephen Greenblatt, *Hamlet in Purgatory* (Princeton, 2001), p. 240.

[29] Stubbes, *The Anatomie of Abuses*, s.p.

[30] 'The Translators To the Reader', in *The Holy Bible, Conteyning the Old Testament and the New* (London, 1611), facsimile edition (Peabody, MA, 2010), sig. B2v.

[31] Shaheen, *Biblical References in Shakespeare's Plays*, p. 34.

Meantime, however, history attached further meanings to this word family. Neither Hamlet nor Polonius in the fictive world of the play could have been aware of our present-day associations of *holocaustum*, an ancient term cognate with the Greek ὁλοκαύτωμα used by the Septuagint, and of course neither Shakespeare nor his audience or readership could have divined the widespread, if controversial, twentieth-century afterlife of the term from its first isolated occurrences in 1933, 1938, 1939, 1941 and 1942 to its gaining wider currency from the late 1950s onwards,[32] the metaphorical application of the ancient Hebrew religious notion of whole burnt offering to the extermination of latter-day Hebrews together with Gipsies, homosexuals and other victimized categories in the camps, gas chambers and crematoriums. The ballad, quoted by Hamlet, alludes to Jephthah's sacrifice in the book of Judges, and one of the most influential translations of the Bible, the Vulgate, rendered that sacrifice with a word, *holocaustum*, that came to designate (many centuries later and by the accretion of new, yet not unrelated meaning) a twentieth-century genocide. If I may coin a much-needed term for the birth and formation of allusions in such a belated and maybe anachronistic manner, Hamlet's reference is a striking example of an *accretive* allusion, unintended, but with grave consequences for interpretation. For a moment the ensuing new perspective shows the possible future of Ophelia as repeating the fate of Jephthah's daughter, yet not only as the biblical example of *holocaustum* but also as the first victim of what was to be called *the* Holocaust. I know that some try to discredit or even condemn the making of any such connection between the two meanings of the word, the old biblical one signifying a religious ritual and the new one designating atrocities in twentieth-century European history, but their arguments, though displaying solid data selected from the history of the word's usage, are based on a logic that is flawed and leads to false conclusions. True, the word had already been used in English at the beginning of the century to denote all sorts of catastrophes man-made or natural (whether by fire or not), and its first applications to the mass-murder

of Jews by the Nazis were not a product of theological thinking,[33] but these premises are not sufficient for the conclusion that the biblical word could not shape the meaning of its modern likeness, or that it is mistaken and harmful (if not downright wicked) to assume that it did. True, it is an 'etymological fallacy' to assume that a word's original meaning would forever fix its 'correct sense',[34] and I accept the thesis quoted here from Samuel Johnson that '[t]he original sense of words is often driven out of use by their metaphorical acceptations', but one should not omit the other half of Johnson's sentence either, which nevertheless insists that the former sense 'must be inserted for the sake of a regular origination', and his additional remark that knowing 'the primitive ideas of these words . . . the figurative sense may be commodiously deduced'.[35]

Even if those who applied the phrase *holocaust* in the 1930s and early 1940s did not mean to use it with theological implications, some of them (including the chief rabbis of Palestine and England) must have been aware of its biblical origin, and at any rate the word could not help bringing along some of its old connotations. It is worth recalling J. L. Austin's linguistic insight from the mid-1950s that words hardly ever shake off their formative pre-history, they do not shed their former meaning completely; indeed, they come to us 'trailing clouds of etymology' (as the new-born child comes 'trailing clouds of glory' in Wordsworth's Immortality Ode). Austin is right to conclude that withstanding yet also governing any changes or extensions of a word's meaning

---

32 Philologos, 'Roots of the Holocaust: On Language', *The Jewish Daily Forward*, 16 September 2005. http://forward .com/articles/2793/roots-of-the-holocaust/*; James E. Young, *Writing and Rewriting the Holocaust: Narrative and the Consequences of Interpretation* (Bloomington and Indianapolis, 1990), p. 200.

33 Jon Petrie, 'The Secular Word HOLOCAUST: Scholarly Myths, History, and 20th Century Meanings', *Journal of Genocide Research*, 2.1 (2000), 31–63.

34 Petrie, 'The secular word HOLOCAUST', p. 36.

35 Samuel Johnson, 'Preface' [to A Dictionary of the English Language, 1755], in *Johnson on the English Language*, ed. Gwin J. Kold and Robert DeMaria, Jr (New Haven and London, 2005), p. 92.

'there will still persist the old idea', an inherited notion usually in the form of some etymologically coded 'pictures or *models* of how things happen or are done'. This legacy of the word's past may be half-forgotten but it is effectively shaping the applications of the word even when the new phenomenon it is applied to is so remote, and has become so important for us in its own right, that the inherited model would distort rather than elucidate its features.[36] The thesis (also couched in Wordsworthian language) that 'no word ever achieves entire forgetfulness of its origins'[37] may unwittingly confirm the much earlier observation (by Hermann Paul in 1880) of how our mind retains old meanings that subconsciously influence our thinking;[38] it also chimes in with Theodore Thass-Thienemann's later view that whenever the new meaning of a word replaces the old one it is due to some connection, they must have something in common, and this may help us understand the way symbolic language works.[39] Yet we should add that no word ever achieves entire forgetfulness of its *afterlife* either, so it is worth investigating what happens when the biblical word *holocaustum* appears in a new context, trailing clouds of its former and later etymological history and inducing associative shortcuts in the mind of a modern reader. Moreover, although those referring to a series of atrocious crimes by the Nazis as 'the Holocaust' hardly ever meant it (strictly speaking) as a religious sacrifice, there were theologians, both Jewish and Christian, who followed the inherited biblical logic and interpreted the Holocaust as a sacrifice pointing back to its origins in the Old Testament and, metaphorically, in Jesus's example.

OPHELIA AS JEPHTHAH'S 'HOLOCAUSTUM': FROM THE BIBLE VIA HOLOCAUST THEOLOGY TO *HAMLET*

The accretion of meanings that turned Hamlet's biblical reference into an accretive allusion implies discrepancies, both ancient and anachronistically modern, that deepen some of the central problems of *Hamlet* and adds further paradoxes to its interpretive richness. Obviously, neither Jephthah's daughter nor Ophelia fits the requirements of *holocaustum* proper. As the Geneva Bible formulates it: "'If his sacrifice *be* a burnt offring of the herde, he shal offer a male without blemish, presenting him of his owne voluntary wil at the dore of the Tabernacle of the Congregacion before the Lord."' (Leviticus 1: 3). The text unambiguously confines this type of offering to animals (bull, sheep, goat, fowl) and this in itself underlines the strikingly unusual, even if not unprecedented, situation created by Jephthah's vow. Moreover, the criteria for the animal to be offerable provide a bitterly ironic correspondence or contrast when applied to Jephthah's daughter and Ophelia. As human beings, neither fits into the first and most basic category of this description (or, rather, prescription), but they are not male either (as Isaac was). Symptomatically, the female human being as burnt offering clashes even with the most practical socio-economic reason for the tradition of sacrificing a male animal: whereas in livestock-raising societies female animals were precious for their milk products and their role in breeding, and the males were considered expendable,[40] it is repeatedly stressed that Jephthah's daughter 'had knowen no man' (Judges 11: 39), so she was sacrificed before she could be a mother, and Ophelia was driven to death before she could breed, too. On the other hand Jephthah's daughter and Ophelia fit the requirement of being unblemished, both as characters and in the sense of being intact as virgins. As regards the criterion of voluntariness on the part of the person who brings the offering to the Tabernacle, Jephthah himself, though unhappy about his former vow, presents his daughter 'of his owne voluntary wil' and, unlike Abraham, he does it not in order to obey the

---

[36] Austin, 'A Plea for Excuses', pp. 201–3.

[37] Austin, 'Three Ways of Spilling Ink', *Philosophical Papers*, p. 283.

[38] Hermann Paul, *Prinzipien der Sprachgeschichte* (Tübingen, 1960), p. 25.

[39] Theodore Thass-Thienemann, *The Interpretation of Language*, 2 vols. (New York, 1973), vol. 1, pp. 81–2.

[40] Milgrom, 'Comment: The Burnt Offering: Name, Antiquity, Function', p. 174.

Lord's command, but to fulfil a vow that he had initiated without any external pressure whatsoever. This is exactly what George Buchanan's *Jephthes sive Votum* (1554) emphasizes when the priest urges the father not to ascribe his own cruel deed to God because He did neither demand nor condone the making of the vow, an arbitrary act of sheer human folly: 'infandum scelus / qui perpetrare spondet, ultro adfectibus / stultis suisque paret ille insomniis. / proinde voti quicquid illud est, deum / crudelitati desine adscribere tuae.'[41] ('He who binds himself to carry out unspeakable crime obeys without compulsion his own dreams and foolish feeling. So whatever that vow of yours, cease to associate God with your cruelty.')[42]

The great question is how the *function of holocaustum* proper, implied in Judges and defined in Leviticus, relates to the sacrifice of Jephthah's daughter and the death of Ophelia, and how do the meanings ascribed to this term, from the Septuagint and the Vulgate up to the sixteenth century and beyond, confirm, qualify or subvert the attribution of this function. Originally the burnt offering was meant primarily as a ploy to make amends so that the Lord's wrath ceased: 'And he shal put his hand vpon the head of the burnt offring and it shalbe accepted to *the Lord*, to be his atonement' (Leviticus 1:4). When 1:19 adds that 'the Priest shal burne all on the altar: *for* it is a burnt offring, an oblatió made by fire, for a swete sauour vnto the Lord', the marginal note of the Geneva Bible explains the sweetness thus: 'Or a sauour of rest, which pacifieth the angre of the Lord'. But if so, then the Lord must have been either angry for something, hence the need for a burnt offering presupposed some kind of sin (idol worship, betrayal of the true faith, moral corruption) which was to be punished by Him, or maybe (as in Jephthah's case) there was a confrontation of human powers which could be settled in favour of one of the parties, so the burnt offering was a means to ensure that God's might would be wielded against the other side. A whole burnt offering or *holocaustum* as the supreme kind of sacrifice, meant to be a means of reconciliation between sinful man and wrathful God, had often reminded commentators of the sacrifice of Jesus

for mankind. The first complete Hungarian translation of the Bible, published in 1590, attached a marginal note to Leviticus 1: 9, next to the Hungarian phrase 'egészlen égő áldozatúl' ('as a whole burnt offering'), interpreting it as a prefiguring of Christ's sacrifice: 'The burning of the entire body for a sacrifice, the specific type of sacrifice called holocaustum, exemplified the sacrificing of Jesus Christ in his entire being, because he was entirely devoted to something and sacrificed himself for us, otherwise we would have been lost entirely in body and soul alike.'[43] The implied meaning of expiation is still there: the death of Christ as a *holocaustum* was meant for the sins of mankind. When the term was applied to Nazi mass-murder, some biblical-minded thinkers could not but follow the implied biblical logic and interpreted the Nazi crimes as either a divine punishment, an indication of a wrathful God turning away his face or a divine instrument for purifying the world. (However, the term seems to have confirmed this logic rather than having created it; for example in Hungary several rabbis were preaching in this vein during or shortly after the Second World War, decades before the new meaning of the word holocaust gained currency in the country.) This was one of the starting points leading to what came to be called *holocaust theology*, a body of thought elaborated to come to terms with 'the' Holocaust in a way that would make theological sense. Needless to say, many of the survivors protested against the application of both parts of the composite term because they suspected their mutual tendency to imply some kind of theodicy and they did not want to see any transcendental meaning, let alone justification, in mass-murder.

Even nearer to Hamlet's allusion to the Jephthah story, some Jewish and Christian theologians resorted to the original biblical meaning of

---

[41] George Buchanan, *Tragedies*, ed. P. Sharratt and P. G. Walsh (Edinburgh, 1983), pp. 50–1.
[42] Buchanan, *Tragedies*, pp. 83–4.
[43] *Szent Biblia az-az: Istennec Ó és Wy Testamentvmanac prophétác es apostoloc által meg iratott Szent könyuei*, transl. Károli Gáspár (Vizsoly, 1590). Translation mine.

holocaustum as burnt offering, a certain type of ritual *sacrifice* in their attempts to theologize what came to be called the Holocaust. In *The Face of God after Auschwitz*, Ignaz Maybaum quoted the word of God from the book of Jeremiah calling Nebuchadnezzar, the destroyer of Jerusalem, 'my servant' (Jeremiah 27: 6), and concluded that Hitler could also be considered God's servant, otherwise contemptible yet used as God's instrument 'to cleanse, to purify, to punish a sinful world'.[44] Maybaum was fully aware of the biblical meanings of ritual burnt offerings: his previous book, in 1959, was *The Sacrifice of Isaac*, and he always emphasized that the Akedah, the binding of Isaac, was the heart of Judaism precisely because there followed no human sacrifice. When he applied the analogy of sacrifice to Auschwitz, he was retaining its traditional religious logic and implications, though avoiding the term *holocaust* and foregrounding the atonement: 'The innocent who died in Auschwitz . . . atone for evil and are the sacrifice which is brought to the altar and which God acknowledged favourably. The six million, the dead of Auschwitz and of other places of horror, are Jews whom our modern civilisation has to canonise as holy martyrs; they died as sacrificial lambs because of the sins inherent in Western civilisation. Their death purified Western civilization . . .'[45] Whereas Maybaum professed all this as a lesson different from yet compatible with the cross as the emblem of Christianity,[46] Ulrich Simon's *A Theology of Auschwitz* (1967) based the analogy of sacrificial offering on the example of Jesus. Sacrificed on the cross, it was through Jesus that 'the tremendous themes of atonement were translated from temple ritual and annual observance to a celestial sanctuary', hence one can 'appropriate this pattern partly for the victims of Auschwitz' who 'enter into the supreme sacrifice by the way of a sharing analogy'.[47] Simon is not hesitant to call this a *holocaust*, interpreting it 'in the great tradition of prophetic expectation and priestly ritual', in the full theological meaning of the term. 'This holocaust is no less a sacrifice than that prefigured in the Scriptures. Here again the circle closes, and the lives of the many are given

for the sins of the world.'[48] Talking about the Holocaust like this, it is hardly possible to separate original and accreted meanings, yet it is clear that the implications of Jesus's sacrifice differ from that of Jephthah's daughter. The claim that the innocent who died in Auschwitz *atone for* evil (Maybaum) and were *given for* the sins of the world (Simon) seems to imply the *do ut des* formula latent in all burnt offerings and probably in any sacrifice,[49] but such a reductive similarity cannot do justice to their significant differences and does not provide a sufficient explanation for their motivation either.

Should we try to apply such meanings, original or accreted, of *holocaustum*, to Ophelia's death? More importantly, and to borrow Hamlet's word, what 'follows' when we do it and how does it affect the play's interpretation? In the light of the ominous term *holocaustum* we can re-imagine Ophelia's death by water metaphorically as death by fire, only to face the disturbing question that has always been implied in *holocaustum*, even more so since the twentieth-century accretion of its meanings: how could the ascending smoke of her incinerated body be 'a swete savour' to the Lord? Did it really ascend to the Lord, or did it go astray after we have lost sight of it, just as עלה (*'ala*), the Hebrew verb cognate with the noun עלה (*'ola*) translated as *holocaustum*, could mean not only 'ascend' but also 'disappear' (e.g., Genesis 17:22, 35:13; Exodus 16:14)?[50] And if the ascending fragrance was meant to pacify and reconcile a wrathful God, what was the cause of divine anger in the world of the play? And if there is a divine consent behind each and every event, as the play implies in the

44 Ignaz Maybaum, *The Face of God after Auschwitz* (Amsterdam, 1965), p. 67.
45 Maybaum, *The Face of God after Auschwitz*, p. 84.
46 Maybaum, *The Face of God after Auschwitz*, p. 67.
47 Ulrich Simon, *A Theology of Auschwitz* (London, 1978), pp. 84–5.
48 Simon, *A Theology of Auschwitz*, pp. 83–4.
49 Cf. Gerhard von Rad, *Old Testament Theology*, trans. D. M. G. Stalker, 2 vols. (New York and Evanston, 1962), vol. 1, pp. 255–6, 259–60; Milgrom, *Leviticus 17–22*, pp. 1587–8.
50 Milgrom, 'Comment: The Burnt Offering: Name, Antiquity, Function', pp. 172–4.

biblical reference to the fall of a sparrow, then how does this apply to Ophelia's death, especially as seen in the light of the *holocaustum* of Jephthah's unnamed daughter and the many daughters and sons, named and unnamed, of the twentieth century? And if Ophelia's death can be contemplated as one belonging to all these, should we ask whether it was a sacrifice and thus had a real meaning, as sacrifices have always been supposed to have, or should we abhor even the thought of it, denying that there can be a theology of any *holocaustum* when applied to human beings? Finally, if Jephthah's daughter, Ophelia and the victims of Auschwitz are all to be seen as examples of an ancient sacrifice, how can they maintain their uniqueness, a trait so important to some interpreters that they stubbornly refuse to admit even the possibility of any historical precedent or later comparison? Are we to conclude that nothing can ever be a 'pattern, precedent', let alone a 'lively warrant' for anybody 'to perform the like'? Or is it just the opposite insight that we should learn here, namely, that human suffering, though always unique, is never unprecedented, neither is the human desire to make sense of it, and we still belong to a long tradition that has desperately sought to find some dignified meaning even in the ascending smoke of burning human flesh? All in all, we can be grateful that Hamlet's biblical reference, taken as an accretive allusion of multiple origins, raises these difficult, maybe unanswerable, yet troubling questions that further problematize one of Shakespeare's most intriguing plays.

THE ELEPHANTS' GRAVEYARD REVISITED: SHAKESPEARE AT WORK IN *ANTONY AND CLEOPATRA, ROMEO AND JULIET* AND *ALL'S WELL THAT ENDS WELL*

CATHERINE BELSEY

I

'Origins and Originality', the clever and provocative topic of this volume, has prompted me to reflect on the meaning of both terms in their relation to our activities as Shakespeare scholars. If Shakespeare's writing is not original, what is? And yet, paradoxically, the affirmation of absolute originality would rule out any origins for the work beyond the writer's own mind, and we know that very few of the plays originate solely in Shakespeare's domed head. Most of them are derivative in one significant way or another. How could it be otherwise? Writing, any writing, is unthinkable outside the existence of shared conventions of storytelling or staging, genre and decorum, not to mention the language itself in which they are intelligible. In that sense, all writing finds its origins somewhere else and its limited originality resides in its difference from what has gone before. Moreover, the places where writing originates are not themselves moments of pure origin. Habits of narrative, theatre, propriety, meaning emerge from previous practices in an infinite regress.

We can, however, artificially freeze that unceasing process for inspection by comparing a new work with a predecessor. And to that end, I want to add my voice to pleas for a return to Shakespeare's sources. In the version of 'Shakespeare and the Exorcists' published in 1985 Stephen Greenblatt commented that source study was 'as we all know, the elephants' graveyard of literary history', a place where old scholars go to die.[1] The remark

was partly ironic: he was about to expand on the relationship between *King Lear* and a known source, Samuel Harsnett's *Declaration of Egregious Popish Impostures*. At the same time, the observation pointed to the way the sources identified have so often remained inert in the process of interpretation, dead bones uncovered in the living text but with few implications for its final shape. Much of our ambivalence towards the tradition of attending to Shakespeare's reading stems from the weakness of that focus in explaining his work.[2] Greenblatt's essay well and truly brought Harsnett to life, if not precisely as a source, but since then source study has continued to decline, to the point where Arden 3, for example, has virtually replaced it with critical insights and performance history.[3] (I have had to keep my copies of Arden 2 to retain easy access to the dates of the plays and earlier versions of their plots.) I have nothing against critical insights or performance history, and have

---

[1] Stephen Greenblatt, 'Shakespeare and the Exorcists', in *Shakespeare and the Question of Theory*, ed. Patricia Parker and Geoffrey Hartman (New York, 1985), pp. 163–87; p. 163. The comment was not included when the essay was republished in *Shakespearean Negotiations* (Oxford, 1988), pp. 94–128.

[2] Greenblatt, 'Shakespeare and the Exorcists', p. 165; Steven Mentz, 'Revising the Sources: Novella, Romance, and the Meanings of Fiction in *All's Well, That Ends Well*', in *All's Well, That Ends Well: New Critical Essays*, ed. Gary Waller (New York, 2007), pp. 57–70; p. 57.

[3] Cf. Douglas Bruster, *Shakespeare and the Question of Culture: Early Modern Literature and the Cultural Turn* (New York, 2003), pp. 167–90; esp. pp. 173–5.

contributed in a modest way to both. But comparison with the sources is where we catch Shakespeare at work. It's what he changes that throws into relief what makes him Shakespeare. (Please note that 'Shakespeare' includes not only the playwright but also the collaborators, scribes and compositors, as well as members of the company, who may have had a hand in producing the texts available to us.)

A source is a source to the degree that it resembles Shakespeare's text. But it is a source, and not the work itself, to the degree that it differs from that text. In those differences we can find Shakespeare's hand, his limited originality (limited because the differences themselves may well be derived from other sources in a profusion of intertextual filiations). We discard a precious asset if we opt to ignore the sources. In the hope of persuading anyone who remains to be convinced, let me offer three rather different examples of the kind of thing I mean. In the process, I risk rehearsing much that is already familiar. I hope readers of *Shakespeare Survey* will think I do so in a good cause.

II

First, Antony's beard. It is well known that Shakespeare's account of Cleopatra's first meeting with Antony echoes Plutarch's, or rather Sir Thomas North's translation of Plutarch's *Life of Marcus Antonius* (*Antony and Cleopatra*, 2.2.200–36).[4] In this instance, the editor of Arden 3 prints Plutarch's version, or most of it, in the notes at the foot of the page – and comments, 'Closely though he follows this passage, Shakespeare also modifies and develops it. By comparing the two extracts we have an opportunity to observe his imagination working on his material.'[5]

Exactly. So let's do that. Here Shakespeare makes a virtue of necessity. The first encounter between his protagonists, the moment when Antony falls in love, is crucial to Shakespeare's story, as it is to Plutarch's. But it would be impossible to do justice on the early modern stage to the spectacle Plutarch describes and, in any case, the event belongs in the past, before the action of the play begins. *Antony and Cleopatra* is particularly given to such analepses

and they rely on reminiscence.[6] There were precedents. In Book 2 of the *Aeneid* the hero tells the history of the Trojan War as a set-piece narrative at the court of Dido, and in Shakespeare's play Enobarbus will narrate the meeting between the Egyptian queen and the general. Like Dido's Carthaginians, his Roman audience, Maecenas and Agrippa, are eager to hear a first-hand version of the story.

The parallels between Shakespeare's version and Plutarch's are close. Students looking for differences, on the other hand, notice a distinction between biography and poetry. The biographer lists the properties employed, emphasizing the production values of the pageant: his Cleopatra puts herself on display. First, Plutarch specifies the colour scheme: the poop was gold, the sails purple and the oars silver; the oars, meanwhile, kept stroke to the sound of music. For her person, it was 'layed' under a pavilion of cloth of gold of tissue; Cleopatra was 'attired like' Venus as she appears in pictures; the little boys were 'apparelled as' painters portray them; her attendants were 'apparelled like' mermaids and Graces. Plutarch's Cleopatra is putting on a show: the entire impression is of wealth in the service of art.

Shakespeare allows the element of pageantry to be inferred but reduces the role of the painters and costume designers. Instead, his emphasis is on the *inability* of the arts to match the ineffable reality. Cleopatra herself 'o'erpictures' the work of the painter, just as she 'beggars' the description of the poet. While Plutarch's Cleopatra mimics art, Shakespeare's surpasses it. In Plutarch Cleopatra's

---

[4] Unless otherwise indicated, Shakespeare references are to *The Arden Shakespeare Complete Works*, ed. Richard Proudfoot, Ann Thompson and David Scott Kastan (London, 2011).

[5] William Shakespeare, *Antony and Cleopatra*, ed. John Wilders (London, 1995), 2.2.201–28n. 'The two passages are worth detailed comparison in order to see how fine prose is alchemized into great poetry' (William Shakespeare, *The Tragedy of Antony and Cleopatra*, ed. Michael Neill (Oxford, 1994), 2.2.198–233n). Like Arden 2, Neill's edition includes extracts from Plutarch as an appendix.

[6] The play incorporates the past into the present from the beginning. Philo's opening speech contrasts what was with what is (1.1.1–10). See also, for example, 1.3.34–8; 1.4.57–69; 2.2.187–93; 2.5.15–23; 3.6.1–19; 3.11.35–40; 3.13.87–90.

desirability is implied by the allusions to Venus, Cupid, the mermaids; Shakespeare leaves the references in place but also sexualizes everything else, including the props. His barge burns; the winds are love-sick for the sails; the water is excited by a beating from the oars; the tackle swells at the touch of the women's hands.[7] Plutarch's citizens flock to see the queen, leaving her Roman visitor alone in the imperial seat in the market-place; in Shakespeare, the air would have gone to gaze at her too, were it not that nature abhors a vacuum.

So far, so familiar. Teachers of Shakespeare may well have covered this ground with their students a dozen times. As the class can see, out of what is presented as historical fact, Shakespeare makes a succession of metaphors and their effectiveness is registered by the fictional audience. 'O, rare for Antony!' exclaims Agrippa, 'Rare Egyptian!' (2.2.212, 225). But other elements that do not come from Plutarch begin to indicate the intervention of the fictional teller, Enobarbus. In his account, the great warrior – *whistles*: 'Antony, / Enthroned i'th'market-place, did sit alone, / Whistling to th'air' (221–3). The image is suddenly absurd: in Egypt, representing the imperial power, the 'triple pillar of the world' (1.1.12), accustomed to performing before huge crowds, idly plays at indifference when his audience deserts him for the competition.

The source extract given in the notes in Arden 3 stops here but Enobarbus is not done yet. In both accounts Antony invites Cleopatra to supper; she reverses the invitation and Antony politely accepts. According to Plutarch, he is profoundly impressed by the sumptuous fare and the splendour of the lighting. In the play Enobarbus tells a different story:

> Our courteous Antony,
> Whom ne'er the word of 'No' woman heard speak,
> Being barbered ten times o'er, goes to the feast,
> And, for his ordinary, pays his heart
> For what his eyes eat only.   (*Antony*, 2.2.232–6)

Antony falls in love: he pays with his heart for a meal consumed purely by his eyes; his gaze is captivated just like the citizens', just as the air's

would be. Evidently, desire for Cleopatra is a leveller: no one, nothing, however powerful, however commonplace, is immune to it. Moreover, Antony can't eat – like a teenager anxious in the presence of his idol. And he has his beard trimmed ten times, like the same adolescent hovering by the bathroom mirror. What, meanwhile, are we to make of the fact that Antony never says no to a woman? Is it that courtesy does not refuse a lady, or that he cannot turn down any overture from the opposite sex?

The register has switched abruptly from the grand to the everyday: whistling is not imperial; barbers do not belong in heroic verse; an 'ordinary' is an unimposing tavern meal. And the effect is mocking. Enobarbus the plain soldier integrates a sceptical point of view into the record of a legendary love affair. Plutarch, narrating in his own voice, judges and records, but he separates judgement from incident, commentary from the event; while no anecdote is too small to escape his attention, the story is often there to support or exemplify a prior assessment of character. And Plutarch has no patience whatever with the 'pestilent plague and mischiefe of Cleopatraes love',[8] although he does concede the charm of her conversation and the courage of her death. Shakespeare's soldier, by contrast, decries his general in the vocabulary that tells his story. The difference is one of degree, of course: no narrative delivered in words can be wholly impartial. But Enobarbus does not even pretend to be bound by the facts. Did Antony actually whistle, playgoers might wonder, or is this a case of un-poetic licence? *Ten* trips to the barber's? Did he really eat *nothing* at the feast? But then, we didn't literally suppose the winds were love-sick or the waves enjoyed their beating. Hyperbole is at work in both cases, but here it acts in the service

---

[7] Possibly this imagery echoes elements of Dido's promise to repair the Trojan ships (*Dido, Queen of Carthage*, in *The Complete Works of Christopher Marlowe*, ed. Fredson Bowers, vol. 1 (Cambridge, 1981), 3.1.113–33). See Janet Adelman, *The Common Liar: An Essay on 'Antony and Cleopatra'* (New Haven, 1973), p. 181.

[8] Geoffrey Bullough, ed., *Narrative and Dramatic Sources of Shakespeare*, 8 vols. (London, 1957–75), vol. 5, pp. 254–321; p. 283.

of irony: if the account of the spectacle inflates the queen's enchantment, the tale of Antony's capitulation diminishes the general.

The practice of integrating a judgement of another character's conduct into a narrative within the play is characteristically Shakespearian. Richard II disparages Bolingbroke's courtship of the people as he goes into exile: 'Wooing poor craftsmen with the craft of smiles. . . . Off goes his bonnet to an oyster-wench' (*Richard II*, 1.4.28–31). The first we hear of Desdemona's elopement is that she is 'Transported' in the care of a mere gondolier 'To the gross clasps of a lascivious Moor' (*Othello* 1.1.122–4). In these cases it is not simply that opposed points of view confront one another: there is plenty of that in Kyd and Marlowe. Instead, an alternative assessment informs the narrative offered to playgoers of events they do not see.[9]

Because in these instances the detraction is ascribed to a fictional figure, it cannot be attributed to Shakespeare as *authoritative*: the scepticism of Enobarbus might be persuasive – until we remember that it will ultimately lead to heartbreak.[10] In other words, Shakespeare has invented the unreliable narrator, usually associated with the nineteenth-century novel. As Wayne Booth puts it, 'I have called a narrator *reliable* when he speaks for or acts in accordance with the norms of the work (which is to say, the implied author's norms), *unreliable* when he does not.' But we should note that 'Sometimes it is almost impossible to infer whether or to what degree a narrator is fallible.'[11]

While a negative is hard to prove, I cannot think where Shakespeare might have learnt to do this. There had been lying narrators, Virgil's Sinon, who fools the Trojans, for one. Ovid's *Heroides* take the point of view of the women who write the letters; Chaucer to varying degrees adapts the *Canterbury Tales* to the values of their tellers, or shows the reader his dream worlds though the eyes of a naïve reporter who cannot be relied on to make sense of what he sees. Rabelais narrates in character as, nearer home, does Thomas Nashe. But I should be glad to know of an earlier instance where a fictional storyteller so inflects the tale that

the point of view challenges evidence to be found elsewhere in the same work.

Or perhaps it doesn't. As narratologists recognize, 'Many texts make it difficult to decide whether the narrator is reliable or unreliable, and if unreliable – to what extent. Some texts – which may be called ambiguous narratives – make such a decision impossible, putting the reader in a position of constant oscillation between mutually exclusive alternatives.'[12] Uncertainty about how far to trust the narrator's judgement invites the audience to choose a position of its own, to look out for evidence elsewhere in the play that supports or rebuts the view put forward. *Antony and Cleopatra* incorporates this process into the scene itself. Maecenas, silent hitherto, does not echo Agrippa's thigh-slapping enthusiasm for Cleopatra. On the contrary, Antony must leave her, he declares (2.2.243). 'If beauty, wisdom, modesty can settle / The heart of Antony, Octavia is / A blessed lottery to him' (251–3). The general has just gone off to confirm his alliance with Caesar's sister when Enobarbus intervenes to remind playgoers of Cleopatra's magical power to seduce. Do the exchanges between these Romans not condense the undecidability of the play as a whole? Impossible not to feel reservations about Antony's

---

9   In view of the discrepancies between the Chorus and the play, James Hirsh identifies the Chorus of *Henry V* as an unreliable narrator, noting a similar strategy in Marlowe's choruses: 'Shakespeare's Stage Chorus and Olivier's Film Chorus', in *Shakespeare on Screen: The Henriad*, ed. Sarah Hatchuel and Natalie Vienne-Guerrin (Mont-Saint-Agnan, 2008), pp. 169–92.

10   'He persistently questions the sincerity of the passions, but when he follows his reason, he dies of a broken heart' (Adelman, *The Common Liar*, p. 24).

11   Wayne C. Booth, *The Rhetoric of Fiction* (Chicago, 1961), pp. 158–9; p. 160. In this respect Booth appears to contrast the novel with Shakespeare, where he finds 'persistent norms' (pp. 141–2). Modern narratology continues to refine the concept of the unreliable narrator but still in relation to the novel (see James Phelan, *Living to Tell about It: A Rhetoric and Ethics of Character Narration* (Ithaca, NY, 2005), esp. pp. 49–53). I am grateful to Marina Lambrou for advice on current work in narratology.

12   Shlomith Rimmon-Kenan, *Narrative Fiction: Contemporary Poetics* (London, 2002), p. 104.

dotage; equally impossible, surely, not to succumb to the play's imagery of desire, increasingly exalted as the hero's folly rebounds on his fortunes.[13]

Part of Shakespeare's enduring appeal must be the reluctance of the plays to resolve the questions they raise. Love, which elicits the most transcendent verse, also consistently arouses scepticism. If *Romeo and Juliet* gives a voice to Mercutio, while *Troilus and Cressida* makes a place for Thersites, the comedies, required to tip the balance in favour of romance by the genre they themselves invent, include nonetheless a Theseus or a Ganymede, who will have none of it – and *Shakespeare* remains enigmatic. Is that, in the end, the difference between *Antony and Cleopatra*, on the one hand, and its source on the other? Plutarch, gossipy, judgemental, busily enumerates Antony's virtues and vices. The play, by contrast, has the power to keep us guessing – and perhaps reflecting – if not on the value of love, on the nature of drama, which makes space for more than one narrative voice.

III

Perhaps Shakespeare had no need to learn from elsewhere about unreliable narrators. Conceivably, it just seemed inevitable that a storyteller would have an investment in the tale. Shakespeare's originality – if that is what it is – becomes visible in *Antony and Cleopatra* at the point where the play is faced with the challenge of a double genre switch to incorporate narrative back into drama and is thus required to confront its divergence from North's Plutarch. In my second example, concerning Phaeton's wagon, the sources present a different sort of problem and the originality lies in Shakespeare's talent for making a silk purse out of a sow's ear. Juliet's exclamation of impatience for her wedding night is well known and justly admired:

> Gallop apace, you fiery-footed steeds,
> Towards Phoebus' lodging. Such a waggoner
> As Phaeton would whip you to the west
> And bring in cloudy night immediately.
> (*Romeo and Juliet*, 3.2.1–4)

Not everyone is so familiar, however, with the humble origins of this passage in the sources. Here, first, for comparison, is the equivalent moment in William Painter's prose narrative *Romeo and Julietta*, translated more or less literally from the French version: both lovers are looking forward to the onset of night, 'for euery minute of an houre seemed to them a Thousand yeares, so that if they had power to commaund the Heauens (as Iosua did the Sunne), the Earth had incontinently bene shadowed wyth darkest Cloudes'.[14]

Shakespeare keeps the clouds and the urgency, but the oddity in this passage is Joshua, one of the Nine Worthies, who famously fought the battle of Jericho. On another occasion Joshua arrested the progress of the sun across the sky. When the people of Gibeon, who knew a conqueror when they saw one, chose to make peace with Israel rather than fight, five Middle-Eastern kings combined to punish the Gibeonites for their perfidy. No sooner had God put the kings to flight with a hailstorm, than Joshua ordered the sun to stand still, and the moon delayed her rising until the Gibeonites as Israel's allies had had a chance to avenge themselves fully on the enemy forces (Joshua 10:12–14).

But the intertextual analogy doesn't hold. First, far from hastening the night, Joshua prolonged the day; second, the motive for his intervention

---

[13] For analysis of the uncertainty the play provokes, see Adelman, *The Common Liar*, pp. 14–52, as well as Anne Barton, '"Nature's Piece 'Gainst Fancy": The Divided Catastrophe in Antony and Cleopatra', in *Essays, Mainly Shakespearean* (Cambridge, 1994), pp. 113–35; esp. pp. 126–30.

[14] William Painter, *Rhomeo and Iulietta, The Second Tome of the Palace of Pleasure* (London, 1567), fos. 179v–202v, fo. 186r. Opinions vary on whether Painter constitutes a source for the play. Bullough concedes that Shakespeare must have known Painter but believes Arthur Brooke's *Romeus and Juliet* was Shakespeare's 'main and perhaps sole source' (Bullough, *Sources*, vol. 1, p. 274). In my view, there are enough minor parallels with the play to suggest Painter's contribution. For a translation of Pierre Boaistuau's version of the story, the basis for both Painter's and Brooke's renderings, see *Romeo and Juliet before Shakespeare: Four Early Stories of Star-Crossed Love*, ed. and trans. Nicole Prunster (Toronto, 2000), pp. 85–122. Joshua (p. 96) does not appear in Boaistuau's own Italian source.

in the temporal cycle is military and vengeful: it has nothing to do with love. To his credit, Arthur Brooke seems to have seen the difficulty when he reinscribed the French version as the heroic poem *Romeus and Juliet*: Joshua is a sore thumb. Brooke opts for a more appropriate account of the longed-for adjustment of chronology. His readers will imagine the lovers' impatience, he thinks:

For my part, I do gesse eche howre seemes twenty yere:
So that I deeme, if they might have (as of Alcume we
  heare)
The sunne bond to theyr will, if they the heavens
  might gyde,
Black shade of night and doubled dark should straight
  all over hyde.[15]

This time the puzzle is Alcume. It seems likely that the compositor, not a classical scholar and doing his best with Brooke's handwriting, must have misread 'Alcmene' or Alcmena, one of Jupiter's many sexual conquests. The king of the gods suspended the passage of time when he shared Alcmena's bed, postponing the sunrise in order to spend more time with his lover.

We can now put Joshua behind us in favour of Alcmena. She takes us into the territory of passion, at least: Jove is interfering with chronology for the sake of sex, as Shakespeare's Juliet would if she could. But his project is to hold back the dawn, not bring on the night – and we are still some way from Phaeton. Alcmena was probably familiar to Brooke, as well as to Shakespeare, from Chaucer's *Troilus and Criseyde*, where a woman laments the dawn of day: Criseyde, partly anticipating Juliet's next words, asks the night to stay over the two of them for as long a time as when Almena (everyone seems to have trouble with this name) lay by Jove.[16] And Criseyde goes on to paraphrase one of the great sources of such love poems appealing for the delay of the sunrise, *Amores* 1.13. Alcmena features in Ovid's *aubade*, although she remains unnamed (lines 45–6).

This poem, recently translated by Marlowe, brings in a new component – command of the horses that draw Aurora's chariot across the night sky in symmetry with the sun god's by day.[17] Ovid's lover, who wants to prolong the hours of darkness, urges Aurora to rein in her steeds with her rosy hand (line 10). If she were leaving *her* lover, she would tell them to slow down: '*lente currite, noctis equi*'.[18] As all specialists in early modern drama know, that line had taken on a new and shocking currency in the early 1590s, when it reappeared in the final, agonized speech of Doctor Faustus (line 1935).[19]

Alcmena made another striking appearance, this time in 1595, up to a year before the conjectural first performance of *Romeo and Juliet*. The bridegroom of Spenser's *Epithalamion* appeals to the night itself to be calm, 'Lyke as when Jove with fayre Alcmena lay' (line 328).[20] Juliet, too, will go on to address the night directly, and in words that at once echo and transform an earlier passage of Spenser's poem. In *Epithalamion* the bridegroom's appeal, like Juliet's, is for the sun to go faster:

Ah when will this long weary day have end,
And lende me leave to come unto my love?
How slowly do the houres theyr numbers spend?
How slowly does sad Time his feathers move?
Hast thee O fayrest Planet to thy home
Within the Western fome:
Thy tyred steedes long since have need of rest.
              (lines 278–84)

Although the mood is different, here are impatience, the sun god and his horses heading home to the west.[21] Moreover, in the poem the bride is

---

[15] Arthur Brooke, *The Tragicall History of Romeus and Juliet*, in Bullough, *Sources*, vol. 1, pp. 284–363, lines 823–6.

[16] F. N. Robinson, ed., *The Works of Geoffrey Chaucer* (London, 1957), pp. 385–79, 3.1427–8.

[17] The sun god's horses appear in Brooke but to arrest the night of love (line 919).

[18] Run slowly, steeds of night (*Amores* 1.13.40).

[19] Marlowe, *Doctor Faustus*, The Complete Works, vol. 2.

[20] *The Yale Edition of the Shorter Poems of Edmund Spenser*, ed. William A. Oram *et al.* (New Haven, 1989), pp. 659–79. All references are to this edition.

[21] The structure of Spenser's poem follows the epithalamium of Catullus 61 with its refrain of '*abit dies*' (the day passes). For a discussion of the line of descent, see Gary M. McCown, '"Runnawayes Eyes" and Juliet's Epithalamium', *Shakespeare Quarterly*, 27 (1976), 150–70.

led to her bed with 'silken courteins' (line 303). 'Spread thy broad wing', the bridegroom urges, 'over my love and me, / that no man may us see, / And in thy sable mantle us enwrap' (lines 319–21). Juliet's reasons for wanting night to 'Spread' her 'close curtain' so that Romeo remains 'unseen' are more pressing, perhaps, but she too seeks night's 'black mantle' to hide the lovers' embraces (*Romeo and Juliet*, 3.2.5, 7, 15).

As Jove might have been pleased to note, I have slowed down time to a crawl in order to disinter this elephant dust. Traces of some or all of these allusions, lying around in Shakespeare's textual memory, must have reassembled themselves, perhaps in an instant, converting Brooke's invocation of Alcmena into a plea for the sun god to hurry his steeds towards the west. So evident is the influence of Spenser that it might seem possible to dispense with the intermediaries of Chaucer and Ovid. But Chaucer offers the young woman as speaker, while Ovid contributes speeding horses. His poem also registers a wish for the horses to fall from the sky (*Amores* 1.13.29–30), perhaps indirectly suggesting a link with Phaeton. Above all, there is nothing 'weary' about Juliet's impatience, nothing urgent about Spenser's. We have only to add the king's eagerness to confront his enemies from Marlowe's *Edward II*, 'Gallop a pace, bright *Phoebus*, through the skie' (4.3.43)[22] and, in a final touch of genius, the contrast between steady, commanding Apollo and reckless Phaeton.

Phaeton featured early in the Elizabethan grammar-school curriculum as the son of Apollo, who insisted on driving the sun god's chariot and lost control of the horses, fatally dropping the reins so that they ran wild.[23] If their unrestraint bore on expectations of a wedding night, Phaeton's rashness might take the audience back to Romeo's dangerous intervention in the quarrel with Tybalt. Juliet knows nothing of this yet but she, like Phaeton, is already defying her father's judgement. When Elizabethan schoolmasters reached Ovid's story, no doubt they insisted on the consequences of the boy's wilfulness as a moral lesson to their own youthful charges, in accordance with the educational advice of Erasmus.[24] Ovid's

Phoebus urges his son to spare the lash; Shakespeare's Phaeton uses it, risking disaster.[25] Ovid gives Apollo's horses flaming feet, Arthur Golding calls them 'firiefooted',[26] and so we finally arrive at Juliet's lines as we have them.

From the evidence, we might be forgiven for saying that there is not one original word in these four lines of Shakespeare. On a hint perhaps from Painter and definitely from Brooke, Shakespeare composes Juliet's speech by appropriating words, phrases and ideas from Chaucer, Spenser, Marlowe and Ovid, as well as Ovid's English translator. But what do we mean by originality, if not the lateral thinking that puts together out of existing materials a brand new combination distinct from its predecessors? In this case a patchwork of borrowings joins to evoke the mixture of intensity, excitement and anxiety that attends a wedding night, perhaps any wedding night, but certainly one conducted in secret, against parental authority, that will also turn out to be overshadowed by the husband's banishment.

Perhaps most original of all, a decisively Shakespearian vocabulary redefines the relationship between playgoers and the Ovidian pantheon. In *Romeo and Juliet* Phoebus and Phaeton are both rendered workaday. We might expect the sun god to spend his nights in a palace but Shakespeare calls it a 'lodging' (at least in Q2).[27] The word covers any sleeping place: it is familiar, casual. In both Quartos Phaeton is a 'wagoner'. Ovid describes the sun's chariot as made of gold and silver and

---

22 *The Complete Works of Christopher Marlowe*, vol. 2.
23 Ovid, *Metamorphoses*, 2.1–328. He was also a recurring figure in Shakespeare's own plays, most obviously in this context *Richard II*, 3.3.178–9.
24 T. W. Baldwin, *William Shakspere's Small Latine and Lesse Greeke*, 2 vols. (Urbana, 1944), vol. 1, p. 609; vol. 2, p. 195.
25 I am grateful to Duncan Salkeld for a discussion of some possible contemporary resonances of Phaeton's whip.
26 Ovid, *Metamorphoses*, 2.392; *Ovid's Metamorphoses: The Arthur Golding Translation*, ed. John Frederick Nims (New York, 1965), 2.491.
27 Q1, which has 'mansion', is substantially less precise on Phaeton: 'Such a wagoner / As Phaëton would quickly bring you thither', *The First Quarto of Romeo and Juliet*, ed. Lukas Erne (Cambridge, 2007), 11.2–3.

adorned with precious jewels; the dramatist, how-ever, names this triumphal coach for what it has in common with a cart.[28] This is the same Shake-speare who would soon make the dawn stand on tiptoe (3.5.10) and would go on to call the now marble-constant queen a 'lass' (*Antony and Cleopatra* 5.2.314), while elsewhere he identifies Echo as a 'babbling gossip' (*Twelfth Night* 1.5.276). That ability to combine distance with proximity and make grandeur look unassuming is special to Shakespeare.

IV

If my first example of Shakespeare's originality was formal and my second textual, the third and final one is structural and it concerns Bertram's recalcitrance. *All's Well That Ends Well* was based ultimately on Boccaccio's novella of Giletta of Narbonne and known to Shakespeare in Painter's translation. The dramatist has introduced any num-ber of differences but my concern is Bertram's story.

Boccaccio's tale belongs to Giletta. A resource-ful young woman pursues the man she wants, earns the respect of the tenants by the way she runs Bel-tramo's estate when he flees from an unwelcome marriage, and arranges to meet what he thinks are impossible conditions: the possession of his ring and his child. Beltramo's point of view barely fea-tures in the narrative. But the switch to drama changes that: once there are actors on the stage, it is best to give them something to do. Bertram's story is largely Shakespeare's invention.

But not entirely. In the tale of Giletta, pro-saic in the main, with elements of verisimilitude, Shakespeare has recognized the shape of an old wives' tale about the clever heroine who over-comes obstacles, solves riddles and marries the prince.[29] The play duly aligns itself more closely with fairy tale by reducing the probability of the events it depicts. Giletta's cure of the king's fistula will take up to eight days; it depends on a powder of herbs. Helena's, by contrast, will take no more than twenty-four hours; there is no mention of the treat-ment; her intervention is altogether more magical. Where Giletta is rich and sought after, Helena is poor, a Cinderella figure, but one who will leave home to make her fortune, just like any number of woodcutters' children who eventually make their way to the castle. Helena does not set out to run the estate and impress the tenants: her plan is sim-ply to solve Bertram's riddle. While Giletta repeats the bed trick until she can be sure she is preg-nant, Helena is confident that one hour with her husband is enough to guarantee conception.

In Beltramo, meanwhile, Shakespeare found a young man whose error of judgement led him to leave his home and those who loved him, until experience restored him to his senses. Bertram's story, devised in symmetry with Helena's fairy tale, invokes another ancient, minimalist genre, the parable of the Prodigal Son, who 'took his journey into a far country, and there wasted his substance with riotous living'. The young man was reduced to eating husks with the pigs. 'And when he came to himself', Luke's gospel records, he went home to his father, who forgave him and killed the fatted calf in his honour.[30]

The biblical parable mainly concerns the indig-nation of the virtuous older brother, who has never

---

[28] Golding's preferred term is 'Chariot' but he calls Phaeton 'the Wagoner' (2.394). The range of reference for *wagon* was wider in the period: the vehicle could also carry people (*OED* 2), as well as produce and artillery (*OED* 1), but chariots were generally more stately. Phoebus drives a wagon in Spenser's *Faerie Queene* at 1.5.44 and to accommodate such instances *OED* includes a 'poetic' usage (*OED* 2c).

[29] The case has been familiar since W. W. Lawrence, *Shake-speare's Problem Comedies* (New York, 1931), pp. 32–77. For more recently available analogues see 'Kate Crackernuts', 'The Wise Little Girl' and 'Three Measures of Salt', all in *The Virago Book of Fairy Tales*, ed. Angela Carter (London, 1990).

[30] Luke 15:11–32 (Bishops' Bible). The Geneva Bible has 'he toke his iorney into a farre country, and there he wasted his goods with riotous liuing' (13). Barbara A. Mowat points out that Shakespeare was especially drawn to Luke's Gospel and that eleven of his plays allude to the Prodigal Son: 'Shake-speare Reads the Geneva Bible', in *Shakespeare, The Bible and the Form of the Book*, ed. Travis deCook and Alan Galey (London, 2012), pp. 25–39; p. 26. Helen Wilcox sees the parable as the model for the conclusion of the play: 'Shake-speare's Miracle Play? Religion in *All's Well, That Ends Well*', in Waller, ed., *All's Well, That Ends Well*, pp. 140–54; p. 152.

had a fatted calf killed for *him*, and the point in the context is that there's more joy in heaven over one sinner that repents than over ninety and nine who have no reason to repent (Luke 15: 7, 10). But the story of the younger son took on a life of its own in the sixteenth century as an instance of the youthful inclination to riotous living that was, even so, not beyond redemption. *The Interlude of Youth*, a moral play dating from the early years of the century, had run to at least three editions by the time Shakespeare was five.[31] Its protagonist, pleased with his good looks and physical prowess, is happy to be led into bad company by Riot personified. The play was evidently popular enough to be worth rewriting in a Protestant – and more prolix – version called *Lusty Juventus*, where the title page characterizes the work: 'Liuely describyng the frailtie of youth: of nature, prone to vyce; by grace and good councell traynable to vertue'. Here the good counsel culminates in the parable of the Prodigal Son (lines 1077–83), causing the hero, still called Youth, to forsake delinquency at once.[32]

Painter's translation of Boccaccio gave Shakespeare very little to go on, but it indicates that Beltramo was young – the same age as Giletta, who has just become old enough to marry. Offered her hand by the king, Beltramo reacts 'skornefully' to the prospect of a marriage incompatible with his noble stock. And he delivers his riddle 'chorlishly'.[33] Coincidentally or not, the protagonist of *The Interlude of Youth* rebuffs good advice with verbal abuse and is encouraged by Pride to disdain his social inferiors:

> think ye come of noble kind.
> Above all men exalt thy mind.
> Put down the poor, and set nought by them.
> Be in company with gentlemen. (lines 342–5)

Youth isn't offered a poor physician's daughter to marry, but we can guess how he would react under the tutelage of vice. Instead of taking up his role as a husband, Bertram does his best to seduce a young woman. When Pride suggests that Youth take a wife, Riot thinks a mistress would be better, and on the basis, no doubt, of the elder brother's complaint that the Prodigal has devoured his father's wealth

with harlots, Youth goes off to the tavern with Pride's sister, Lechery, until he learns better from Humility and rapidly repents.

If early modern plays are to be trusted, the parable of the Prodigal Son was a favourite source of decoration. Middleton's Dick Follywit is to sleep, appropriately enough, surrounded by bed hangings 'with the story of the prodigal child in silk and gold. Only the swine are left out... for spoiling the curtains' (*A Mad World, My Masters*, 2.2.6–8).[34] More economically, when Mistress Quickly fears she will be reduced to pawning her tapestries, Falstaff suggests replacing them with wall paintings. 'The story of the Prodigal' is one possible theme (*2 Henry IV*, 2.1.140–7) and, in a rare example of continuity, it turns out that the hostess has taken note of this idea. Falstaff's chamber in Windsor 'is painted about with the story of the Prodigal, fresh and new' (*The Merry Wives of Windsor*, 4.5.6–7). The plays give no indication of how the parable was illustrated but wall paintings of three and a half scenes from five of the life of the Prodigal Son were executed in about 1600 at Knightsland Farm, Hertfordshire. The first extant scene shows the young man feasting in the tavern with Lechery,[35] so it

---

[31] 1532–3; 1557–9; 1566–9. See Ian Lancashire, ed., *Two Tudor Interludes: The Interlude of Youth, Hickscorner* (Manchester, 1980), pp. 1–5. Quotations are from this edition.

[32] R. Wever, *An Enterlude Called Lusty Iuventus*, ed. Helen Scarborough Thomas (New York, 1982), probably written in the 1540s and printed 1547–53, 1562–8, 1568–75 (Thomas, pp. xi–xxxix).

[33] Bullough, *Sources*, vol. 2, pp. 389–96; pp. 391, 392.

[34] *Thomas Middleton, The Collected Works*, gen. eds. Gary Taylor and John Lavignano (Oxford, 2007).

[35] Reproduced in Tara Hamling, *Decorating the 'Godly' Household: Religious Art in Post-Reformation Britain* (New Haven, 2010), pp. 155–7. See also a valance at Hardwick Hall, Anthony Wells-Cole, *Art and Decoration in Elizabethan and Jacobean England* (New Haven, 1997, Fig. 468). Since the European contribution to elite decoration makes it almost impossible to isolate native iconography, a long tradition of continental representations of the Prodigal Son among the harlots may also be at work here; see Alan R. Young, *The English Prodigal Son Plays: A Theatrical Fashion of the Sixteenth and Seventeenth Centuries* (Salzburg, 1979), pp. 27–54. I am grateful to Stuart Sillars for advice on Shakespeare's visual world.

seems that the popular story has influenced representations of the parable.[36]

We know Shakespeare was familiar with *The Interlude of Youth* or, at least, its hero as a generic type, since young Tarquin appeals to an explicitly theatrical precedent as he prepares to rape Lucrece. 'It is time enough to be good / When that ye be old', urges Pride (*Youth*, 645–6). 'Respect and reason', Tarquin convinces himself, 'wait on wrinkled age.... / My part is youth, and beats these from the stage' (*Lucrece*, lines 275–8).[37] There is a more distant echo in the Sonnets, when the poet complains that his friend has succumbed to his own mistress, corrupted by 'thy beauty and thy straying youth / Who lead thee in their riot' (41.10–11). The nearest analogue in the plays is Prince Hal, whose father complains that 'Riot and dishonour stain the brow / Of my young Harry' (*1 Henry IV*, 1.1.84–5; cf. *2 Henry IV*, 4.4.63–4), while the prince is in the tavern with Falstaff, 'That villainous abominable misleader of youth' (*1 Henry IV*, 2.4.456).[38]

This is the context in which Bertram repudiates respect for his surrogate father, disdains a wife of humble birth and chooses instead to journey into a far country in the dubious company of Parolles, whose 'inducement' encourages the corruption of 'a well-derived nature' (*All's Well That Ends Well* 3.2.88–9),[39] only to pursue an illicit sexual relationship. The play repeatedly insists on how young he is: too young to inherit, so that he is a ward of court; too young to go to the wars without the king's permission. He is a 'rude boy' (3.2.81), a 'Proud, scornful boy' (2.3.152). When the king first welcomes Bertram to the court, he calls him 'Youth': 'Youth, thou bear'st thy father's face' (1.2.19). Is it possible that that mode of address had a resonance for early modern audiences that it has lost for us? Eventually, when Bertram comes home, his mother will urge the king to make allowances for his 'Natural rebellion done i'th' blade of youth' (5.3.6).

In a line of descent from the Youth plays, a number of riotous young husbands were redeemed by good wives from illicit liaisons, or beggary, or both on the early seventeenth-century stage.

Among these plays, *The London Prodigal*, printed in 1605, roughly when we think *All's Well* was new in the repertoire, was ascribed on the title page to William Shakespeare, although to my knowledge recent scholars have not (yet) claimed it for the canon. Young Flowerdale sinks lower and lower into financial disgrace until the unexpected loyalty of the woman he married for her money shames him into sudden repentance.[40] Bertram's humiliation, however, is more protracted. In an ironic addition to the traditional story, when the young man comes home penitent and forgiven, his welcome by the king – as stand-in for his father – is interrupted in *All's Well* by the sudden reappearance of Helena's ring and Bertram's arrest on suspicion of murder, closely followed by Diana's suit for breach of promise, and Bertram's succession of lies to evade justice. The entry of Helena stands to exonerate him and Bertram's 'O pardon!'

---

[36] Lechery ('Abhominable Liuing' in *Lusty Juventus*) features as 'the strumpet wind' in Graziano's Prodigal Son conceit (*The Merchant of Venice*, 2.6.14–19).

[37] *Lusty Juventus* was still sufficiently familiar in 1599 to be worth parodying in *Histriomastix*, where Juventus, led on by the Devil, declares that he is 'the prodigall child' (*The Plays of John Marston*, ed. H. Harvey Wood, 3 vols. (Edinburgh, 1939), vol. 3, pp. 243–302; p. 265), while the troupe of players in *Sir Thomas More* (1595) include *Lusty Juventus* in their repertoire. (I owe these references to Alan C. Dessen.) Oddly enough, however, Shakespeare's brief allusion suggests acquaintance with the older play (or a lost intermediary), where Youth repeatedly threatens his good counsellors with violence. Riot, the word that links so many of the Prodigal Son references, is the Vice in *Youth* but does not feature in *Lusty Juventus*.

[38] J. Dover Wilson, *The Fortunes of Falstaff* (Cambridge, 1943), pp. 17–25.

[39] Cf. 4.5.1–3. Bullough notes the parallel between Parolles and Falstaff as misleaders of 'Lusty Juventus' but does not develop the analogy with the Youth plays (*Sources*, vol. 2, p. 387).

[40] The heroes of these Prodigal husband plays all repent unreservedly. For discussion of the links with Shakespeare's play, see Robert Y. Turner, 'Dramatic Conventions in *All's Well That Ends Well*', *PMLA*, 75 (1960), 497–502; W. David Kay, 'Reforming the Prodigal: Dramatic Paradigms, Male Sexuality, and the Power of Shame in *All's Well That Ends Well*', in *Re-Visions of Shakespeare: Essays in Honor of Robert Ornstein*, ed. Evelyn Gajowski (Newark, DE, 2004), pp. 108–27.

(5.3.307) is at once a plea and an announcement. But now, across the conventional reconciliation, falls the shadow of the notorious 'If', an apparent qualification of his contrition which is not found in the sources or the analogues: 'If she, my liege, can make me know this clearly / I'll love her dearly, ever, ever dearly' (5.3.314–15).

What do we make of this 'If'? It seems Bertram is calling on Helena to convince him. Alternatively, last year's RSC production dissolved the 'if' in a happy ending. This too seems to me a possible reading. There are strong *if*s ('If all the world were paper', when it evidently is not) and weak *if*s ('if that's how it stands', when it evidently does). Bertram's *if* need not mark incredulity. But either way, an *if* specifies conditions, and Bertram apparently still doesn't see that he has no right to impose his.

On the other hand, since *if* registers uncertainty, suspending assent or denial, it also backs away from confrontation. When Touchstone riffs on quarrels, he invokes an *if* to avoid conflict. One of the parties to a dispute, he explains, had only to think of an *if*, and 'they shook hands and swore brothers. Your If is the only peacemaker; much virtue in If' (*As You Like It*, 5.4.99–101). Perhaps, then, who has what right is not the issue at the end of *All's Well*. In the parable the father is God and divine forgiveness demands unreserved contrition. But it may be that secular human relations are coming to seem less absolute, less fit to be held to this ideal standard.

Bertram's *if* is addressed to the king in what is effectively a court of law, and he promises amendment on the basis of full understanding: 'If she, my liege, can make me know this clearly . . .' Know what? Know the whole story, perhaps, including his own part in it?[41] The comedies end in justice, including the imposition of penalties, perhaps to excess in the case of Malvolio or Shylock. But new questions dominate a number of the later plays: what is to be done in the face of continuing human fallibility? The issue of whether and when to forgive works its way most notably through *Measure for Measure*, *King Lear*, *The Winter's Tale* and *The Tempest*, not to mention *Timon of Athens*. 'The rarer action is / In virtue than in vengeance', declares Prospero loftily. 'They being penitent . . .' (*The Tempest*, 5.1.27–8). But they are not: Sebastian and Antonio do not show the least sign of remorse.[42] Even so, truth and reconciliation can seem a better way forward than the relentless pursuit of punishment for past offences. Must injury always be paid for by pain or guilt in an economy of debt sanctified as justice? If not, perhaps Lafew models the ending of *All's Well* in its difference from both the parable and its early modern reinscriptions, when he takes responsibility for the exposed but *un*repentant Parolles: 'though you are a fool and a knave you shall eat' (5.2.53).

Whatever we think about that, there are no ultimate origins, only lines of descent. We can pay attention to resemblance or difference, the one ultimately unthinkable without the other. My case has been that when we neglect the sources, we sacrifice a way to catch Shakespeare at work and, if we look for Shakespeare's originality, it's in the changes he makes that we are most likely to find it.

---

[41] 'Restorative' justice brings offenders face-to-face with the implications of the offence, makes them *know clearly* what they have done and how it has affected their victims. There is some evidence that this is more effective than conventional punishment in averting recidivism.

[42] It is conceivable that they silently indicate repentance but the text suggests not: 5.1.75–9, 126–33.

'EVERY LIKE IS NOT THE SAME': TRANSLATING SHAKESPEARE IN SPANISH TODAY

ALFREDO MICHEL MODENESSI

Para Sarah, alma mía

At the end of a decisive scene in *Julius Caesar*, after the haughty dictator invites his future killers to go to the Capitol 'like friends', Brutus deplores the hypocrisy surrounding his 'best lover':

> That every like is not the same, O Caesar,
> The heart of Brutus earns to think upon!
> (2.2.135–6)[1]

Brutus' concern with how 'likeness' and 'sameness' relate to individual integrity contrasts strongly with the fast pace of collective action unfolding around him. His assimilation in the conspiracy does not lack hubris, however: he is as given as Caesar to placing himself above the rest. In this, he closely resembles the 'true original', the self-centered *title* character of a tragedy where Brutus ends up being the *tragic* character. Being quite 'like' Caesar but 'not the same', Brutus is an outstanding exercise in characterological fluidity and contrast – or, if you please, in 'intra-dramaturgical' translation.

Among much else, *Julius Caesar* displays men striving to distinguish themselves from each other – for example: 'If I were Brutus now, and he were Cassius...' (1.2.302); 'I am no orator, as Brutus is' (3.2.213), and so on. But, with Brutus, comparisons often problematize notions of *integrity*: as in the aside above, or his deeply flawed 'Let's be sacrificers but not butchers' (2.1.173). One echo is especially interesting: in battle, Cato plays a 'translation' of Brutus and, being found a mere stand-in, re-affirms the integrity of 'his lord' by telling Antony that, if found, 'alive or dead', Brutus will

be found 'like Brutus, like himself' (5.4.26). When found, however, that paradigm of integrity *is* dead.

Brutus repeatedly detaches himself from his peers in absolute ways. To paraphrase: 'I am not like Antony; he loves games and parties. And I am not like you, Cassius, because I am never afraid and never wrong.' Ironically, in his final scene, he is surrounded by 'poor remains of friends' (5.5.1) whose names we hear for the first and only time. This near-absolute isolation stems from his being absolutely sure of his integrity, even though this monolithic certainty comes into question before the battle, when, speaking with his dark mirror (or inverted likeness, also known as Cassius), Brutus admits that he cannot stay true to his doctrine against self-slaughter. Apparently, claims to absolute integrity are contingent and relative, after all – like absolute claims, in general. In passing, Shakespeare again illustrates how 'every like is not the same'.

Associating that line with translating is useful, as many still hold the obsolete assumption that a translation seeks an impossible, and pointless, 'sameness' with its source, instead of doing what a translation invariably does: derive *and at once* differ from its source while enabling it to exist across languages, cultures and ages. Oddly, most who assume translation means 'sameness' also presume it to be necessarily subservient. Translating, however, does not entail mechanically producing self-defeating

---

[1] References are to Shakespeare's *Complete Works*, ed. Jonathan Bate and Eric Rasmussen (Basingstoke, 2007).

replicas but different, yet akin, new artefacts. A translation is therefore an exercise in originality, the outcome of a creative process that demands being deeply in touch with the source so as to grasp its energies and effects, in order to enable and effect them anew through another semiosis in another milieu. Translating allows cultural goods to function in manifold guises inside equally differentiated and ever-changing settings. And, in spite of the complex acts involved, what the translator does to the source cannot affect the source in any material way: its constitutive signs remain intact and therefore notions of translation as 'loss' or 'deformation' are sterile. The source, instead, is given new, different life: 'The translation will truly be a moment in the growth of the original, which will complete itself in enlarging itself.'[2]

'YOURS IS AS FAIR A NAME'

The boldest act of artistic originality ever can bring this into better perspective. In 1573, Paolo Caliari, 'Il Veronese', was interrogated by the Inquisition about a painting entitled *The Feast at the House of Simon* or *The Last Supper*, which he had made for the Basilica of Saint John and Saint Paul in Venice.[3] One inquisitor questioned Veronese's display of eccentric figures around a solemn subject: 'At the *Last Supper*, does it seem fitting to paint buffoons, drunkards, dwarfs, and similar vulgarities?'[4] 'No, milords', Veronese answered, 'that is wrong; but I am obliged to follow my masters'. 'What have your masters done?', the inquisitor inquired. Veronese rebounded: 'Michelangelo in Rome, for example, painted the Heavenly Host in the nude and in different poses – '. But the inquisitor would not budge: 'Because of this you maintain that it is good and decent?' Veronese yielded: 'Illustrious Lords, I do not want to defend it' – which was very wise, Galileo-wise, as it were, forty years before the latter faced his inquisitors. Veronese was given three months to 'correct' his painting. But in much less he made a totally new work. Only, he did it without painting a new one or making the slightest physical change to his original. The painting remained the same *object*. Veronese simply

gave it a different title: *The Feast in the House of Levi*. Thus, by exercising originality upon his own original and upon a shared origin, he made a work of art anew, cancelled inquisitorial objections, and gave himself and his work a new lease on life.

This famous case illustrates what translating is about, not what it is. Materially, there is not a *new* painting, but there is a *different* painting, an original if there ever was, except that it is the *same* object. Significantly, the 'original' *Last Supper* remains literally and historically embedded in the 'new original'. And another original, the dynamic cultural cluster known as 'The Last Supper', is also embedded in it. All coexist, in inter-creative flux, for, as Veronese acknowledges, he did *like* his masters. Moreover, if copies are made of the second original, copies will likewise be made of the first, because all simultaneously become part of the common cultural flux, sharing the origin and ensuing narratives in their own, differentiated but intertwined, ways.

'The superstition concerning the inferiority of translations derives from a negligent experience', says Jorge Luis Borges, discussing the inherent instability of artistic endeavours and the ensuing illusion of originality: 'There's no good text which doesn't seem invariable and definitive when executed a sufficient number of times.'[5] Significantly, this illusion of originality emerges in full in early modern times, when works of art are not considered absolutely original but, to the contrary, as a counterfeit, man-made, part of history: 'originality is itself a relative quality'.[6] These relational views on

---

[2] Jacques Derrida, 'Des Tours de Babel', *Difference in Translation*, ed. Joseph F. Graham (Ithaca and London, 1985), p. 188. This echoes Walter Benjamin's 'Die Aufgabe des Übersetzers', of course.

[3] Now in the Gallerie dell'Academia. View at www.wga.hu/support/viewer_m/z.html

[4] Based on Elizabeth G. Holt, *A Documentary History of Art* (New York, 1960), pp. 69–70.

[5] Jorge Luis Borges, 'Las versiones homéricas', in *Discusión* (Madrid, 1976), p. 90 (trans. Ángel-Luis Pujante).

[6] David Quint, *Origin and Originality in Renaissance Literature* (New Haven, 1983), p. 5.

literary production imply that translations respond in their particular historic and cultural terms to the demands of aesthetic experience. Borges, again: 'Owing to my congenital practice of Spanish, *Don Quixote* is a uniform monument, whose only variations are provided by the editor, the book-binder and the typesetter; thanks to my opportune ignorance of Greek, the *Odyssey* is an international library of works in prose and verse.'[7] Regardless of their perceived quality, translations are transcultural practices sustaining creative relationships with their 'originals' (in translation studies better described as *sources*), not performing parasitical or subservient roles. A translation is an *event*, evanescent by nature, like a performance, and it will not usually become fixed and translatable – although it has done so, more often in earlier than in modern times. Moreover, a translation *is* single and unique yet entirely provisional and alternative, like Veronese's painting (or paintings). As a multidimensonal creative interaction across cultures, translating may then be legitimately called 'trans-creating'.

Conceptually, 'transcreation' is attached to the Brazilian poet and translator Haroldo de Campos and to the Indian poet and translator Purushottama Lal.[8] Both identified the source as the dynamic totality of an efficient experience and its translation as consequently made to allow the circulation of the source's energies – social, political, artistic – in a separate culture, via a new and necessarily removed vehicle: 'appropriating the source's historicity as an imaginative construction of a living tradition is, to a certain extent, an act of usurpation'.[9] This again implies that translating pertains to the life of an original not only as a performative act effected *after* the original, but also as an efficient cause *for* the 'original' to persist and evolve in ways unrestrained by its native history and language.

'THE SKIES ARE PAINTED WITH UNNUMBERED SPARKS'

Starting with Wyatt and Surrey, a similar understanding of translation was fundamental to what became prime materials and tools for Shakespeare – 'imitation' being the word of choice.[10] This is too well-known but must be brought into specific focus. I am not referring to a purported acquaintance of Shakespeare with works in Italian[11] but to the power of translation to inform cultural-identitarian formations. According to Michael Cronin, the construction of the English nation and empire constituted 'an exercise in translation'.[12] This *translational* formulation is illustrated by the 'translation' of the act of translating and its products into 'originals', effected by emerging and expanding host nations where translators were '*forging* the vernacular that would be . . . adequate to the ambitions of the new body politic. In other words, the forging of a new national identity implies the forgery of translation, the reading of translation as if it were the original.'[13] This harmonizes with another effect of translation: an enhanced linguistic self-awareness, which is critical, since the effects of translating do not pertain only to its outcomes, in linear fashion, but to its being a transformative cultural energy, even in feedback fashion.

To give a personal example: all patient readers know this:

> My galley, charged with forgetfulness,
> Through sharp seas, in winter nights doth pass
> 'Tween rock and rock; and eke mine enemy, alas,
> That is my Lord steereth with cruelness . . .

---

[7] Borges, 'Las versiones homéricas', p. 90.

[8] Representative texts would be Haroldo de Campos, "Da tradução como criação e como crítica", *Metalinguagem: Ensaios de teoria e crítica literaria* (Petrópolis, 1967), pp. 21–38; and Purushottama Lal, *Transcreation* (Calcutta, 1996).

[9] Haroldo de Campos, 'Tradução, ideologia e história', in *Remate de Males*, ed. Iuma Maria Simon (Campinas, 1984), p. 240 (my translation).

[10] See Ronald L. Martínez, 'Francis, Thou Art Translated: Petrarch Metamorphosed in English, 1380–1595', *Humanist Studies & the Digital Age*, 1.1 (Winter 2011), pp. 80–108; and Alison Cornish, *Vernacular Translation in Dante's Italy* (Cambridge, 2010).

[11] See Jason Lawrence, *'Who the devil taught thee so much Italian?': Italian Learning and Literary Imitation in Early Modern England* (Manchester, 2005).

[12] Michael Cronin, *Translation and Identity* (London and New York, 2006), p. 97.

[13] Cronin, *Translation and Identity*, p. 103.

And all likewise know it to originate here:

> Passa la nave mia colma d'oblio
> per aspro mare, a mezza notte, il verno
> enfra Scilla e Caribdi; et al governo
> siede'l signore, anzi'l nimico mio . . .

All acquainted with the history of English verse likewise appreciate how Wyatt's originality renders the mythical Mediterranean monsters as solid though nameless rocks and rocks of seas probably colder and closer to his heart, achieving a ground-breaking English transcreation of Petrarch's inter-culturally long-lasting picture of the lover as a ship lost in the tempest of despair, an image that traversed all Europe.[14]

This instance of transcreation teaches much about the Italian and the English despairing lovers. But it also teaches much about a Spanish cousin of theirs – or, vice versa, the Spanish cousin teaches much about them. This is the translational experience I meant: when I read Wyatt's sonnet for the first time (an original in its own right and tradition) that was not my *first* time. I knew the sonnet, and loved it, thus:

> Pasa mi nave el mar, de olvido llena,
> a media noche, y en cruel invierno,
> por Scila y por Caribde, y al gobierno
> preside el señor mío, que es mi pena; . . . [15]

In Spanish, indeed, not in Italian. That experience placed Wyatt's poem under a peculiar light, and also made me brush up my Petrarch and pursue the experience of the 'true' original, *another* original experience, irrespective of historical precedence. For the Spanish sonnet that I read first was and remains an original – as a translation, in the sense outlined earlier, but also as the original *experience* of the poem, one that, for me, preceded, and hence continues to bear upon, all experiences of sonnets that are alike but, fortunately, not the same.

Underlying this is the fact that translation engenders or reinforces 'forms of creativity, ranging from national and other identity formations to literary and linguistic resourcefulness'.[16] Thus, the experience of Petrarch's sonnet in Spanish remains an original also regarding the instruments and energies that inform it, which in turn have informed my craft as a translator on both ends: as a reader-interpreter and as a writer-translator. For we also know where the vigour of the sweet Italian forms led in early modern England: to the dissemination of its tropes and related resources, to the inception of the stuff that dreams would be made of, the poetic input to Shakespeare's drama, his 'potential action in rhythmical progression'.[17] That Shakespearian stuff, even in its least refined shapes, is what translators look to translate – in a way, *back* to its sources.

'TEAR HIM FOR HIS BAD VERSES!'

Despite the *foundational* role of translation in the culture and tradition within which Shakespeare developed, misconceptions still abound, often voiced with an unwarranted baritone of authority. Here is a scholar, discussing Shakespeare movies, and showing typical and self-evident proprietary prejudices: 'what if the language is not English? Kozintsev directed a magnificent *King Lear* derived from the Russian translation of Boris Pasternak. The original poetry will have been lost, but . . . the translation was, after all, written by a highly respected national poet.'[18]

---

[14] In England, apart from the usual suspects – e.g. Spenser's *Amoretti*: 34, 63 and 64, or Shakespeare's 116.5–8 – there are witnesses ever since Chaucer, of course; see Martínez, 'Francis Thou Art Translated'.

[15] This excellent version of Petrarch's most quoted sonnet in the sixteenth century (*Rerum vulgarium fragmenta* 189) is by the Spanish grammarian, philosopher, poet and translator Francisco Sánchez, 'El Brocense' (1523–1600); see complete at http://hemerotecadigital.bne.es/issue.vm?id=0005273775&search=&lang=es.

[16] Roshni Mooneeram, *From Creole to Standard: Shakespeare, Language, and Literature in a Postcolonial Context* (Amsterdam and New York, 2009), p. 135.

[17] Mary Snell-Hornby, 'Theatre and Opera Translation', in *A Companion to Translation Studies*, ed. Piotr Kuhiwczak and Karin Littau (Clevedon, 2007), p. 111.

[18] James M. Welsh, 'What is a "Shakespeare Film", anyway?', in *The Literature/Film Reader: Issues of Adaptation*, ed. James M. Welsh and Peter Lev (Lanham, 2007), p. 107.

Similar instances of blatant misconceptions are more to my point, however, for, although coming from a choir more wanting in knowledge, they have the added interest of being 'friendly fire'. Below are two website comments about a production of *The Tempest* staged in Mexico from my translation in 2011:

Some lines penned by Shakespeare were used literally – which was clear thanks to his characteristically rich poetic language. However, phrases from the crudest Mexican lexicon were also included, and sexual innuendos, which made the show stoop to vulgarity. What? Wasn't Shakespeare enough?

The show was disappointing and offensive, for these characters, Trinculo and Stephano, weren't funny – though to the common people they were: they seemed elated with their pranks and coarse language. I'm not easily shocked by obscene puns, but to adapt a novel [*sic*] to Mexican jargon just for laughs isn't just absurd, it's insulting to the author's memory, and to the few of us who are not vulgar.[19]

For these refined Mexicans, I am evidently no 'respected national poet'.

Here, again, is the ingrained bias that Shakespeare is a supreme commodity of 'high' culture. But more striking and significant to me are, on the one hand, the readiness with which these compatriots identify a connection between *The Tempest* and *our* common culture only in what they decry as *my* degradation of *their* Shakespeare and, on the other, their intense self-denial. Centuries of (ongoing) coloniality lie behind this. Horrified by Shakespeare's foul mouth (although heretofore unacquainted with it), these Calibans, wishfully thinking themselves Prosperos, needfully de-translate Shakespeare's foulness back to the Caliban-translator, deeming the only parts of our common language that they deign recognize as *ours* unworthy to serve the genius of the *universal* genius – evidently inaccessible to them *but* in translation. What did they expect a Mexican translation to pursue, other than making Shakespeare available to *our* here and now? Moreover, what one calls 'Mexican jargon' was not such. Undeniably Mexican, instead, were the rhythms of speech, the syntax and the turns of phrase, so intended, first and foremost, to suit Mexican performing voices and bodies, and then the ears of mainly Mexican audiences. These comments stem from deeply rooted identitarian issues and, concomitantly, from not finding in my work, and in the performances therefrom, the supposedly 'higher', *colonial* norms until late unquestionably used to translate Shakespeare into Spanish.[20]

Proprietary views like these ignore that the capacity of Shakespeare to originate cultural production is itself the outcome of multiple exercises of originality that effect 'Shakespeare' distinctively; i.e. no staging, edition, declamation, derivation and so forth exists without interaction with, and intervention in, texts already much intervened in and interacted with. Translating Shakespeare is one of many ways Shakespeare is effected. The questions, then, as with any other dramatist, are how and what for. The general answers are clear. Translating a play means enabling an event from the potential event inscribed in the source: the translation must be apt for performance; it must set voices and bodies into effective action. And of course, you must know what you are doing and do it responsibly. The specifics are trickier.

'A FEVER WHEN HE WAS IN SPAIN'

Three collections of Shakespeare's 'Complete Works' have been recently published in Spanish. The first, 'Shakespeare by Writers', started in 1999, edited by the Argentinean Marcelo Cohen for Norma of Colombia. This collection features all-new versions, each by a 'writer with translating experience' (a questionable premise), all in verse and prose but in largely different styles, and of notoriously uneven quality, as many want

---

[19] http://criticonteatrounam.tumblr.com/post (my translations). Fortunately, these comments were a minority.

[20] See my '"A double tongue within your mask", Translating Shakespeare in/to Spanish-speaking Latin America', in *Shakespeare and the Language of Translation*, ed. Ton Hoenselaars (London, 2004), pp. 240–54.

indispensable linguistic and academic skills.[21] Despite being mostly by Latin Americans, the majority of these versions use what I call 'mock-Golden Age' Iberian Spanish.[22] The second was published in 2010, by Losada of Argentina, edited by Pablo Ingberg. This collection, in verse and prose, combines previous work – even fifty years old[23] – with new texts, also of uneven quality. Tellingly, this collection is virtually all written in mock-Iberian Spanish although *all* the translators are Latin American. The latest was published in Spain by Random House in 2012, edited by Andreu Jaume, mostly reprinting existing texts made in Spain and Latin America, several from the two above. Nearly all, again, are written with Iberian norms. Thus, regarding Latin America, all three collections perpetuate the stale and unwarranted assumption that Shakespeare is best rendered in a 'prestigious' Iberian or pseudo-Iberian variety of our common language, at times debatably termed 'neutral'[24] – notions that nowadays even Spaniards deem pointless.

In 2014, however, the distinguished Spanish scholar and translator Ángel-Luis Pujante completed one long, and historic, project, started as a solo enterprise in the 1980s: a consistent rendering of all the plays openly translated into Iberian Spanish, now published in Madrid by Espasa. This collection neither pretends to be written in any other sort of Spanish nor shuns to thus identify its main readership. Pujante in the end wrote over twenty-seven translations. I am honoured to say I contributed four, so I am obviously no impartial judge. But my schizoid nature licenses the academic in me objectively to affirm that this is the most reliable collection ever, in terms of content and style, sound and solid from scholarly and translational perspectives, mostly due to the sustained work of one outstanding, responsible and creative professional.

First, since the translators of Shakespeare into Spanish returned to the use of verse roughly in the last quarter of the twentieth century, after many decades of mostly shunning it, no collection using verse and prose in keeping with the sources has stayed true to its principles as consistently or rendered more cohesive results. As noted, all three collections above stem from a variety of sources and eras and feature a wide range of hands and quality levels. All texts in Pujante's collection, instead, are made according to a flexible version of Schlegel's principles,[25] a method which Pujante has ensured rigorously underpins his own translations and those by his only two collaborators, invited in the latter stages: first, Salvador Oliva, a Catalonian poet who has translated all of Shakespeare into his native language, and then me, a Mexican.

With strict attention to content, all the translations in this series feature prose for prose and verse for verse, the latter line by line. Therefore, nearly all the translations contain exactly as many lines of verse as their sources. Set forms and metres other than iambic pentameter are treated case by case, always rhyming in strictly similar patterns. For instance, Prospero's epilogue appears in Spanish octosyllabic couplets with assonant rhyme, but sonnets are rendered in hendecasyllables (or alexandrines, where applicable) with perfect rhyme in the Shakespearian scheme. The main variation on Schlegel's model is that, where there is blank verse, we use as few as seven- or as many as fifteen-syllable lines.

Rendering a line for a line addresses a common issue in English–Spanish translation. A speech in prose from *The Merchant of Venice* is Pujante's choice example:

[21] See my 'Traducir la alteridad a la alteridad, español mediante. Posibles Shakespeares en Latinoamérica', in *Escrituras de la traducción hispánica*, ed. Verónica Zondek and Amalia Ortiz de Zárate (Valdivia, 2009), pp. 39–70.

[22] '"A double tongue within your mask"', p. 246.

[23] For instance, the editor's odd 'completion' of Pablo Neruda's *Romeo and Juliet* and Emir Rodríguez Monegal's *Twelfth Night*, both made in 1964.

[24] See Juan Jesús Zaro, 'La traducción de Shakespeare en la América de lengua española: entre la tradición y la transculturación', in *Traducción y representaciones del conflicto*, ed. Alonso Icíar, Alba Páez and Mario Samaniego (Salamanca, 2015).

[25] See Ángel-Luis Pujante, 'The Schlegel Model and Shakespearean Translation in Spain', in *Lengua, traducción, recepción*, ed. Rosa Rabadán, Trinidad Guzmán and Marisa Fernández (León, 2010), pp. 541–53.

Nerissa. . . . they are as sick that surfeit with too much, as they that starve with nothing; it is no small happiness, therefore, to be seated in the mean. Superfluity comes sooner by white hairs, but competency lives longer.

(1.2.3–6)

In 1929, Luis Astrana-Marín rendered it thus:

Aquéllos a quienes la hartura da indigestiones están tan enfermos como los que el vacío les hace morir de hambre. No es mediana dicha en verdad la de estar colocado ni demasiado arriba ni demasiado abajo; lo superfluo torna más aprisa los cabellos blancos; pero el sencillo bienestar vive más largo tiempo.

Performing arts are time/space-specific events: economy and precise rhythms are crucial. If brevity is the soul of wit, here English is the wittier tongue, as prolixity often hinders bringing Shakespeare effectively into Spanish. Astrana-Marín's text features fifteen more words than the English but, more significantly, it almost doubles the number of syllables: it is too long, dull, unsuited for stage-delivery, even in Spain. But this is also due to misunderstanding the role of semantics in translating. Significantly, Nerissa's sententiousness is missing, as this text strives more to provide a veiled explanation of its source's *lexis* than a speech proper for stage delivery. This simple fact presides over our task: translating a play entails writing a play, an artefact that efficiently informs and generates performance; hence, what is translated is not a certain meaning but speech acts, *units of dramatic praxis* enabling effective live performance before living audiences. Pujante's method strictly achieves this by exercising dynamic, well-balanced fidelity, one that stays true to praxis, not just to 'sense'. It starts with command of the source, of course, in all dimensions.

Take Warwick insulting Suffolk in *2 Henry VI*: 'Pernicious blood-sucker of sleeping men!' (3.2.227). Roberto Appratto offers this: '¡*Vampiro pernicioso de durmientes*!'.[26] There is nothing semantically or historically challenging in the line, and yet here is a *vampire* in a Shakespearian context. Moreover, preceding this line are 'word-for-word' misconstructions of the previous phrases 'this fearful homage' and 'give thee thy hire' (3.2.225–6)

which undermine what might otherwise be commended in this translation: economy. Instead, in Pujante's collection the line reads '¡*Maligna sanguijuela de quien duerme!*': the proper term for 'bloodsucker' (leech), as well as using idiomatic Spanish phrases for the previous lines and a hendecasyllable. The first requisites of fidelity, then, are observed: attention to sense in historical context, in economic fashion.

But pure semantics are only part of a speech act. Take a case from the famously hard *Love's Labour's Lost*, Holofernes' convoluted extrametrical sestet:

The preyful princess pierced and pricked a pretty
   pleasing pricket;
Some say a sore, but not a sore, till now made sore with
   shooting.
The dogs did yell, put 'L' to sore, then sorrel jumps
   from thicket;
Or pricket sore, or else sorrel; the people fall a-hooting.
If sore be sore, then L to sore makes fifty sores o' sorrel.
Of one sore I an hundred make by adding but one
   more 'L'.   (4.2.45–50)

Shakespeare must have had a blast devising this hunk of abstruseness, but I wonder if any Anglophone ever has fun with it except for the combination of its *noise* with the gifts of a good actor having already shown that this pedant speaks more for pomp than sense. Translating is a complex reading/writing process, not a linear job where reading comes first, ceases, and then writing starts. Where must 'fidelity' to the source's semantics yield to a creative engagement with the dramatic speech act? The principle is clear: understanding semantics, together with all other components, contributes to establishing the dramatic effect but it is not the central factor. Overrating semantics will inevitably stymie drama. Take this version in apparent assonant couplets by Delia Pasini:[27]

---

26 *Enrique VI, parte 2*, in William Shakespeare, *Obra completa III: Dramas históricos* (Barcelona, 2012), p. 157 (previously published in the collection 'Shakespeare by Writers').
27 *Trabajos de amor perdidos* (Buenos Aires, 2007), p. 103 (now also in the 'Complete Works' of the publishing house Losada).

La depredadora princesa perforó y pinchó un lindo y
    agradable cervato;
unos dicen cervatillo, si bien hasta ahora ileso, pues al
    cazarlo quedó herido.
Los perros ladraban. Pon una L al cervato, y un gran
    ciervo salta del mato;
ciervo, cervatillo, o, si no, cervato. Los cazadores
    lanzaron unos gritos.
Si al cervato hieres, entonces una L lo hace cincuenta
    veces más crecido,
y de un cervato yo hago cien, si agrego otra L al
    cervatillo.

This is not even a semantic transcription, although it aims to be. Holofernes' speech is pedantic and abstruse but not senseless. This text hardly makes sense, as the critical elements in the puns are exclusive to English; i.e., in English 'sore' plus 'L' equals 'sorrel', etc.; but in Spanish '*cervato*' plus '*L*' means nothing, period. Moreover, for a real translation of its pedantry, Holofernes' speech demands using verse efficiently. These lines merely gesture at verse, exceeding all Spanish metrical standards, randomly fluctuating between seventeen and twenty-four syllables, and wanting accentual rigour; consequently, rhymes do not rhyme.

Instead, if the translation targets dramatic praxis, the 'challenges' posed by Holofernes' text are next to naught. I translated *Love's Labour's Lost* for Pujante's collection as *Afanes de amor en vano*. His rule for jokes and puns is that all must be based on their sources as closely as possible, but self-sufficient – a policy observed to the point that notes on wordplay are practically non-existent in the collection. To translate this, then, I had only to devise pedantic wordplay fireworks in solid metre and rhyme, making cryptic sense concerning a Princess, deer-hunting and dogs. I hope to have achieved this through a burst of alliterative paronomasia in Spanish hexadecasyllables with perfect rhyme, playing with the differences between young and grown-up deer – reinscribing a Shakespearian pun between 'hind': 'deer'/'*ciervo*', and 'hind': 'servant'/'*siervo*' – but more with the differences in Spanish pronunciation between the /s/, /z/ and /c/ sounds, as well as with the words

for account (*cuenta*), if (*si*), yes (*sí*), without (*sin*), fifty (*cincuenta*), and one hundred (*cien*):

La predatoria princesa cazó una pieza preciada.
– ¿Un cervato, dice el siervo? ¡Ciervo con pinta
    opulenta! –
Corrieron sus perros prestos tras la presa apresurada,
que, fuese cervato o ciervo, contaba con cornamenta.
La que caza cobra y cuenta: cuanto caza cobra atenta,
y si cuenta, sí que cuenta: cincuenta o cien, o sin
    cuenta.[28]

The presumed problems in Holofernes' silly sestet become a cipher. If anything, the lengthy metre and alliterative excess *help*, not hinder, in emulating their sound and their fury because, here, the sense and sensibility matter much less. Wordplay is 'an exercise of virtuosity to no profit, without economy of sense or knowledge',[29] and since paronomasia stems from acoustic clusters in synchronous operation rather than from semantic knots, it enables the dramatist (and the translator) to work with sound above sense. Moreover, the purposeful pronunciation challenges of this version provide readers and listeners of Spanish with different experiences depending on their region. In Spain, /c/ and /s/ before /i/ are strongly distinguished, which creates a clear contrast between '*cin*cuenta' (fifty) and '*sin* cuenta' (countlessly); but they are not distinguished in Latin America, and hence cause the *opposite* effect. It may be argued that this case is exceptional. Granted. But it shows the need to carefully balance meaning with form.

Two more typical instances prove another point about Pujante's method: regardless of which hand was at work, the method and rigorous supervision of the head translator resulted in consistent, reliable, readable, and speakable versions. Here is a small piece from *Richard II*:

> *King.* I'll give my jewels for a set of beads,
> My gorgeous palace for a hermitage,
> My gay apparel for an almsman's gown,

---

[28] *Afanes de amor en vano*, in William Shakespeare, *Teatro completo II: Comedias y tragicomedias* (Madrid, 2012), p. 253.
[29] Jacques Derrida, "Proverb: 'He that would pun...'", in John P. Leavy, ed., *Glassary* (Lincoln, 1986), p. 17.

My figured goblets for a dish of wood,
My sceptre for a palmer's walking staff,
My subjects for a pair of carved saints
And my large kingdom for a little grave . . .

(3.3.148–54)

rendered thus by Pujante:

Mis joyas las daré por un rosario,
mi palacio señorial por una ermita,
mis vistosos trajes por gabán de limosnero,
mis copas decoradas por un plato de madera,
mi cetro por bordón de peregrino,
mis súbditos por dos tallas de santos
y mi ancho reino por una estrecha tumba . . . [30]

Pujante delivers content very closely, with great economy, and in a solid combination of Spanish metres: hendecasyllables, dodecasyllables (a major Spanish tradition) and alexandrines very aptly bring Richard's voice from one King to his 'other self' in another language.

Now, from *3 Henry VI*:

King. This battle fares like to the morning's war,
When dying clouds contend with growing light,
What time the shepherd, blowing of his nails,
Can neither call it perfect day nor night. (2.5.1–4)

translated as follows, in the same collection, with the same criteria, but by me:

Esta batalla imita la guerra matinal
entre las sombras moribundas y la aurora,
cuando el pastor, soplándose las palmas,
no puede aún decir si es día o noche. [31]

Although translated by two different hands, the similarities between the two passages regarding closeness to original content, rhythms of speech, and verse-use show that the method unifies the overall results, providing the collection with strong stylistic consistency and performability, mostly fostered by the strict rule of rendering a line for a line.

But translating a line for line makes no difference if done carelessly. In *Love's Labour's Lost*, for example, Navarre reads this sonnet:

So sweet a kiss the golden sun gives not
To those fresh morning drops upon the rose,

As thy eye-beams, when their fresh rays have smote
The night of dew that on my cheeks down flows:
Nor shines the silver moon one half so bright
Through the transparent bosom of the deep,
As doth thy face through tears of mine give light;
Thou shinest in every tear that I do weep:
No drop but as a coach doth carry thee;
So ridest thou triumphing in my woe.
Do but behold the tears that swell in me,
And they thy glory through my grief will show:
But do not love thyself; then thou wilt keep
My tears for glasses, and still make me weep.

(4.3.16–29)

The version below, again by Pasini, presumably meant to 'respect the sense', does not give Navarre a sonnet to read, but a sequence of long lines randomly ranging from fourteen to eighteen syllables, with a puzzling scheme of assonant rhymes, one of which is missing:

El sol resplandeciente no da un beso tan dulce	a
a las frescas gotas que cada mañana a la rosa mojan	b
como el fulgor de tus ojos cuando sus rayos tocan	b
la noche de rocío que por mis mejillas fluye.	a
Al brillar, ni la luna de plata tanto resplandece	–
en el reflejo que el mar a través de sus olas transparenta	c
como lo hará tu cara cuando mis lágrimas encienda.	c
Brillas en cada lágrima que vierto al recordarte	d
y, más que lágrimas, carruaje son para llevarte.	d
Así, triunfal, cabalgas erguida sobre mi dolor.	e
El llanto que me arrasa detente a contemplar	f
y él revelará tu gloria a través de mi aflicción.	e
Pero tú no ames, pues así podrás conservar	f
mis lágrimas como espejos y aun mi llanto provocar. [32]	f

This is not strict verse, let alone the hendecasyllables historically adopted to induct sonnets into Spanish. Likewise, against the apparent aim to privilege content, the final lines are misinterpreted. More importantly, this precludes dramatic praxis:

---

[30] *Ricardo II*, in William Shakespeare, *Teatro selecto I* (Madrid, 2008), p. 179.

[31] *Enrique VI, tercera parte*, forthcoming in William Shakespeare, *Teatro completo III: Obras históricas* (Madrid, 2015).

[32] *Trabajos de amor perdidos*, pp. 111–2.

here no one can play or hear Navarre's sonnet because there is none, as perceptive readers can tell.

Praxis being the main criterion, I translated thus:

> No besa el áureo sol con tal encanto
> el néctar de la rosa en la alborada,
> como de mis mejillas limpia el llanto
> el fresco resplandor de tu mirada;
> ni la luna de plata se refleja
> en el fondo translúcido del mar,
> como atraviesa el agua de mi queja
> la luz de tu semblante. Al llorar,
> en mis lágrimas viajas, y montada
> en mi pena celebras tu victoria.
> Mira mi faz, de lágrimas colmada:
> allí verás la estampa de tu gloria.
> Mas no adores tu imagen, pues querrías
> por espejo tener lágrimas mías.[33]

This is a strict Spanish sonnet, hendecasyllabic with perfect rhymes. As required by Pujante, the rhyme scheme is English – somewhat rare but not unheard of in Spanish. And this proved far more challenging than Holofernes' silly sestet, as here I had to compress and abstract content to make it fit and function within the Spanish verse. Shakespeare's content *is* there, not literally but quite closely and *pragmatically*: here verse not only says what the original text says but more importantly, effects in Spanish the poetic-dramatic effects for which it was devised.

Other instances of wicked verse in *Love's Labour's Lost* also demand special care. Boyet's characteristic affectedness is well served by the see-saw of extra-metrical couplets with caesura:

> His tongue, all impatient to speak and not see,
> Did stumble with haste in his eyesight to be.
> All senses to that sense did make their repair,
> To feel only looking on fairest of fair.   (2.1.243–6)

Again, Spanish prosody can match the effects of Shakespeare's verse quite well. Here, I employed assonant alexandrines – which in Spanish have a natural caesura – to render Boyet's bi-membered flamboyance:

> Ansiosa porque habla, mas no puede mirar,
> su lengua ansiaba, torpe, sus ojos alcanzar,
> y todos sus sentidos, reunidos en la vista,
> a la bella de bellas rindieron pleitesía.[34]

More challenging is dialogue in couplets that flow naturally while being highly artificial. In these lines by Rosaline, enjambment and caesura play major roles towards her closing sarcasm:

> We four indeed confronted were with four
> In Russian habit. Here they stayed an hour,
> And talked apace; and in that hour, my lord,
> They did not bless us with one happy word.
> I dare not call them fools; but this I think,
> When they are thirsty, fools would fain have drink.
> (5.2.387–93)

Here – as in the entire collection wherever there are couplets – assonant dodecasyllables, a distinctly Spanish metre that fosters ironic delivery, do the trick:

> Las cuatro, es verdad, hemos visto a cuatro
> rusos, que una hora entera han pasado
> charla que te charla, sin que sus discursos
> tuvieran sentido, provecho ni gusto.
> No me atreveré a llamarlos necios,
> mas si falta el agua, hay necios sedientos.[35]

The consistent results of Pujante's method throughout the collection suggest nothing new: that the dramatic goal of the lines is primordially inscribed in *rhythm*, with semantics framed by it. 'Meaning' is not irrelevant, just not as central as usually assumed. The three translators in Pujante's collection worked, so to speak, 'outside-in': from frame to field. Significantly, these translations in Iberian Spanish are proper for stage delivery: they lead voices and bodies to perform with rhythmical economy – especially if those voices and bodies belong to *Spaniards*.

---

[33] *Afanes de amor en vano*, p. 257.
[34] *Afanes de amor en vano*, p. 242.
[35] *Afanes de amor en vano*, p. 280.

TRANSLATING SHAKESPEARE IN SPANISH TODAY

'TRULY, SIR, IN RESPECT OF A FINE WORKMAN . . . '

Before final considerations, a disclaimer. I have elsewhere insisted – for performative and political reasons – that Latin American translators of Shakespeare use local varieties of Spanish, dropping the blind and pointless habit of producing texts that resonate with colonial notes.[36] Although I pointedly observe those principles in my own stage practice, my contributions to Pujante's collection are in Iberian Spanish because they are meant for the Spanish market, and I was trusted to do them that way. And so I did them, with no illusions that they would be appropriate for stage purposes in my region or country.

As suggested above, however, differentiating between Iberian and Latin American versions is vital. Spanish is used by 500 million people. Three quarters are Latin American (one quarter Mexican), while ten percent reside in Spain and another ten in the USA.[37] It is crucial to have texts for and from all Spanish voices and bodies and ears. The differences may not seem big to some, but they are. In *The Tempest*, for instance, Gonzalo's first speech,

> Beseech you, sir, be merry; you have cause –
> So have we all – of joy, for our escape
> Is much beyond our loss. Our hint of woe
> Is common: every day some sailor's wife,
> The masters of some merchant and the merchant
> Have just our theme of woe . . .   (2.1.1–6)

reads thus in Pujante's translation:

> Alegraos, Majestad, os lo ruego. Tenéis
> motivo para el gozo, como todos: salvarnos
> cuenta más que lo perdido. La desgracia
> que sufrimos es corriente: cada día, esposas
> de marinos, dueños de barcos, mercaderes,
> también tienen motivo de dolor . . . [38]

In mine, yet unpublished, made in prose for a Mexican stage-production, it reads thus:

Le ruego que se alegre, Majestad; no le faltan razones, como a nadie: habernos salvado importa más que lo perdido. Nuestra desgracia no es única: cada día, las esposas de marinos, los dueños de barcos mercantes y los mercaderes también tienen por qué sufrir.

Apart from a negligible difference in length, these versions, basically matching in semantics, feature the most evident contrasts between Iberian and Latin American Spanish. First, the conjugations and pronouns for the second person and then, when voiced, the also important lack of distinction in pronunciation between /s/ and /z/ (and /c/ before /i/ and /e/) that characterizes Latin Americans. But more significantly, and less visibly, there are differences in rhythms of speech, turns of phrase and concepts of time, impossible to detail here, but culturally fundamental.

Other important contrasts can be better appreciated in more specific types of language. Take Falstaff's diatribe against Hal in *1 Henry IV*:

'Sblood, you starveling, you eel-skin, you dried neat's tongue, you bull's pizzle, you stock-fish! O for breath to utter what is like thee! You tailor's-yard, you sheath, you bowcase; you vile standing-tuck –   (2.4.185–187)

This is Pujante's rendering:

¡Voto a . . . ! ¡Tú, famélico! ¡Tú, piel de anguila, lengua de vaca curada! ¡Tú, vergajo! ¡Tú, bacalao seco! ¡Ah, más aliento para decirte lo que eres! ¡ Tú, vara de sastre! ¡Tú, funda! ¡Tú, vaina! ¡Tú, daga empinada . . . ![39]

Mexican spectators would not respond well to this frankly Iberian version. But they did to mine, made for the 2012 '37 plays/37 languages' festival, and as yet unpublished:

¡Carajo! ¡Tú, muerto-de-hambre! ¡Pellejo de anguila! ¡Lengua de buey en salmuera! ¡Chicote de verga de toro! ¡Bacalao reseco! ¡Ojalá tuviera el aire para decirte lo que

---

[36] See my 'Of Shadows and Stones: Revering and Translating "the Word" Shakespeare in Mexico', *Shakespeare Survey 54* (Cambridge, 2001), pp. 152–64.

[37] See *El español, una lengua viva. Informe 2013*, Instituto Cervantes (Madrid, 2013): http://eldiae.es/wp-content/uploads/2013/06/2013_espanol_lengua_viva.

[38] *La tempestad* (Madrid, 1997), p. 65.

[39] *Enrique IV, partes I y II* (Madrid, 2000), p. 108.

eres! ¡Vara de sastre! ¡Funda de estoque! ¡Vaina marchita! ¡Puñalito quebradizo...!

These versions achieve similar general effects for very different audiences. Yet a contrasting glance would show that only one word, '*Chicote*', is lexically exclusive to Latin America, while the rest mean basically the same on both sides of the Atlantic. But many carry potentially different innuendos. The contrast is not due, then, to specific regional *lexis* (much less to 'jargon') but to *praxis*: the uses each culture makes of the language, channeled in diverging syntax. For example, '*puñalito*' means the same ('little dagger') anywhere in Spanish, and betokens a characteristically Latin American predilection for diminutives. But only in Mexico does it carry a homophobic double sense. Here it is employed to help Mexican Falstaff do what Shakespeare's Falstaff does: accusing Hal of being thin and lacking in 'manhood'.

Significantly, two of my contributions to Pujante's collection I had already translated for Mexican stagings: *Love's Labour's Lost* and *The Comedy of Errors*.[40] Thus, I have made two totally different versions of each play, in highly contrasting kinds of Spanish and medium. A glance at the Mexican *Love's Labour's Lost* may provide an idea of the great differences. That text, entitled *El vano afán del amor*, was made in prose, except for crucial rhyming parts, which I rendered strictly: sonnets for sonnets, and so forth. One piece I treated differently, however: Holofernes' sestet. The convoluted Iberian version above actually stemmed from my as yet unpublished Mexican text, but the latter was less elaborate from the start:

> Nuestra Princesa, certera,
> ha cobrado un cervatillo,
> que llama así el zafio pillo,
> pues confundirnos quisiera.
> Los canes le hacen correr,
> y nota el cortejo todo
> que la presa queda a modo,
> ¡como cantar y coser!
> La que caza, cuando cobra,
> canta tanto cuanto cuenta:

> su canto crece y, contenta,
> la cuenta crece de sobra.

Also, this was only the first and closer version, as for the final stage-script I devised wordplay on fishing instead of deer-hunting, since the play happened on a beach. Apart from thus illustrating the joyfully unstable nature of stage-translation, this version shows how translating the passage is feasible without emulating its metre and scheme – in other words, here I did not apply a method like Pujante's, but freely yet economically used perfect octosyllables, the fundamental Spanish metre, seasoned with wordplay. It worked: audiences laughed at the pompously cryptic pedant.

Ultimately, what is significant about translating Shakespeare plays twice, very differently, into the same language for separate but mutually understanding markets, is that the effects of Shakespeare's texts can be well matched on either side of the Atlantic by many diverse means, but never without the care and responsibility earlier outlined. How I differ from Pujante's criteria in my own practice proves that the translator's vehicles may be independent of the source's evident literary aspects but not so of its performative demands. Whatever the translator's choices, they must be made to obtain a firm grip on the text's performative energies.

Doubtless, in Shakespeare the strongest of these energies which the translator must confront is blank verse: its variety, its flexibility, its unchecked productivity. One last example is required. In 2013 Pujante and I had our respective translations of *Julius Caesar* staged at the same time, his in Spain, mine in Mexico – a strange coincidence. His text goes back twenty-five years; mine to 2011. Here are our entire translations of Antony's 'O pardon me, thou bleeding piece of earth...' (3.1.273–94), his on the left, mine on the right:

---

[40] My Mexican version in prose and occasional verse of *The Comedy of Errors* was staged in 2007 as *La comedia de los errores* and remains unpublished; my translation for Pujante's collection is called *La comedia de los enredos*, in William Shakespeare, *Teatro completo II: Comedias y tragicomedias* (Madrid, 2012), pp. 163–218.

¡Perdóname, sangriento pedazo de barro
por tanta dulzura con estos verdugos!
Escombro eres hoy del hombre más noble
que vio la luz en el curso de los siglos.
¡Ay de la mano que vertió tu augusta sangre!
Sobre estas heridas (cuyas bocas mudas
sus labios rojos abren invocando
mi voz y mi palabra) aquí profetizo:
Caerá una maldición sobre los miembros humanos;
la furia interna y la cruel guerra civil
angustiarán a todas las partes de Italia;
serán tan comunes la sangre y el estrago
y tanta atrocidad habrá que presenciar
que las madres sonreirán al ver a sus criaturas
destrozadas por las manos de la guerra,
pues tanta barbarie ahogará la compasión.
Y marchará en son de venganza el espíritu de César,
con Ate a su lado salida del infierno,
y, soltando a los perros de la guerra,
gritará en estas tierras con voz soberana '¡Muerte!';
y el hedor de esta infamia llegará hasta el cielo
con cadáveres podridos implorando sepultura.

¡Perdóname, despojo de tierra ensangrentada,
por ser dócil y amable con estos carniceros!
Eres las ruinas del hombre más noble
que haya existido en la marea del tiempo.
¡Ay de la mano *que derramó esta sangre incomparable!*
Ante tus heridas – bocas mudas
cuyos labios rojos piden
el sonido de mi voz – hago esta profecía:
una maldición *consumirá la carne de los hombres;*
la furia de una cruel guerra civil
abatirá cada región de Italia;
la sangre y destrucción serán tan habituales,
y habrá tantas imágenes atroces,
que hasta las propias madres sonreirán al ver a sus criaturas
destazadas por las manos de la guerra,
pues la barbarie sofocará a la compasión.
Y el espíritu de César – rabioso por vengarse,
con Ate junto a sí, recién salida del infierno –
con voz de rey *ha de gritar: "¡Que nadie quede vivo!"*
y en todas partes soltará los perros de la guerra,
hasta que el hedor de este sucio crimen llegue al cielo,
mientras se pudren los cadáveres, implorando sepultura.

Pujante's criteria have hardly changed since he got started, with good reason: they work very well. There are several dodecasyllables in this text and, when the speech requires it, he uses longer lines. Some take the form of the sweet Italian hendecasyllable, and others play close to or exactly as alexandrines. As shown above, the flexibility of his method, modified from Schlegel's, permits the translations in Pujante's edition to match Shakespeare's blank verse well, without prolixity. Here the last lines do quite what Shakespeare's last lines do, proving the efficacy of the method again, especially with regard to Shakespeare's famous blending of short and long words and vowels, which in this case bring Antony's prophecy down from the intense height of lines 292–3:

Cry havoc and let slip the dogs of war,
That this foul deed shall smell above the earth.

to the conclusive long descent of 294:

With carrion men groaning for burial.

I, on the other hand, always render Shakespeare's blank verse in prose for my Mexican stage versions. But it is a kind of prose that I intend to be fully yet freely 'rhythmical', and has proven quite effective in performance. In this case, to illustrate, I have broken my 'rhythmical prose' for Antony according to Shakespeare's lines. Overall, my text achieves effects much like those in Pujante's. Printed as prose, however, on the page my unpublished version will seem much longer but in fact it is only twelve syllables longer. This is because my prose contains much hidden and, as it were, *undisciplined* verse, either as speech units that actually read as proper verse lines or as lines embedded in longer speech units.

For clarity, above I have marked *hendecasyllables* in italics and **alexandrines** in bold type, although practically every speech unit corresponds to a particular form of Spanish verse. Thus, within my prose there are about ten hendecasyllables, some embedded in longer units, and several alexandrines, most of which share with the hendecasyllables the fundamental stress on the sixth beat, creating a network of accents that I like to think of as helpful for performance. Significantly, some of it came from working with the actor playing Antony, from the privilege of translating for the actor and the actor's voice, as I often fortunately can. But, as I noted, none of this is planned or pursued *strictly*. Do these things 'translate' themselves to a translator's ear and make the host language look into its own resources for empathetic 'accents yet unknown' to inform this exercise in ephemeral originality and creation of ephemeral originals called 'translating'? I doubt it. But I cannot say why I doubt it.

What I do know is that when translators responsibly and knowledgeably bring Shakespeare's works into our different yet intertwined worlds, by means of long shared and long cultivated means, we act out of care, out of love. Our ways and resources are not alien to Shakespeare and Shakespeare is not alien to us: his own means come from, and inhabit, vastly shared intercultural energies that meet in the creative act of translation and make the ever expanding intercultural library named Shakespeare a splendid, manifold reality.

READING ORIGINALS BY THE LIGHT
OF TRANSLATIONS

TOM CHEESMAN

The first half of this article discusses the idea that translations, considered as texts, as editions and as interpretations, can help Shakespearians re-read the original. The second half discusses some new technologies which attempt to put that idea into practice.

I

The recent upsurge of interest in non-English Shakespeares, coinciding with a 'cultural turn' in Translation Studies, has – as Ton Hoenselaars puts it succinctly – led to 'Shakespeare without *his* language' being mostly interpreted as 'Shakespeare without his *language*'. The 'verbal component' of translation, 'the original core business involving the interaction of foreign languages', is losing out to other cultural components: those which are more easily transferred back into Anglophone discussions.[1] Ruth Morse also calls for new attention to literary-theatrical translations as texts, not just as documents of their original culture, but as pragmatic aids to reading the original: 'the translation of metaphor may help the native speaker to alert herself to secondary (or even primary) associations in a text'; translations 'can be just as thought-provoking when they arouse reservations'; they can 'preserve what has been lost from the original' by change in English (the you/thou distinction is among her examples).[2] Dirk Delabastita goes further. He points out that 'every translation [including every interlingual adaptation] incorporates or constitutes an act of total interpretation' of the original, and that translators are often 'superbly

sensitive readers', who are less likely than native speakers of English to overlook the significance of 'misleadingly familiar patterns' in the original. This means that 'translations present a vast exegetical potential', overlooked by Anglophone editors and critics (and teachers and theatre practitioners). Translations, he says, ought to be deployed 'as key witnesses of the diverse ways in which certain passages *can* be read and *have been* read'.[3]

This is a striking thought. An edition which incorporated translators' readings would be a great advance on the editions we have and are getting, which arbitrarily confine their sources to English. Delabastita reminds us that Shakespeare's translators were inevitably aware of his texts' 'ambiguities, puns, and quibbles' long before the scholars:

not . . . that all [individual] translators [fully] understood these subtle puns or ambiguities as such, but different translators appear to have disambiguated puns in different ways, so that the [aggregate] picture emerges of readings that are complementary in their respective partialities. The mere collation of such incomplete translations or 'mistranslations' thus produces a

---

[1] Ton Hoenselaars, 'Translation Futures', in *Shakespeare Survey* 62 (Cambridge, 2009), pp. 273–82; p. 275. I thank Margaret Tudeau for the invitation to take part in her stimulating seminar, 'Lost in Translation', at ISC 2014, and Balz Engler for sharing his expertise in comments on a draft of this article.

[2] Ruth Morse, 'Reflections in Shakespeare Translation', *The Yearbook of English Studies*, 36 (2006), 79–89; pp. 79, 81, 82.

[3] Dirk Delabastita, 'More Alternative Shakespeares', in *Four Hundred Years of Shakespeare Translation in Europe*, ed. A. Luis Pujante and Ton Hoenselaars (Newark and London, 2003), pp. 113–33; p. 24. Original emphasis.

surprisingly accurate sense of the possible semantic range of Shakespeare's words. If translations, through their easy availability and their interpretive explicitness, are among the most valuable documents for exploring both the interpretive history of a Shakespeare text and its semantic virtualities, why is it that editors (and critics) are not taking note of them?[4]

It is a good question.

There is a sort of precedent, but not a happy one. In the 1870s and 1880s, Horace Howard Furness took note of translations in several volumes of his *New Variorum* edition. Sometimes he simply reprinted parallel translations of a sample passage, without comment. In an appendix to *Othello*, titled 'Can Shakespeare Be Translated?', he presented thirty-five versions of Iago's 'mandragora' lines (3.3.334–7), in eight European languages.[5] His only comment, at the end of the series of quotations, was: 'Let me not be understood as citing these translations in any carping, critical spirit. They are all good, and some of them admirable, as exact and literal as is possible. Where they have failed, they have failed because they *must*.'[6] Furness combines smug certainty that Shakespeare's poetry *cannot* be translated – that is, not at all *well* – with an impressive show of his own linguistic skills: 'I could continue the series in Russian, in Polish, in Bohemian, and in Hebrew, – not, however, as examples of translations, for my having in these languages is as a younger brother's revenue, but as illustrations of the universality of Shakespeare's presence in every land, and in every tongue.'[7] A 'translation', for Furness, is a text which he can read: anything else is just an 'illustration' of universality. This is a key point and it largely answers Delabastita's question. Even if Shakespeare's editors are beginning to overcome Furness's ideological insularity (and even if they acknowledge both Delabastita's point that translations are editions[8] and Balz Engler's that editions are translations),[9] they cannot actually read actual translations or certainly not all the translations they would need to read; and what they cannot read they are not comfortable working with.

Furness printed samples from translations, only in order to underline that none was worth reading.

The ruse worked; no Anglophone editor since has paid even that much attention to translations. Perhaps the profession is ready now to move on. But it will be necessary to demonstrate a pragmatic gain to be made from engaging with translations, sufficient to justify the intrinsic challenge. International collaborations are necessary between scholars with expertise both in Shakespearian originals and in translations. The clincher could be Delabastita's immodest proposal. Translations are not just documents of the translating cultures and of intercultural dynamics (although that is sufficient reason to be interested in them). As interpretations, they can be put to work, serving readers of the original – and in the process fomenting those readers' linguistic curiosity.

To implement Delabastita's suggestion, a network of specialists must help editors tap translations' 'vast exegetical potential'. Here 'help' implies 'translate': in order to contribute to the understanding of a crux in English Shakespeare, renderings of it in other languages must be made accessible in English, that is, at least back-translated and glossed, and ideally subjected to more detailed commentary. We will return to this tricky point. 'Help' also means, pragmatically, obtaining copies of translation texts. Delabastita exaggerates the 'easy availability' of translations. Collecting them, with necessary information about their contexts, can be far from straightforward. Here Morse's work on the quasi-canonical French translations by François-Victor Hugo is instructive. His texts have the status of classics but his copious scholarly, critical and polemical work, essential to

4 Delabastita, 'More Alternative', p. 124. Cf. his study: *There's a Double Tongue: An Investigation into the Translation of Shakespeare's Wordplay, with Special Reference to 'Hamlet'* (Amsterdam and Atlanta, 1993).

5 Horace Howard Furness, ed., *Othello. The New Variorum Edition* ([Philadelphia, 1886], facs. repr. New York, 2000), pp. 453–8.

6 Furness, *Othello*, p. 458.

7 Furness, *Othello*, p. 458.

8 Delabastita, 'More Alternative', pp. 122–3.

9 Balz Engler, 'The Editor as Translator', in *Shakespeare Survey* 59 (Cambridge, 2006), pp. 193–7.

his original edition, has been utterly forgotten. Basic book history data is lacking. She notes that even the greatest libraries have failed to collect translations systematically.[10] An important start in plugging the information deficit was made by the bibliographies in 33 languages assembled by the 'Shakespeare in Europe' project at Basel University.[11] But quite aside from the arbitrary 'European' limitation of that particular project, it largely restricted itself to print publications. Many translations of great interest are not and never were in print. Vast numbers of manuscripts and typescripts are scattered in public, theatre and private archives – never mind audio-visual materials. What is more, the task is never-ending. New translations and adaptations are being created at an accelerating rate, in more and more languages – some print-published, most not. And finally, merely accessing a text is never enough: readers need information about its contexts of origin and use in order to assess it and its textual choices.

Would the investment pay off in terms of new and better understandings of the original? Take the first major crux in *Othello*, Iago's description of Cassio as 'A fellow almost damned in a fair wife' (1.1.20). The phrasing – 'to damn', in the passive, with the preposition 'in' and a noun for a person (or class of persons) (and a marital 'wife' or 'wife' meaning woman?) – is so unusual that no clear meaning can be construed. Furness devotes five pages to Anglophone and German editors' and commentators' ingenious proposed emendations and glosses, finally admitting defeat.[12] ('The text cannot be altered, and opinions are often just an expression of despair at that.')[13] For Michael Neill, the line expresses Iago's misogyny and sexual envy of Cassio, but its 'precise reference . . . remains unclear': he suggests Cassio is either about to marry and suffer the consequences; or 'a ladies' man'; or having an affair with a married woman.[14] Balz Engler, on the other hand, neatly explicates 'damned in' as either 'damned because of' or 'transformed into' (citing Macbeth's 'damn thee black', 5.3.11).[15] German translators, between them, offer all these interpretations. Their

predominant reading is Engler's second, taking 'wife' to mean 'woman':[16] Cassio is effeminate, 'damned [to be / by being turned] in[to] a woman'. Wolf Baudissin's *Othello* in the Schlegel-Tieck edition (1832, and countless revisions) gives: 'zum schmucken Weibe fast versündigt', approximately meaning: 'sinned [so as] almost to [become] an attractive woman'. This German phrasing is strange too, if not so ambiguous as the original. Most later translators express the same basic idea. The closest version perhaps is: 'fast in ein schönes Weib verdammt' ('almost damned into a beautiful woman', Friedrich Gundolf, 1909). Some simplify: 'anzusehen wie ein Weib' ('like a woman to look at', Erich Engel, 1939); 'ein femininer Schönling' ('an effeminate pretty-boy', Christian Leonard, 2012). Others elaborate: 'der durch Zufall / nicht als ein hübsches Weib auf diese Welt kam' ('who by chance was not born into the world as a pretty woman', Hans Rothe, 1955); 'Der Teufel / hat fast ein schönes Weib aus ihm gemacht' ('The devil almost made a beautiful woman out of him', Erich Fried, 1972); 'n verdammter Schwulenschönling, n Tuntentalent. Kapp ihm den Schwanz und du hast n einwandfreies Blowjobluder' ('A damn fairy-pretty-boy, a faggot-talent. Cut off 'is cock 'n' you

---

[10] Ruth Morse, 'François-Victor Hugo and the Limits of Cultural Catalysis', in *Shakespeare Survey 64* (Cambridge, 2011), pp. 220–30; p. 224.

[11] 'Sh:in:E' (edited by Markus Marti and others) at https://shine.unibas.ch/home.html (2000–2007).

[12] Furness, *Othello*, pp. 5–10. Furness notes that Alexander Schmidt, in revising Baudissin's 'Schlegel-Tieck' (1832) translation of *Othello* for the edition of the Deutsche Shakespeare-Gesellschaft in 1877, 'avails himself of a translator's privilege' and cuts the line (p. 11). Wieland (in 1766) and Schiller and Voss (in 1805/6) had done the same before. Bibliographic details for translations cited in this paper are at www.delightedbeauty.org/vvvclosed (at: Corpus = 'Othello, German, Act 1 Scene 3). Back-translations are my own.

[13] Franz Kafka, *The Trial*, trans. Mike Mitchell (Oxford and New York, 2009), p. 157 (translation adapted TC).

[14] Michael Neill, ed., *Othello. The Oxford Shakespeare* (Oxford and New York, 2006), p. 197.

[15] Balz Engler, ed., *Othello. Englisch-deutsche Studienausgabe* (Munich, 1976), p. 35.

[16] Interference may be a factor: German 'Weib' primarily means 'woman'.

gotta total blow-job-bitch', Feridun Zaimoglu and Günther Senkel, 2003). Among alternative, minority readings: 'schon zum Pantoffel fast verdammt' ('already almost damned to [be under] the slipper [of a housewife]', Otto Gildemeister, 1871); 'dem mal ein Weib zum Schicksal wird' ('for whom a woman is going to be fateful one day', Frank Günther, 1992); 'Schürzenjäger' ('skirt-chaser' i.e. 'ladies' man', Oliver Karbus, 2006).

This sample of a few versions of a crux raises problems for the potential deployment of translations as exegetical aids. First, it is not always obvious what the translations mean, any more than their original. Arguably the best translations – certainly for exegetical purposes – convey some of the original's ambiguity, at the risk of exceeding it, multiplying the uncertainty. They have their own 'semantic virtualities'. Back-translations into English must struggle to convey the sense aptly and fully, never mind the equally essential tone and style; and as for prosody, rhythm, 'Klangmalerei' ('sound-painting', a word that sounds effectively in German and is partially translatable as 'onomatopeia') – only with luck. Second, a translation tradition has its own dynamic of intertextual influence and imitation, resistance and differentiation, which skews the distribution of Delabastita's 'complementary . . . respective partialities'. In this case, the Baudissin/Schlegel-Tieck reading – the 'canonical, tacitly evolving'[17] 'original' for the German poetic-theatrical tradition – predominates. It is noteworthy that Engler's *Studienausgabe* text (in the tradition of explicatory and philological prose versions, whose original is Wieland) gives precisely the reading that is not found in Baudissin: 'fast verdammt . . . wegen einer schönen Ehefrau' ('almost damned . . . because of a beautiful married woman', Balz Engler, 1976).[18] Third, in a Shakespeare translation tradition, paratexts are paramount: annotations, notes, discussions in commentaries. Translators may or may not consult Anglophone editions, but they certainly consult German editions;[19] as often as translations rewrite (or plagiarize) previous translations,[20] they rewrite editors' notes and glosses. Karbus (cited above) has most likely taken his reading from Neill. A

variorum edition including translations as readings might have a high level of redundancy.

2

Nevertheless, if one gathers a fair number of translations in a given language, and if the texts are electronic, it becomes possible to do things which should interest even those who cannot read the translations, as well as those who can. Overviews of translation traditions, for example, in time-maps of metadata – where and when a work's translations, of what kinds, were created and published, and who was involved. Such online, interactive maps can also afford access to the texts, or samples of them, and information about them.[21] The maps can be populated with further data, e.g. about performances, with video links, and so on. That could be a relatively 'populist' approach. More technically, we can apply computational analysis to compare translations. Stylometry measures occurrences of highly frequent words, to identify unconscious authorial stylistic fingerprints. Such techniques are well known from forensic author attribution studies. Applying them to the comparison of translations has been pioneered by Jan Rybicki and colleagues.[22] Their software

---

[17] Morse, 'Reflections', p. 79.

[18] The bilingual *Studienausgabe* resumes the earlier German philological tradition: Nicolaus Delius's critical edition with German notes, often offering translations: *Complete Works* (Elberfeld and Leipzig, 1854–60, reprinted as late as 1898), the declared basis of Furnivall's *Royal* and *Leopold* editions; Alexander Schmidt, *Shakespeare-Lexicon* (Berlin, 1902) and Leon Kellner, *Shakespeare-Wörterbuch* (Leipzig, 1922), both still valuable; Schmidt's work is digital at www.perseus.tufts.edu.

[19] Translators now draw less often on the *Studienausgabe* than on the easily accessible explicatory translations, facing English texts, in the cheap Reclam editions, e.g. the *Othello* of Hanno Bolte and Dieter Hamblock (Stuttgart, 1985).

[20] See Maik Hamburger, 'Translating and Copyright', in *Shakespeare and the Language of Translation*, ed. Ton Hoenselaars (London, revised edition, 2012): pp. 148–67.

[21] See Stephan Thiel's 'Othello Map' at: http://othellomap.nand.io (2012).

[22] See https://sites.google.com/site/computationalstylistics/. The site is maintained by Jan Rybicki, Maciej Eder and Mike Kestemont.

script 'stylo' creates a graphic which visualizes comparable works forming clusters of genre and of period style. All prose explicatory versions of *Othello* (from Wieland to Bolte and Hamblock) form a cluster, clearly set apart from all the poetic-theatrical texts. All versions of the twenty-first century or the later nineteenth century form clusters, clearly set apart from all other versions. Certain particular texts are shown to be linked by common stylometric measures, indicating genealogical, intertextual relations of imitation, dependency or indeed plagiarism.[23]

Such visualizations of 'distant readings'[24] offer starting-points for exploratory investigations. These help us to see – quite literally – the convoluted histories of remediation which lie between each rewriting and its various, unstable sources.[25] But they concern translations as documents of their cultures, much more than their relations to their 'original source', to the so-called 'untranslated' Shakespeare.[26] Can we put translations to work as sources for the interpretation of original texts or passages? Can a comparison of the textual variations between different translations be put to work as a resource for *discovering* difficult original passages?

Before I answer that, another detour into original and translated wordings. Elsewhere I have discussed, at length, differing translations into German and French of a notorious couplet from *Othello* – the Duke's parting couplet, spoken to Brabantio: 'If virtue no delighted beauty lack, / Your son-in-law is far more fair than black' (1.3.289–90).[27] (I am also 'crowd-sourcing' versions of the couplet in *all* languages: some 200 so far, old and new, in 30 languages, including 'Englishes' – glosses, accounts of performances, literary rewritings, etc.)[28] The lines make enormous demands on translators: 'virtue', 'delighted', 'fair' and 'black' are all polysemic, ambiguous in the context, echoing other passages which amplify that ambiguity; the Duke's rhetoric, his intended meaning, mood and effect (sententious, humorous, chiding, commanding, complicit?) are ambiguous. The racist ideological assumption is offensive in many contexts, obliging translators to disambiguate ideologically, either constructing the Duke as a racist, or as an anti-racist, or (more rarely) finding a way to re-ambiguate which is pertinent to their cultural context. Not only 'race', but ideologies of gender, kinship, ethics, aesthetics, social hierarchy and political power are all in play in Shakespeare's fourteen words. The difficulties increase for translators whose translation strategy or norm demands formal correspondence, so they must produce a rhyming, scanning couplet, and for those seeking to 'archaicize' their text but, willy-nilly, writing in and for their own time. Translators' varying solutions make each version of the couplet a microcosmic illustration of their interpretation of the play, their translation strategy, and their cultural political times.

What can be called the 'strongest' translations (by analogy with Harold Bloom's notion of 'strong' poets in relation to their precursors)[29] are rewritings which disrupt translation traditions, performing readings of their own creative contexts. The

---

[23] Tom Cheesman and Jan Rybicki, 'Stylometric Analysis of 40 German Versions of *Othello*', at: https://sites.google.com/site/delightedbeautyws/outputs/exhibition or: http://tinyurl.com/vvvex (2014).

[24] See: Franco Moretti, *Distant Reading* (London, 2013).

[25] See further: Tom Cheesman, Kevin Flanagan, Jan Rybicki and Stephan Thiel, 'Six Maps of Translations of Shakespeare', in *Un/Translatables: New Maps for Germanic Literatures*, ed. Bethany Wiggin et al. (forthcoming 2015).

[26] Dirk Delabastita, 'Shakespeare', *Routledge Encyclopedia of Translation Studies*, ed. Mona Baker and Gabriela Saldanha (London and New York, 2nd edn, 2009), pp. 263–9.

[27] Tom Cheesman, 'Thirty Times "More Fair than Black": Othello Re-Translation as Political Re-Statement', *Angermion*, 4 (2011), 1–52; and '"Far More Fair Than Black": Mutations of a Difficult Moment', in *The Cambridge Guide to the Worlds of Shakespeare*, vol. 2, ed. Bruce R. Smith (forthcoming 2015).

[28] See www.delightedbeauty.org (2010–). New contributions to this collection are always welcome. I am grateful to Jürgen Gutsch for introducing the project to the worldwide contributors to *William Shakespeare's Sonnets, for the First Time Globally Reprinted. A Quatercentenary Anthology*, ed. Jürgen Gutsch and Manfred Pfister (Dozwil, 2009).

[29] '... strong poets make [poetic] history by misreading one another, to clear imaginative space for themselves': Harold Bloom, *The Anxiety of Influence: A Theory of Poetry* (Oxford, 2nd edn, 1997), p. 5.

only German woman to have translated *Othello* (so far) writes: 'Wenn nie der Tugend lichte Schönheit fehlt, / ist Eure Tochter hell, nicht schwarz, vermählt' ('If virtue never lacks bright-lit beauty, / your daughter is brightly, not blackly, married', Hedwig Schwarz, 1941). A translator persecuted by the Nazis, returned to Germany after the war, writes: 'Zählte bei Menschen nur der innre Schein, / würden wir dunkler als Othello sein' ('If people's inward appearance alone [were all that] counted, / we would be darker than Othello', Hans Rothe, 1955). A translation making both the play and the Duke anti-racist has: 'Gäbs helle Haut für Edelmut als Preis, / Dann wär Ihr Schwiegersohn statt schwarz reinweiß' ('If light skin were a prize for noble-mindedness, / then your son-in-law would be pure white instead of black', Frank Günther, 1992) – here 'pure white' is a sarcastic emphasis, indicating that the Duke disavows the racist equation of whiteness and virtue. Another has: 'Ein Fremder wird zum Freund durch Tapferkeit / Mach Frieden mit dem Schwiegersohn, nicht Streit' ('A stranger becomes a friend through bravery / Make peace with your son-in-law, not strife', Christian Leonard, 2010). A translation making the Duke a neo-fascist has: 'Solange männliche Tugend mehr zählt als Schönheitsfehler, kann man sagen, Ihr Schwiegersohn ist eher edel als schwarz' ('So long as male virtue counts more than blemishes, one can say your son-in-law is more noble than black', Zaimoglu and Senkel, 2003). Such translations make sense as performative readings, cultural interventions in their particular contexts. Can they even be termed 'interpretations', manifesting the original's 'semantic virtualities'? Can they help readers understand the original? Surely not, if 'original' means a finished thing; only if we mean 'originator of differences'. But then we are well beyond what Delabastita formulated as 'a surprisingly accurate sense of the possible semantic range of Shakespeare's words'.

A slightly different proposal would be this: diverse versions can contribute to a new reading of the original in terms of their *differential variability* at the level of *passages*. Consider another short passage, this one provoking far less variation in translations. Brabantio's 'Here is the man, this Moor' (1.3.71) is not a difficult half-line to translate. Only 'Moor' can pose a problem. The closest German equivalent, the traditional translating term, is 'Mohr', which is just as archaic as 'Moor'. 'Maure', also archaic, signifying a north African rather than sub-Saharan physiognomy, was used by Rothe and Schwarz in the mid-twentieth century. Since about 1990 (only!), translators often use non-archaic alternatives. 'Schwarzer' ('black man') is current and neutral (first used in this passage by Frank Günther, 1992). 'Neger' (back-translatable as 'negro' or 'nigger') is current and derogatory (first used by Werner Buhss, 1996). Another strategy is omission ('Here comes the man', first used by Christian Leonard, 2010). Translators make such choices either consistently for 'Moor' throughout the play (including the subtitle), or in varying combinations, so that their choices in various speeches convey their interpretation of the characters' attitudes, as well as, implicitly, what the writers think the audience will expect and want and/or be outraged by. Hermann Motschach (1992) gives Brabantio this line: 'Da steht der Mann, der schwarze Teufel' ('There stands the man, the black devil') – making an interpretation explicit. But overall, translations of this short passage vary little, compared with the variation in translations of the Duke's 'delighted beauty' couplet. In any set of variant translations, levels of variation vary, passage by passage. This simple observation can be exploited to interesting effect, with digital technology.

I have collected over fifty different German translations and theatrical adaptations of *Othello*, from Christoph Martin Wieland (1766) to Frank-Patrick Steckel (2014),[30] so far. Most are printed books, but fourteen are unpublished theatre scripts, ranging in date from 1939 to 2010.

---

[30] Not in the online database at time of writing: Steckel's *Die Tragödie von Othello, dem Mohren von Venedig / The Tragedie of Othello, The Moore of Venice* (Buchholz, 2014; facing Folio text). Jette Steckel's production at the Deutsches Theater, Berlin, 2009/2011, credited F.-P. Steckel's translation.

Four are study translations in explicatory, 'prosaic prose'; the rest are intended for leisure/pleasure reading and theatrical performance, using verse or (in some recent adaptations) poetic prose. Nine are versions of the Baudissin 'Schlegel-Tieck' text, including the electronic text in the German Project Gutenberg collection (c.2000).[31] These differ to a surprising degree. ('The great thing about a translation is that you do not need to treat its decisions with respect.')[32] So far, thirty-eight versions of Act I, scene 3 have been digitized with sufficient textual accuracy (correcting the output of optical character recognition processing against scanned page images) to be published online. At the 'Version Variation Visualization' (VVV) website,[33] readers can consult all the versions of this sample scene in parallel text views, side-by-side with an English 'original' – more exactly, a 'base text', compiled for the purpose from the MIT electronic text,[34] collated with Neill's edition for additional material and commoner modern readings.

All versions have been aligned with the 'base text', speech by speech; speech prefixes too are aligned. Software enabling 'multi-translations'[35] to be segmented and aligned in this way – a machine-assisted process – was developed by Kevin Flanagan. Software enabling readers to explore the resultant aligned corpus through interactive visual interfaces was developed by Stephan Thiel and his team (Studio Nand, Berlin).[36] At our VVV site, a visual 'barcode' is displayed, representing a text's speech-structure, in order to help readers both navigate within and compare texts. It appears as a narrow vertical strip, divided into horizontal bars of varying thickness: bars represent speeches, and thickness represents length in words. These 'barcode' representations enable readers to compare at a glance the speech-structures of a base text and its translations. We can see exactly where versions reduce or cut, add or expand or re-order material. This mode of 'slightly distant' reading, representing a scene or a play as a patterned image of the formal structure as represented (usually) in typography, can be compared with the practice of holding a page or two of script at arm's length, in order to 'see the rhythm' of a passage of dialogue.[37] Scale of view makes the difference. A 'scalability' which far exceeds that of print on paper is a key virtue of digital representations. We can smoothly, fluidly zoom in and out between close and closer, distant and more distant readings. The other virtue we can exploit is that a digital surface can carry many optional marks. With menus and filters we can represent all sorts of computational analyses or diagnoses of machine-readable features of texts or corpora, as marks *on* the texts.

Here at last we come to the point where translations may shine new light on the original. Eddy and Viv are algorithms which compare, select, rank and mark text. Eddy (so called because translations are eddies in the stream of transcultural history) compares the wording of versions, segment

---

31 The German e-text was transcribed from Hans Jürgen Meinerts's edition of 1958, then collated with an English Gutenberg Project e-text, presumably www.gutenberg.org/files/1531 (a transcript of an unidentified edition). Where they did not align, material was added (from where?). The volunteer editor was probably Ruediger Wenig, a multiply-aliased slam poet and media design consultant, who first published German e-Shakespeare at www.william-shakespeare.de (c.2000) before donating it to the Gutenberg Project.

32 Morse, 'François-Victor Hugo', p. 222.

33 See www.delightedbeauty.org/vvv. The limitation to one scene is also due to my agreement with copyright holders, who (for a modest fee) permit use of the texts, subject to a variable public access restriction.

34 At http://shakespeare.mit.edu. The VVV base text is yet another unauthorised variant edition.

35 Stig Johansson, 'Between Scylla and Charybdis: On Individual Variation in Translation', *Languages in Contrast*, 11 (2011), 3–19.

36 Thiel's work includes visualizations of Shakespeare's English play-texts, experimentally combining algorithmic readings with views of text structures ('Understanding Shakespeare: Towards a Visual Form for Dramatic Texts and Language', at www.understanding-shakespeare.com, 2010) and an interface for exploring the text of *Macbeth* using a table of lemmas (headwords) ranked in order of their differential frequency in that play, compared to the Shakespeare corpus: www.tinyurl.com/macbthe, 2014. This will make sense to readers of Jonathan Hope and Michael Witmore, 'The Language of Macbeth', in *Macbeth: The State of Play*, ed. Ann Thompson (London, 2014), pp. 182–208.

37 My thanks to Peter Holland for this observation.

by aligned segment,[38] and so measures the relative distinctiveness of each version of each segment. Viv ('variation in variation') then maps the results of Eddy's comparisons onto the original's segments, as a visual mark. In the 'Eddy and Viv view' of *Othello* 1.3 at the VVV site, readers can retrieve all the translations of any chosen segment of the English base text (together with machine back-translations, which are of limited value). They can also order these segments in various ways, including – and this is original – by distinctiveness or unpredictability, as measured by Eddy. At the same time, the English text is displayed, annotated, segment by segment, by the Viv algorithm, showing us the extent to which the translations of each segment vary – the range of distinctiveness or unpredictability. This is the most conceptually experimental feature of our work so far, and perhaps the most interesting for readers who are interested in translations but cannot read them.

Recall the examples of the Duke's couplet and Brabantio's words. Eddy the algorithm compares all versions of every segment, simply in terms of which words (spellings) each one uses. If a version of a segment mostly uses words which many other versions of the segment also use, it will score a *low* Eddy value. Versions which mostly use words which few or no other versions also use in that segment will score a *high* Eddy value. When Eddy ranks all versions of Brabantio's 'Here comes . . .' in order of distinctiveness, Motschach's wording automatically comes top. In this way Eddy picks the more 'original', more distinctive translations out of the crowd: a very useful function for readers of many translations. Eddy is less useful in comparing versions of the Duke's couplet, because they vary so much. Nearly all of them have high Eddy values. But this is where Viv becomes useful. Viv is the average (essentially) of all the Eddy values for versions. The Viv value is assigned to the original segment, on the basis of analysis of its translations. The higher the Viv value, the more translations differ, the more translators disagree about how to translate that segment. In the Eddy and Viv view, the Viv values are represented as a variable colour highlight on the English base text. The darker

the colour, the higher the Viv value, the more translators differ or disagree. Brabantio's words are light-coloured; the Duke's couplet is dark. So Eddy and Viv between them use translations to identify difference-provoking, difficult passages in the original Shakespeare text.

The mathematics is complex. We have developed several versions of the Eddy and Viv formulae. The algorithms currently use word spellings but it might be better to use lemmas. It might be better to exclude highly frequent 'function words'. Segment length is a crucial factor: the longer the segment, the more variation is likely, all else being equal. Adjusting results for that factor is tricky. The initial results are (in information theoretical terms) 'noisy'. But this is an experimental work in progress. Nor is it the aim to identify some objective 'truth' about texts. Numerical Eddy or Viv values do not represent *quantities*; the numbers express *relations* which are themselves *indicative* – and of what, we are still finding out. The aim is to enable and instigate new kinds of exploratory investigations of texts in the light of their translations. Here are some initial results for *Othello*, Act 1 scene 3.

These results are based on analysis of a sub-corpus of fifteen twentieth-century poetic-theatrical German versions of *Othello*. We selected these because the stylometric analysis showed the importance of period style and genre differences, so we hypothesized that a time-limited and genre-limited analysis should give less 'noisy' results. I excluded versions derived from Baudissin, explicatory prose versions and also adaptations with extensive omissions, contractions, expansions and additions, which would all introduce noise. This left the following versions in the VVV database: Gundolf (1909), Schwarz (1941), Zeynek (1948), Flatter (1952), Rothe (1955), Schaller (1959), Schröder (1962), Fried (1972), Swaczynna (1972), Laube (1978), Rüdiger (1983), Motschach (1992), Günther (1992), Buhss (1996), Wachsmann (2005).

---

[38] All speeches are defined as segments; we can also choose to define as a segment any string of words which interests us. We can also 'tag' segments as any kind of 'type'.

Table 1 Othello 1.3 by 15 C20 German translations. Highest Viv values. Running order.

Rank	Viv	
2	1.06	*Duke* There is no composition in these news That gives them credit. (l.1)
8	0.94	*First Senator* Indeed, they are disproportioned; My letters say a hundred and seven galleys. (l.2)
4	1.00	*Duke* Nay, it is possible enough to judgment: I do not so secure me in the error, But the main article I do approve In fearful sense. (l.9)
10	0.93	*Duke* To vouch this, is no proof, Without more wider and more overt test Than these thin habits and poor likelihoods Of modern seeming do prefer against him. (l.106)
9	0.94	*A Senator* But, Othello, speak: Did you by indirect and forced courses Subdue and poison this young maid's affections? Or came it by request and such fair question As soul to soul affordeth? (l.110)
6	0.95	*Duke* I think this tale would win my daughter too. Good Brabantio, Take up this mangled matter at the best: Men do their broken weapons rather use Than their bare hands. (l.170)
3	1.05	*Duke* And, noble signior, If virtue no delighted beauty lack, Your son-in-law is far more fair than black. (l.289)
7	0.95	*Brabantio* Look to her, Moor, if thou hast eyes to see: She has deceived her father, and may thee. (l.292)
1	1.13	*Iago* If thou dost, I shall never love thee after. Why, thou silly gentleman! (l.306)
5	0.96	*Roderigo* Wilt thou be fast to my hopes, if I depend on the issue? (l.361)

The analysis includes whole speeches only and excludes segments of fewer than 50 or more than 500 characters, because results for very small or large segments are noisiest. This left a set of some 50 speeches. Table 1 shows those with the ten highest Viv values, in running order (with speech prefixes and first line numbers), alongside absolute rank and rounded Viv values.

It is gratifying to see the Duke's couplet – and Brabantio's reply to it, too – both 'discovered' by the algorithms as passages provoking much variation. In other speeches, archaisms and obscurities demand paraphrase in any language ('composition', 'disproportioned', 'possible . . . to judgment', 'likelihoods of modern seeming', 'be fast to my hopes'). But doubt creeps in. Are these translational challenges really greater than others in the text, not shown here? Wherein lies the particular provocation in the Senator's 'But, Othello, speak . . .', or the Duke's 'I think this tale . . .', or Roderigo's 'Wilt thou be fast . . .'? All are susceptible of multifarious translations – but more so than other speeches?

These initial results look like an artefact of factors other than the original text: the very limited sample, the exclusions mentioned and, above all, what we can speculate about the behaviour of translators and observe about cultural-linguistic constraints on them. Regarding translators' behaviour, it would be no surprise (but rather interesting for Translation Studies) if further studies confirmed that they tend to translate speeches at the beginning of a scene (as here), or speeches by a character of singular importance in a scene (here the Duke), most diversely. Certainly we can explain along these lines why Brabantio's 'Look to her' couplet (which presents little by way of translational challenge, compared with the Duke's) is very diversely translated: because it is a very conspicuous passage, calling for a verbal tour de force. Shakespeare translators are motivated by the desire to achieve distinction – to rewrite differently from, more originally than their precursors and rivals.[39]

---

[39] The will to achieve 'distinction' (as the term is used in Pierre Bourdieu's sociology of culture) underlies difference in retranslations in many accounts, e.g. Sameh Hanna: 'Othello in Egypt: Translation and the (Un)Making of National Identity', in *Translation and the Construction of Identity*, ed. Juliane House *et al.* (Manchester, 2005), pp. 109–28. Jan Mathijssen (seemingly unaware of Bourdieu) proposed a similar model: 'The Breach and the Observance: Theatre Retranslation as a Strategy of Artistic Differentiation, with Special Reference to Retranslations of Shakespeare's *Hamlet* (1777–2001)' (PhD diss., Utrecht, 2007).

Therefore they put in most effort where it is most likely to be noticed. But then the absence of Othello and Desdemona from this table is odd: surely translators ought to invest in writing their parts more distinctively?[40] As for cultural-linguistic constraints, what propels Iago's speech to the number one spot here is probably the fact that the quasi-oxymoronic phrase 'silly gentleman', though neither really archaic nor obscure, is peculiarly difficult to render into German, generating a great diversity of paraphrases, as does the colloquial exclamation 'Why'. We might well say, after the Duke, 'There is no composition in these numbers that gives them credit' – at least, not yet as news about the original.

A glance at the eight speeches found to have *lowest* Viv value in the same analysis (Table 2, ranked low to high) is dispiriting at first. It immediately suggests a problem with the adjustment for segment length: most of these speeches are of one length, as most in Table 1 are of another.

Ranked eighth from bottom here is Desdemona's 'That I did love the Moor...', with lines which have provoked much commentary and would seem likely to provoke variant translations – but Eddy and Viv find variation is low. Reading the translations, it turns out that several standard options for 'visage' and 'mind' are quite evenly distributed, and no translator attempts the kind of original rewriting we saw with the Duke's couplet. On reflection, the putative discovery of 'original non-difficulty' in Table 2 seems rather more plausible than the putative discovery of 'original difficulty' in Table 1. In the sequence of 'low Viv' speeches, characters are taking care to express themselves clearly; even if very emotional, they are controlling that emotion; or issuing a crisp command (the Duke); or, in Iago's case, speaking as if to someone who is slow on the uptake. For all the deficiencies of this preliminary analysis, we can begin to see how it might inform readings by students and players, if not yet editors and critics.

Eddy and Viv have a lot more work to do. We need larger text samples (the whole of *Othello*, more plays), more translations, more languages. If translators into different languages encounter different sets of challenges rooted in the linguistic resources of their target languages and cultures, rather than in the original, then in an analysis of a multi-lingual multi-translation corpus, the impacts of target cultural-linguistic constraints should be spread more evenly across the original text.[41] We must improve correction for segment length difference. It will make sense to work on more comparable units (e.g. couplets, other comparable word-strings or n-grams). We can also look for correlations between translation diversity and individual words, word-classes, semantic word-sets and grammatical features. This would open the way to exploring patterns of repetition and coherence both within translations and in their originals.

Eddy and Viv is only one line of possible digital experimentation. The general aims are broader: to make translations visible and accessible to new kinds of reading. The comparison of translated versions can resemble the editorial work of collating witnesses and prior editions. We can envisage digitally visualized, translingual variorum editions.[42] But as with editorial work, this is not an end in itself. The humanistic purpose is to facilitate future re-readings and rewritings. That will include comparing variant English versions of 'untranslated' (always-already translated) Shakespeare. True, texts are only one component of translation. They are not even a sine qua non of cultural translation: 'Shakespeare' travels very well as rumours of stories by and about him, pictures and clips, tags and snatches in worldwide folklores, memories of private and public performances, 'appropriations, adaptations, and afterlives'.[43] But

---

40 The limitation to speeches of under 500 characters is not a factor here. Viv gives (for instance) Othello's 'Let her have your voices...' (1.3.260–74), with the obscure 'comply with heat' passage, a very average value (0.86). The great set-piece 'Her father loved me...' (127–69) scores 0.8.

41 Pavel Drábek and Tomáš Kačer have a Czech Shakespeare translation corpus; Vladimir Makarov and colleagues have a Russian one. We intend to collaborate.

42 Ben Fry's visualisation of the variorum edition of *On the Origin of Species* was a prime inspiration for our project: http://benfry.com/traces (2010).

43 In the proceedings of the 9th World Shakespeare Congress, 24 papers are grouped under this subtitle. Only one concerns

Table 2 *Othello* 1.3 by 15 C20 translations. Lowest Viv values. Running order.

Rank	Viv	
7	0.77	*Brabantio* So did I yours. Good your grace, pardon me; Neither my place nor aught I heard of business Hath raised me from my bed, nor doth the general care Take hold on me, for my particular grief Is of so flood-gate and o'erbearing nature That it engluts and swallows other sorrows And it is still itself. (l.52)
6	0.77	*Desdemona* My noble father, I do perceive here a divided duty: To you I am bound for life and education; My life and education both do learn me How to respect you; you are the lord of duty; I am hitherto your daughter: but here's my husband, And so much duty as my mother showed To you, preferring you before her father, So much I challenge that I may profess Due to the Moor my lord. (l.179)
4	0.77	*Brabantio* God be wi' you! I have done. Please it your grace, on to the state-affairs: I had rather to adopt a child than get it. Come hither, Moor: I here do give thee that with all my heart Which, but thou hast already, with all my heart I would keep from thee. For your sake, jewel, I am glad at soul I have no other child: For thy escape would teach me tyranny, To hang clogs on them. I have done, my lord. (l.188)
8	0.76	*Desdemona* That I did love the Moor to live with him, My downright violence and storm of fortunes May trumpet to the world: my heart's subdued Even to the very quality of my lord: I saw Othello's visage in his mind, And to his honour and his valiant parts Did I my soul and fortunes consecrate. So that, dear lords, if I be left behind, A moth of peace, and he go to the war, The rites for which I love him are bereft me, And I a heavy interim shall support By his dear absence. Let me go with him. (l.248)
1	0.79	*Duke* At nine i' the morning here we'll meet again. Othello, leave some officer behind, And he shall our commission bring to you; With such things else of quality and respect As doth import you. (l.279)
3	0.78	*Roderigo* It is silliness to live when to live is torment; and then have we a prescription to die when death is our physician. (l.308)
2	0.79	*Iago* O villainous! I have looked upon the world for four times seven years; and since I could distinguish betwixt a benefit and an injury, I never found man that knew how to love himself. Ere I would say, I would drown myself for the love of a guinea-hen, I would change my humanity with a baboon. (l.311)
5	0.77	*Iago* Thou art sure of me: – go, make money: – I have told thee often, and I re-tell thee again and again, I hate the Moor: my cause is hearted; thine hath no less reason. Let us be conjunctive in our revenge against him: if thou canst cuckold him, thou dost thyself a pleasure, me a sport. There are many events in the womb of time which will be delivered. Traverse! go, provide thy money. We will have more of this tomorrow. Adieu. (l.363)

translators as re*writers* are key agents, whether they try to transfer the original faithfully, or cannibalize it gleefully. They are routinely under-credited and increasingly invisible (at least Furness *saw* and *printed* their work). Their languages are misunderstood as transparent windows onto an 'original' meaning, or silently back-translated, or left out of the discussion altogether, if only because transporting the difference translation makes across another language gap is hard work.

Rejection of or indifference to translations is not a purely Anglophone vice, rooted in the imperialistic global predominance of English. Jacques Derrida resoundingly endorses the privileging of

translation: Martin Hilský, 'Shakespeare's Theatre of Language: Czech Experience', in *Renaissance Shakespeare: Shakespeare Renaissances*, ed. Martin Procházka, Michael Dobson, Andreas Höfele and Hanna Scolnicov (Newark, DE, 2014), pp. 171–80.

the original as a law-giving act of genius, when he compares several French versions of Hamlet's 'The time is out of joint' (1.5.189):

The translations themselves thus find themselves '*out of joint*'. *However* correct and legitimate they may be and whatever *right* one may acknowledge them to have, they are all disadjusted, as it were unjust in the gap that *affects* them. This gap is within them, to be sure, because their meanings remain necessarily equivocal; then in their relation to one another and thus in their multiplicity; finally or first of all in their irreducible inadequacy to the other language and to the stroke of genius of the event that makes the law, to all the virtualities of the original.[44]

Recall Delabastita's 'semantic virtualities'. Here Derrida cites French translations precisely in order to help himself mine the original's meaning-potential. But he continues: 'The excellence of the translation cannot help. Worse, and this is the whole drama, it can only aggravate or seal the inaccessibility of the other language.' The drama of translation, for Derrida, as for Furness and for most Shakespeare scholars, is that of the Fall; the original 'other language' is Eden or Arden. The

original is the law; translations are transgressions. Yet a few pages later Derrida comes back to 'the apparently disordered plurivocity (which is itself "out of joint") of these interpretations', to note that they are all, after all, 'authorized', for what makes an origin is the power to originate:

Is it possible to find a rule of cohabitation under such a roof, it being understood that this house will always be haunted rather than inhabited by the meaning of the original? This is the stroke of genius, the insignia trait of the spirit, the signature of the Thing 'Shakespeare': to authorize each one of the translations, to make them possible and intelligible without ever being reducible to them.
(22)

All we have of the haunting Thing is translations in one sense or another. Bring the translations proper – the original rewritings – under one roof, and they will surely tell us new ghost stories.

---

[44] Jacques Derrida, *Specters of Marx: The State of the Debt, the Work of Mourning and the New International*, trans. Peggy Kamuf (New York and London, 1994), p. 19 (translation adapted TC).

'MY NAME IS WILL': SHAKESPEARE'S SONNETS AND AUTOBIOGRAPHY

STANLEY WELLS

I once wrote on Twitter that the more I read Shakespeare's sonnets, the more difficult I find them. To which an unknown follower, flatteringly assuming that I was an undergraduate, responded with 'Finals are going to be fun, then.'

There are many reasons for the difficulties that I experience with the Sonnets. It is partly that many of them are highly intellectual poems written in an exceptionally dense and demanding style. I have problems too with the complex interrelationships among the sonnets and with the challenge of reading consecutively a large number of short poems, some clearly interrelated, whether in subject matter or by syntactical links, some not. Continually one has to make a fresh start after the apparent finality of a couplet. But many of my difficulties relate directly to the theme of this volume, the poems' origins and their originality.

The vexed question of their origin – where they came from – may be asked in what we might call the geographical, or physical, sense of 'Where did Thomas Thorpe get the manuscript that lies behind his 1609 publication?' Did Shakespeare himself negotiate its publication – possibly for ready money – or did Thorpe somehow acquire a manuscript (or possibly two manuscripts, one containing the sonnets, the other 'A Lover's Complaint') from someone other than Shakespeare who may not have had the author's permission to part with it? It is an important question because if Shakespeare authorized the publication, that would imply that he had signed off on the collection, regarding it as a finished and publishable work, whereas if publication was unauthorized the volume could more rationally be thought of as an open-ended collection of poems which had accumulated over the years, which might have continued to grow after 1609, and which the author might even have regarded as too personal to be published. The ordering may be Shakespeare's – I think there are good reasons to suppose that it is – but the numbers could have been inserted by a scribe or by someone in the printing house.

The Arden editor, Katherine Duncan-Jones, is one of the primary exponents of the belief that publication *was* authorized. She addressed the question in her wonderfully well-researched 1983 article 'Was the 1609 *Shake-speares Sonnets* really unauthorized?'[1] There she demonstrates that Thorpe was not, as had been suggested, an unscrupulous publisher who would have been likely to print a surreptitiously obtained manuscript against its author's wishes, and concludes that it is reasonable to suppose that he received a finished manuscript from Shakespeare himself. She has sustained this position, writing in the 2010 revision of her 1997 Arden edition that 'there is good reason to believe that the 1609 Quarto publication was authorized by Shakespeare himself'.[2]

An obvious objection to this is the fact that the dedication appears over Thorpe's initials, not over Shakespeare's name (as in the narrative poems). To

---

[1] *Review of English Studies*, 34 (1983), 151–71.
[2] *Shakespeare's Sonnets*, ed. Katherine Duncan-Jones, The Arden Shakespeare (London, 2010), p. 33.

get round this, she hypothesizes that Thorpe wrote the dedication on Shakespeare's behalf because plague had driven the poet out of London. Thorpe, it would seem, had more boldly – or foolhardily – stayed behind. 'The hasty departure of the author', she writes, 'and his prolonged absence, rather than any kind of conspiracy or deception, probably account for Thorpe's being the signatory of the dedication.'[3] In her biographical study, *Ungentle Shakespeare*, too, she writes confidently that Shakespeare sold 'the valuable and much laboured-over text . . . surely for a good sum', to Thorpe, and that the dedication was 'signed by Thorpe, but authorized by Shakespeare'.[4]

Colin Burrow, in the Oxford edition published in 2002 (between the two versions of the Arden), is less confident about the state of the manuscript that Thorpe printed and of its provenance. Certain 'features of the printed text', he notes, 'suggest that the copy from which Eld's compositors worked may have been hard to read or that it may not have been finally revised'.[5] And whereas Duncan-Jones is willing to believe that 'The "book" sold to Thorpe may have taken the form either of an autograph manuscript or of an authorially corrected scribal transcript',[6] Burrow thinks the manuscript was a scribal copy, possibly written in more than one hand.[7]

My own view is that publication was not authorized. This is partly because the title page (like the Stationers' Register entry) is written, as it were, in the third person – 'Shakespeare's Sonnets, never before imprinted'. 'Shakespeare's Sonnets' is also the running title, and the volume bears a dedication followed by the initials of its publisher, not of its author. All this makes me believe that Thorpe published the poems without Shakespeare's authority. I see no reason to suppose that Shakespeare chose the dedicatee. And the theory, which has also been advanced, that 'Mr W. H.' is a misprint for 'Mr W. S.', standing for Master William Shakespeare, is surely absurd – why should a publisher, then or now, dedicate a book to the man who wrote it?

This does not, however, require us to doubt that Shakespeare is responsible for the order in which the sonnets are printed. To judge by the most reliable dating studies, that order does not correspond to their dates of composition. That is a crucial factor in discussion of whether the Sonnets were conceived as a whole. The fact that the collection includes a number of clearly interconnected groups of poems, such as those encouraging a young man to procreate, and the last twenty-six, which contain all those with female addressees, along with a number of other subsections such as those poems that have been supposed to refer to a rival poet or poets – all this favours the supposition that someone who knew the poems extremely well put them in their present order. This is most likely to have been Shakespeare himself, re-arranging them for his own satisfaction (like a boy with a stamp album), for perusal by one or more private friends, or, just possibly, with the thought in mind that he might eventually offer them for publication. I am not greatly attracted by the theory that he was inhibited by shyness from doing so until after his mother died, in September 1608, but I do suspect that he regarded the collection as a whole as something that he preferred to keep under wraps. The posthumous publication of John Donne's *Songs and Sonnets* in 1633 suggests itself as a parallel. I am happy to believe that Shakespeare wrote 'A Lover's Complaint' and that he would not have objected to its appearing along with the sonnets, though I am not convinced that it is integral to the collection.

A different aspect of the poems' origin is their relationship to sonnet sequences written during the 1590s in the wake of the publication of Sir Philip Sidney's *Astrophil and Stella*. In the book that I co-authored with Paul Edmondson ten years ago we argued that Shakespeare's sonnets do not form

---

[3] *Sonnets*, ed. Duncan-Jones, p. 11.

[4] Katherine Duncan-Jones, *Ungentle Shakespeare: Scenes from His Life* (London, 2001), p. 217.

[5] William Shakespeare, *Complete Sonnets and Poems*, ed. Colin Burrow, The Oxford Shakespeare (Oxford, 2002), p. 92.

[6] *Sonnets*, ed. Duncan-Jones, p. 40.

[7] *Sonnets and Poems*, ed. Burrow, p. 93.

a unified sequence but that they are a collection of disparate poems, some of them closely inter-related, though written (as chronological studies show) over a long period of time. As I have said, studies of chronology (as well as common sense) also show that they were not written in the order in which they are printed; so they are more prop-erly regarded as a miscellany than as a sequence.[8] This view is surely supported by the indisputable fact that not all the poems in the volume are love sonnets. Indeed, 146 – 'Poor soul, the cen-tre of my sinful earth...' – would not be out of place among Donne's Holy Sonnets. It is, says Duncan-Jones, 'Shakespeare's only explicitly reli-gious poem'.[9] And 129, 'Th'expense of spirit in a waste of shame', is a philosophical meditation on love and lust written in the third person which, though it can be related to other poems in the col-lection, can stand entirely on its own and would, moreover, seem completely out of place in a con-ventional sonnet sequence of the 1590s.

Furthermore, although we concur that all the sonnets clearly addressed to or written about a male person occur among the first 126 of the poems in order of printing, we dispute the common assump-tion that they are addressed to only one young man (or boy – 'sweet boy', 108, 'my lovely boy', 126), supporting our argument (which had been notably anticipated by Heather Dubrow[10]) by demonstrat-ing on the evidence of pronouns and forms of address that only twenty of these poems can con-fidently be said to be addressed to a male, and that many of the earlier-printed poems, including some of the most intensely amatory, could equally well relate to either a male or a female. I do not find it easy to overcome my own preconceptions about this. Just as it is difficult to get out of the habit of referring to the sonnets as a sequence (which, in the most basic, etymological sense of a series of poems that follow one another, they are) rather than as a collection or a miscellany, so also I often need to make a conscious effort in reading many of the first group of poems to think hard about whether the gender of the addressee, or of the per-son referred to, is ascertainable. Take for example Sonnet 27, in which the poet tells how, exhausted after a hard day's work, he lies awake thinking and writing in absence to a loved one:

> For then my thoughts, from far where I abide,
> Intend a zealous pilgrimage to thee,
> And keep my drooping eyelids open wide,
> Looking on darkness which the blind do see.

Traditionally this poem, and the subsequent son-net, which links with it in sense – 'How can I then return in happy plight, / That am debarred the benefit of rest...' – are regarded as poems addressed to the supposed male friend, but there is nothing in them to gender the addressee; Germaine Greer is fully justified in suggesting not merely that they do not have to be addressed to a male but that they could even be expressive of what she calls 'the loneliness and anxiety, the frustration and disap-pointment' that Shakespeare may have felt as he rode away from his wife and family.[11] (The same may be true of Sonnets 50 and 51, both of which take place, as it were, on horseback.)

These propositions seem to me to be self-evident – but old beliefs die hard. It is still all too common to hear reputable scholars and crit-ics rolling out the old fallacies about 'the young man of the sonnets' and basing whole arguments on the totally erroneous assumption that there is undisputedly only one young man, whether fic-tional or not. This idea is encouraged by Thorpe's dedication to 'the only begetter of these ensu-ing sonnets', whatever 'begetter' may mean and on whatever authority he may have said it, but is refuted by the contents of the volume. It perme-ates Hyder Rollins's monumental New Variorum edition of 1944,[12] and afflicts many currently circu-lating editions. Even in the revised Arden of 2010 (which does not refer to our study) Duncan-Jones

---

[8] Paul Edmondson and Stanley Wells, *Shakespeare's Sonnets*, Oxford Shakespeare Topics (Oxford, 2004), esp. pp. 49–51.

[9] *Sonnets*, ed. Duncan-Jones, p. 408.

[10] '"Incertainties now crown themselves assur'd": The Politics of Plotting Shakespeare's Sonnets', *Shakespeare Quarterly*, 47 (1996), pp. 291–305.

[11] Germaine Greer, *Shakespeare's Wife* (London, 2007), p. 261.

[12] *A New Variorum Edition of Shakespeare: The Sonnets*, ed. H. E. Rollins, 2 vols. (Philadelphia and London, 1944).

writes that 'more than four-fifths of the sequence [sic] is devoted to celebrating a [sic] fair youth', and she devotes a large part of her introduction to identifying William Herbert, Earl of Pembroke 'as the dedicatee and addressee [sic] of *Sonnets*'. [13] Colin Burrow, who allows that many of the earlier printed poems 'carefully skirt around even giving a fixed gender to their addressee', nevertheless also slips into referring to 'poems to the young man'. [14] David Ellis, in a book, *The Truth About William Shakespeare* (2012), which aims pugnaciously to take a hard-headed attitude to Shakespeare biography, writes of the sonnets as 'a story in which the poet is continually contrasted with *a beloved male younger than himself*' (p. 75) and of '*the man* to whom most of the sonnets were predominantly or exclusively addressed' (p. 79). [15]

These questions are of the highest importance to an understanding of the sonnets both as poetry and as the most personal of all Shakespeare's writings, the only ones that might give us direct access to his private thoughts and perhaps even to his daily existence. Are they indeed, as Wordsworth wrote in 'Scorn not the Sonnet', the 'key' with which 'Shakespeare unlocked his heart'? To liberate the sonnets from the notion that individual poems in the collection are necessarily subordinate to an overall design enables us to examine individual poems, or small groups of clearly interrelated poems, in their own right. To acknowledge that Shakespeare might have written love poems to and about a variety of persons, including past lovers, has fascinating consequences for biographical studies. And it is supported by the statement in Sonnet 31 (which is ungendered) 'Thou art the grave where buried love doth lie, / Hung with the trophies of my lovers gone.' Many critics have protected the poet's reputation (thus implicitly acknowledging that the poem may be autobiographical) by saying that the word 'lovers' 'need not', as Duncan-Jones puts it in her note on this poem, 'carry any erotic charge', but doesn't the word 'trophies' imply some form of amatory conquest? Burrow seems to think so. In his fascinating note on the same poem he suggests 'there is something at once resurrective and vampiric in the way the beloved makes life from

buried former loves'. To recognize, however, that not all the poems are straightforward love poems is also to extend the potential breadth of reference of the volume. An example is Sonnet 26, beginning

> Lord of my love, to whom in vassalage
> Thy merit hath my duty strongly knit,
> To thee I send this written embassage
> To witness duty, not to show my wit.

Duncan-Jones glosses 'this written embassage' as 'the sonnet itself' but it might equally refer to a written gift which the sonnet accompanied. Capell, in 1780, when the Sonnets were only just beginning to be taken seriously, remarked on the resemblance between this poem and the dedication to *The Rape of Lucrece*. [16] Both the poem and the dedication refer to the poet's 'love' for the person addressed, and to his 'duty', and indeed Rollins finds that this resemblance became the starting point for the theory that Southampton is not only addressed in this poem but is the addressee of all the male-oriented sonnets. To my mind abandonment of the concept that the sonnets have a single male addressee gives strength to the theory that Shakespeare wrote this sonnet to accompany the manuscript of *Lucrece* when he sent it to the Earl.

There are also at least three sonnets which make me suspect the existence of a portrait of a lover of the poet as an external reference, and which embolden me to make an association again with Southampton. One such sonnet is 20, 'A woman's face with nature's own hand painted / Hast thou, the master-mistress of my passion', which is immediately followed by the poem beginning 'So is it not with me as with that muse / Stirred by a *painted* beauty to his verse'. And three poems later comes 24, beginning 'Mine eye hath played the painter, and hath steeled / Thy beauty's form in table of my

---

[13] *Sonnets*, ed. Duncan-Jones, pp. 52–69.

[14] *Sonnets and Poems*, ed. Burrow, p. 135.

[15] David Ellis, *The Truth About William Shakespeare: Fact, Fiction, and Modern Biographies* (Edinburgh, 2012).

[16] See Rollins, *New Variorum Edition*, note to Sonnet 26.

heart. / My body is the frame wherein 'tis held, / And perspective it is best painter's art.' ('Table' could mean the canvas or board on which a painting was done.) The poem continues with references to 'the painter', his 'bosom's shop', and other words associated with painting: 'glazed', 'drawn', 'art' and 'draw'. The sonnets' order of printing does not of course necessarily correspond to their order of composition, but it is at least suggestive that only two poems later comes 26, which may have accompanied the presentation manuscript of *Lucrece*. Anyone who has seen the portrait of the Earl of Southampton identified in 2002 and looking singularly androgynous can surely be forgiven for suspecting a connection between the sonnets that reference painting and the Earl. It has to be emphatically said, however, that to associate *some* of the poems with Southampton does not require us to suppose that he is the only male presence behind the poems.

In 1598 – before many of the poems in the 1609 volume were composed, if we accept chronological studies by Macdonald P. Jackson and others – Francis Meres wrote of Shakespeare's 'sugared sonnets among his private friends'. Did he mean simply that Shakespeare let some of his friends read poems that he had written purely out of an impulse to create pleasing verbal artefacts, or might Meres have meant that the poet was showing intimately personal poems only to friends who would recognize their links with Shakespeare's closest personal relationships? The phrase 'sugared sonnets' had been used in a cryptic poem published four years previously by Richard Barnfield, whom Meres calls his friend, which forms part of Barnfield's sequence *Greene's Funerals*. There, curiously referring, it would seem, to Marlowe as 'Malta's poet' – i.e. the author of *The Jew of Malta* – Barnfield writes that his muse 'seldom sings' 'sugared sonnets'.[17] The association of this phrase with the two best known homoerotic poets of the period is intriguing; might 'sugared sonnets' have implied poems that were homoerotic in tone? And perhaps we should remember that the word 'sonnet' did not necessarily mean poems in the 14-line form with which it is now most generally associated.

Writers on the Sonnets often invoke a dichotomy between literary convention and personal experience, simplistically suggesting that the poems are either 'literary exercises' on the one hand or autobiographical documents on the other. If we think of them as a series of individual poems or groups of poems written over a long period of time – perhaps as much as 27 years – we may gain insights into the range of reasons why in any given poem Shakespeare may be seen to be writing as a professional poet concerned to create a verbal artefact either for its own sake, or as a literary exercise, or for fun, or as a professional task – and perhaps to make money – or on the other hand in order to work out for himself in poetic form matters of deep and essentially private personal significance.

There is of course an element of poetic convention behind all these poems in the very fact that they adopt the conventions of sonnet form deriving ultimately from Petrarch and Dante. Shakespeare plays with this point of origin in 130, 'My mistress' eyes are nothing like the sun', as if to imply the existence of a poem which makes that comparison. Sonnet 21, too, beginning

> So is it not with me as with that muse
> Stirred by a painted beauty to his verse,
> Who heaven itself for ornament doth use,
> And every fair with his fair doth rehearse

similarly defies poetic convention in its claim that the poet's beloved – whether male or female – though 'as fair / As any mother's child', is nevertheless 'not so bright as those gold candles fixed in heaven's air'. The first of these poems, 'My mistress' eyes', is printed among the late-numbered group and is clearly about a woman, whereas 'So is it not with me . . .', which is ungendered, is printed among the earlier group.

In spite of the undeniable literariness of the form, there are remarkably few identifiable specific literary sources for Shakespeare's sonnets. The two most derivative are 153 and 154, both based on a single Greek epigram. Here unquestionably

---

[17] Richard Barnfield, *The Complete Poems*, ed. George Klawitter (Selinsgrove, 1990), p. 73.

Shakespeare is writing with a literary model before him, but where he read the epigram, and whether he read it in Greek, in Latin translation, or even in someone else's English version, remains a mystery in spite of numerous attempts to solve it. Burrow (p. 117) writes of these two sonnets as 'alternative versions of each other and of a poem (which Shakespeare might have encountered in any one of a multitude of disguises)' without, however, identifying any of these disguises. And Duncan-Jones in her edition (p. 422), conjecturing that they may be based on a lost English version of the epigram translated by Ben Jonson, nevertheless admits that they 'seem closer to the Greek original than to any of the [surviving] Latin or vernacular adaptations of it'. A simple, possibly simplistic explanation would be that Shakespeare translated it himself from the Greek, but neither Duncan-Jones nor Burrow allows for this possibility. In my lecture to the World Shakespeare Congress in 2011 I made what seems to be the original suggestion that these two poems might even be 'schoolboy exercises in translation undertaken by a young man who was obliged to study Greek at school but did not take it much, if any, further than classroom level'.[18] This would place them close in date to the Anne Hathaway sonnet, 145. Whether this is so or not, it seems to me that the derivative nature of these two poems invalidates any attempts to link them to Shakespeare's life, such as the common suggestion that the references to baths, which are present in the original poem, show that he visited the city of Bath to be treated for a venereal disease, or that he took mercury baths in London.

Beyond this, identifiable literary sources for the sonnets are confined to a few echoes of Ovid, especially in the opening lines of 60 – 'Like as the waves make towards the pebbled shore . . .', a generalized debt to Erasmus's 'Epistle to Persuade a Young Gentleman to Marriage' in those of the sonnets that encourage procreation, and a surprisingly small number of classical allusions, such as the references to Adonis and Helen in 53 and to Mars in 55. In sheer density of literary allusiveness the Sonnets are surely less obviously 'literary' than most, perhaps any, of the plays.

Let me now embark on a kind of taxonomy of the sonnets. Some of them may be thought of as generalized love poems which, though they might spring from personal emotion, nevertheless would not be out of place in a collection that either had no identifiable personal referent or that was written as it were for public consumption, the poet wearing his heart on his sleeve – or appearing to do so – like the professional sonneteers. Examples are: 29, 'When, in disgrace with fortune and men's eyes . . .'; 39, 'O, how thy worth with manners may I sing . . .'; 40, 'Take all my loves, my love, yea, take them all . . .'; 53, 'What is your substance, whereof are you made . . .'; 60, 'Like as the waves make towards the pebbled shore . . .'; and, among the later printed group, 128, 'How oft, when thou, my music, music play'st', and 107, beginning

> Not mine own fears, nor the prophetic soul
> Of the wide world dreaming on things to come,
> Can yet the lease of my true love control,
> Supposed as forfeit to a confined doom . . . .

This is a magnificent declaration of love that even readers not in the know about its ungendered addressee, or about the 'peace' to which it appears to refer, may enjoy; the points of reference in the lines beginning 'The mortal moon hath her eclipse endured', lost to us, may have been intelligible to at least some general readers at the time.

All these poems are romantic in tone. Another, which also is intelligible without special knowledge on the part of the reader, is the determinedly anti-romantic 151, 'Love is too young to know what conscience is'. Like 146 it has as its topos the contrast between soul and body, but whereas that poem treats its subject matter in spiritual terms, this one does so with explicit, not to say lewd frankness:

> My soul doth tell my body that he may
> Triumph in love; flesh stays no farther reason,
> But rising at thy name doth point out thee
> As his triumphant prize. Proud of this pride,

[18] 'Shakespeare: Man of the European Renaissance', in Martin Procházka et al., eds., *Renaissance Shakespeare: Shakespeare Renaissances* (Newark, DE, 2014), p. 6.

He is contented thy poor drudge to be,
To stand in thy affairs, fall by thy side.
   No want of conscience hold it that I call
   Her 'love' for whose dear love I rise and fall.

The final couplet gives power of speech to the poet's penis.

As you might expect, the Variorum commentary on this poem makes intriguing reading. In a 1937 book entitled *The Sonnets of Shakespeare: A Psychosexual Analysis* one H. McC. Young wrote that the poem is 'so frankly physiological as to violate even the shreds of taboo that Professor Freud has left us'. Hyder Rollins comments 'The majority of readers pass this sonnet by in silence, and probably most readers fail to understand it.'[19] There are of course parallels to its sexual frankness in the plays, as for example in the scene in *Love's Labour's Lost* in which Boyet and the ladies of the court jest bawdily about pricks and masturbation of a man by a woman, provoking Maria to say, understandably, 'you talk greasily, your lips grow foul.' (4.1.131–6). Shakespeare might have written the sonnet for publication as a corrective to sentimentalizing poems. In any case it demands to be taken into account in any investigation into Shakespeare's mind and imagination.

Other poems, while not being especially intimate, invite us to identify the poet with Shakespeare himself because of what we know about aspects of his life. Sonnet 23, for instance, beginning 'Like an imperfect actor on the stage' and including reference to 'my books', does not have to have been written by a bookish actor, but our knowledge that Shakespeare was such a man personalizes it for us. And the obvious pun on Hathaway identified by Andrew Gurr, and the somewhat less obvious one on Ann suggested by Stephen Booth,[20] in the couplet of the octosyllabic Sonnet 145 –

'I hate' from hate away she threw,
And saved my life, saying 'not you'

are surely enough to identify this as a private poem written in Shakespeare's youth, and therefore also,

incidentally, as evidence that he had ambitions as a writer well before he left Stratford.

Attempts to link the sonnets to Shakespeare's life sometimes hinge on decisions as to whether language is being used metaphorically or literally. Obvious examples are what might be interpreted as allusions to physical disability in Sonnets 37, 66, 89 and (possibly) 90. Should we believe that Shakespeare was literally 'made lame by fortune's dearest spite', and did he actually 'halt' because of lameness (89) – an interpretation which might lead to the suggestion that he wrote Richard III as a role for himself to play? René Weis is the most recent biographer to accept this reading.[21] I suspect the allusions are metaphorical, not literal, but there is no definitive answer. I feel less diffident about dismissing a suggestion by Martin Green referring to the sonnet beginning 'Why didst thou promise such a beauteous day / And make me travel forth without my cloak?' Green took this to mean that Shakespeare had contracted a venereal disease as a result of not wearing a condom – a 'cloak' – during a 'brief intimacy' with his friend – 'he was not one hour mine' (Sonnet 33), and suggests that John Shakespeare manufactured such items out of leather and sold them under the counter of his glover's shop.[22] He writes 'The puns on quondam in Shakespeare's plays reveal this familiarity with the condom', undeterred by the fact that the word 'condom' is not recorded until *c.*1706.

The first seventeen of the poems as printed (one has to say this because it is all too common for scholars to slip into writing as if the order of printing were also the order of composition) are perhaps also the most clearly interrelated group in the

---

19 *New Variorum Edition*, ed. Rollins, note to Sonnet 26.
20 A. J Gurr, 'Shakespeare's First Poem: Sonnet 145', *Essays in Criticism*, 21 (1971), 321–6; Stephen Booth, *Shakespeare's Sonnets: Edited with Analytic Commentary* (New Haven, 1977), p. 501.
21 René Weis, *Shakespeare Revealed: Decoding a Hidden Life* (London, 2007), pp. 185–92.
22 *The Labyrinth of Shakespeare's Sonnets: An Examination of Sexual Elements in Shakespeare's Language* (London, 1974), p. 24.

collection. They all play loving, sometimes rapturously eloquent (but occasionally irritable) variations on the theme of persuading a young man to marry and beget a child – or even, in Sonnet 6, to beget ten children:

> That use is not forbidden usury
> Which happies those that pay the willing loan –
> That's for thyself to breed another thee,
> Or ten times happier, be it ten for one.

(Am I alone in finding the notion that a young man might wish to multiply himself by the going rate of usury rather funny?) There is an element of technical virtuosity here, as if Shakespeare were flexing his poetical muscles in a series of exercises in creating variations on a theme. But that does not preclude their being strongly personal poems. It has been suggested that they might have been written to commission from a parent anxious that his or her son was not getting down to the task of perpetuating the family line, and various potential aristocratic candidates for this position have been suggested. Indeed in the television film *A Waste of Shame*, scripted by William Boyd with the Arden editor as adviser, we see Shakespeare visiting the Countess of Pembroke, played by Zoë Wanamaker, and carrying a sheaf of sonnets, identified ingeniously as 'one for each of [her son's] years', which the poet hands over to her for ready cash even before he has met her beautiful and flirtatiously seductive son, who enters the room as Shakespeare is about to leave. But the idea that the impetus to write poems addressed to a young man he had never met came purely as the result of a commission is surely negated by the intensity of personal affection displayed in the poems, which express admiration not just of the addressee's beauty but of his 'gracious and kind [presence]', which address him as 'love' and 'dear my love', (13) and in which the poet speaks of himself as 'all in war with time' for love of the youth (15). And would it have been seemly for a commissioned poet to advise the young man, who 'buries his content' within his 'own bud', and who has 'traffic with [him]self alone' (4), to stop masturbating and start copulating?

> Thou that art now the world's fresh ornament
> And only herald to the gaudy spring,
> Within thine own bud buriest thy content,
> And, tender churl, mak'st waste in niggarding.

For me, all this adds up to the belief that these opening sonnets spring from a strongly personal impulse, that they were not written either to commission or for publication, that they could have been written to or about more than one young man, and that they are essentially private poems.

These so-called 'procreation' sonnets are at least fully intelligible without a specific point of reference. Other sonnets are not. An obvious example is 125, beginning 'Were't aught to me I bore the canopy', where the point of reference is lost to us. It is not, however, so obviously intimate that the poem might not, in its time, have been intelligible at least to Shakespeare's 'private friends' if, for example, he had actually borne a canopy in a court procession.

This is not true, it seems to me, of the poems generally taken to refer to rivalry between their author and another poet. Why, putting it crudely, should people have been expected to pay good money for a book in which they would be puzzled by references to the 'proud full sail' of some unidentified poet's 'great verse', to 'a better spirit' (80) and to 'some affable familiar ghost' (86), references which must have been as unintelligible to most people in Shakespeare's time as they have been to generations of subsequent commentators? I suppose you might say that this is coterie verse, which the poet knew would have only limited intelligibility but which readers not in the know might have enjoyed puzzling over, but at the very least this is clearly poetry with strong autobiographical content.

A rather similar air of mystery arises from the sub-group opening with 'Full many a glorious morning' (33), where the poems appear to allude to an unexplained series of shifts in an emotional relationship. First the poet forgives his 'sun' for withdrawing some unexplained favour; then it appears that the friend has apologized, that the poet still feels aggrieved – 'I have still the loss' – but finally the friend's tears of penitence bring him round – 'ransom all ill deeds'; then the poet 'brings in sense' to account for some intriguingly unexplained 'sensual fault'; then even more opaquely he refers to a 'separable spite', also unexplained but sometimes identified as a penis, that 'steal[s] sweet hours from love's delight'; then consoles himself for his own 'lameness' but takes pleasure in the friend's 'abundance'; then expresses gratitude that the friend inspires his 'muse'; then says it is acceptable for them to be apart because that means he can 'entertain the time' with 'thoughts of love'; and then segues into a poem (40) which in conjunction with 41 starts a new thread implying that the friend (or should we say 'a friend'?) has stolen the poet's (female) lover: 'when a woman woos, what woman's son / Will sourly leave her till he have prevailed?' If these poems were written for public consumption, all one can say is that the poet is singularly incompetent as a storyteller.

In speaking of Sonnet 129, 'Th'expense of spirit in a waste of shame', I said that it would seem completely out of place in a conventional sonnet sequence of the period. This is even more true of some of the last-printed group of poems – it's tempting to call them a group, as they include all that are clearly addressed to a woman, but this is true of only seven of them. The poet speaks of his mistress – if indeed there is only one mistress – in conflicting and conflicted terms. The parodic 'My mistress' eyes' – taking up a phrase in Sonnet 127, 'My mistress's eyes are raven black' – denies her the conventional attributes of a poetical love object but ends with a declaration of love which is all the more powerful for the volte-face that it expresses:

> And yet, by heaven, I think my love as rare
> As any she belied with false compare.

But other poems in this group are cryptic in allusions to a love triangle –'Beshrew that heart that makes my heart to groan / For that deep wound it gives my friend and me' – and expressive of a love-hate relationship that is totally at odds with conventional love poetry.

Even more explicitly autobiographical are those poems which pun on the poet's own name. 'My name is', he declares, not Christopher, nor Henry, nor Edward, not even Mary or Elizabeth Regina, let us note, but 'Will'. Nowhere else does Shakespeare identify himself so emphatically. And nowhere else – not even in 151 with its reference to an erection – does he write with such unabashed sexual frankness. Sonnet 133, pretty clearly addressed to a woman, speaks of an anguished triangular affair:

> Me from myself thy cruel eye hath taken,
> And my next self thou harder hast engrossed.
> Of him, myself, and thee I am forsaken -
> A torment thrice threefold thus to be crossed.

Then 135, beginning 'Whoever hath her wish, thou hast thy Will', uses the word 'will' 13 times, and does so, sometimes with grotesquely lewd punning, in at least five distinct senses: object of desire, the poet's own name, desire, vagina and penis. The poem that follows it, 136, uses the word five times and ends 'my name is Will'. The two poems that follow, though they do not pun on 'will', continue the theme. In 137 the poet castigates himself for thinking that 'a several plot' which his heart knows 'the wide world's common place' and, in 138, admitting that he suppresses truth by believing his mistress's lies, he bitterly acknowledges his folly:

> Therefore I lie with her, and she with me,
> And in our lies by lies we flattered be.

* * *

I have suggested that Shakespeare's sonnets fall into several main categories. The last two in the collection as printed are literary exercises in the purest sense. Two of the poems parody the sonnet convention. One sonnet –146 – is a religious meditation, another –129 – a philosophical study. Some of the poems display no necessarily personal reference but would be at home in any collection of love poetry of the period. Others may be more or less identifiably related to Shakespeare's personal experience but would nevertheless have been intelligible and enjoyable to contemporary readers who did not know him. One – the Hathaway poem – is identifiable as a personal love poem. The sonnets advocating marriage seem to me to be poems written altruistically to a young man whom Shakespeare loves deeply but with no expectation of physical reciprocity. And finally there are some poems that seem so intimately personal, not to say confessional, that I find it difficult not to see them as highly original poems that are autobiographical in origin and which Shakespeare wrote primarily for himself, to help him to clarify his mind and emotions about personal dilemmas and rivalries in love.

These poems reveal a man who was at various times of his life caught up in emotional and sexual entanglements with more than one male (man or boy, one of whom was also a poet) and with more than one woman; a man of conscience who experienced transcendent joy and happiness in love but who suffered as the result of other people's infidelities, and who was tormented with profound jealousy, guilt and remorse about his own behaviour. 'She that makes me sin / Awards me pain', he writes in 141; 'Love is my sin', and his mistress's lips 'have sealed false bonds of love as oft as mine, / Robbed others' beds' revenues of their rents' (142).

In other words I, like Wordsworth, and whatever Browning may have thought, see some of these poems as keys with which Shakespeare did indeed unlock his heart – though I suspect he intended the keys to remain in his own pocket.

TRACINGS AND DATA IN *THE TEMPEST:* AUTHOR, WORLD AND REPRESENTATION

JANET CLARE

To say anything original about the origins of Shakespeare's plays is a daunting task and the same may be said of his originality. Since the rise of the scholarly edition with its critical apparatus, successive generations of editors have combed the play-texts, alerting the reader to Shakespeare's debts to classical and historical sources and to intertextual links. Critics have identified the proverbial, biblical, classical appropriations which constitute the rich verbal textures of his plays, implicitly endorsing Ralph Waldo Emerson's observation that there is no pure originality. All minds quote.[1] Apart from such localized borrowings, historicisms, new and old, have brought to light actual and possible features of the ambiance in which Shakespeare was working, reminding us that plays, like other literary artefacts, are conditioned by pre-existing discourses. Origins of his work have been found in such diverse forms of cultural productions as the English mystery plays, the revenge plays of Seneca, the popular repertory of the Queen's Men, Virgilian epic, Italian *novelle*, and the chronicles compiled by Holinshed and his predecessors. This is far from an exhaustive list. Shakespeare's works, possibly analysed more than any other literary artefacts, reveal that he was highly eclectic, magpie-like, in his collection and use of materials, shrewdly identifying their dramatic possibilities.

An attempt to trace back Shakespeare's plays to their sources of origin can be a prelude to a process of locating the text's moments of originality, offering a clue as to why Shakespeare's plays are so much richer and more emotionally and psychologically

engaging than those of many of his contemporaries. A comparison between Shakespeare's *King Lear* and the older, anonymous version performed by the Queen's Men offers us some idea of Shakespeare at work as he revises and re-visions the play in a totally different dramatic idiom. It is possible to be awed by the sheer brilliance of his addition of the Fool to the previous stage version. Kings had fools and the role of the Fool is not original to drama. In bringing the Fool into his version of the Lear story, Shakespeare creates an edgy, liminal presence whose role as foil for Lear offers the actor so much scope for individual interpretation.

In general, though, originality seen as the residue when sources are subtracted from the text is a limited formula primarily because it does not touch on originality understood as the way data are assimilated, reconceptualized and reconfigured. I introduce data here in the literal sense of things that are known, assumed by or given to a writer. This seems to me a useful term of reference for the diverse materials absorbed by Shakespeare, taking us away from the rather narrow concept of 'source', with its verbal connotations, uniformly used in mid to late twentieth-century editions of his plays. Moreover, as I will argue, it is a particularly apposite term in discussing *The Tempest*, the subject of this article, a late play which does not evince a remodelling of existent narratives or

---

[1] Ralph Waldo Emerson, 'Quotation and Originality', in *Ralph Waldo Emerson*, ed. Richard Poirier, Oxford Authors (Oxford, 1990), pp. 427–39; p. 427.

dramaturgy, as other plays by Shakespeare do. At the end of his career, Shakespeare was composing with a remarkable freedom, drawing on literary materials, accumulated theatrical experience and responding creatively to new-world discoveries.

Our way of thinking of originality as spontaneously or independently creating is historically affected by Romantic theory, whereas, as we know, Renaissance ideas were differently orientated and inflected. Echoing the author of Ecclesiastes, John Florio in the preface to his translation of Montaigne posits that there is 'no new thing under the Sunne':

What is that that hath beene? That that shall be . . . What doe the best then, but gleane after others harvest? Borrow their colours, inherite their possessions? What doe they but translate? perhaps usurpe? At least collect?[2]

For Florio, all writing is a matter of gleaning, borrowing and translating. Everything that is will become something else in the composition of another and still be nothing new. Creativity amounts to no more than collecting and translating, even scraping together the residue of what others have left. There is, of course, an element of special pleading here. Reducing the claims of purportedly original writing enhances the claims of translation (though in one respect this is a self-defeating manoeuvre since it downgrades all writing).

Other Renaissance writers responded more positively. Tasso, for example, claims that the newness of a poem is not in the fictitiousness of a subject unheard before, but in the fine complication and resolution of its fable. Citing the commonly handled stories of Thyestes and Medea, Tasso observes that by treating them differently authors turn them from common property into their very own and from something old into something new.[3] Often poets and playwrights used images of colour and of texture to differentiate their work from that of others, entailing notions of originality. Skilled writers weave new patterns with old and familiar strands, while lesser writers merely patch together materials from one or several sources, creating what we might regard as bricolage. On this basis, insults

and praise were bestowed on fellow playwrights within a comparatively small theatrical community. Thomas Lodge, for example, had accused the playwright turned anti-theatrical polemicist, Stephen Gosson, of patching up his plays with orations taken from Cicero.[4] Shakespeare's lines, according to Ben Jonson, were richly spun and fitly woven, evoking images of both colour and texture.[5] Robert Greene, on anticipating that his re-telling of Susanna's story from the Apocrypha might be judged derivative, stressed that he had added his own colours to the narrative.[6] Making antecedent material one's own, on this account, is a creative act and can be seen as a moment of originality. If source material is reconstructed within a new and different context, it is no longer the same.

Renaissance assertions of what constitutes originality have a certain affinity with modern theories of intertextuality. Gilles Deleuze and Félix Guatarri, for example, posit the cultural book as an assemblage that establishes connections between certain multiplicities drawn from three orders: world, representation and author. Defining the cultural book, Deleuze and Guatarri see it as necessarily a tracing of itself, a tracing of previous books by the same author, a tracing of other books however different they may be, an endless tracing of established concepts and words, a tracing

---

[2] Michel de Montaigne, *The Essayes, or Morall, Politique and Millitarie Discourse of Lord Michaell de Montaigne*, trans. John Florio (London, 1603), A5r-v.

[3] Torquato Tasso, *Discourses on the Heroic Poem*, trans. Mariella Cavalchini and Irene Samuel (Oxford, 1973), p. 28.

[4] Thomas Lodge, *A Defence of Poetry, Music and Stage-Plays* (London, 1853), p. 28. For a more detailed discussion of Renaissance debates on imitation and borrowing, see Janet Clare, *Shakespeare's Stage Traffic: Imitation, Borrowing and Competition in Renaissance Theatre* (Cambridge, 2014), pp. 3–11.

[5] 'To the Memory of My Beloved, The Author Master William Shakespeare And What He Hath Left Us', in *The Cambridge Edition of the Works of Ben Jonson*, ed. David Bevington, Martin Butler and Ian Donaldson, 7 vols. (Cambridge, 2012), vol. 5, 638–42.

[6] See Robert Greene, 'To the Right Honorable and Vertuous Ladie, the Ladie Margaret, Countesse of Darbie', *The Myrrour of Modestie* (London, 1584).

of the world, past and present with a potential futurity.[7] Conjoined and to an extent overlapping with the notion of data, the idea of textual tracings is particularly useful in dealing with those plays, *A Midsummer Night's Dream, Love's Labour's Lost* and *The Tempest*, which have been identified as Shakespeare without sources.[8] The assertion was made at a time when source study was more narrowly conceived, but the point remains that, unlike many of Shakespeare's plays, in these there is no narrative or dramatic template or sustained engagement with history. *The Tempest* is not self-evidently turning something new from something old, although it does reconceptualize localized borrowings. It has tracings of Shakespeare's earlier work, tracings of plays by other playwrights, plays of sorcery and conjuration, and it borrows passages from Montaigne and Ovid. I would add that it may be conjoined with cosmographic fictions of new-found lands and their inhabitants. The proposition that I wish to investigate is that originality lies in the way connections are established between such tracings of author, world and representation, that is, in the way Shakespeare uses his data.

As with later works of other writers and artists, *The Tempest* has a quality of self-haunting. Wilson Knight demonstrated many decades ago that from first to last Shakespeare's work displays a preoccupation with the sea and tempests.[9] Wilson Knight stressed the symbolic use of the tempest, whereas my emphasis would be on its use as a dramatic device. Plots turn on ships that miscarry at sea: in *The Merchant of Venice* Antonio's argosies are thought to be gifted to the sea and in *Measure for Measure* Fredrick, Marianna's brother, is lost at sea, leaving her without her dowry. Storms sever families, a device used in *Twelfth Night* and *The Comedy of Errors* to multiply comic confusions or loss of identity, whereas in *The Tempest* the association of storms and shipwreck deepens into a more profound meditation on the vicissitudes of chance, fortune and providence. In contradistinction from these earlier natural tempests, the storm of *The Tempest* is supernatural, the work of a magician and designed to dramatize the interplay of chance and choice governing its survivors.

In presenting the play's catalyst as supernatural, *The Tempest* taps into a culture of magic and sorcery and is in dialogue with other sorcery plays. In his ground-breaking introduction to *The Tempest* in the Arden second series, Frank Kermode suggested that the play represents distinct if not binary approaches to magic, with Prospero's art being that of supernatural virtue while Sycorax practises the darker arts, inherited by Caliban.[10] This reading is arguably informed by a late nineteenth-century to mid-twentieth-century idealization of Prospero, to the extent of relating Prospero's curtailment of the betrothal masque – 'our revels now are ended' – with Shakespeare's valediction to the theatre. Such a view has, in turn, been called into question by colonial readings of the play emphasizing, amongst other matters, Prospero's subjugation and exploitation of Caliban. Even without the perspectives of postcolonial theory, the identification of Prospero exclusively with white magic needs to be questioned. Indeed, later editors have noted that the lines of demarcation between the two sorcerers are rather more blurred.[11] Prospero's speech casting-off his magic (5.1.33–57) is a paraphrase of Medea's

7 Gilles Deleuze and Félix Guattari, *A Thousand Plateaus; Capitalism and Schizophrenia*, trans. Brian Massumi (Minneapolis, 1987), p. 24.

8 Stanley Wells, 'Shakespeare Without Sources', in *Shakespearean Comedy, Stratford-Upon-Avon Studies 14* (London, 1972), pp. 58–75. Although he does not use the term 'dramaturgy' – not current in Anglophone criticism in the 1970s – Wells examines dramaturgical resemblances between the three non-source plays and concludes that they 'betray a preoccupation on the part of the dramatist with his own art' (p. 69).

9 G. Wilson Knight, *The Shakespearian Tempest* (Oxford, 1932; repr. London, 1953). For Wilson Knight, the tempest was a suggestive and variable symbol; at the same time, tempests and sea-imagery are 'less flexible than other fictional realities', see Introduction, pp. 1–19; p. 13.

10 *The Tempest*, ed. Frank Kermode, The Arden Shakespeare, 6th edn (London, 1961), pp. xlvii–li.

11 See *The Tempest*, ed. Stephen Orgel, The Oxford Shakespeare (Oxford, 1987), pp. 20–3; *The Tempest*, ed. David Lindley (Cambridge, 2002), pp. 45–6; and *The Tempest*, ed. Virginia Mason Vaughan and Alden T. Vaughan, The Arden Shakespeare, 3rd ser., rev. edn (London, 2011), pp. 62–6, 288n50. See also Jonathan Bate, *Shakespeare and Ovid* (Oxford, 1993), pp. 251–5.

incantations in Book Seven of Ovid's *Metamorphoses* in which the sorceress calls on supernatural powers to assist her in producing potions and spells to extend the life of Jason's father. Her lines and their frenzied context of a Bacchanalian orgy contaminate Prospero's 'art', inviting us to associate its mysteries with darker powers.[12] Not only are Prospero's lines effective theatre poetry, giving Ovid's lines new life, through their incantatory power and association they are also a chilling reminder that supernatural power can never be entirely benign. As Mary Beard reminds us, Medea, a witch from Colchis, was on the terrifying margins of the Greek world.[13] The sorceress's incantations are re-territorialized, but for a Jacobean audience, familiar with its Ovid, they bring something of the territory with them.

It could be said that Prospero would have no cause to renounce his 'art' if he did not think there was something questionable about it. The play's epilogue works hard to suppress all the equivocal associations of conjuration aroused in the very act of its renunciation. At the play's close, Prospero turns to petitionary prayer as Faustus could never do. It is perhaps not a coincidence that the play was performed at Court on one of the residual Catholic feasts, All Saints, 1 November. The saints offered protection to the pure and aid to the penitent with the collect of the day appealing for 'grace' to follow the 'blessed saints in all virtuous and godly living'.[14] Not only Prospero but also Caliban, who, with Stephano and Trinculo, has sought to usurp supernatural power, seeks mercy. The line in Caliban's exit speech – 'I'll be wise hereafter, and seek for grace' (5.1.294–5) – is curious. Kermode glosses 'grace' as 'pardon' or 'favour', and editors link Caliban's statement with an urge to seek forgiveness from Prospero. But in the context of the epilogue and the occasion of court performance the resonances are deeper. While to seek for the divine gift of grace is perhaps theologically naïve, in keeping with character, the evocation of grace at this moment is suggestive, perhaps indicating that in recognizing his woefully wrong choice of god and object of worship, Caliban is also rejecting the powers of magic.

Indeed, I would argue that *The Tempest* registers its culture's anxieties about sorcery and the arts of magicians and enchanters which are, for example, manifest in James Mason's treatise, *The Anatomie of Sorcerie*, published in 1612, a year after the production of *The Tempest*. Mason roundly condemns sorcerers as agents of the devil who conspire to counterfeit miracles.[15] Magic is founded neither upon reason nor common sense, even though those that use it 'seem to make an art of it'.[16] Throughout the text Mason assumes that the grace of working miracles is a spiritual gift, counterfeited by magicians, witches, sorcerers, all of whom are instructed by the devil who, in return, offers 'riches, honours, pleasure, health'.[17] Mason is, for example, emphatic about the work of the devil in the calling of 'rain, clouds, thunder' and it is the devil's ministers, the sorcerers, who use the same 'outward meanes' as the 'servants of God have used in such like cases'.[18] The devil works such effects by natural means whereas true miracles are 'effected by the divine power of God only', and designed for 'the glory of God, and the edification of his Church'.[19] The impossibility of differentiating between the true and the false is what contributed significantly to equivocal responses to magic since both, according to Mason, are a source of wonderment. Confronted with the conundrum, Mason's only resort is to claim – with some qualification – that 'it is more than probable, that miracles are now ceased'.[20]

James Mason described miracles – both those that were right and true and those false or

---

[12] Publius Ovidius Naso, *The XV Bookes entytuled Metamorphosis, translated out of Latin into English meeter by Arthur Golding*, (London, 1567), 'the seventh book', M3r.

[13] Mary Beard, 'Domestic Violence', review of Euripides' *Medea*, National Theatre, *TLS*, 1 August 2014, p. 17.

[14] *The Book of Common Prayer, the Texts of 1549, 1559, and 1662*, ed. Brian Cummings (Oxford, 2011), p. 387.

[15] James Mason, *The Anatomie of Sorcerie. Wherein the Wicked Impietie of Charmers, Inchanters, and such like, is discovered and confuted* (London, 1612), p. 22.

[16] Mason, *The Anatomie of Sorcerie*, p. 46.

[17] Mason, *The Anatomie of Sorcerie*, pp. 55–6.

[18] Mason, *The Anatomie of Sorcerie*, p. 17.

[19] Mason, *The Anatomie of Sorcerie*, p. 64.

[20] Mason, *The Anatomie of Sorcerie*, p. 4.

feigned – as works which 'seemeth impossible to be wrought by any natural force', and 'thereby moveth admiration'.[21] The theatre is in the business of moving admiration, and acts of magic, real and feigned, naturally translate with all their equivocal cultural associations to the stage. In *2 Henry VI* sorcery is equated with treason. Eleanor, Duchess of Gloucester employs the conjurer Bullingbrook and the witch, Margaret Jordan, to foretell her fortune. The conjuration with its magic circle, the raising of spirits and the effects of thunder and lightning has, in fact, been set up by York to trap Eleanor and it ends abruptly with the entry of York and Buckingham and the arrest of Eleanor for treason. The most powerful precedent of what the stage could do with conjuration and the dangerous arts of the conjurer was offered by Marlowe's *Dr Faustus*, the property of a rival company to Shakespeare's, a tragedy which, according to its editors, aroused in its audience a 'pleasurable terror' from the uncertainty as to whether all the devils on stage were real or not.[22] First published only in 1604, *Dr Faustus* was republished in 1609 with a variant title page in which the new publishers were keen to stress that not only was Faustus's history tragical, but that his life and death were 'horrible'.[23] Faustus's thwarted quest for knowledge and his boasts that the practice of the concealed arts will lead to his earthly canonization and imperial rule are a source of deep tragic irony. What we see on stage is a series of cheap thrills and diversions. Magic – performed off-stage – exploits popular lore and mythic associations and the audience has to take on trust that Faustus has been taken on a cosmographical expedition, Medea-like, in a chariot drawn by dragons. And the same could be said of Prospero's off-stage Medea-like magic or necromancy, his allegation that he has 'bedimmed the noontide sun', split the trunks of oaks, uprooted pines and cedars, opened graves and 'waked their sleepers' (5.1.33–57).

Irreverent, daring and cautionary treatments of theatre magic predate *The Tempest*. If Marlowe represented the conjurer in thrall to the devil and the awfulness of the magic arts, in *The Alchemist* Ben Jonson, the year before *The Tempest* was performed, depicted the come-uppance of the would-be conjurer, and the sham nature of alchemy.[24] Shakespeare's theatrical memory, though, goes further back. In *The Tempest*, as in *Cymbeline*, there is a recollection of what is now an obscure Elizabethan entertainment, *The Rare Triumphs of Love and Fortune*, performed before the Queen in 1587.[25] The pageant sets up an illustrated debate about the relative powers of love and fortune, and presents the thwarted love of Hermione (a man) and the King's daughter, Fidelia. Hermione's father, Bomelio, the wronged, exiled courtier – a prototype for Belarius in *Cymbeline* – has turned to magic, like Prospero, as a means of righting wrong, a situation which so alarms Hermione that he sets about burning his father's books and warning the audience at the same time:

My father thereupon devised how he might
Revenge and wreak him self on her, that wrought him
    such despite
And therefore I perceive he strangely useth it,
Inchaunting and transfourming that his fancy did not
    fit.
As I may see by these his vile blasphemous Bookes,
My soule abhores as often as mine eye upon them
    lookes
What gaine can countervaile the danger that they bring,
For man to sell his soule to sinne, ist not a greevous
    thing? . . .
In ransacking his Cave, these Bookes I lighted on:
And with his leave Ile be so bolde whilste he abroad is
    gone
To burne them all: for best that serveth for this stuffe
I doubt not but at his returne to please him well enough

[21] Mason, *The Anatomie of Sorcerie*, p. 16.
[22] See *Doctor Faustus A- and B- texts (1604, 1616)*, ed. David Bevington and Eric Rasmussen (Manchester, 1993), pp. 48–50; p. 50. The play had belonged to the Admiral's Men with Edward Alleyn playing Faustus.
[23] *The Tragicall History of the horrible Life and death of Doctor Faustus* (London, 1609).
[24] For a discussion of these two plays see Harry Levin, 'Two Magian Comedies: The Tempest and The Alchemist', *Shakespeare Survey 22* (Cambridge, 1969), pp. 47–58.
[25] The entertainment has been cited in relation to *Cymbeline*, but not to *The Tempest*. See *Cymbeline*, ed. Martin Butler (Cambridge, 2005), p. 13 and Clare, *Shakespeare's Stage Traffic*, p. 235.

And Gentlemen I pray, and so desire I shall
You would abhor this study, for it will confound you
all.[26]

And so the scene ends with the unambiguous message: dabbling in magic is a bad thing, bringing the soul into jeopardy.

Later plays are not so explicitly admonitory. Between *The Rare Triumphs of Love and Fortune* and *The Tempest*, *Dr Faustus* has intervened in the dramatic tradition. The motif of burning 'blasphemous books' is taken up and strikingly intensified in Faustus's desperate last words as the devils prepare to carry him off to hell: 'I'll burn my books! – Ah, Mephostophilis!' Prospero does not burn his books; he drowns them to ensure that they don't get into the wrong hands. Yet, his renunciation of magic creates a theatrical frisson. This is his Faustian moment or Shakespeare's Marlovian one, a conjuration for the theatre. Elsewhere, Prospero's sorcery is of a different or rather more indeterminate order. As commentators have observed, his art conspires with the artistry of the playwright, employing his puppet spirits to achieve a desired end. He creates the illusion of the storm which initiates a set of circumstances devised to induce penitence and a restitution of power. Charms and acts of magic are performed by Ariel on stage in accordance with Prospero's instructions – the spirit's descent as a harpy and the betrothal masque – and these masque-like moments are surely designed to enchant: an enchanting art to offset the darker aspect of enchantment.

The novelty of *The Tempest* is in conjoining sorcery and the occult to a new-world context. Confronted with magical practices in the New World, the Europeans transferred their own anxieties about sorcery onto indigenous populations, a natural and perhaps inevitable way of responding to things not previously encountered. In *The New Found Worlde or Antarctike*, a translation by Thomas Hacket, published in 1568, of *Les singularitez de la France Antarctique, autrement nommée Amérique* by the royal cosmographer André Thevet, the author condemns the error and ignorance of the indigenous 'wilde men', who superstitiously believe that their dreams will actualize and trust in 'prophets' to interpret them. In the chapter 'Of false prophets and magicians, that are in this country of America, the which invoke and call upon wicked spirits', it is acknowledged that the Americans have not been the first to practise magic, and that, until the coming of Christ, it was 'common in many nations'.[27] Two kinds of magic are introduced at this point, one of which is most damnable, 'full of enchantments, words, ceremonies and invocations', the other 'to seke out and know heavenly things'. Yet, examples of the latter are rather sparse and vague, confined to those of the three magi, who visited the infant Christ, and the respect paid to magic in the Persian Empire. According to Thevet, one type of magic may be more vicious ('vitieuse') than the other 'mais toutes deux pleines de curiositie'.[28] Hacket expands a little, both forms are 'naught and full of curiosity'.[29] Author and translator seem to be aware that in condoning any kind of magic they are on dangerous ground and, in the blurring of the two forms, the text betrays signs of self-censorship.

The phantom island of *The Tempest* is the perfect setting for the projection of both old and new worlds, connecting the ancient European fascination with magic and the powerful presence of magic in the new world. Of all the locations of Shakespeare's plays, that of *The Tempest* is the only one that remains unspecified. Following the epilogue and before the 'names of the actors', the Folio editors describe the scene as 'an un-inhabited Island'.[30] This paratextual detail is interesting in furnishing a possible European perspective according to which Sycorax, Caliban and Ariel do not

---

[26] *The Rare Triumphes of Love and Fortune*, 1589, F1v, *The Malone Society Reprints*, prepared by W. W. Greg (Oxford, 1930).

[27] *The new found worlde, or Antarctike, wherin is contained wonderful and strange things . . . written in the French tong, by that excellent learned man, master Andrewe Thevet* (London, 1568), H2r–H8v.

[28] *Les singularitez de la France Antarctique, autrement nommée Amérique* (Paris, 1558), R4r.

[29] *The new found worlde*, H6v.

[30] The only other play in the Folio to include any paratextual reference to location is *Measure for Measure* and here it is the specific location of Vienna.

count as people and therefore the voyagers can make the island their own.

The Tempest, as has been often noted, has echoes and shadowy presences of other texts: the essays of Montaigne, Virgil's *Aeneid* and Ovid's *Metamorphoses*. We may conjecture that some members of Shakespeare's audience would have recognized another work in Gonzalo's evocation of his primitive ideal of a new world:

> For no kind of Trafficke
> Would I admit: No name of Magistrate:
> Letters should not be knowne. Riches, poverty,
> And use of service, none. Contract, Succession,
> Bourne, bound of Land, Tilth, vineyard none:
> No use of Metal, Corn, or Wine, or Oyle.
> No occupation; all men idle, all:
> And Women too, but innocent and pure:...
> All things in common Nature should produce
> Without sweat or endeavour: Treason, fellony,
> Sword, Pike, Knife, Gun, or neede of any Engine
> Would I not have: but Nature should bring forth
> Of its owne kinde all foyzon, all abundance
> To feed my innocent people.   (TLN 857–74)

As is well-known, Gonzalo's projection of an ideal commonwealth is modelled closely on a passage from another New World text, Montaigne's essay 'Of the Canniballes'. Montaigne's description of the Brazilian Indians, who inhabit 'Antartic France', emphasizes their lack of corruption when compared with the economy of the old world:

It is a nation, would I answer *Plato*, that hath no kinde of traffike, no knowledge of Letters, no intelligence of numbers, no name of magistrate, nor of politike superioritie; no use of service, of riches or of povertie; no contracts, no successions, no partitions, no occupation but idle; no respect of kindred, but common, no apparell but naturall, no manuring of lands, no use of wine, corne, or mettle. The very words that import lying, falshood, treason, dissimulations, covetousness, envie, detraction, and pardon, were never heard amongst them.[31]

'Of the Canniballes' is not based on experience, but on an assortment of travellers' tales and cosmographical fictions. It is only in the conclusion to the essay that Montaigne offers any first-hand evidence, namely in recording the voices of three Indians he encounters in Rouen. In the brief, almost abrupt, conclusion to the essay, he recounts the surprise of the Indians that a boy king (Charles IX) should be obeyed and their shocked reaction to the manifestations in France of extreme luxury and of extreme poverty. In first praising the cannibals and then in recording their moral criticism of Europe, Montaigne's work is a radical critique of ethnocentricity: 'I am not sorie we note the barbarous horror of such an action, but grieved, that prying so narrowly into their faults we are so blinded in ours' (k4v).

Where Shakespeare's play and Montaigne's essay connect is a shift away from eurocentrism towards an understanding of cultural relativism. Both the supposedly civil power of the Old World and the primitivism of Caliban have their darker side. But, as with Shakespeare's appropriation of Ovid's Medea, this is a moment of imaginative refiguring. On recollecting 'Of the Cannibals' or working with lines transcribed in a commonplace book, Shakespeare, we may suppose, recognizes words that he could transfer to Gonzalo, enabling the character to develop as he utters them. The words are now projected in an entirely different way, as a purely personal statement of an aristocratic, paternalistic figure as his idea of a perfect society. In dialogue with Alonso and Sebastian, the lines take the shape of a good-natured, though naïve wish-dream, and in that respect they differ from their apparent 'source'. The articulation of words by a particular character in a given situation with every semblance of naturalness or spontaneity is a creative act and represents on Shakespeare's part, not an act of cribbing, but a creative one of recognition and imagination. In recycling Montaigne's words in this context Shakespeare adds dramatic irony: the island is far from Gonzalo's Edenic vision, and the irony is intensified by the murderous proclivities of his detractors.

The idea of originality as knowing how to reconceptualize material in another context is far

---

[31] Michel de Montaigne, *The Essayes, or Morall, Politike and Millitarie Discourse of Lord Michaell de Montaigne*, trans. John Florio (London, 1603), Chapter 30, 'Of the Canniballes', K3v.

removed from Romantic notions of Shakespeare's plays as autonomous works of art, products solely of the imagination. Characteristic is Coleridge's claim that *The Tempest* addresses itself to the imaginative faculty, together with his belief that the interests of the play are independent of all historical facts and associations. For Coleridge the play could only be understood by employing the 'moved and sympathetic imagination' and accepting that as reader/audience 'we choose to be deceived'.[32] Critical perspectives come and go and come again into fashion: it is difficult, however, to imagine a contemporary assertion of such a kind after more than a century of historically grounded scrutiny. *The Tempest* is a play that is adjusting to the changing world. Much has been made in his composition of *The Tempest* of Shakespeare's intervention in the English colonial enterprise. The ill-fated expedition to Virginia in 1609, documented by William Strachey and Silvester Jourdain, in which the Admiral's ship was wrecked in a violent storm and stranded in the Bermudas, has been taken as stimulating the scenario of the play.[33] In a short pamphlet published soon after his return from Virginia, Jourdain describes the crew's survival, the temperate and hospitable climate of the Bermudas, and the company's resumption of the voyage to Virginia on reconstructing their vessel. Notably, Jourdain refutes the popular view of the Bermudas as 'a most prodigious and inchanted place',[34] an assumption, somewhat paradoxically, conveyed in the title page's alternative name for the Bermudas, the Isle of Devils. The latter designation conveys something of Prospero's view of the island before his magic counters that of Sycorax. Unlike the pamphlet, however, the play does not dispel the notion of enchanted new worlds. *The Tempest* goes beyond the simple and matter-of-fact account of survival and escape offered by Jourdain, responding, as it does, to the fantastic and fabulous aspects of new-world exploration. We lose a strand of the play's historical texture if we separate it from its cosmographical moment. *The Tempest* belongs at least as much to the European cosmographical revolution, to the writing of Amerigo Vespucci, André

Thevet and others as it does to the colonizing ventures of the Virginia Company.

The island of *The Tempest*, with a topography of bogs and fens which does not entirely match its supposed location in the Mediterranean, and inhabited by spirits, devils and witches, corresponds to the fantastic places recorded by the cosmographers. Caliban, with his dreams from which he does not want to wake, and Trinculo and Stephano, who take Caliban for a sea-monster, are akin to the natives and seafarers who populate accounts of the cosmographers' New World exploration. Miranda in her wonderment, 'O brave new world', reacts like a European discovering the New World either directly or at second hand. Shakespeare gives an original twist to the phrase: it is, of course, the Old World that Miranda is describing in these terms. If anything corresponds to the New World of popular imagination it is what is for her the old world of her island home. Any audience would see the point of Prospero's response, ''Tis new to thee', and share his perspective. By reversing new and old, her response together with his reaction create a paradigm for a knowing, wary attitude which could be projected on to the naïve, astonished, marvelling, credulous responses to the New World of early modern cosmography. *The Tempest* has made wide use of such diffuse materials and now, just for a moment, tellingly invokes a worldly-wise and illusion-free realism which casts an unfashionably pragmatic light on the wishful dreams of better worlds and the cosmographers' fantasies.

It is a relatively straightforward if arduous task to unearth quotation and borrowing in Shakespeare's plays. It is less easy to define originality or to demonstrate it in practical terms. From classical

---

[32] Samuel Taylor Coleridge, *Shakespearean Criticism*, ed. Thomas Middleton Raysor, 2 vols. (London, 1960), vol. 1, pp. 113–23.

[33] Kermode offers a detailed discussion of the Bermuda pamphlets and critical responses to them, see *The Tempest*, Arden, 6th edn, xxvi–xxxiv.

[34] Silvester Jourdain, *A Discovery of the Barmudas, otherwise called the Ile of Divels* (London, 1610), p. 8.

authority to contemporary cultural theory, originality is conceived of figuratively in metaphors of weaving, painting and organic growth. The Romantics used the image of the great poet as godhead. Emerson, in the essay I quoted from at the beginning of this essay, appears to be having it both ways, employing the organic metaphor of a forest decomposing for the composition of the new, while firmly on the side of genius in his claim that the bard speaks not his own but the word of some god.[35] Geological metaphors of sedimentation, whereby a heterogeneous collection of materials forms a largely homogeneous layer to create sedimentary rock, may also prove illuminating in relation to Shakespeare's playmaking in his last work.[36] Whatever figurative language is employed, *The Tempest* is a remarkable work of appropriation and assimilation of data. In its direct and spectral connections, the play integrates relations between author, representation, contemporary or near-contemporary plays, echoes of Ovid and Montaigne, and the worldly and other-worldly concerns registered in new-world texts and tales of magic and sorcery, spirits and devils. Therein lies its originality.

---

[35] Emerson, 'Quotation and Originality', pp. 437, 438.

[36] A metaphor suggested by some of the passages in Deleuze and Guatarri, see *A Thousand Plateaus*, pp. 41–2.

SHAKESPEARIAN GESTURE: NARRATIVE AND ICONOGRAPHY

FARAH KARIM-COOPER

...the *Hand* that busie instrument, is most talkative, Whose *language* is as easily perceived and understood, as if a Man had another mouth or fountain of discourse in his Hand.[1]

John Bulwer's *Chirologia: or the Natural Language of the Hand* (1644) is one of the earliest cultural histories of gesture. In it, Bulwer observed that to interpret gesture one must study the hand first and then its most important function: communication. The hand was not constructed merely to conduct manual labour. It was, in Bulwer's estimation, a sophisticated tool designed for discourse and apprehension and perhaps *the* dignifying feature of the human body. Bulwer assembles a range of gestural theories, charting their origins from classical, Biblical, medieval and continental sources in order to argue that the hand is as capable, if not more so, of emotive communication as the tongue; the hand, to him, is a kind of microcosmic version of the person to whom it is attached. He goes so far as to suggest it has its own voice – the 'busie' instrument refers not to a hand that is doing or conducting activities but one that is gesticulating during speech. He imagines the hand as another mouth – a corporeal fusion that exemplifies the infinite number of semantic units that could be produced by it.

The culmination of Bulwer's enquiry into the hand and its communicative function was his later works *Philocophus: or, the deafe and dumbe mans friend* (published in 1648), a polemical and educational treatise stipulating the importance of educating the

deaf, and his unpublished manuscript, *Philocophus, or the Dumbe mans academie, wherein is taught a new and admired art instructing them who are borne deafe and dumbe to heare the sound of words with their eie.* This synesthetic model was inspired by and drawn from Spanish writer Juan Pablo Bonet's 'sign language manual' published in Madrid in 1620. Bulwer seems to have intended to introduce and establish sign language in England. Bulwer's *Chirologia* is important to any study of the hand in early modern England, not just because of the plates illustrating the gestures he decodes (Illustration 3) and that provide some insight into a broad cultural vocabulary of gestures in the early modern period, but also because of the emphasis on the hand as a crucial signifying agent of the body. Bulwer does make some dubious claims about the universality of gestures for which critics like Michael Neill have taken him to task.[2] When Bulwer suggests that commercial trade between nations and ethnicities is conveniently lubricated by the universal signs of the hand, for example, he does not take into account the possibility of multiple gestural dialects that are contingent upon class and culture.

Theorists like Bulwer were also aware that gesture was a crucial semiotic feature of art,

---

[1] John Bulwer, *Chirologia, or the Naturall Language of the Hand* (London, 1644), p. 1.

[2] See Michael Neil, '"Amphitheaters in the Body": Playing with Hands on the Shakespearian Stage', in *Shakespeare Survey 48* (Cambridge, 1996), pp. 23–50.

3. John Bulwer, *Chirologia* (1644)

reflecting human interaction and the visual artic- ulation of emotion. E. H. Gombrich argues that art 'makes use of gestures that have their mean- ing in human intercourse', suggesting that the artist closely observes social exchanges in order to imitate them. Art manuals and treatises of the period counsel artists about the various methods of capturing what are otherwise fleeting actions of the human body.[3] Giovanni Lomazzo's *Curi- ous Arte of Paintinge, Caruinge and Buildinge*, trans- lated into English by Richard Haydocke in 1598, defines Painting as 'an arte, which with propor- tionable lines, and colours answerable to the life, by obseruing the Perspective light, doeth so imi- tate the nature of corporall things, that it not onely representeth the thicknesse and roundnesse thereof upon a flat, but also their actions and gestures, expressing moreouer diuers affections and passions of the minde'.[4] It was the job of the artist not only to imitate gestures but, in doing so, to capture the 'affections and passions of the minde'. The impli- cation here is that the gestures of the hand demon- strate the emotional and psychological status of the gesturer. Lomazzo later expounds upon the ways in which representations of the body will determine the gazer's interpretation of the subject's passions. Significantly, according to this and other art man- uals, an artist must have some prior knowledge or understanding of humoral psychology, anatomy (of course), and the ways in which perception pro- duces particular emotions, 'all which being Philo- sophically vnderstood', the translation reads, 'bring with them a certaine knowledge of all actions and gestures, to be imagined in bodies, by vertue of which they may be put in practise. Which knowl- edge, if it be behouefull in any artificer, then surely is it most requisite in a Painter.'[5]

Because, according to Lomazzo, the body is altered by the passions experienced in the mind, painters must be wary of these fluctuations so that rather than that pictures to appear 'like dreames, or works done hap-hazard', they should rather be 'true and liuely representations of the his- tory intended'.[6] These passionate manifestations of the body can influence or shape the emo- tional responses of those around it and thus the gestural relationship between subjects in a paint- ing must reflect a life-like and animated discourse. According to such a theory, gestures act as emo- tional transmitters not only reflecting the mind of a single gesturer but also producing the same emo- tion and, perhaps, gesture in another. Whether an expression of identity or an emotional transmitter, gestures were signs.

J. A. Burrow observes that in the medieval period, there was a 'scholastic tradition which con- sidered non-verbal messages as part of a general theory of signs, *signa*'.[7] St Augustine identified two types of signs: natural and given (*signa naturalia* and *signa data*); gestures as well as facial expressions are 'involuntary' or natural 'signs of emotion'.[8] With given signs, 'the signer intentionally gives, or trans- mits, them in order to communicate something'.[9] In St Augustine's own words: 'when we nod, we give a sign just to the eyes of the person whom we want, by means of that sign, to make aware our wishes. Certain movements of the hands sig- nify a great deal. Actors, by the movement of their limbs, give certain signs to the cognoscenti and, as it were, converse with the spectators' eyes . . . . All these things are, to coin a phrase, visible words [*verba visibilia*].'[10] Later in the 1640s, Bulwer would make a similar observation: 'gestures' are 'naturall signes'.[11]

In both oratory and acting, subtlety of ges- ture could indeed provide the cues for response that are conditioned by the 'smoothness' or polish of the performance. Certainly, Quintilian, while

---

[3] E. H. Gombrich, *The Image and the Eye: The Psychology of Pictorial Representation* (New York, 1982), p. 66.

[4] Giovanni Paolo Lomazzo, *A Tracte Containing the Artes of curi- ous Paintinge, Carvinge & building*, trans. Richard Haydocke (London, 1598), p. 13.

[5] Lomazzo, *A Tracte Containing the Artes*, p. 14.

[6] Lomazzo, *A Tracte Containing the Artes*, p. 15.

[7] J. A. Burrow, *Gestures and Looks in Medieval Narrative* (Cam- bridge, 2004), p. 1.

[8] Burrow, *Gestures and Looks*, p. 2.

[9] Burrow, *Gestures and Looks*, p. 2.

[10] St. Augustine, *De Doctrina Christiana*, 11.5, cited in Burrow, *Gestures and Looks*, p. 2.

[11] Bulwer, *Chirologia*, p. 2.

recognizing that gestures revealed aspects of the self, made clear distinctions between everyday gestures and those belonging to performance. The 'opposition . . . between *vulgaris* and *ex arte* . . . points to some mental distinction between commonly used gestures and those appropriate to more formal contexts'.[12] In doing so, Quintilian acknowledges the emotional truths that the hands can reveal:

For other parts of the body merely assist the speaker, whereas the hands themselves virtually speak. Or is it not the case that we use them to demand, promise, summon, dismiss, threaten, entreat, show aversion and fear, question and deny? Do we not use them to express joy, sorrow, hesitation, guilt, regret, measure, quantity, number and time?[13]

Quintilian's description of hand gestures 'does not constitute a highly specialized system of movements; it is in fact little more than a catalogue based upon the existing practices of conversational gesticulation at Rome'.[14] Therefore, it is not unlikely that gestures, 'like linguistic stylistic devices, are able to exert a persuasive effect, whether their subtleties are consciously appreciated by the audience or not'.[15] This is clearly a point that Bulwer suggests is true when he implies that there is a strong connection between thought, the heart and the hand, 'that a holy thought can no sooner inlarge the erected Heart, but it workes upon the *Hands*'.[16] Even modern gestural theory would corroborate the synchronous relationship between the hand and the mind or gesticulation and thought.[17]

Significantly, theories about the relationship between hands, hearts and thoughts have been developing since antiquity, featuring in philosophical discourses in the early modern period and as part of psycholinguistic studies now. To understand this relationship in Shakespeare we can assess how the ubiquity of representations of hand gestures in art and on stage helped provide a visual vocabulary of gestures and meaning. What I want to explore in this article, then, is how we might investigate the meaning of gestures and gestural exchanges not as they are performed but rather as they are described

to us in instances of Shakespearian narrative and dramatic narrative reporting. Theatre historians have not yet been able to identify with certainty a gestural system used by actors in the sixteenth- and seventeenth-century commercial playhouses. Other than what we can infer from stage directions and gestural indicators within the speeches and dialogue, it is difficult to argue that there was a definitive and codified template of stage gestures that early modern actors deployed either stylistically or naturalistically. The Bulwer plates are misleading when it comes to our understanding of gestures as they were performed in the commercial playhouses of early modern London. The classical differentiation between the performance of gestures in everyday life and the performance of gestures on stage may, therefore, *not* be a reasonable difference to apply to Shakespearian performance. Rather, a more productive route might be a consideration of the medieval and Renaissance iconographic origins and pictorial representations of hand movements together with how gestures are described, expressed and felt (both by characters and readers/audience) in narrative sequences in the plays and in the poems of Shakespeare.

I will focus on two gestures described in Shakespeare, one involuntary and one deliberate; one by an individual gesturer, the other interpersonal, involving an exchange between two characters. I will discuss their iconographic counterparts and argue that gestural meanings are traceable and variable, not consistently able to be determined; I will suggest, moreover, that the context of a gesture is paramount to an interpretation of its meaning in a text.

---

[12] J. Hall, 'Cicero and Quintilian on the Oratorical Use of Hand Gestures', *Classical Quarterly*, 54 (2004), 143–60; p. 150.

[13] Quintilian, *Institutio Oratoria* 11.2.85–6, cited in Hall, 'Cicero and Quintilian', p. 150.

[14] Hall, 'Cicero and Quintilian', p. 149.

[15] Hall, 'Cicero and Quintilian', p. 149.

[16] Bulwer, *Chirologia*, p. 24.

[17] See David McNeill, *Hand and Mind: What Gestures Reveal about Thought* (Chicago and London, 1992).

SLEEPING WOMAN — HEAD RESTING ON HAND

The first gesture I want to focus upon occurs in *The Rape of Lucrece*, Shakespeare's narrative poem describing the dangerous desires and resulting violation produced involuntarily by female virtue. Tarquin's increasing desire for Lucrece is provoked not just by her ideal physical beauty, but by the virtue that manifests her beauty through her body:

> When at Collatium this false lord arrived,
> Well was he welcomed by the Roman dame,
> Within whose face beauty and virtue strived
> Which of them both should underprop her fame.
> When virtue bragged beauty would blush for shame;
>   When beauty boasted blushes, in despite
>   Virtue would stain that or with silver white.[18]
>
> (50–6)

Her perfect complexion of what the narrator calls 'beauty's red and white' glistens – as 'silver white' suggests. The lustre is a result of the glow that is produced upon the skin, in neo-Platonic terms, because of a truly virtuous mind. It is her face and the flickering between white and red (her intermittent blushes) that begins to provoke Tarquin's lust. But it is when her body becomes animated by her emotions that we see Tarquin's desire increasing to genuinely dangerous levels. When he narrates her husband's victories, 'Her joy with heaved-up hand she doth express, / And wordless so greets heaven for his success' (111–12). This emotional gesture demonstrates the perfect union in Lucrece between bodily comportment and interiority. Her virtue is trustworthy as the attention to the correspondences between her actions and her feelings throughout the poem imply.

The gesture I want to examine more closely occurs later in the poem, but is curiously an involuntary one: 'Her lily hand her rosy cheek lies under, / Coz'ning the pillow of a lawful kiss' (386–7). The violation of Lucrece begins with Tarquin stealing into her chamber and witnessing her body vulnerable, asleep and effigy-like. What is significant about the narrator's attention

to her hands is that it suggests that silent, involuntary gestures help to install Tarquin's sexual desire. Lucrece's unconscious gesture here invokes a familiar artistic and literary motif of sleeping women. The sleeping woman trope dates to antiquity – the most famous example being the 'sleeping Ariadne' (Illustration 4). This pose is one that had been admired for centuries. The Roman poet Propertius in the third elegy in Book I of the *Elegies* describes a sleeping woman from the point of view of her lover:

> – So Cynthia, breathing slumber, lay in bed
> With her unconscious hands beneath her head
> When I returned tipsy feet one night
> With link-boys waving flares to give me light –[19]

The tradition of depicting a woman asleep and being watched posits a woman as an object lying vulnerable, assailable and, in her statue-like stillness, the site upon which a man might meditate upon the desirability of her body, all the while, paradoxically, appreciating her virtue. We learn in the next passage of *Lucrece* that,

> Without the bed her other fair hand was,
> On the green coverlet whose perfect white
> Showed like an April daisy on the grass,
> With pearly sweat resembling dew of night.
>
> (393–6)

Lucrece here has no conscious control over where her hands are lying, what position they are in: one under her cheek and the other resting upon the 'green coverlet'. The narrator couches the description within common poetic tropes of beauty, 'lily' hands, 'April daisy on the grass', emphasizing her beauty; its signification of her virtue, of course, fundamentally leads to the violation of her body.

---

18 William Shakespeare, *The Rape of Lucrece*, in *The Norton Shakespeare: Romances and Poems*, ed. Stephen Greenblatt, Walter Cohen, Jean E. Howard and Katharine Eisaman Maus (New York and London, 1997).

19 G. S. Tremenheere, trans., *The Elegies of Propertius* (London, 1923), cited in Udo Kultermann, 'Woman Asleep and the Artist', *Artibus et Historiae*, 11 (1990), pp. 129–61; p. 134.

4. Roman art: Ariadne Sleeping. Vatican, Museo Pio-Clementino.

Like her face, the hands of a woman were tasked with manifesting evidence of chastity. In addition to the conventional poetic tropes that detail facial perfection, we learn that hands were also crucial in the construction of ideal beauty during the early modern period. Featuring as a ubiquitous trope in love poetry, the white hand of the mistress is often the site upon which the lover projects and concentrates his physical desire. It is the only part of her body that a suitor is allowed to touch, albeit within the strict ritualistic codes of courtship. Because the hand played a crucial part in courtship, its physical appearance would naturally be subject to the same idealistic standards of beauty as the face. Agnolo Firenzuola's Florentine treatise *On the Beauty of Women* (1541) paints a verbal portrait of the perfect beauty in the form of a dialogue.

He catalogues each part of the body, including the hands:

The hands . . . ought to be white, especially on the upper side; large and somewhat full, the palm a little hollow and shadowed with roses. The lines must be clear and quite distinct, well marked, not tangled nor crossed. The mounds of Jupiter, Venus, and Mercury must be quite distinct, but not too high. The line of the intellect must be deep and clear and not crossed by any other line. That hollow between the index finger and the thumb should be well set, without wrinkles, and of a lively color. Fingers are beautiful when they are long, straight, delicate, and slightly tapering toward the end, but so little as to be scarcely perceptible. Fingernails should be clear and like balas rubies tied with flesh-pink roses and pomegranate leaves; not long, not round, nor completely square, but with a fine shape and a very slight curve; bare, clean, well kept, so that a little white crescent at their base is always visible. At the top the nail should extend past the flesh of the finger the thickness of a small knife, without the least suspicion of a black rim at the tip. The hand as a whole ought to be delicately soft, as if we were touching fine silk or the softest cotton. And this is what we wanted to say about the arms and the hands.[20]

The specificity in the description here reminds us how important appearances of hands were, and, therefore, of the importance of the movement and placement of women's hands in social discourse. Thus, the appearance and gestures of the hand participated in a social vocabulary that helped to identify class, sexual status, modesty, virtue and character.

Compellingly, Lucrece's gesture reminds the reader of the vulnerability of the sleeping body. In doing so, it alludes to the range of sleeping woman gestures that had been depicted in print, in sculpture and in paint over the centuries with female purity, virtue or sainthood as the context, some images with which Shakespeare might have been familiar, some he may not. He may have had no knowledge, for example, of Carpaccio's *Dream of St Ursula* but I want to pause on it to alert the reader to the potential parallels within the narrative context of Lucrece's sleeping gesture. St Ursula's story was well known in early modern England. She was the Romano-British saint who was famously martyred when, on a pilgrimage with 11,000 virgins, she was intercepted by the Huns and killed; in the chronicle version adapted in 1509, her virtue and beauty incite the lust of the 'rural rebelle' who, when rejected, shoots an arrow into her brain.[21] In Carpaccio's painting (part of a series depicting St Ursula's life) she is visited in her dream by an angel, who is there to foreshadow her impending martyrdom. The main point I wish to consider is how her posture highlights her interiority. The hand resting on the cheek, whether awake or asleep, is a pose redolent of contemplation, virtue and, in some contexts, melancholy; in depictions of women, sometimes these meanings are fused, as might be evident in Artemisia Gentileschi's portrait of the sleeping, melancholy Mary

Magdalene (*c.*1621–22).[22] The melancholy is foregrounded by the over-flexible wrist, the palm facing down, and her cheek resting on the back of the hand.

Lucrece's rape and her subsequent lamentations establish her as virtuous victim but she is also melancholic plaintiff. Her eventual suicide, then, concretizes her martyrdom as a Roman heroine. Whether or not Shakespeare was familiar with Carpaccio's painting matters less for my purposes than the story of the dream itself, which was a familiar feature of the legend. The sleeping woman resting her head upon her hand was part of the cultural idiom of gesture that was associated with ideals of female beauty and virtue and frequently depicted in relation to tragic narratives of rape and martyrdom.[23]

Curiously, the hand gestures of the unconscious Lucrece are framed by a sub-narrative of the hand in the poem. Shakespeare establishes the heroine's hand as an agent of involuntary seduction in a set of complex references. What is consistent is that Lucrece's gestures are not pre-fabricated, studied courtly gestures. Instead, her hands consistently gesture to reflect her true emotions. We saw her hands manifesting her virtuous jubilation, a gesture that captured Tarquin's imagination. Later he recalls how she took him by the hand when she feared for Collatinus's life, reporting 'And how her hand, in my hand being locked, / Forced it to tremble with her loyal fear' (260–1); her trembling hand simulates for him a sexual encounter of which she is unconscious. Extraordinarily, touching a woman's

20 Agnolo Firenzuola, *On the Beauty of Women*, trans. Konrad Eisenbichler and Jacqueline Murray (Philadelphia, 1992), p. 67.
21 Anonymous, *Here begyn[neth] y lyf of saynt Vrsula after y[e] cronycles of englo[n]de* (London, 1509), sig. Aviiir.
22 This painting is held in the Cathedral, Sala del Tesoro, Seville, Spain and can be viewed at www.artemisia-gentileschi.com/magdalen2.html
23 Other depictions include Lodovico Carracci's *The Dream of Catherine of Alexandria* (*c.*1593) in the National Gallery of Art, Washington D.C. and Paolo Veronese's *The Dream of St Helena* (1575–8) in the National Gallery London; both illustrate virtuous women sleeping whilst holding or resting their heads in their hands.

hand was a far more intimate gesture than it is now; it enacted a degree of intimacy we have not, in modern terms, entirely comprehended. Later still, as Tarquin is stealing towards her room, he encounters another productive symbol – a surrogate for the lady's hand and a potential final warning:

And being lighted, by the light he spies
Lucretia's glove wherein her needle sticks.
He takes it from the rushes where it lies,
And gripping it, the needle his finger pricks,
As who should say 'This glove to wanton tricks
    Is not inured. Return again in haste.
    Thou seest our mistress' ornaments are chaste.'
                                            (316–22)

Gloves convey a network of symbolic meanings for early moderns. Although it is beyond the scope of this article to explore these here, I can propose that, in this moment, the needle pricking Lucrece's glove has more than the obvious sexual connotation as it also signals the impending puncture wound in the Roman lady's honour. Her virtue as symbolized by the glove, though, ignites further Tarquin's violent desire; the glove then flickers for the reader between its status as chaste ornament and erotically-charged symbol.

Gloves were fetishistically erotic in some contexts, indicating a woman's flesh while covering it. Castiglione's Count in *The Book of the Courtier* (1528) discusses women's hands, saying 'they leave a very great desire to see more of them, and especially if covered with gloves'.[24] He expresses a particular wish to see the gloved hand as it will provoke an erotic curiosity that seems to be at the heart of the sexual desire paradoxically provoked by female virtue. Evelyn Welch argues that during the early modern period gloves, in addition to indicating status, were accessories that provoked desire: 'the woman's hand entering or exiting the glove was presented [in art] as a highly sensual act'.[25] Equally, the practice of exchanging gloves as love tokens or personalized gifts further eroticized and objectified the hands. The Spanish Humanist, Juan Luis Vives, shares his advice about how a woman must behave when she goes out in public and, curiously, is emphatic about what parts of her body she should cover up. Vives worries about the provocative effects upon men who see the parts of a woman's body that are particularly desirable, including the hand: 'some wanton men seeing the part of the body not used to be seen, are set on fire therewith. Whereto were gloves ordained, but to hide the hands, that they should not appear, except it were in work?'[26] Thus the physical appearance and positioning of the hand was important in this period to the production of desire. Because it was a visible part of flesh of the female body, covered only by gloves and, at times, makeup; 'as one of the few areas of flesh visible lower down the body, [the hands] were an important locus for attention'.[27]

As I have been arguing, in *Lucrece* the narrative of the rape is punctuated by a carefully conceived composition of hand gestures that develop the emotional trajectory of the tragedy, the central image being that of her cheek resting unconsciously upon her hand. In her supplication, appealing to Tarquin not to commit the rape she heaves up her hands again, but this time in an appeal to his conscience, not knowing how powerfully her 'heaved up hands' had aroused him earlier. After the rape, 'She, desperate, with her nails her flesh doth tear' (739), enacting the gesture of deconstructing her beauty, focusing her despair and shame upon her hands and her face, the natural sources of her beauty. She later addresses her 'poor hand' directly as it quivers, leaving it to do the deed of expunging her guilt and shame by taking her life: 'For if I die', she says to her hand, 'my honour lives in thee, / But if I live, thou liv'st in my defame' (1032–3). Lucrece takes back control of her hands, the hands that unconsciously provoked and framed her violation.

---

[24] Baldesar Castiglione, *The Book of the Courtier*, trans. Leonard Eckstein Opdycke (New York, 2005), p. 52.

[25] Evelyn Welch, 'Art on the Edge: Hair and Hands in Renaissance Italy', *Renaissance Studies*, 23(2009), 241–68; p. 260.

[26] Juan Luis Vives, *The Instruction of Christian Woman*, trans. Richard Hyrde (London, 1547), fo. 39v.

[27] Welch, 'Art on the Edge', p. 260.

'HE TOOK ME BY THE WRIST'

In *The Passions of the Minde*, Thomas Wright explains that 'the gesture of the body may be reduced unto these heades: motions of the eyes, pronuntiation, managing of the hands and bodie, manner of going'.[28] If we pay close attention to the body, he argues, we can interpret the internal gesticulations of the heart. The notion that gestures manifest thoughts and emotions crops up time and again in medieval and early modern psychological theory. What Bulwer and other theorists of the period repeatedly offer is a way of perceiving the movements of the body as an unfolding of the self: 'there riseth no passion in the soule', observes Nicolas Coeffeteau in 1621, 'which leaveth not some visible trace of her agitation vpon the body of man'.[29] Given the relationship between the emotions and their 'visible traces upon the body', we might ask how thought, emotion and gesture can be explored by examining a device in which Shakespeare explores this crucial dialectic: *narratio*. This rhetorical device defined in *The Dictionary of Sir Thomas Elyot, Knight* as a 'narration or report of thynges that are doone',[30] is often evident in Shakespeare when the dramatist wants us to *hear* about a highly charged gestural exchange. David Bevington observed that Shakespeare sometimes chooses to convey an emotionally profound moment through gestural language rather than gesture itself.[31] What I would like to do here is explore just what the impact might be of such moments by focusing on one example from *Hamlet* and tracing, again, its correspondences in visual representations.

In Shakespeare's gestural *narratio* we hear about past bodily events through re-collective reporting; it is in these spaces where we see a specific Shakespearian notion of gesture and how it conveys emotion:

He took me by the wrist and held me hard,
Then goes he to the length of all his arm,
And with his other hand thus o'er his brow
He falls to such perusal of my face
As a would draw it. Long stayed he so.
At last, a little shaking of mine arm,

And thrice his head thus waving up and down,
He raised a sigh so piteous and profound
That it did seem to shatter all his bulk
And end his being. That done, he lets me go,
And, with his head over his shoulder turned,
He seemed to find his way without his eyes,
For out o' doors he went without their help,
And to the last bended their light on me.

(2.1.88–101)[32]

What Ophelia describes to her father in full is a gestural performance of Hamlet's grief and pretence of madness. Traditionally, this moment has been interpreted as Hamlet's way of conveying his fictive madness to Ophelia, knowing full well she will report it. And I am not arguing against that. But I want to consider how Hamlet relies upon Ophelia's 'kinesic intelligence' to interpret his emotional state and in turn incorporate it. 'Kinesic intelligence', defined by Ellen Spolsky, refers to 'our human capacity to discern and interpret body movements, body postures, gestures, and facial expressions in real situations as well as in our reception of visual art.'[33] Spolsky suggests that this '"intelligence" stems from "our sense of the relationship of parts of the human body to the whole, and of the patterns of bodily tension and relaxation as they are related to movement"'.[34] We might ask to what extent Shakespeare would have depended upon the 'kinesic intelligence' of his audience when gestures are communicated

---

[28] Thomas Wright, *The Passions of the Minde* (London, 1601), p. 210.

[29] Nicolas Coeffeteau, *A Table of Humane Passions*, trans. E. Grimeston (London, 1621), p. 17.

[30] LEME http://leme.library.utoronto.ca/search/results.cfm accessed 13–07–2014.

[31] David Bevington, *Action is Eloquence: Shakespeare's Language of Gesture* (Cambridge, MA, 1984).

[32] William Shakespeare, *The Tragedy of Hamlet Prince of Denmark*, in *William Shakespeare: The Complete Works*, ed. Stanley Wells and Gary Taylor, John Jowett and William Montgomery (Oxford, 1986).

[33] Guillemette Bolens, *The Style of Gestures: Embodiment and Cognition in Literary Narrative* (Baltimore, 2012), p. 1.

[34] Ellen Spolsky, 'Elaborated Knowledge: Reading Kinesis in Pictures', *Poetics Today*, 17 (1996), p. 159, cited in Bolens, *The Style of Gestures*, p. 1.

aurally through narrative as well as when they are performed on stage. Regardless of whether or not we hear a gesture, see it performed or view a representation of one in art, we rely on our own motor memory of gestures, particularly tactile gestures, as we come to understand or interpret their meaning in artistic contexts.

'Gesture analysis in literature' forces us to 'take into account narrativity as a decisive parameter.'[35] When it comes to Shakespeare's dramatic examples, however, the first question we have to ask is why is a particular gesture or gestural exchange described to the audience rather than performed? There are several examples of gestural *narratio* in Shakespeare, such as the description in *The Winter's Tale* of Perdita's touching reunion with her father (5.2), or Portia's reiteration to Brutus of his anxious gestures that she interprets as marital negligence in *Julius Caesar* (2.1). While it is generally accepted that some emotions, too deeply felt, are inexpressible, do we have to consider the prospect that certain emotions or emotional exchanges are instead un-performable? In considering these questions and this passage from *Hamlet*, I want to isolate the wrist grasp to suggest that some gestural moments in Shakespeare have resonances beyond the theatre and to argue for the possibility that this particular narrated gesture is poignantly deliberate. How does the wrist-grasp gesture contribute specifically to the emotional trauma Ophelia experiences through this encounter? What broader cultural meanings might it evoke and what, if anything, can its ubiquitous visual correspondences within religious and secular iconography tell us about this moment in *Hamlet*?

It is a physiological fact that if the wrist is held hard, the hand is rendered immobile. Thus, as Corine Schleif has suggested, this gesture has ritualistic beginnings that 'generally denoted a relationship in which a weaker person was subjugated to or dependent upon a stronger person'.[36] A brief survey of some examples of this gesture reveals that, at its most basic, it was a gesture of intervention and hierarchy. Numerous *danses macabres*, such as Hans Holbein's sequence of woodcuts (1526)

or the Abbot and Bailiff examples from *La danse macabre* (Paris, 1486), show death sometimes rather cheerfully grasping his victims by the wrist. In such instances the wrist grasp demonstrates a hierarchical structure that highlights the helplessness or sense of incapacitation humans experience when faced with the inevitability of death. The gesture also occurs in images of Christ grasping Adam and Eve or sinners by their wrists in depictions of the harrowing of hell or Christ's descent into limbo; in this context, it symbolizes and celebrates Christ's intervention in the salvation of mankind, while keeping in view the subordinate position of humans in relation to the divine.[37]

Conversely, depictions of the last judgement might illustrate a demon or Satan grasping a sinner by the wrist as is figured in a detail of a winged demon in Hieronymous Bosch's *Last Judgement* (1504). It was a gesture that, again depending upon context, had meanings ranging from protection to violent intentions. We see it in literary and artistic portrayals of martyrdom. For example in Caravaggio's *Martyrdom of Saint Matthew* (1599–1600) we see an image of the saint being grasped, somewhat aggressively by the wrist, recalling the perpetual association between martyrdom and gestures of power.[38]

What is compelling is just how often this gesture is deployed in artistic contexts to illustrate female subordination. This type of depiction appears in religious iconography and is found within pictorial narratives of the Creation, the Fall and Expulsion. Marjorie O'Rourke Boyle's study of touch provides examples of the creation of Eve, noting that at times God holds her by the wrist or pulls

---

[35] Bolens, *The Style of Gesture*, p. 25.

[36] Corine Schleif, 'Hands that Appoint, Anoint, and Ally: Late-Medieval Donor Strategies for Appropriating Approbation through Painting', *Art History*, 16 (1993), 1–33; p. 18.

[37] In addition to the example discussed here, there are countless more depictions of this gesture in 'harrowings' from across Europe throughout the middle ages and early modern period.

[38] A copy can be viewed at http://en.wikipedia.org/wiki/The_Martyrdom_of_Saint_Matthew_(Caravaggio).

5. Harrowing of Hell (1240)

her from Adam's side by her wrist.[39] This gesture establishes, in such contexts, womankind's subjectivity in light of divine creation; the immobilization of the hand that this gesture emblematizes may even invoke prophetically the admonition not to touch the forbidden fruit. It is thus a disabling grasp that recalls the biblical link between the creation of woman and the fall of mankind, generated by the touching hand.

Another context for this grasp is even more unsettling. In her analysis of medieval rape imagery, Diane Wolfthal identifies common visual tropes designed to signal that a rape was either about to occur or had already taken place. There are numerous examples from medieval iconography: such as the Rape of Dinah from the Pamplona Bible, or the story of the Levite's concubine in the Book of Judges, depicted in the Morgan Bible, where the host presents the concubine, grasping her wrist, to a gang of rapists. We see this again in a sixteenth-century German *album amicorum* where Lucrece, in attempting to prevent her own rape, grasps Tarquin's wrist, while he is, in turn, forcefully grasping hers. Wolfthal argues that this gesture is so often 'employed as a sign of sexual attack' that it became a metonym or shorthand visual signal of the act of rape itself;[40] and this seems to be the case throughout the early modern period, as mid-seventeenth century depictions of the rape of Tamar by her half-brother indicate.[41]

I am not suggesting Hamlet is like God or Christ or a rapist nor that Ophelia is necessarily a martyr, but the rich and complicated history of this gesture can illuminate some of these meanings that constellate around it when we see it or, as in Shakespeare, hear it described. What is clear is that by using this gesture, Hamlet deliberately inflicts or transfers his grief and perhaps even pain upon Ophelia. The highest number of pins found in an early modern outfit were more often than not concentrated around the neck to hold a ruff in place and around the wrists to attach cuffs to the sleeves, on male as well as female clothing. Thus to take someone by the wrist and hold them hard would arguably be a painful gesture.

Hamlet's gesture is disturbing, then, for a number of reasons. Typically, gestural exchanges between lovers are ritualistically conventional. Bulwer says that the hand is a central feature upon which the intentions of both lovers are inscribed: 'lovers', he remarks, 'I know not by what amorous instinct, next to the face direct their passionate respects to the Hand of those they love'.[42] By intruding Tarquin-like into Ophelia's chamber and grabbing her wrist, Hamlet inverts the usual function of the hand in the socially encoded exchanges between lovers. Ophelia's narrative report here tells us about an extreme intervention that is inflected with violence. More broadly, this gesture is also a metaphorical reminder of one of the chief concerns of the play: incapacitation. Thus Hamlet's own sense of immobility and Ophelia's by tactile association is emblematized in the description of the seizure of a wrist.

To conclude, there may be more to a gesture than a fleeting action of the body. As I suggested earlier, it is perhaps unfruitful to attempt to reconstruct precisely what actors did with their hands on stage, but we may acquire a sense of the visual and emotional impact of certain gestures when we hear or read how Shakespeare describes them to us. Why are audiences asked only to imagine certain gestural encounters in the plays? Why are we not allowed to witness the passionate expressions of reunions or traumatizing exchanges? Many early modern theorists provided external portraits of the emotions as they would appear on the body, developing a standardized bodily vocabulary of the emotions. As we have seen, the Renaissance visual tradition and early modern discourses on the hand

---

[39] See Marjorie O'Rourke Boyle, *Senses of Touch* (Brill, 1998) and Hieronymus Bosch's *The Garden of Earthly Delights* (1490–1510) in the Museo del Prado, Madrid http://en.wikipedia.org/wiki/The_Garden_of_Earthly_Delights.

[40] Diane Wolfthal, '"A Hue and a Cry": Medieval Rape Imagery and Its Transformation', *Art Bulletin*, 75 (1993), 39–64; p. 42.

[41] www.bergerfoundation.ch/wat1/picture?ref=6323–3042–3157.64&type=medium.

[42] Bulwer, *Chirologia*, p. 117.

contribute to this vocabulary, which with some 'kinesic intelligence' can be applied to narrative contexts. By charting the iconographic histories of certain gestures, I have tried at the very least to complicate the meanings of gestures as they are described in narrative poetry and the gestural exchanges reported to us in the plays, so they can be read as decisively complex encounters, expressing the deepest and perhaps most un-performable emotions in human nature.

THE ORIGIN OF THE LATE RENAISSANCE DRAMATIC CONVENTION OF SELF-ADDRESSED SPEECH

JAMES HIRSH

INTRODUCTION

One of the most conspicuous and artistically important features of late Renaissance English drama was that soliloquies by characters engaged in the fictional action represented self-addressed speeches as a matter of convention. The dramatists most responsible for the establishment and early development of the convention in the late 1580s and early 1590s were Thomas Kyd, Christopher Marlowe and Shakespeare. By the mid-1590s it had become an overwhelmingly dominant convention. All important late Renaissance dramatists employed it with remarkable frequency and consistency, and it remained in effect until the closing of the theatres in 1642. Plentiful, unambiguous, varied, conspicuous and overwhelmingly one-sided evidence demonstrates that this was the governing convention. The present essay will present a catalogue of the relevant evidence in three plays that were landmarks in the establishment of the convention: *The Spanish Tragedy*, *Dr Faustus* and *Richard III*. Providing this huge catalogue of evidence would have been unnecessary were it not for the startling and significant fact of cultural history that a great many post-Renaissance commentators have assumed that soliloquies in late Renaissance drama were typically meant to represent speeches knowingly addressed by characters to playgoers. This fundamental error about the artistic practices of Shakespeare and his fellow dramatists has led to misunderstandings about major themes of plays of the period and about the hypothetical, implied psychologies of individual characters.

Many post-Renaissance scholars, including many compilers of reference works, adopt the simple, one-step, labour-saving method of defining the theatrical term *soliloquy* on the basis of the etymology of the word, as a speech (*loqui*, 'to speak' in Latin) uttered when a character is alone (*solus*) on stage. This is a patently wrong-headed procedure. There is no chance that late Renaissance dramatists tailored their dramatic practices so they would conform to the etymology of a word, particularly a word that had not yet come into common usage in England as a theatrical term. Imagine the immense labour that biologists could save themselves if, instead of carefully examining the properties of the pineapple plant to determine its relationship to other plants, they simply defined *pineapple* as a cross between a pine tree and an apple tree on the basis of the etymology of the word. The above definition-by-etymology of *soliloquy* excludes *by fiat* the large number of soliloquies that occur when another character is on stage, such as Juliet's soliloquies in the balcony scene when, unbeknownst to her, Romeo is eavesdropping. Some other scholars define the term *soliloquy* as a passage knowingly addressed by a character to playgoers. Their definition excludes by fiat the huge number of soliloquies in late Renaissance drama that contain conspicuous, unambiguous markers of *self*-address, such as Hamlet's 'O heart, lose not thy nature!' (3.2.382). Each of these definitions employs an a priori, unempirical procedure that relieves the definition-maker of the hard work of surveying, analysing and categorizing a sufficiently large number of soliloquies in plays of the era to discern the actual practices followed by dramatists.

The findings presented here were arrived at on the basis of a systematic survey of the actual practices of late Renaissance dramatists.[1] The working definition of *soliloquy* I employed at the outset of this investigation was 'a dramatic passage with the distinguishing feature that the character portrayed by the actor who speaks the words does not intend them to be heard by any other character'. This definition was devised to leave the question *at whose hearing do characters direct such speeches?* to be answered by *evidence* not by fiat. The definition was also devised to leave the question *in what contexts do such speeches occur?* to be decided by evidence not by fiat. That soliloquies in late Renaissance drama were designed to represent self-addressed speeches is a *finding* reached after a laborious investigation, not an a priori definition. An *aside* is defined herein as 'a speech that a character guards from the hearing of at least one other character'. Many scholars have attempted to define the terms *soliloquy* and *aside* so that they will be mutually exclusive. This has sown confusion, like the confusion that would be sown if someone tried to define the terms 'Canadian' and 'carpenter' so that the concepts would be mutually exclusive. The dramatic practices of late Renaissance drama have been obscured by the failure to recognize that soliloquies and asides were overlapping rather than mutually exclusive categories. Characters frequently guard soliloquies in asides from the hearing of other characters.

THE SPANISH TRAGEDY

The Spanish Tragedy (circa 1586) is pervaded by evidence that soliloquies represented self-addressed speech rather than audience address. Three kinds of evidence of self-address often occur independently and often in combination: (1) a character addresses himself by name, title, alias or epithet, or addresses a feature of his own consciousness; (2) a character addresses himself by a second-person pronoun; (3) a character issues a command clearly directed at himself not at playgoers. In the following

catalogue of evidence, each unambiguous marker of self-address is in bold-face type.

HIERONIMO **Hieronimo, beware, thou** art betrayed,
And to entrap **thy** life this train is laid.
Advise thee therefore, **be** not credulous:
This is devised to endanger **thee**,
That **thou** by this Lorenzo shouldst accuse,
And he, for **thy** dishonor done, should draw
Thy life in question, and **thy** name in hate . . .
Then **hazard** not **thine** own, **Hieronimo**,
But **live** t'effect **thy** resolution.[2]   (3.2.37–47)

LORENZO Now to confirm the complot **thou** has cast
Of all these practices . . .   (3.2.100–1)

PEDRINGANO Now, **Pedringano, bid thy** pistol
hold.   (3.3.1)

SERBERINE Here, **Serberine, attend** and **stay thy**
pace,
For here did Don Lorenzo's page appoint
That **thou** by his command shouldst meet with him.
        (3.3.23–5)

PEDRINGANO Now, **Pedringano**, or never, **play** the
man!   (3.3.29)

LORENZO This works like wax; yet once more **try thy**
wits.   (3.4.60)

HIERONIMO **Hieronimo**, 'tis time for **thee** to
trudge . . . .
Away, Hieronimo, to him **be** gone: ['Away' is used
as a command.]
He'll do **thee** justice for Horatio's death.
Turn down this path, **thou** shalt be with him
straight;
Or this, and then **thou** need'st not take **thy**
breath . . .
Here's the king, nay, **stay**.
        (3.12.6–23) [He commands himself to 'stay'.]

---

[1] For this survey of evidence, see my book *Shakespeare and the History of Soliloquies* (Madison, NJ, 2003), chapters 4–7; for additional detailed analyses of how the convention operated in particular episodes, see the series of articles I have published on such matters since 1981.

[2] Thomas Kyd, *The Spanish Tragedy*, 2nd edn, ed. J. R. Mulryne, in the New Mermaids series (London, 1989).

HIERONIMO Then, **stay, Hieronimo, attend** their
will . . .
Strike, and **strike** home, where wrong is offered
thee . . .
If destiny **thy** miseries do ease,
Then hast **thou** health, and happy shalt **thou** be;
If destiny deny **thee** life, **Hieronimo**,
Yet shalt **thou** be assured of a tomb;
If neither, yet let this **thy** comfort be . . .
No, no, **Hieronimo, thou** must enjoin
Thine eyes to observation, and **thy** tongue
To milder speeches than **thy** spirit affords,
Thy heart to patience, and **thy** hands to rest,
Thy cap to courtesy, and **thy** knee to bow,
Till to revenge **thou** know, when, where and how.
(3.13.4–44)

ISABELLA **Isabella, rent** them [i.e. boughs] up
And **burn** the roots. (4.2.8–9)

HIERONIMO **Bethink thyself, Hieronimo,**
Recall thy wits, **recompt thy** former wrongs
Thou has received by murder of **thy** son;
And lastly, not least, how Isabel,
Once his mother and **thy** dearest wife,
All woe-begone for him, hath slain herself.
Behooves **thee** then, **Hieronimo**, to be
revenged . . .
On then, **Hieronimo, pursue** revenge.
(4.3.21–9) ['On' is used as a command.]

A fourth unambiguous marker of self-address is
an apostrophe in the sense of 'an address to an
imaginary listener'. It would be incongruous to
address an *imaginary* listener in a speech knowingly
addressed to *actual* listeners. On very rare occasions
a character uses an apostrophe as a highly artificial
rhetorical device in a speech intended to be heard
by other characters. If soliloquies were meant to
be speeches to playgoers, apostrophes would be as
rare in them as they are in speeches directed at the
hearing of other characters. In fact, apostrophes
are vastly more common in soliloquies than in
speeches intended to be heard by other characters.
This huge differential is evidence that soliloquies
were self-addressed, not audience-addressed.
Instances in which a character addresses an
imaginary audience by name, epithet or pronoun,
or gives an imaginary audience a command, occur
frequently in soliloquies in *The Spanish Tragedy*.

HIERONIMO **O earth**, why didst **thou** not in time
devour
The vild profaner of this sacred bower?
O poor Horatio, what hadst **thou** misdone,
To lesse **thy** life ere life was new begun?
O wicked butcher, whatsoe'er **thou** wert,
How could **thou** strangle virtue and desert?
(2.5.26–31)

HIERONIMO Or what might move **thee**,
Bel-Imperia,
To accuse **thy** brother, had he been the mean?
(3.2.35–6)

PEDRINGANO And **hold on, Fortune**! Once more
favour me;
Give but success to mine attempting spirit,
And **let** me shift for taking of mine aim! (3.3.2–4)

LORENZO'S PAGE Alas, **poor Pedringano**, I am in a
sort sorry for **thee**, but if I should be hanged with
thee, I cannot weep. (3.5.17–19)

HIERONIMO Wast **thou, Lorenzo**, Balthazar and
thou,
Of whom my son, my son deserved so well? . . .
O false Lorenzo, are these **thy** flattering looks?
Is this the honour that **thou** didst my son?
And **Balthazar**, bane to **thy** soul and me,
Was this the ransom he reserved **thee** for? . . .
Woe to **thy** baseness and captivity,
Woe to **thy** birth, **thy** body and **thy** soul,
Thy cursed father, and **thy** conquered self!
And banned with bitter execrations be
The day and place where he did pity **thee**!
(3.7.42–66)

BEL-IMPERIA. **Accursed brother, unkind**
murderer,
Why bends **thou** thus **thy** mind to martyr me?
Hieronimo, why writ I of **thy** wrongs,
Or why art **thou** so slack in **thy** revenge?
Andrea, O Andrea, that **thou** sawest
Me for **thy** friend Horatio handled thus. (3.9.5–10)

HIERONIMO And **Balthazar**, I'll be with **thee** . . . ,
And **thee, Lorenzo**! (3.12.22–3)

HIERONIMO Pha! **keep your** way.
(3.14.167) [an apostrophe to departed characters]

ISABELLA **Hieronimo, make haste** to see **thy**
son, . . .

Make haste, **Hieronimo**, to hold excused
Thy negligence in pursuit of their deaths . . .
Ah nay, **thou** dost delay their deaths,
Forgives the murderers of **thy** noble son. (4.2.26–33)

Yet another unambiguous marker of self-address is an assertion or non-rhetorical question that would not make sense if the character addressed it to playgoers. After discovering the corpse of Horatio, Hieronimo asks in a soliloquy,

Who hath slain my son? (2.5.18)

Playgoers know the answer to this question and are sympathetic to the character who asks it. If playgoers believed that the character knowingly addressed this question to themselves, they quite appropriately would have shouted out 'Lorenzo!' and 'Balthazar!' If playgoers were under the impression that Hieronimo could *see* them, it would have followed logically that he could *hear* their shouted responses to his question. And yet Hieronimo shows no sign of having heard answers shouted out by playgoers. Similarly, in a soliloquy in 3.7 Hieronimo asks a question about Pedringano,

Help he to murder mine Horatio? (40)

If playgoers believed that the character addressed this question to themselves, they quite appropriately would have shouted out 'Yes!' And yet Hieronimo again shows no sign of having heard such a response. Indeed, at no point in any soliloquy in the play does any character ever acknowledge the presence of playgoers.

Grand totals for *The Spanish Tragedy*. Unambiguous markers of self-address in soliloquies: **144**. Unambiguous markers of audience address: **Zero**.

It is not coincidental that the same play that established the convention of self-addressed speech also includes two characters, the Ghost of Andrea and Revenge, who are on stage throughout the play eavesdropping on the other characters. The on-stage eavesdroppers can see and hear the other characters, but those other characters show no awareness of the on-stage eavesdroppers. Kyd implicitly established a partial analogy between the on-stage eavesdroppers and playgoers. Just as Andrea and

Revenge eavesdrop on the other characters, playgoers eavesdrop on all the characters including Andrea and Revenge. Just as none of the other characters shows any awareness the presence of the on-stage eavesdroppers, none of the characters, not even the on-stage eavesdroppers, shows any awareness of playgoers. Like the on-stage eavesdroppers unperceived by the other characters, playgoers eavesdrop on the entire action, including soliloquies, and are unperceived by any of the characters.

Aware that many playgoers had memories of earlier plays in which characters who were engaged in the fictional action explicitly addressed playgoers, Kyd went to extraordinary lengths to establish in no uncertain terms and with obsessive repetition that, in this play, soliloquies represented self-addressed speeches rather than speeches knowingly addressed by characters to playgoers. At the time of its first performance, Kyd's extensive use of unambiguously self-addressed speeches and exclusion of audience-addressed speeches by characters engaged in the action was boldly original. The play became one of the most influential plays in the period, and its most widely imitated element was the device of self-addressed speech.

DOCTOR FAUSTUS

With its pervasive and unswerving insistence that soliloquies within it represented self-addressed speech, *The Spanish Tragedy* might have been a curious anomaly in theatrical history were it not for the fact that other dramatists enthusiastically followed Kyd's lead. Another key figure in the establishment of the convention was Christopher Marlowe, who was at the time Kyd's close friend. There are almost as many markers of self-address in the A-text of *Dr Faustus* (circa 1591) as in *The Spanish Tragedy*.[3]

---

3 Christopher Marlowe, *'Doctor Faustus' and Other Plays*, ed. David Bevington and Eric Rasmussen (Oxford, 1995). Even though the A-text (1604) is probably a truncated version and may contain material by a collaborator, I have used it as the basis for analysis because many of the additional passages in the longer 1616 B-text were probably inserted by other dramatists after Marlowe's death.

DRAMATIC CONVENTION OF SELF-ADDRESSED SPEECH

The play begins with a long choral speech that is explicitly addressed to playgoers. That speech is immediately followed by a soliloquy in which Faustus addresses himself by name five times and which contains 31 other unambiguous markers of self-address:

Settle thy studies, **Faustus**, and **begin**
To sound the depth of that **thou** wilt profess.
Having commenced, **be** a divine in show,
Yet **level** at the end of every art,
And **live** and **die** in Aristotle's works.
Sweet *Analytics*, 'tis **thou** hast ravished me! . . .
Then **read** no more; **thou** has attained the end. . . .
Bid *On kai me on* [being and not-being, that is, ontology] farewell. **Galen, come!** . . .
Be a physician, **Faustus**. **Heap** up gold,
And **be** eternized for some wondrous cure. . . .
Why **Faustus**, hast **thou** not attained that end?
Is not **thy** common talk sound aphorisms?
Are not **thy** bills hung up as monuments . . . ?
Yet art **thou** still but Faustus, and a man.
Wouldst **thou** make man to live eternally . . . .
Physic, farewell. Where is Justinian? . . . [The question would not have made sense if addressed to playgoers.]
Jerome's Bible, **Faustus**, view it well. . . .
        Divinity, adieu! . . .
Here, **Faustus**, **try thy** brains to gain a deity. (1.1.1–65)

In this speech Marlowe emphatically depicts a character engaged in the process of *making up his mind*, not a character in the profoundly different rhetorical and dramatic situation of *explaining* himself to thousands of strangers. The juxtaposition of the first two speeches of the play sets up a conspicuous direct comparison between audience-addressed speeches – henceforth relegated to choral characters who do not participate in the fictional action and to epilogues after the action has concluded – and self-addressed speeches by characters engaged in the fictional action. Like Kyd, Marlowe was *training* playgoers to understand and accept the new convention.

Faustus's soliloquies elsewhere in the play are also pervaded by markers of self-address:

Faustus, begin thine incantations,
And **try** if devils will obey **thy** hest,

Seeing **thou** hast prayed and sacrificed to them. . . .
Then **fear** not, **Faustus**, but **be** resolute,
And **try** the uttermost magic can perform. (1.3.1–15)

Now, **Faustus**, must **thou** needs be damned,
And canst **thou** not be saved. . . .
Away with such vain fancies and **despair**! ['Away' is used as a command.]
Despair in God and **trust** in Beelzebub.
Now **go** not backward. No, **Faustus**, **be** resolute.
Why waverest **thou**? . . .
To God? He loves **thee** not.
The god **thou** servest is **thine** own appetite. . . .
What god can hurt **thee**, **Faustus**? **Thou** art safe;
Cast no more doubts. . . .
Why shouldst **thou** not? Is not **thy** soul **thine** own?
    Then **write** again. (2.1.1–69)

What art **thou**, **Faustus**, but a man condemned to die? . . .
Confound these passions with a quiet sleep. . . .
Then **rest thee**, **Faustus**, quiet in conceit.
        (4.1.126–131)

In the presence of other characters in 5.1, Faustus explicitly addresses himself,

Where art **thou**, **Faustus**? **Wretch**, what hast **thou** done?
Damned art **thou**, **Faustus**, damned! **Despair** and **die!** . . . .
Accursèd **Faustus**, where is mercy now? (5.1.47–62)

In these lines Faustus is not depicted as holding up his side of a conversation with the other characters. Either Faustus guards these self-addressed speeches from the hearing of the other characters, or he is so overwhelmed by despair that he has momentarily become oblivious to their presence.

Faustus's last speech in the play contains two long soliloquies (separated by a prayer and followed by words directed at the hearing of Lucifer and Mephistopheles) that resemble his first in the density of unambiguous markers of self-address:

Ah, **Faustus**, / Now hast **thou** but one bare hour to live,
And then **thou** must be damned perpetually.
Stand still, you ever-moving **spheres** of heaven . . . .
Fair **nature's eye, rise, rise again**, and **make**
Perpetual day; or let this hour be but

A year, a month, a week, a natural day . . . .
See, see where Christ's blood streams in the
   firmament! . . .

                  and **see** where God
Stretcheth out his arm and bends his ireful brows!
Mountains and **hills, come, come** and **fall** on me,
And **hide** me from the heavy wrath of God! . . .
Earth, gape! O, no, it will not harbor me.
You stars that reigned at my nativity, . . .
Now **draw up** Faustus like a foggy mist . . .
That when **you** vomit forth into the air,
My limbs may issue from **your** smoky mouths,
So that my soul may but ascend to heaven . . . .
                        (5.2.57–89)

Why wert **thou** not a creature wanting soul?
Or why is this immortal that **thou** hast? . . .
No, **Faustus, curse thyself. Curse** Lucifer,
That hath deprived **thee** of the joys of heaven.
O, it strikes, it strikes! Now, **body, turn** to air,
Or Lucifer will bear **thee** quick to hell.
O **soul, be changed** into little waterdrops,
And **fall** into the ocean, ne'er be found! . . .
Ugly **hell, gape not.**   (97–114)

In the context of this play, Faustus's repeated commands to 'see' (70, 74) are unambiguously self-directed. In his soliloquies in the play up to this point, Faustus has given himself a huge number of commands (28 to be exact) of many different sorts: Settle, begin, be a divine, level, live, die, read no more, Bid, Be a physician, Heap, be eternized, view, try, begin, try, fear not, be resolute, try, [do] Away with, despair, Despair, trust, go not, be resolute, Cast, write, Confound, rest.

The verb in one of those commands, 'Jerome's Bible, Faustus, *view* it well' (1.1.38), contains a close synonym of 'see' and is unambiguously addressed to himself not to playgoers. Conversely, Faustus never elsewhere in the play issues a command unambiguously addressed to playgoers. Indeed, he never shows any awareness of their presence. Elsewhere in late Renaissance drama the command to 'see' and similar commands occur in explicitly self-addressed speeches, as in the passage already quoted in *The Spanish Tragedy*, the landmark play that initiated the convention:

See, see, O see thy shame, Hieronimo.

Alert late Renaissance playgoers would have been in no doubt that in this play every command in a soliloquy was directed by the speaker either at himself or at an imaginary audience in an apostrophe (such as 'Mountains and hills, come, come and fall on me'). After issuing commands to 'see' in the course of this very speech, Faustus issues two commands addressed explicitly to his own soul. That Faustus's commands to 'see' represent self-address is also unambiguously implied by the dramatic situation. Faustus is intensely fixated on his own perception, on what *he* sees as a sign of the imminent commencement of his own hellish torment for all eternity. He does not take time out from the overwhelming horror of his own predicament in order to serve as a tour-guide for a large group of strangers, helpfully alerting them to a visual phenomenon that they might find interesting, and playgoers do not in fact see what Faustus sees.

Soliloquies spoken by other characters also contain unambiguous markers of self-address. In a soliloquy guarded in an aside from the other characters on stage, the Knight addresses an apostrophe to Faustus:

Ay, marry, **Master Doctor**, now there's a sign of grace in **you**, when **you** will confess the truth.   (4.1.46–7)

Near the end of 5.1, the Old Man addresses an apostrophe to Faustus who has just exited,

Accursèd **Faustus, miserable man,**
That from **thy** soul exclud'st the grace of heaven.
                   (5.1.110–11)

After speaking for seven lines while alone on stage earlier in the same scene, Wagner notices the entrance of other characters. He then says in a soliloquy now guarded in an aside from the hearing of the entering characters,

        See where they come.   (8)

Having already heard another character in the play unambiguously direct a huge number of commands at himself, alert late Renaissance playgoers would have been in no doubt that Wagner's direction to 'see' constituted yet another self-directed command. The reason that Wagner makes a point of telling himself to take note of the entrance of other characters is to remind himself that, from the moment other characters arrive, he must actively guard any further self-addressed speeches in asides or else those speeches would be overheard. Successfully guarding a soliloquy required attention and skill. In numerous episodes in late Renaissance drama, a character becomes so preoccupied by what he is saying to himself in a soliloquy, initially guarded in an aside from the other characters present, that he becomes oblivious to the presence of those characters, lowers his guard and the other characters begin to hear him talking to himself.[4]

At no point in the play does any character engaged in the action ever address playgoers. A speech in the middle of the play bears the prefix 'Wagner' in the 1604 Quarto, but in its content and style it does not resemble other speeches by that character and does resemble choral speeches elsewhere in the play. Most editors label the speech the third Chorus. A likely explanation for the speech prefix is that the actor who played Wagner doubled as the Chorus.

The play ends with a juxtaposition that replays in reverse order the juxtaposition that began the play. The play began with a choral speech explicitly addressed to playgoers followed by a speech by a character engaged in the fictional action that was dense with markers of self-address (36 in the first 65 lines). The final speech of the play is a Chorus. That example of explicit audience address by a character not engaged in the fictional action is immediately preceded by a long speech by Faustus containing two soliloquies that are dense with markers of self-address (41 in 51 lines). Once again, Marlowe went out of his way to set up a direct contrast between self-addressed speech by a character engaged in the action and audience-addressed speech by a choral character who does not interact with the characters who are engaged in the fictional action.

Grand totals for *Doctor Faustus*. Unambiguous markers of self-address in soliloquies: **131**. Unambiguous markers of audience address in speeches by non-choral characters: **Zero**.

RICHARD III

The third key figure in the establishment of the convention was Shakespeare, and *Richard III* (circa 1592) was a landmark in his original, imaginative, daring and subtle employment of the convention. Most post-Renaissance performers and commentators have convinced themselves that Richard's soliloquies were designed to represent speeches knowingly addressed by the character to playgoers. Their Richard is a sociable fellow who keeps a large group of strangers informed about his motives and plans and who makes jokes for their amusement. This Richard is demonstrably at odds with Shakespeare's character. Post-Renaissance performers and commentators who maintain that Richard is aware of the presence of playgoers have blinded themselves to a large number of conspicuous, unambiguous, varied and wholly one-sided pieces of evidence.

The soliloquy that opens the play superficially recalls opening monologues in plays written before *The Spanish Tragedy*, in which a character who later participated in the action explicitly acknowledged the presence of playgoers and informed them of the initial dramatic situation, but the similarity turns into a striking and profound contrast. At no point in the speech does Richard acknowledge the presence of playgoers, and at the end of the speech he explicitly and unambiguously addresses the contents of his own mind:

> **Dive, thoughts,** down to my soul. (1.1.41)

---

[4] For example, Luciana asks Dromio (of Syracuse), 'Why prat'st thou to thyself?' (*Comedy of Errors*, 2.2.196). In the presence of Lucius, Portia initially guards a soliloquy in which she apostrophizes Brutus. She becomes so preoccupied with her imaginary audience that she ceases to guard the soliloquy adequately in an aside and then, realizing that she has been careless, expresses in a soliloquy that is now well-guarded her concern that the boy may have overheard her soliloquy (*Julius Caesar*, 2.4.41–4).

Richard's next soliloquy in the play, which occurs later in the opening scene, contains five unambiguous markers of self-address. His apostrophe to his just-departed brother would be incongruous in a speech knowingly addressed to playgoers:

> **Go tread** the path that **thou** shalt ne'er return:
> Simple plain **Clarence**, I do love **thee** so
> That I will shortly send **thy** soul to heaven.
>
> (118–20)

Richard's soliloquies elsewhere in the play contain unambiguous markers of self-address. In the second scene he addresses an imaginary audience,

> **Shine out, fair sun.** (1.2.249)

In the third scene, he cautions himself,

> But **soft**, here come my executioners.
>
> (1.3.338)

'Soft' here means 'take care'. Richard must take care to guard in asides any further self-addressed speeches, or else the entering characters would overhear him. In the process of waking up in 5.5, he initially addresses figments of his dreaming imagination:

> **Give** me another horse! **Bind** up my wounds!
>
> (131)

The same speech contains other unambiguous markers of self-address. Fully awake, he addresses a component of his mind:

> **O coward conscience**, how dost **thou** afflict me?
>
> (133)

Richard asks and answers a clearly self-addressed question:

> **Is there a murderer here?** No. Yes, I am. (138)

If playgoers had thought that Richard were asking *them* the question, they quite appropriately would have shouted out, 'Yes!' That would have destroyed the dramatization of a radical, *unaided* shift in Richard's own perception. In Shakespeare's version, Richard's initial response to his own question is to deny his guilt, but then he acknowledges his guilt to himself. If, on the other hand,

Richard's question had been knowingly addressed to playgoers, Richard's 'No' would not have been a response to his own question, but rather a response to playgoers' affirmative response to his question. His reversal from 'No' to 'Yes' would not have been a recognition that he reached *on his own* but rather an expression of agreement with the viewpoint already expressed by playgoers. The post-Renaissance assumption that soliloquies represented audience-addressed speeches disrupts the psychological and moral implications of the dramatized action created by Shakespeare. Immediately after acknowledging his guilt to himself, Richard issues a command directed at himself and then recognizes its illogicality:

> Then **fly**! What, from myself? (139)

A later passage is a tour-de-force of self-directed speech:

> **Fool, of thyself speak** well. – **Fool, do not flatter.**
>
> (146)

In a single line Richard twice addresses himself by a self-denigrating epithet, addresses himself by a second-person pronoun and gives himself two commands.

That Richard's soliloquies represent *self*-address rather than audience-address is a crucial feature of his characterization. Instead of the public-spirited post-Renaissance figure who exerts himself to entertain a large gathering of strangers, Shakespeare's Richard is a relentlessly antisocial loner. Early in the play, he is bursting with self-conceit about his daring, cleverness and wit. He does not need to *share* his cleverness with anyone else. He does not need anyone else's validation. He gleefully reviews his schemes in self-addressed speeches simply because he delights in speaking about and thereby also hearing about the cleverness of his manipulations. It is enough for him that *he* knows how clever he is. He makes jokes for his *own* amusement. He forms temporary alliances that serve his purposes but has no genuine friends. He flatters Buckingham about the intimacy of their relationship simply because Buckingham's support is useful. At the first sign that Buckingham is less than a fully committed henchman, Richard ceases to confide in him. Shakespeare's relentlessly antisocial Richard is a much more disturbing figure than the post-Renaissance friend of playgoers.

Soliloquies by other characters also contain numerous unambiguous markers of self-address. Margaret's soliloquies guarded in asides from the hearing of other characters on stage in 1.3, for example, contain no acknowledgement of playgoers but instead contain a series of apostrophes addressed to her fellow characters:

[apostrophe to Queen Elizabeth] **Thy** honor, state, and seat is due to me. . . .
[apostrophes to Richard] **Out, devil**! . . . / **Thou** killed'st my husband. . . .
Ay, and much better blood than his or **thine**. . . .
A murd'rous villain, and so still **thou** art. . . .
Hie thee to hell for shame, and **leave** this world,
Thou cacodemon; there **thy** kingdom is.   (112–44)

In a soliloquy at the beginning of 4.4 Margaret gives herself a command and addresses herself by pronoun and by name:

> **Withdraw thee**, wretched **Margaret**.   (8)

A moment later, in a soliloquy guarded in an aside from the hearing of the Duchess of York and Queen Elizabeth, Margaret addresses an apostrophe to Elizabeth's recently murdered sons:

> **Hover** about her, **say** that right for right
> Hath dimm'd **your** infant morn to agèd night.
>   (15–16)

Just as Richard apostrophizes Clarence immediately upon Clarence's departure in 1.1, the Second Murderer apostrophizes the First immediately upon the exit of the latter in 1.4:

> **Go, coward** as **thou** art.   (274)

As noted above, in soliloquies guarded in asides Margaret apostrophizes other characters on stage in 1.3 and 4.4. Buckingham engages in the same sort of activity in 3.2:

HASTINGS Nay, like enough, for I stay dinner there
[the Tower].

BUCKINGHAM And supper too, although **thou**
know'st it not.   (116–17)

In this apostrophe in a soliloquy guarded from the hearing of Hastings, Buckingham gloats in the knowledge that the unsuspecting Hasting will shortly be arrested. In a soliloquy that occupies an entire scene, a Scrivener comments on a disturbing situation. He has just finished writing out the official indictment of Hastings even though Hastings has already been executed. In the course of this speech, he says,

> And **mark** how well the sequel hangs together.
>   (3.6.4)

Taken utterly out of its context in this play and its context in theatrical history, the Scrivener's command to 'mark' might seem ambiguous: is it self-addressed? or is it knowingly addressed by the character to playgoers? In the context of this particular play and in the context of English Renaissance drama of the 1590s, however, the passage is not ambiguous. By the time Shakespeare wrote *Richard III*, regular playgoers had become very familiar with the convention of self-addressed speech. Commands synonymous with the command to 'mark' occur in explicitly self-addressed speeches in earlier plays ('See, see, O see thy shame, Hieronimo'). Furthermore, as shown above, there are numerous markers of self-address in this very play, including unambiguously self-directed commands ('Dive, thoughts'). There are no counterbalancing examples of unambiguously audience-addressed speeches by characters in the play. In these contexts and in the absence of unambiguous overriding of the by-now familiar convention, experienced playgoers in the 1590s would have assumed as a matter of course that the Scrivener's command to 'mark' was self-directed. In subsequent plays the command to 'mark' occurs in explicitly self-addressed speeches, such as 'Tom away. / Mark the high noises, and thyself bewray / When false opinion . . . / In thy just proof repeals and reconciles thee' (*History of King Lear*, Scene 13, 103–06), that is, 'Listen to rumours of great events and reveal thy true identity when false accusations have been refuted.' Furthermore, instead of being dramatized as a public speaker, the Scrivener is dramatized as engaged in the much more psychologically interesting activity of coming to terms with his own predicament in private. He is morally astute enough to recognize that an injustice has been committed against Hastings. In the course of the soliloquy, he *talks himself into* keeping his mouth shut because speaking up would be dangerous. The hypothetical implied psychology of the character would be hopelessly muddled if this decisive moment of his private moral life were turned into a public speech delivered by the character with the purpose of bringing playgoers up to speed.

In the 1623 Folio the following stage direction is printed before a soliloquy guarded in an aside by Richard:

Speakes **to** *himselfe*. (TLN 792 (at 1.3.316 in *The Oxford Shakespeare*))

This clearly refers to the *character*, not the actor (who speaks to be heard by playgoers). A similar stage direction occurs in *The Merchant of Venice*: '*Bassanio comments on the caskets to himself*' (3.2.62sd). The obvious reason that such stage directions do not occur in later plays is that by the mid-1590s they had become superfluous. The convention of self-address had become established by countless conspicuous, unambiguous markers in the *dialogue* of almost all plays written after *The Spanish Tragedy*. Such markers continued to pervade soliloquies until the closing of the theatres in 1642. Nowhere in the Folio or in any quarto edition of any play by Shakespeare does any counterbalancing stage direction ('Speakes to auditors') occur in conjunction with any soliloquy spoken by a character engaged in the action.

At no point in *Richard III* does Richard or any other character acknowledge the presence of playgoers. Some commentators have argued illogically that Richard's comparison of himself to the Vice character of morality plays ('Thus like the formal Vice, Iniquity, / I moralize two meanings in one word', 3.1.82–3) implies that he knows that he is merely a character in a play. It implies nothing of the sort. Real human beings often compare themselves to fictional characters. A dramatist whose goal is to depict human behaviour will occasionally depict a character who compares himself to a fictional character without any suggestion that the character who makes the comparison knows that he is himself merely a character.

Grand totals for *Richard III*. Unambiguous markers of self-address in soliloquies: **44**. Unambiguous markers of audience-address: **Zero**.

SOME IMPLICATIONS AND RAMIFICATIONS OF THE CONVENTION

It is certain that playgoers understood and enthusiastically accepted the convention of self-addressed speech. If they had not done so, Shakespeare would not have gone on to employ the convention so consistently, so conspicuously, so frequently and so imaginatively in plays of all genres for the rest of his career. If playgoers had not enthusiastically accepted the convention, other dramatists would not have taken up the device and created countless demonstrably self-addressed speeches in plays of all genres. By the mid-1590s the convention of self-addressed speech had overwhelmed and eclipsed the convention of medieval and early Renaissance drama whereby characters engaged in the fictional action acknowledged the presence of playgoers. Providing playgoers with the voyeuristic pleasure of eavesdropping on the most private moments of an enormous variety of characters, the convention of self-addressed speech became a hallmark of drama for the next half-century.

Once the convention was established explicitly, consistently and insistently by Kyd, Marlowe and Shakespeare, dramatists no longer had to familiarize playgoers with the convention. By the mid-1590s, dramatists could employ the convention *implicitly* on the assumption that experienced playgoers were already familiar with it. Evidence that soliloquies represented self-addressed speeches continued to pervade later plays simply because self-addressed speeches are apt to contain evidence of self-address. Experienced playgoers encountered unambiguous instances of the convention in operation in every play or nearly every play they attended. Dramatists competed with one another to employ the convention in novel, sometimes convoluted eavesdropping episodes, including explicitly overheard soliloquies, implicitly overheard soliloquies, explicitly overheard soliloquies that are incompletely guarded in asides, implicitly overheard soliloquies incompletely guarded in asides, explicitly feigned soliloquies, implicitly feigned soliloquies, situations in which an eavesdropper overhears himself addressed in an apostrophe in a soliloquy by another character and so on.[5]

Such convolutions would have been impossible if soliloquies had gone back and forth between self-address and audience-address. If that had been the case, it would have been necessary to establish unambiguously in each case the transition between self-address and audience-address, but evidence for these hypothetical transitions is conspicuous by its absence. Also, if a character had once shown awareness of playgoers, it would not have made sense for the character subsequently to address himself as if playgoers did not exist.

Any convention can be overridden in a given case by an unambiguous signal. Such exceptions do not undermine the convention as long as the number of instances in which the convention is unambiguously maintained greatly outnumber the instances in which the convention is unambiguously overridden. In this particular case the evidence is staggeringly lopsided. In the three plays surveyed above, there are 319 distinct, unambiguous markers of self-address and not a single unambiguous marker of audience-address by a character engaged in the action. The convention was so important to dramatists of the period that they very rarely overrode it. Rarity of evidence can be a form of evidence if that rarity is conspicuous. The vast majority of plays by important dramatists in the period contain numerous unambiguous markers of self-address and no unambiguous markers of audience-address by characters engaged in the action. As a result, an experienced late Renaissance playgoer would have assumed that any particular soliloquy represented self-address as a matter of course *unless the convention was unambiguously overridden*. Audience-address in late Renaissance drama was strictly segregated from the fictional action, relegated to choral characters who do not interact with the characters in the fictional world and to epilogues in which an actor addresses playgoers after the fictional action has concluded.

Some people mistakenly think of all conventions as arbitrary and pointless restrictions on an artist's freedom. Rather than hamstringing late Renaissance dramatists, the convention of self-addressed speech spurred their imaginations. Without this convention, many of the most memorable and thought-provoking episodes in plays of the period would not have come into existence.

The convention of self-addressed speech enabled writers to dramatize a character's *relationship with himself*. It enabled dramatists to depict characters engaged in an enormous variety of *self*-directed actions: self-congratulation, self-justification, self-denigration, self-manipulation, self-deception, etc. Characters are depicted in the processes of *making* decisions, *formulating* plans, *obsessively reviewing* traumatic events, etc. By contrast, an audience-addressed speech would dramatize how a character relates to a large group of strangers. Instead of depicting a character in the process of making up his mind, an audience-addressed speech would depict a character engaged in *announcing* a decision to playgoers. Anyone genuinely interested in the issue of how selves were fashioned in the late Renaissance should be interested in the fact

---

[5] Instances of each of these types of situations are discussed in *Shakespeare and the History of Soliloquies* and my articles on the topic, especially 'Guarded, Unguarded, and Unguardable Speech in Late Renaissance Drama', in *Who Hears in Shakespeare?*, ed. Laury Magnus and Walter Cannon (Madison, NJ, 2011), pp. 17–40.

that soliloquies, which occur frequently and conspicuously in plays of all genres and which often depict a character intensely focused on the process of self-fashioning, were designed and understood as self-addressed speeches rather than as speeches that the character knowingly addressed to thousands of strangers. The self depicted in each of these passages is *the most private self* of the character. If these speeches had been knowingly addressed by the character to thousands of playgoers, they would have each represented the character's *most public self*. It is a fascinating and profoundly disturbing feature of Richard's psychology that in the early part of the play he is gleefully self-isolated. That pathological feature of his hypothetical psychology is destroyed by the sentimental assumption that Richard regards playgoers as genuine confidants whom he strives to entertain. The vast number of self-addressed speeches in English drama from *The Spanish Tragedy* to the closing of the theatres in 1642 constitute an enormous common endeavour by many dramatists to explore diverse ways in which individuals fashion themselves *in their most private moments*. As a result of the demonstrably false assumption by most post-Renaissance commentators that soliloquies in late Renaissance drama represented public speeches by the character, those commentators have blinded themselves to this major undertaking by dramatists of the period.

Shakespeare and some other dramatists were adept at incorporating dialogue-like elements in self-addressed speeches. Some soliloquies dramatize an overt conflict or subtle differentiation between distinct *sub-divisions* of a character's mind. Richard, for example, insults his 'coward conscience'. These soliloquies dramatize a character engaged in a dialogue with himself. In some soliloquies the character gives voice to one impulse and then gives voice to a conflicting impulse. In other cases, one soliloquy by a character gives voice to one side of an internal debate, and another soliloquy gives voice to a conflicting viewpoint. The two soliloquies are in dialogue with one another. In some cases an attitude expressed by a character in a soliloquy is conspicuously at odds with actions of the character. This incongruity implies that the soliloquy gave voice to only one component of the character's mind and that some conflicting, unvoiced attitude actually governs the character's behaviour. The convention of self-address thus enabled the dramatization of a profound and disturbing insight into human psychology: that, instead of having a unitary essence, a person's mind or self is composed of distinct parts that can come into conflict or into competition with one another for supremacy. A further dialogue-like feature of countless soliloquies is the presence of apostrophes. Each apostrophe constitutes one side of an imaginary dialogue with another character or personified entity. As a result of these techniques, many self-addressed speeches are as dramatic and dynamic as exchanges between characters.[6]

The vast array of unambiguous evidence of self-address by characters engaged in the fictional action and the conspicuous rarity of unambiguous evidence of audience-address by such characters demonstrates that late Renaissance dramatists and playgoers were fascinated by what a character might say when she thought she had only herself for an audience and that dramatists and playgoers were not interested in what a character might say if she knew that she was merely a character in a play.

EVIDENCE VERSUS ORTHODOXY

Some assertions about cultural history are purely speculative; they can be neither proven nor disproven because insufficient evidence is available to decide the issue or because the evidence is ambivalent. But some assertions about cultural history can be proven or disproven because sufficient evidence is available and that evidence is clear-cut. The issue raised in this essay is a prime example of the latter. Plentiful, unambiguous, conspicuous, varied and

---

[6] For a detailed account of the issues raised in this paragraph, see my article 'Dialogic Self-Address in Shakespeare's Plays', *Shakespeare*, 8 (2012), 312–27.

overwhelmingly one-sided evidence demonstrates beyond a reasonable doubt that in this period, soliloquies by characters engaged in the fictional action were meant to represent self-addressed speeches as a matter of convention. Counter-evidence is conspicuous by its extreme rarity or doubtfulness.

The evidence is so plentiful, unambiguous, conspicuous, varied and one-sided that my presentation of so much of that evidence here would have been superfluous were it not for the startling and significant fact of cultural history that many post-Renaissance commentators, including some of the most eminent and influential scholars of recent decades, have made unsubstantiated pronouncements in no uncertain terms that soliloquies in late Renaissance drama typically represented addresses to playgoers:

In most [of Shakespeare's] tragedies, the protagonists confide in the audience.[7]   (Janet Adelman)

Richard of Gloucester...remains the punning, self-expressive ambidexter directing, in continuous contact with the audience, his own murderous rise to the throne.[8]   (Robert Weimann)

There are very few absolute rules with Shakespeare, but I personally believe that it's right ninety-nine times out of a hundred to share a soliloquy with the audience. I'm convinced it's a grave distortion of Shakespeare's intention to do it to oneself.[9]   (John Barton)

Henry IV speaks in soliloquy, but as is so often the case in Shakespeare, his isolation only intensifies the sense that he is addressing a large audience: the audience of the theater.[10]   (Stephen Greenblatt)

Shakespeare's greatest originality in *Richard III*... is the hero-villain's startlingly intimate relationship with the audience. We are on unnervingly confidential terms with him.[11]   (Harold Bloom)

Richard [of Gloucester] will often speak to the audience in soliloquy, confiding in us his real plans and thoughts.[12]   (Marjorie Garber)

Some commentators have argued illogically that if a soliloquy contains information useful for playgoers to have, this is evidence that the speech was performed as knowingly addressed by the character to playgoers. Every speech in every play contains some sort of information useful for playgoers to have, but that is not evidence that every speech in every play is knowingly addressed by the character to playgoers. One should not confuse the *dramatist's* purpose of informing playgoers with the *character's* purpose in speaking. Hieronimo and Faustus review recent events not as a service to playgoers but in order to come to terms with their situations. Richard reviews his clever schemes not as a service to playgoers but to demonstrate *to himself* his intellectual superiority to others. Many soliloquies in which characters review their situations, motives or plans contain unambiguous markers of self-address. Faustus's first soliloquy, in which he reviews his situation, contains 36 unambiguous markers of self-address and no unambiguous markers of audience address. Richard's opening soliloquy, in which reviews his situation, contains no unambiguous markers of audience-address and concludes with two unambiguous markers of self-address: 'Dive, *thoughts*, down to my soul'. Some scholars have made another fundamental mistake, that of confusing the purposes of the *actor* and the purposes of the *character*. Every actor in every play speaks to be heard by playgoers, but this is not evidence that the character portrayed by the actor is represented as having the same intention.

Countless successful post-Renaissance productions of Shakespeare's plays have staged soliloquies as speeches knowingly addressed by characters to

---

[7] Janet Adelman, *The Common Liar: An Essay on 'Antony and Cleopatra'* (New Haven, CT, 1973), p. 50.

[8] Robert Weimann, *Shakespeare and the Popular Tradition in the Theater: Studies in the Social Dimension of Dramatic Form and Function*, ed. Robert Schwartz (Baltimore, 1978), p. 159.

[9] John Barton, *Playing Shakespeare* (London, 1984), p. 94.

[10] Stephen Greenblatt, *Shakespearean Negotiations* (Berkeley, CA, 1988), p. 54.

[11] Harold Bloom, *Shakespeare and the Invention of the Human* (New York, 1998), p. 70.

[12] Marjorie Garber, *Shakespeare After All* (New York, 2004), p. 133.

playgoers. This has no bearing on the issue of what these passages were designed to represent in the late Renaissance. Evidence generated in later periods of cultural history cannot be used to make a determination about an issue in an earlier age. Stage conditions and aesthetic tastes change. Thousands of successful post-Renaissance productions of Shakespeare's plays have cast actresses in the roles of women characters, but this cannot retroactively change the fact supported by the surviving body of evidence that in their original productions those parts were played by boys or men. There is vastly more evidence of the sorts catalogued above proving that soliloquies in late Renaissance drama were designed to represent self-addressed speeches as a matter of convention than there is evidence of any sort that women characters were portrayed by male actors in the period.

Most current theatre professionals and scholars *prefer* the theatrical device of audience-address to the device of self-addressed speech and have projected their personal taste anachronistically onto late Renaissance drama by blinding themselves to the vast array of evidence that inconveniently contradicts their preference. This blindness has resulted in profound misconceptions about the hypothetical psychology of countless individual characters as well as profound misconceptions about late Renaissance perspectives on psychology, selfhood, individuality, artistic representation and many other matters.

In *Shakespeare and the History of Soliloquies*, I supplied a huge array of unambiguous, conspicuous and varied evidence from plays by Kyd, Chapman, Marlowe, Shakespeare, Dekker, Middleton, Jonson, Marston, Webster, Fletcher, Massinger and Ford demonstrating that soliloquies in late Renaissance drama represented self-address as a matter of convention. In a review of the book in *Modern Language Review*, Lucy Munro dismissed that finding as 'over-dogmatic' on the basis of a single example of supposed audience-address in a play by Edward Sharpham, a very obscure writer.[13] The quarrel of those who want to believe that audience-address by characters engaged in the fictional action was a

conventional 'original practice' of late Renaissance drama is with the evidence. It is the evidence – the vast amount of unambiguous, conspicuous, varied and overwhelmingly one-sided evidence – that is uncompromising.

How is it possible that, in spite of conclusive evidence that soliloquies in late Renaissance drama represented self-addressed speeches as a matter of convention, countless post-Renaissance commentators have somehow convinced themselves and their readers that these speeches typically represented audience-address? The sad answer to that question is that, unlike most other fields of scholarship, our field is not yet a *discipline*. What provides discipline in most other fields is *evidence*. In those fields, as soon as a theory is proposed, scholars (usually including the proposer of the theory) conscientiously *test* it. They diligently search for evidence *both for and against* the theory. A theory is not accepted as valid, even by the theorist himself, unless and until it survives this rigorous testing process. If evidence is discovered that conflicts with the theory, the theory is discarded or altered to account for the evidence. If a systematic survey of representative evidence demonstrates the validity of a theory, the theory is accepted even if it is at odds with cherished beliefs. The professional training of scholars in those fields instils them with intellectual curiosity about whether their theories are valid or not. Graduate students are taught techniques of rigorously testing hypotheses. In the field of cultural history, however, many theories that have never been rigorously tested are nevertheless regularly repeated and routinely applied as if their validity were beyond question. Instead of the theory being tested against the evidence, the evidence is tested against the theory. If the evidence conflicts with a cherished belief, the evidence is dismissed or simply ignored. Theories that have been demonstrated to be invalid by systematic surveys of evidence are not

---

[13] Lucy Munro, *Modern Language Review*, 102 (2007), 210–11; p. 211.

winnowed out. Conversely, theories that have been validated by such surveys of evidence are dismissed or ignored if they conflict with cherished beliefs. In fields of study that are disciplines, these procedures are recognized as 'confirmation bias', and scholars are enjoined to avoid them. While many cultural historians are empiricists, there is at present no profession-wide obligation imposed on proponents of theories to test them rigorously against evidence.

READING IN THEIR PRESENT: EARLY READERS AND THE ORIGINS OF SHAKESPEARIAN APPROPRIATION

JEAN-CHRISTOPHE MAYER

The literary appropriation of Shakespeare's works is generally considered to have originated in the eighteenth century. With an unprecedented number of Shakespearian editions on the market, multiple heated debates between their editors, the undeniable rise of readers and the increasing use of Shakespeare to promote local and national political agendas, it is obvious that the Georgian era stands out in Shakespearian cultural history.[1] Nonetheless, this article will argue that significant readerly and literary appropriation practices began at the turn of the sixteenth century, at about the same time as the first appearance of Shakespeare's works in print.[2]

The most recent research suggests that not only has the place of Shakespeare's works on the early modern publishing market been largely underestimated but also that his first readers (along with his spectators) played a crucial role in the playwright's rise to fame. As Lukas Erne observed recently, 'Shakespeare's arrival in the book trade was sudden and massive.' Likewise, for John Jowett, it is clear that '[b]y 1600 Shakespeare had become the most regularly published dramatist'.[3] Moreover, scholars have gathered an indisputable wealth of evidence of early ownership and collecting of Shakespeare's works.[4] Thus, the already large early circulation of Shakespeare in print was to lead to an equally substantial number of attempts to come to terms with his works and dissect them in their printed form. In fact, to have a more balanced and more historically accurate view of the processes which led to the dissemination of his works throughout society, one should pay closer attention to the *origins* of

Shakespearian literary appropriation. While the number of copies of Shakespeare's works in circulation was a crucial factor, Shakespearian appropriation was also aided by other early modern cultural influences and practices.

Indeed, and as will become apparent in the opening section of this article, those who first bought, collected, marked up and extracted Shakespeare's printed works were encouraged to do so

---

[1] For a classic study on Shakespeare's cultural presence in the eighteenth century, see Michael Dobson, *The Making of the National Poet: Shakespeare, Adaptation and Authorship, 1660–1769* (Oxford, 1992).

[2] For an informed and balanced definition of the concept of appropriation in Shakespeare studies, see Douglas Lanier, *Shakespeare and Modern Popular Culture* (Oxford, 2002), p. 5.

[3] Lukas Erne, *Shakespeare and the Book Trade* (Cambridge, 2013), p. 18; John Jowett, *Shakespeare and Text* (Oxford, 2007), p. 8.

[4] See for instance, Erne, *Shakespeare and the Book Trade*, pp. 224–30; p. 214, or Alan Nelson, 'Shakespeare and the Bibliophiles: From the Earliest Years to 1616', in *Owners, Annotators, and the Signs of Reading*, ed. Robin Myers, Michael Harris and Giles Mandelbrote (London, 2005), pp. 49–73. Recent debates have revealed that reprint rates for plays may have been higher than we had previously thought. Thus, this could be an indication that playbooks were desirable items. See the series of position papers and responses in *Shakespeare Quarterly*: Alan B. Farmer and Zachary Lesser, 'The Popularity of Playbooks Revisited', *Shakespeare Quarterly*, 56 (2005): 1–32 (this was written partly in response to Peter Blayney's influential: 'The Publication of Playbooks', in *A New History of Early English Drama*, ed. John D. Cox and David Scott Kastan (New York, 1997), pp. 383–42); Alan B. Farmer and Zachary Lesser, 'Structures of Popularity in the Early Modern Book Trade', *Shakespeare Quarterly*, 56 (2005), 206–13; Peter Blayney responded in 'The Alleged Popularity of Playbooks', *Shakespeare Quarterly*, 56 (2005), 33–50.

because of the self-reflexive elements they found in play-texts. In turn, readers' engagement with the text could lead them to form judgements on the works and even to express their critical tastes. This again (as we shall see in a second section) goes against the grain of the commonly held opinion that literary 'taste' was really an eighteenth-century invention. Multiple self-reflexive elements show that dramatists, and in particular Shakespeare, knew why their contemporaries were reading and dissecting plays. Through an exploration and analysis of one of the most frequent early practices of literary appropriation – commonplacing – the next part of this article will explain how Shakespeare's works were so effectively and creatively dispersed throughout society. Furthermore – and again contrary to usual assumptions – the practice of commonplacing did not disappear at the outset of the eighteenth century but in fact survived and renewed itself during the Georgian era.[5] Finally, I shall attempt to dispel another myth – that Shakespeare's works did not play a meaningful part in readers' lives during the early modern era. The article will close on a number of short case studies which prove that some early modern individuals were developing their sense of self through their reading, annotating, transformation and use of Shakespeare's words. In sum, the aim of this article will be to draw more attention to early material reflecting intellectual and emotional engagements with the playwright's text, which, from the very beginning, set Shakespearian appropriation on a momentous and specific path.

DRAMA AND (LITERARY) NOTE TAKING

What transpires from the literary play-texts which have reached us is the fact that dramatists were well aware that their readers could mine their works. Ben Jonson's Sir Politic Would-be, in *Volpone*, famously collects '*notes / Drawne out of Play-bookes*', and, as will appear later, this was the case for a fair number of Jonson's contemporaries.[6] Professional writers such as Nashe, Chapman,

Webster and of course Jonson kept table-books, that is, portable notebooks. Yet it is interesting and paradoxical to observe that the very people who gleaned extracts from plays or other works sometimes ridiculed the frequent practice of commonplacing. Jonson's Sir John Daw describes Aristotle as 'a mere common place-fellow' in *Epicoene*. In his university play, Thomas Tomkins has the character of Anamnestes cast aspersions on 'studious Paper-wormes and leane Schollers' who 'furnish vp common place-bookes with other mens faults'.[7]

Shakespeare also stages note-takers in at least two of his plays and, for all we know, may himself have kept such notebooks.[8] Again, the tone is humorous and verges on social satire. Extracting was clearly a source of inspiration but also a touchy subject, in the sense that it posed the question of the originality of creative writing with acuteness. Professional writers and amateur readers could well be seen as upstart crows, beautifying themselves with others' feathers, to gloss Robert Greene.[9] In *Love's Labour's Lost*, the two pedants Sir Nathaniel (a curate) and Holofernes (a schoolmaster) are ridiculed for their abuse of Latin phrases and their obscure fragmented language. Sir Nathaniel has a 'table-book', which he brings out absurdly (5.1.16).[10] Moth remarks that 'They have been at a great feast of languages and stolen the scraps' and

---

5 See David Allan, *Commonplace Books and Reading in Georgian England* (Cambridge, 2010).

6 Ben Jonson, *Volpone, or The Fox* (London, 1607), sig. M2r, act 5, scene 4. STC 14783.

7 Ben Jonson, *Epicoene or The silent Woman. A Comoedie. Acted in the yeere 1609. By the Children of her Maiesties Revells*, in *The Workes of Benjamin Jonson* (London, 1616), p. 543, act 2, sc. 3. STC 14751. Thomas Tomkins, *Lingua, or the Combat of the Tongue, And the five Senses for Superiority. A pleasant Comoedie* (London, 1607), sig. E4v, act 3, scene 2. STC 24104.

8 See the section 'Appropriation as Displacement' below, p. 151, on commonplacing.

9 Robert Greene, *Greenes, Groats-worth of Witte, bought with a million of Repentance* (London, 1592), sig. F1v. STC 12245.

10 Some 'table-books' were erasable and the material gathered in them could then be transferred and classified in a commonplace book. See Peter Stallybrass, Roger Chartier, J. Franklin Mowery and Heather Wolfe, 'Hamlet's Tables

Costard is also under the impression that 'they have lived long on the alms-basket of words' (5.1.36–9). In the opening scene of the play Biron had already warned against the so-called credit gained from books: 'Small have continual plodders ever won, / Save base authority from others' books' (1.1.86–7). The King of Navarre's answer to him is ironical but deeply revealing of the fundamental paradox which I have already identified: 'How well he's read, to reason against reading!' (1.1.94). Writing some four decades later, Thomas Fuller voiced similar views quite wittily: 'I know some have a Common-place against Common-place books and yet perchance will privately make use of what publickly they declaim against.'[11]

Readers of *Hamlet* in quarto could likewise witness a character somewhat ambiguously taking notes on the unfolding of the drama. Hamlet kept a 'table book' and yet in the same speech (after hearing his dead father's injunction to remember him) he decides first that 'from the table' of his 'memory' he will 'wipe away all trivial fond records, / All saws of books [that is, all sententious sayings]' (1.5.98–100),[12] only to jot down a commonplace in his notebook a few moments later: 'My tables – meet it is I set it down / That one may smile and smile and be a villain' (1.5.108–9). One senses here a conflict between 'natural memory' (the brain) and 'artificial memory' (the notebook), a conflict which, in Elizabethan terms, ought to be a dialectic between two types of memory which should really work together, one making up for the failings of the other. Nonetheless, in Shakespeare, these two forms of memory are often set one against the other. In the case of Hamlet their conflict betrays a fundamental dilemma between the character's desire to be a self-sufficient autonomous individual and his recourse to a common method of making sense of the world through the formulation of philosophical topics or places.[13] This notion of conflict between the self and the world seems to me to be essential in understanding the processes through which early readers approached books, configured them and appropriated them.[14] I shall return to commonplacing later on in this essay to consider how

Shakespeare's works themselves became the focus of this practice.

APPROPRIATION AND TASTE: THE BEGINNING OF SHAKESPEARIAN LITERARY CRITICISM

As we have seen, Shakespeare's plays were self-consciously aware of the appropriation processes to which they could be submitted. These processes could in turn involve a measure of critical judgement – a fact that has either been overlooked or underestimated. I will not be concerned here with early printed responses to Shakespeare, which have been addressed by a number of scholars,[15] but with

---

and the Technologies of Writing in Renaissance England', *Shakespeare Quarterly*, 55 (2004), 379–419; p. 411.

[11] Thomas Fuller, *The Holy State* (1642), cited by Peter Beal, '"Notions in Garrison": The Seventeenth-Century Commonplace Book', in *New Ways of Looking at Old Texts, Papers of the Renaissance English Society, 1985–1991*, ed. W. Speed Hill (Binghamton, 1993), pp. 131–47; p. 139.

[12] This is a passage which caught the imagination of Abraham Wright, a seventeenth-century reader, who also makes a note of Hamlet's promise to 'wipe away all triuiall fond records' in his commonplace book, *Excerpta Quaedam Per A. W. Adolescentem* (British Library Add. MS. 22608, printed in part in James G. McManaway, *Studies in Shakespeare, Bibliography, and the Theater* (New York, 1969), p. 288).

[13] In Sonnet 122, the opposition is compounded by the acceptance of the 'tables' (or note books) as a 'gift', but also by the poet's insistence on natural memory: 'Thy gift, thy tables, are within my brain / Full charactered with lasting memory' (1–2). In *Cymbeline*, Giacomo also uses a table book to prepare his plot against Posthumus, but then he too suddenly stops writing and finds the inspiration in himself: 'No more. To What end? / Why should I write this down that's riveted, / Screwed to memory?' (2.2.42–4).

[14] Neil Rhodes writes helpfully of 'a conflict between uniqueness and commonness' in *Hamlet*, in *Shakespeare and the Origins of English* (Oxford, 2004), p. 157.

[15] See, for instance, C. M. Ingleby et al., *The Shakspere Allusion-Book: A Collection of Allusions to Shakspere from 1591 to 1700*, 2 vols. (London, 1909); Charles Witney, *Early Responses to Renaissance Drama* (Cambridge, 2006); Stanley Wells, 'Allusions to Shakespeare to 1642', in *Shakespeare Beyond Doubt: Evidence, Argument, Controversy*, ed. Paul Edmondson and Stanley Wells (Cambridge, 2013), pp. 73–87.

amateur readers. Contrary to what one might suppose, early readers could judge a play by evaluating the various qualities of its characters, its style and its plot. This last element, which, in modern terms, might translate as the 'pitch' of a script, was especially important. Church of England clergyman Abraham Wright (1611–1690) is famed for the notes he took on several plays around 1640. In a manuscript now preserved by the British Library, he commends *Othello* for meeting both literary and dramatic high standards in the following terms: 'A very good play, both for lines and plot, but especially ye plot'.[16] Wright himself had done some acting while at Oxford in the 1630s and he was the author of a play, *The Reformation*, which is now lost. He was a man who, in the words of Tiffany Stern, was 'also interested in how plays worked as performance texts for he is analysing them with an eye to the audience'.[17]

Conversely, a more literary-oriented person could find a good plot insufficient and the play a poor read, if it was devoid of other qualities. A late seventeenth-century reader of Shakespeare's fourth folio (1685) notes in his commonplace book that 'the plot [of *The Merry Wives of Windsor*] is good, but yᵉ characters & persons of yᵉ play so mean, yʳ witt & language & conversation so plain, that 'tis scarse worth reading'.[18] Others were even more radical and deemed some plays totally unfit for note taking. This is the opinion of another reader – possibly an early seventeenth-century clergyman – who writes in his commonplace book: 'The tragedy of King John. & Richard the 3ʳᵈ: Tamburlaine, vertumnus, ye 4 Prentises haue nought worthy excerping.'[19]

One of the earliest and lesser-known literary critical responses to Shakespeare's style can be found in William Scott's treatise, *The Model of Poesy*, which Gavin Alexander, in his recent edition of the treatise, has dated to the summer of 1599.[20] Born *c.*1571 and deceased in or around 1617, Scott had read Shakespeare's *Rape of Lucrece* (1594) and his *Richard II* (1595). Like many of the readers to whom I will be referring in this article, he only had access to the quarto editions of Shakespeare's plays, which, as I have pointed out in the introduction, seemed to be in wider circulation and use than was previously thought. Scott was a law student at the Inner Temple when he wrote this treatise, a scribal manuscript now in the British Library (Add. MS. 81083), which also comprises a partial translation of the poem of the Creation by the French Protestant poet Du Bartas, *La sepmaine*. Scott's *Model of Poesy* was dedicated to Sir Henry Lee and was also no doubt an attempt in part to demonstrate his talents and seek future employment or patronage. The title of the treatise recalls Sidney's *Defence of Poesy* (1595), but while Sidney viewed popular theatre generally as being too basic for his standards, Scott judged that both of Shakespeare's works were 'well-penned' (pp. 45 and 53). He does however find Shakespeare somewhat excessive at times, thus anticipating what neoclassically inspired authors would write about him. Much of the treatise has to do with appropriateness of style and rhetoric. Thus, it is not surprising to find *The Rape of Lucrece* commended for its fitting *imitatio*: 'it is as well showed in drawing the true picture of Lucretia, if it be truly drawn, as in imitating the conceit of her virtue and passion' (p. 12). *Lucrece* is mentioned again as a graceful instance of the heroic together with the

16 British Library MS. Add 22608, cited in Arthur C. Kirsch, 'A Caroline Commentary on the Drama', *Modern Philology*, 66 (1969), 256–61; p. 257. Plots were indeed of paramount importance for theatre people and all performance-oriented readers. See Stern, *Documents of Performance*, pp. 1–35. Some readers also kept manuscript plot lists. See, for proof that this was a lasting practice: Folger Library MS. S.a.9, Plots of plays and romances summarized by John Howe Chedworth, 4th Baron, *c.*1775.

17 Tiffany Stern, *Documents of Performance in Early Modern England* (Cambridge, 2009), p. 8.

18 Bodleian MS. Eng. Misc. c. 34, cited in G. Blakemore Evans, 'A Seventeenth-Century Reader of Shakespeare', *Review of English Studies*, 21.85 (1945), 271–9; p. 274.

19 Bodleian MS. Eng. Misc. D. 28, cited in Guillaume Coatalen, 'Shakespeare and other "Tragicall Discourses" in an Early Seventeenth-Century Commonplace Book from Oriel College, Oxford', *English Manuscript Studies, 1100–1700*, 13 (2007), 120–64; p. 137.

20 William Scott, *The Model of Poesy*, edited with an introduction and commentary by Gavin Alexander (Cambridge, 2013), p. xxviii. All references will be to this modern spelling edition and will be given in the text.

Mirror for Magistrates, *Rosamond* and *Peter's Denial* (p. 20). Further on in the treatise, in a passage dealing with the superabundance and excess of conceits and of *copia* in general, one passage of Shakespeare's narrative poem does not fare so well. Scott quotes the line 'The endless date of never-ending woe', describing it as 'a very idle, stuffed verse in that very well-penned poem of Lucrece her rape' (p. 53).

Scott, it is true, is mostly focused on poetry and rhetoric. Therefore, it is not entirely perplexing to find him quoting Shakespeare's *Richard II* to illustrate a point about the power of amplification. He cites John of Gaunt's speech in 1.3.227–32,

> Shorten my days thou canst with sullen sorrow,
> And pluck nights from me, but not lend a morrow;
> Thou canst help time to furrow me with age,
> But stop no wrinkle in his pilgrimage;
> Thy word is current with him for my death,
> But dead, thy kingdom cannot buy my breath.
>
> (p. 66)

For Scott, amplification is a means of impression on 'the mind of the reader': 'Sometime our amplification is by heaping our words and, as it were, piling one phrase upon another of the same sense to double and redouble our blows that, by varying and reiterating, may work into the mind of the reader' (p. 66). It is obvious that Scott sees Shakespeare's *Richard II* with the eyes of *a reader* and not those of a playgoer. In this way, Scott turns Shakespeare into a *literary* author, or indeed a poet, rather than a playwright – an interesting turn in the early modern literary criticism of Shakespeare and a feature which will reappear as we examine the work of other annotators in a later part of this article.

Yet, far from offering a dry rhetorical interpretation of Shakespeare's *Richard II*, Scott is also interested in how characters deal with their emotions and how this is conveyed to the reader: 'Sometime the person shall be so plunged into the passion of sorrow', writes Scott, 'that he will even forget his sorrow and seem to entertain his hardest fortune with dalliance and sport, as in the very well-penned tragedy of *Richard the Second* is expressed in the King and Queen whilst / They play the wantons with their woes' (p. 45). Like other annotators, Scott has mixed up two passages. In the play, Richard is talking to his cousin Aumerle. It is only in the next scene that the queen comes on stage to speak words that echo Richard's: 'What sport shall we devise here in this garden / To drive away the heavy thought of care?' (3.4.1–2). Coalescence and criss-crossing are frequent phenomena among annotators.

The most annotated First Folio in the world by an early reader (now part of the Meisei University Shakespeare Collection in Japan) has some interesting revelations to make in the field of literary criticism, even though its extensive annotations, covering every single page of the volume, have often been dismissed as merely repetitive of Shakespeare's text. In fact, a fair number of notes disclose some of the tastes of this early to mid seventeenth-century reader. For instance, the annotator is twice dismissive of the mechanicals in *A Midsummer Night's Dream* – he calls them 'doltish personages of a comedie' (TLN 282–347)[21] and notes a little later that they are involved in 'doltish preparation for a shew' (TLN 851–916). When Justice Shallow, Justice Silence and Falstaff meet for dinner in *2 Henry IV*, the reader writes in the margin 'foolish talke at the Iustices supper' (TLN 3021–79). However, he seems to find some of Shakespeare's epilogues more to his taste – he records in the margin 'Conceiued feares and losses happilie remoued Intricassies cleered and Ioyfullie ended' for *The Merchant of Venice*, or 'good epilogue' for *As You Like It* (TLN 2760–96, and Finis).

Other marginalia show him coming to terms with the aesthetic world of some of the plays. For him, the gist of Jaques's famous speech (2.7.139–43) is that 'The world is the stage of mens changeable fortunes' and that 'many parts [are] played by one man' (TLN 1097–159). In *The Winter's Tale*, in the scene where the statue of Hermione comes to life, the annotator is well aware that Shakespeare is theatrically playing with fire. Indeed, according to

---

[21] For a greater degree of precision, I will refer to Charlton Hinman's Through Line Numbers (TLN), which Akihiro Yamada also uses in his edition of the marginalia.

him, what the characters are witnessing are 'Things so Incredible as may make the beholders to beleeue they are done by witchcraft' (TLN 3254–319). However, it is probably the marginalia in *Henry V* that show him working hard to understand what artistic deal Shakespeare is trying to strike with his audience. Just before the Prologue, he writes this perceptive note in short hand: 'The auditours Imagination must supplie the strangenesse of Incredible representations of the stage' (TLN 19–36 and 61–85).[22] Confronted with the Chorus in Act 3 (which begins with 'Thus with imagined wing our swift scene flies / In motion of less celerity / Than that of thought . . . '), he appears less sure of himself. Nevertheless, still earnestly groping for meaning, he writes tentatively, 'Imagination must conceiue the suddane changes and actions of the stage' (TLN 1007–66).

While it is easy to dismiss these statements as primitive forms of literary criticism, they are, notwithstanding, extremely valuable traces of a living and feeling individual's meeting with the world of Shakespeare's plays and prove, like the other extracts we have examined, that the literary and critical reception of Shakespeare among amateur readers began earlier than we had perhaps imagined.

APPROPRIATION AS DISPLACEMENT: COLLECTING AND COMMONPLACING SHAKESPEARE

As Shakespeare's works gradually exceeded the bounds of the Elizabethan and Jacobean entertainment business to enter the sphere of printed literature, they began to stir critical interest and his words and lines became collectible items. This was indeed an era when people collected words and sentences in the way in which nowadays we would collect stamps in albums, or aggregate data from the World Wide Web. Commonplacing – that is the collecting and classifying of excerpts used to garnish one's own speech, or writing with other people's thoughts and words – was a widespread practice stemming in great part from classical education, where much was based on *imitatio* and the gleaning of wisdom from classical writers.

With the rise in prestige of vernacular literature, some early commentators began to regard Shakespeare as the exemplar of English writers and as a font of wisdom and of *sententiae*. In his famous 1668 essay *Of dramatick poesie*, John Dryden reported that John Hales, a very distinguished Greek scholar, had declared, 'That there was no subject of which any Poet ever writ, but he would produce it much better treated of in *Shakespeare*.'[23] The word 'subject' recalls the Aristotelian 'topic' or the *loci communes* of ancient rhetoric. Such arguments on the nature of Shakespeare's genius would of course help establish him as a national author, one who could shake off the yoke of classical tradition. Likewise, in the preface to his tragedy *The Loyal General* (published in 1680), Nahum Tate wrote to Edward Tayler, 'I cannot forget the strong desire I have heard you express to see the Common Places of our Shakespear, compar'd with the most famous of the Ancients.' Tate also mentioned John Hales, the Greek scholar, who, according to him, had asserted, 'That since the time of Orpheus and the Oldest Poets, no Common Place has been touch'd upon, where our Author [Shakespeare] has not perform'd as well.'[24] The idea that Shakespeare's writing is built around a unique network of commonplaces, that it relies upon a personal cluster of *topoi*, lives on today.

---

22 After reading Shakespeare's fourth folio (1685), one late seventeenth-century reader did not seem to be too disconcerted either by Shakespeare's appeal to the imagination. In his notes on *Much Ado About Nothing*, he wrote in his commonplace book that 'I see no reason why an action of 5 days may not be represented in 2 hours as well as an action of one in ye same time. or why we may not as well conceive every act to take up a day as 2 hours. since neither can be done without ye Help of an imagination willing & consenting to be cheated & deceived' (Bodleian MS. Eng. Misc. c. 34, cited in Blakemore Evans, 'A Seventeenth-Century Reader of Shakespeare', p. 274).

23 This was also an attack on Ben Jonson's art. John Dryden, *Of dramatick poesie* (London, 1668), p. 48. Wing D2327.

24 Nahum Tate, *The loyal general a tragedy: acted at the Duke's* (London, 1680), sig. A4r. Wing T193. See also Rhodes, *Shakespeare and the Origins of English*, pp. 172–3.

Not so long ago, the distinguished critic Emrys Jones observed that 'It is often as if, at some deep level of his mind, Shakespeare thought and felt in quotations.'[25] The recent discovery of a dictionary, John Baret's 1580 *Alvearie*, with notes supposedly written in Shakespeare's hand, has reawakened the dream that there may have been a commonplace book composed by Shakespeare.[26]

It is true that Shakespeare could write with apparent ease in this vein but, as we have already noted, at times even he appears to distance himself from tradition. For instance, part of the humour attached to the character of Polonius comes from his use and abuse of standard wisdom. It is no coincidence, for that matter, that an astute early seventeenth-century reader by the name of Edward Pudsey, who had undoubtedly been trained in his school years to recognize commonplaces and *sententiae*, should seemingly take Polonius's sayings at face value and wish to include them in his commonplace book.[27] Pudsey copied them almost word for word, often simply by transforming the verse into prose and getting rid of speech prefixes and oral structures. Thus Portia's lines in Act 5, scene 1 (lines 107–8) of *The Merchant of Venice* are commonplaced under the title 'Season' and read simply as 'many things by season seasond are to their right prais and true perfection' (p. 5). Pudsey proceeds in a similar fashion with some of the material he lifts from *Titus Andronicus*: to lend a universal, commonplace value to Shakespeare's lines he turns questions into direct style, cuts the verse line and adds 'If' at the beginning of some of the lines (p. 8). Moreover, he had a sharp eye for rhetorical figures as testified for instance by his use of the word 'Simile' to classify a passage from *The Merchant of Venice* (p. 6).

Nevertheless, decontextualizing and turning dramatic style into prose are not systematic features of commonplacing readers. In *Merchant* Pudsey retains Portia's speech prefix (p. 3),[28] which illustrates the fact that he is not constantly in search of the universal and the transferable, but that he also takes an interest in Shakespeare's characters. His notes on *Much Ado About Nothing* reveal that,

far from discarding dialogue as being uninteresting or difficult to reconfigure, he extracts it, condensing this dialogue considerably (p. 42), and shows a visible interest in repartee (p. 46).

Similarly, James Whitehall had a curiosity for characters, context and oral dialogue. His miscellany, now kept by the William Salt Library in Stafford (Hand Morgan Collection 308/40), contains Shakespeare extracts which predate the

[25] Emrys Jones, *The Origins of Shakespeare* (Oxford, 1977), p.21.
[26] That these notes are actually by Shakespeare remains highly uncertain. John Baret, *An aluearie or quadruple dictionarie, containing foure sundrie tongues: namelie, English, Latine, Greeke, and French. Newlie enriched with varietie of wordes, phrases, prouerbs, and diuers lightsome obseruations of grammar. By the tables you may contrariwise finde out the most necessarie wordes placed after the alphabet, whatsoeuer are to be found in anie other dictionarie: which tables also seruing for lexicons, to lead the learner vnto the English of such hard wordes as are often read in authors, being faithfullie examined, are truelie numbered. Verie profitable for such as be desirous of anie of those languages* (London, 1580), STC 1411. For more information on this specific copy, access: http://shakespearesbeehive.com/.
[27] The *Hamlet* extracts appear on both sides of one of four leaves now detached from a miscellany compiled by Edward Pudsey (1573–1613). They date from the 1600s and these leaves (together with extracts from *Richard II, Richard III, Othello, Much Ado About Nothing* and parts of *Romeo and Juliet*) were separated from the overall MS. (Bodleian MS. Eng. Poet. d. 3) and are now preserved by the Shakespeare Birthplace Trust Record Office, shelfmark ER 82. Most of these extracts (apart from the *Othello* excerpts) were reproduced (not always accurately) in Richard Savage's *Shakespearean Extracts from 'Edward Pudsey's Booke'* (Stratford-upon-Avon: John Smith, 1888). The passage cited here is from pp. 57–9 of Savage's edition. For readers' ease of reference, further citations will refer to this edition and the page numbers will be given in the text. Savage's omissions or errors will, however, be indicated in the notes. Edward Pudsey's commonplace book is one of the most extensive of the period. Pudsey seems to have cared about its preservation as much as he cared about his books. In his will drawn up in 1609 and proved in 1613, he wrote this injunction to his executors concerning his son Edward, 'that all my books bee safe kept for him, especially my note books' (cited by Juliet Mary Gowan in 'An Edition of Edward Pudsey's *Commonplace Book* (c. 1600–1615) from the Manuscript in the Bodleian Library' (M. Phil., University of London, 1967), p. 18). See also Edward Pudsey's entry in the *ODNB*.
[28] Savage omits this prefix in his transcription.

publication of the First Folio.[29] For example, Whitehall lifted a line from Act 5, scene 3 of *Richard II*, 'feare & not love begets his penitence' adding in brackets 'q^dold Yorke to the kinge against his sonne Aumerle' (fo. 97r). On folio 160r of his notebook, Whitehall also began what was to become a long section entitled 'Joci', where he collected amusing phrases and jokes, as well as aphorisms. Among these are to be found plots or summaries of some of Chaucer's *Canterbury Tales*.[30] A feature of many of these extracts and stories is that they involve imaginary dialogue, frequently ending with the expressions 'quoth he', 'quoth she', thus pointing to the fact that Shakespeare's extractors also mingled the playwright's lines with other stories and phrases belonging to that semi-oral culture of circulating aphorisms, proverbs, unusual sentences, paradoxes and entertaining narratives.

Other early readers went even further by reconfiguring the printed text of the plays in ways that would re-inject life into Shakespeare's language – these were creative transformations which went well beyond commonplacing. In his notes on *The Merchant of Venice* William How, a mid-seventeenth-century transcriber, transforms one of Gobbo's lines ('He hath a great infection, sir, as one would say, to serve' (2.2.119–20)) into 'He has an infection to serue you' (fo. 7), thus lending more impact and ultimately more life to the line (Folger MS. V.a.87). Such transformations are also ways in which literature can be potentially recirculated into more common everyday vernacular language. Even when Shakespeare is seemingly at his best in his use of a so-called 'natural style', William How sometimes manages to produce a snappier, more dynamic version. Thus, Nim's lines in *Henry V* ('I dare not fight, but I will wink and hold out mine iron. It is a simple one, but what though? It will toast cheese' (2.1.6–8)) are rephrased and reduced to a single and more dynamic expression: 'Heres a sword will serue to tost cheese on' (fo. 7). Similarly, in his notes on *Much Ado About Nothing* Edward Pudsey turns Claudio's indirect comment on Benedick ('And never could maintain his part, but in the force of his will' (1.1.221–22)) into a

direct address to someone: 'Yo^w cannot maintayne y^r argum^t but in ye force of yor will' (p. 35), a phrase which again carries more pith and can be re-injected into real-life situations.

OWNING AND DISOWNING SHAKESPEARE – FINDING THE SELF IN SHAKESPEARE

This brings us to consider how early modern individuals' everyday aspirations influenced their reading and how literature in turn played a concrete role in their lives. In the winter of 1663, John Ward, vicar of Stratford-upon-Avon, wrote the following entry in his diary: 'Remember to peruse Shakespears plays and bee versd in *them that* I may not bee ignorant in *that* matter:' (Folger MS V.a.292, fo. 140r). Shakespeare was a stone in the edifice of knowledge that Ward was trying to build for himself. One could also detect a fear of ignorance in this statement ('that I may not be ignorant') which may be related not only to the need for self-improvement but also to preoccupations linked to social standing. In modern terms, Ward was conscious of the social and cultural capital that could be gained by reading the 'right' authors.

This preoccupation with social standing and 'rank' is common among many early modern individuals interested in Shakespeare. Famous for the notes he took in his journals on *Macbeth*, *Cymbeline*, *The Winter's Tale* and possibly *Woodstock*, after allegedly seeing them on stage *c.*1611, London astrologer and physician Simon Forman also wrote an autobiography in them, adding drawings of his coat of arms and several versions of his genealogy, before turning his own life into a literary romance: 'But we will leave them all and speak

---

[29] The first set of Shakespeare extracts was probably written around 1609 (cf. 1609 date fo. 97v), the second set possibly around 1611 (cf. fo. 164r).

[30] *The Wife of Bath's Tale, The Merchant's Tale, The Reeve's Tale, The Miller's Tale* [end of the story], *The Friar's Tale* (fo. 173v).

of the wonderful life of the said Simon', added Forman unabashedly.[31]

Similarly, James Whitehall, who copied extracts from Shakespeare's *Richard II* (fos. 97r-v), *The Merchant of Venice* (fos. 98r-v) and *1 Henry IV* (fos. 176v-178r), vented his frustration in his miscellany at not getting promotion as an academic at Christ Church, Oxford, despite his repeated attempts (e.g. fo. 50v, fo. 55v).[32] Like Forman, he begins a chronology of his life and his ancestors (fo. 65v) and various drawings of his coat of arms appear on the front and back inside covers of his notebook, as well as in the manuscript itself, where Whitehall explains the origins of the arms (fo. 71r) and later dwells on how his surname should be spelt ('howe our name hath been written', fo. 73). It is obvious that through his own writings and those of others (including Shakespeare) Whitehall had set out on a quest for personal identity.

His notebook can at times appear to be a bizarre mix. Indeed, the large literary section in it is preceded by some 'observ[ations]: for dyet' (fo. 60r), in which he records his illnesses and the physical and mental effects of various foods on him. Yet one should look beyond the oddity to consider that a miscellany is precisely a reflection of the multifariousness of existence and sometimes of the difficulty in finding the right recipes for living.

Another miscellany will further illustrate this point. Bound in vellum wrappers from a twelfth-century theological manuscript, the Huntington Library's Danby Manuscript (HM 60413) is a miscellany which was inscribed and added to by members of the Danby family of Kirby Knowle, North Yorkshire *c.*1570-*c.*1625. The volume contains two quotations from Shakespeare's *Othello*, which are mixed with remedies, household hints, legal forms, land rental, as well as poems, epigrams and *sententiae*. In a volume where medical remedies and recipes – including recipes for making red wax, ink, or 'to make the face fayre' (fo. 39) – are so prominent, the *Othello* quotations may appear to be slightly at odds at first glance. Yet they too are remedies of sorts.

Lifted from the opening scene of *Othello*, the first extract begins just after Iago voices his dissatisfaction with Othello in front of Roderigo, concluding precisely with these words: 'Why, there's no remedy. 'Tis the curse of service' (1.1.34). The remedy offered by Iago no doubt struck the reader. Stripped of its context and of its speech prefix, the passage in question can be construed as a general consolation in such situations: 'O sir content you, / I follow him to serve my turne upon him, / wee cannot be all masters, nor all masters, / Cannot be truly followed . . .' (fo. 80).[33] Similarly, the second extract can be seen as a recipe for living a better and more contented life. Also divested of its context and speech prefix, the passage originally spoken by the Duke in 1.3.198–208 is partly cut and copied under the first quotation. This time the word 'remedy' actually appears, thus confirming the status of the two extracts in the miscellany:

> When remedyes are past, the greifes are ended
> by seeinge the worst, which late on hopes depended
> to mourne a mischeife that is past & gone
> is the next way to draw more myscheife on . . .
>
> (fo.80)

These extracts are proof that literature, and Shakespeare in particular, did serve a purpose in people's lives and that the playwright's first readers were well aware of it. As Margaret Cavendish's 'young Lady' would point out later in the century, play reading was conducive to a better understanding of human nature: 'Pray give me Play-Books, or Mathematical ones; the first, said she, discovers and expresses the Humours and Manners of Men, by which I shall

---

[31] Cited in A. L. Rowse, *Simon Forman: Sex and Society in Shakespeare's Age* (London, 1974), p. 268. For a more recent account of Forman's life and work, see Barbara Howard Traister, *The Notorious Astrological Physician of London: Works and Days of Simon Forman* (Chicago and London, 2001).

[32] Incidentally, a great number of literary anthologies and manuscripts originated at Christ Church, Oxford, especially during the first half of the seventeenth century. The college encouraged literary composition. See, especially, Arthur F. Marotti, *Manuscript, Print, and the English Renaissance Lyric* (Ithaca and London, 1995), p. 32.

[33] The whole extract corresponds to 1.1.41–55 in the modern Oxford edition.

know my self and others the better, and in shorter time than Experience can teach me.'[34]

If we return to Whitehall's miscellany to look at the nature of many of the extracts in the self-styled literary section of his notebook, we notice a distinct interest in passages dealing with the subject of love. The section begins with Sidney's *Arcadia* which Whitehall appears to have read in its 1598 edition. This was a work of some influence on him, since no fewer than seventeen pages are devoted to it in his notebook (fos. 88r to 95r and 98r). Many of the passages copied concern love, like those he lifted from John Marston's *The Dutch Courtesan*, when Freewill speaks these romantic words to Beatrice in Act 2, scene 1 of the play: 'So could I live in desert most vnknowd, / your selfe to mee inough were populous' (fo. 95r). Revealingly, Whitehall has added in the bottom margin this indication for future reference and use: 'for soliciting'.[35]

Whitehall's choice of Shakespearian passages indicates that he had a preference for Shakespeare the romantic poet rather than for Shakespeare the tragedian. This is partly the image that the playwright has in popular culture at the present time and it is interesting to witness its early development, all the more so as the plays chosen by Whitehall, *The Merchant of Venice* and *Richard II*, do not stand out as being particularly romantic, at least to our eyes. Arthur Marotti has also noted a natural tendency in collectors of verse to be interested in the subject of love.[36] They were often young (Whitehall was in his early thirties) and had received a university education.

In *The Merchant of Venice* Whitehall focused on passages spoken respectively by Portia and Bassanio in Act 3, scene 2:

> you have devided mee
> one halfe is yours: *the* other halfe yours,
> mine owne I would say : but if mine then yours
> and so all is yours. O these naughty times
> put barrs betweene the owners & their rightes (fo. 98r)

> you haue bereft mee of all wordes,
> : onely my bloud speakes to you in my vaines (fo. 98v)

In *Richard II*, the romantic effect of the passages is mainly achieved through the extraction and partial decontextualization, as the lines were of course spoken in sad or rather tragic contexts. Whitehall has transcribed (with a number of variations from the text of the 1597 Quarto edition)[37] the parting words of Richard and his queen, as she is about to leave for France in Act 5, scene 1 of the play:

> The*n* count *the* miles with sighes
> Come, come, in wooing my sorrowe lets be breiff
> since winding it there is such length of greif
> one kisse shall stop our mouthes, ^wiche at last part^
>   and dumbly part
> [added in other ink: 'thus let mee take your heart.']
>   Thus give I mine & thus I take thy heart.
> Queene.   Give mee mine owne againe twere no
>   good part
> to take on mee to keepe & kill thy heart
> Wee make grief ^woe^ wanton with this fond delay;
> Once more adue [adieu], *the* rest let sorrowe say.
>   (fo. 97)[38]

The *Richard II* extracts end with a passage taken from a slightly less dramatic scene (5.3) where the Duchess of York begs Henry IV to forgive her son Aumerle's potential treason:

> Oh king beleeve not this hardhearted man
> Love loveing not it selfe none other can.. qd duchess
>   (fo. 97v)

Intriguingly, the *Richard II* excerpts are immediately followed by lines of love poetry which are dated 1609 and may well be by Whitehall. There is

---

[34] Margaret Cavendish, *Natures picture drawn by fancies pencil to the life being several feigned stories, comical, tragical, tragi-comical, poetical, romantical, philosophical, historical, and moral: some in verse, some in prose, some mixt, and some by dialogues* (London, 1671), p. 408. Wing N856.

[35] The Marston extracts outnumber the Shakespearian passages in Whitehall's diary. This may have been because Marston's fashionable satirical vein made him more collectible as an author.

[36] Marotti, *Manuscript, Print, and the English Renaissance Lyric*, p. 75.

[37] All the quarto editions after this one (STC 22307) have 'doubly part' instead of Q1's 'dumbly part'.

[38] These last two lines are actually spoken by King Richard.

reason to believe that Shakespeare the love poet may have inspired him. Indeed, the following broken lines seem to indicate some attempt at improvising rather than copying:

> I ~~loved~~ you
> you had my heart} before I was aware.

Then the hesitant composition is turned into:

> you stole my heart before I was aware

However modest, these lines demonstrate that our early seventeenth-century Oxford academic had adopted the practices of other extractors who transformed Shakespeare's text and wrote varieties of 'answer poems'.[39] More importantly, Whitehall was not only finding inspiration through Shakespeare and other authors, but also finding his *own* words through literature. His notebook, which was pocket-sized, no doubt accompanied him on part of his journey through life, helping him to sketch what we might call a scribal identity waiting to be translated, as the case might be, into words and action.

CONCLUSION

Marking and extracting – poaching on Shakespeare's lands – classifying his language and reworking it are activities that triggered endless textual circles and involved constant changes of spheres: Shakespeare's words journeyed from the labile sphere of the manuscript to the communal and ephemeral world of the performance text, to the partial fixity of the printed book (thus entering the world of literature), before going on another circle. Indeed, readers extracted the publicly printed text into their semi-private manuscripts in order to transform and reuse Shakespeare's language on other spoken and public occasions, or they shared it with their relatives and friends, sometimes creating select social circles, where manuscript circulation fostered a sense of community. They could also glean extracts whose purpose was to answer pressing personal questions.

In this way, appropriation was not solely a way of 'stealing' another person's words. In its early modern form, it was an activity that was driven both socially and existentially. Appropriation was a way for readers to learn the words of a common language, the language of a certain 'class' of citizens or the language of society at large. Readers were perfecting a social or professional rhetoric, constructing the self and the self's relation to others and in doing so, they began, consciously or unconsciously, to set the standards of taste and literary aesthetics.

So why were Shakespeare's works marked out and extracted? Such practices were of course far from being limited to Shakespeare or to dramatists in general (the manuscript circulation of John Donne's work throughout society being a case in point).[40] However, in Shakespeare's case, explanatory factors include of course the amount of cultural capital which could be gained by reading the works of an author who, as the First Folio and some of the preceding quartos make abundantly clear, was associated through his company not only with prestigious and influential aristocratic and royal circles but also with so many other poets and dramatists – those whom Heminges and Condell call his 'friends' in their famous address 'To the great Variety of Readers'. Another hypothesis would be one to which we have already alluded – Shakespeare's talent for what Tiffany Stern has called 'play patching', that is, his gift not only for plotting but also for offering the linguistic nectar sought after by readers, like the bees in Erasmus's well-known parable on reading. After all, was he not called by his contemporary Francis Meres, in a book that appeared during his lifetime, a 'Honie tong'd' and 'mellifluous' writer producing 'sugared' lines? The upstart crow, who, like other writers, naturally beautified himself with others' feathers, knew how to give back too. If, as Lukas Erne has argued, Shakespeare 'anticipated a readership' for his

---

[39] Answer poems were relatively frequent in anthologies and miscellanies (Marotti, *Manuscript, Print, and the English Renaissance Lyric*, p. 160).

[40] See Marotti, *Manuscript, Print, and the English Renaissance Lyric*, p. 147 and his *John Donne: Coterie Poet* (Madison, NJ, 1986).

plays,[41] he may have realized that his success was also tied to the potential ease with which readers, playgoers and authors like Meres, would be able to detach, alter and circulate his words in a commonplace book culture that would in fact continue right up to the end of the eighteenth century. Thus, Shakespeare's originality and ability to be absorbed and appropriated lies, at least in part, in the potential for replication of his words, a replication which, as we have seen, was an obvious source of pleasure but which could also become a transformative textual and existential experience.

---

[41] Erne, *Shakespeare and the Book Trade*, p. 123.

SHAKESPEARE OUT OF TIME (OR, HUGO TAKES DICTATION FROM THE BEYOND)

RUTH MORSE

If many of us began with a desire to listen to the dead, few of us have attempted it through psychical research. Even fewer are likely to be acquainted with those who achieved their desire, and fewer still with those who were great French poets, novelists, dramatists and political campaigners. This article can thus only be about Victor Hugo's engagement with Shakespeare, an author of great importance to him, not least as legitimation for his own work. Hugo had discovered *King John*, and therefore Shakespeare, during the festivities for the coronation of Charles X, by listening to Charles Nodier and his friends reading aloud. At this point the young Hugo was a Royalist Catholic whose Odes supported the restored Bourbon monarchy (1824). He was soon the acknowledged leader of a group of mainly young writers who recognized him as the leader of the Romantic movement, which came late to France. Stimulated, like Berlioz, by a touring Shakespeare company who played set scenes in English, Hugo was inspired to write his closet drama, *Cromwell* (1827).

The programmatic introduction to Hugo's play invoked the hitherto often despised name 'Shakespeare' as a weapon against the moribund post-classical French theatres, with their narrow repertoire, archaic speaking style and closed caste of actors. French Romanticism is often dated from the first night of Hugo's melodrama, *Hernani* (1830), which caused rioting in the theatre (and became one of Verdi's transformations of Hugo). Not much later, having moved steadily left, Hugo became a politician who spoke in support of freedom of thought and expression and against the death penalty. He was an early and unusual architectural preservationist: when Notre Dame Cathedral was practically derelict Hugo's romantic and gothic novel, *Notre Dame de Paris: 1482* (1831), initiated the movement to protect and preserve its medieval architecture as well as the medieval street plan around it. In 1848 he was a good Parliamentarian, on the side of law and order; by 1851, when Paris resisted Napoleon III's coup d'état, he had to hide, then flee, and was among the first to be proscribed. In his – and his sons' – almost twenty-year exile in the Channel Islands he reinvented himself as a post-romantic almost-surrealist; he fought best as a writer, railing against the elite's ignorant dismissal of its impoverished masses and creating in fiction what he had failed to achieve in fact. His polemical resistance began with the outraged satirical pamphlet, *Napoléon le Petit* (1852, banned) and, ten years later, finally left *Les Misérables* (1862) as his fictional testimonial to the terrible slaughters at the barricades not of 1851 but the July Revolution of 1832, those 'trois glorieuses' days which deposed the last Bourbon king in favour of the moderate Louis Philippe. All Hugo's life he rewrote his own history into the history of France and the world's, i.e. Europe's, literature, and his long fight to defend Shakespeare always defended his own redesign of French poetry, fiction and the theatre.

Like Dickens, but much longer lived, Hugo was a tough, sexy genius, whose self-representation as a loving father (and later grandfather) erased the domestic tyrant who kept his family tied to his purse strings, who prevented his sons from gaining independence through education or placement in a profession and who maintained a devoted mistress who acted as his secretary and companion for fifty years. In a world which still believed that the great writer was necessarily a good man, a sage and a model to be emulated, his parallel life was scrupulously hidden by his admirers for decades. So, too, his executors would suppress his *spiritism*, the séances in Jersey which are my main subject. The material that follows, though known to many French scholars and admirers of Hugo, has not called itself to the attention of Shakespearians either in France or elsewhere.

I. THE HUGO CIRCLE IN JERSEY

In September 1853, Hugo and his family, at the suggestion of a visiting friend and fellow writer, Mme de Girardin, started table tapping, not to be confused with 'tipping'. The fashion for both was American and had recently taken off in Paris as a kind of society game – *fluidomanie*, Daumier called it; our familiar ouija board was almost forty years in the future. Not everyone was caught up in the fad: many of the politically committed found the fashion a distraction from more urgent subjects, and an initially sceptical Hugo distanced himself from what was going on in Marine Terrace. For three days nothing happened; their enthusiastic visitor thought this an equipment failure, and searched the shops to find a *guéridon parleur*, a small round three-legged table, which they placed on a larger square table so they could sit comfortably while two of them each held a leg.[1] Still nothing happened.

Jersey was full of exiles and spies; inside Marine Terrace there were servants whose presence required their employers' discretion. All the Hugo family were gathered in the large house just beyond St Hélier: Victor-Marie and his wife, Adèle; their sons, Charles and Victor (later François-Victor to distinguish himself from his father), and their surviving daughter, Adèle (all in their twenties), and their great friend Auguste Vacquerie. Vacquerie was not only one of Hugo's admirers and a political comrade of Hugo's sons, but also the brother of Hugo's deceased son-in-law, Charles Vacquerie. At the beginning of an exile of uncertain extent,

Hugo was writing what became *Les Chatiments*; young Victor was preparing the ground-work for his great edition and translation of Shakespeare; Charles was working towards his own ambitions as a novelist.[2] The children had learned English, but Hugo himself had none when he arrived in Jersey, and when he left Guernsey after all those years of banishment he had not much more, having lived entirely in French, in the bosom of his family and the bosoms of his French mistresses, of whom the most important, Juliette Drouet, was established in a house not far away. She was an important copiest, not only for Hugo, but for Charles as well. She was, of course, never present in Marine Terrace, the fiction of her non-existence being required by *les convenances*. This lightning sketch of the *dramatis personae* matters, because of the provenances of the transcripts of the séances, taken from dictation at the time or copied subsequently by various of these actors.

Hugo's post mortem reputation was carefully managed by his acolytes, and table-tapping conversations with spirits from the Beyond were not obviously calculated to enhance it. His executors suppressed many things about Hugo, not least his astonishing libido. So, too, the executors suppressed Adèle's mental illness, which resembled the psychosis of her uncle, Hugo's brother, Eugène – thus evading the revelation of hereditary madness in the family. It may be worth recalling that when

---

[1] Graham Robb, *Victor Hugo* (London, 1997) p. 331. Subsequent references will be by author's name in brackets in the text. The short section on the séances is to be found on pp. 330–41; see especially p. 339 for the explanation of the strangely titled and otherwise incomprehensible 'Ce Que Dit la Bouche de l'ombre' ('What the Mouth of Darkness says'), which was the result of that Spirit's private communication to Hugo. See also Jean Hovasse, *Victor Hugo*, 2 vols. (Paris, 2001, 2008). Bracketed references are to the second volume. Hovasse's engagement with the séances is in 2.2 'Au Bord de l'infini'; he throws light on some of the obscurities of Hugo's *William Shakespeare* (1864).

[2] See my 'Not Shakespeare: François-Victor Hugo and the limits of cultural catalysis', in *Shakespeare Survey* 64 (Cambridge, 2011): pp. 220–30 and my chapter on father and son in *Great Shakespeareans*, vol. 14 *(Hugo, Pasternak, Césaire, Brecht)*, ed. Ruth Morse (London, 2013).

André Gide was asked who was the greatest poet of the nineteenth century he replied, 'Victor Hugo, hélas'. Cocteau's view, by contrast, was that 'Victor Hugo était un fou qui se prenait pour Victor Hugo' (a madman who thought he was Victor Hugo).

After the silence of the first three days, something did indeed happen, on 11 September 1853, the anniversary of the day on which Hugo (then on annual holiday with Juliette Drouet) had by chance seen in a provincial paper news of the boating accident which drowned his daughter, Léopoldine Hugo Vaquérie, and her husband. The first Spirit to address the gathered mortals announced itself as 'fille' [daughter].[3] Auguste Vaquerie and Charles Hugo – the bereaved brothers – were each holding one of the table legs. Knock by knock, the spirit, Léopoldine, responded to their questions that she was happy, in the Light, and that to join her they must love. This was the opening of the floodgates, whose keeper that night, and subsequently, was Charles Hugo. Messages from a beloved dead child, spouse or sibling has long been a spiritualist cliché: the Summoned come with comfort, in a 'now' for the living that is timeless in the Beyond. Léopoldine could not restore the break, but her spirit could confirm her peace. *Cui bono?* Graham Robb dismisses the likelihood that anyone would impersonate a dead child as a practical joke, but practical jokes are often acts of aggression against the oppressor. Though I am not sure how far what started as a comforting (perhaps) deception may have run out of control, the evidence suggests that Charles, supposedly the most receptive of them, was for once in his life the driving force. Rumours in the house of seeing a headless snooper nosing about in Hugo's papers may have been Charles, doing research for yet another evening of surprises. The participants recorded who was present, who held a leg, took dictation, asked the questions, left the room. The participants were sometimes astonished when Charles returned to the Table after apparently being upstairs in his room, only to pick up the middle of a conversation he could not have heard. But the word 'eavesdropping' is relevant here and there is no proof that Charles

had retreated out of earshot. His brother, François-Victor, would have nothing to do with the supernatural amusements and regularly left the house when they took place. Charles retained his post of chief medium, even when they proposed to speed things up with a spinning needle stuck in an alphabetical card. Apparently the Table – always cranky – refused. Of course 'it' did. For eighteen months the Table was the evening activity, often lasting all night.

In the Hugo dining room appeared – or, at least, knocked – the spirits of Torquemada and Machiavelli, before André Chénier came to discuss their craft and sullen art. The evident pleasure of those exchanges was simpler, and more polite, than some of the obstreperous and impatient Beings, including Androcles' Lion and Balaam's Ass, the Shadow of the Tomb, and a series of abstract ideas who spoke without recourse to ectoplasm. After a few cursory excursions into post mortem existence, what the group of exiled writers wanted was to discuss writing. There were also arguments about religious belief and belief in what was happening which spilled into family correspondence and therefore survive. Mme Hugo maintained that the Spirits were proof of the existence of God and the importance of Christianity; the spirits retaliated by telling her to leave the room. There is no

---

[3] All translations are mine. Massin's edition (see n.6) is a composite of numerous copies of the original transcripts, some commented, some not. So, while he labels each source, he does not explain his preferences; for the first night we have Vaquerie's annotated copy of the transcripts and his memories, published in his *Miettes de l'histoire* (Paris, 1863) as well as an extract from Adèle Hugo's *Journal de l'exil*, ed. Frances Vernor Guille, 4 vols. (Paris, 1968–2002). Guille recounts the extraordinary rediscovery of some 4,000 pages left behind in Hauteville House, Guernsey, to which the Hugos moved when expelled from Jersey – and bought by an English collector twenty years after Hugo's death and the family's departure. All the editors correct and normalize spelling. Hovasse assembles several witnesses and gives their various testimonies (Hovasse, pp. 206–22). The Hugo Research Centre of Université Paris-Diderot (Sorbonne-Paris-Cité) maintains a useful website: http://groupugo.div.jussieu.fr/Recherches_indexees/Querygroupugo.aspx.

evidence that Hugo knew Blake, but the shared interest in a post-Christian religion with a difference made itself apparent. There were, additionally, 'automatic' drawings (Hovasse II.16, 263ff).

Among its other functions, the Table offered a writers' discussion group ready to analyse draft work. Hugo's own desire was proof of the essential, abstract, coterminous genius of writers who participate in a single creative spirit of which he was the current, and culminating, avatar. One might call this an answer to essentialism which turns Great Truths into a Cloud of Knowing. Hugo himself kept journals, wrote letters, worked on his drafts. His daughter's *Journal de l'exil* reports on her father's doings and sayings, as did other family members.[4] Visiting friends in the Hugo circle were involved in regular contact with their connections in Paris and their letters contain hints of what was happening. For example, the two men who became Hugo's executors were close friends: Vacquerie corresponded with Paul Meurice, still at liberty in Paris. This does not mean that the transmission of the primary sources is straightforward. In Vacquerie's memoir, *Les Miettes de l'histoire*, he rewrites some of the paranormal experiences at a distance, as if describing things he had heard about rather than experienced. The existence of the transcripts was known – indeed, copies were made – but the four original notebooks were kept hidden. Victor Hugo, Théophile Guérin and Auguste Vacquerie had been frequent secretaries who recorded what the spirits dictated. Juliette Drouet made fair copies of the *Livre des Tables* ('Table' Book) held by Hugo, and Hugo himself rewrote the experience in his *William Shakespeare* as if he, too, had known of the séances only at second hand; he did not leave the notebooks to the Bibliothèque nationale with his other papers, and it was only after 1897 that Meurice leaked the news of the four notebooks' existence but did not publish them. Vacquerie had died in 1895, Meurice in 1905, after which point there is no certainty of what happened.[5] The surviving transcripts and copies, entirely in French, remain paleo- and bibliographical nightmares. 'Cahier Trois' surfaced briefly, and was exhibited at the Maison Hugo in Paris, its provenance labelled 'Hugo heirs'; it then disappeared again. One of the Cahiers was later auctioned at Drouot on 11 April 1962. Today, almost all that remains are copies in various hands from the original *Livre des Tables*. Two more or less coy publications were superseded by the massive chronological edition of Hugo's work.[6] There is some identification of the sources, but the section editor explained, 'Pour les copies plus modernes, nous n'avons pas jugé bon de chercher à identifier les scribes, ou même de distinguer entre eux' [For more modern copies, we have not thought it right to identify the scribes, or even to distinguish among them] (Massin, 1184).

II. CONVERSATIONS WITH SHAKESPEARE

Out of time, Babel releases its hold, though it may just be the courtesy of the spirits. On 13 January 1854, in the presence of Hugo and Vacquerie, with Mme Hugo and Charles holding the table legs, there was movement, and someone asked

---

4 Adèle Hugo recorded his fears that the transcripts would make him a laughing stock (*Journal de l'exil*, 7 February 1854).

5 In *La Tribune de Lausanne* of 19 February, Meurice proposed to publish the four notebooks and offered some extracts. Nothing came of this announcement, and the Notebooks were handed on to Gustave Simon. See the discussion paper given by Patrice Boivin to the 'Groupe Hugo' in 2000. Their site is a mine of information on Hugo: http://groupugo.div .jussieu.fr/Groupugo/doc/09–06–20boivin.pdf (last accessed 9 September 2014).

6 These two early publications of the séances are partial in both senses. A first, slightly embarrassed, selection, *Chez Victor Hugo: Les Tables tournantes de Jersey*, ed. Gustave Simon (Paris, 1923) and then *Ce Que Disent les tables parlantes: Victor Hugo à Jersey*, ed. Jean Gaudon (Paris, 1963). Neither volume gives clear source references to the surviving notebooks nor do they indicate editorial intervention. The séances, more complete, were edited by Jean and Sheila Gaudon, and are in the 'Documents' section (with some MS references) at the end of volume IX (pp. 185–55), which will be the main source here, in brackets in the text (e.g. Massin, 185), of Victor Hugo, *Oeuvres Complètes: édition chronologique publiée sous la direction de Jean Massin* (Paris, 1967–70). Of the participants in the Jersey séances, Auguste Vacquerie is quoted in Massin, 1168 from *Les Miettes de l'histoire* (Paris, 1863).

'Ton nom?' And the spirit replied, 'Shakespeare'. On this occasion Hugo asked if the decision to join them was his own? Shakespeare replied, 'Oui' (Massin, 1280ff).

On 22 January 1854, Hugo asked if Shakespeare would tell them what meeting took place, what happened in the tomb, on 23 April 1616. Shakespeare replied that he kissed the nascent Corneille, and when Hugo reminded him that he did not ask about 1606 (birth of Corneille), but 1616, which was when Cervantes died, Shakespeare responded with a brief history of time:

Quand on meurt on prend tout à coup l'âge de tous les morts, c'est-à-dire de l'éternité. Dans le ciel il n'y a ni premier ne dernier venu. Tous ont une seconde de vie, et cette seconde dure cent millions d'ans. Demander à un mort: Combien y a-t-il de temps que tu es dans le ciel? C'est demander à un rayon: combien y a-t-il de temps que tu es dans le soleil? Une âme est une soeur qui n'a pas d'aînée. L'infini n'est pas l'aîné de l'amour. L'éternité n'est pas l'aînée du génie. Tous les grands esprits sont jumeaux. Dante n'est pas le cadet d'Eschyle . . . . Shakespeare n'est pas le petit frère, Job n'est pas le grand.　　　　(Massin, 1280f)

[When we die we are suddenly the same age as all the dead, that is, eternal. In heaven there is no first comer, nor last. All have a second of life, and that second lasts a hundred million years. Ask the dead, how long have you been in heaven? It's to ask a beam of light, how long have you been in the sun? A soul is a sister who has no older one. The infinite is not the elder of love. Eternity is not the older sibling of genius. All the great consciousnesses are twins . . . . Dante is not Aeschylus's younger brother. Shakespeare is not the little brother, nor Job the big.]

Hugo left the room, and Mme Hugo asked Shakespeare why, when André Chénier had told them *he* was still writing in the Beyond, Shakespeare was not. He replied,

La vie m'a couronné. Elle a décapité Chénier. Chénier a encore quelque chose à dire à la vie. Moi, je ne parle plus qu'à Dieu ou en son nom. Shakespeare est le père de son oeuvre, Chénier est l'orphelin de la sienne.
　　　　(Massin, 1281)

[Life crowned me. It decapitated Chénier. Chénier still has something to say to Life. I no longer speak except to God or in his name. Shakespeare is the father of his work. Chénier is the orphan of his.]

This conversation was interrupted by the arrival of Job, who agreed with Shakespeare, explaining to his listeners that 'Shakespeare was right to tell you: doubt is the basis of all human works. Yes, Don Juan is doubt. Hamlet doubts with Don Juan; Don Quixote weeps, Don Juan laughs, Hamlet smiles, and all three suffer' (Massin, 1282; Hovasse, 265).

All their conversations continued to be in French. Shakespeare's conclusion is that we (that is, we authors) make 'le drame', and God completes it. This sounds like Hugo of the famous preface to *Cromwell*, that extraordinary essay which finds a way around neoclassical ideas of tragedy, in which Hugo first adumbrated some of what Shakespeare is now telling him, confirming what he knows. In fact, one of the spirits who speaks is *Le Drame* itself, in case there was any doubt that it existed as real. At nineteen Hugo had already reversed the French *idée reçue* of Shakespeare – perpetrated by his bugbear, Voltaire – and written that Aeschylus is the Shakespeare of Athens ('Eschyle est le Shakespeare d'Athènes'). He had read no Shakespeare. Yet, partly through Scott's romances, he learned – or at least he legitimated via Shakespeare – a new dramatic practice for the French stage.

On the evening of 25 January 1854, Mme Hugo and a visitor were holding the table legs when Shakespeare announced himself (Massin, 1284f). Almost immediately the Spirit appeared to be unable to communicate and insisted that Mme Hugo be replaced by Charles. There followed a difficult conversation in which lines of poetry are exchanged. At this point the speakers are not identified, but the surviving manuscripts are in the hands of Charles or his father. The evenings devoted to Shakespeare continue into February, though they were interspersed with visits from other Spirits, including Molière and Aeschylus.

To the *guéridon parleur* in Marine Terrace came not only once-living individual spirits, not only spirit ideas, but also spirit abstracts such as, say, Criticism. *La Critique* (the spirit of criticism) arrived to characterize Shakespeare as 'un plongeur de l'âme', a 'deep-soul diver'. On 19 September 1853, Criticism, this time more irascible, went on to dictate,

L'âme humaine avant Shakespeare était une mer insondée. Eschyle avait eu tout de la mer, la tempête, le vent, l'éclair, l'écume, le roc, le ciel, tout excepté le perle; Shakespeare a plongé et il a rapporté l'amour.

(Massin, 1226)

[Before Shakespeare the human soul was an unsounded sea. Aeschylus had had everything of the sea, storm, wind, lightning, foam, rocks, skies, everything except the pearl; Shakespeare dove and brought back love.]

Of course, what else? Out of time, Shakespeare composes the correct number of syllables with rhyming couplets. On 22 January 1854 Shakespeare acknowledged the superiority of French: 'La langue anglaise est inférieure à la langue française' (Massin, 1283). That may explain why his verse invited editing or amendment, which his French listeners discussed with him. He accepted their corrections, asking Hugo to alternate lines with him, and, in all humility, says, 'I like your line better' (Massin, 1285–6). Later, Shakespeare dictated many lines of poetry, himself or through the medium of another spirit, via Le Drame. The logic of this is impeccable: if all writers are coterminous, what Le Drame speaks through them can be spoken by them or by Le Drame; Adèle Hugo's journal reports them labelling as 'Shakespeare' what appears in the transcripts to be spoke by Le Drame. This is of a piece with Hugo's chronology-free universalism. Unlike Criticism, Shakespeare was gentlemanly – not Voltaire's impression of him – and at one point when the living feel tired and want to retire to bed, they ask him if he will return. Yes, he says, Wednesday night at nine in the evening. In the event, 9 p.m. seems to be his regular slot.

In the absence of the original notebooks it is risky to generalize. It is safe to notice that the Table was often irascible and would frequently tell Mme Hugo to leave the room, preferring Charles to hold a leg rather than a recording pen. Mme Hugo's presence seemed to bring the spirits out in a kind of ranting piety, but even Shakespeare goes

on about the glory of God, which comforted Mme Hugo, always wanting to turn her Deist husband back to orthodox Catholicism. He also tells the mortals that they are chosen (Massin, 1300), though he is just as quick to let them know if they err in listening. After days of alexandrines, Auguste Vacquerie and Charles Hugo seem to have had an idea that Shakespeare might be persuaded to give them a play. Vacquerie asks,

Shakespeare, laisse-nous te demander une chose immense. Vous venez à nous pour faire faire un pas au genre humain. Ce livre que vous nous dictez remuera sans doute toutes les pensées. Mais il y a quelque chose de la plus puissant encore que le raisonnement du livre, c'est l'émotion du théâtre. Là, tous sont pris, la foule comme l'élite; celui qui ne sait pas lire comme celui qui sait écrire, l'instinct grossier, comme l'intelligence délicate. Il suffit d'avoir des yeux pour pleurer. Le livre, c'est l'esprit du vrai; le drame, c'en est le corps crucifié et sanglant; c'est le dieu qui fait toucher ses plaies. Tu le sais, toi qui fais saigner Othello sur les siècles. Eh bien, veux-tu nous dicter un drame? Ce sera peut-être une grande fatigue pour toi; c'en sera sûrement une énorme pour nous. Mais toute fatigue nous sera chère pour ajouter un frère et un collaborateur à cet éternel groupe de civilisateurs émus que tu nommes Othello, Hamlet, Lear, Roméo, Richard III. Veux-tu?

(Massin, 1302)

[Shakespeare, let us ask you for something immense. You come to us to make humanity take a step forward. The book you are dictating to us will doubtless stir all thinking. But there is something yet more powerful than the logic of the book: the emotion of the theatre. There, everyone is carried away, the crowd like the elite; the illiterate like he who knows how to write; gross instincts like delicate intelligence. It is enough to have eyes to weep. The book is the spirit of truth; the drama is its crucified and bloody body; a god who invites us to touch his wounds. You know it, you who bleed Othello over the centuries. So, would you dictate a play to us? It will perhaps be terribly tiring for you; it will surely be enormously fatiguing for us. But all fatigue will be dear to us if it adds a brother and a collaborator to that eternal band of emotionally stirred civilizers you call Othello, Hamlet, Lear, Romeo, Richard III. Will you?]

And Shakespeare replies, 'Oui', and that he will be ready in a month. Furthermore, he goes on,

163

La création a deux phases: l'invention et l'exécution. Colomb trouve l'Amérique en une nuit, il met des mois à la conquérir. La mer, le vent, la tempête veulent à chaque moment lui voler son monde, c'est-à-dire son enfant. Et plus que la mer, plus que le vent, plus que la tempête, les matelots conspirent contre lui. Eh bien, les mots sont les matelots de l'idée. Ils la servent et ils se révoltent contre elle. Le style est le mousse de l'esprit, il faut qu'il monte à tous les cordages, à tous les agrès, à tous les mâts de la majestueuse pensée en pleine mer.

(Massin, 1302)

[Creation comes in two phases: invention and action. Columbus finds America in a night, he spends months conquering it. At any moment the ocean, winds, storms, all want to rob him of his world, that is, his child. And worse than the ocean, worse than the wind, worse than the raging storm, his sailors conspire against him. Well, words are the sailors of the idea. They serve it and the revolt against it. Style is the spirit's cabin boy, it must climb all the lines, all the bars, all the masts of majestic thought in the open sea.]

This is where they call it a day – or a night. It was two o'clock in the morning.

Still they persevered. On 5 March, Vaquerie misunderstands Shakespeare's correction of a line, and Shakespeare asks him,

Comprendrais-tu: 'Vous fites le pardon le jour de la douleur'?

[Vacquerie] Tu as raison, j'avais tort, je comprends maintenant.

[They continue until Hugo interjects] 'Ce serait un très beau vers: Vous fites du pardon l'autre nom de douleur'.

Shakespeare corrects, 'Vous pensiez au pardon en écrivant: douleur / Un ange lut pardon, vous écriviez douleur'.

Hugo replies, Je trouve ce vers plus beau que la strophe. A ta place, je referais la strophe, et je retournerais le vers ainsi: 'Vous écriviez douleur, un ange lut pardon'. Trouve-tu que j'ai raison?   (Massin, 1304)

[S.] Oui.

[S. Do you understand 'You made forgiveness the day of grief'?

VH. That would be a very beautiful line: you made forgiveness the other name of grief. Why don't you like it?

S. You were thinking of forgiveness in writing: grief / An angel read pardon, you wrote grief.

VH. I think that line more beautiful than the stanza. In your place, I'd remake the stanza, and I'd turn the line like this: You wrote grief, an angel read 'forgiveness'. Do you think I'm right?

S. Yes.]

Time, for those in it, passes. The 23rd of April comes and goes without a sign. Then, on the 27th, not Shakespeare, but Le Drame, appears and the play, or some of the play, is eventually dictated (here the loss of the relevant notebooks makes any generalization difficult).

The play is a little like one of those fairy-tale special-effects fantasies of the Paris Opera: it opens with two stars which quickly resolve into huge globes which recognize each other as Heaven and Hell. A series of Spirits assure the living that Shakespeare will return, but it is Le Drame who reappears to describe a continuing argument between Heaven and Hell, set in the France of Louis XV. On the 29th Hugo notes that the scenes are very like something he wrote during the preceding October (Massin, 1366; Hovasse, 302–4). After speeches too long ever to be performed, the dramatic location changes to a peasant wedding. But the lovers are spied upon, and the play metamorphoses into a melodrama in which a king-seducer comes to destroy the young people's happiness.

Then the absence of Charles Hugo produced an interruption (which seems not to have raised suspicion), until, on 12 May the plot took its inevitable turn – into something more like Hugo's own *Hernani* than anything else. By 28 May Le Drame submitted to interrogation by Vacquerie, who wanted to know why Le Drame claims what was to have been Shakespeare's play as his own: Le Drame explains that all playwrights are one in Le Drame. The play then petered out. Hovasse shows the relations between what the Table said and what existed already in Hugo's drafts. He writes that Hugo had 'assurément' [surely] read these drafts aloud to his family audience (Houvasse, 303).

The séances had lasted only about eighteen months, and stopped in part because Hugo became increasingly nervous about word getting out, particularly to the authorities; additionally, one of his less balanced acolytes seems to have turned up to the séances with a pistol (or so implied Vacquerie). It may simply be that Hugo had had enough of such time-consuming nights.

In our time, it is a temptation to send up people such as Hugo and his circle. These are far from being the only people to believe themselves in direct relation with The Bard.[7] 'Do you know that we, much more than the English, are your compatriots?' asks Hugo [Sais-tu que nous sommes bien plus tes compatriotes que les Anglais (Simon 143)]. 'Oui', replies Shakespeare. This is far from the only place that Hugo, that controlling *monstre sacré*, seeks Shakespeare's deference, which, in his time, he gets. The questions the Hugo circle put to his spirit were current contemporary artistic concerns, as we read from the answers they summoned Shakespeare to give. They assume that of course Shakespeare writes like they do. Or would have done. What has moved me most, reading the records of the séances, is the demand that the past acknowledge and confirm the present – especially Hugo's place in its eternity. There is an insistence upon artistic simultaneity which is only about Time insofar as it innocently absorbs its historical differences in now, that ever-present timelessness in which an all-seeing, because timeless, God himself dwells.

Those Shakespearian answers have been more various than asking for someone to take dictation, and while in such a presentation the comedy – for us – is unavoidable, the intent is also serious, and has ramifications for criticism, especially reception, and biography, though most of those ramifications focus on Hugo. We are not looking at art forgery, which dates so quickly we wonder why it ever fooled anyone. Nor did Hugo control La Table, since there were always two people holding its legs, and Hugo was seldom one of them. He was evidently stimulated and disturbed by the séances. It must be remembered that Charles, his older son, fancied himself a writer, as did Auguste Vacquerie, who wrote a 'Falstaff' for the stage with Paul Meurice. Is this a *folie à famille*? Group psychosis? Certainly today strange things happen over the ouija board, not just in college dorms, but we seldom hear of long-dead legendary animals popping up, such as Balaam's ass or Androcles' lion. It was exciting, with its whiff of sulphur and the risks of being exposed to public ridicule. There is a strong sense of recruitment to Hugo's ideas about art and to Mme Hugo's certainty that heaven is Catholic – though of the participants only she was devout. As the Hugos trade verse-lines with Shakespeare, we discover the Spirit interrupting himself to ask Hugo to finish his stanza. As we might predict, Shakespeare preferred Hugo's

Morts nous nous écartons, humbles, sous les étoiles,
Nous nous cachons, rêveurs, derrières nos tombeaux.
Et, là, nous regardons l'immensité sans voiles ... [pause]
[Hugo completes:] L'astre éternel éteint les terrestres
    flambeaux.
[Shakespeare had completed:] Sur nos astres éteints
    allumer les flambeaux (Massin, 1285 [slightly
    compressed])
    [Dead, we step aside, beneath the stars, in humility,
We hide ourselves, dreamers, behind our monuments.
And there we see unveiled immensity ...
[Hugo] The eternal star quench the earthly torches
[Shakespeare] On our quenched stars light the torches]

I choose this passage, with its typical Hugolian unclarities, because of its phoenix-like variants. Shakespeare recognizes time passing, and new poets springing from his ashes. Hugo's similar line offers something a bit more patricidal. His new star (by implication, of course) becomes the poet for all time; by this is meant, of course, Hugo, not Shakespeare. After death, perhaps, out of time, all great souls share their creative spirit, as conduits for the divine. In life they suffer that they may write, afterwards they discover that they have somehow already written more. Hugo found the exchanges of poetry disturbing, because what Shakespeare was dictating seemed uncannily close to what

---

7 Jeffrey Kahan's recent book is devoted to anglophone spiritualists; see his *Shakespiritualism: Shakespeare and the Occult, 1850–1950* (Houndmills, Basingstoke, 2013). The final sentence of Kahan's Introduction does, however, overlap with Hugo's own universalist sense that all great poets were and are one.

he himself was writing at the time. He even put some drafts into sealed envelopes so as to protect himself from any accusation of plagiarism – a rare sensibility at the time.[8]

Never one to reject good ideas (especially his own), Hugo was at one point delighted by a spirit's advice that he instruct his heirs to space out the publication of his posthumous works – the strategy of Mme Valérie Eliot *avant la lettre*. This became the strategy of Meurice and Vacquerie, and the transcripts – the most complete we are likely to see – published in the Chronological Edition appeared only in 1968. Graham Robb calls Hugo's transcriptions of the Table's pronouncements a case of automatic writing, through which he improved what the tapping seemed to spell out (Robb, 331f), but his idea that Charles was released into ventriloquizing his father seems more convincing. That Hugo was 'almost insanely gullible' (Robb, 334) is harsh and might be anachronistic. Hugo was a great one for sonorous juxtapositions; and we might remember that at the close of *Dream* Theseus's view about lunatics, lovers and poets may be as far off the mark as his refusal to take seriously the young people's descriptions of their night. Nor, of course, was Hugo alone in the spiritist pastime. Only François-Victor held constantly aloof. Charles was almost always one of the two table-leg holders since he was the most fluid of the circle; since Hugo was often absent from Marine Terrace, it seems to me probable that the controlling figure was Charles; that François-Victor knew, or guessed what Charles was doing, while, for the rest of the family their most successful medium appeared ready to exhaust himself for their good. Perhaps the hand that rocks the table rules the world.

Sceptical or not, anyone reading these transcripts might take the following observations into account. First, Hugo's domination of his family and friends was extraordinary, and all three children, as well as his wife, resisted, at some cost. Adèle, the surviving daughter, was equally brought up to wait and serve; she was beautiful and a talented musician, but entirely at the beck and call of her father, who involved her in secretarial work and recording his table talk – including 'table talk' that he

composed for her journal. Like her uncle, Hugo's brother, Adèle eventually suffered a long breakdown, and was incarcerated for the rest of her long life. She was the only one to outlive Hugo. The older son managed to marry and produce the son who inspired *The Art of Being a Grandfather* (he lived to squander Hugo's huge fortune); the younger did not, and, having lost one love to tuberculosis, refused a marriage his father attempted to arrange, to die in his forties of kidney failure. Mme Hugo managed a brief revenge in an affair with Hugo's close friend, Sainte-Beuve.

Second, the table-tapping episode contains numerous oddities, not least that, having enlisted Shakespeare in his theatrical revolution, Hugo exchanged the most straightforwardly classical alexandrines with him. Perhaps that is what poets do in their spare moments out of time, but it certainly reduced Shakespeare to an avatar of Hugo rather than the other way around. Shakespeare was not the only poet to join the workshop: the verses produced by the spirit of André Chénier, who was executed during the Terror (and who was published posthumously), resemble standard French verse that is unsurprising in someone (or the spirit of someone) so much closer to mainstream French poetry. It should be said, however, that other spirits, some not human, also dictated their verse.

Third, the readers and writers gathered around the table had no idea what Shakespeare sounded like; their contact was only with translations which

---

[8] In one of the transcripts in Hugo's hand he adds a note recognizing that the spirit of Molière repeats a line he, Hugo, had already penned (Massin, 1332). On 23 and 24 March he annotates his own copy of the transcriptions to record a night of care and composition in which he includes in his sealed envelope the four matches he struck in order to light his candle – as a kind of proof that his muse was his own. *The Journal d'exil* contains, for example, 'La révélation des Tables me gêne beaucoup. Si le sujet de la pièce de Shakespeare roule sur la transformation successive d'un méchant en un juste, elle pourrait se rencontrer avec un livre que j'ai fait il y a cinq ans . . . . (recorded 13 May 1854, p. 223). The Table's revelations trouble me considerably. If the subject of Shakespeare's play turns on a bad man's transformation by degrees into a good one, it could encounter the same thing in a book I wrote five years ago.

corrected and improved his 'barbaric' structure and style, whether it was Ducis adapting for the Comédie française or the aureate multi-volume effort by LeTourneur (who knew neither English nor the London stage, but published and improved text from 1776–83 that was subsequently updated for republication by other 'translators'). Neither did they know French Shakespeare (improved) in the study or adapted for the stage by Ducis, among others; what they knew was 'Shakespeare', a French writer whose main function had been to propose a counter to Neoclassicism and to have announced Romanticism to come. In the Hugo household only François-Victor had first-hand knowledge of Shakespeare in English. The Spirit of Shakespeare with whom they conversed was already a Frenchman.[9]

---

[9] Without Supriya Chaudhuri's invitation to participate in a Panel at the Shakespeare Association of America conference in 2014, Hugo's paranormal experiences might have remained a well-kept French secret. I thank her and Coppélia Kahn for their generous reading. In metamorphosing that talk into something rather more serious, I have called upon long-suffering friends: Stefan Collini, Peter Holland, Russ McDonald and R. N. Watson.

BETRAYAL, DERAIL, OR A THIN VEIL: THE MYTH OF ORIGIN

BI-QI BEATRICE LEI

'Is this Shakespeare?' is the reaction to many contemporary performances, particularly non-Anglophone productions. After roughly two decades of scholarly deliberation on foreign Shakespeare, local Shakespeare, native Shakespeare and, more recently, global Shakespeares (plural), authenticity remains a stubborn issue, and questions of fidelity to the early modern origin continues to qualify creative attempts to update, indigenize, stylize and popularize Shakespeare. While some plainly un-Shakespearian elements – artificial lighting, special effects, anachronistic costumes and so on – are widely used and generally accepted on stage and screen, critical demand for loyalty to the text tenaciously persists. For many, the quintessence of Shakespeare inheres in his brilliant language, and any theatrical or cinematic production that adopts a translated, modernized, simplified or significantly excised text is indelibly debased. For others, Shakespeare's structure, characterization, humanism or ambiguity is similarly sacrosanct. Thus an adaptation may well be judged to be lacking, due to its omission of a subplot, a two-dimensional portrayal of a character, its propagation of racism or sexism or its black-and-white morality.[1]

Conversely, the quest for authenticity has led some scholars and theatre artists to pursue 'original practices' or 'original pronunciation'.[2] While these painstaking endeavours have indeed achieved educational and promotional effects and on occasion rendered refreshing performances, the search for 'origin' cannot but be futile. Contemporary performance of Shakespeare, even in archaic language and period dress, on a bare stage and with minimal technology, has inevitably been filtered through our culture, assumptions and preoccupations. Despite the best of intentions to be faithful, whatever we can conceive, imagine and execute exposes our values, aesthetics and limitations no less than the Bard's. As Antony Tatlow maintains, the past is a culture of its own, and our engagement with Shakespeare is 'necessarily intercultural'.[3]

Our Shakespeare, an intercultural hybrid of past and present, foreign and native, thus has multiple 'origins'. This practice is by no means modern or 'original' – Shakespeare did as much to Plutarch and Holinshed. Rather than censuring a contemporary production for departing from its Shakespearian source, it is more productive to investigate what causes such variance and what effect it achieves. It is time to leave behind the moral judgment implied by an authenticity test. Polonius advises his son: 'This above all: to thine own self be true, / And it must follow, as the night the day, / Thou canst not then be false to any man' (*Hamlet* 1.3.78–82). Can this serve as a compass

---

[1] An example is Alan Ying-Nan Lin's critique of *Bond*, 'Appropriating *The Merchant of Venice*: On the Adapting Strategy of *Bond* and Its Problems (Nuojie *Weinisi shangren* shilun *Yueshu de gaibian celue yu suo yinfa de wenti*)', *Taipei Theatre Journal* (*Xiju xuekan*), 14 (2011), 85–108.

[2] See the discussion of 'original practice' by Jeremy Lopez, 'A Partial Theory of Original Practice', in *Shakespeare Survey 61* (Cambridge, 2008), pp. 302–17.

[3] Antony Tatlow, *Shakespeare, Brecht, and the Intercultural Sign* (Durham, NC, 2001), p. 1.

for Shakespearian translators, theatre directors and filmmakers?

SHAKESPEARE BETRAYED

Not all seem bothered by this issue of authenticity. Indeed, some openly defy it. A most notable example is the 'Cardenio Project', an experiment in cultural mobility orchestrated by Stephen Greenblatt.[4] Greenblatt recounted how Shakespeare and Fletcher collaboratively lifted the story of Cardenio from Cervantes' *Don Quixote* and transmuted it to create a new play. Greenblatt and Charles Mee undertook a similar task to transform Shakespeare and Fletcher's work, this time self-consciously exploring how cultural context figures in creation and re-creation, yielding the modern comedy *Cardenio*. Theatre companies around the world were then invited to rework these materials passed down from Cervantes, Shakespeare and Fletcher and Lewis Theobald, to Greenblatt and Mee. The only stipulation was that local theatres should not give a direct performance of the translated texts but must rewrite them into a form that fits their own cultural circumstances. So far the play has been remodelled in Japan, India, Croatia, Egypt, Brazil, Poland, Serbia, Turkey, South Africa, Spain and Taiwan. Each production is manifestly different from Greenblatt and Mee's original, and also from the others.

Akio Miyazawa, playwright and director of the Japan production entitled *Motorcycle Don Quixote*, contends that cultural mobility depends on 'misunderstanding'.[5] In his 'un-Shakespearean' play set in an industrial quarter of contemporary Yokohama, 'Bardolatry, self-Orientalism, and Japonism were hardly recognizable and neither was the text of Greenblatt and Mee'.[6] Perng Ching-Hsi, co-playwright of Taiwan's variant, takes the demand for localization as a call for betrayal. '[T]his kind of betrayal', he claims, 'highlights the adaptors' truthfulness to their vision of their own culture. Betrayal thus becomes a different form of loyalty.'[7]

Hence the title of the Taiwan adaptation – *Betrayal*.[8] In the style of *xiqu* (traditional Chinese opera), the performance features period costumes, arias backed by a live orchestra, choreographed movement and martial arts, presenting a visual and aural experience markedly distinct from realist drama. With spectacular sword fighting against 'miracle warriors' and flying peach petals that emit a fragrance with paralysing effects, some scenes recall Ang Lee's award-winning film *Crouching Tiger, Hidden Dragon*. Indeed, the play diverges from its sources still more radically. Beyond the bare bones of the plot, of two young couples going through a series of pre-marital disruptions and complications, nothing follows Greenblatt and Mee's original play, or even Shakespeare and Fletcher's. The language, plot, characters, setting and themes are all changed. Male anxiety and jealousy, the axis of Greenblatt and Mee's comedy, vanishes entirely.

The story involves four fictive empires: Xuanwu, Canglong, Zhuque and Baihu. The play starts with preparation for a wedding celebration, between Xuanwu's Princess Yulan and Xingyuan, a prominent Canglong nobleman. Decreed by the Xuanwu Emperor, this marriage promises to strengthen the alliance between the two countries. But a vengeful royalist of Zhuque, a kingdom toppled by the joint force of Xuanwu and Canglong fifteen years ago, steals the bridegroom

---

[4] See the Cardenio Project's official website (www.fas.harvard .edu/~cardenio/index.html). A more detailed account of the creative process is in Stephen Greenblatt, 'Theatrical Mobility', in *Cultural Mobility: A Manifesto*, ed. Stephen Greenblatt *et al.* (Cambridge, 2009), pp. 75–95.

[5] Greenblatt, 'Theatrical Mobility', p. 91.

[6] Mika Eglinton, 'Metamorphoses of "Shakespeare's Lost Play": A Contemporary Japanese Adaptation of *Cardenio*', *Shakespeare*, 7 (2011), p. 340.

[7] Perng Ching-Hsi, 'Foreword', *Betrayal (Beipan)*, by Perng Ching-Hsi and Chen Fang (Taipei, 2013), p. vii.

[8] There were two separate productions, by Chinese Culture University's Department of Chinese Drama in 2013, and by Rom Shing Hakka Opera Troupe in 2014. Both productions used the same script, with minor changes. As my discussion is not on the theatrical aspects of these two productions – music, performance style, acting, design, etc. – I do not distinguish them but speak of *Betrayal* as the play-text. The text quoted is from the published bilingual script.

away to incite dissent. Fearing the Emperor's wrath, Xingyuan's father assigns his younger son Shiyuan to console the deserted bride. Meanwhile, the abducted Xingyuan meets his jailor Yixiang, the orphaned Zhuque Princess brought up by the royalist. Each of the four protagonists ends up falling in love with the wrong person.

Parallels exist between *Betrayal* and *Cardenio* – the green world setting, the disrupted wedding celebration, the misaligned loves, a generation gap, a fixation on food with natural ingredients, etc. Despite a superficial resemblance, however, *Betrayal* presents an immensely different world inhabited by characters much larger than life – not only aristocrats but also moral paragons and martial heroes. Xingyuan is skilled in the legendary Canglong Fencing Methods, and Yixiang practices the ancient art of divination. Instead of love's oaths, Shiyuan and Princess Yulan exchange government agendas and defence strategies during their first encounter, in the form of a duet:

Shiyuan. First come people, then the sovereign king.
  Encouragement of agriculture tops th' agenda.
  Give people time to rest; reduce their tax,
  Wipe out corruption, form a moral government.
Princess. It takes stability at home to fend off foes
    abroad.
  Promote the worthy to help rule the land.
Shiyuan. When granaries are filled with crops,
  Enlist civilians for the troops.
Princess. If citizens' morale is high,
Shiyuan. We can with ease encroachers crush.[9]

They continue on to where to station their respective armies to best attack their enemy Baihu from two sides. The scene ends with the stage direction: 'The two start a discussion, gesturing variously and making military maneuvers on the sand table.'[10]

In *Betrayal*, love and marriage connect not only two individuals and two families, but also two nations, two cultures, two economies (the agricultural Canglong and the nomadic Xuanwu), and two armies. This bond benefits the rulers, their dynasties and their peoples alike. Love and marriage also unite enemies. The knot between Xingyuan

and Yixiang, incidentally, resolves an ancient feud between Canglong and Zhuque, and pacifies rebel forces. In order to marry Yixiang, Xingyuan surrenders his first-born privileges and consents to a life in the country; his self-inflicted exile redeems his father's sin. These are values entirely foreign to Greenblatt and Mee, to their 'midsummer comedy of love',[11] and to their twenty-first-century American, democratic, middle-class ethos. Even in Taiwan, where arranged marriages are not extinct, these assumptions seem quite unrealistic.

This intricate relation between love and politics may sound reminiscent of Cervantes and Shakespeare's early modern Europe. Indeed, Shakespearian leitmotifs abound in *Betrayal*. Yixiang, for example, notably takes after Miranda of *The Tempest*, who also suffers bereavement and danger as a child and leads a secluded life for twelve years. Ferdinand in turn figures in Xingyuan, who finds physical labour for love's sake to be sweeter than courtly leisure, and Prospero in the royalist Old Man, who threatens revenge on his enemy's son. Princess Yulan, a woman deprived of the freedom to choose her mate, also has numerous Shakespearian predecessors. Do the playwrights 'betray' Greenblatt and Mee only to yield to higher authorities, to return to Shakespeare and Fletcher, and even Cervantes?

According to the playwrights, it is traditional Chinese culture that prescribes these alterations. Confucian ethics – loyalty, filial piety and fraternity – have as much or more weight than any individuals' pursuit of happiness and freedom.[12] In this cultural framework, Xingyuan's fathers thinks it is 'absolutely absurd', 'disloyal and unfilial' and 'a clear case of betrayal' to resist a marriage decreed by the emperor and arranged by the father.[13] Shiyuan

---

9 *Betrayal*, p. 34.
10 *Betrayal*, p. 34.
11 Tagline from the poster of the production by the American Repertory Theater (www.fas.harvard.edu/~cardenio/us-home.html).
12 Perng Ching-Hsi and Chen Fang, post-performance discussion of *Betrayal* (Taipei, 18 May 2014).
13 *Betrayal*, p. 68.

6. Shiyuan and Princess Yulan discuss governing policies and defence strategies in *Betrayal* (Taipei, 2013)

and Princess Yulan have developed mutual affection in Xingyuan's absence, but violating the hierarchy prescribed by birth order, let alone disobeying one's father and king, is utterly inconceivable. He vehemently protests: 'Far be such wild fancy on my mind; / Heaven knows my truthful heart!'[14]

Thanks to a benevolent authority, here Princess Yulan and her father, the many difficulties are resolved and the play closes with a happy ending attributed to 'providence'.[15] National security, political stability, patriarchy and even marital bliss can all be achieved by an individual's submission to the established power structure – there exists no real conflict between public and private good, between right and beneficial. History is written by the victors: Xuanwu and Canglong's allied military operation, defensive or offensive, is righteous.

The provocative Baihu, 'a frightful bully',[16] no doubt deserves retaliation, but how different is Baihu's aggression from the allies' butchering of the Zhuque people, which caused the orphaned Yixiang to bewail 'The homeland shattered, families dispersed'?[17]

Although the title 'betrayal' seems to suggest the opposite, the play is most conservative in its unreserved support of hierarchy, feudal order and the powers that be. Propagating Confucian ethics appropriated to serve the ruling class, the play significantly rewrites both its source and the sources

14 *Betrayal*, p. 58.
15 *Betrayal*, p. 74.
16 *Betrayal*, p. 33.
17 *Betrayal*, p. 41.

of its source. It corrects Shakespeare and Fletcher (and Cervantes) by presenting a world without class conflict, lust, deception or evil. It also scorns the frivolity and folly of love under the sway of 'fast-food culture' as depicted by Greenblatt and Mee. Love does not turn the protagonists of *Betrayal* into fools, dreamers or sceptics; quite the opposite, love and a subsequent dynastic marriage procure an empire's security, prosperity and continuity. There is no room for jesting. Nothing, indeed, can be more serious.

In this instance, revision of source materials does not necessarily entail liberation from ideology, nor approximation to real life. Instead, nostalgia for an old order and past beauty creeps in. While didacticism is part of *xiqu* traditions, the play is exoticized with martial arts and ancient astrology and divination – elements derived from fantasy literature and films. Rather than 'Chinese', *chinoiserie* may better describe the play, which projects an imagined, idealized past, embellished with cultural totems.

SHAKESPEARE DERAILED

While betrayal implies a choice, derailments tend to be accidental. Despite the best of intentions, even when Shakespeare's original story and characters are largely preserved, de-contextualization can take us off the rails. Connotations often get dropped or altered in linguistic and/or cultural translation. Consider Shakespeare's Sonnet 18. In contrast to some Shakespearian sonnets employing puns, metaphysics, topical allegory or financial imagery, Sonnet 18 is rather straightforward, reiterating the timeless *carpe diem* motif. Associations for 'summer', however, are not universal. In tropical regions for instance, the long baking summer evokes a set of feelings contrary to sheer delight and momentary beauty, and anyone can be more lovely and temperate than a tropical summer's blazing sun or raging typhoons. Teaching the sonnet to my Taiwan students thus poses a challenge – although the literal meaning of the poem can be easily conveyed, the intensity of the speaker's emotion does not communicate well.

If summer, a natural concept, can get lost in transit, it only gets more complicated when the text involved is embroiled in issues of race, religion, history and politics. *Bond*, an adaptation of *The Merchant of Venice* by the Taiwan Bangzi Company, presents just such a case.[18] While fairy-tale elements abound, *The Merchant of Venice* is nonetheless a profoundly 'local' play, deeply embedded in a specific culture at a particular historical moment. The conflict between Antonio and Shylock epitomizes the ethnic, religious and social tension in early modern Europe, documenting the alienation of the Jews, the decline of feudalism and the rise of a new economy. Can this play travel smoothly?

Performed in the style of *bangzi*, a regional form of *xiqu*, the play's visual and aural aspects generally conform to its theatrical tradition. Sinicization is the governing principle in the story's transmutation. It is reset in China's Song Dynasty (AD 960–1279), and Venice becomes the fictional Prefecture of Nisi, based on the capital city of Kaifeng. The Duke of Venice reincarnates as Judge Bao; other characters also acquire new names and titles according to Chinese conventions. To make room for arias, the subplots involving Jessica and Lorenzo and between Lancelot Gobbo and his father are excised, and some minor characters, such as Portia's undesirable suitors, are reduced.[19] Other than formal adaptation and pragmatic condensation, the playwrights took pains to preserve Shakespeare and even tried to reproduce some wordplay.[20]

---

[18] Written by Perng Ching-Hsi and Chen Fang and directed by Lu Po-Shen, *Bond* (*Yueshu*) premiered in Taipei in 2009, with two scenes previewed at the British Shakespeare Association's conference in London earlier that year. A condensed version was also performed at the Shakespeare Association of America's 2011 meeting, followed by more performances in the USA. A recording of the play's performance in Taipei, with bilingual subtitles and supporting materials, is available at the Taiwan Shakespeare Database (www.Shakespeare.tw). Unless otherwise noted, citations of the play are from Perng Ching-Hsi and Chen Fang, *Bond* (Taipei, 2009).

[19] See Perng Ching-Hsi, 'Bonding *Bangzi* and the Bard: The Case of Yue/Shu (Bond) and The Merchant of Venice', *Shakespeare in Culture*, ed. Bi-qi Beatrice Lei and Perng Ching-Hsi (Taipei, 2011), p. 140.

[20] See Perng, 'Bonding *Bangzi* and the Bard', pp. 142–4.

This all seems to promise a seamless transfer. The hub of four major canals located a few miles south of the Yellow River, Kaifeng was well connected by waterways, not unlike Venice. A bustling metropolis populated by over a million people, Kaifeng in the Song Dynasty attracted merchants and traders from India, Persia, Arabia, Central Asia and Europe through different branches of the Silk Road. Jews formed a vibrant community in the city. They called themselves followers of the Israelite religion (*Isileye jiao*), but were also known as 'the Sinew-Plucking Sect' (*Tiao jin jiao*) for keeping kosher, and as 'Blue-Hatted Hui' (*Lanmao huihui*), as opposed to the 'White-Hatted Hui' (*Baimao huihui*), the Muslims. The first synagogue, called 'Purity and Truth Temple' (*Qing zhen si*), was built in 1163, and was renovated many times before finally succumbing to a flood in the mid-nineteenth century. Several stone inscriptions dated from 1489 remain, documenting Kaifeng's Jewish settlement over the centuries.[21]

To present Shylock as a Kaifeng Jew, however, would not serve the play's purpose. The Song emperors had an open-door policy to foreign merchants and traders, and there was no trace of legal, social or political discrimination or persecution against the Jews. In the international city of Kaifeng, Jews lived side by side with practitioners of Buddhism, Daoism, Islam, Manichaeism and ancestor worship and folk religion. There was simply no deep-rooted anti-Semitism to move the plot. Nor would Shylock's usury be condemned. That he charges interest for loans would not raise any Chinese eyebrows – it was and is taken for granted.

How to label Xia Luo, the alienated Shylock figure, thus posed a challenge. The playwrights' first thought was to make him a Chinese minority – in addition to Han Chinese, which comprises 91.5% of China's 1.3 billion people, there are fifty-five ethnic groups officially recognized by the PRC.[22] But this scheme proved entirely untenable in China's political environment. Geng Yuqing, the production's music director from China, knew too well that a play thematizing and intensifying ethnic conflict within Chinese society would undoubtedly be barred from the Chinese market, given the sensitive issues surrounding China's racial minorities today.[23]

A second identity was then proposed – *dashiren*, namely someone from Dashi. The term Dashi probably derived from the Persian word Tajik.[24] In China's Tang and Song Dynasties, it was used as a collective term for Arabia and Persia. Dashi merchants and traders came to China primarily through maritime routes, importing a vast variety of commodities, among them spices, herbs, rhinoceros horn, ivory and precious stones. Accepted as harmless aliens in Chinese society, they were free to dress, eat and pray in their own way, and suffered no specific legal discrimination.[25] This scheme has a major advantage: Dashi is an archaic term only used in history textbooks. It invokes exotic imagination but not geographic, ethnic or religious reality.[26] Few can locate the Dashi Empire on today's world map, vaguely knowing only that it refers to somewhere in southern or western Asia.

As a Dashi moneylender, Xia Luo stands out for his exotic looks – he alone wears a curly beard, gowns and hats heavily embroidered in darker shades and ethnic patterns, and extravagant

---

21 The Kaifeng Jews have attracted much scholarly interest. Important studies include the many articles in Roman Malek, ed., *Jews in China: From Kaifeng . . . to Shanghai*, Monograph Series 46 (Sankt Augustin, 2000), and Xu Xin, *The Jews of Keifeng, China: History, Culture, and Religion* (Jersey City, 2003). The stone inscriptions were translated into English and analysed in Tiberiu Weisz, *The Kaifeng Stone Inscriptions: The Legacy of the Jewish Community in Ancient China* (Bloomington, 2006).

22 'Han Chinese Proportion in China's Population Drops: Census Data', *Xiahua Net* (news.xinhuanet.com/english2010/china/2011-04/28/c_13849933.htm).

23 Chen Fang, *Shakespearean Xiqu: Cross-Cultural Adaptation and Interpretation (Sha xiqu kuawenhua gaibian yu yanyi)* (Taipei, 2012), p. 53.

24 Michael Dillon, *China's Muslim Hui Community: Migration, Settlement and Sects* (Richmond, VA, 1999), p. 12.

25 Jonathan Neaman Lipman, *Familiar Strangers: A History of Muslims in Northwest China* (Seattle, 1997), pp. 25–30.

26 Perng, 'Bonding *Bangzi* and the Bard', p. 141.

7. Wang Hai-ling as Xia Luo the Dashi moneylender in *Bond* (2009)

jewellery.[27] His origin, however, is conveniently imprecise. He is thus disassociated from contemporary politics, domestic or international – he is not to remind us of Xinjiang, Tibet, India, Iran, Iraq, Israel or Syria. The same strategy of antiquation is applied to Xia Luo's faith. He recounts only an oath he has sworn by his 'god', no more than a pretext for the pursuit of his pound of flesh.[28] Beyond this, his religious practice is never mentioned. In the play's English translation he is consistently called a Saracen, presumably a Muslim, but similarly vague. Significantly, it is not Xia Luo's foreign identity or his faith but his greed that makes him a target of collective hatred and contempt. Soon after the play starts, a dialogue between two merchants reveals that Xia Luo charges compound interest at thirty-three per cent, a usurious rate by any standards. For his voraciousness, an exclusively moral problem, Xia Luo is condemned as a dog, a shark and a cannibal who devours both flesh and bone. His race and religion in turn become irrelevant and merely decorative.

If Shylock becomes a Saracen usurer from Dashi, what about the Venetians/Christians, the mainstream in Shakespeare's original? In the play they are dubbed as *zhongyuanren*, literally people from *zhongyuan*. Interchangeable with *zhongzhou* (central state) or *zhongtu* (central land), *zhongyuan* (central plain) denotes the lower reaches of the Yellow River. It is the cradle of Han civilization and the home of ancient capitals. Broadly defined, *zhongyuan* comprise of regions directly governed by centralized Chinese governments and dynasties, as opposed to questionable borderlands, vassal states and foreign countries. Notably it does not denote any specific political entity at any historical moment, nor any religious affiliation. Like Dashi, the term *zhongyuan* well serves the set purpose of depoliticizing and dehistoricizing.

Nevertheless a problem arose. Before the troupe departed for a preview of the court scenes in London in 2009, I was invited to see the dress rehearsal and could not help frowning while reading the English subtitles projected on a screen. Xia Luo is charged as an alien attempting to 'spill Chinese blood' and to 'seek the life of a Chinese citizen'.

The court spares Xia Luo's life, an act that illustrates the 'Chinese principle of forgiveness', but seizes his entire fortune and orders that he 'immediately become a naturalized Chinese'. While many of these lines closely follow Shakespeare's original – only replacing 'local', 'our', and 'Christian' with 'Chinese' – I somehow felt that I was reading China's current-day propaganda about unrest caused by Uyghur or Tibetan separatists labelled as terrorists. Upon this, my sympathy for An Yibo (Antonio) and Ba Wuji (Bassanio), who in tears sang a heart-wringing farewell duet a moment ago, suddenly froze.

'Chinese' is an inclusive term: it covers five thousand years of history and is a race, a culture and a language. Yet, it inevitably recalls a modern political entity, the People's Republic of China with the world's largest military, a regime which the West often criticizes for totalitarianism, state-led nationalism, Han chauvinism, human rights violations and suppression of religion. Audiences might take an acute interest in such topical associations and overlook the play's other equally important themes, of love, marriage, patriarchy, friendship, homosociality, economy, etc. I understood that this was not the playwrights' intention and thus suggested the current translation of 'Cathay' and 'Cathayan' to keep the play grounded in the fictional realm.[29]

Intriguingly, unintended and unexpected derailments happen both in transferring Shakespeare to another cultural context and in translating the adaptation back into English. With cultural references lost on each leg of the trip, the final product is a morality play unmoored from any specific history

---

27 According to Lin Heng-zheng, the play's costume designer, Xia Luo's dress combines elements from Persia, Assyria, Miao (a minority in southwestern China) and India. See 'Costume Design Ideas' (*Fuzhuang sheji gainian*), in the premiere program of *Bond* (Taipei, 2009), n.p.

28 *Bond*, p. 39. In actual performances, the 'god' is said to be the God of Wealth (*Caishenye*), a deity in popular religion, though the English translation remains unspecified.

29 In the script published in 2009, 'China' and 'Chinese' still figure in some passages. At the play's performances to American audiences in 2011, they all read 'Cathay' and 'Cathayan' (or simply 'local') respectively.

or reality. While *Bond* speaks Chinese, employs a Chinese setting, and conforms to Chinese theatrical conventions, it enacts a story that resonates in any society and appeals to any audience. Endeavours to 'localize' Shakespeare, in this case to Sinicize Shakespeare, inadvertently end up as universalization, dehistoricization and depoliticization.

SHAKESPEARE UTILIZED AS A THIN VEIL

Foreign, intercultural and global Shakespeare is often called 'Shakespeare without English' or 'Shakespeare without his language'. What happens when Shakespeare's language is preserved? Does that necessarily imply a 'straight', faithful production? According to Jan Kott, Shakespeare speaks in the present tense, and representation of Shakespeare can exhibit provocative visions of our contemporary world.[30] Even verbatim Shakespeare does not guarantee the same dramatic action – in sooth Shakespeare's language can just be a thin veil, barely covering oppositional messages the adapters hope to convey. This is manifested in two adaptations of *Macbeth*, made in Taiwan in 2011 and in Thailand in 2012 respectively. It was not planned, but the two bear many interesting parallels.

The Thai film *Shakespeare Must Die* depicts a theatre group's staging of *Macbeth*. The Shakespearian text is translated into Thai word for word, with very few edits. The dialogue between Ross, an old man, and Macduff (2.4) is presented in full, with only four lines involving place names removed. The 'English scene' (4.2) is chiefly preserved, with Macduff and Malcolm's discussion of the divine rights of kings intact. This is rarely done today, if at all. Some Shakespearians who watched the screening at the Asian Shakespeare Association's inaugural conference in Taipei actually complained that the film was being too textually faithful to the original and bordered on tedium, with the lines delivered at an emphatically slow pace, making the film three full hours long. Ing K, the film's director, protested that it was not tailored to the taste of scholars who knew the play by heart. This is the first and only Thai language Shakespearian film, and she neither

wanted nor could afford to offer anything less than the full *Macbeth*. Educated in the UK, she first encountered Shakespearian drama when she was fifteen. She declares that her purpose is to introduce Shakespeare to her Thai compatriots, who get precious little of him in formal education and almost none in live theatre. She rebuffs any accusations of politically motivated criticism, *lèse-majesté* and hate speech by saying her film came directly from Shakespeare.[31]

The Taiwan production is my *Macbeth: A Political Allegory*, presented at the seventh Chinese Universities Shakespeare Festival hosted by the Chinese University of Hong Kong. Linguistic faithfulness was a requisite and not a choice. Overtly educational in purpose, the Festival has very strict regulations in terms of language – a production must use Shakespeare's original English, with no added dialogue.[32] A copy of the adapted script must be submitted in advance. To ensure accurate pronunciation by the actors – college students from China, Hong Kong, Macao and Taiwan – the organizers provide an audio CD for each finalist team, a slow, word-by-word, undramatic reading of the adapted script by a native speaker of English. English proficiency also comprises twenty per cent of the judging criteria.

Faithfulness to Shakespeare's original makes the play resonate with contemporary politics and yet

---

[30] Jan Kott, *Shakespeare Our Contemporary* (New York and London, 1974). Also see Dennis Kennedy, 'Introduction: Shakespeare without His Language', in *Foreign Shakespeare: Contemporary Performance*, ed. Dennis Kennedy (Cambridge, 1993), pp. 8–9.

[31] Ing K, post-screening discussion of *Shakespeare Must Die* at the Southeast Asian Film Festival held on 2 May 2014 (www.youtube.com/watch?v-0kVe085TJvI). Also see Colleen Kennedy, 'Interview with Ing K, Director of *Shakespeare Must Die*: A Great Feast of Languages', *Shakespeare Standard* (http://theshakespearestandard.com/interview-with-ing-k-director-of-shakespeare-must-die-global-shakespeare-news/).

[32] The first purpose the Festival lists on its official website is 'to promote appreciation of literature in English (particularly the works of William Shakespeare who is considered the finest writer in the language)' (www.eng.cuhk.edu.hk/shakespeare/aboutus2_mission.php).

paradoxically elevates it above our reality. Thematizing usurpation, regicide and tyranny, *Macbeth* can be perceived as quite subversive and thus politically sensitive. When presented as a king – and not a head of a gang or an owner of a restaurant – the title character threatens to evoke our despotic and corrupt politicians and foment resistance. Shakespeare's foreign identity, temporal distance and status as world classics, however, can serve to dissociate his Scottish story from a modern political reality. Adherence to his archaic, poetic language lifts Shakespeare further above us.

Macbeth resonates for both Thailand and Taiwan, each with a former leader convicted of corruption and abuse of power. Thailand changed from absolute monarchy to constitutional monarchy in 1932, but democracy has proved unstable, with nineteen coup d'états since. Thaksin Shinawatra, descended from a rural northern province, was elected as the Prime Minister in 2001 and re-elected in 2005. A controversial leader accused of policy corruption and tax evasion, he was overthrown by a coup in 2006, and subsequently fled into a self-imposed exile. Thaksin's 'red-shirts' supporters, largely rural poor from the north, have struggled with his urban, elite 'yellow-shirts' opponents, with frequent street protests and building occupations that often turn violent. In Taiwan, officially the Republic of China, democracy is more than nominal: thirty-eight years of martial law was lifted in 1987. But the society is no less divided, between the grassroots, pro-independence 'pan-green' and the pro-Chinese 'pan-blue'. In the same year as Thaksin's ousting, a mass campaign was launched to depose President Chen Shui-bian, a 'green' politician from the south, but he managed to stay in office. After his second term ended in 2008, he had to face indictment, and is now serving a twenty-year sentence for corruption. In both Thailand and Taiwan, die-hard supporters claim that the trials of Thaksin and Chen were politically motivated, and whether in jail or in exile, the two former leaders continue to exert influence and agitate society.

The Shakespearian text of *Macbeth*, faithfully adapted, provides then enormous scope for association. In *Shakespeare Must Die*, *Macbeth* is the play-within-the-play staged in a small playhouse. The characters are dressed in traditional Thai style, with King Duncan in royal yellow and with a tall pointed crown, carried around in a sedan chair. All roles keep their Shakespearian names, but Scotland, England and Ireland become fantastical Atlantis, Xanadu and Shangri-la. With simple lighting and minimal effects, the performance is spare and almost amateurish, and the audience seems dispassionate. As the play progresses, the real world collides with fiction, with the same actor playing both Macbeth on stage and the dictator Mekhdekh, dubbed as 'Dear Leader', in the contemporary outside world. The same applies to Lady Macbeth and Khunying Mekhdekh. Shakespeare's original lines for the Macbeth couple are split, some spoken on stage, others in the real world. To further confound theatre and reality, simplistic recordings of raw stage performance are interspersed with cinematic, realistic shootings.

The epiphany arrives when the power of art is fully realized across the fourth wall by the artists, the spectators and the censors alike. The in-film audience quietly watches the show until Macduff appears with Macbeth's head. They then rally and begin shouting 'Get out, Mekhdekh!' A secret police figure, who had fiercely interrogated the director during intermission, leads an angry crowd into the playhouse to attack the audience and actors alike. A horrifying lynching scene follows, as the fanatic crowd hangs the director and mutilates his corpse, while waving their fists and shouting 'Get out, Macbeth! Shakespeare must die!' Here 'Macbeth' no longer points to the regime being criticized, but the critique itself. Shakespeare, symbolizing art that reveals truth, must be killed. The film ends with 'Dear Leader' appearing on television announcing emergency rule, and the actor playing Malcolm beaten and thrown into jail, to be greeted by his fellow actors as 'King of Scotland', the first time a real place name is mentioned in the film as fiction ceases to be fiction.

Sponsored by Thailand's Ministry of Culture under an anti-Thaksin government in 2010, the film was banned by the same Ministry in 2012, under the government led by Yingluck Shinawatra,

(a)

(b)

8. 'Dear Leader' Mekhdekh with blood-stained hands in *Shakespeare Must Die* (2012)

Thaksin's sister, because it 'has content that causes divisiveness among the people of the nation'.[33] While the film follows Shakespeare closely in its language – K claims that 'every syllable in that [English] scene is straight from Shakespeare' – its visuals vividly recall Thailand's contemporary history. The lynching scene echoes a real event, of a student demonstrator lynched in the 1976 uprising. The film incorporates stock footage of recent red-shirt demolition, striking images of an aged king, and a mob wearing red shirts and headbands. Other parallels with the Thaksin regime include the dictator's bloody suppression of dissidents and his final appearance on television.

While attributing the use of documentary footage to the film's low budget, and the excessive use of red to Thai theatre convention and to the bloody nature of Shakespeare's play, K does not evade the film's engagement with Thai politics. Like Shakespeare's Ross and Macduff, she laments: 'Thailand is in the worst mood in my living memory; the very dust in the air is filled with rage, hate, grief and helplessness.' She argues for the necessity to remember a nation's tragic past: 'As with Germany and the Nazis, we need to show it to our children; we need to remember it always, not to perpetuate the bitterness, but to remember not to go back there again.'[34]

Manit Sriwanichpoom, the film's producer, appealed vigorously to the authorities to have the ban lifted. His argument resorts to Shakespeare's universality: the story is well known to all English-speaking school children, and cinematic versions are dispersed 'all over the world – India, Japan, Taiwan, you name it'.[35] All came to nought, but the process was made into a documentary entitled Censor Must Die, released in 2014. Ironically, the banning of Shakespeare became headlines in international media and the film's best advertisement, promoting K's anti-propaganda, anti-censorship message.

In contrast, the Taiwan adaptation encountered neither censors nor censure, from school or government authorities funding the production or the Festival's organizers and sponsors. Although

every word spoken came from Shakespeare's original, the strict runtime and cast regulation set by the Festival – a maximum of twenty minutes and no more than three actors – licensed liberal cutting and merging of roles, and hence enabled the construction of a new play. Heralded by a snare drum, the curtain opens to reveal a huge election campaign sign reading 'Yes! Macbeth'. The three witches appear as Enthusiasts, prophesying Macbeth's advancement. With a quick costume change behind the poster, an actor reappears as Macbeth, deliberating whether this message is good or ill, and his inner conflict is externalized, with the confirmation lines assigned to his wife:

> Macbeth. If it were done when 'tis done,
> Lady Macbeth.   then 'twere well
>   It were done quickly:
> Macbeth.   if the assassination
>   Could trammel up the consequence,
> Lady Macbeth.   and catch
>   With his surcease success; that but this blow
>   Might be the be-all and the end-all here
>
>   (1.7.1–5)[36]

Lady Macbeth hands her husband a pistol, with which he goes back stage. In total darkness a gunshot is heard, followed by the siren of an ambulance. Two Lamenters start a duet 'O horror, horror, horror!' (2.3.73), declaring their shock and grief. Macbeth crawls in, apparently seriously wounded. Checking to see that nobody is watching, however, he gets up unharmed, shakes off his blood-stained shirt, and puts on a jacket

---

33 From the official website of *Shakespeare Must Die* (www.shakespearemustdie.com/search/label/3%20Press%20Release).

34 Ing K, 'Director's Statement' (behindsmd.blogspot.com/2012/03/directors-statement.html).

35 Manit Sriwanichpoom, 'Press Release' (www.shakespearemustdie.com/search/label/3%20Press%20Release). To my knowledge, there is no cinematic adaptation of *Macbeth* from Taiwan.

36 The full performance video with bilingual subtitles, along with supporting materials including the director's notes and the judges' comments, is available at the Taiwan Shakespeare Database (www.Shakespeare.tw).

9. Macbeth and Lady Macbeth conspiring, against the background of a large election campaign sign in *Macbeth: A Political Allegory* (2011)

lowered from on high. Newly attired, he struts proudly about stage, with money showering on him, and the Lamenters' chorus ending 'Bleed, bleed, poor country' (4.3.32). In the next scene a businesswoman-like Collaborator escorts Lady Macbeth in, cleverly discerns her hint for a bribe – 'Naught's had, all's spent' (3.2.6) – and presents her with rich jewellery. Macbeth walks in frowning upon the newspapers he is reading, fretting how to be 'safely thus' (3.1.50). The two women hand him a US passport, telling him to 'Be bloody, bold, and resolute' (4.1.95) and to 'take no care / Who chafes, who frets, or where conspirers are' (4.1.106–7).

In response to this dishonest and corrupt ruler, lines by various Shakespearian characters are mixed and matched to create three new roles: a despairing green-shirt Pessimist, an indifferent light-blue-shirt Passivist, and an impassionate red-shirt Activist, all gathering under the old campaign sign, now smeared with the graffiti '$hame'. Urged by the Activist, they join forces to pull down the poster, thus symbolizing Macbeth's deposition. Desperately shouting 'Arm, arm, and out' (5.5.44) on his mobile phone, Macbeth is caught by two police officers. The play ends with him handcuffed and thrown into jail, to be 'the show and gaze o' the time' (5.10.24).

The play is packed with parallels to Taiwan politics. Governing rather by ideology than with prudence and judgment, Chen had a bumpy first term, and it was doubtful that he would get a second chance. On the day before the 2003 election, Chen was reportedly shot in the stomach. Presumably a politically-motivated assassination attempt, this unprecedented incident shocked all and rumours began to spread. The next day, it was revealed that Chen's injury was slight, but the election was already over, and Chen narrowly won by 0.2%. Many believed that the shooting was staged to win sympathy votes, especially after the subsequent police investigation failed to clarify many mysteries surrounding this case. Started thus, Chen's second term was further plagued by corruption scandals centred on himself and his wife, dubbed 'the Imelda Marcos of Taiwan' for her love of brand-name fashion and fine jewellery, leading to large protests by the 'red-shirts'.[37]

The audience in Hong Kong, primarily local high school and college students, understood the topical reference perfectly and cheered for it, especially because nothing of the like had ever been attempted at the Festival which, bearing the colonial legacy of English education, encourages creative stylization, but not wild interpretation, of Shakespeare. But the play is more than a satire. In the programme notes I wrote:

While presenting the tragedy of regicide and tyranny in verbatim Shakespearean lines, this production can also be seen as an allegory of contemporary politics, of Taiwan and elsewhere, from Southeast Asia to the Middle East, from Africa to Latin America. Though foreign and 400 years old, *Macbeth* is relevant because ambition is not a Scottish or Jacobean prerogative – it predates human history and is ubiquitous in modern times, manifest in obnoxious usurpation and abuse of power, in shameless political foul play, and in crafty manipulation of popular sentiment. Today's counterparts of the Macbeth couple may not have absolute authority to command obedience, but they would not be short of willing collaborators, who benefit from their greed and corruption. What is being eliminated in their scandalous play may not be a divinely ordained monarch, but peace, order, law, justice, liberty,

trust, morality, and public welfare, and we, not unlike Macduff, Ross, Lennox, or the anonymous Old Man, suffer enormous anger, frustration and anguish caused by an incompetent, short-sighted, and dishonest leadership which is wholly faith-based.

As I went on to introduce this production at international occasions, I was told that numerous analogues exist, in India, Korea, Malaysia, the Philippines and Vietnam.

Interestingly, the only 'censure' the play encountered was from the judges of the Festival, namely the Shakespearians. One remarked: 'It is not really a presentation of Shakespeare's *Macbeth* but rather a new play'; another called it 'a kind of visual *Macbeth* poem, or fantasia on Shakespeare's play, rather than a strict performance of it'.[38] As the director, I have no objection to these comments. Rather, I take them as compliment. Indifference or even resentment towards local and international politics has led my students to read *Hamlet* and *King Lear* as family drama, and *Macbeth* as a criminal and ghost story. If my unconventional adaptation has raised consciousness in their political responsibility, it has not been done in vain.

Intentional or accidental departure from source materials, though proscribed by Shakespeare contests and questioned by some Shakespearian scholars, has led to varied and vibrant productions, naturalist or stylized, conservative or radical. More often than not, Shakespeare is employed selectively. He serves as one of the multiple, contending origins for each production – along with the target society's cultural tradition, history and politics – and does not always triumph when clashing with other components. Featuring betrayal, derailments or thinly veiled political agenda, is our Shakespeare

---

[37] When this article was originally written, Taiwan's ex-leader Chen Sui-bian was in jail. He was granted medical parole in January 2015, after serving six years of a twenty-year sentence.

[38] The remarks are by Geoffrey Borny and Peter Holbrook respectively. Their comments, along with those of John Gilles, are online at the Festival's official website (www.eng .cuhk.edu.hk/shakespeare/publicdetail.php?id=55).

still Shakespeare? Or shall these productions be categorized and assessed only as 'Shakespearian-flavoured' original plays?

On food labels, ingredients are listed in descending order of predominance by weight, and as a percentage. Shakespeare, however, is not like potatoes or a fruit, which can be quantitatively measured to authenticate crisps or juice. Even the ample use of his very words – the only measurable Shakespeare – cannot ensure adherence to his early modern suppositions or freedom from local and contemporary engagement. The world is all before us, and what avails to linger? Perhaps it is time that we leave behind the quest for the Shakespearian origin and just embrace our Shakespearian destiny.

GLOBAL SHAKESPEARES, AFFECTIVE HISTORIES, CULTURAL MEMORIES

JYOTSNA G. SINGH AND ABDULHAMIT ARVAS

I

If Shakespeare imagined the 'world as a stage', contemporary globalizing trends have further transformed his works into richly peopled worlds of varied cultures and communities. The Renaissance itself, as demonstrated in recent scholarship, is now viewed as a 'Global' Renaissance in which travel, trade and militarism generated complex, though often asymmetrical, economies of exchange – cultural, economic, sexual and religious, among others.[1] And within this context, critics are increasingly drawn to historical mediations, charting the Bard's works as they have traversed through varied cultural formations, idioms, languages and contexts. In fact, the plays have become plural and multifarious, moving beyond the page and stage into film and digital formats: thus in the past decade, we have witnessed postcolonial Shakespeare, Chinese Shakespeare, Bollywood Shakespeare, Japanese Shakespeare and, as we discuss here, Kurdish and Kashmiri Shakespeare – all rapidly proliferating into a movement labelled 'Global Shakespeare'.[2]

In its overarching aim, this article examines how the intercultural imperative of Shakespearian dissemination is both global – in extending its reach to yet newer parts of the world – and local, in the sense of attending more closely to indigenous, native cultures and geo-politics. More specifically, our interest lies in exploring the *affective* possibilities of a global Shakespeare as a trans-historical brand – becoming 'native' to other cultures, while

dramatizing affective histories and cultural memories in voices and agents that *exceed* the canonical

[1] Among recent studies on the global early modernity, see Jyotsna G. Singh, 'Introduction', in *A Companion to the Global Renaissance: English Literature and Culture in the Era of Expansion* (London, 2010), pp. 1–28; Jerry Brotton, *The Renaissance Bazaar: from The Silk Road to Michelangelo* (Oxford, 2002); Jonathan Burton, *Traffic and Turning: Islam and English Drama, 1579–1624* (Newark, DE, 2005); Gerald MacLean, *Looking East: English Writing and the Ottoman Empire before 1800* (New York, 2007); Daniel Vitkus, *Turning Turk: English Theater and the Multicultural Mediterranean, 1570–1630* (New York, 2003), among others.

[2] In the past decade, early modern studies has been increasingly engaged with the global 'travels' of Shakespearian works via translations, adaptations, and radical revisions in texts and performances on stage and screen. Selected studies that have given direction to this movement are as follows: Christy Desmet and Robert Sawyer, eds., *Shakespeare and Appropriation* (New York, 1999); Martin Orkin, *Local Shakespeares: Proximations and Power* (New York, 2005); Sonia Massai, *World-wide Shakespeares: Local Appropriations in Film and Performance* (London, 2005); Craig Dionne and Parmita Kapadia, eds., *Native Shakespeares: Indigenous Appropriations on a Global Stage* (Burlington, 2008); Alexa Huang, *Chinese Shakespeares: Two Centuries of Cultural Exchange* (New York, 2009); Mark Thornton Burnett, *Shakespeare and World Cinema* (Cambridge, 2010); Journals such as *Borrowers and Lenders, Journal of Shakespeare and Appropriation*, and the *Global Shakespeare Journal* – as well as the MIT pioneering digital site under the directorship of Peter S. Donaldson and Alexa Huang provide a collaborative project, 'The Global Shakespeares Video & Performance Archive' that offers online access to performances of Shakespeare, while demonstrating the diversity of the worldwide reception and production of Shakespeare's plays. To see these diverse productions, see http://globalshakespeares.mit.edu/about/

uses to which the works are put.[3] How does the interaction with local knowledges via 'travelling' Shakespeares mediate and interact with the universalizing claims of dominant ideologies – of the state/nation, of global progress, of an immutable human nature and of a timeless Shakespearian canon itself? 'Resistance', 'subversion', 'appropriation', 'decolonization', 'cultural translation' – often evoked in binaries – are familiar terms in the critical scholarship of the past decade; however, the increasingly transnational globalizing trends are no longer typically invested in binaries of self and other, and colonial and postcolonial, as Martin Orkin succinctly puts it: the 'knowledges' and responses of North Americans and Europeans are 'partly irreversibly hybridized as a result of colonialism, and more recently globalization and its effects'.[4] This article aims to further explore the implications of these current trends of 'going native' focusing on affective possibilities of a global Shakespeare, not only as becoming 'native' to and harnessing affective histories from other cultures, but also how these non-western contexts – 'local knowledges from non-metropolitan locations' – produce new interpretive possibilities within Shakespearian language, meaning and context.[5]

We examine three case studies of Shakespeare 'going native', dramatizing affective histories and cultural memories in voices and agents that *complicate* the traditional canonical uses to which the works are put.[6] These 'Global Shakespeares' include a recently released Indian film version of *Hamlet*, *Haidar* (2014); a staged performance of a Kurdish *Hamlet* in Turkey and the Netherlands; and *King Lear* performed by children, staged outdoors in a Syrian Refugee camp (2014). By focusing on the mobilizations of emotional energies – with attendant cultural echoes – within the native, local materials, we can map the political, not simply in modes of governance, militarism, commerce or diplomacy, etc., but rather, the political as it is suffused by desires, fantasies and the imagination, as Begoña Aretxaga explains in her article, 'Maddening States'. Bringing to the fore an interconnection between the political and affective – a condition Aretxaga defines as the 'feeling state' –

we can see how the state is not an aseptic image of rational micro-practices, but a state suffused with affect. What articulates the excess fantasy of the state (the fantasy of statehood, the fantasy of total control, the fantasy of appropriation of the other, the fantasy of heterosexual domesticity) appears as a major component of political life and a key factor in the deployment of state power under the signs of nationalism, unity, etc.[7] Thus keeping in mind these intersections between the political, affective and the aesthetic, in each of these case studies of 'going native', we illuminate and map the 'affect worlds' or evocations of sensory, oral, emotional effects/affects that shape figures, events, languages and the politics of the Shakespearian adaptations as defined by Ananya Jahanara Kabir.[8]

---

[3] Dionne and Kapadia's discussion of Shakespeare 'going native' provides an important frame for this essay. 'Shakespeare is the site of contest for those peoples who seek to express their identities in complicated ways next to and against British literary traditions. Shakespeare is "native" – the place to which one returns – when rethinking the possibility of resistant forms of self and culture in the postcolonial context' (2). For more on 'Native Shakespeares', see their 'Introduction', pp. 1–18.

[4] Martin Orkin, *Local Shakespeares: Proximations and Power*, (London, 2005), p. 3. For a further discussion of local and global engagements and negotiations of Shakespearian works and their meanings, see, pp. 1–7.

[5] Orkin argues against the 'present readiness of constituencies within the Shakespeare metropolis to disseminate the Shakespeare text . . . to any location and to harvest the attending profits'. Instead, he calls for attending to 'local knowledges' that may 'offer additional opportunities for thinking about Shakespeare's plays' (p. 2).

[6] Dionne and Kapadia, *Native Shakespeares*, p. 2. This is our central formulation, also mentioned earlier.

[7] Begoña Aretxaga, 'Maddening States: On the Imaginary of Politics', appeared posthumously in *Annual Reviews in Anthropology*, 32 (2003), 393–410. She helps us to understand how 'the state becomes a social subject of everyday life . . . That is to ask about bodily excitations and sensualities, powerful identifications, and unconscious desires of state officials; about performances and public representations of statehood; and about discourses, narratives, and fantasies generated around the idea of the state' (p. 395).

[8] Ananya Jahanara Kabir, 'Affect, Body, Place: Trauma Theory in the World', in *The Future of Trauma Theory*, ed. Gert Buelens, Sam Durrant and Robert Eaglestone (London, 2014), pp. 72–3.

Moving beyond a search for a coherent or teleological correspondence between the text and performative/cinematic contexts, while charting the cultural memory formations in these global encounters, we hope to illuminate some aspects of what Ric Knowles defines as a multi-layered contextualized 'thickness' whereby we take 'the larger function [of the productions] within their own cultures into account'.[9]

II

Travel itself almost inevitably invokes a complex, hybrid and dynamic process, one that can destabilize familiar epistemologies and their attendant categories of difference, as James Clifford theorizes: travel involves a scrambling of locations, whereby the 'taint of locations' by class, race, gender, etc. is replaced by an emphasis on 'travel encounters as sites of cross-cultural knowledge' and underpinned by a dynamic reappraisal of a 'history of locations and a location of histories'.[10] Applying Clifford's terminology to global, multicultural and cross-cultural performances as well scholarship on Shakespeare's 'travels' – in its wide-ranging approaches and affects/effects – one can see how this movement has brought the Bard's status as a cultural icon of Western humanist culture under scrutiny. However, as the global, more cosmopolitan reach of Shakespearian scholarship – drawing on earlier inflections of 'Postcolonial Shakespeare' and 'Shakespeare as Empire' – is growing, so the question arises whether this 'popularity' of multicultural and, indeed, multi-media Shakespeare should be read in cautionary terms, for instance, within the context of what Rosie Braidotti defines as the 'paradoxes' within the 'post-industrial culture'. Within her formulation globalization on the one hand evokes the end of history and ideology amidst a return to typically neo-liberal belief in an 'immutable and unmovable "human nature" allegedly catered for by . . . advanced capitalist services'. On the other hand, our global culture also marks a 'euphoric celebration of new technologies, new economy, new lifestyles . . .'[11] Thus, is the global Shakespeare movement an inevitable

product of the political economy of post-modernity, which favours 'a proliferation of differences, but only within a strictly commercial logic of profit and under the sign of a universal, global culture [supposedly] easily accessible to all'?[12] Such questions increasingly shape, or are at least useful in examining, contemporary Shakespearian scholarship, performance and pedagogy today. A well-articulated programme of study, for instance, has been launched by Queen Mary, University of London and the University of Warwick (in joint collaboration) as the 'Global Shakespeare Project'. The aim of this programme is 'to engage with, critique, and develop ideas of globalisation, interdisciplinarity and translation that inform a new approach to the study of Shakespeare. Global Shakespeare is committed to the idea of the "student as producer" and you will be invited to work with leading Shakespearians in the production of new knowledge in the field.'[13]

While these goals will no doubt bring to light new dimensions of 'traveling Shakespeares' within 'a history of locations and locations of history', as Clifford articulates, another endeavour called the 'World Shakespeare Project' (WSP), based in the US, laudably aims to literally disseminate Shakespeare in worldwide travels via 'real time' encounters with Shakespeare, as stated on its webpage: 'Experimenting with new technologies that allow real-time interaction between students and faculty

---

9 Ric Knowles, *Reading the Material Theatre* (Cambridge, 2004), p. 12. While we do not directly apply his theoretical framework drawn from theatre semiotics, cultural studies and materialist analysis, we keep in mind his emphasis on the complexity of contextualization, especially in 'the ways in which theatrical and cultural determinants have worked together (or against one another) in specific instances' (p. 22). See 'Introduction', pp. 1–23.

10 We draw on James Clifford's problematization of the concept of travel as a context for approaching Shakespeare's travels. For a full discussion of Clifford's theory of travel, see *Routes: Travel and Translation in the Late Twentieth Century* (Cambridge, 1997), pp. 16–17.

11 Rosie Braidotti, *Transpositions* (Cambridge, 2006), p. 2.

12 Braidotti, *Transpositions*, p. 8.

13 www2.warwick.ac.uk/fac/cross_fac/iatl/activities/projects/globalshakespeare/pgsudy/whatnext.

worldwide [via teleconferencing], the WSP offers an alternative pedagogical experience. Regardless of location, race, religious creed or financial status, students and faculty share live interactive classroom exchange. Shakespeare's universal narratives provide the common currency. Alternative voices populate this artistic and cultural exchange as languages and regional dialects resonate through its community. The WSP provides the platform – the virtual global "stage" – for these alternative Shakespeares.'[14] A recent article describes the project with a citation from Sheila Cavanagh of Emory University, the WSP director: 'It's very different talking about *The Merchant of Venice* with kids in India who have seen their parents beaten up by moneylenders, or thinking about marriage expectations in *The Taming of the Shrew* with young people in Morocco', she says.[15] Projects such as the WSP can measure some success by the exposure of disparate, and often disadvantaged, communities to both Shakespeare and to some digital know-how; but if (as it states on its website) the WSP represents 'universal narratives of Shakespeare as a common currency', the relationship between metropolitan modes of knowledge and 'alternative voices' seems conceptually problematic and flawed in its aims. WSP is, after all, a metropolitan constituency with its attendant constraints, disseminating Shakespeare from Western perspectives. We want to explore, in terms set by Orkin, Dionne and Kapadia, and others, what happens when natives claim the Bard directly and via *non-metropolitan* modes of knowledge and experiences.

III

Shakespeare going global is clearly the currency of our increasingly worldwide educational and cultural market, as is evident from the projects outlined above or, in another instance, the MIT-based Global Shakespeares Video & Performance Archive (see n. 2). However, these (and other) endeavours still face the challenge of mediating the global disseminations of an iconic Shakespeare, even while attending to the local contexts of adaptation, translation and appropriation of the Bard

'going native'. Keeping these tensions in mind, we chart three case studies of Shakespeare becoming 'native' to or engaging with other non-Western historical recuperations of 'affect worlds' embedded in cultural palimpsests. We argue that these productions, on the one hand, create new interpretive possibilities within Shakespearian language and meaning and, on the other hand, use Shakespeare specifically to engage with globalization and its attendant, frequently violent, dislocations and displacements of peoples, races and cultures. Our focus is on how these specific renderings of each cinematic/theatrical production enables a cultural translation that works both ways, illuminating and complicating both the Shakespearian text and the other/alien culture and history with which it engages. In each study, as stated earlier, we hope to capture voices and agents that are 'in excess' of the familiar, 'universal' Shakespearian universe and as a result even go further in exploring aspects of what Bertolt Brecht describes as the 'material value' of the classics (*Materialwert der Klassiker*), whereby 'the prime value of the classics lay in their being raw material, a quarry to be plundered in the way the Vandals had sacked ancient Rome', an approach that involved 're-mounting or reassembling' the classic work.[16]

Case study 1: Hamlet/Haidar *(India, 2014)*

'All of Kashmir is a prison', Haider (Shahid Kapoor) says in the film version of *Hamlet* (in Hindustani), and the script co-authored by the director, Vishal Bhardwaj, and Kashmiri journalist, Basharat Peer, depicts its draconian repressions on its inmates. Shakespeare's *Hamlet* is largely staged within firmly demarcated interiors or the

---

[14] www.worldshakespeareproject.org/.

[15] 'Shakespeare in the South: Pageants Faded', *The Economist*, 20 October 2014. Online edition, http://www.economist.com/blogs/democracyinamerica/2014/10/shakespeare-south.

[16] For a fuller account of Brecht's approach to adaptation and appropriation, see Wilhelm Hortmann, *Shakespeare on the German Stage: The Twentieth Century* (Cambridge, 1998), pp. 81–3.

battlements of the King's castle, except for the gravediggers' scene. On stage, the outside world has a spectral presence, with news about Ophelia's drowning and the scene representing Hamlet's forced travel to England where he never arrives. If 'Denmark is a prison', the world of the court certainly implies the walls closing in on it, reminiscent of a prison, as for instance famously evoked by another foreign film adaptation, Kozintsev's Russian *Hamlet*. *Haidar*, in contrast, blasts open the world of interiors initially evoked by the police bombing of the young Haidar's family home; then the film moves across fast-changing vistas, taking us from dark interiors of traditional houses, to blasted ruins of bombed out homes, torture chambers in prisons, scenic landscapes of trees and lakes, and a striking snowy graveyard reminiscent of the gravediggers' scene in Shakespeare's play.

'In my film, in a way, Kashmir becomes *Hamlet*', observes the director of *Haidar* in a recent interview. 'The human conflict in Kashmir drew me. I've set *Haidar* in 1995, when militancy was at its peak. I wanted to observe the human tragedy . . . *Haidar* is an extension of what I began in *Maqbool* and *Omkara*.'[17] The conditions of the militant struggle depict a world violently exposed in ruins in which any refuge, safety, or for that matter, any psychic interiority for the melancholy protagonist or for the denizens of occupied Kashmir seems out of reach. The film dispenses with Hamlet's soliloquies and, instead, evokes some scattered lines depicting the hero's angst before various audiences: '*hum hain ki nahin hain*' ('do we exist or do we not?'), Haidar and the demonstrators raise as their slogan of protest (Illustration 10). In 1995, the *New York Times* reported on this militancy, 'For India, ruling Kashmir has come down to something like an occupation: an army and police force of at least 300,000, bunkers everywhere . . . Kashmiri human rights groups say two-thirds of the 30,000 people killed in the five-year conflict have been civilians.'[18] A powerful scene with which the film opens depicts security forces gathering around the house of Haidar's parents (while he is in college). From a distance, seated inside an armoured jeep, a man with his face covered searches the men's eyes for hints of guilt. With a nod or hand gesture they may be spared, and can walk on. Or, if he beeps the horn, as he did when Haider's father stood before him, the security takes them away and they vanish.[19] In this case, the doctor father who treated militants (we learn later) had already been betrayed by his brother, smiling, deceitful Khurram Meer/Claudius (Kay Kay Menon), who is one of the government informants and collaborators.

This is just one of numerous, almost endless scenes of militaristic state power with its paraphernalia of surveillance and check-points, with people disappearing and being tortured, producing powerful emotions of fear and terror in the Kashmiri crowds — and in us as viewers. Basharat Peer, one of the script writers, a Kashmiri himself, explains the genesis of his adaptation of *Hamlet* in Kashmir in terms of a specific, horrific practice: 'a policy deployed by the Indian state was to create a militia of several thousand men, Kashmiris, with a license to kill really let loose on a population and told to kill the militant groups and their sympathizers because they were part of the society, they knew who worked, how and they knew everyone. *And to me, the question of a brother*

---

[17] 'Interview with Director Vishal Bhardwaj', in *Indian Express* 5 October 2014, Harneet Singh http://indianexpress.com/article/entertainment/bollywood/kashmir-is-the-hamlet-of-my-film/. It is useful to note, as one critic observes, that Bhardwaj 'uses his plays to reflect the violence and vicissitudes of modern India. *Maqbool*, an adaptation of *Macbeth*, was set in the Mumbai underworld; *Omkara* transported *Othello* to the feudal badlands of northern India. His latest effort, a loose adaptation of *Hamlet* called *Haidar* takes place in Kashmir during the turbulent 1990s.' Vaibhav Vats, 'Bollywood Takes on the Agony of Kashmir through Shakespeare', *New York Times, India Ink*, 27 October 2014.

[18] *New York Times* reporting by John Burns cited by Omar Waraich, '*Kashmir in Hamlet*', http://roadsandkingdoms.com/2014/hamlet-in-kashmir/.

[19] Basharat Peer, who co-wrote the script of *Haidar*, in his earlier book, *Curfewed Nights* (New York, 2010), pp. 38–45, tells readers of crackdowns where Indian soldiers would surround a village and summon its male residents to be paraded in front of a masked man who would determine their fate with a mere glance. The powerful scene near the start of the film was inspired by this anecdote.

Do we exist or do we not?

10. Haidar on left with street demonstrators.

betraying a brother, that the unit of a family is torn into two – the moment we thought of "Hamlet";[20] this is the 'affect-state' in action, enacting the 'fantasy of statehood, the fantasy of total control, the fantasy of appropriation of the other' with confident state actors like the informant and aspiring politician Khurram Meer/Claudius and Parvez/Polonius, a sinister policeman, feeling little compunction in their opportunism, even if it harms their own kin.[21]

While some critics have suggested that the film is 'deficient in the *Hamlet* department', others more aptly observe how the film has infused Shakespeare with new suggestive, affective possibilities by transplanting some of his poetic imagery and language onto re-imagined, re-contextualized visuals, and not merely reproducing the literal action with dialogues: 'The setting is one of the reasons *Haidar* works. It is true to the haunting opacity of Shakespeare's most opaque of tragedies, but the Kashmir canvas is potent.'[22] For instance, a creative way of

translating the original ambiguity of Shakespeare's play is by replacing the literal ghost of Hamlet's father with the presence of a phantasmal militant, hiding his bruises under dark glasses aptly called *Roohdar* (Ghost-person), played by the charismatic actor, Irfan Khan. He brings the message of revenge

[20] 'New Shakespeare Movie Puts *Hamlet* in Kashmir', Interview with the Basharat Peer, who adapted and co-wrote the script, www.npr.org/2014/10/25/358789984/new-shakespeare-movie-puts-hamlet-in-kashmir.

[21] Aretxaga, 'Maddening States', p. 395.

[22] Sanjukta Sharma, Film Review, *Haidar*. 1 October 2014. *Live Mint* praises the film for 'transmuting Shakespeare's poetic imagery and the atmosphere that his verses conjure into recontextualized visuals' and considers it a success, www.livemint.com/Leisure/NLNfyiXDL31Dq9zF0NZU8N/Film-review–Haidar.html Rachel Saltz in her review. 'Shakespearean Revenge in Violent Kashmir' does not consider *Haidar* the 'equal of Mr. Bhardwaj's other Shakespeare films', *New York Times*, 2 October 2014, www.nytimes.com/2014/10/03/movies/haider-puts-an-indian-twist-on-hamlet.html

(*Intiqam*) from Hamlet's dead father (Dr Meer) whom he knew in the torture chambers of the Indian military:

> Haidar mera intiqam lena mere bhai se
> Uski dono aankheno mein goliyan dagna
> Jin Aankhon se usne tumhari maa pe fareb dale the
> Aur Maa? –Use Allah ke insaaf ke liye chor de
>
> [Hamlet, take revenge on my brother.
> Shoot him in his eyes – those eyes with which he
>   seduced your mother.
> And your Mother? Leave her to the justice of God
>   (Allah).]

In doing away with the supernatural horror of the original play, the director rejects the contrivance of suspense and horror, highlighting instead the commonplace traumas of Kashmir, an 'affect-world' depicted in sensory terms throughout the film – death, loss, poignant hauntings of everyday life in the brutal war. Roohdar's resonant voice and poetic re-creation of Haidar's dead father's presence is perhaps the centrepiece of the themes of death, loss, revenge and tragedy in the film.

Haidar's rendering of Gertrude/Ghazala (Tabu) is perhaps most remarkable in the centrality of her role in the film, as well as in cross-pollinating the Oedipal dimensions of Hamlet's obsession with his mother's virtue in Shakespeare's play with the Indian Oedipal mother-son relationship, the staple of Hindi/Bollywood cinema. The charged erotic relationship is even given a backstory of the mother-son bonds in childhood, and some intimations of her un-erotic marriage to his father. She is also depicted as a figure of empathy and, until Haidar is able to find his father's grave to confirm his death, her fate is similar to scores of Kashmiri wives of missing men; they are called 'half-widows', not free to marry, though in Ghazala's case, she quickly submits to the seductions of Khurram/Claudius before they marry. The 'mirth in funeral, dirge in marriage' which casts a shadow on Gertrude here transposes into the more local condition of the 'half-widows' who are surreptitiously breaking the same codes of loyalty. Familiar, Shakespearian effects/affects are captured in striking scenes, as for instance when Hamlet returns from college and we watch him spying on his mother and uncle in an intimate playful moment of song and laughter, followed by an emotionally wrought scene between mother and son. The final scenes of *Haidar* take place in a graveyard in a long snowy expanse of hillside.

Here among the graves, we witness the burial of Arshia (Ophelia) who goes down the same path of a breakdown and suicide as well as the climactic, violent revenges played out within a larger battle of militants versus the security forces. As mentioned at the outset, there is no return to a world of interiors or to any sustained sense of interiority throughout the film. Hamlet reflects on the transience of life ruminating on an unidentified skull as a *memento mori*. These final scenes reinforce the public, mass 'graveyard' that is Kashmir and end literally in a series of blasts and plot twists but in ways that undermine the traditional 'revenge' plot. In the final moments Ghazala warns her son that revenge only produces revenge and tells him, 'we must gain freedom from revenge [*Intiqam*]'.

Haidar is obviously not an authentic *Hamlet* in its adaptations from the original; but reading the play via the contextual 'thickness' of the Kashmir tragedy – within a draconian State in which the opaque protagonist, Haidar, loses all emotional and psychic security – helps us to rethink 'all of Denmark as a prison'. In Brechtian fashion, Bhardwaj and Peer ransack and reassemble the original work in order to harness the traumatic cultural memories of the Kashmir conflict – one that is not entirely resolved even today and has, in fact, become exacerbated with the rise of the Hindu right wing that projects India as a purely 'Hindu' nation.[23] Thus the final vision of the film inflects the Kashmir tragedy with postcolonial South Asian history, in a poetic epilogue recited (during the credits) from a poem 'Intisaab', by noted Pakistani poet, Faiz Ahmed Faiz, who is also the social conscience of the sub-continent:

---

[23] The Hindu right and jingoistic nationalists really went after the film. They ran a campaign on Twitter encouraging a boycott of *Haidar*, as an anti-national film that shows the Indian army in a negative light.

Intisaab (Dedication)
(A dedication) to this day
And to this day's sorrow.
Today's sorrow that disdains the blossoming garden of
    life,
To the forest of yellow leaves –
the forest of yellow (dying) leaves that is my country,
to the assembly of pain that is my country . . . [24]

If Shakespeare's tragic, poetic representations in *Hamlet* gave us a distinct emotional language to understand the disintegration of the characters caught up under the surveillance state of Kashmir in *Haidar*, the same play has also enabled an evocative and affectively charged rendering of Kurdish cultural memories and identities in our next case study of a Kurdish *Hamlet*.

Case study 2: A Kurdish Hamlet *(Turkey and the Netherlands, 2012)*

The first Shakespeare production in the Kurdish language, *Hamlet*, staged in the city of Diyarbakir/Amed (2012) by director Celil Toksöz made history. Incorporating into the Shakespearian play-text the affective repertoire of Kurdish music, dance, costumes and language, this adaptation brought to life the shared cultural memories of the Kurdish peoples. Kurds, as we learn from contemporary headlines, are scattered across several countries, Turkey, Syria, Iraq and Iran, as well as within a large diaspora, and have a history of struggles against political and cultural repression. Produced by Theatre RAST (Amsterdam, the Netherlands) and in cooperation with the City Theatre and the Cultural Department of the City of Diyarbakır, a centre of Kurdish culture in the Southeast of Turkey, this version of *Hamlet* was translated into Kurdish (in the most commonly spoken Kurdish dialect, *Kurmancî*) by Nawa Kemir. The Kurdish *Hamlet* has so far been staged in the Netherlands, Sweden and many cities in Turkey such as Diyarbakir, Ankara and Izmir, drawing great attention from the public – both Kurdish and Turkish – and the mainstream Turkish media.[25] Indeed it was a celebratory moment for the director, actors and the translator, as well as for

Kurdish and Turkish politicians who attended the play and applauded the production, evoking the recent peace negotiations between the Turkish state and the Kurds.[26]

It was in this atmosphere of a revival of the Kurdish language and culture in Turkey that Shakespeare's *Hamlet* in particular became a means for the director to declare a unique Kurdish identity not only to the Turks but also to the world at large. Here we have another example of Shakespeare 'going native', in this case representing the world of *Hamlet* in a distinct Kurdish setting, deploying traditional Kurdish music, folk dances, costumes and songs, adding contextual depth to the canonical work. The play is translated onto the stage through an appropriation and addition of local Kurdish elements to the play. Some soliloquies are transformed into songs, new lyrics have been written by Toksöz and the music, too, is composed specifically for the show and performed live on stage by a five-piece orchestra playing traditional Kurdish instruments. The plot and the characterizations do not deviate much from Shakespeare's text and a preoccupation with revenge based on remembrance remains intact. The ghost of the father motivates the young Hamlet for revenge by connecting it to 'honour' (*namus*), calling Hamlet's future revenge a form of honour-killing. Gertrude's guilt, or Hamlet's relationship with his mother, with its possible incestuous implications, is of less concern for this performance. The characters are all familiar,

---

[24] See www.bollymeaning.com/2014/09/aaj-ke-naam-lyrics-translation-haider.html. Accessed 12 December 2014.

[25] For press coverage of the performances in mainstream Turkish newspapers see, for example, 27 November 2012 issues of *Hurriyet, Radikal, Yeni Safak*.

[26] The play came at a time when the 'Kurdish conflict', which had been long ignored by the Turkish state since the foundation of Turkish Republic in 1923, was in the process of resolution through peace negotiations and the Turkish State was beginning to recognize the Kurdish language and ethnic identity. Many Turkish and Kurdish members of the Parliament attended the performance in the playhouse, Sinasi Sahnesi, in the capital city Ankara on the 27 November 2012, and the Turkish government was represented by the Minister of Culture, Ertugrul Gunay. For more on Kurdish conflict see n. 28.

except for Rosencrantz and Guildenstern who are now the male and female Ros and Gul. The play imagines *Hamlet* in a Kurdish setting with a feudal Kurdish ruler (*mir*) instead of a European court. The older Hamlet is *Mir* Hamlet and Prince Hamlet becomes Hamlet *Mirza*. Thus, interestingly, while Shakespeare's 'Denmark' (as many of his other locales) does not represent a distinct cultural or national milieu, the Kurdish elements in this production evoke a recognizable locale based on non-metropolitan knowledge and culture, while making it available to the growing global audience and market for Shakespeare's plays. To what extent was this adaptation and translation of *Hamlet* a Brechtian form of ransacking classics? It does not radically alter the incidents and language of the play, as occurs in *Haidar*; instead the Kurdish *Hamlet* simply 'travels' to an unfamiliar, non-western world, though with a Brechtian political agenda of giving recognition to the repressed Kurdish linguistic and cultural agenda, creating a contextual thickness to the familial and political drama of the play.

In its re-assemblage of Shakespeare's *Hamlet*, then, the Kurdish play reworks the metadramatic elements of the canonical text into an innovative framing device that enacts the appropriation of the Bard's play by agents of the Kurdish culture. In effect, *Hamlet* itself becomes a play-within-a-play about a celebration of Kurdish culture. The curtain opens with two storytellers, a man and woman on stage, introducing the story to the audience. As they discuss and consider what story to narrate, the male storyteller says he has a new and beautiful (*tezeye, pir xweşe*) story in contrast to the well-known, too familiar Kurdish stories the woman wants to deliver. 'Nave çîrokame Hamlet e' ('our story is called *Hamlet*'), he announces, it is 'the story of prince Hamlet of Denmark (*mirzaye Denmark'e*) written by an English playwright called Shakespeare'. Of course Shakespeare's *Hamlet* is not new, and probably today it is the most adapted story, on stage and screen, in the western world. It is also familiar to Turkish audiences. However, in such a self-reflexive move, the play stresses *that it is the first Shakespeare in the Kurdish language*, thus *new* for Kurds to hear it in their long repressed, native

tongue. Seeing an English play in the Kurdish language with Kurdish settings, costumes and songs strengthens the affective relation between the play and the Kurds, between the Kurds and their native language.

Moving on, in their introduction to the play, the storyteller also calls Shakespeare a friend of Ahmad Khani, the prominent Kurdish writer from the seventeenth century. Making a connection between Shakespeare and the celebrated Kurdish author, the Kurdish *Hamlet* not only imagines the Bard as a native friend to the beloved author Khani but also situates the production in an affective literary world within repressed cultural histories of Kurdishness and the Kurdish language. Actually these two storytellers themselves are a part of this affective memory of the Kurdish experience of preserving their literary culture. They recall on the modern stage the role of the earlier figures of the *Dengbej*, who were, until very recently, wandering Kurdish storytellers and played a significant role in Kurdish folk and literary culture, belonging to a tradition that goes back to pre-Islamic times. While the Kurdish language was repressed and outlawed, the *Dengbej* faced criminalization and were under strict surveillance by military forces to prevent the transmission of the Kurdish language, especially after the 1980s. Thus the narrators on stage in the Kurdish *Hamlet* evoke immediate associations for Kurdish (and some Turkish) audiences with the Kurdish oral tradition in literature, culture and history. In fact, these two figures on the stage act as *Dengbej* characters mediating between the stage and the audience, and between the global, canonical play and the local histories of the Kurds.

These two narrators are also meaning-makers in their self-reflexive commentary and intrusions into Shakespeare's plot itself. For instance, they direct the audience's attention and emotional reactions to the world of *Hamlet* to that of the Kurds. At one point they intervene and query if Shakespeare is actually Kurdish because the story is so familiar and touching. The affective world of the play makes the storytellers and the audience seek proximities in human emotions, experiences, histories and tragedies. On the one hand the storytellers

11. Hamlet's first appearance on stage.

highlight the affective engagements between a foreign play and a local culture, but on the other hand they make sure that the Kurdishness is not missing in their retelling of Shakespeare's *Hamlet*. In Hamlet's first appearance on stage, while storytellers introduce each player to the audience, Hamlet comes on stage with a book in his hands, moves forward, and says 'to be or not to be' in English (Illustration 11).

In contrast to all the other characters standing behind him in traditional Kurdish dress, Hamlet wears a white shirt and black leggings that highlight his protruding genitalia. Upon seeing this, the female storyteller interrupts the play, asking '*Gro ev kîye?*' ('Who is this man?'). When the other storyteller identifies him as Hamlet, she protests, exclaiming what kind of clothing he is wearing, making his genitals visible in an 'inappropriate and shameless' way. She asks him to go backstage at once, get appropriately dressed, and come back on

stage. Hamlet follows her order and, like all other characters, he appears in traditional Kurdish clothes for the rest of the play (Illustration 12).

The storytellers change Prince Hamlet the Dane and his 'to be or not to be' in English to Hamlet the Kurd with his '*hebûn an nebûn*' in Kurdish. In sum, through such interventions by the two storytellers, the production *self-reflexively* highlights the significance of Kurdish elements – clothes, music and dance – in translating *Hamlet* to the Kurdish stage. Using *Hamlet* as a means to express Kurdish cultural difference, yet highlighting affective proximities, the production therefore puts into dialogue the global and the local and lets prince Hamlet travel onto the Kurdish stage through his transformation into a Kurdish noble.

The Kurdish *Hamlet* therefore plays a significant role in the process of creating a national identity and generating recognition of long-repressed Kurdishness in Turkey. On the webpage of the

12. A scene of festivity set in Mir Hamlet's court. Characters are dancing a Kurdish dance (*Govend*). Live musicians are present on the stage throughout the play, and Hamlet is in his Kurdish dress. Screenshot from the Amsterdam premiere of the play, *YouTube*.

Theatre Rast, the company that produced the play, the director of the play, Celil Toksöz, explains his decision to produce the Kurdish *Hamlet* on stage via a telling anecdote:

I remember reading an article in a Turkish newspaper once, in which a politician dismissed my language, Kurdish, as a 'language spoken in the mountains'. Answering a question from the journalist why Kurds weren't allowed to be taught in their own language in schools, he said: 'But Kurdish is not a real language, is it? You can't perform *Hamlet* in Kurdish, can you?' That remark has stuck with me ever since.[27]

Transitioning from the multi-ethnic Ottoman Empire to a national republic, the new Turkish Republic, founded in 1923, put Turks and the Turkish language at the very centre of its nation-building process. In this process, the Turkish Republic generated a policy of 'Turkification', a policy that suppressed and marginalized all other ethnic identities and languages in Turkey by confining the use of those languages to the private sphere and erasing them from public and political domains.[28] Toksöz refers particularly to the post-Republican, specifically post 1980s nationalism

[27] For the interview, and a documentary record of the premiere, see www.youtube.com/watch?v=V_7vugzZVO0 which is also where screenshots are from. All translations from Turkish, Kurdish and Hindi are ours, unless otherwise stated.

[28] The early republican policy of Turkification and nationalism continued in the following decades with official prohibition of the Kurdish language, Kurdish names, Kurdish publications and Kurdish music – the latter two would be set free only after 1990s. Yet the Turkish state recently began to give ear to the demands of Kurdish people after the Justice and Development Party rose to power, starting what is called the resolution process in 2010. This new process of negotiating with the Kurds resulted in publications in Kurdish, Kurdish translations, a state-sponsored television channel broadcasting in Kurdish, the appearance of Kurdish music videos on TVs and initiation of Kurdish language and literature departments in universities. For more on language reforms, and the association between the Turkish language and nation-state building in Turkey, see Senem Aslan, 'Citizen, Speak Turkish: A Nation in the Making', *Nationalism and Ethnic Politics*, 13 (2007), 245–72; Ilker Aytürk, 'Turkish Linguists against the West: The Origins of Linguistic Nationalism in Atatürk's Turkey', *Middle Eastern Studies*, 40.6 (2004), 1–25; Füsun Üstel, *Imparatorluktan Ulus-Devlete Türk Milliyetçiliği: Türk*

that denied Kurdish identity and culture, classified as 'inferior Turks' or 'Turks who lived in mountains', and associated 'savagery' and 'wildness' with the Kurdish people. In fact, some Turkish politicians and intellectuals claimed that the Kurdish language was not and could not be a completely separate language, but a corrupt form of the Turkish language, the mountain peoples' language in other words. And since supposedly inferior language cannot narrate a work like *Hamlet*, it is uncivilized. By defining the Kurdish language as a derivative, savage form of the Turkish language, this discourse 'othered' Kurdish people as rude, barbarous mountain folk.

This history of denial makes the Kurdish *Hamlet* an even more significant success because the play, as the director notes, provided him with an avenue to announce the distinct Kurdish culture and language that can give voice to *Hamlet*. As Dionne and Kapadia note, 'Shakespeare is a site for those peoples who seek to express their own identities, in complicated ways, with, next to, against British literary traditions. Shakespeare is "native" – the place to which one returns – when rethinking the possibility of resistant forms of self and culture in the postcolonial context.'[29] In this instance, the global Shakespeare, therefore, becomes a site of negotiation for the local Kurdish people to legitimize their once-criminalized cultural identity and language in Turkey and Europe.

Case study 3: King Lear *in the Zaatari Syrian refugee camp (Jordan, 2012)*

The production of *King Lear* performed by children in a Syrian refugee camp draws attention to the particular tragedy of the Syrian civil war, with its vast numbers of displaced children, seen through the prism of Shakespeare's seminal work. According to Ben Hubbard in his live story in the *New York Times*, this was the Zaatari Refugee Camp in Jordan: 'on a rocky patch of earth in this sprawling city of tents and prefab trailers, the king, dressed in dirty jeans and a homemade cape, raised his wooden scepter and announced his intention to divide his kingdom. His elder daughters, wearing

paper crowns and plastic jewelry, showered him with false praise, while the youngest spoke truthfully and lost her inheritance.'[30] Wide coverage followed this event as a human-interest story in major news outlets such as the *New York Times*, *Times of Israel* and *France 24*. The cultural capital associated with Shakespeare's name gave a widespread currency to the plight of a vulnerable population of children, deprived of education and other fundamental rights. Shakespeare is not unfamiliar in the Middle East or to the Arabic language, yet this

---

Ocakları, 1912–31 (Istanbul, 1997); Yilmaz Çolak, 'Language Policy and Official Ideology in Early Republican Turkey', *Middle Eastern Studies* 40.6 (2004), 67–91; Huseyin Sadoğlu, *Türkiye'de Ulusçuluk ve Dil Politikaları* (Istanbul, 2003). On repression and prohibition of Kurdish language and its relation with the rise of the Turkish nation state, see Abbas Vali, 'The Kurds and Their Others: Fragmented Identity and Fragmented Politics', *Comparative Studies of South Asia, Africa and the Middle East*, 18 (1998), 82–95; Ahmet Içduygu, Yilmaz Çolak, and Nalan Soyarık, 'What is the Matter with Citizenship? A Turkish Debate', *Middle Eastern Studies*, 35.4 (1999), 187–207; Kerem Öktem, 'Incorporating the Time and Space of the Ethnic 'Other': Nationalism and Space in Southeast Turkey in the Nineteenth and Twentieth Centuries', *Nations and Nationalism*, 10 (2004), 559–78, and his 'The Nation's Imprint: Demographic Engineering and the Change of Toponymes in Republican Turkey', *European Journal of Turkish Studies*, 7 (2009); Senem Aslan, 'Incoherent State: The Controversy over Kurdish Naming in Turkey', *European Journal of Turkish Studies*, 10 (2009); Amir Hassanpour, *Nationalism and Language in Kurdistan, 1918–1985* (San Francisco, 1992).

29 Dionne and Kapadia, *Native Shakespeares*, p. 2.

30 Ben Hubbard. 'Behind Barbed Wire, Shakespeare Inspires a Cast of Young Syrians', *New York Times*, 31 March 2014, www.nytimes.com/2014/04/01/world/middleeast/behind-barbed-wire-shakespeare-inspires-a-cast-of-young-syrians.html?_r=0. Jodi Rodoren, 'A Lost Generation: Young Syrians Struggle to Survive', *New York Times*, 8 May 2013: 'As the Syrian civil war rages into its third year, nearly one-third of the population of 22 million inside Syria needs humanitarian help, and 1.4 million have fled their homeland altogether. Of about 500,000 seeking shelter in Jordan, about 55 percent are under 18. Their troubles and challenges – years out of school, trauma from having witnessed the killing of relatives, sexual abuse – mirror those of their peers struggling to survive in tents and hideaways in Turkey, Iraq, Lebanon and Syria's own shattered communities.' www.nytimes.com/2013/05/09/world/middleeast/syrian-refugees-in-jordan-struggle-to-survive.html

13. Children as actors and their audience in the *Lear* production at the Zaatari refugee camp for Syrian refugees in Jordan.

seemingly minor event of Syrian children clearly produced an affective charge that infused both *Lear* and the location of performance with reverberations that extended far and beyond the civil war. We are forced to consider (in Clifford's formulation) the 'history of the location of the desert camp, and the location of history' in this production of *Lear* that serves as a *witness* to the mass dispossession of children, which in turn echoes Lear's own dispossession and the plight of the denizens of the storm, their 'houseless heads and unfed sides / [their] looped and windowed raggedness'. A sense of the stark poignancy of the youngsters' performance is evident in the account below (Illustration 13):

The sun blazed on the day of the performance, staged on a rocky rectangle of land surrounded by a chain-link fence topped with barbed wire. The 12 main actors stood in the middle, while the rest of the cast stood behind them, a chorus that provided commentary and dramatic sound effects. The audience sat on the ground. When each of Lear's first two daughters tricked him with false flattery in elegant, formal Arabic, the chorus members yelled 'Liar! Hypocrite!' until the sisters told them to shut up. And when the third sister refused to follow suit, the chorus members yelled 'Truthful! Just!' until the king told them to shut up.[31]

The Syrian actor-turned-director Nawar Bulbul, from the Syrian city of Homs, adapted and modified the play to make it more suitable for the children. His aim was not to make a political statement, nor to re-map the political coordinates of *Lear*. As he explains: it 'has nothing to do with politics and the Syrian uprising. I only took the roots of the story – that there is a dying king who wants to divide his realm among his three

---

[31] Hubbard, 'Behind Barbed Wire'; see also fn 30.

daughters. Two of them are liars and the third is honest. I focused on the comparison between lying and telling the truth.'[32] A simple fable distinguishing between truth and lies. And thirteen-year old actor Majd Ammari utters in classical Arabic the thunderous lines 'Blow, winds, and crack your cheeks! Rage! Blow!' He rails in a storm, calling on the sky to send down 'sulphurous and thought-executing fires' to 'singe my white head!' The stark simplicity of the production was a result of the literal deprivation of life in the refugee camp, but nonetheless the director stressed the historic convergence of events in the *Lear* performance:

Putting on one of Shakespeare's classics with a group of children in a refugee camp was nothing short of a crazy gamble. But the craziest thing of all is that they exceeded my wildest expectations.

I did this because I wanted to show that these children are not worthless and that they aren't condemned to stay on the fringes of society. I wanted to show that they have something real to contribute. I wanted to prepare the show for the International Theatre Day on March 27 (2014). In my opinion, the refugees living in Zaatari have as much right to celebrate this day as anyone anywhere. My original idea was simple. I just wanted to release the children from the mess created by grown-ups, the war that put them on the path to exile and poverty. To me, it doesn't make any sense when people talk about a 'revolution' in Syria . . . but bringing theatre into a refugee camp, that's a real revolution![33]

* * *

These three case studies draw on a range of affective experiences of distinct cultures and locales; they call for 'thick' contextual layers, revealing the political, civil war and refugee displacements in Syria/Jordan, the brutal military occupation in Kashmir and cultural and political dispossession of the Kurdish peoples in Turkey and elsewhere. To elaborate, the production of *King Lear* by the stateless Syrian children produced as a morality fable tugged at the conscience of the Western media; the Kurdish *Hamlet* on stage disrupted the Turkish state's singular linguistic and cultural project of Turkishness; and in the most recent, *Haidar*, Shakespeare's poetic palate has given us a new emotional language to understand the militaristic surveillance state that governed Kashmir during its civil unrest in the 1990s (with continuing instability today). Politics and politicians rarely provide a language beyond platitudes for understanding or mediating conflicts, violence and injustice; thus, it is befitting that we reach to Shakespeare to provide us with ways of imagining and shaping the intractable world in which we live, both locally and globally.

---

[32] 'Young Syrians Bring Lear to Life in a Refugee Camp', *Israel Times*, www.timesofisrael.com/young-syrians-bring-lear-to-life-in-refugee-camp/#ixzz3JYdE8M2C.

[33] 'Syrian Refugee Children Stage *King Lear*', http://observers.france24.com/content/20140331-syria-jordan-shakespeare-refugee-camp-zaatari.

SPINACH AND TOBACCO: MAKING SHAKESPEARIAN UNORIGINALS

PETER HOLLAND

I. SPINACH

On 19 January 1940, the Fleischer Studios released a new short animated film. Lasting six minutes, twenty-eight seconds, the usual length of one of their shorts, but unusual in its subject matter, *Shakespearian Spinach* was the first and only Popeye cartoon to be concerned with Shakespeare in performance.[1] Most Popeye cartoons, though by no means all, work with a formulaic template. In this one, the management of the Spinach Theatre have sacked Bluto for his hammy performance and replaced him with Popeye in the role of Romeo. Furious, Bluto makes attempt after attempt to sabotage the production – the scene under way is of course the 'balcony' scene. Eventually he takes Popeye's Romeo costume and nails him into a box. Popeye escapes, dresses in another Juliet costume and takes Olive's place as Juliet. Bluto shifts the action to 'Death Scene', as it is labelled on-stage, and apparently kills Popeye. Revived by munching a wreath made of spinach, Popeye beats up Bluto to the audience's delight and exhaustion, ending with Bluto, now in the Juliet costume, knocked-out in the ruins of the balcony and Olive and Popeye embracing.

As Lanier rightly notes, there are references to 'only two familiar lines from the balcony scene . . . as well as two key scenes from the play, the balcony scene and the crypt scene, both converted to slapstick violence'.[2] Nonetheless, it seems to me that *Shakespearian Spinach*, as a moment of cultural definition of Shakespeare performance, is surprisingly and intriguingly complex.

It was, of course, only a matter of time before the *Popeye* series would tackle Shakespeare. It had, for instance, played with the performance of classical music as early as 1935 in *The Spinach Overture* with Popeye as conductor. But *Shakespearian Spinach* was part of director Dave Fleischer's analysis at this time of live performance in relation to animation and *its* representation of liveness, for animation confronts liveness in an idiosyncratic way. The short in this sequence that has most intrigued animation scholars is *Puttin on the Act*, released a few months after *Shakespearian Spinach* on 30 August 1940, an unusual episode since it has no Bluto and no spinach. Popeye is at home rocking Swee'Pea when Olive rushes in brandishing a copy of a newspaper with a headline 'Vaudeville Coming Back!'. And, indeed, in 1940, live variety performances were again being programmed alongside films. Popeye heads off to

This article was first given as a paper at the International Shakespeare Conference in Stratford-upon-Avon in 2014. My thanks to all the many helpful questions and comments after the paper.

[1] My thanks to my colleague Don Crafton for introducing me to *Shakespearian Spinach* and for much advice on early animation. The film is available on YouTube but by far the best version is as part of a series of DVDs that include Popeye cartoons remastered and uncut with helpful commentary from historians of animation: *Popeye the Sailor, 1938–1940* (Warner Brothers, 2008), 2-DVD set. The film has been almost entirely ignored by Shakespeare scholars, except, of course, for a brief listing by Douglas Lanier in his extraordinary catalogue of 'Film Spin-Offs and Citations' in Richard Burt, ed., *Shakespeares after Shakespeare*, 2 vols. (Westport, CT, 2007), 1: 132–365, item 1127, p. 268.

[2] Lanier, 'Film Spin-Offs and Citations', p. 268.

the attic and dusts off his vaudeville costumes and the rest of the short is a set of variety turns as they get ready to perform in vaudeville again. With Swee'Pea as call-boy, we have a dance routine, a body-building act, Popeye impersonating Jimmy Durante, Stan Laurel and Groucho Marx, a balancing act, and an adagio dance. The bubble bursts when Swee'Pea points out the date on the newspaper, not 1940 but 1 August 1898; 'Olive', says Popeye, 'we're too late!' and the short ends.

Puttin on the Act gives Popeye and Olive a history: the stars of their own show had, as it were, started out in vaudeville. The cartoon characters have a backstory in performance, what Donald Crafton calls 'earlier pre-stardom lives' creating an 'authenticity' through their demonstration of their 'old shtick' as if the 'toon actors' are 'living stars'.[3] *Shakespearian Spinach* does not posit the *Romeo* production at the Spinach Theatre as past lives for the stars. Instead, it is simply another setting for the template triangle with its inevitable resolution. But it documents a placing of film and especially animation in relation to classical theatre and its connections with other forms of live performance. When Bluto pulls from the wings a stand and turns the page to show the sign 'Death Scene', we might see it as a reference to the placards that, at this time, were thought to have been displayed as scene locators in the early modern theatre, as for instance in Olivier's *Henry V* film (1944), where a page-boy as call-boy displays such a sign to the audience at the Globe. But we can also see it as an example of the signs announcing each act in vaudeville, analogous to the ones Swee'Pea will change in *Puttin on the Act*. Assumptions about early modern performance and the practices of variety converge.

These ambiguities of location are apparent in the short's first sequence, as Bluto arrives at the theatre. The building has traces of a Spanish Colonial style in its exterior, like the Pasadena Playhouse, built in 1925, which, for Hollywood, was the epitome of theatre as high culture. But, just as American English uses 'theatre' both for live performance spaces and for film, unlike the British English distinction between 'theatres' and 'cinemas', so the Spinach Theatre, with its marquee signage and

ticket office centralized under the front canopy, could as easily be a movie theatre and its auditorium style, with boxes, is not able to be defined as uniquely appropriate to *live* performance, given the extravagance of interior décor in mid-century picture-houses. It is the technology of production that separates film from theatre and Bluto's actions serve to display it, from follow-spots to lightning machines and snow, technologies not new to 1940 theatre but rather belonging to an earlier era of effects, when they existed at all. I leave out here the rising and falling balcony that operates as a reference to a fairground 'Test Your Strength' machine and which is a lovely fantasy of a piece of set.

But Bluto's first actions on entering the theatre, pulling fly-lines to reveal a succession of drop-cloths, also define the state of theatre. It is not marked by the advertisement on the front-cloth ('We do asbestos we can') something I certainly remember from UK theatres in the 1950s and which here is parallelled by the final match of Olive and Popeye embracing with the couple painted onto the two curtains advertising 'Use non-skid lipstick'. Instead it is the increasingly tatty cloths that Bluto raises that show theatre's effective poverty. Patched and mended, looking on one cloth as if they are a gigantic pair of oft-repaired bloomers, they represent more than the reality of stage-cloths viewed up close and suggest that theatre is now in a permanently declining state of make do and mend. There is nothing painted on most of them, only the signs of wear, and, startlingly, when the last is flown out, we see straight through the back-wall of the theatre into the street with pedestrians, a policeman and honking traffic. In one sense this is a scene-dock door left open but it is also a statement of the reality beyond and behind the stage, a reality from which a text like *Romeo and Juliet* is here sharply disconnected, unlike the 'authentic' reality of film or even animation. Shakespeare is the unreal against which animation and the world beyond and behind the theatre is placed.

---

[3] Donald Crafton, *Shadow of a Mouse* (Berkeley, 2013), pp. 128–9.

The sets of this *Romeo* are of course stock rep material but they can metamorphose into something that is no longer two-dimensional so that a punch from Popeye can send Bluto flying into the cloth depicting a landscape of the Capulet garden but where the lake instantly becomes real and Bluto lands with a splash, turning the flat cloth into a three-dimensional space that marks film's refusal of the planes of falsity that theatre needs in order to produce its own distinctive possibilities of redefining fictive locations. I want to suggest that a moment like that turns theatre into film in its transformation of landscape drop-cloth into landscape as location at the point at which the stereotype of cartoon violence most denies the real. Only in cartoons or cartoon-derived movies can a single punch send someone flying yards into a lake.

Perhaps most significantly, the audience is mostly in evening dress (bow-ties and tuxedos for the men) but, at some moments, it is clear that not all the audience are dressed up to the nines. While the front row is always wealthy and predominantly elderly, there are also younger people, women in ordinary dresses, men in sports-jackets with a turtle-neck sweater beneath. The social exclusivity of theatre as high culture is being denied here – or is it a sense of the conflict between the theatre audience and the cinema audience watching *Popeye* now being reinserted into the action? The audience at the Spinach Theatre is nearly as much a social cross-section as at The Globe.

Of course the action of *Romeo* in *Shakespearian Spinach* is reduced to its popular culture essentials. There is even less here than is squeezed into the wonderful 2003 Nextel advertisement, a 30-second *Romeo* with cellphones (where Juliet awakes with the words 'Better now' and Friar Laurence rings down the curtain with 'Kids!').[4] The Popeye *Romeo* equals nothing more than a balcony scene and a death scene (without tomb or crypt but with an off-stage crate which serves as a coffin substitute into which Bluto can nail Romeo, neatly removing Popeye's Romeo costume as he does so). The Shakespeare text becomes merely two lines: first, 'Romeo, Romeo, wherefore art thou, Romeo?', misunderstood as 'where' as usual

and explained by her hand-prop of a telescope to find him, as, in the following, non-Shakespearian line, her attempt to hear if he responds to her 'Answer me, my Romeo' is explained by her producing an ear-trumpet through which to hear his response; and, second, 'Parting is such sweet sorrow' which, here, is Popeye to a comatose, cross-dressed Bluto at the cartoon's end. And, if we might reasonably expect the experience of Shakespearian tragedy to be emotionally exhausting, it is the speed of Popeyes' pummelling of Bluto that leaves the Spinach Theatre's audience completely collapsed in limp response to the spectacle. This slapstick violence, rather than *Romeo*'s expected violence of sword-play and poison, works on this audience far beyond the normal range of spectator response.

But what is most striking is not this extreme compression or fragmentation but the unacknowledged transformation of the play into opera, for this version of the balcony scene is sung as an operatic duet. The choice of musical source and referent is not an expected one. This is not, say, Gounod's *Roméo et Juliette* pressed into dramatic service. As I suspect the 1940 cinema audience would have realized but few will grasp now, the Romeo-Juliet duet is sung to 'Ach! So fromm', Lyonel's aria from Flotow's opera *Martha* (1847). If Flotow's opera has dropped almost completely from sight now, it was a staple of the operatic repertory across the US in the late nineteenth and early twentieth century, and this aria was the best-known and very popular number from it – and I emphasize 'popular' as going far beyond the elite audience of opera. Indeed, it is still well-known among the elite opera audience: a YouTube clip of Pavarotti singing it in 1989 as an encore at a concert has the audience applaud in recognition as soon as the orchestra has played a bar or so of the introduction.[5] It was most often sung in Italian, as 'M'apparì tutt'amor',

---

4 See the transcript in Marjorie Garber, *Shakespeare and Modern Culture* (New York, 2008), p. 60; the advertisement is available on YouTube, e.g. www.youtube.com/watch?v =IHGWFWpMZyk, accessed 10 October 2014.

5 See www.youtube.com/watch?v=lnQCD1_pj7w, accessed 10 October 2014.

as Pavarotti does and also, on YouTube, Schipa, Gigli, Domingo and others. Fritz Wunderlich and Jonas Kaufmann, unsurprisingly, opt for the original German. The words in *Shakespearian Spinach* are not the usual English translation of the libretto but there are allusions, so that Flotow's text Englished to 'Like a dream, bright and fair'[6] becomes 'Like a beam from above' and so on. And, since the words sung in opera are assumed to be usually impossible to hear, Olive can simply sing her anger at Bluto to the notes of her part without in any way disrupting the performance: 'Get out, scram, / Clumsy ham. / You're a monkey with a beard.' We hear it but the theatre audience does not notice.

I cannot see any connection between *Martha* and *Romeo* other than that the opera is set in that kind of Merrie England – its subtitle is *The Fair at Richmond* – that might be seen as Shakespearian. Fleischer's point is, I take it, no more than that popular, accessible opera and popular Shakespeare belong in the same cultural stratum – this is, after all, about the last moment at which opera or at least its most popular arias are still able to be seen as an art-form enjoyed by a broad social cross-section and, in that sense, properly aligned with Shakespeare. Reducing *Romeo* to two lines and references to two scenes is the same as reducing *Martha* to its single highlight.

2. TOBACCO

Popeye serves here as a mid-twentieth-century text that fragments Shakespeare to use him to comment on the cultural positioning of theatre, not remaking him with originality but accepting what was currently being made in repertory Shakespeare companies' productions all over America, where balconies and landscape drop-cloths were still the norm. Theatre vs. film (here animated film) is complexly re-imagined. The originality of film is superimposed on the unoriginality of theatrical origins. Here Shakespeare is a site of unoriginality in performance through the conventions of repetition. But the twenty-first-century phenomenon I want to turn to next and for which I have not found earlier examples is the remaking of a different text

into a Shakespearian form, Shakespearianizing, if you will, to create a new original from a work with a different origin – hence making out of it a work deliberately unoriginal. As I was researching for this article, I read Michael Billington's review of the stage production of *Shakespeare in Love* in London, which he opened with 'I've often attacked our modern mania for turning movies into plays.'[7] What I want to look at and begin thinking about here is the current mania for turning movies into Shakespeare, of making an unoriginal and not very Shakespearian play out of film. This craze is markedly different from the long tradition of using Shakespeare for parody, from Poole's *Hamlet Travestie* (1810) onwards, even though there are ways that, all unknowingly, the works share certain characteristics with Poole's play.

Poole's play is a travesty of *Hamlet*; it does not seek to turn something else into Shakespeare. The burlesque tradition makes something out of Shakespeare; it does not make something into Shakespeare. There are not, so far as I know, mid-nineteenth-century attempts to turn *Oliver Twist* into Shakespearian blank verse. So what is happening in the recent and successful sequence? It includes a revision of Quentin Tarantino's *Pulp Fiction* as *Bard Fiction* by Aaron Greer, Ben Tallen and others (first performed in 2009), Adam Bertocci's *Two Gentlemen of Lebowski* (published 2010) from the Coen Brothers' *The Big Lebowski*, and Ian Doescher's *William Shakespeare's Star Wars* trilogy (published 2013–14), *Verily, A New Hope*, *The Empire Striketh Back* and *The Jedi Doth Return*, the first volume of which reached number 12 on the *New York Times*' hardcover fiction list.[8] And I ought to explain that 'Tobacco' in my title is simply an allusion to Chewbacca in *Star Wars* as

---

6 See, e.g., F. von Flotow, *The Opera of Martha* (Boston, n.d.), p. 170.
7 www.theguardian.com/culture/2014/jul/24/shakespeare-in-love-theatre-review, accessed 24 July 2014.
8 www.nytimes.com/2013/07/21/books/review/inside-the-list.html?_r=0, accessed 24 July 2014. By October 2014, the trilogy was available as a boxed set – or, accurately, as the 'Royal Imperial Boxed Set', complete with poster – on the analogy of boxed DVD collections as much as book sets.

well as to Popeye's pipe. The sequence seems to have begun in 2007 with a mash-up of *Twelfth Night* and George Romero's 1968 film *Night of the Living Dead*, a 45-minute show often performed for Hallowe'en. All share a base in a cult film, one with an enormous fan-base that – and this is the problem – may or may not be theatre-going and Shakespeare-aware as well as film-obsessed. These versions, dubbed 'neo-Shakespeare' by Paul Rogalus,[9] negotiate between small theatre companies, desperate to attract a different audience to live performance, and the gathering of fan communities as public demonstration of their fandom. In some ways, the productions connect to the decades-long phenomenon of late-night screenings of *The Rocky Horror Picture Show* (1975) for which audiences dress up and perform with the movie in a variety of forms, singing along, shouting comments, creating jokes with added dialogue.[10]

We could just define this kind of work as mash-up and leave it at that. But the epitome of mash-up is YouTube[11] where brevity is key and the unit of film-text is often the trailer that is then recut and mashed-up with other materials. I can see *Shakespearian Spinach* as a form of mash-up *avant la lettre*. For the longer expanse of novels we could use, say, the huge success of Seth Grahame-Smith's *Pride and Prejudice and Zombies* (2009), published by Quirk Books who also publish Doescher's trilogy. Others will have to tell me whether such parody can sustain itself across 320 pages – I have not put myself through the pain of reading it. In the thin stream of Shakespeare novel mash-ups, there is Christopher Moore's astonishingly vulgar reworking of *King Lear* with sprinklings of *Macbeth* as *Fool* (2009), in which Pocket, Lear's Fool, ends up married to Cordelia and ruling France. I emphasize here the paucity of such works. My recent check on the extraordinary fan-fic site *Archive of Our Own* produced about 1300 mash-ups, fan-fic and slash fic pieces based on Shakespeare's works, ranging from a few hundred words to over 15,000, but a search for Harry Potter lists over 62,000 pieces.[12]

The conjunction of Shakespeare and screenplay in *Bard Fiction* is the outcome of a wiki, a piece of collaborative writing begun in 2009 under the title the *Pulp Shakespeare Project*, and devoted, as the wiki site states, 'to the reconstruction of William Shakespeare's play *A Slurry Tale*, which curiously resembles Quentin Tarantino's film *Pulp Fiction*'.[13] It was first performed in a one-hour version by Tedious Brief Productions – tag-line 'We make plays that are often ten words too long'[14] – at the Minnesota Fringe Festival in 2009 and then in an expanded version in Chicago in 2012, while a different version, *Pulp Shakespeare*, performed by Her Majesty's Secret Players, won a 'Best of Fest' award at the 2011 Hollywood Fringe and was selected for the 2012 New York City Fringe Encores series. Collaborative writing, then, produces a fluid text of various extents – which makes the project sound distinctly early modern. Tedious Brief Productions went on to create *Tempests*, a mash-up of *Aliens* and *The Tempest*, with, as it were, Miranda in the Sigourney Weaver role of Ripley. Good though *Bard Fiction* is, I shall not have more to say of it.[15]

By comparison with the long gestation of a wiki-based collaborative drama, Bertocci's adaptation of the Coen Brothers' *The Big Lebowski* was drafted in a single weekend. Unlike *Bard Fiction*, written for fringe performance, *Two Gentlemen of Lebowski* is now unperformable, simply because 'any and all adaptation rights' in the film are 'reserved to the Coen Brothers and to Universal

9 Paul Rogalus, 'The Bard, the Knave and Sir Walter: Adapting a Modern Cult Movie into a Neo-Shakespearean Play', in Zachary Ingle, ed., *Fan Phenomena: The Big Lebowski* (Bristol, 2014), pp. 64–71; p. 65.

10 See Sal Piro and Michael Hess, *The Official Rocky Horror Picture Show Audience Par-tic-i-pation Guide* (Livonia, MI, 1991) and Sal Piro, *"Creatures of the Night": The Rocky Horror Picture Show Experience* (Redford, MI, 1990).

11 See Stephen O'Neill, *Shakespeare and YouTube* (London, 2014).

12 http://archiveofourown.org/works/search?utf8=%E2%9C %93&work_search%5Bquery%5D=harry+potter and http://archiveofourown.org/works/search?utf8=%E2%9C %93&work_search%5Bquery%5D=shakespeare, accessed 24 July 2014.

13 http://pulpbard.wikispaces.com/home 24 July 2014, accessed 24 July 2014.

14 http://www.tediousbrief.com/, accessed 24 July 2014.

15 My thanks to Ben Tallen of Tedious Brief Productions for kindly providing scripts of *Bard Fiction* and *Tempests*.

Pictures' and therefore, as the adaptation's website insists, 'For avoidance of doubt: This means that the author is not able to grant stage rights.'[16] Self-described as 'a viral phenomenon' and outlined online, with an allusion to the Reduced Shakespeare Company's Shakespeare mash-up, as 'The compleat history of a viral phenomenon (abridged)',[17] the version was performed in New York in 2010 but the online script had to be removed at the insistence of the rights holders and future performances are unlikely. Incidentally, the apparent endorsement of Bertocci's play by the Royal Shakespeare Company of the work as a 'hysterical amalgamation', quoted in many online references, turns out to be a comment in Peter Kirwan's performance history section of the Bate and Rasmussen edition of *Two Gentlemen of Verona*.[18]

Also unlike *Bard Fiction*, which is unpublished, *Two Gentlemen of Lebowski* was published by Simon and Schuster, a fact of considerable significance because Bertocci's play has a full-scale commentary, which Bertocci has described as 'the funniest part of the thing'.[19] The commentary is deliberately formatted to mimic the lay-out of the facing-page annotation and illustrations placed within a ruled box in the Folger Shakespeare Library edition by Barbara Mowat and Paul Werstine also published by Simon and Schuster. As reading text, then, Bertocci's mash-up defines itself as not only transforming the Coen Brothers' screenplay but also as a commentary on the characteristics of the Shakespeare scholarly commentary as something helpful but also at times desperate, as in his gloss on 'sexton' as 'not a sexual reference, for once',[20] something Bertocci learned about through taking three Shakespeare classes as part of his minor in English at Northwestern University. Since a primary location of fandom is among current or former college students, the intersection with their experience of Shakespeare in edited texts like the Folger Shakespeare Library series is immediately a source of the comic. And the Folger editions' endearing use of images from early texts can be turned by Bertocci, at times brilliantly, into further punning.

We can see, though Bertocci probably could not, that this echoes the games that Poole played

in *Hamlet Travestie* in 1810, producing notes supposedly by Pope, Dr Johnson and others, like the marvellous discussion of 'a rope of onions', with Johnson's note expressing gratitude to 'a lady celebrated at once for her literary acquirements, and for her culinary accomplishments'.[21] But Bertocci's text and the jokes in the commentary also depend on knowing the screenplay for *The Big Lebowski*, often in minute detail. Take, for instance, the image of a beaver captioned 'A beaver picture' (p. 146). Nothing explains what the illustration is doing here but Jack Treehorn, a character in the film who here becomes Jaques Treehorn, is a pornographer and hence 'beaver pictures' are what he makes. Even more complexly clever is the note on the apparently bizarre line 'I still read Ben Jonson manually' on the same page: 'by hand. The Knave may be affirming his literacy here; he can read, and write or copy text by hand, and thus has no need for the dramatic wonders of Treehorn's theatre' (p. 146). Throughout the film there are threats made by the Nihilists, a group of comic German blackmailing terrorists – to castrate the other Lebowski, the Dude, to cut off his 'Johnson'.[22] 'I still read Ben Jonson manually' is an adaptation of the Dude's line 'I still jerk off manually'[23] and therefore explains Bertocci's Treehorn's next line, a neat *Hamlet* quotation, 'Ay, there's the rub'. But the commentary note on 'rub', 'obstacle', while accurate for the quotation, deliberately ignores

---

[16] www.runleiarun.com/lebowski/viral.shtml, accessed 24 July 2014.

[17] www.runleiarun.com/lebowski/viral.shtml. Compare Adam Long et al., *The Compleat Works of Wllm Shkspr (Abridged)* (New York, 2000).

[18] Jonathan Bate and Eric Rasmussen, eds., *The Two Gentlemen of Verona* (London, 2011), p. 105.

[19] Zachary Ingle, 'Fan Appreciation No. 2 Interview with Adam Bertocci', in Ingle, ed., *Fan Phenomena: The Big Lebowski*, pp. 58–63; p. 61.

[20] Adam Bertocci, *Two Gentlemen of Lebowski* (New York, 2010), p. 62.

[21] John Poole, *Hamlet Travestie* (London, 1810), p. 87.

[22] See, e.g., Ethan Coen and Joel Coen, *The Big Lebowski* (London, 1998), p. 73: 'Tomorrow vee come back und cut off your chonson.'

[23] Coen and Coen, *The Big Lebowski*, p. 99.

the joke on masturbation, while depending on the reader knowing, without needing to be told, how the screenplay has been reworked here.

Fans of a cult movie know the screenplay by heart and *The Big Lebowski* is nothing if not a cult movie. Indeed, for many, including Jenny Jones, the author of one encyclopedic study, it is 'The Greatest Cult Film of All Time'. Actually, I do not know another cult film that has generated its own cult – the Church of the Latter-Day Dude, led by the Dudely Lama, with, by 2012, 140,000 self-ordained priests,[24] and also an analysis of it as a pseudo-gospel.[25] Alongside the gatherings of fans at Lebowski Fests, dressed as characters in the film or as allusions to features of the screenplay – appearing, for instance, in white Russian fur outfits to suggest the Dude's favourite drink, White Russians – comes a remarkable pseudo-academic analysis in collections of fan essays, often strikingly learned, that are packaged as college text books[26] or volumes whose echoes of how academics publish are striking, not least when published by a respected university press.[27] Sophisticated analysis in film studies is often no more acute or theory-aware than the pieces collected in *The Year's Work in Lebowski Studies*, which is, reassuringly, a one-off volume, not an annual publication.

But Bertocci layers another form of knowledge over his version for, as well as writing in blank verse, he incorporates allusions to, he claims, all of Shakespeare's plays and his website offers a checklist so that the reader can tick them off.[28] Some are obvious but also rapid. In the encounter between the Chorus, 'The Stranger' in the film, and the Knave, the film's 'Dude', a few lines of screenplay dialogue yield allusions to *Henry IV*, *Othello*, *Macbeth*, *Richard III* and *The Winter's Tale* in the adaptation:

Chorus. What sayst thou, Mistress Quickly? Hast thou a goodly beverage, brew'd of sarsaparilla-root?
Mistress Quickly. [without] As brew'd in the city of the base Indian.
Chorus. Ay, there's a good one. How fares the Knave?
The Knave. So foul and fair a day I have not seen.
Chorus. Such a day, I mark thee, whereupon the winter of our discontent is ne'er made glorious summer. A

gentleman wiser than myself did say that on some such days, thou exits, pursued by a bear, and on others, the bear exits, pursued by you.   (pp. 121–3)

The last sentence, gifted by the screenplay's 'Wal, a wiser fella than m'self once said, sometimes you eat the bar and sometimes the bar, wal, he eats you',[29] allows the commentary to pun on the screenplay's replication of a cowboy accent: '*bear*: a stocky mammal reputed to consume and be consumed by humans . . . Here, the word might also be "bar," an obstacle or impediment' (p. 122).

Ian Doescher plays with such lightly hidden allusions too, calling them 'Easter Eggs', like the inside jokes hidden in computer programs. From Nietzsche's Übermensch staring into the abyss to the story of *Oedipus*, from *Star Trek* ('To boldly go where none hath gone is wild!') to the fact that the actor who played Lando advertised Colt 45s with the slogan 'Colt 45: it works every time' ('A colt is ridden best by kindly rider. / I know 'tis true: it worketh ev'ry time.'), and even HMV's dog Nipper: 'Now seems it plain to me that Vader doth / Perform the part of docile dog unto / The sick'ning whinny of his Master's voice', Doescher's range of references is wide.[30] I particularly like the allusion to the motto of the US Postal Service in *The Empire Striketh Back*, 'For neither snow nor ice nor gloom of Hoth / Shall stay my rescue of my

---

[24] Jenny M. Jones, *The Big Lebowski: An Illustrated, Annotated History of the Greatest Cult Film of All Time* (Minneapolis, 2012), p. 191.
[25] Cathleen Falsani, *The Dude Abides: The Gospel According to the Coen Brothers* (Grand Rapids, MI, 2009).
[26] Oliver Benjamin, ed., *Lebowski 101* (Abide University Press [sic], 2013).
[27] Edward P. Comentale and Aaron Jaffe, *The Year's Work in Lebowski Studies* (Bloomington, IN, 2009).
[28] See www.runleiarun.com/lebowski/checklist.pdf, accessed 10 October 2014. It is worth noting that the website's domain name, runleiarun, is an allusion to an animated film parody mash-up of *Star Wars* and *Run Lola Run* (*Lola rennt*) that Bertocci made in 2003.
[29] *The Big Lebowski*, p. 78.
[30] All are explained at http://geekylibrary.com/2014/06/26/secrets-the-easter-eggs-in-the-william-shakespeares-star-wars-trilogy/, accessed 26 July 2014

greatest friend',[31] and the double self-reference in this passage with its acrostic on Yale and allusion to Doescher's own M. Div. from Yale Divinity School:

Han.	You shall for sure discover what is right
	And proper, when I blast apart thy frame.
C-3PO.	Lo, 'tis forbidden, Gen'ral Solo, for
	E'en droids aren't masters of divinity.[32]

One accident of naming produces an apparent allusion. In *A New Hope* one of the red squadron pilots is named Biggs Darklighter but in *Verily, A New Hope* this becomes in effect an Easter Egg for Murray Biggs, the Yale professor with whom Doescher studied and who, for all three volumes, Doescher gratefully acknowledges, 'improved my Shakespearean pastiche'.[33] I dread to think what it was like before his help. It is easy, far too easy, simply to mock and therefore patronize Doescher's poor verse-writing. But I want to make two moves here. One is to see how Shakespeare allusions are being embedded in his text and the route towards revealing them. The other, at the end of this article, is to see here and in Bertocci's work what Shakespeare means for them, what is their understanding of 'Shakespearian' of which these are 'neo-Shakespearian' forms, what, in sum, we might see as their understanding of the value-added that Shakespeare provides to the fan's pleasure in the originating text (film or screenplay). These forms depend on a fundamental imbalance between their consumers' (readers' or spectators') knowledge of Shakespeare and of the source-text. Reading *The Two Gentlemen of Lebowski* without knowing *The Big Lebowski* well is pointless but there is no need to read *The Two Gentlemen of Lebowski* with a knowledge of their antecedents from Verona, beyond the title itself.

Understanding Doescher's approach to the kinds of presences that Shakespeare has in his trilogy is complex. On the one hand there are allusions that are designedly obvious;

Enter Luke Skywalker, *holding stormtrooper helmet.*
Luke. Alas, poor stormtrooper, I knew ye not,
. . . What manner of a man wert thou?
A man of inf'nite jest or cruelty?[34]

As Doescher comments, Yorick and the skull 'is probably the image we associate most with Shakespeare' and therefore he 'couldn't resist writing a similar moment for Luke [Skywalker]'.[35] I will return in a moment to the extraordinary source of that comment in a moment. On the other hand, there are ones that might give some of us just a moment's pause for explanation. The opening of *The Jedi Doth Return*, for instance, 'Cease to persuade, my grov'ling Jerjerrod, / Long-winded Moffs have ever sniv'ling wits',[36] alludes to Valentine's lines, 'Cease to persuade, my loving Proteus: / Home-keeping youths have ever homely wits' (*The Two Gentlemen of Verona*, 1.1.1–2) – and Doescher does nothing to recreate the repetition of 'home' in Shakespeare's line. There is no suggestion here that somehow Darth Vader is like Valentine or Jerjerrod like Proteus. Instead, as with the openings of the two previous versions, Doescher wants to allude directly to the opening of a Shakespeare play, 'Now is the summer of our happiness / Made winter by this sudden, fierce attack!' and 'If flurries be the food of quests, snow on.'[37]

Reading Doescher's blank verse shows up what he conceives of as the principal characteristics of Shakespeare's language. But Doescher has helpfully provided his own analysis, available online for each volume on the publisher's website as an 'Educator's Guide', each a pamphlet of twenty pages or so. I am still trying to puzzle out what the pedagogical circumstances might be within which there would be an Educator in need of such a guide and, indeed, much of Doescher's style, addressed

---

[31] Ian Doescher, *William Shakespeare's The Empire Striketh Back* (Philadelphia, 2014), p. 20.

[32] Ian Doescher, *William Shakespeare's The Jedi Doth Return* (Philadelphia, 2014), p. 87.

[33] Ian Doescher, *William Shakespeare's Star Wars: Verily, A New Hope* (Philadelphia, 2013), p. 173.

[34] Doescher, *Verily, A New Hope*, p. 124.

[35] 'William Shakespeare's Star Wars' Educator's Guide, p. 11 at www.quirkbooks.com/sites/default/files/editor_uploads/ShakespeareStarWars_EducatorsGuide.pdf, accessed 26 July 2014.

[36] Doescher, *The Jedi Doth Return*, p. 10.

[37] Doescher, *Verily, A New Hope*, p. 10 and Doescher, *The Empire Striketh Back*, p. 10.

to a hypothetical 'you', presupposes that it is a naïve reader who needs this help, not a teacher in search of classroom assistance. But perhaps it is not wrong of Doescher to imagine that teachers, trying to stimulate their class towards at least a liking for Shakespeare, might use such a popular culture adaptation as a lure. For each Shakespeare play he quotes/transforms/alludes to, Doescher provides a two-sentence summary and a 'Great film version' or two to watch. Then he parallels his source with his adaptation and its context.

For my concerns, more intriguing than this are his list of 'some quick and easy elements you'll find in Shakespeare's plays, all of which can be found in' his adaptation, a list of 'Shakespearean devices' he has used and his substantial explanation of how blank verse operates.[38] The first, elements in Shakespeare, includes 'minimal stage directions', glossing for asides and soliloquies (including the curious idea that 'The longest soliloquy by a Shakespearean character is 63 lines, spoken by the character Canterbury in Act 1, scene 2 of *Henry V*'[39]), and the notion that 'Each play is in five acts' which was, he strangely seems to think, 'the usual structure of plays in Shakespeare's times' because of 'ancient Roman plays, many of which also had five acts'.[40]

Doescher's account of blank verse assumes that every foot is iambic, with no room for any trochees whatsoever. This gives him pause over the frequently necessary word 'stormtrooper' which cannot have two initial strong stresses by his rules and must therefore be stressed on the middle syllable. Throughout this there is plainly a hope – verily, a new hope – that reading his pastiche will encourage his readers to read Shakespeare, a hope that may be far more forlorn than that in his first volume's title. I cannot work out whether Doescher's belief that reading his versions will lead to reading Shakespeare is naïve or hubristic.

Reading Doescher is often like reading early Shakespeare, especially the *Henry VI* plays. Some of this is the sheer regularity of the metrical structure of his blank verse, though his enjambment is often looser even than late Shakespeare. But it is partly an assessment consequent on those 'devices' he so oddly accumulates. Here is the full list: anaphora,

extended metaphor, stichomythia, songs, extended wordplay, premonitory dreams (Clarence's) and moral fable, for which his example is Hamlet on the king going 'a progress through the guts of a beggar' but for which his examples from his own work sound more like Othello's narrative of the origins of the handkerchief. The dense frequency and extent of his anaphoric structures are even greater than in early Shakespeare and the rarity of weak endings to his blank verse, albeit slightly more common in the later two adaptations, adds to the constriction on metrical experiment.

But it is also frustrating that Doescher knows so little. So, for instance, in constructing love dialogue for Han Solo and Princess Leia, Doescher proudly notes that he copies the quatrain forms of *Romeo and Juliet* but he has never noticed – and Murray Biggs seems not to have pointed out to him – that Romeo and Juliet speak sonnets, complete and truncated, with the result that Doescher's lovers are not modelling or speaking all unaware that their speech has been modelled on the Petrarchan implications, positive and negative, of love-sonnets.

Just occasionally, there is an experiment which offers a larger clue to Doescher's conception of the Shakespearian and its purpose in his work. In *Star Wars*, R2-D2 is a droid, the short one, who never speaks but only beeps. Doescher gives him noises that are always firmly in iambic pentameter: 'Beep, meep, beep, squeak, beep, beep, beep, meep, beep, whee!'[41] Then, when R2-D2 is alone, he is able to speak:

> Around both humans and the droids I must
> Be seen to make such errant beeps and squeaks
> That they shall think me simple. Truly, though,
> Although with sounds oblique I speak to them,
> I clearly see how I shall play my part,
> And how a vast rebellion shall succeed
> By wit and wisdom of a simple droid.[42]

---

[38] *William Shakespeare's Star Wars' Educator's Guide*, p. 2.
[39] *William Shakespeare's Star Wars' Educator's Guide*, p. 2.
[40] *William Shakespeare's Star Wars' Educator's Guide*, p. 2.
[41] Doescher, *Verily, A New Hope*, p. 15.
[42] Doescher, *Verily, A New Hope*, p. 15.

In the course of the trilogy R2-D2 grows into a concerned and active thinker, a strategist for the rebels and a sharply percipient analyst of what is happening. As Doescher describes it, '[t]he plucky little droid is the fool of the trilogy – a fool not in the modern sense but in the Shakespearean sense: a knowing presence who aids the action even though he seems rather simple', and Doescher gives him the Epilogue to the entire trilogy, in which there is another Easter Egg, this time an acrostic reading 'Episode VII Cometh'.[43]

It is time to take two steps back. The first step would be towards the nature of fandom and our place within it. Recognizing that the materials I am working on depend on at least one kind of fan in the concept of its readership, the fan of the cult film, we can worry about our place within this. Fan studies are often concerned to distinguish between the fan and the academic. But Henry Jenkins, a principal figure in the study of fans and of convergence culture, describes himself as an 'Aca-fan', 'a hybrid creature which is part fan and part academic', and sees his own writing, including the brilliant study of British TV fans *Textual Poachers* (1992), as an attempt to bridge between the two, hoping, as he puts it, 'to find a way to break cultural theory out of the academic bookstore ghetto'.[44] That there is also a link between our academicism and fandom is clear. As Michael Dobson put it in comparing fans of the RSC and the England football team, they share 'doggedly masochistic brand loyalty and the self-loathing pathology of fandom . . . trivia, lists, fanzines and collections of souvenir programs'.[45] If the distinguishing features of fandom include attending conventions and accumulating souvenir materials, often, in the high-brow fan, materials that are offered as ironic commentary on the subject, then almost all Shakespeare scholars must be fans as well as academics, with the strict proviso that, unlike fans at Comic-Con and Lebowski Fest, we do not dress up as characters in our beloved works. Fandom connects intrinsically with the geek, the dork and the nerd. One recent interview with Ian Doescher is on a website called 'geeky-library', described as a site of 'book reviews and

news for geeks like us'.[46] Adam Bertocci, on a page on his website that serves as an addendum to *Two Gentlemen of Lebowski*, discusses at length the font used because 'I'm a typography dork, you see. My publisher doesn't do those sorts of pages (I nearly wept when I learned this).'[47] And we can see how these terms function as popular expressions of academic study, the obsessive, self-absorbed, neurotic world in which we live as well as work. Indeed, the failure for most academics to distinguish between life and work might function as a central feature of the neurotics of fandom. One direction for this work would be to see how Lebowski fans and *Star Wars* fans might intersect with Shakespeare aca-fans. As Roberta Pearson asks, as she thinks about high-cultural fans, the most understudied groups of fan communities, 'which of the appellations would fans/buffs/enthusiasts/ devotees/aficionados/cognoscenti/connoisseurs of J. S. Bach, William Shakespeare, Sherlock Holmes, and *Star Trek* accept, and which not?'.[48]

There is much to be done on Shakespeare fandom. But the other step seems more important for now. The creation of these works depends on a perceived connection between the two groups, Shakespeare and cult movies. As Adam Bertocci notes, asked by an interviewer whether he was inspired by mash-ups like *Pride and Prejudice and Zombies*,

I think the difference between those books and mine is, my book works better the more you know about the 'classic' source – this project is how close Shakespeare

---

43 Doescher, *The Jedi Doth Return*, p. 159.

44 http://henryjenkins.org/aboutmehtml. See Henry Jenkins, *Textual Poachers*, 20th anniversary edition (London, 2012).

45 Michael Dobson, 'Watching the Complete Works Festival: the RSC and its Fans in 2006', *Shakespeare Bulletin*, 25.4 (2007), 23–34; p. 24.

46 http://geekylibrary.com/2014/06/18/a-chat-with-ian-doescher-best-selling-author-of-shakespeares-star-wars/, accessed 28 July 2014.

47 http://www.runleiarun.com/lebowski/type.shtml, accessed 24 July 2014.

48 Roberta Pearson, 'Bachies, Bardies, Trekkies, and Sherlock-ians', in Jonathan Gray *et al.*, eds., *Fandom* (New York, 2007), pp. 98–109; p. 98.

and *The Big Lebowski* are, not about how much Austen and zombies contrast.[49]

There are Shakespeare and zombie narratives, for instance the film *Zombie Hamlet* (John Murlowski, 2012) about the making of a film of *Hamlet* where the Southern matron financing the film requires zombies to be included to widen the potential audience demographic, or *Rosencrantz and Guildenstern Are Undead* (Jordan Galland, 2009), where a production of *Hamlet* reveals a conspiracy of Shakespeare, the Holy Grail and vampires. Both are comic parodies; neither suggests a convergence of rather than a contrast between Shakespeare and vampire.

What begins to become apparent, the more I read work on *The Big Lebowski*, is how frequently Shakespeare is invoked and therefore the extent to which Adam Bertocci is tapping into a popular cultural assertion of the Shakespearianness of the Coen Brothers' film. It is not simply the frequency that matters but rather the ways in which that invocation is made by radically different kinds of commentators. Here, for example, at one end of the spectrum, is Roy Preston, owner of a shop in Manhattan entirely devoted to Lebowski merchandise, on the central figure of the Dude:

And what about the Dude himself? Isn't he an archetypal character? . . . Audiences have always loved to root for this sort of character. If you held up a drawing of Shakespeare's Falstaff (wasn't he after all just an Elizabethan abider?) next to the Dude, you would probably see a rather striking resemblance. Both are portly, bearded white men prone to a love of beverage . . . (Falstaff was so popular in his day that Queen Elizabeth I demanded the character be brought back for two more plays – much as fans today are always clamoring for the Coens to do a sequel to *Lebowski*.)[50]

Ignore, if one can, the turning of myth into history and the doubling of the Queen's demand; forget for a moment the idea that one could have a drawing of Falstaff. What we are dealing with is not only advanced Fluellenism – all overweight drunks are the same – but also a deep belief in the way all audiences' desires indicate not tradition or influence but the presence of a cultural

archetype. Bertocci, who makes the same comparison between the Dude and Falstaff, sees Falstaff as a 'jovial, iconoclastic, dissolute genius' and, in quoting Harold Bloom on Falstaff's 'comprehensiveness', sees the Dude plainly adumbrated.[51]

Here are Tyree and Walters, co-authors of a fine British Film Institute 'Film Classics' book on the film, very self-consciously and awkwardly trying to work with the analogy between Shakespeare and *The Big Lebowski*:

Lebowski is a bit like a Shakespeare comedy, if only in the light-hearted sense that it celebrates life and love, ultimately endorsing marriage and ending with nuptials or sexual reproduction: in the end, Walter and the Dude embrace and go bowling, restoring equilibrium to their strange bachelor relationship.[52]

Ignore here the overly positive view of the ending of Shakespeare comedies and forget whether you can identify one that ends with sexual reproduction, for they are trying to connect Shakespeare comedy with the *absence* of marriages in prospect at the end of the film and the Stranger's line in the film's quasi-epilogue that 'there's a little Lebowski on the way'[53] or as Bertocci reworks it: 'But then, the fellow wise is like to know / That on the way's a little Lebowski / Perpetuating human comedy / Down through the generations' (I rather like the line 'Perpetuating human comedy' which is rhythmically sophisticated).[54]

In an earlier article, titled 'Is it Okay to Read the Coen Brothers as Literature?', Tyree and Morgan Meis seem even more desperate:

Like a Shakespeare comedy, *The Big Lebowski* not only becomes funnier during each screening, it also yields

[49] Ingle, 'Fan Appreciation No. 2 Interview with Adam Bertocci', p. 59.

[50] Jones, *The Big Lebowski: An Illustrated, Annotated History*, pp. 170–1.

[51] Bertocci, *Two Gentlemen of Lebowski*, p. 200.

[52] J. M. Tyree and Ben Walters, *The Big Lebowski* (London, 2007), p. 88.

[53] Ethan Coen and Joel Coen, *The Big Lebowski*, p. 140.

[54] Bertocci, *Two Gentlemen of Lebowski*, p. 193.

such an intricately threaded carpet of motifs that it begins to look pretty deeply piled.[55]

The apparently bizarre image is an allusion to the film's concerns with the tatty rug that, in the Dude's view, 'really tied the room together'.[56] For Tyree and Meis, there are two explicit references to Shakespeare in the film. The first is a rereading of the voice-over prologue and Stranger's epilogue as 'a throwback to outdated devices of cinema and the Renaissance stage',[57] so that the Prologue's ironies become deliberate undercutting of a form that, by quoting the opening Chorus of *Henry V* as their exemplar of the heroic mode, can here be seen as redefined: 'sometimes there's a man – I won't say a hee-ro, 'cause what's a hee-ro? – but sometimes there's a man . . . who, wal, he's the man for his time'n place, he fits right in there . . .'[58] There is here a common assumption – Doescher makes the same one – that the Chorus is a frequent enough device to be seen as quintessentially Shakespearian.

The second is much more effective as an argument for allusion. In Walter's funeral oration before the scattering of the ashes of his much-abused friend Donny, an oration which ends in magnificent bathos when the wind blows the ashes not into the ocean but all over the Dude, Walter ends with 'Goodnight, sweet prince'.[59] As Walter's pompous but moving speech redefines his relationship to Donny so that we can agree with the judgement of John Goodman who played Walter that 'It's definitely a buddy picture',[60] so the scene, through the quotation from Horatio, brings together the gravediggers' comedy and the messy reality of rotting corpses and skulls with the far more romanticized death of Hamlet. Donny is no prince nor is anyone in the film, but the citation's metamorphosis of him is both ridiculous and admirable.

The Coen Brothers play wryly with Shakespeare. 'Roderick Jayne', Oscar-nominated as editor of *Fargo*, described how he later helped them with the title for *The Man Who Wasn't There*:

They had solicited my advice, they now told me, because they thought that, being British, I might know some 'Shakespearean stuff' that 'might work' . . . I . . . proposed *My Hearth is Gas* . . . . Ethan . . . asked, 'Is that from the sonnets?'[61]

Roderick Jayne does not exist – he is a pseudonym used by the Coen brothers.

But for Bertocci, Shakespeare is not only 'the greatest writer who ever lived' but also someone who, '[i]f *The Big Lebowski* had premiered in 1598, . . . would have ripped it off by 1603'.[62] Bertocci, himself ripping off *The Big Lebowski*, generates a text that, in turn, can be seen as alluding to Shakespeare through its source text, as if, every time someone sees Bertocci's Sir Donald as Sir Andrew Aguecheek and his Sir Walter as Sir Toby Belch, the Shakespeare analogy is reinforced by its truthfulness in relation to the film's Donny and Walter.

As well as these kinds of local interconnections, what is often argued is that the tonal range of the Coen Brothers' film is more than a simple analogue to Shakespeare's need to respond to the social dynamics of his playgoers. For an academic like Paul Rogalus Shakespeare and the Coen Brothers, as well as Quentin Tarantino, share the mixture of comedy, obscenity, violence, traditional plots and that (to me, incomprehensible) notion of the creation of 'timeless, universal characters'[63] precisely in order to appeal to 'the masses', defined in current terms by Rogalus as 'both the filmgoing public at large, as well as the more sophisticated film students and scholars, the viewers looking for more'.[64]

---

[55] Morgan Meis and J. M. Tyree, 'Is it Okay to Read the Coen Brothers as Literature?', *Gettysburg Review*, 19 (2006), 61–73; p. 66.

[56] Ethan Coen and Joel Coen, *The Big Lebowski*, p. 9.

[57] Meis and Tyree, 'Is it Okay to Read the Coen Brothers as Literature?', p. 68.

[58] Ethan Coen and Joel Coen, *The Big Lebowski*, p. 4.

[59] Ethan Coen and Joel Coen, *The Big Lebowski*, p. 137.

[60] Meis and Tyree, 'Is it Okay to Read the Coen Brothers as Literature?', p. 69.

[61] Meis and Tyree, 'Is it Okay to Read the Coen Brothers as Literature?', p. 61.

[62] Bertocci, *Two Gentlemen of Lebowski*, p. 199.

[63] Paul Rogalus, 'The Bard, the Knave and Sir Walter', p. 69.

[64] Paul Rogalus, 'The Bard, the Knave and Sir Walter', p. 69.

At least this models a commercial process of production. Doescher, in describing the Shakespearian qualities of *Star Wars*, establishes a direct connection – at least of sorts – through Joseph Campbell's once popular *The Hero with a Thousand Faces*,[65] a book that uses Shakespeare to support its universalist argument in comparative mythology: George Lucas read Campbell and saw that his drafts of *Star Wars* were 'following classic motifs' and rewrote to make the screenplays conform more consistently to Campbell's models.[66] So, since Campbell uses Shakespeare to define his notions of character archetypes, Doescher can, by his lights, easily list comparisons between the characters of *Star Wars* and Shakespeare:

C-3PO and R2-D2 observe and comment on the action like Rosencrantz and Guildenstern. Chewbacca is as untamable as Caliban. Lando is as smooth and self-interested (at first) as Brutus. Obi-Wan Kenobi is like a wise Prospero . . . Jabba the Hutt enjoys a diet worthy of Falstaff.[67]

And he can add to that bland themes that are supposedly parallel: parent/child relationships, villains, destiny and fate, colourful supporting players, wise magus and fatherly ghosts and so on. In the end, what is crucial about Shakespeare for Doescher, far more than for Bertocci, is not merely the structures of high cultural value so well explored by Kate McLuskie and Kate Rumbold[68] but familiarity as a sign of a value which Doescher calls 'relevance'. He is happy to assert Shakespeare's popularity as comparable to *Star Wars* but also as constituting a set of cultural expectations of adequate sophistication: 'All well-rounded post-modern cultural connoisseurs are expected to have at least a passing familiarity with both sets of stories.'[69] In the high-volume sales of fan-linked products, Doescher's work itself proves to be powerfully perceived by its consumers as relevant, thereby in turn making Shakespeare relevant in the all-about-me world inhabited by the young demographic of fans.

But what, finally, is the positioning of this Shakespeare work as drama in theatre, performed or unperformable? Can the post-modern cultural connoisseurs who enjoy Bertocci and Doescher fill theatres and revive a supposedly dying art, supposedly in a terminal state of decline both in 1940s *Shakespearean Spinach* and now? For Paul Rogalus, 'the cult success of recent neo-Shakespearean stage adaptations . . . suggest that contemporary stage theatre in the twenty-first century is not dead; rather, it simply needs captivating, universal characters that a modern audience can know and love'.[70] I am not sure that *Two Gentlemen of Lebowski* is the route to the salvation of live theatre, the spinach that will give new strength to theatre as Popeye. In Stratford-upon-Avon at least the Spinach Theatre is in good health. The unoriginality of neo-Shakespeare, for all that it taps so superbly into the cult film demographic and its substantial intersection with a college-educated audience, limits the healthful effects of such makings. We can see its origins all too plainly but its originality is too temporary to sustain life, even for Popeye.

---

[65] Joseph Campbell, *The Hero with a Thousand Faces* (New York, 1949).

[66] Quoted Doescher, *Verily, A New Hope*, p. 170.

[67] Doescher, *Verily, A New Hope*, p. 171.

[68] Kate McLuskie and Kate Rumbold, *Cultural Value in Twenty-first-century England* (Manchester, 2014).

[69] Doescher, *Verily, A New Hope*, p. 171.

[70] Paul Rogalus, 'The Bard, the Knave and Sir Walter', p. 70.

REN FEST SHAKESPEARE:
THE COSPLAY BARD

ANDREW JAMES HARTLEY

That engaging with Shakespeare is an engagement with history is a critical commonplace which has attained the status of dogma as a necessary corrective to older ideas of universality and transhistoricity. Historicist modes of study thus operate on the assumption that, if no attempt at contextualization within the originary cultural moment was a Bad Thing, then total immersion in that moment must be a Good Thing, even when predicated on the sophisticated notion that re-creation of that moment is theoretically impossible and that all we can do is reach for something which is always receding. Historicist scholarship as an endeavour is paradoxically both doomed and essential to any solid understanding of the plays, so we become Sisyphus or Tantalus, striving for the unachievable, thirsting for what we cannot reach.

For centuries, theatrical Shakespeare provided an alternative, blithely presentist in its approach, feeling little need to footnote itself in terms of what things meant in 1599, but some version of new historicism in literary study is now echoed in theatres, and has been since Poel and Bridges-Adams in the early twentieth century. Today it takes the various guises of theatre companies and spaces which claim to somehow model early modern theatrical forms in the present. Some of these are meticulously researched and inventive. Though I am wary of any claim to theatrical value or credibility based on what was or might have been, such approaches can, of course, be immensely interesting and revelatory. But what of performed Shakespeare which partakes of bad history? I

mean not the loose, vague or shoddy 'history' which is used to bolster the less credible forms of so-called 'original practices' productions, but those less straight-faced, less serious, less 'authentic' versions of staged Shakespeare which no scholar would ever take for their more historically respectable cousins? What about Renaissance Festival Shakespeare?

There are over fifty Renaissance Fairs or Festivals in the United States. Most only appear for a few weeks of the year, even where they have permanent bases, and some are itinerant. Among the smallest are the Virginia Renaissance Festival, Camelot Days in Florida, and the Middlefair Renaissance Festival in Hillsboro, Texas which draw crowds of about ten thousand people each season. Most are considerably larger, attracting a hundred thousand annually, while the festivals in Georgia, Arizona, Colorado, Louisiana, Maryland, Michigan, Pennsylvania, Southern California (the Renaissance Pleasure Faire) and Scarborough (Texas) all draw double that number. The Minnesota Renaissance Festival in Shakopee boasts 320,000 people a year, and the Texas Renaissance Festival in Plantersville is attended by over 600,000 people annually.[1] Most of these are characterized by ersatz medieval settings outdoors, and offer folk arts, games and activities, numerous stalls selling food and drink, leather or metal work and other crafts, clothes, curios and

---

[1] I draw these numbers from the press releases, websites and Wikipedia entries for each festival, and their precision should thus be taken with a grain of salt.

books.[2] They all provide entertainment – music, dancing, singing and forms of martial combat, particularly jousting tournaments – usually in designated performance spaces. The whole faire or festival has a performative feel, of course, and in addition to the strolling jesters, mayors, knights and royalty who tour the site constantly, engaging in 'period' banter with the customers, there are many paying attendees who cosplay (dress up – usually in fantasy/scifi inspired home-made costumes – about which, more later). Shakespeare – manifested in a variety of forms – is a frequent element of these faires and festivals.

The Faire/Fest event is inherently theatrical, not least in that it all functions as a thinly veiled fiction, and that the version of historical authenticity on display is almost entirely and self-consciously bogus. The whiff of historicity is wheeled out occasionally to sell products or claim status, but the ambience of these places and the people who frequent them (many of whom attend repeatedly in a single season or visit more than one festival location a year) is close to the spirit of the Society for Creative Anachronism and the fantasy convention, which is a spirit of play.

This is not to say that the festivals do not claim a historical and educational component even when there is not much to the argument. The Escondido Renaissance Faire, which used also to have a Shakespeare festival, is a case in point:

'This festival is a recreation of a 15th or 16th century English country village,' said Dick Wixon, founder of Gold Coast Festivals. 'Queen Elizabeth is the reigning queen. We try to give the visitors a look into the lives of people during that time. We have three stages of live entertainment. We also have battles, treasure hunts, storytelling and parades on the street during the day. We like to involve the public in all of the activities so that they can feel a part of everything. We want to immerse people in everything that is going on, the entertainment scenarios and impromptu entertainment on the streets. This is a living history recreation and we want people to have a good time and leave feeling that they have learned something about that time in history.... It's an older park full of large oak trees, and very much like what you would see if you went to England.'[3]

This is, of course, preposterous. But it is also merely marketing, and it is difficult to imagine that many who go mistake all this faux pageantry for history, however old the trees, and even the marketing blurbs themselves rarely make the historical case too rigorously (Elizabeth is the queen, but it's fifteenth or sixteenth century? We are glimpsing the lives of people from the period through treasure hunts and stage combat?). This is history in the sense that Disney's Epcot cultural centre is cultural geography and is easily dismissed as lacking seriousness when compared to venues – such as theatres – which wear more rigorous research on their sleeves. But as I will argue in this essay, history is not actually the goal of the Ren Faire's Shakespeare, and the performances generated there function quite differently from those at more conventionally historicist venues.[4] As such they enact a different kind of negotiation with the past, one which – paradoxically – creates a greater sense of cultural immediacy and engagement.

Some faires and festivals are partnered with actual theatrical companies who stage legitimate Shakespeare productions on the festival site: Suitcase Shakespeare, for instance which tours various festivals,[5] or the Arizona Shakespeare Festival whose *Much Ado* was staged at the Grand Canyon

---

[2] Most of the vendors have online presences which provide income when the festival is not in session and many travel from one venue to another, often showing up at fantasy/scifi conventions as well as Renaissance Festivals.

[3] http://www.utsandiego.com/sponsored/2013/oct/09/escondido-renaissance-faire-gold-coast-festivals/

[4] I'm using this admittedly simplistic catch all term to denote any theatre which in its physical layout, performance style or production model harkens back to some notion of original playing conditions as a marker of their purpose and their professional or commercial identity.

[5] Suitcase Shakespeare have played at:

Bristol Renaissance Faire	Kenosha, Wisconsin
Chicago Fringe Festival	Chicago, Illinois
Custer's Last Stand Festival	Evanston, Illinois
Janesville Renaissance Faire	Janesville, Wisconsin
Waupace Arts on the Square Festival	Waupaca, Wisconsin
Chippewa Valley Renaissance Faire	Chippewa Falls, Wisconsin
Stronghold Olde English Fair	Oregon, Illinois
Shakespeare on the Edge Faire	New Glarus, Wisconsin

Renaissance Faire this summer.[6] Where such productions occur they tend to have the aesthetics of the faire: bare-bones outdoor stages and some version of period costume. The plays selected usually favour the crowd-pleasing comedies played 'straight' and involve an element of knock-about and, where possible, an emphasis on the physical which includes sword play. Acting leans to the presentational, but also to the interactive where the audience is concerned, and the result is something closer to panto than to the psychologically realist performance style which typifies mainstream Shakespeare production in the US in more traditional (non-historicist) venues.

Such formal productions of full plays at Ren Faires/Fests is, however, unusual. Elsewhere, Shakespeare is usually an element in the brief (15–20 minute) performances which appear in the course of the day on side stages: sonnets delivered as rap, famous scenes played for laughs, pastiche and burlesque of various kinds, and a more generally pervasive sense of Shakespeare as repository of olde worlde earthiness, wisdom and, for want of a better term, *thenness*: that sense of a generalized past which seems simpler, clearer and more desirable than the present.

But in addition to formally staged shows, Shakespeare is also a frequent element in the constant street theatre of the faire. Sometimes you get the man himself in full Bardic attire mingling among the masses, swapping quotations, anecdotes and historical tidbits along the lines of those period re-enactors-cum-guides employed by tourist venues such as Hampton Court, but who might also be found at Shakespeare's birthplace or the Globe, blending history lesson, dramatic re-enactment and simple play. Sometimes prospective visitors are invited to contribute plot points which the Shakespeare impersonator weaves into a story of his own, as is suggested by this advertisement for the 22nd Annual Folsom Renaissance Faire & Shakespeare Festival (2014):

Celebrating The 22nd Anniversary Of The FAIRE!!! The rising young star of London's theater scene, Will Shakespeare, faces a scourge like no other: a paralyzing bout of writers block while the great Elizabethan age of entertainment unfolds around him. Will is without inspiration on material. What Will needs is a muse and, in an extraordinary town whilst on progress with Her Most Royal Majesty, Queen Elizabeth, he finds himself surrounded by numerous quirky characters who draw him into an amazing, dramatic adventure of action and love. Their stories make their way into his plays and into our hearts. The theme of the Faire is Shakespeare's Muse.

Over October 18th and 19th, the Folsom City Lions Park will be transformed to a delightful Elizabethan town filled with myriad characters and vignettes resembling those of Shakespeare's plays we so dearly love. In addition, over 900 costumed entertainers and over 100 shopkeepers and artisans will add to the ambiance of the Faire. The Festival will be the ultimate Renaissance bash, a lively Dionysian party, where the guests enjoy turkey legs, exotic food, and drink as they banter with the myriad performers filling the streets. The event sports one-of-a-kind shows, music, and comedy.[7]

History is on show here, but it is faux history or, better, *play* history, and I particularly like the conflation of turkey legs and exotic food, since turkeys (being New World birds) would have been exotic indeed to the Elizabethans. This version of Shakespeare's world is predicated on its (play) historical exoticism not to the (imaginary) Elizabethans but to the (actual) twenty-first century Americans and it is their engagement in Shakespeare's act of creation which is crucial. Something similar takes place at Much Ado About Sebastopol (Florida) where, according to Rydell Downward, the artistic director,

We have Will Shakespeare as an interactive street character, who sits and writes, interacts with our audience, recites sonnets, and is part of a scripted stage show featuring Elizabeth and her court. In addition, he uses members of the Queen's court as actors to read and perform 'newly composed' scenes, usually 'Pyramus and Thisbe' from *Midsummer Night's Dream*, but also the famous balcony scene from *Romeo and Juliet*, and scenes from *Much Ado About Nothing*, *The Merry Wives of Windsor*,

---

[6] www.azshakes.com/

[7] Folsom seems to be continuing a tradition begun at the Ardenwood Shakespeare Festival and Renaissance faire last advertised in very similar terms in 2010.

and others. On occasion he'll pull members of the audience to read minor roles in these scenes. We have also featured the drama departments of local schools performing various Shakespeare scenes, instructed in the street prior by The Bard himself.[8]

This interactive approach to Shakespeare, something frequently set up in order to be defused in more traditionally historicist performance in which audience participation is heavily circumscribed for fear of disrupting the show, grows in part out of the performance conditions of the faire in which the stakes are so usefully low. Impromptu stagings involving improvisation are less like productions and more like audience-driven rehearsals. This means that performers can try more, risk more, play more and, if it does not work, they can give it another go when the next group sidle into range. I would like to give closer attention to one particular ensemble who tour festivals and faires all over the Eastern seaboard. This pitch is from their website:

NICKEL SHAKESPEARE GIRLS

William Shakespeare's words come alive for the young and old. Find us in the lane, name ANY play written by Shakespeare and we will perform a 30-second selection from that play just for you! Our presentation is sometimes a fight, sometimes upside-down, sometimes dramatic, but always with maximum energy and wild amounts of fun! [9]

Nickel Shakespeare take a fast and physical approach, particularly in their impromptu street work, though they also do forty-minute stage shows whose content they describe as:

- Pants & Poise: Meet many of Shakespeare's leading ladies
- All the World's a Stage: Selections from the 'greatest hits'
- The Lunatic, the Lover & the Poet: Romance, infatuation and true love
- Little Fooleries: Shakespeare's clowns amuse and beguile
- Complete Works: All 39 plays in about 35 minutes. Fast. Furious. Fun.[10]

The approaches taken to their street performance pieces do not necessarily grow out of close-reading and have no historical justification, emerging instead from what seems most arresting in contemporary performance terms. In the words of Rebecca Blum, the company's managing director,

We figure out what we will do with each piece organically. Most of our stuff is based on what text members of the troupe already know. We will listen to the text and play with it to see if anything fun comes out of it. Sometimes, all it takes is a little physicality to make a piece more interesting. For example, we perform our most popular *Titus Andronicus* speech [Titus's 5.2 lines prior to killing Chiron and Demetrius beginning 'Hark, villains, I will grind your bones to dust...'] while doing a hand-balancing pose that has one of us upside down with a face between the speaker's legs. The pose has nothing to do with the play, but it looks strange and that makes the speech more engaging to people who may have never heard it before.[11]

If this seems whimsical to the point of irresponsibility, it might be worth remembering that many actors use other methodologies (emotional recall, say) which a textually or historically driven scholar might find bizarre or irrelevant. In this particular instance it accesses something of the passage's blood-thirsty excesses in ways at once strange and unsettling, while – in having the voice come from between a woman's legs – supply a troubling visual image to accompany the lines about the victims' unhallowed dam swallowing her own increase, so that the utterance seems to enact the moment it promises (5.2.190–1). Whatever else it does, this approach foregrounds something common to Nickel Shakespeare's attitude generally and

---

[8] Private e-mail correspondence with author (25 June 2014).
[9] This suggests they also do full productions: www .vacationsmadeeasy.com/NewYorkNY/articles/ TheNewYorkRenaissanceFaireatSterlingForestinTuxedoNy .html. The Nickel Shakespeare girls have toured many festivals, past venues are listed here: http://nickelshakespearegirls .com/performance.html.
[10] http://www.nickelshakespearegirls.com/performance.
[11] All quotes from Blum come from e-mail correspondence with the author made between 8 and 22 June 2014.

14. Nickel Shakespeare – Anna Gettles, Kacey Schedler and Rebecca Blum – performing one of their 'flippy' scenes at the Carolina Renaissance Festival.

complicates the Ren Fest model, because its focus is on an end result defined by effectiveness in the present, rather than being a harkening back to something which might have been successful at some past origin point. For all its historical trappings, Ren Fest Shakespeare is finally, and honestly, interested in contemporary playability, not in exploration of or justification by the past.

Nickel Shakespeare emerged from Carmen-Maria Mandley's training at Shakespeare & Company and Dell'Arte, and the playing style emphasizes high energy clowning and physical theatre. Their street theatre selections (the 'Shakespeare juke box' generated by audience requests which gives them their name) take a variety of forms including speeches incorporating hand-balancing (which they call 'Flippy Ones' because most of the time someone is upside down), fights, story-theatre (acting out the speech), and choral work. One of their *As You Like It* offerings is Celia's 1.3 speech declaring her love for Rosalind and how she will follow her cousin into banishment, risking death rather than staying in her father's court. Of it Blum says, 'It immediately occurred to me that it might be funny to have Celia accidentally beat up Rosalind while delivering this speech. So we choreographed it that way. I introduce the piece by stating that Celia's devotion to Rosalind may go "a little too far", and it works really well.'

Light and silly Shakespeare is still Shakespeare, and may in broad strokes access a playably valid take on the text. Celia's devotion to Rosalind need not be presented as sentimental or psychologically realist, and Nickel Shakespeare's broad-brush comedy may offer a legitimate critique of Celia's overly demonstrative fascination with her more captivating cousin as well as playing to the tastes of the Faire/Fest crowd. But the point is not that such approaches may have merit as *readings* so much as that this is Shakespeare in the world, or one part of it at least, and as such it shapes and responds to mainstream culture's notion of what Shakespeare is.

The Faire is a rather over-stimulating environment with lots of diversions and distractions, most of them emphasizing play, and so the company uses serious monologues sparingly, producing them only when they know they have a receptive group (either by prior experience or stated willingness to hear/see something darker or more reflective). It seems to me that the suitability of lighter, more comic material also speaks to the day-lit actor-audience dynamic, and that this is something more 'serious' historicist theatres wrestle with. While there are virtues to not controlling audience focus with stage lights, many audiences miss both the prompt to attention and the dignified aesthetic of conventionally darkened theatres in ways that make the production feel fundamentally less polished, less serious, and this is partly, I suspect, why so many historicist venues lean towards the playful and glib. Why else might an otherwise 'straight' production

of *King Lear* at the Staunton Blackfriars in 2006 begin with a curtain speech in which Lears' three daughters – in costume and a grotesque version of the roles they are about to play – feature Charlie's Angels gags and other frivolity? Why does Atlanta's Shakespeare Tavern (another self-described 'Original Practices', or OP, theatre) play so much of its tragedies for laughs? Why, in the earliest days of the Globe, were the audience encouraged to hiss and throw bread at the French during *Henry V*? For all their claims to how the historicist space buys a kind of authenticity, there is frequently a kind of embarrassment about such places from the performers themselves, a lack of faith in the notion that the project is, in fact, serious. Or is it us? And by 'us' I do not mean academics who have a vested interest in taking what is performed seriously. I mean we as representatives of the mainstream culture, who are, perhaps, too inculcated by other modes of theatre to be able to take day-lit, actor-driven performance as anything but trivial and disposable entertainment.

Twenty-first-century audience members have evolved towards solipsism and, in spite of the rhetoric to the contrary, the sharing of light by actors and audiences creates a community with a limited emotional range. A bored audience for *Hamlet* in a darkened auditorium is relatively shrouded in ways that tend to individualize them, shield them from each other's feelings, and tears shed in the dark are private, even when you are sitting next to a stranger. This is not the case for shared-light audiences for whom the behaviour of individual members (sleeping, muttering, joking at inopportune moments) is far more distracting, in ways presenting serious and constant risk to the atmosphere of gravitas most tragedies depend upon. It is striking that wildly successful interactive productions such as Punch Drunk's *Sleep No More* require audience members to go masked so that, even as they share light with the performers, they are crucially shielded from other audience participants and granted a particular kind of privacy. Shared-light audiences are largely reserved for sporting events where the brand of interactivity and the performance of emotion is different, and the dynamic works well at the Ren Faire, even if it limits the range of performance on offer.

Not everyone at the faire wants to experience Shakespeare, of course, and some will deliberately shy away, but the Nickel Shakespeare members have a wealth of stories in which people who professed boredom or hostility towards Shakespeare were won over, and the company says that 'A huge part of our mission is to educate people without them knowing it.' What they want their audiences to learn is simply that Shakespeare can be approachable, can be fun, and in this the immediacy of the actor/audience dynamic is crucially and pointedly unhistorical. Their sense of being 'flippy' is not just about physically upending actors: it is also about taking the 'preconceived notions people have about how Shakespeare is to be performed' and turning them on their heads. Part, of course, of what they are flipping, is the gendered casting of the original playing conditions, Nickel being an all-female troupe. This reinforces a contemporaneity to their educational mission which in some senses renders the past irrelevant, something to be inverted, something which has to be aggressively countered and redressed for twenty-first-century social mores. As Blum says:

What we do is try to bring to the masses what we think is appealing about Shakespeare and present it in a more engaging way than it has been presented to them in the past. Unfortunately, the passionless presentations of Shakespeare is an epidemic in our country. We don't believe in reading the plays, we believe in experiencing them. That is what we try to do for people – remind them that Shakespeare can be (and should be) fun.

'Fun' perhaps sells the company short, but it emphasizes, once more, the present, not the past, which makes sense since the audience – however much they are playing at being in (a version of) the past are absolutely of the present. Audiences, including those at historicist theatres, always are. Nickel's rhetoric of fun and immediacy is, of course, familiar, something many companies espouse, and much of what makes these particular performances different from those in conventional theatres is that the audience is, in a sense,

accidental. The crowds who experience Nickel did not go to see Shakespeare but to experience the Faire, though something about the demographic makes them better suited to be audiences for Shakespeare than, say, the crowd at a business convention or sporting event. This is not about Shakespeare's curiously persistent – even unique – tendency to span high and low culture simultaneously. It is about a particular manifestation of Shakespeare in a particular subcultural group.

Let us be clear. Faire/Fest Shakespeare is largely silly, innocuous stuff and anyone looking to see serious explorations of the poetry, plays, the man or his times should probably look elsewhere. But whatever its limitations it is not mere nostalgia and is rarely taken, as I already suggested, as history in the ways claimed by more respectable historicist theatres. The Faire/Fest world is fantasy history and fantasy Shakespeare, and you are as likely to see people dressed as wizards, elves and fairies as you are medieval lords and ladies (about which, more in a moment). Suffice it to say that this is Shakespeare as geek culture and, while it may be neither especially good art nor especially good history, I am unconvinced that fixing one of those components would necessarily fix the other. Indeed, I suspect the opposite might be the case. I have seen a lot of productions at historicist theatres where claims to authenticity bolster tedious and unimaginative shows, shows whose structuring 'concept' is the quasi-historicist claim not to have one. I am not, of course, suggesting that good art is transhistorical, though I do think that it often tends to an immediacy which at least appears to be unmediated by the temporal, nor am I suggesting that what is historical cannot function as art. My point is that the goals of art and history are, if not actually antithetical, different, and we would do well to keep them separate so that successes in one area cannot be misread as successes in the other. This is a frequent confusion and one which is common – even central – to the OP movement, though it seems to me that where OP Shakespeare works as art (which it certainly can do) it does so in spite of the project's historical valences, not because of them, and that claims to historicity often function simply as branding ('We do it with the lights on').

Indeed, the very flippancy (or flippiness) of Ren Fest Shakespeare might be its strongest suit. It rarely claims to be serious art, and is not generally (so far as I can tell) taken for it, nor – for all the straight faced Days of Yore press releases – is it generally taken for history. How can it be when it stands shoulder to shoulder with pirates, Klingons and hobbits? What it works as – and this is perhaps something other theatres and academics might take note of – is entertainment of the more playful sort. It is also a marker of what people think Shakespeare is and what sorts of people (beyond academics and serious theatregoers) gravitate to him/it by choice.

Because Shakespeare, for many, is part of the world glanced at in the Ren Fest, a world which is not simply an idealized version of a lost past, but which is defined quite self-consciously by fantasy and play. That play may extend to actual productions, but it is generally something more allusive, tied more directly to role-playing in a nebulously Shakespearian tradition (Ren Fest as forest of Arden). It is a place to which you go to be someone else, someone made up, a fantasy performance in which the audience is the world around you, a place in which you surround yourself with people who share your peculiar interests and celebrate them outside the workaday world of the mundane. It is, in the terms of the Faire world, Shakespeare as cosplay.

Cosplay blends fandom, craft work and performance art, practitioners building and wearing costumes at specific locations including Ren Fests and fantasy/scifi conventions, parades and photo shoots. Levels of professionalism vary wildly, as does how much is scratch built. Some cosplayers make money from their work and are professional invitees at said conventions where they model their costumes and present on construction techniques, but most are hobbyists, pouring vast amounts of time, money and creativity into what they make. Experienced cosplayers have the skills and resources of a theatre's design and production unit, being experts at drafting, cutting, sewing, make-up and prop construction. At its best, the results are dazzling, equal to the best that theatres or movie studios produce, and cosplay emblematizes geek culture not just in its focus on fantasy and science fiction but in its manifestation of labour, of commitment, of the desire to live one's interests rather than merely observe them from a distance.

Shakespeare does not naturally lend itself to actual representation in cosplay because, even when the form does not depend on replicating, tweaking or combining extant costumes from other media (movies, comic books etc.), it does depend upon dramatic visuals which are not inherently present in Shakespeare's text. A Hamlet – black clad, equipped with skull – might be a rare but not terribly interesting exception and, as a friend pointed out, might be mistaken for Jim Butcher's Harry Dresdon, or someone from George Martin's *A Game of Thrones*. Once in a while, you might glimpse someone cosplaying a Shakespeare character or Shakespeare himself, but any such are massively outnumbered by the elves, Trekkies, stormtroopers and Doctor Whos (all fourteen of them).

Yet there is a palpable overlap between the 'geek' subculture and non-academic Shakespeare, a curious little nexus where fandoms bleed together, and which goes some way to explaining Shakespeare's persistent presence in the various marginal spaces of that sub-culture. Partly, it is that there is something vaguely Shakespearian about cosplay itself – the impulse not so much to disguise as to embrace a playful self-fashioning which allows one to explore interests, desires or aspects of one's personality that are usually private, like Viola finding a new brand of autonomy and self-possession through the paradoxical constraints of masculine attire. Cosplay is more than dress-up: it is the performance of one's wit and skill and creativity in the form of a character or idea the cosplayer finds compelling; and with the clothes comes a suitable attitude, a costume-specific affect which leaps to the fore when the wearer poses for pictures. It might not be theatre in the conventional sense but it certainly is performance, and a liberating one which permits a demure Rosalind to swagger as Ganymede. Cosplay does not affirm absolute transformation like Tamburlaine discarding his shepherd's weeds, rather it is holiday wear or the donning of a mask, something done in fun which brings pleasures and discoveries of its own before returning, enriched, to ordinary reality.

But done also because Shakespeare seems to stand in for an adventurous version of history and literature which is bound to fantasy. Though generalization about such things is perilous, geek culture is sometimes defined by being the intersection of intelligence, specialist knowledge and social awkwardness. This intersection produces particular kinds of focused interest and enthusiasm often manifested in ways the larger culture considers excessive. Geek space is naturally populated by the bookish, the solipsistic and the imaginative, so a certain Bardic gravitational pull makes a kind of sense. But I wonder if there is more to it than that, that Shakespeare has always been thought of in these terms in ways Marlowe and Jonson, for instance, never were. Shakespeare was a purveyor of romance, not just in terms of love stories, but in the medieval sense which includes magic, providence, sprites, ghosts, witches and fairies but also, and more generally, a version of history as a kind of idealized fantasy. While Jonson and Middleton were drawn to the contemporary immediacy of their own urban surroundings, Shakespeare was more at home in the exotic, the imaginative. Even when he was trying to write satire in a play like *Merry Wives*, he could not resist turning the final act into a reprise of the fairy world of *A Midsummer Night's Dream*, the workaday realism of laundry hampers turning into the stuff of mythic fertility figures and the fairy denizens of a haunted forest. Yes, the audience is in on the joke, but that does not take away from their revelling in the theatrical magic of the episode, the fanciful whimsy which propels the play to its unexpectedly harmonious ending. The heart of Shakespeare's plays is frequently play itself, play which mines the imagination, spinning it into the strange, unearthly and fanciful stuff of ghosts and witches, of sorcerers, gods and other agents of the supernatural which defy conventional realism and what would come to be called 'common sense', sometimes working

at the level of plot, sometimes as little more than delighted and digressionary tangent, like Queen Mab bursting from Mercutio in a joyous cascade of finely detailed irrelevance. Shakespeare was from the outset 'Fancy's child', not schooled in the classics so much as nurtured by those Warwickshire wilds where (in Jonson's slightly condescending phrase) he warbled his wood-notes and, however inadequate, prejudiced or superficial such assessments may be, they persist into the present: geeks (myself included) are drawn to Shakespeare because they see him as one of their own.

If there is something to such a view (something small, perhaps, no bigger than the agate stone on the forefinger of an alderman), then the Shakespearian presence in the Ren Fest world is the manifestation of the way the people of that world have built a home for Shakespeare, or a version of him, which is as valid as the homes we have built for him in theatres and English departments. This is a Shakespeare which runs, Puckish, free from academia, free even from some of the calcification of high literary culture, a live Shakespeare, a momentary, present Shakespeare, a Shakespeare of imagination, of invention, of play: Shakespeare for geeks. Shakespeare as geek.

In academia we may forget the extent to which we are, by the standards of the larger culture, Shakespeare *fans*.[12] It is a troubling word which suggests, perhaps, an uncritical enthusiasm with which most of us would not be comfortable. But the world of fandom is not nearly as unselfconscious or unthinking as might appear from the outside, and fandom frequently yokes a range of diverse and sometimes hostile opinions. Indeed, fandom is less about enthusiasm and more about

[12] In his piece for *Jezebel* on Shakespeare and cosplay, Chris Braak talks about the geek desire to live in the world of the material which fascinates them rather than being satisfied by merely watching the TV show or – in this case – the play. In an amusing aside he wonders aloud whether Harold Bloom dresses up as Hamlet and offers passers-by his skull for fondling, or whether he frequents Ned-Alleyn-themed bars. I can offer no definitive evidence either way. http://jezebel.com/5787630/what-is-geek-culture-aka-why-isnt-shakespeare-cosplay-more-popular.

investment, investment in something which speaks to us in ways often quite idiosyncratic. Conventions, like academic conferences, unite fans over given commonalities, but they then subdivide repeatedly within those commonalities; they factionalize, not just over areas of preference, but over interpretation and ideology. A generation of fans schooled in the cultural studies classrooms of the last three decades apply theories of gender politics to the Steven Moffat era of *Doctor Who* as vehemently as they do to *Macbeth*.

Shakespeare is not merely a field of scholarly discourse or conventionally theatrical enterprise. He, or rather it, is a field of play, of imaginative invention where the stakes are not scholarly or otherwise professional, but recreational. As academics, of course, we know this already. It is a significant portion of the appeal which fills our classes and our theatre audiences. Yet we persist in applying the apparatus of one field (the academic) as judgemental criteria for another (the recreational, the playful), evaluating the latter according to how well it passes for the former. So when we invoke history in the context of Shakespearian performance we tend to slide into familiar assessment models rooted in the original performance conditions even when our own theoretical sophistication steers us away from the idea that such conditions can or should be the goal of production. It is telling that the reconstructed Globe has retreated from its rhetoric of authenticity grounded in an essential pastness, embracing instead a notion of the playhouse as an experimental (and in certain respects post-modern) space. This seems to me both smart and honest, though it remains to be seen whether their rhetorical self-presentation can trump the pursuit of that historical authenticity which many audiences (and, of course, tourists) seem to want or even need.

Shakespeare's theatrical value is historically mediated and complicated, but that does not mean that history should be an end in itself, and the Ren Fest model illustrates ways in which companies can exploit those vaguer historical associations while keeping their eyes front and forward looking. Geeks are drawn to the arcane, the marginal.

That is part of what makes them geeks: a delight in knowledge of things outside the mainstream. But geeks are also – in the most positive of senses – fantasists, people who revel in the unreal, the imaginary, and deem it important. This is, perhaps, where academics are most obviously geeks, because they embrace the reading of plays written four hundred years ago as something of the most urgent and vital importance. And if that alone does not make us geeks, then the fact that most of our non-academic neighbours find such conviction slightly baffling, or flat-out crazy, does.

Fantasy conventions, Ren Fests and other geek gatherings tend to be tolerant, upbeat places and, though not without their controversies and problems, are premised upon being a safe space for like-minded people, people frequently ostracized by main stream culture. That geek culture has moved steadily into the mainstream in the last decade or so complicates this sense of community somewhat and has created various backlashes and in-fighting over what 'real geeks' are, but such things tend to be marginal, and the overall mood remains that of a celebration of things loved. It makes sense to me that Shakespeare should be a part of that culture not as a manifestation of anything approaching real history but as another aspect of the fantastic, imaginative and dynamically present intersection of the intellectual, the arcane and the playful which demarcates so much of geek life.

Since Ren Fest history is fantasy, it is not a serious attempt to understand the past, but a guise with which to play in the present, though this too, one might argue, is a very Shakespearian notion of history, one which invokes the past in order to simultaneously step out of and explore a present whose veil is no more concealing than the mantle of Romanness which disguises *Julius Caesar's* expressly Elizabethan crowds. Original Practices productions and other forms of historicist Shakespeare may be dignified by better (in most cases) notions of history, but in their defiance of the temporal immediacy of theatre – their tendency to self-justify according to museum models of thenness and authenticity – they risk a greater fallacy than does the self-consciously frivolous Ren Fest model which knows its history is spurious. Both approaches recognize and exploit Shakespeare's pastness and both seek to provide a bridge to what that pastness was or might have been. Both have their strengths and their weaknesses as ways of addressing what Shakespeare is or signifies but, while one offers academic respectability, its implicit claims to essential correctness seems to me far more problematic as a mode of theatre than does the Ren Fest model's emphasis on Shakespeare as fantasy, as cosplay.

'DEAD AS EARTH': CONTEMPORARY TOPICALITY AND MYTHS OF ORIGIN IN *KING LEAR* AND *THE SHADOW KING*

KATE FLAHERTY

I know when one is dead and when one lives;
She's dead as earth

(King Lear, 5.3.258–9)[1]

In an interview about his Indigenous Canadian production of *King Lear* for the National Arts Centre (2012), director Peter Hinton shares a pointed anecdote about these resonant lines. He describes how August Schellenberg, the Montreal-born Metis actor playing Lear, said in rehearsal that the words were 'hard to say'. 'Why?' asked the director. 'Because the earth isn't dead', replied the Indigenous performer. And so, by Hinton's account, began a journey of 'opening up the play in a new way'.[2] For two reasons this anecdote of cultural collision offers an ideal departure point for an essay which considers the cultural work undertaken by an Australian Aboriginal adaptation of *Lear*. First, the anecdote crystallizes how the appropriative process produces unexpected alignments and dissonances between the embedded cultural norms of the play-texts and those of its adapters. Second, it is an excellent example of one of several para-discourses which, when combined with the play and production, can contribute to a thick description of its function as a cultural entity. Cued by these factors I take as my theoretical foundation what James C. Bulman has identified as

the radical contingency of performance – the often unpredictable, often playful intersection of history, material conditions, social contexts, and reception that destabilises Shakespeare and makes theatrical meaning a participatory event.[3]

The Shadow King – an Australian reworking of Shakespeare's *King Lear* by Tom E. Lewis and Michael Kantor – is by no means the first production to draw Shakespeare's evocation of Albion's origins into a topical Indigenous present. Stage adaptations such as Peter Hinton's *Lear* for the National Arts Centre and, before it, David Gardner's 'Eskimo *Lear*' have sought to recalibrate the content and theatrical conventions of the play to articulate aspects of local Indigenous experience.[4] *King Lear* offers an attractive proposition for such projects of exploring First Nations identity, particularly in postcolonial contexts where that identity has been fractured by the collective trauma of invasion, displacement and disenfranchisement. For *Lear* is itself a nation-founding myth replete, as

---

[1] This and all subsequent references to William Shakespeare's *King Lear* are taken from R. A. Foakes, ed., Arden Shakespeare edition (London and New York, 1997).

[2] Peter Hinton is interviewed by Suzanne Keeptwo in a podcast found at nac-can.ca/en/podcasts/hinterviews/king-lear (accessed 28 August 2014).

[3] J. C. Bulman, 'Introduction: Shakespeare and Performance Theory', in *Shakespeare, Theory and Performance*, ed. J. C. Bulman (London and New York, 1996), p. 1.

[4] David Gardner directed an 'Eskimo *Lear*' in 1961/2 which experimented with an 'Eskimo' setting but did not use Indigenous performers. Arguably this amplified the sense of the 'Eskimo' as the cultural 'other' rather than taking up *Lear* as a tool for exploring Indigenous concerns. See David Gardner, 'Canada's Eskimo Lear', *Theatre Research in Canada*, 7 (1986). Mark Houlahan also writes persuasively about *King Lear* in the native and settler Oceanic imaginary: '"Think about Shakespeare": *King Lear* on Pacific Cliffs', in *Shakespeare Survey 55* (Cambridge, 2004), pp. 170–80.

such myths always are, with many jagged hooks of topicality.

However, what is seen as innovation in connecting *Lear* to the topical, localized present finds a direct precedent in its first known performance. Scholarship of the past twenty years, stimulated by the authorial revision cataclysm, has illuminated many sources of early modern contemporary contextual interplay with the play.[5] Pointedly, Leah S. Marcus argues that the 1608 Quarto and the 1623 Folio represent distinctly 'localised' versions of the play. The 1608 Quarto, announced on its title page as having been 'played before the Kings Majestie at Whitehall vpon S. Stephans night' is, Marcus argues, more than the Folio 'permeated with details relating to the Project for Union' because of the contemporary exigency of that concern. 'In *King Lear*', she contests, 'James I's notions about the organicism of Britain under the king as head are themselves put on trial.'[6] The establishment of the revision hypothesis has thereby lifted a veil on the degree to which Shakespeare's dramaturgy is inflected by contemporary topicality. For the purposes of this essay it is relevant to note that *King Lear* in performance seems to retain this capacity to 'put on trial' facets of the present-day political and cultural status quo. Moreover, the animating tension between nation-founding narrative and contemporary topicality has very recently commended *Lear* as an ideal fictive conveyance into indigenous mythic imaginaries. In Australia this constitutes a new development in indigenous appropriation of Shakespeare; one that moves away from casting Shakespeare as an icon of British culture to be alternately revered and resisted, and one that moves towards harnessing the drama's inner dynamics and contradictions for new purposes.

* * *

The Three Sisters is the name of a rock formation in the majestic wilderness of the Blue Mountains National Park west of Sydney (Illustration 15). It is the region's most popular sight, attracting thousands of visitors to the precipice-perched Echo Point every week. Its popularity owes to its name and ancient story: a father, to protect his daughters

from an attacking tribe, turned them into stone but lost the magic that would return them to flesh. His daughters are literally 'dead as earth'. Anyone who stands on the edge of the cliff at Katoomba can appreciate the enigma that eddies within that statement just as 'waterfall' eddies within the word 'Katoomba'. A father overreaches the limits of his own power by translating his daughters into land and pays the price in desolate grief. Which origin do we ascribe to this mythic narrative? Who owns it? The common ground between this story and Shakespeare's *King Lear* is abundantly clear and many similar meeting places are offered at the intersections of narrative-rich Aboriginal cultures and the source stories to which Shakespeare gave such durable dramatic identity. It is surprising, then, that Australian productions of Shakespeare's plays have so rarely tapped the underground stream of archetypes and originary narratives which feeds both Indigenous Dreaming and Shakespeare's plays.[7] More often, in productions which include Aboriginal actors, the distinction between imperial colonizer and colonized peoples provides the torque. This has important cultural uses: Shakespeare has been deployed to dramatize the injustices of invasion and oppressions of white settlement in Australia. The oppositions offered within the plays' narratives – the Montagues versus the Capulets, Prospero versus Caliban and Duke Frederick versus Duke Senior – invite translation into nuanced

---

[5] The well-verified assertion that the Quarto and Folio *Lears* are based on distinct documents – both of authorial provenance – and that the Folio *Lear* thereby represents a purposeful dramatic revision of the play is most fully explored in Gary Taylor and Michel Warren, eds., *The Division of the Kingdoms: Shakespeare's Two Versions of 'King Lear'* (Oxford, 1983). Uncritical conflation of Quarto and Folio texts has since been eschewed as editorial practice but, puzzlingly, persists in theatrical production.

[6] Leah S. Marcus, *Puzzling Shakespeare* (Berkely, Los Angeles and London, 1988), pp. 148–9, 153.

[7] A notable exception is the all-Indigenous *A Midsummer Night's Dream* directed by Noel Tovey for the Sydney Theatre Company in 1997. This production deliberately linked the *Dream* with the pre-history of Australia's Indigenous peoples referred to as 'the Dreaming'. See Kate Flaherty, *Ours As We Play It: Australia Plays Shakespeare* (Perth, 2011), pp. 171–3.

15. The Three Sisters.

dramas of settler versus Indigenous cultures. However, it is arguable that this binary and competitive conception of culture paradoxically reinstates Shakespeare as the oppressive yardstick of cultural achievement. *The Shadow King* is a radically new use of Shakespeare by Indigenous artists in Australia to the extent that it exploits the shared imaginative territory of originary myth, and internalizes oppositions offered by the play as explorations of intra-cultural, not just inter-cultural, crises.

The Shadow King is an Australian Indigenous adaptation of Shakespeare's *King Lear* developed by director Michael Kantor and Indigenous artist and performer, Tom E. Lewis, for Melbourne's Malthouse Theatre and the Melbourne Festival in 2013. In 2014 it toured to festivals in Australia's major cities. The adaptation process involved several members of the all-Indigenous cast translating the play into a variety of Indigenous languages including Kriol (Australian 'creole' developed from a once widespread Australian pidgin which is still used in the Northern Territory (NT)) and Gupapuyngu (a Yolngu language spoken in

parts of Arnhem Land, NT). Very little of the original text was retained — by Kantor's account only four lines — but prominent episodes in Shakespeare's drama, both by sequence and content, were directly shadowed by *The Shadow King*.[8] Importantly, by locating itself linguistically and geographically in the Northern Territory this production side-stepped the impulse in mainstream white Australian culture to represent Indigenous culture and political crises as a set of generalized 'problems' in

---

[8] Matthew Westwood, 'Campfire King Tom E. Lewis Delivers an Indigenous Version of King Lear', *The Australian*, 5 October 2013. In an interview Kantor explained that the last four lines of the play were retained (Michael Kantor, interview with K. Flaherty, 21 October 2014). One important omission was the character of Kent whose 'moral weight' was, by Kantor's account, supplied by the Fool (Michael Kantor, interview with K. Flaherty, 21 October 2014). *The Shadow King's* Fool (Kamahai Djordan King), unlike the Fool of Shakespeare's play, haunted the performance as a spirit beyond his disappearance in 3.6 and, although he was announced by Lear as 'hanged', reappeared to speak a version of Edgar's final speech.

favour of dramatizing a specific, localized tragedy of 'two families being torn apart'.[9] Added to this, just as the play itself militates against a clear resolution, so, according to Tom E. Lewis, the piece was more of a 'question' than an attempt to 'bash some didactic line'.[10]

In Sydney, where I attended, the production was staged in the prestigious Carriageworks venue – a converted train workshop in the now decommissioned railway yards in Redfern.[11] The set comprised freestanding bleachers in an unimaginative end-on configuration to a lit space of red earth floor and surrounded by a cavern of darkness.[12] Audience members entered to see a group of women sitting together on the ground doing handcrafts at stage left, a band of three musicians clustered around a drum-kit downstage right, and wide, parallel steel rails in the floor. On these rails the major set feature arrived. In the words of the stage directions, 'The "machine" – part mining equipment, part road train, comes to life, it swings around, headlights blinding the audience, and slowly trundles downstage.'[13] The front face of this set feature comprised a raked, rust-coloured platform with a central set of stairs to a higher platform. It served variously as a piece of mining machinery, a truck and the porch of both Goneril's and Regan's homes – distinguished by the stills and looped video projected onto the screen behind it (Illustration 16).

This Lear's 'darker purpose' was selling land to a mining company. The hubris of his action in its disregard for the traditional belief that the 'land owns us and not we it', and the rapacity that it both reflected and unleashed, provided a credible starting place for Lear's trajectory – one which was both recognizable and new.[14] In the early part of the production, Tom E. Lewis as Lear wore a white suit, black shirt with embroidered white coils, black cowboy boots and a gold crown that looked like a cardboard party hat. He used the front of the structure as a stage to strut his wealth in this garish 'outback' style. The mood of the performance – combining live music and singing – was one of brash ambition and amusement on the part of the audience. This was undercut by the Fool's

introductory commentary which figured land as a living and violable entity:

First let's meet a man, the martja, martja for one of us mob!
    Big one la the community, proper regon mijelf, with a nod and a wink, if you know what I mean.
    He bin callem but meeting to let everyone know his plans . . . and this land, this buru, this pindan, im screams at what he willdo! (*Shadow King*, p. 2)

Cordelia (Rarriwuy Hick) continued this figuration in her explanation to Lear of her response of 'Najing' to the love test he used as part of his division project:

I'm not lookin round bla big fortune, specially not from this blood money, and I gottim no smooth word, but I know where I stand, and I sabi what's important . . . and I know you can't gibbit me what you don't own.
    (*Shadow King*, p. 5)

That the land 'screams' and that gains made from selling it for mining is 'blood money' immediately implies a tradition of regard for land as living. Despite being of the play's younger generation, Cordelia, therefore, appeared as a guardian of traditional culture rather than a transgressor of convention. Her outrage was directed less at Lear's betrayal of herself in the staged love competition and more at his betrayal of sacred country which encompassed all betrayal. Indeed all instances of disrespect

---

9 Michael Kantor, interview with K. Flaherty, 21 October 2014.
10 Quoted by Westwood, 'Campfire King'.
11 Redfern is home to one of Australia's largest urban Aboriginal populations. Regarded equivocally as a centre of black pride and identity, and as a troubled zone of socio-economic disadvantage it was recently the subject of a two-season television drama – *Redfern Now*, broadcast by the Australian Broadcasting Corporation in 2012 and 2013.
12 Set design by Paul Jackson, Michael Kantor and David Miller.
13 This and all subsequent references to *The Shadow King* script are to *The Shadow King Working Script 6*, Sydney Remount, January 2014. For access to the script of *The Shadow King* I am indebted to the generous assistance of Michael Kantor, Mark Pritchard and Malthouse Theatre, Melbourne.
14 *Fool.*   Dis land imm noma blong la you.
        It is you who blong na this land.   (*Shadow King*, p. 64)

16. Clockwise from left: Jada Alberts (Goneril), Tom E. Lewis (Lear), Natasha Wanganeen (Regan), Rarriwuy Hick (Cordelia).

were linked to land – a deliberate emphasis born of Lewis's very specific imaginative connection with the play:

When you talk of lands, and all the land councils, and the hypocrisy in society based on bullies who would steal other people's country without any respect, it's written in the books, in the white-fella book, Lear story.[15]

The metaphorical evocation of land as a living entity was further amplified by the production's physical aesthetics. Lear's abstract carving up of territories on a map took on potent materiality in the red earth of the set. As a consequence, dust offered a pervasive synecdoche for origins, land, country and cultural connection. The earth took on animation or life as it was worn by the characters: Lear's white suit was tainted with red dust; Edgar (Damion Hunter) sifted the earth through his fingers and painted his body with white clay

when transforming himself into Tom the bush sprite (Illustration 17), and the female Gloucester (Frances Djulibing) after her apparent 'fall' from the cliff rose coated in dust. Exposure to the elements, earth included, took on a nuance which both echoed and seasoned Shakespeare's *Lear*'s bracing encounter with nature. Tom/Edgar's journey into the wilderness was a kind of initiation rite which instilled in him wisdom and strength. His paradoxical return, as it were, to his ritualistic origins as a spirit figure made new sense of the play's contemplation of mortality. 'Unaccommodated man' was not a debasement of human potential but a thing of power, pride and beauty – a thing rendered immortal through its literal and narrative connection with the earth. As such Tom haunts Lear as a spectre of the connection with the land that he has lost.

[15] Quoted by Westwood, 'Campfire King'.

17. Kamahai Djordan King (Fool), Damion Hunter (Edgar).

For Lear, as for Edgar, exposure to the storm was less an 'unnatural' crisis than a point of reconnection with the physical world in what Kantor described as his journey from 'hubris to humility'.[16] The fearful thing about Lear's ejection from civilization was not his exposure to the natural elements but his exposure to the brutality of Edmund (Jimi Bani), Regan (Natasha Wanganeen) and Goneril (Jada Alberts) – members of his own community whose avarice had resulted in profound disrespect for the land and their elders. These pursued him as if pursuing wild pig or kangaroo – from the back of a truck with spotlights blazing – bearing knives and clubs and wearing pseudo-military garb. As the hunters stood on the upper platform the screen behind them played footage of their spotlights picking out Lear in his frantic attempts to escape through long grass in the rain.[17] This scenario offered effective Australian shorthand for white redneck blood-lust and mechanized brutality but was here deployed with a radical self-reflexive twist.

In *Lear* and in *The Shadow King* land ownership and division are intimately connected with more abstract qualities of legacy. Land is emblematic for what one generation passes down to the next. In Shakespeare's era Lear's decision to divide his kingdom between his daughters would have reverberated with the horror of the recent dynastic and civil conflicts now known as the Wars of the Roses. In *The Shadow King*, the point that bore most emphasis was the inborn Indigenous connection between land and lore. Lear's error lies in attempting to translate his land into hard currency and, in doing so, failing to transmit to the next

---

[16] Quoted by Westwood, 'Campfire King'.
[17] Film design by Natasha Gadd, Rhys Graham and Murray Lui.

generation collective wealth of traditional culture that is intimately connected with country. To illustrate this point I turn to Bruce Chatwin's famous *The Songlines*, in which the author's knowledgeable interlocutor describes the Indigenous relationship between land and narrative as follows:

In theory, at least, the whole of Australia could be read as a musical score. There was hardly a rock or creek in the country that could not or had not been sung. One should perhaps visualize the Songlines as a spaghetti of Illiads and Odysseys, writhing this way and that, in which every 'episode' was readable in terms of geology.

By singing the world into existence . . . the Ancestors had been poets in the original sense of *poesis* meaning 'creation' . . . the man who went 'Walkabout' was making a ritual journey. He trod in the footsteps of his Ancestor. He sang the Ancestor's stanza without changing a word or note – and so recreated Creation.[18]

The notable emphasis on fidelity to the original – 'without changing a word or note' – provokes questions about respect and source text which are broached below. For the present purpose, Chatwin's work helps to illuminate the conundrum of trading traditional lands – particularly for ecologically scarring exploitation such as open-cut mining – as the risk of displacing the narratives embedded within them.[19] In August Schellenberg's words: 'the earth's not dead'; it is alive with the narratives of its origins.

Lear's failure of transmission which results in unbridled greed and brutality received an inverted echo in Gloucester's family. Gloucester (Frances Djulibing) was a custodian of traditional culture and Edmund (Jimi Bani) its searing critic (Illustration 18). He wanted nothing but to throw off the trappings of traditional culture which for him represented superstition and hypocrisy:

My father they called a violent man, made him and I leave town, but violence can't be banished when it's in the soil and wind. This whole town is stained with rape and brutality, and yet they call me 'bastard' and 'lowlife', 'guttawah' when I'm smarter and stronger than legitimate family. Why do they call as [sic] bastards 'lowlifes'?

(*Shadow King*, p. 9)

In the Indigenous terms of the play Edmund is of the 'wrong skin'. His struggle laid bare the experience of discrimination and domestic turmoil within an Aboriginal community and so, again, resisted the totalizing conceptions of Aboriginal culture frequently peddled by mainstream Australian culture. A troubled individual emerged, whose bitter insight about the conventional bias that would brand him 'base', 'bastard' and 'illegitimate' opened up a sympathetic breach in the established order, which – in *The Shadow King*, as in *Lear* – is an oppressive patriarchal one. The crushing realization, however, is that his subsequent path of vengeful brutality is a literal dead end for himself and for his community.

To use Shakespeare to stage this moral complexity as part of an internal cultural struggle – as this production did through Jimi Bani's charismatic performance – breaks new ground in Australian theatre. Addressing the audience from downstage in the production's version of Edmund's 'Why "bastard"?' speech, Bani dared the audience to take a cynical view of traditions of kinship and country and explained the logic of his own 'darker purpose'. In doing so he was part of what Kantor described as the production's objective to 'represent on stage the complexity of contemporary Indigenous life in those small communities'. By Kantor's account, moving away from the familiar narrative

---

18 Bruce Chatwin, *The Songlines* (London, 1997; first published London, 1987), pp. 13–14. Chatwin frames his endeavour with diffidence: 'My reason for coming to Australia was to try to learn for myself and not from other men's books, what a Songline was – and how it worked. Obviously I was not going to get to the heart of the matter, nor would I want to' (p. 3). By his own admission Chatwin's account is limited, as all narratives are, by personal frames of reference and priorities. Insofar as it is an iconic attempt to apply Western European conceptions of geographically embedded narrative (Shakespeare's Stratford, Homer's *Odyssey* among them) to arrive at new insights on originary story-making in indigenous culture, it is very pertinent to this essay. It is also, as a seminal instance of the form 'travel writing', a kind of originary tale in its own right.

19 Although over 50 per cent of Australian Aboriginals are urban dwellers, the vast majority still trace important aspects of identity to the specific 'country' of their ancestors.

18. Jimi Bani (Edmund), Frances Djulibing (Gloucester).

of white oppression – a narrative nevertheless implicitly present in the giant piece of mining machinery – to one which shows difficulties and violence within an Aboriginal community, relied on great 'bravery and gumption' in the performers: 'they had to bear the brunt of it. They're responsible for their communities, and representing their communities on stage is really important.'[20] Any estimation of this bravery can only be increased by awareness that the same performers were refused taxis on their first day of rehearsal in Melbourne and racially abused on a tram – incidents which received wide media coverage.[21] The task of 'representing' Indigeneity – both for Indigenous communities and to the rest of Australia – is fraught with danger, and the artists of *The Shadow King* took a deliberate step into the cross-fire.

Frances Djulibing's performance as Edmund's mother, 'Gloucester', affectively collapsed the distinction between performing as, and being, a revered custodian of a traditional Indigenous culture. As a female performer and as a native speaker of the Gupapuyngu language, Djulibing contributed to the production a forceful expression of the link between land, lore and eldership, and a counterweight to Edmund's cynicism. Djulibing's distinctive prop was the 'dilly bag' – a small bag woven of plant fibres which she wore dropped to her waist on a strap around her neck. The dilly bag in itself is a resonant emblem of women's importance in culture because it confounds the accustomed division of work and the sacred.[22] The

[20] Michael Kantor, interview with K. Flaherty, 21 October 2014.

[21] www.abc.net.au/news/2013–05–02/aboriginal-actors-racially-abused-in-melbourne/4664752 (accessed 28 November 2014).

[22] Diane Bell, 'Person and Place: Making Meaning of the Art of Australian Indigenous Women', *Feminist Studies*, 28:1 (Spring, 2002), 99.

dilly bag is traditionally woven by women and used for tasks such as gathering food, but it is also strongly associated with sacred relics and transactions between the spirit world and humans.[23] In *The Shadow King*, the dilly bag was implicitly the repository of traditional culture and, in particular, of stories. Reinforcing this link, the violence committed on Gloucester (in this version Goneril and Regan gouged out her eyes) was accompanied by the tearing up of the dilly bag. Gloucester had her physical sight and symbolic role as a 'seer' violated at once:

Gloucester. (in amongst her screams of pain) Bayngu yurr munha ga barrimirr.   (Nothing, darkness, and fear) The ground is cursed. My dilly bag has been ripped and the red earth poured down to the ground. I can smell the ashes under my feet. The wind is blowing them away. I hope I can still hear my ancestors calling me.
Edgar! Wanha ngarraku yothu Edgar?
                                        (*Shadow King*, pp. 43–4)

Djulibing/Gloucester's custodianship role took on further significance at the point where Tom led her to the apparent brink of a cliff – here imagined through screen footage as a gorge in Djulibing's own Katherine region. To see her stately figure crumple and become coated in dust was to wonder if she could ever rise again. And yet she did, with a song composed by herself in her own language – a chant, strong and dry as if born of the dust itself – which remade her as does Gloucester's resolve to 'bear / Affliction till it do cry out itself / "Enough, enough", and die' (4.6.75).

For me the parallel poetry of this moment provided the most moving experience of the piece. This was no doubt partly because I carry strong traces of the 'original' poetry in my auditory memory and was able to hear the interwoven music of translation from moment to moment. Other commentators disagree. 'Could we not have an Aboriginal *Lear* that cleaved more closely to Shakespeare's language and dramatic structure?' asked reviewer Cameron Woodhead while conversely applauding actors' performances that 'wrest a fierce sense

of ownership of the story'.[24] From the perspective of co-creator Michael Kantor 'when you hear the Kriol, it re-finds the poetry... It's hard to read but the lyricism and rhythm is so close to Shakespeare. Almost by chance it's reclaimed the poetry.'[25] To my uneducated ear there was certainly poetic serendipity in certain aspects of the translation. The simple use of the pronoun 'im' – particularly when applied to the 'Lear story' and to land – conferred an animate, self-determining quality upon story and country, effectively crystallizing the raison d'être of the piece. Likewise, the use of the terms 'Daddy one' with reference to Lear seemed efficiently to encode a sinister patriarchal order. This lure of syntactical curiosity and half-understood but fully felt utterance mirrors the experience of many modern-day audiences of Shakespeare and suggests that poetic apprehension is not reliant on utter comprehension.

While the use of Indigenous languages did not distance me as an audience member, there were two aspects of the production that did undercut, to a significant degree, the strength and dynamism of its connection with its audience. The blunt end-on configuration of stage to audience space directly undermined the communal oral storytelling encounter which other aspects of the production sought directly to cultivate. The Fool opened the performance with engaging direct address to the audience:

Let me tellembut you wan mili mili,
(He holds up the book) one of <u>your</u> dreamtime stories,
but tonight we gunna make im one of ours...
It's one of those mili milis gutta king, crowns and
    kingdoms,
Kind of like what we gottem eya – this kingdom on
    which we jidan,
this place, this buru that we are, and share.
                                        (*Shadow King*, p. 1)

---

[23] Ian Keen, 'Ancestors, Magic and Exchange in Yolngu Doctrines: Extensions of the Person in Time and Space', *Journal of the Royal Anthropological Institute*, 12 (2006), p. 521.
[24] Cameron Woodhead, 'Theatre Review: The Shadow King', *The Age*, 18 October 2013.
[25] Westwood, 'Campfire King'.

His distinction of 'yours' and 'ours' constituted a lightly barbed acknowledgement of the predominant racial demographic of the audience but at the same time, a convivial invitation to share space and story. However, this potential was undermined by the deadening effect of the audience being ranged in geometric rows like a television or lecture audience. We were not in any sense 'in the picture'. I was sitting in the front row but never felt close to the action which was too often 'projected' into the blank middle distance of a darkened auditorium the way it would be from a Victorian picture stage. I later learned that this shortcoming owed little to the artists' lack of vision and everything to the inflexibility of Australian performance venues. Kantor explained that his original impulse was to do it in the round 'with just the red earth floor' but that the constraints on a touring production prohibited this. In Darwin the production was mounted in the round, without a set and was well received.[26]

A thrust-stage configuration and an evenly lit space might be advocated as the 'original' physical conditions upon which Shakespeare's dramaturgy was predicated; but in the case of *The Shadow King* there are grounds more relative to the production's own aims to advocate for them. There is a pressing imperative to augment the Indigenous oral storytelling tradition by allowing the performers to speak directly to the audience. In an interview Tom E. Lewis described the story of *Lear* as 'taking us back into our cultural dynasties', and suggested that 'because we have that opportunity, we can create the Lear dynasty in my campfire'.[27] The intimate access implied by Lewis could have been achieved by having the audience gathered *around* the performance space (and was, fittingly, accomplished in the Darwin, NT production). As it was, however, the actors had to move artificially facing outwards, from left to right and back again along the rigid perimeter of stage edge thereby reinforcing the sense of distinct territories and cultural difference. This, moreover, generated a parodic air of the Broadway musical which, to give him credit, Tom E. Lewis used to his advantage as he flaunted his new wealth, but which in general muted the force

of topical reference and distanced the energies of the performance from the audience.

Another distancing aspect of the performance was its base note of misogyny. Exposing and redressing ingrained forms of discrimination was, as discussed above, well within the ambit of the production. However, there was one moment in the Sydney performance where the Fool sided disturbingly with Edmund in his violence towards Regan. In the script the complex episode is preceded by Regan's expression of regret for her violence towards Gloucester. Edmund responds:

> I think it's a little too late for tears and regret . . . Look, We have our own future to look after, on our land now, and with what's in your belly, that land is will give and give for generations, just as we planned it. But you have to learn who's the daddy-one now . . . If I want my woman on all fours I'll have her on all fours!
> *(Edmund suddenly seems threatening and dangerous, and with a glint in the eye, he leads Regan off the stage)*
> (*Shadow King*, p. 47)

In the Sydney performance, Edmund actually knocked the pregnant Regan down and pursued her as she scrambled off-stage. At this point the script continues:

> *The Fool appears around the corner, a noose still around his neck*
> Fool. (*pointing to where Regan has just left*) Serves you right, you devilish shrew, cursed by them crimes you have committed. A woman deformed by hatred and rage is more horrifying than the debil himself.
> (*Shadow King*, pp. 46–7)

It was very unclear to me why the 'ghost' Fool, who acts as a mediator for the audience and a moral guide to Lear, should at this point align himself against the admittedly criminal Regan but *with* the much more sinister Edmund by whom he has just been hanged! This strangeness is amplified by the fact that Regan has expressed remorse for her crimes and that Edmund's response is a threat of vindictive rape. The only explanation offered is that

---

[26] Michael Kantor, interview with K. Flaherty, 21 October 2014.

[27] Tom E. Lewis quoted by Westwood, 'Campfire King'.

a '*woman* deformed by hatred and rage is more horrifying than the devil'; and, it would seem, more
deserving of vindictive violence than a man who
fits the same description.

As the stage configuration dilemma and the
dissonant chord of misogyny in *The Shadow King*
reflect, Shakespeare adaptation projects are prone
to both oversight and over-determination. This in
turn brings to light the ignorance and embedded
biases of the target culture(s) and so turns the tables
on the idea that any updating of Shakespeare's
presumed imperialist values constitutes moral
progress. Discourses of reception reflect such confusion positioning *The Shadow King* as digressing
provocatively from the 'original' and, at the same
time, re-capturing its essence. Significantly, the
production's innate concern with preservation
of traditional culture nuanced and amplified its
treatment of the concept of the 'original' in ways
that would not obtain in an Anglo-Australian
production of *Lear*. Recent Australian *Lears* in
their attempts radically to distance themselves from
what they (mis)understand as the 'original' bear
this out.[28] However, by dramatizing an Indigenous
conceptualization of land ownership, *The Shadow
King* also challenged embattled postures of cultural
ownership to arrive at a new conception of story
which is particularly pertinent to drama. The
emerging proposition is that no-one owns Shakespeare's plays, but that they in some measure possess
us as humans.[29] Conflating the problematics of
land ownership and cultural possession, as this
production has prompted me to do, has generated
some experimental analysis, not only of the production itself, but of the para-discourse by which it
is framed. It is worth noting that Lewis's and other
commentators' understandings of the cultural work
accomplished by the production are not identical.
In many respects the project is a living template for
reconciliation through artistic collaboration. The
short video used to tell the story of the collaboration's origins underscores this.[30] However, in the
published rhetoric around cultural possession even
Kantor and Lewis seem subtly at odds.

Director Michael Kantor was quoted as wondering 'wouldn't it be interesting for Indigenous
culture to *grab* the canon, the white man's dreaming, the white man's songline?' (emphasis mine).[31]
Reviewer Matthew Westwood conceptualizes the
project in similar terms: 'a cast of black actors *claiming* and reimagining the white man's culture'.[32] In
a similar vein, Cameron Woodhead, reviewer for
The Age, commends the cast for 'wresting' a 'fierce
sense of ownership of the story'. The pervasive
discourse of 'grabbing', 'wresting' and 'claiming'
echoes the cultural oppositions which, as I outlined earlier, formed the basis of many previous
adaptations of Shakespeare's plays which starred
Indigenous performers. The persistence of this
language begs the question of whom the work
is to be 'wrested', 'claimed' or 'grabbed' from.
Shakespeare scholars are the obvious candidates
and one reviewer claims that 'Kantor reckons the
Shakespeare scholars would "rip us to shreds".'[33]
Is violently contested territory the only available
paradigm for Shakespeare in Australia?

A kind of answer to this question can be found
in Tom E. Lewis's more poetically nuanced and
less defensive understanding of possession – both
of land and stories:

If we disrespect, we lose the story . . . From the beginning
we've got to be true to the story that we're doing. It will
make you respect a lot of things. The story is taking
us back into our cultural dynasties. . . . We don't want to

---

[28] Instances in point are Barry Kosky's iconoclastic expres-
sionistic *Lear* for Bell Shakespeare (1998) and Rachel Mc-
Donald's *Queen Lear* for the Melbourne Theatre Company
(2012).

[29] This sentiment is articulated by two other directors of
indigenous *Lears* discussed above. David Gardner director of
the 'Eskimo *Lear*' opines that 'Shakespeare's poetry belongs
to us all.' See Gardner, 'Canada's Eskimo Lear'. Peter Hinton, director of the all-aboriginal Canadian *Lear*, argues that
'Shakespeare doesn't belong to the colonisers . . . it belongs
to all of us. Shakespeare offers something to humans.' Podcast
at nac-can.ca/en/podcasts/hinterviews/king-lear (accessed
28 August 2014).

[30] (www.malthousetheatre.com.au/show-listing/the-shadow-
king/ (accessed 13 July 2014).

[31] Westwood, 'Campfire King'.

[32] Westwood, 'Campfire King'.

[33] Andrew Stephens, 'Lear Takes on New Territory', *Sydney
Morning Herald*, 5 October 2013.

take it away from the old story, . . . but you've got the old mob playing an old story in a new version: that's good little triangle isn't it?[34]

Played out in the discourse surrounding the project are two polarized attitudes towards cultural heritage: the post-modern, western attitude that is about toppling dynasties, and an Indigenous voice which holds in tension respect for traditional cultures with the imperative of making them live in the present. While the rhetoric of violent appropriation reasserts the anticipated binaries of cultural possession borne of the assumption that culture is a static relic, Lewis's words imply a fluidity and a shared imaginative territory which to some extent 'owns us' and not we it: '"*Lear* is constructed like a songline", Lewis says, describing how its layered stories run like tributaries into a larger river.'[35] For Lewis, Shakespeare's play offers a path like a songline, across a narrative-rich country. The 'spirituality' in *The Shadow King* was, for him, 'found in the way it explores relationships to country'. Walking the path of embedded narratives is a way of respecting the country – in his conception a shared path and a shared country: 'we have a beautiful country, both of us, black and white', he says. 'We are going to lose it if we don't mind it.'[36] The generosity of Lewis's view cuts across the territorial boundaries unintentionally reinstated by mainstream Australian cultural rhetoric and is perhaps most eloquent in what he describes as his 'dream' for the production – to take it back to Shakespeare's own country: 'I'd love to do that, give them back the book and say thank you to them . . . Do you ever thank the Pom in our country? Thank them for *Lear*.'[37]

As is the case in many settler and postcolonial contexts, in Australia there is a substantial history of using Shakespeare in performance to articulate and explore the issues of invasion, displacement, discrimination and, more subtly, of land ownership, eldership, oral story-telling traditions, spirituality and magic. These discourses offer themselves in Shakespeare's plays and are readily accommodated to dramatize specific conflicts in the local context. Three mainstage productions in the year 1999 provide key examples. Simon Philips directed a production of *The Tempest* for the Queensland Theatre Company which pitted white colonial settlers, evocatively indicated as First Fleeters by redcoats and muskets, against a native Caliban.[38] Neil Armfield directed a production of *As You Like It* for the Belvoir Street Theatre in Sydney which cast Indigenous performer Deborah Mailman as Rosalind, giving her arbitrary exile to Arden a particular valence of displacement.[39] Finally, La Boite Theatre and Kooemba Jdarra Indigenous Performing Arts collaborated in a production of *Romeo and Juliet* directed by Sue Rider which cast the Capulets as Indigenous and the Montagues as white Euro-Australians. As Emma Cox has argued, each of these productions 'examined the operations of racial divisiveness and prejudice and enacted narratives of reconciliation between Indigenous and Euro-Australians both on and offstage'.[40] The important intercultural work that Shakespeare has been harnessed to accomplish in Australia is indisputable. The groundbreaking development I have identified in *The Shadow King* is the use of Shakespeare by Indigenous artists for intra-cultural, self-reflective purposes. This constitutes a further step away from conceptualizing indigineity, either obliquely or directly, as a set of familiar problems that have to do with the past, and towards populating the stage with stories from the topical, living present. In particular, *The Shadow King* made *King Lear* about the internally contentious Indigenous issue of dividing and selling off traditional lands for mining ventures. Connected with this it tackled the issue of intergenerational schism – loss of identity through loss of lore and loss of respect for stories – pointedly centred on the production's

---

34 Westwood, 'Campfire King'.

35 Andrew Stephens, 'Lear Takes on New Territory'.

36 Andrew Stephens, 'Lear Takes on New Territory'.

37 Westwood, 'Campfire King'.

38 Emma Cox, 'Reconciling Shakespeare and Indigeneity in Australia: Star-cross'd Communities and Racial Tempests', *Australasian Drama Studies*, 44 (2004), 78–94.

39 Kate Flaherty, *Ours As We Play It: Australia Plays Shakespeare* (Perth, 2011), pp. 144–50.

40 Cox, 'Reconciling Shakespeare', p. 78.

female Gloucester. In allowing such detailed treatment of Indigenous intra-cultural topics the production arrived at new and surprising alignments between Shakespeare's *Lear* and Australian Indigenous culture. Rather than reinforcing longstanding cultural opposites, this production, and particularly Tom E. Lewis's aspirations for it, took the contemporary predicament of composite culture as its origin and demythologized schism, even as it appropriated a blended mythological imaginary to do so.

The death of Cordelia is, without a doubt, the most potent point of fusion between Shakespeare's *King Lear* and any context of production. Successive ages have staged it as nihilistic or redemptive in accordance with the mood of their cultural moment or, in the case of Nahum Tate's durable adaptation, omitted it altogether. In *The Shadow King* Cordelia died and was grieved piteously by her father. Just prior to her death, while locked in a very realistic prison cell with Lear and Gloucester, she quipped in a wry tone that 'at least we not the first of our mob to end up in here' (*Shadow King*, p. 57). This grim throwaway operated as a jagged hook of topicality – hauling into focus a vast and recent history of abuse, discrimination and death of Indigenous Australians.[41] Cordelia's death provided sobering synecdoche for what has been irretrievably lost and indelibly damaged through Australia's settlement process and its persistent echo of

disadvantage for its native peoples: 'Never, never, never, never, never!' (*Lear*, 5.3.307, *Shadow King*, p. 63). Gloucester's poignant question lingers in the air: 'Is this the end of the world?' (*Shadow King*, p. 63). However, the chord of devastation was also radically nuanced by an implication of shared responsibility: Lear's 'What did I do? What have I done!' (p. 63). Unlike Shakespeare's Lear, this shadow king probes his own conscience at the brink of mortality; he seeks to know what he as an individual owns in the tragedy. This sets *The Shadow King* apart from all Australian productions and adaptations of *Lear* by making crisp its faint ring of redemption in the hope for a reconciled future. The very existence of *The Shadow King*, the hospitality and new use it offered for Shakespeare's *Lear* narrative, and especially the way it dramatized story and country as valuable, shared entities that own us and not we them, produced an experience-tempered but hopeful outlook. In short, if Cordelia is 'dead as earth', the story is far from finished.

---

[41] In the wake of a staggering number of Aboriginal deaths in prison, many of them suicides, a 1991 Royal Commission was held into Aboriginal deaths in custody. It found that 14 per cent of Australia's prison population was Aboriginal. Today 26 per cent of Australia's prison population is Aboriginal. Only 2.5 percent of Australia's general population is Aboriginal. For a synopsis see www.abc.net.au/news/2013–05–24/death-in-custody-report-alarms-indigenous-leaders/4712056 (accessed 4 September 2014).

SHAKESPEARE AND THE IDEA OF NATIONAL THEATRES

MICHAEL DOBSON

O for a muse of fire, that would ascend
The brightest heaven of invention:
A kingdom for a stage, princes to act,
And monarchs to behold the swelling scene!

(*Henry V*, 1.0.1–4)

I begin with the Chorus's speech from the start of *Henry V* (1599), not just because it is one of the best beginnings ever written for anything, but because it is central to my topic in ways that are both intellectual and autobiographical. What I want to do in this article is look at three propositions according to which different national theatre institutions have emerged, and in particular the extent to which those different theatres have plausibly appealed to Shakespearian precedent. In the process I will be glancing at some theatres in continental Europe, in North America and in Australia, but I will mainly be concentrating on Ireland and the more-or-less United Kingdom, where these rival rationales for nationalized theatre have overlapped and competed in particularly interesting ways. One incidental, local symptom on which I will be touching has been a long-standing rivalry between Stratford and London as imagined natural homes for live Shakespeare: even Daniel Rosenthal's immense history of the metropolitan National Theatre, after all, *The National Theatre Story* (2013), begins with the arresting claim that it all started in Stratford: 'The National Theatre story begins in 1564, with the birth of William Shakespeare.'[1] If the playwright himself ever had an inkling that he was part of such a story, it was surely when he wrote the opening of *Henry V*,

as, feigning to find his own company's current venue (whether it was the Curtain or the Globe) inadequate to the play's epic national aspirations, Shakespeare pictures an entire country transformed into an auditorium for his drama. In essence, most of the remainder of this article will sketch an account of how that fleeting vision was and wasn't realized over the three centuries that followed Shakespeare's death, closing with one instance in which the three different paradigms I am going to outline strikingly converged. There will then be a post-war epilogue and a shameless endorsement.

My autobiographical reason for starting from the prologue to *Henry V* is simple: those were the first words I ever heard spoken from a Stratford stage, in the old 1932 Shakespeare Memorial Theatre, which in 1961 had become the Royal Shakespeare Theatre. They were spoken by Emrys James, in Terry Hands' glorious 1975 RSC production of *Henry V*, with Alan Howard in the title role.[2] In the course of drafting this article I realize that I have returned to questions which have preoccupied me on and off since I was at school. Including the RSC, I encountered three very different putatively national theatre institutions before I went to

---

This article is adapted from the script of an inaugural lecture given at the Shakespeare Institute on 14 October 2014: a full version, copiously illustrated, can be watched on YouTube at http://youtu.be/2EsBzdaX5cc.

[1] Daniel Rosenthal, *The National Theatre Story* (London, 2013), p. 3.
[2] On this production, see especially Sally Beauman, *The Royal Shakespeare Company's Centenary Production of 'Henry V'* (London, 1976).

university, and the question of how and why they each counted as national is one which definitely puzzled me at the time.

Chronologically, the RSC was the second of these institutions. I was brought to see them in a bus all the way from Bournemouth, along with the rest of my grammar school's O-level cohort, since I was given to understand that a compulsory national examination about one of the works of our national poet and an educational visit to a state-subsidized performance of it were part of my birthright as a freeborn Briton. Quite apart from the intense pleasures of Hands' production itself – I remember thinking: I must try to find some excuse for spending more time here – there was a definite excitement in knowing that I was sitting in a playhouse which people read about in *The Guardian* and *The Times*, rather than just in the *Bournemouth Echo*. Here, I was told, nationally significant theatre happened. It was a far cry from the first national theatre I had visited, during a family holiday in the late 1960s: the Siamsa Tíre National Folk Theatre of Ireland, in Tralee.[3] As far as I can remember, we and an audience of fellow-tourists saw a song-and-dance show in Gaelic which presented an idealized, nostalgic vision of unspoiled peasant life, complete with picturesque supernatural beliefs and country dancing: a sort of hyper-Celtic *Fiddler on the Roof*. There was definitely a whitewashed cottage on stage, which is one reason I was reminded of Siamsa when I first visited my third national theatre, the NT itself, a couple of years after my O-level introduction to Stratford.

Denys Lasdun's bunker-like complex on the South Bank, I admit, did not look particularly rustic, and in what sense this concrete building was more national and less royal than the red-brick Royal Shakespeare Theatre I wasn't sure. The set of the show we watched, however, looked much like a big-budget version of Siamsa's, since my A-level group had been brought to London – incidentally, by the best teacher of English and drama ever, Wendy Williams – to see a play which had been written for another national theatre altogether, the Abbey in Dublin. Seventy years earlier, the premiere of Synge's *Playboy of the Western*

World had been famously heckled in Dublin by an audience who had expected a much more rosy and Siamsa-like portrayal of Irish country life from their national stage than this play about the hero-worship of a parricidal braggart. At a matinee in the Olivier in 1977, however, it was received in near-silence, one more expertly-curated safe state-approved classic. Despite taking place in an auditorium named after one of the great Henry Vs, this theatrical experience seemed a long way from that play's imagined super-Globe. So in what ways, I wondered, did the RSC, the Abbey, Siamsa and the National, all founded three centuries after Shakespeare's time, each offer, if not a kingdom for a stage, then stages for kingdoms, or at least stages for one kingdom and for one neighbouring republic?

I. ROYAL

The earliest proposition about national theatres is perhaps the simplest. Proposition one, then: serious drama such as the Shakespeare canon is an expression of cosmopolitan high culture – court culture – and is best encouraged and supported from above by royal patronage. This is certainly a view Shakespeare would have recognized, even if it wasn't very consistently or wholeheartedly endorsed by the sovereigns he served, and it sends us back once more to those monarchs beholding the swelling scene.

By the time the warlike Harry is assuming the port of Mars five or six lines into the Chorus's prologue, the notion of a platonic super-stage with royals for its actors is already metamorphosing into a more Homeric vision in which real warriors contend in the theatre of war under the eyes of godlike spectators. Something of the combined impression that results – of theatre as national spectacle and theatre as arena of international conflict – is taken up in Ben Jonson's commendatory poem elsewhere in the First Folio: 'Triumph, my Britain! Thou hast one to show / To whom all scenes of Europe

---

[3] On this organization and its history, see www.siamsatire.com

homage owe.'[4] For Jonson, all playwrights seem to be engaged in a sort of perpetual competitive Cultural Olympiad, in which the Shakespeare canon represents a decisive goal for Britain against 'all scenes of Europe'. Jonson is elsewhere in the poem keen to stress the royal endorsements Shakespeare received in his lifetime – his plays 'so did take Eliza, and our James' – and one historical factor behind both this couplet and the prologue to *Henry V* is the extent to which, at the time they were written, rival Renaissance princes were indeed deliberately investing in drama as a source of prestige. By 'scenes of Europe' Jonson may imply 'national traditions of theatre across the continent', but he also means quite literally 'European playhouses', many of which had been specifically built to demonstrate the technological sophistication and cultural mastery of royal patrons. The most influential may have been those built for the Gonzaga dynasty in Mantua: here under the patronage of Duke Vicenza in 1607, at around the time Shakespeare was working on *Pericles*, Monteverdi staged *L'Orfeo*. The court theatres of Renaissance Italy were opera houses in embryo, temporarily imitated in court entertainments in England (thanks largely to the well-travelled Inigo Jones), but a far cry from the sorts of public, commercial playhouses for which Shakespeare was writing.

Designed to produce an environment in which every detail of the spectacle is under complete artistic and technological control, these baroque structures turned out to be equally suitable, once the vogue for fancy-dress gods and heroes singing endless repeats had finally passed, for the purposes of bourgeois realism. The Teatro della Pergola in Florence, for instance, built for Gian Carlo de'Medici in 1656, is now most famous as a venue for opera (in 1847 it saw the premiere of Verdi's *Macbeth*), but when Nicky Watson and I visited it (during one of those indispensable research trips to Tuscany which one feels coming on from time to time), the play we saw was Goldoni's orthodox neoclassical comedy *La Bottega del Caffè*, and it seemed perfectly at home. These are playhouses better suited to Goldoni or Molière than to Shakespeare, and it is suggestive in this connection that after Molière's

own company became the first true national theatre in Europe – when the Comédie Française was established by the decree of Louis Quatorze in 1680 – they played for many years in a royal auditorium, within the Tuileries palace.[5] They are still, of course, based at a formerly royal site, by the Palais Royal, in another classic opera-house-style auditorium, the Salle de Richelieu (1799).

Royal patronage just wasn't like this for Shakespeare: although James adopted Shakespeare's company as the King's Men, and was happy to provide red cloth when they served as extras in royal processions,[6] he did not build or endow the Globe or the Blackfriars. British Renaissance princes were cheapskates by comparison to their Italian and French counterparts, prepared to hire common players to perform in unadapted halls much like those which such companies might have encountered at the Inns of Court or in provincial towns. Shakespeare might have fantasized in *The Tempest* (1611) about a technologically sophisticated Italian prince who can produce a sort of opera full of simulated deities to impress his daughter and her fiancé but, despite their occasional participation in court masques, his company's day-by-day experience was much more like that of the players he had depicted in *Hamlet* (1600). Though they have often played at Elsinore before, the 'best actors in the world' have been competing unsuccessfully in the urban theatrical marketplace against all-boy companies, and they now seem to be on perpetual tour.

When the Stuarts eventually did support the establishment of opera-house-like baroque theatres in London, after the Restoration, they did so not by paying up themselves but by awarding a duopoly, rigging the market so as to make the

---

[4] Ben Jonson, 'To the memory of my beloved, the author, Master William Shakespeare...', in William Shakespeare, *Mr William Shakespeares comedies, histories and tragedies...* (London, 1623), A4 r-v: v.

[5] See e.g. Charles Maurice, *Le Théâtre-Français, monuments et dépendances* (Paris, 1860).

[6] See the much-studied document in the Public Record Office, LC 2/4/5 reproduced (with some unacknowledged alterations) in Samuel Schoenbaum, *Shakespeare: A Documentary Life* (Oxford, 1975), p. 196.

two new exclusive indoor playhouses artificially profitable. Although Charles II's court occasionally frequented both of these theatres, his successors took less and less interest, and the royal decrees by which the King's Company and the Duke of York's Company had been established in 1660 were soon treated as heritable commercial property, in which speculative investors might purchase shares. Shakespeare's own company was nominally royal from 1603 onwards and after the Civil Wars so were the two Theatres Royal, but they weren't national in the same sense that the Comédie Française was national. In fact by the mid-nineteenth century, the two royal patent houses, Drury Lane and Covent Garden, engaged in a relentless commercial struggle for an ever lower common denominator of popular taste, were widely regarded as a national disgrace, unworthy of Shakespeare or of his present-day successors. Across the rest of the continent, the royally supported court theatres of different kingdoms and princedoms eventually metamorphosed into the national and civic theatres of republics, constitutional monarchies and cities; but in Britain the Theatres Royal were destined to become the problem to which a national theatre had to be proposed as the solution.

2. EMBODIED

This is not to say that Drury Lane in particular was always regarded as unfit to be a shrine of the national drama. For one key period in the mid-eighteenth century, indeed, it was regarded as Shakespeare's natural posthumous home, but this was not because of the Hanoverian kings who nominally patronized it but because of the actor-manager who actually ran it. One quite different paradigm for the establishment of a playhouse's national status, which has haunted all successive attempts to produce a national theatre in Britain, was pioneered by someone whose inspired publicity campaigns in London and in Stratford continue to resonate in both. According to this proposition, the national drama is the expression of a single legitimate theatrical tradition, and in order to be properly national a theatre has to be the professional

base of someone who personally embodies that tradition.

In France, the Comédie Française is still known as 'la maison de Molière', and a statue of Molière stands in its foyer accordingly;[7] in England, those different theatres which have claimed to be the home of our classical theatre have all been houses of Shakespeare, but usually houses of Shakespeare as compèred in a mode pioneered by the person who supplied Drury Lane with the statue of Shakespeare which now lurks in one neglected corner of its foyer, namely David Garrick. I first explored the story of how Garrick managed to convince the world that he was Shakespeare's representative on earth more than twenty years ago,[8] but what I hadn't appreciated until researching this article was how powerful the Garrick paradigm has remained down the centuries since the actor-manager's death in 1779.

To recap at terrible speed: throughout the period of the two patent houses, theatre managers were always anxiously aware that once upon a time the drama had been at once more popular and more artistically reputable than it had become, and the shorthand for that awareness, articulated in prologues, epilogues and cartoons, was the vengeful Ghost of Shakespeare. In the cartoon 'The Rival Printers', 1734, published to satirize the unseemly struggle over publishing rights to the Shakespeare canon then in progress between the firms of Tonson and of Walker, in the centre of Covent Garden, there rises in the midst of the degraded world of modern popular entertainment – dancing dogs, prize-fighters and all – the disapproving ghost of Shakespeare, to remind us that we can do better than this.[9] In 1741 a comparably reproachful-looking statue of Shakespeare was put up in Westminster Abbey, but in the same theatrical season an actor from Lichfield took London by storm to

---

7 On this piece of branding, and on Shakespeare's place in the Comédie Française repertory, see Estelle Rivier, *Shakespeare dans la maison de Molière* (Paris, 2012).
8 See Michael Dobson, *The Making of the National Poet: Adaptation and Authorship, 1660–1769* (Oxford, 1992), chapter 4.
9 British Museum, 1868, 0808.3522.

set the ghost's spirit at rest. David Garrick was already co-starring with a copy of the Westminster Abbey statue as an uncredited understudy in a show called *Harlequin Student* even before his sensational official debut as Richard III, and he would spend much of his career posing with it. Soon established as the definitive Hamlet of his generation, Garrick (almost literally) cast Shakespeare as the Ghost. Standing in front of the statue, most famously while reciting his 1769 Jubilee ode, first in Stratford and then in his play *The Jubilee* at Drury Lane, Garrick claimed to be the rightful Prince who was Shakespeare's true executor. In case anyone still hadn't got the point by 1769, Garrick's badge as Steward of the Stratford Jubilee resembled the miniature which he carried as Hamlet in the closet scene, bearing an image of Shakespeare and the line 'We shall not look upon his like again'; variations appeared on souvenir products too. Declaring his loyalty to Shakespeare in countless manifesto prologues, from his first season as manager of Drury Lane in 1747 onwards, Garrick advertised his peerless actorly technique and his equal facility in comedy and tragedy as a Shakespearian versatility – see, for instance, Sir Joshua Reynolds' famous portrait *David Garrick between Comedy and Tragedy* (1760–1).[10] The supreme show-off of his age, Garrick even sometimes played the comic rustic Scrub on the same bill as he played King Lear. When he commissioned Roubiliac to make a statue of Shakespeare for the Temple of Shakespeare which he proprietorially built in his garden at Hampton, Garrick allegedly posed for it himself. So of course a legitimating statue of Shakespeare was much in evidence on stage and off at Drury Lane in Garrick's time; and for a while the one he had co-starred with on-stage in shows such as *Harlequin's Invasion* and *The Jubilee* even stood outside on the portico, like a pub sign. This is the theatre, it once declared, in which Garrick speaks for Shakespeare: 'Sacred to Shakespeare was this spot designed', he declaimed in the prologue that opened the 1750 season, 'To pierce the heart and humanize the mind'. It isn't surprising, I think, that some histories of the National Theatre claim quite erroneously that the institution was all Garrick's idea.[11]

The trouble with this paradigm, as with that of hereditary monarchy, precisely as dramatized by *Hamlet* itself, is that it is prone to succession crises. What was to happen after Garrick died? The idea that any truly national theatre has to be the home of Shakespeare's ghost, best represented on earth by a great Hamlet and forever associated with Garrick, certainly proved a haunting one. In the unidentified frontispiece 'Consecrated to the Memory of David Garrick',[12] presumably produced within a short time of Garrick's death in 1779, Tragedy looks suitably distraught while even Comedy shows how the gaiety of nations has been eclipsed. Comedy and Tragedy appear again in a 1782 painting by George Carter, *The Apotheosis of Garrick*, now in the RSC's collection. Garrick, having appeased, cherished and befriended the ghost of Shakespeare in life, is now off to join him for all eternity, cheerfully waved off by his Drury Lane colleagues towards the Bard who has long been awaiting him in Parnassus.[13] When a club was founded in London in 1831 to campaign for the moral and artistic reformation of the national drama, it was inevitably called the Garrick Club.[14] Over the next century, countless theatres around the world similarly invoked Garrick's name, most famously the one established in the Charing Cross Road in 1889, where Arthur Bourchier and Violet Vanbrugh would in time stage up-market Shakespeare for Shakespeare's sake.

---

[10] Now on display at Waddesdon Manor: see www .museumnetworkuk.org/portraits/artworks/waddesdon/ img2.html.

[11] See e.g. Aleks Sierz, 'The National Theatre', in David Scott Kastan, ed., *The Oxford Encyclopaedia of British Literature* (Oxford, 2006), pp. 82–95; p. 82.

[12] A copy is catalogued in the Folger as ART File G241 no.42 (size XS).

[13] For a reproduction of this image, currently not on show, see http://www.bbc.co.uk/arts/yourpaintings/paintings/ the-apotheosis-of-garrick-54891. On Garrick and art see Shearer West, *The Image of the Actor: verbal and visual representation in the age of Garrick and Kemble* (Basingstoke, 1991).

[14] On the club's history see its expensive website at http:// www.garrickclub.co.uk/

They were outdone, however, at the Lyceum. A cartoon in *Punch* on 8 June 1895, captioned 'What a Knight We're Having!', commemorated a happy occasion in the West End; another great Hamlet, Henry Irving, had followed Garrick's strategy of becoming a national treasure by identifying himself as a true Shakespearian (indeed, Irving commissioned cartoon likenesses of himself between Comedy and Tragedy après Reynolds as part of his PR strategy), with such success that he had just been granted the first theatrical knighthood. In the cartoon it is not Shakespeare but his deputy, however, who materializes from the beyond to pass comment: the ghost of Garrick steps out from between Comedy and Tragedy in a copy of Reynolds's famous portrait on the wall to offer his congratulations ('Congratulate you, Sir Henry! In the name of the Profession! Live long, and prosper!'). In a subsequent *Punch* cartoon, however, 'Princes of the Stage' (1938), anxious times have come for the theatre, as for everyone, a hundred years on from the birth of Irving. The two greatest Hamlets since Burbage, now firmly established as posthumous colleagues, stand on successive stairs on a heavenly staircase reminiscent, in retrospect, of the subsequent Powell and Pressburger film *A Matter of Life and Death*, looking back down towards the earth to wonder fearfully whether they will ever have a worthy successor. 'You followed me, Henry', says David, 'but who comes after?'

They needn't have worried, of course. Hindsight is a wonderful thing: we all know now exactly who would be following them next up that patrilineal staircase of successive great Shakespearian actor-managers. The supreme show-off of his age, he would in time demonstrate his peerless actorly technique and his Shakespearian versatility by playing Mr Puff and Oedipus on the same bill. But at the time of that *Punch* cartoon he had just played Hamlet for the first time, at the Old Vic. He wouldn't get his knighthood, though, until he had played the Dane on film in 1948. It says much about the lasting power of the paradigm for being an embodiment of Shakespearian tradition established in the eighteenth century that, when

Britain finally got a designated national theatre two centuries after the glory days of Drury Lane, the only possible candidate for its founding artistic directorship was someone about as similar to David Garrick as could possibly have been found, Laurence Olivier. (And he would begin his reign as such by directing yet another *Hamlet*.) It's striking, too, that it will only be in 2015, more than half a century later, that the National will for the first time come under the artistic directorship of someone without a conspicuous personal track record as an interpreter of Shakespeare, Rufus Norris. But if the Garrick paradigm turns out to be mighty yet, Norris had better look out: if he doesn't already know the identity of the current knighthood-bearing actor-manager Hamlet conspicuously in the queue for the next stair after Olivier's, he just hasn't been watching *Wallander* or *Thor*.

There is a whole other side to Garrick's legacy, however, partly explored in Ewan Fernie's article elsewhere in this volume, and that is a side which belongs less to the metropolitan conception of a national theatre and more to the municipal. By staging his 1769 Shakespeare Jubilee in Stratford, giving another copy of that trademark statue to its town hall and getting himself declared a freeman of the borough in the process, Garrick had taken the Shakespearian theatre back to its civic roots – since Shakespeare himself had first experienced live drama under the auspices of the local community, whether when his father had licensed visiting players at the Guildhall or when he had himself encountered the non-professional dramatic forms he draws on in his comedies, such as mummings and Whitsun pastorals. Even though the street procession of Shakespearian characters which Garrick planned for Stratford in 1769 had to be cancelled due to torrential rain, it was endlessly staged in Garrick's play about the event *The Jubilee* (in London and elsewhere), and it continues to run and run. The account of Shakespeare's rural belonging which it encodes – heavily reinforced by appeal to the fairy scenes of *A Midsummer Night's Dream* – would permanently colour the Stratford tourist industry,[15] and continue to inflect the subsequent development of Stratford's theatres. In 1827, a Shakespearian procession – at first still called the Jubilee Procession – became a feature of the ever-expanding celebrations of Shakespeare's birthday advocated and organized by the Stratford Shakespeare Club, and that year this costumed parade inaugurated the first of Stratford's Shakespearian theatres, the all-but forgotten Shakespeare Room on Chapel Lane (the foundations of which were recently excavated by the Shakespeare Birthplace Trust).[16] But by then aspects of Garrick's Stratford festivities had already been imitated elsewhere, for the benefit of other civic organizations. 1819, for instance, saw the establishment of the Sheffield Shakespeare Club, which commissioned an annual Shakespearian performance for the benefit of the local community. At its AGM at the Angel Inn in 1821, 'A bust of Shakespeare, crowned with laurels, was appropriately placed over the head of the President', after which the proceedings became a sort of alcohol-enhanced cut-price Jubilee: songs from Garrick's Jubilee Ode were sung, interspersed with toasts. These included 'The immortal memory of William Shakespeare' ('He was a man; take him for all in all, / We ne'er shall look upon his like again'), the Shakespeare Club itself ('We few, we happy few, we band of brothers'), and 'The Memory of David Garrick'.[17] Comparable local societies sprang up elsewhere too: there was a Cambridge Garrick Society as early as 1835[18] and in Australia a Melbourne Garrick Society by 1855. In 1864 they staged a 'Grand Shakespearian Fete' in order to raise money to install a bust of the playwright in their theatre; the event concluded with a 'Grand Shakespearian Tableau'.[19]

Back in northern England, the Stockport Garrick Society, established in 1901, acknowledged its loyalty to the rural Shakespeare Garrick had celebrated in Stratford by displaying a picture of Anne Hathaway's Cottage on its notepaper. In common with its imitators (the Altrincham Garrick Theatre, the Lichfield Garrick Society, and many others), this amateur organization was already doing locally much of the work of a subsidized National Theatre. Its core repertory was Shakespeare, but it also

revived other classics, and staged new plays too, and it also offered extensive educational activities, all under the presidency of the Mayor.[20] There has been an unbroken succession of such civic Shakespearian theatres, amateur and professional, ever since, recognizably traceable to Garrick's festival in Stratford: among recent examples I might cite the inauguration of a statue of Shakespeare to preside over the newly christened Piata William Shakespeare outside the Marin Sorescu National Theatre in Craiova, Romania (2014), the annual birthday rituals associated with the statue of Shakespeare in Lincoln Park, Chicago, and with the statue of Juliet outside the Chicago Shakespeare Theatre, or the ceremonies which inaugurated the new Teatr Szekspirowski in Gdansk in Poland in September 2014 (where, in a nice inversion of the Garrick model, the citizens of Gdansk were invited to process across the stage of the new auditorium and were welcomed by Shakespearian characters).

3. FOLK

Just as importantly, by emphasizing that Shakespeare was a native son of Warwickshire whose plays sprang from the soil of his nation's rural heartland, Garrick not only founded a tradition of regional Shakespeare but he prepared the way for Shakespeare to be assimilated to a quite different proposition for the establishment of national

---

[15] See Nicola Watson, *The Literary Tourist: Readers and Places in Romantic and Victorian Britain* (Basingstoke, 2006), chapter 2.

[16] See *The Mirror of Literature, Amusement and Instruction*, May 5 1827.

[17] *Proceedings of the Sheffield Shakespeare Club . . . By a Member of the Club* (Sheffield, 1829), p. 3.

[18] See Peter Holland, 'Campus Shakespeare', in Andrew Hartley, ed., *Shakespeare on the University Stage* (Cambridge, 2014), pp. 10–26; pp. 16–17.

[19] J. M. Forde & Melbourne Garrick Club & Theatre Royal (Melbourne, Vic.) (1864). *Grand Shakeperean fete by members of the Melbourne Garrick Club in aid of the Statue Fund, on Friday, April 22, 1864*. Retrieved 9 September 2014, from http://nla.gov.au/nla.obj-19617248

[20] See Michael Dobson, *Shakespeare and Amateur Performance: A Cultural History* (Cambridge, 2011), pp. 92–103.

theatres. That proposition is what I am going to call the notion of a folk theatre, exactly as represented nowadays by Siamsa Tíre in Tralee. According to this paradigm, drama should be an expression of traditional immemorial indigenous popular culture, which is to be preserved at all costs from the encroachments of an implicitly foreign, metropolitan or cosmopolitan modernity. For proponents of this model, Shakespeare's works are to be cherished above all as repositories of native wisdom and folklore and of innocently pre-industrial forms of entertainment and festivity. To perform them properly in Elizabethan costume is to celebrate the true vernacular spirit of the English people.

Over the course of the nineteenth century, such enthusiasm for popular, non-metropolitan Shakespeare was animated by the libertarian and egalitarian energies of romantic nationalism.[21] It was in 1847 that Shakespeare's birthplace was bought for the nation, and it was in the revolutionary year of 1848 that the radical Yorkshire publisher Effingham Wilson first proposed the establishment of a state-subsidized national theatre, in a pamphlet called 'A House for Shakespeare'.[22] Having properly consecrated Shakespeare's provincial roots by buying the Birthplace for the people, Wilson urges, Britain should now follow through and provide public funding for live performances of the plays. (In so far as they eventually fulfilled Wilson's demand, then, both the National and the RSC are mere junior subsets of the Shakespeare Birthplace Trust.) The campaign gathered momentum in the run-up to the 1864 tercentenary of Shakespeare's birth, with local amateur groups and others using the occasion as a vehicle for raising funds towards establishing a Shakespeare Memorial National Theatre. In the event, though, the campaign failed, partly due to the squabbles between organizers in London and organizers in Stratford which are so conspicuously absent from the current preparations to mark the 400th anniversary of Shakespeare's death in 2016. Nothing was built in London, though on 23 April 1864 a procession organized by the Working Men's Shakespeare Association did go to Primrose Hill to see the affordable actor-manager Samuel Phelps of Sadler's Wells, the ancestor of the Old Vic, plant a patriotic oak tree (I've looked for it. It died).[23] But the sort of folk-oriented Shakespearian national theatre that might have been established in London under other circumstances can still be seen elsewhere.

The Czech national theatre in Prague, for instance, opened in 1867 as a direct result of efforts which began during local celebrations of the Shakespeare tercentenary in 1864.[24] Determined to have a theatre in which drama would be performed in Czech rather than in the German of their imperial Hapsburg oppressors, this theatre's founders were especially keen to stage a translation of The Winter's Tale – a play whose fourth act, conveniently set in rural Bohemia, is full of authentic rustic folk-dancing. (As the first Czech-speaking public institution in Prague, this theatre remains a charged political locale; famously, Stanley Wells was lecturing there when the Velvet Revolution broke out. A few readers of this journal may regard that as a coincidence.) In other emergent European nations too – Hungary and Romania among them – translations of Shakespeare into tongues hitherto treated as minority languages featured as aspects of political campaigns for self-determination; ominously, one popular play for such völkisch nineteenth-century theatres on the continent was The Merchant of Venice, the one about ethnic exclusion.[25] In 1875, furthermore, in another country with aspirations towards a purer national identity all its own, a special sort of high-art folk-theatre was established, destined to have a large and sometimes unrecognized influence

---

[21] In France, Shakespeare's ghost was invoked in this cause in George Sand's play Molière (1851), when he appears to the founder of the Comédie Française in a dream (among other minatory spectres), urging him to write not for the monarchy but for le peuple.

[22] Rosenthal, The National Theatre Story, pp. 3–4; Geoffrey Whitworth, The Making of a National Theatre (London, 1951), pp. 26–9.

[23] See Richard Foulkes, The Shakespeare Tercentenary of 1864 (London, 1984), pp. 20–1, 42–3.

[24] On this episode see especially the late Zdeněk Stříbrný, Shakespeare and Eastern Europe (Oxford, 2000), pp. 57ff.

[25] See especially Péter Dávidházi, The Romantic Cult of Shakespeare (Basingstoke, 1998).

on the staging of Shakespeare back in England. This was the Wagner Festspielhaus in Bayreuth, a monument to someone whose career as a writer of opera had begun in the 1840s with an adaptation of *Measure for Measure*. It was purpose-built to host festival seasons of a great sequence of works about national mythology, the Ring cycle. When Stratford at last got a Shakespeare Memorial Theatre, in 1879, it definitely looked Germanic, and it was definitely a folk-theatre.[26] Equipped by Ronald Gower with the mandatory statue (nowadays, sadly, exiled to a site between the canal and the A3400), not only did it specialize in playing the history plays as a Ring-like cycle (Yeats explicitly compared Stratford to Bayreuth when he visited while making his own plans for establishing the Abbey),[27] but it went in for folk-dancing and authenticity, as can be seen from the explanatory caption on a postcard from 1900: 'Shakespearean performances take place in the theatre, folk songs, dances and other entertainments are arranged on the banks of the Avon.'[28] The travel writer H. V. Morton would remember its Edwardian actor-manager Frank Benson telling him that

only through Stratford, the common meeting place of the English-speaking world, could we heal the pains of Industrialism and make England happy again. We were to make the whole world happy, apparently, by teaching it to morris-dance and to sing folk songs and to go to the Memorial Theatre. With the splendid faith of Youth we pilgrims believed that England could be made 'mer-rie' again by hand-looms and young women in Liberty gowns who played the harpsichord.[29]

As I've pointed out elsewhere, this structure of feeling has survived among amateur proponents of outdoor Elizabethan-dress Shakespeare around the English provinces.[30] But it's an oddity of recent cultural history that if one wants a professional example of this sort of Shakespearian folk theatre nowadays – full of populist Luddite energy and thatched roofs and recreated costume of the period and country-dancing – one has to go not to Stratford but to central London, to a site on the South Bank opposite St Paul's, just east of the Tate Modern art gallery. The last time I described

Shakespeare's Globe as the folksiest theatre in London I received an abusive e-mail from its artistic director, so I am going to do so again just in the hopes of annoying him. For all the rigour and intelligence of its education and research department, for all the talents of some of the theatre professionals it employs, and for all the cosmopolitanism of its relations with international companies and donors, the default house style at the replica Globe on Bankside has been folksy ever since it opened in 1997.

A CONVERGENCE

Even under the patriotic management of Frank Benson, the Shakespeare memorial theatre that had opened beside the Avon in 1879 apparently wasn't national enough to satisfy Britain's hunger for such a thing – which according to the latest generation of propagandists, such as George Bernard Shaw and William Archer, absolutely had to be based in the imperial capital.[31] A new fund-raising effort was launched and over the first decade or so of the twentieth century it very nearly succeeded. The climax of that campaign was a large and remarkable charitable event which most historians of the National Theatre have preferred to forget.[32] However, it so signally brought into play all three of the propositions I have described so far that it seems the right point at which to bring the main narrative part of this article to a close.

In the summer of 1911, the notions of a royally-patronized Shakespearian theatre, of an embodied Shakespearian theatre, and of the association

---

[26] I am grateful to Ton Hoenselaars for many discussions on the connections between Shakespeare and Wagner, on which I hope he will eventually complete his long-planned book.

[27] W. B. Yeats, 'At Stratford-on-Avon' (1901), in *Essays and Introductions* (New York, 1961), pp. 102–19.

[28] Collection of the author.

[29] H.V. Morton, *In Search of England* (1927: London, 1949), p. 250.

[30] Dobson, *Shakespeare and Amateur Performance*, pp. 161–96.

[31] Whitworth, *The Making of a National Theatre*, pp. 50–1, 164–7.

[32] See e.g. Rosenthal, *The National Theatre Story*, p. 18.

between Shakespeare and authentic Elizabethan dancing all had their apotheosis at once. The largest gathering of people in Shakespearian dress since Shakespeare's own time – some 4,000 of them, variously costumed as eminent Tudors and as Shakespeare's characters[33] – the Shakespeare Memorial National Theatre Ball took place at the Royal Albert Hall on 20 June. It was visibly descended from Garrick's Jubilee; a massively expanded version of the fancy-dress ball which had taken place in Stratford in 1769, it also went to town on its procession. The 1911 event featured a full-scale ceremonial march-past of a full-scale Elizabethan court, cast as far as possible from the direct descendants of courtiers, such as Lord Sackville; this was to be ethnic authenticity not just of style but of genetics. There were also choreographed entries by whole matching sets of aristocratic revellers representing particular plays. Formal photographs survive, for example, of the Duchess of Wellington's party assembled at Apsley House before setting out, dressed as the dramatis personae of *A Midsummer Night's Dream*.

During the set-piece entries at the ball, each such party was preceded by a page carrying a banner, as per the annual Stratford procession, but in the Royal Albert Hall – with a fake Italian sky and mock-Renaissance garden features designed for the occasion by Lutyens – the effect was altogether more glittering. Procession followed procession, each one of them staffed by the cream of London society. In the *Macbeth* group were the former star of the Garrick Theatre and of Stratford, Violet Vanbrugh, as Lady Macbeth, with Lady Baring as Lady Macduff. Still they came. There was Lady Speyer as Silvia, there the young Vita Sackville-West as Katharina, complete with the leather whip which the stage tradition since Kemble had preferred to give to Petruchio. There were some nice fairies from *The Tempest*.[34] Accompanying her friend Ellen Terry and other members of the *Much Ado About Nothing* group was the Stratford conservationist and best-selling novelist Marie Corelli, who had booked a private box.[35] There was Queen Hippolyta, there Queen Margaret. In fact some of the people dressed up as kings and

queens were themselves kings and queens, since the ball was deliberately arranged for the same week as the coronation of George V, so that all those great personages who had come to London from around Europe and around the Empire for one fancy-dress spectacle could come to two. The souvenir publication includes a handy 'List of Royal Guests at the Shakespeare Ball' (pp. 42–4): clearly, for once when Henry V strutted across the stage there really were princes to act and monarchs to behold the swelling scene. And there at the ball too was the ghost of Old Hamlet, since en route to the splendours of the auditorium one passed the mandatory statue of Shakespeare in the foyer.

But although it raised £10,000 the ball looked much more like an exercise in spending and displaying money than one designed to accumulate it, and for all its Tudor dances and its assertions of Shakespeare's popularity it couldn't help but give the impression that the Shakespeare Memorial National Theatre it was trying to found was going to be a fashionable plaything for the elite, like the Royal Opera House. Certainly the large souvenir volume produced and sold a year later, each copy originally tied up in silk ribbons, now has a wistful air.[36] Poignantly, the epilogue to this

---

33 Admittedly, some guests simply wore 'Venetian cloaks' over ordinary evening dress: see H. Hamilton Fyfe, 'The Shakespeare Ball', in *Souvenir of the Shakespeare Memorial National Theatre Ball* (London, 1912), pp. 25–30.

34 See the photographic portraits from the occasion preserved in the National Portrait Gallery archive: www.npg.org.uk/collections/search/set/493/Shakespeare+Memorial+National+Theatre+Ball.

35 Sylvia Morris has conducted further research on Marie Corelli's presence at the ball, and points out that the official souvenir volume appears to downplay the event's interest, despite its London-based project, in Stratford: an unidentified illustration from a contemporary newspaper shows a dance-floor framed on one side by nearly life-size reproductions of Stratford buildings such as Holy Trinity Church and the Birthplace. See http://theshakespeareblog.com/2014/10/remembering-the-days-of-empire-the-shakespeare-memorial-national-theatre-ball-1911/.

36 Very unusually, this book is not in the collection of the Shakespeare Institute library: so I am immensely grateful to have been able to borrow a copy from an honorary senior research fellow of the Institute who happens to embody the

book, by the Shakespearian scholar Israel Gollancz, promises that the remaining money to establish the National in London will surely be raised in the foreseeable future, if only everyone makes one last big push during the impending 300th anniversary of Shakespeare's death, in 1916.[37]

That of course was not, as it turned out, the sort of big push that was going on in April 1916. Of the ball's royal guests, for instance, at the time of the 1916 tercentenary his Highness the Crown Prince of Germany was leading the 5th German Army at the battle of Verdun. His Imperial and Royal Highness the Archduke Charles, meanwhile, had become the heir presumptive to Austro-Hungary on the assassination of his uncle at Sarajevo, and in spring 1916 he was leading the 20th Corps against the Italians. The Crown Prince of Romania, meanwhile, was in 1916 on the eve of entering the war on the opposite side; and the Grand Duke Boris would soon be driven into exile after the assassination of his cousin the Tsar. Back in Britain those bearing more less august titles were coping not just with the war on the continent and at sea but with the ramifications of the Easter Rising in Dublin, an event which Yeats half-feared and half-boasted had been inspired by the repertory of the Abbey Theatre.[38] The royal and the national, the imperial and the folk, were tearing each other apart all over Europe: and in London the piece of land which had been bought for the National, close to RADA in Bloomsbury, had become the site not of a Shakespeare Memorial National Theatre but of a mock-Tudor building leased to the YMCA for the rest and recreation of troops on leave, nicknamed the Shakespeare Hut. In practice it would take this world war and then another after that to accustom Britain to the idea of a welfare state which would include public funding for the arts. It's another oddity of cultural history that if anyone had wanted to visit an Anglophone national theatre during the Second World War they would have had to go to Wagner's Bavaria to do so. At Stalag 383 in Hohenfels in 1942, one of the camp's two auditoriums used for drama by Allied prisoners-of-war was mockingly called 'The National Theatre'. Hence M. N. McKibbin's prescient-sounding remark in

his memoir: 'if you came upon a fellow washing stockings or French knickers in the Stalag laundry you didn't raise an eyebrow. You merely asked him whether he was appearing at the National.'[39] Like any good National Theatre, this one did perform Shakespeare among its musicals, but disturbingly only one play. At the suggestion of the Commandant, who provided the costumes, the prisoners staged *The Merchant of Venice* (but that's an incident I have discussed elsewhere).[40] Back in Britain, as famine, sword and fire continued to crouch for employment, the country built other things than playhouses. The fine portrait relief of Shakespeare carved in oak which now hangs in the entrance hall of the Shakespeare Institute, for instance, comes not from the foyer of a national Shakespearian theatre but from the wardroom of a submarine, HMS Shakespeare (1942–45).

POST-WAR EPILOGUE

Even *Henry V*, however, ends not in bloodshed and despair but with a peace treaty and a betrothal, and I am going to close, as promised, with a post-war epilogue and an endorsement.

Perhaps people are only allowed the institutional changes they ask for when the institutions in question no longer seem to matter quite as much – as in the cases of gay marriage and women bishops. By 1951, the year of the Festival of Britain, when the foundation stone for the National Theatre in London was finally laid on what later turned out to be

---

great national Shakespearian actor-manager tradition in his spare time, namely Gregory Doran.

[37] Israel Gollancz, 'The Shakespeare Tercentenary', in *Souvenir of the Shakespeare Memorial National Theatre Ball*, pp. 21–3. On Gollancz and the tercentenary, see especially Gordon McMullan, 'Goblin's Market: Commemoration, Anti-Semitism and the Invention of "Global" Shakespeare in 1916', in Clara Calvo, ed., *Shakespeare and the Cultures of Commemoration: The 1916 Tercentenary in Britain and Abroad* (forthcoming).

[38] 'Did that play of mine send out / Certain men the English shot?', 'The Man and the Echo', in *Last Poems* (1938).

[39] M. N. McKibbin, *Barbed Wire: Memories of Stalag 383* (London, 1947), p. 85.

[40] See Dobson, *Shakespeare and Amateur Performance*, pp. 140–5.

the wrong site, just to the west of Waterloo Bridge, theatre had long been superseded as the dominant medium of entertainment by film, which would soon be overtaken in its turn by television. As Kate McLuskie and Kate Rumbold point out in their fine book on Shakespeare and cultural value, however, the classical theatre retained its cachet and its relevance in part through a renegotiation of its relation to education.[41] This was already visible in 1951, when some aspects of the seventeenth-, eighteenth- and nineteenth-century paradigms I've outlined were still very much in play too.

In 1951 the civic tradition of the Sheffield Shakespeare Club and the Stockport Garrick Society was still going strong, its educational purpose still to the fore. The Middlesbrough Little Theatre, for example, marked the Festival of Britain by staging *Hamlet*, with its founding treasurer, John Berriman, my grandfather, as the Ghost. There were reduced rates for school parties, an instructive programme note by Tyrone Guthrie, and a local grammar-school girl playing Ophelia, one Wendy Craig.[42] But still more important developments were taking place elsewhere – as, oddly, was almost prophesied by that big book about the ball. One of the whimsical essays which punctuate this volume's series of society portraits and its account of the evening's programme recounts how the author's taxi to the ball broke down outside a Southwark pub, inside which the man he took to be a fellow-guest dressed as Shakespeare and also going to the Royal Albert Hall turned out to be our old friend, Shakespeare's ghost. But Shakespeare himself was not going to the ball: instead he was about to leave London altogether, conducting a sort of immortal coach party – consisting of the ghosts of Aeschylus, Virgil, Dante, Chaucer, Milton and Molière – to Stratford-upon-Avon.[43] If they had happened to travel via Birmingham – perhaps to admire its magnificent civic Shakespeare library, one 1864 tercentenary project which *did* get built – Shakespeare's ghost and his friends might have called at another notable building, also substantially funded by Joseph Chamberlain. The main door of Britain's first great civic university, built in 1900, is surmounted by a whole pantheon of

Western civilization's finest, but the figure in the centre, uniquely marking this as the university of his home region, is Shakespeare. This is the last statue in this article, and the most important: a solemn and inviolable promise from the founders that the University of Birmingham will provide, in perpetuity, unlimited funding for Shakespeare studies. And it was in 1951 that this promise really began to achieve fulfilment.

In Stratford that year the Shakespeare Memorial Theatre had just acquired a new artistic director, Anthony Quayle. As new artistic directors will, Quayle was setting about the history plays, in which he played Falstaff himself.[44] But it was only in the summer that a rather more transformative development was made public, intended to revolutionize the relationship between Stratford's theatres and the world of education. On 5 August 1951, the same few square inches of newsprint in *The Times* announced the debut of two remarkable new measures for the maintenance of Britain's international prestige. One was the Avro 707A, which with only a few modifications would go into production as the Vulcan nuclear bomber: the other, described under the heading ELIZABETHAN STUDIES AT STRATFORD: UNIVERSITY INSTITUTE TO BE FOUNDED, was the Shakespeare Institute.

Located in Stratford so as to produce what *The Times* calls 'a desirable association of study and stage', the Institute took over what had been the ball-goer Marie Corelli's house on Church

---

[41] Kate McLuskie and Kate Rumbold, *Cultural Value in Twenty-First Century England: The Case of Shakespeare* (Manchester, 2014), esp. pp. 148–52.

[42] See Dobson, *Shakespeare and Amateur Performance*, pp. 156–60.

[43] *Souvenir*, p. 17.

[44] My mother-in-law was taken in a school party to see a matinee that spring, from the vertiginous new upper gallery, just as I would be taken to see *Henry V* a generation later, and she well remembers the theatre's new Shakespearian royal carpet, with a pattern depicting all the kings from the history plays, a sample of which (thanks to some work my generous father-in-law did for Axminster a little afterwards) now adorns my office.

Street, Mason Croft. It had mainly been planned by the theatre historian Allardyce Nicoll and the previous Stratford artistic director, Sir Barry Jackson, founder of the Birmingham Rep. The intention was always that the Institute would not only provide a continuing home for the biennial International Shakespeare Conference and the promising journal *Shakespeare Survey*, spearhead research, teach resident postgraduates and teach visiting undergraduates, from Birmingham and from around the world, but that it should also inform and analyse the work of the Memorial Theatre. I don't know whether Nicoll and Jackson imagined in 1951 that the Memorial Theatre would within a decade hugely expand its remit, by royal charter, to become the Royal Shakespeare Company – taking shows to London and on tour, playing other classics alongside Shakespeare, and commissioning new writing too. But in any case, ten years after the foundation of the Institute, the Memorial Theatre became the RSC, and it soon acquired the use of the Aldwych in London,

and in 1963 the new National Theatre Company began to perform at the Old Vic. So after all those three centuries waiting around for a National Shakespeare Memorial Theatre to come along suddenly two had turned up at once.

Nearly forty years after first seeing both the RSC and the National, I am still inclined to think that one of them fulfils more of the long-cherished hopes of the national theatre campaign than does the other; that one of them, to put it another way, is much closer to the heart of its country. Very conveniently, it is also the one that is based much nearer to the Shakespeare Institute. Perhaps quite soon, the sixty-year partnership between the university and the company, scholarship and the stage, may even grow deeper yet: perhaps it may become commonplace and even legal to see their insignia side by side. I could not possibly say. But for now I am very happy to conclude simply by endorsing the work of the Royal Shakespeare Company – our royal, embodied, civic, folk, educational, national theatre.

JOHN RICE AND THE BOYS OF THE JACOBEAN KING'S MEN

DAVID KATHMAN

As one of the actors named in the Shakespeare First Folio, John Rice has long been recognized as a significant figure by historians of the Jacobean theatre. Since the nineteenth century, historians have also known that Rice was a boy actor for the King's Men late in the first decade of the seventeenth century, apparently one of the company's leading boys, to judge by the scant evidence we have. This latter fact is especially significant, because it suggests that Rice may have originated key female roles in some of Shakespeare's late plays. Despite this importance, very little has been known about Rice apart from his appearances in theatrical records, first as a boy in 1607–10 and then as an adult in 1619–25. More than seventy years ago, Edwin Nungezer and G. E. Bentley laid out the few remaining biographical scraps: appearances by Rice in the St Saviour's Southwark token books living 'Nere the Playhouse' between 1617 and 1623, and Rice's appearance as one of two overseers (along with Cuthbert Burbage) of John Heminges's 1630 will, in which Heminges described him as the clerk of St Saviour's Southwark.[1] Rice had apparently quit acting by that time, since he appears in no theatrical records after 1625.

New documentary evidence now makes it possible to bring John Rice's life and acting career into sharper focus. The most significant new evidence is a Chancery deposition given by Rice on 16 October 1626, in which he describes himself as a clerk of St Saviour's, aged thirty-six, implying that he was born about 1590.[2] This information about Rice's age allows us to construct a likely timeline for his career as a boy actor with the King's Men in the first

decade of the seventeenth century. Such a timeline can be informed by the enormous amount of new information that has emerged in recent years about how boys were apprenticed in adult playing companies, and by new information about the specific boys who certainly or probably performed with the Lord Chamberlain's/King's Men between the late 1590s and 1610. Rice's career is interesting in its own right, but it also serves as a useful springboard for a broader discussion of all the actors who may have first played some of Shakespeare's most famous women.

Beyond Rice's stage career, the lawsuit in which he gave his deposition provides fascinating and sometimes heart-breaking detail about the circumstances under which he left the acting profession, circumstances tied to the horrendous plague outbreak of 1625. A full examination of the St Saviour's token books and other records show that Rice was apparently living in the parish as early as 1612, that he married at least three times and had five children and that he remained as St Saviour's parish clerk until the outbreak of the English Civil War, when he was past fifty years old. His will, previously unknown, shows that he died in Sussex in 1654, nearly thirty years after he

---

[1] Edwin Nungezer, *A Dictionary of Actors and of Other Persons Associated with the Public Representation of Plays in England before 1642* (New Haven, 1929), pp. 296–7; G. E. Bentley, *The Jacobean and Caroline Stage*, 7 vols. (Oxford, 1941), vol. 2, pp. 546–7.
[2] The National Archives (TNA) C24/528, Wicharley vs. White.

quit the theatre and a dozen years after the London playhouses where he gained fame were shuttered.[3]

RICE'S CAREER AS A KING'S BOY

In order to put John Rice's career as a boy actor into the proper context, it helps to know how the apprenticeship system of the early modern London theatre worked. Boy actors in the major London-based playing companies were typically bound as apprentices to adult members of the company; they were thus subject to the rules governing all London apprentices, notably a minimum term of seven years. By the early seventeenth century, theatrical apprentices were often bound to adult actors who were members, or freemen, of London livery companies such as the Grocers and Drapers; these boys were legally apprentices in these companies even when their training was entirely on the stage.[4] While training was an important element of theatrical apprenticeships, boys also played the female roles, since women were barred by custom from the English professional stage. Despite the common assumption that early modern theatrical 'boys' were prepubescent (say, eight to twelve years old), recent research has made it clear that the term was used more or less as a synonym of 'apprentice', and that the age range for these boys was roughly the same as that for London apprentices in general. The youngest boys documented playing female roles in the adult companies were thirteen or fourteen, though the all-boy companies that came into vogue around 1600 had members as young as ten. Some apprentices transitioned to male roles in their late teens, while some continued to play female roles until the age of twenty-one or so.[5]

Surviving records of the various London livery companies have made it possible in recent years to pinpoint when many boy actors were apprenticed, and have allowed us to identify previously unknown theatrical boys. John Heminges of the Lord Chamberlain's/King's Men was a freeman of the Grocers who bound ten apprentices in that company between 1595 and 1628, most of whom can be traced on the professional stage. Other members of the Jacobean King's Men, including Robert Armin, Alexander Cooke and John Lowin, also bound apprentices in livery companies.[6] These records, along with other pieces of evidence, allow us to reconstruct much of the roster of King's Men boys in the early seventeenth century, providing important context for John Rice's early career with that company. As we will see below, the evidence suggests that, at least in this company, the most skilled apprentices tended to arrive in clusters separated by seven or eight years, the approximate minimum length of an apprenticeship contract.

Our direct knowledge of John Rice's career as a boy actor comes not from any recent archival discoveries but from three records that have been known for more than a century. The earliest of these is dated 16 July 1607, when the Merchant Taylors' Company of London hosted an elaborate banquet to induct Prince Henry as an honorary member of the company, with King James also being present. As part of the festivities, the Merchant Taylors paid Ben Jonson £20 to devise an elaborate entertainment for the king, in which a ship was lowered from the rafters with three musicians aboard dressed as mariners, singing three songs written by Jonson and set by court musician John Cooper. Before the ship was lowered, 'a very proper child, well spoken, being clothed like

---

[3] TNA PROB 11/234/165v-166.

[4] David Kathman, 'Grocers, Goldsmiths, and Drapers: Freemen and Apprentices in the Elizabethan Theater', *Shakespeare Quarterly*, 55 (2004), 1–49, and David Kathman, 'Players, Livery Companies, and Apprentices', in *The Oxford Handbook of Early Modern Theatre*, ed. Richard Dutton (Oxford, 2009), pp. 413–28, both discuss this system in some detail, with the latter chapter also including discussion of the early modern English apprenticeship system in general.

[5] David Kathman, 'How Old Were Shakespeare's Boy Actors?', in *Shakespeare Survey 58* (Cambridge, 2005), pp. 220–46, presents the robust evidence for the ages of early modern boy actors, which I also summarized in 'Players, Livery Companies, and Apprentices', pp. 426–7, and in 'The Seven Deadly Sins and Theatrical Apprenticeship', *Early Theatre*, 14 (2011), 121–39, esp. pp. 130–2. It has been suggested that adult male actors sometimes played older women such as Juliet's Nurse, but as I discuss in 'How Old Were Shakespeare's Boy Actors?', evidence for such a practice is scant to non-existent.

[6] Kathman, 'Grocers, Goldsmiths, and Drapers', esp. pp. 6–11.

an angel of gladness with a taper of frankincense burning in his hand, delivered a short speech containing eighteen verses, devised by Master Ben Jonson the poet; which pleased His Majesty marvellously well'.[7] The Merchant Taylors' records reveal that the 'very proper child' was John Rice, directed by John Heminges of the King's Men. Among the disbursements for the pageant were forty shillings 'To Mr Hemmynges for his direccion of his boy that made the speech to his Majesty', and five shillings 'given to Iohn Rise the speaker'.[8] Rice was about seventeen years old at the time, demonstrating that the terms 'child' and 'boy' had a significantly broader inflection than they have today.

Rice performed in another royal spectacle honouring Prince Henry three years later, this time alongside a different member of the King's Men, Richard Burbage. On 31 May 1610, the City of London put on an elaborate water pageant on the Thames to celebrate Henry's creation as Prince of Wales, and five days later Burbage and Rice were paid for performing in it and allowed to keep their costumes. Burbage played Amphion, described in Anthony Munday's published account of the pageant as 'a graue and iudicious Prophet-like personage, attyred in his apte habits, euery way answerable to his state and profession, with his wreathe of Sea-shelles on his head, and his harpe hanging in fayre twine before him, personating the Genius of Wales'. Rice played Corinea of Cornwall, described by Munday as 'a very fayre and beautifull Nimphe, representing the Genius of olde Corineus Queene, and the Prouince of Cornewall, suited in her watrie habit yet riche and costly, with a Coronet of Pearles and Cockle shelles on her head'. Michael Baird Saenger has suggested that the King's Men later used these costumes in the original production of Shakespeare's *The Tempest*, with Prospero wearing the Amphion costume and Ariel wearing the Corinea costume when he is dressed as a sea-nymph.[9] Again, it's worth noting that the 'fayre and beautifull Nimphe' was about twenty years old.

The third piece of evidence does not directly involve Rice as a boy actor, but it provides a terminus ad quem to his career as a boy for the King's Men. On 29 August 1611, fifteen months after his appearance in the water pageant with Burbage, Rice was one of twelve signatories of a bond between Philip Henslowe and Lady Elizabeth's Men, a new acting company that had been created four months before the date of the bond. Those twelve signatories – John Townsend, Joseph Taylor, William Ecclestone, Giles Gary, Robert Hamlen, Thomas Hunt, Joseph Moore, Rice, William Carpenter, Alexander Foster, Francis Waymus and Thomas Basse – were apparently sharers in the new company, but they were an unusual group of sharers in many ways.[10] Seven of the twelve are not traceable in any theatrical record before this one, and only one besides Rice (Thomas Hunt) is traceable in any record earlier than 1609.[11] Of the others, Giles Gary had performed in Ben Jonson's *Epicoene* in 1609 with the Children of the Queen's Revels, a company of youths, and the same year he was called a 'boy' when he performed in Jonson's *The Entertainment at Britain's Burse*. William Ecclestone had performed with the King's Men in Jonson's *The Alchemist* (1610) and *Catiline* (1611) at the age of nineteen or twenty and had probably been one of the leading

---

7 Ian Donaldson, *Ben Jonson: A Life* (Oxford, 2011), pp. 238–9.
8 Jean Robertson and D. J. Gordon, 'A Calendar of Dramatic Records in the Books of the Livery Companies of London, 1485–1640', in *Malone Society Collections III* (Oxford, 1954), p. 172.
9 Anthony Munday, *Londons Love, to the Royal Prince Henrie* (London, 1610), sig. C1v, C4; Michael Baird Saenger, 'The Costumes of Caliban and Ariel qua Sea-Nymph', *Notes and Queries*, 240 (1995), 334–6.
10 One copy of the bond, lacking Giles Gary's signature, is Dulwich College MS XVIII, Article 9, and is transcribed in Walter W. Greg, *Henslowe Papers* (London, 1907), p. 111. Another copy, which includes Gary's signature but lacks Francis Waymus's name entirely (in both the text of the bond and the signatures) is Dulwich College Muniments, Series 1, no. 47; it is transcribed in Greg, *Henslowe Papers*, pp. 18–19, and a digital photograph of it is available online at www.henslowe-alleyn.org.uk/images/Muniments-Series-1/Group-047/01r.html.
11 Hunt had been a hired man with the Admiral's Men in the late 1590s, and was later with that company's successor, the Palsgrave's Men, in 1621. Nungezer, *Dictionary*, p. 201.

boys of the King's Men alongside Rice, as we will see below. All this suggests that Lady Elizabeth's Men was organized as a company of young men, many of whom had recently been apprentices. Two years later in March 1613, it merged with the Children of the Queen's Revels, and the combined company continued into the 1630s.[12]

Rice must have been considered an adult when he signed this bond, and so he cannot have been too much younger than twenty-one years old. If the age he later gave in his deposition is accurate, he was born in about 1590 and thus exactly twenty-one in 1611. However, it was not uncommon in that era for ages given in depositions to be off by a year or two, so we cannot be certain in the absence of further documentation. I previously suggested that the actor may have been the John Rice who was baptized in St Bride's Fleet Street on 22 September 1591; the evidence of the new deposition makes that identification less likely, but does not absolutely disprove it.[13] Assuming for the moment that Rice gave the correct age in his 1626 deposition, he would have been sixteen or seventeen when he performed in the 1607 Merchant Taylors' banquet, and nineteen or twenty when he performed with Burbage in the 1610 water pageant.

We thus know when Rice's apprenticeship ended, but when did it begin, and to whom was he apprenticed? Though no direct evidence of Rice's binding survives, a variety of evidence suggests that he was apprenticed in the King's Men in 1603 or 1604, soon after the company (formerly the Lord Chamberlain's Men) was granted a royal patent dated 19 May 1603. Rice would have been thirteen or fourteen years old then, the most common ages for boy actors to be apprenticed; thirteen is the lower limit found in the record, so Rice is unlikely to have been apprenticed before 1603. The minimum length of an apprenticeship term was seven years, so if Rice's move to Lady Elizabeth's Men in 1611 came soon after his term ended, he could have been apprenticed no later than 1604.[14] In any case, he presumably had several years of experience before being selected for the high-profile Merchant Taylors' entertainment in 1607.

The fact that Rice was called John Heminges's 'boy' in 1607 suggests that he was apprenticed to Heminges, though this idea is not without its problems. As we saw above, the Grocers' records show Heminges binding ten apprentices between 1595 and 1628, most of whom also appear in theatrical records, but those records contain no trace of John Rice. This is not necessarily a deal-breaker, though. Heminges bound no apprentices in the Grocers between 26 January 1597, when he bound Alexander Cooke for eight years, and 4 July 1610, when he bound George Burgh, also for eight years. The time of Rice's binding (1603–04) is right in the middle of this thirteen-year span, and it seems likely that Heminges bound at least one apprentice around that time. There was a severe plague outbreak in 1603–04 that closed the playhouses and disrupted regular life in London, so it is possible that Heminges did bind Rice as his apprentice, but the binding was never recorded in the Grocers' records for some reason.[15]

RICE'S PREDECESSORS: COOKE, GOUGH, TOOLEY AND OTHERS

There is considerable evidence that, in addition to the plague closures and change in patronage, the King's Men in 1603–04 were in particular need of

---

12 Nungezer, *Dictionary*, pp. 85, 127; Scott McMillin, 'Jonson's Early Entertainments: New Information from Hatfield House', *Renaissance Drama* n.s.:1 (1968), pp. 153–66. Andrew Gurr, *The Shakespearian Playing Companies* (Oxford, 1996), pp. 397–401, summarizes the company's history during this time, though Gurr's account is not without its problems.

13 Kathman, 'How Old?', pp. 231–2.

14 For thirteen as the minimum age for theatrical apprentices and boy actors in the adult companies, see Kathman, 'How Old?', pp. 244–5, and 'Players, Livery Companies, and Apprentices', pp. 426–7. For seven years as the minimum apprenticeship term, see 'Players, Livery Companies, and Apprentices', p. 415.

15 Kathman, 'Grocers, Goldsmiths, and Drapers', esp. pp. 6–12. Apprentice bindings for all London livery companies were recorded in the Guildhall, but these records were nearly all destroyed by fire in the late eighteenth century, and do not survive before that time except for a few years in the mid-sixteenth century.

new boy actors, because several key members of a previous generation of boys were simultaneously becoming too old to play women easily. One such boy was the above-mentioned Alexander Cooke, who had been apprenticed to Heminges on 26 January 1597 for a term of eight years. Cooke is almost certainly the 'Sander' who appears in the manuscript plot of *The Second Part of the Seven Deadly Sins*, playing the leading female roles of Queen Videna and Progne for the Lord Chamberlain's Men around 1597–98. Thomas Belte, who had been apprenticed to Heminges on 12 November 1595 for nine years, certainly appears in the plot as 'T Belt', playing Panthea (a minor female role) and a servant.[16] Cooke appears to have been one of the leading boys for the Chamberlain's Men in the late 1590s, to judge by the *Sins* plot and his status as Heminges's apprentice, but in 1603 he turned twenty years old, at the upper end of the age range for boys to play women. The same year, he got married (two years before his apprenticeship term was scheduled to end) and also appeared in the cast list for Ben Jonson's *Sejanus*, suggesting that he was transitioning to male roles.[17] In 1604, Cooke appeared for the first time in the token books of St Saviour's Southwark, the parish of the Globe playhouse, living in Hill's Rents. He continued to appear in the token books until 1613, the year before his death, and he had four children baptized in the parish between 1605 and 1614.[18] Cooke became a prominent enough adult member of the King's Men to be listed among the 'Principal Actors' in the Shakespeare First Folio; he was also freed as a Grocer in 1609 and bound an apprentice of his own, Walter Haynes, on 28 March 1610.[19]

Robert Gough is another key boy actor who was reaching the end of his useful career as a boy by 1603. There are no certain notices of Gough in a theatrical context before that year, but he is almost certainly the 'Ro Go' who played the major female roles of Aspatia and Philomela in the *Seven Deadly Sins* plot. On 13 February 1603, Gough married Elizabeth Phillips, the sister of Augustine Phillips, and on 22 July 1603, Thomas Pope bequeathed all of his wearing apparel and arms to be divided

equally between Gough and John Edmonds, who had probably been his apprentices. Gough's marriage, like Alexander Cooke's the same year, shows that he was no longer a boy, and both of these records demonstrate close connections to members of the Lord Chamberlain's Men, connections that must have taken years to develop. Like Alexander

---

[16] For many years the *Seven Deadly Sins* plot was assumed to originate with Strange's or the Admiral's Men in the early 1590s, but in 'Reconsidering *The Seven Deadly Sins*', *Early Theatre*, 7 (2004), 13–44, I argued that the evidence as a whole points to an origin with the Lord Chamberlain's Men in 1597–98. Heminges's bindings of Belte and Cooke in 1595 and 1597 are key pieces of this evidence, but by no means the only ones or even the most important. Andrew Gurr, 'The Work of Elizabethan Plotters and 2 *The Seven Deadly Sins*', *Early Theatre*, 10 (2007), 67–87, challenged this redating, but in '*The Seven Deadly Sins* and Theatrical Apprenticeship', *Early Theatre*, 14 (2011), 121–39, I rebutted Gurr's argument in considerable detail.

[17] He is probably the Alexander Cooke who was baptized in Sandwich, Kent on 15 December 1583, along with a twin sister Anna; see Kathman, 'Reconsidering *The Seven Deadly Sins*', pp. 28–9 and n.49, and Kathman, 'How Old?', p. 230. He is most likely the Alexander Cooke who married Thomazine Wiles on 14 July 1603 in Godmersham, Kent (according to the International Genealogical Index). In any case, he was presumably the 'Mr Cooke and his wiefe' who sent their commendations to Edward Alleyn in a letter by Joan Alleyn on 21 October 1603 (Nungezer, *Dictionary*, p. 102).

[18] London Metropolitan Archive P92/SAV/253 p. 4; /254 p. 5; /255 p. 6; /256 p. 4; /257 p. 7; /258 p. 5; /201 p. 18; /202 p. 18. Nungezer (*Dictionary*, p. 102) notes four of Cooke's token book appearances, but misses four others. These records are available online at http://tokenbookslma .cityoflondon.gov.uk, as photographed, transcribed, and indexed by William Ingram and Alan H. Nelson. Ingram's very useful outline of what token books were and how they were compiled can be found in the 'Manual' section of the site. Essentially, they recorded the purchase of required tokens for Easter communion by all parish residents aged sixteen or above, listed according to the head of each household.

[19] Kathman, 'Grocers, Goldsmiths, and Drapers', p. 8. Since apprentices were not allowed to marry, Cooke must have left his apprenticeship early when he got married in 1603, but if this was so, then it is not clear why the Grocers granted him his freedom in 1609. Such discrepancies are not uncommon in livery company records of this period, suggesting that some companies were sometimes lax in enforcing their own rules.

Cooke, Gough appeared in the St Saviour's token books for the first time in 1604, living in Hill's Rents, a few doors down from Cooke; he continued to appear in the token books until 1624, the year before his death.[20] Gough had five children baptized in St Saviour's Southwark between 1603 and 1614, played minor roles for the King's Men in 1611 and 1616, was a sharer in the company by 1619 and was one of the 'Principal Actors' listed in the First Folio.[21]

Then there is Nicholas Tooley, who is most likely the 'Nick' who appears in the Seven Deadly Sins plot playing a lady and Pompeia. As with Gough, there is no documentary record of his binding as an apprentice, but in his 1623 will he refers to 'my late Mr [master] Richard Burbage', indicating that he had been apprenticed to Burbage. (Tooley had witnessed Burbage's will four years earlier.) Tooley's will also shows that at the time of his death he was living in the home of Richard's brother Cuthbert Burbage and his wife Elizabeth, to whom he expressed 'my love in respect of her motherlie care ouer me'.[22] Mary Edmond made a good (but not ironclad) case that he was the Nicholas Tooley born in Antwerp about 1582–83 to William Tooley, citizen and leatherseller of London, a merchant adventurer who came from a family of Warwickshire gentry and died in late 1583.[23] If this identification is correct, then Tooley was twenty or twenty-one in 1603, at the very upper end of the age range for boys to play female roles. In any case, he was considered an adult member of the company by May 1605, when Augustine Phillips called both Tooley and Alexander Cooke 'my fellow' in his will. Like Cooke and Gough, Tooley went on to be a sharer in the King's Men and one of the 'Principal Actors' listed in the First Folio. Annotations in a copy of the Ben Jonson Folio shows that at some point between 1616 and 1619 he played the jealous husband Corvino in Volpone and the Puritan deacon Ananias in The Alchemist.[24]

Beyond the 'big three' of Cooke, Gough and Tooley, who appear to have been the leading boys of the Lord Chamberlain's Men around the turn of

the century, several other boys of their generation had left the company by 1603–04, and/or were too old to play women by then. Thomas Belte, who as we saw above was apprenticed to John Heminges on 12 November 1595 and played two minor roles (one male and one female) in the Seven Deadly Sins plot, appears in no theatrical record after that plot. This suggests that he never made much of a mark and may have left his apprenticeship early, but even if he did not, his term expired in late 1604, by which time he was twenty-five years old.[25] More conjecturally, the 'Ned' who played the female role Rodope in The Seven Deadly Sins might have been William Shakespeare's younger brother Edmund, as I speculated in 2004. Even if we accept that conjecture, Edmund was twenty-three years old by 1603, and shortly before his death in 1607 he was associated with St Leonard Shoreditch, the parish of the Curtain playhouse; St Giles Cripplegate, the parish of the Fortune; and St Saviour's Southwark, the parish of the Globe.[26] Christopher Beeston

[20] LMA P92/SAV/253 p. 5; Gough's appearance in the 1624 book is LMA P92/SAV/301 p. 23. He moved to Samson's Rents in 1605 (P92/SAV/254 pp. 5, 26) and to Austen's Rents in 1612 (P92/SAV/259 pp. 31, 37). He is listed with a 'wife' in 1607 (P92/SAV/256 p. 27) and 1621 (P92/SAV/299 p. 4), and with a 'wife & daughter' in 1620 (P92/SAV/298 p. 4).

[21] Nungezer, Dictionary, pp. 157–8; E. A. J. Honigmann and Susan Brock, eds., Playhouse Wills 1558–1642 (Manchester and New York, 1993), pp. 68–71; Kathman, 'Reconsidering', p. 29. As with Cooke, Nungezer notes some of Gough's token-book appearances, but also misses some.

[22] Honigmann and Brock, Playhouse Wills, pp. 124–8, esp. p. 125.

[23] Mary Edmond, 'Yeomen, Citizens, Gentlemen, and Players: The Burbages and Their Connections', in Elizabethan Theater: Essays in Honor of S. Schoenbaum, ed. R. B. Parker and S. P. Zitner (Newark, DE, 1996), pp. 30–49, esp. pp. 36–9.

[24] Nungezer, Dictionary, pp. 374–6; James A. Riddell, 'Some Actors in Ben Jonson's Plays', Shakespeare Studies, 5 (1969), 285–98.

[25] Belte was baptized in Norwich on 16 April 1579, the son of Thomas Belte, minstrel, who had been expelled from Norwich with his family in late 1594. See Lawrence Manley, 'Thomas Belte, Elizabethan Boy Actor', Notes and Queries, 252 (2007), 310–13.

[26] Kathman, 'Reconsidering The Seven Deadly Sins', 29–30; Nungezer, Dictionary, pp. 314–15; Wayne H. Phelps,

was certainly with the Lord Chamberlain's Men in 1598, when he performed with them in Ben Jonson's *Every Man In His Humour* and he is probably the 'Kit' who played three minor roles in the *Sins* plot around the same time. Beeston was eighteen years old in 1598, the age of an older apprentice, though he may have been a covenant servant bound to Augustine Phillips for a term shorter than seven years, given that Phillips called Beeston 'my servaunt' in his will.[27] Beeston had left to join the Earl of Worcester's Men by 1602 along with John Duke and Robert Pallant, who had been hired men with the Chamberlain's Men, and he went on to become a famous and influential theatrical entrepreneur.[28]

Finally, there is John Edmonds, who was probably apprenticed to Thomas Pope and appeared alongside Robert Gough in Pope's will in 1603, as noted above. Edmonds gained control of half of Pope's shares in the Globe and Curtain playhouses after marrying Mary Clark alias Wood, to whom Pope had bequeathed the shares; the marriage must have happened soon after Pope's death in August 1603, since a son of John Edmonds, 'player', was baptized in St Saviour's on 6 January 1605.[29] He appears in the St Saviour's token books starting in 1606, living in Langley's Rents, and he continued to live there until 1624, with further children of John Edmonds, 'player', being baptized in the parish in 1607 and 1615. Despite his financial interest in the Globe, Edmonds never became a sharer in the King's Men as an actor; instead, in 1618 he shows up in a travelling version of Queen Anne's Men, a company with which he was connected much earlier through Robert Pallant. Edmonds lived next door to Pallant in Langley's Rents from at least 1609 until Pallant's death in 1619, after which Pallant's widow Ann was living with John and Mary Edmonds in 1620, and Dorothy Pallant (presumably another relative) was living with them in 1621.[30] As noted above, Robert Pallant was a hired man with the Lord Chamberlain's Men in the late 1590s, when Edmonds was (probably) an apprentice with the company, but he moved to Worcester's Men in 1602 along with Beeston and Duke, and subsequently spent most of his career with that company's successor, Queen Anne's Men.[31] Edmonds must have made the move to join his former fellows at some point, perhaps after his apprenticeship term ended. No doubt opportunities in the Chamberlain's/King's for former apprentices were limited in 1603–4, especially with Cooke, Gough and Tooley joining the company as adults at the same time. The actor may be the John Edmunds, son of Simon Edmunds, who was baptized at St Matthew Friday Street, London, on 4 August 1583, which would make him a near-exact contemporary of Alexander Cooke.[32]

'Edmund Shakespeare at St Leonard's, Shoreditch', *Shakespeare Quarterly*, 29 (1978), p. 422. Edmund was buried in the St Saviour's Southwark parish church on New Year's Eve 1607, presumably due to the influence of his brother William, and he appeared in the 1607 St Saviour's token book, though his name is crossed out (LMA P92/SAV/256, p. 6).

27 Honigmann and Brock, *Playhouse Wills*, pp. 72–5. In 1596, around the same time Beeston may have been bound, Edward Alleyn of the Admiral's Men signed seventeen-year-old Richard Perkins (a year older than Beeston) to a three-year contract as a covenant servant. See David Mateer, 'Edward Alleyn, Richard Perkins, and the Rivalry Between the Swan and the Rose Playhouses', *Review of English Studies*, 60 (2009), 61–77.

28 Kathman, 'Reconsidering *The Seven Deadly Sins*', pp. 26–7; Nungezer, *Dictionary*, pp. 36–8. Duke and Pallant both appear in the *Seven Deadly Sins* plot, and Duke appears in the 1598 *Every Man In His Humour* cast list alongside Beeston (Kathman, 'Reconsidering *The Seven Deadly Sins*', pp. 22–4).

29 Nungezer, *Dictionary*, p. 128; G. E. Bentley, 'Shakespeare's Fellows', *TLS*, 15 November 1928, 856; David Kathman, 'The Burial of Thomas Pope', *Notes & Queries*, 53 (2006), 79–80.

30 LMA P92/SAV/255 p. 36; /257 p. 40; /259 p. 46; /291 p. 19; /293 p. 22; /294 p. 21; /295 p. 24; /296 p. 23; /297 p. 24; /298 p. 24; /299 p. 26; /301 p. 23.

31 Nungezer, *Dictionary*, pp. 263–4.

32 A. M. Bruce Bannerman, ed., *The Registers of St Matthew, Friday Street, London, 1538–1812 and the United Parishes of St Matthew & St Peter Cheap, Marriages, 1754–1812* (London, 1933), p. 9. The fact that Edmonds does not appear in the *Seven Deadly Sins* plot is a minor strike against the idea that he was a Chamberlain's boy in the late 1590s, but he could have been bound after that production, or he could have been unavailable for some reason.

RICE'S FELLOW BOYS IN THE KING'S MEN, 1603–1611

With Cooke, Gough and Tooley (and possibly Edmonds) all becoming too old to play women by 1603–04, the newly christened King's Men needed to recruit a new generation of boys. John Rice was one of them, as we have seen, but who were the others? Who were the boys who performed with Rice during his heyday as a performer of female roles, during the time when Shakespeare was writing such plays as *King Lear* and *Antony and Cleopatra*? This is not a simple question to answer, since explicit documentary evidence is scarcer than it became in the following decade. There are no relevant apprentice binding records dating from 1603–04, such as those for Cooke and Belte in 1595–97 and for the next generation of King's Men boys starting in 1610–11. The only apprentice binding by a member of the King's Men to be recorded in a livery company between 1597 and 1610 came on 15 July 1608, when Robert Armin bound James Jones in the Goldsmiths. Jones did not serve out his full term with Armin, for three years later, on 10 July 1611, he was re-apprenticed in the Drapers to the player William Perry, who was then probably with the Children of the Queen's Revels and was definitely a member of Lady Elizabeth's Men two years later.[33] Even so, Jones might have been available to play female roles in some of Shakespeare's latest plays, assuming that he stayed with the King's Men during the whole three years between his bindings.

A few previous scholars doing broader studies of Chamberlain's/King's Men personnel have tried to reconstruct the company's roster of boys during this period, most notably T. W. Baldwin in 1927 and David Grote in 2002. Both Baldwin and Grote made some reasonable inferences, along with others that we can now see to be highly improbable or flat-out wrong. Baldwin, for example, knew about the records we saw earlier involving John Rice, so he correctly identified Rice as one of the company's leading boys in the years leading up to 1611. Baldwin also believed that John Edmonds was a near contemporary of Rice's who played Cleopatra in the original production of *Antony and Cleopatra*, but he was unaware that Edmonds was a married father by 1605, before that play was written. Baldwin also believed that James Sandes was a contemporary of Rice who played important female roles up to 1613, but Sandes appears to have been nearly a decade older, as we will see below.[34] Grote also correctly identified Rice and suggested (quite plausibly, as we will see) that William Ecclestone was another of the company's leading boys. But he also argued that George Birche was a key boy from 1604 to 1611, being unaware that Birch was apprenticed to John Heminges in 1610 and still playing female roles in 1616–19.[35] While a certain amount of speculation is still inevitable, new evidence along with other clues now allow us to reconstruct the company's roster of boys during this period more confidently and to eliminate some actors who might at first glance seem to be likely candidates.

Augustine Phillips's 1605 will provides some of the most obvious clues, though in the end it is not as helpful as it might at first appear. In addition to his bequests to various 'fellows' in the King's Men, including William Shakespeare, Phillips bequeathed forty shillings and various items to Samuel Gilburne, 'my Late Aprentice', and forty shillings and musical instruments to James Sandes, 'my Aprentice', to be paid at the expiration of his apprenticeship indenture. The phrasing here indicates that Gilburne had already served out his term of apprenticeship and graduated to adult roles; he presumably became a sharer, since he is listed

---

33 Kathman, 'Grocers, Goldsmiths, and Drapers', pp. 12, 18.

34 Thomas Whitfield Baldwin, *The Organization and Personnel of the Shakespearean Company* (Princeton, 1927), pp. 277–9, 422–5. Baldwin based much of his analysis on an inaccurate assumption that theatrical apprentices were typically bound at age ten for terms of eleven years, and on the assumption that the *Seven Deadly Sins* plot dates to March 1592. This led him to believe that Alexander Cooke, for example, was a decade older than we now know Cooke actually was.

35 David Grote, *The Best Actors in the World: Shakespeare and His Acting Company* (Westport, CT, 2002), pp. 135–6, 145, 195, 238–51. For Birche, see Kathman, 'Grocers, Goldsmiths, and Drapers', pp. 8–9.

among the First Folio 'Principal Actors', but he appears in no other theatrical records, so he probably died young.[36] James Sandes was still Phillips's apprentice in 1605, so it is natural to wonder whether he may have been part of the class of 1603–04 along with Rice, as Baldwin believed. However, previously unknown evidence makes this unlikely. Sandes also appears in the nuncupative (oral) will of William Sly of the King's Men, dated 14 August 1608, and it turns out that both Augustine Phillips and William Sly had connections to the Sands family apart from James. A Jane Sands married Phillips's former servant Christopher Beeston in 1602, and a Cicely Sands married the player Robert Browne in 1594; the Brownes became very close friends with William Sly, who bequeathed his share of the Globe playhouse to Robert and most of the rest of his estate to Cicely and their daughter Jane.[37] Cicely and Jane Sands were sisters, the daughters of Anthony Sands, who had an estate in Hawkshead, Lancashire but was living in St Leonard Shoreditch outside London when Cicely and Jane were born (in 1576 and 1583 respectively).[38] Given the connections noted above, and the rarity of the name, our James Sands is extremely likely to be the child of that name who was baptized in Hawkshead in December 1581, the son of Charles Sands.[39] This would make him twenty-three when Augustine Phillips made his will, presumably near the end of his apprenticeship term, and several years past the time when he could have played female roles.

Things are more promising when we turn to William Ecclestone. As we saw earlier, Ecclestone performed with the King's Men in the original productions of Ben Jonson's *The Alchemist* in 1610 and *Catiline* in 1611, according to the cast lists in the 1616 Jonson Folio, but on 29 August 1611 he signed a bond for the newly-formed Lady Elizabeth's Men alongside John Rice. He was still with that company two years later when he performed in *The Honest Man's Fortune*, but he soon returned to the King's Men, performing with them for many years, and was one of the 'Principal Actors' listed in the First Folio.[40] While no record directly says that Ecclestone was a boy with the King's Men, that conclusion is extremely likely given what

we now know about his age. William Ecclestone was the son of John Ecclestone, citizen and merchant taylor of London, who died in 1604 and had his will proved in the Commissary Court of London. Because John Ecclestone was a freeman of London who died with minor children, one-third of his estate was put into a trust, with the money to be distributed to his children once they turned twenty-one. William Ecclestone claimed his 'orphan's portion' of £14 on 26 May 1612, meaning that he was at least twenty-one years old by that date, and was probably not much older than that.[41] This means that he was about nineteen or twenty when he performed in *The Alchemist* and *Catiline* for the King's Men – the age of an older apprentice, too young to be an adult sharer. The previously noted annotations in a copy of the Jonson Folio shows that at some point between 1616 and 1619 Ecclestone played the 'angry boy' Kastril in *The Alchemist*, and this would have been an entirely appropriate role for him to have played in

---

[36] Nungezer, *Dictionary*, p. 153.

[37] Honigmann and Brock, *Playhouse Wills*, pp. 80–1; Mark Eccles, 'Elizabethan Actors IV: S to End', *Notes and Queries*, 238 (1993), 165–76, esp. p. 165.

[38] Christopher Matusiak has traced the history of the Sands (Sandys) family in 'Robert Browne, Christopher Beeston, and the Continental Use of Queen Anne's Men's Plays', a paper written for the 2009 Shakespeare Association of America meeting. Anthony Sandys' 1591 will, which mentions Cicely, Jane and their brother Edwin, is Lancashire Record Office DDSA 30/2/1. The relevant St Leonard Shoreditch parish register was formerly Guildhall Library MS 7493, and is now LMA P91/LEN/A/001/MS07493.

[39] H. S. Cowper, ed., *The Oldest Register Book of the Parish of Hawkshead, Lancashire, 1568–1704* (London, 1897), p. 43. James Sands was presumably related to Cicely and Jane, but the exact relationship is not clear; no other Charles Sands appears in the Hawkshead register, or in the pedigree of Anthony Sandys' immediate family in J. Hall Pleasants, 'The Lovelace Family and its Connections: Sandys of Furnace Fells, Lancashire', *Virginia Magazine of History and Biography*, 29 (1921), 227–43.

[40] Nungezer, *Dictionary*, p. 127.

[41] Mark Eccles, 'Elizabethan Actors II: E-J', *Notes and Queries*, 236 (1991), 454. John Ecclestone's will is LMA DL/C/B/004/MS9171/020, f.36v, indexed in Marc Fitch, ed., *Index to Testamentary Records in the Commissary Court of London, Volume III, 1571–1625* (London, 1985), p. 133.

the original 1610 production, as a nineteen-year-old.[42] If Ecclestone was an apprentice in 1610 and 1611 but left for Lady Elizabeth's later in 1611 when his term expired, just as John Rice did, this implies that he was bound in 1603–4, around the same time as Rice. In fact, the death of Ecclestone's father in 1604 would have been an appropriate occasion for this, since it was not uncommon for newly orphaned boys to be bound as apprentices or otherwise put into service.[43] All this evidence puts us on fairly solid ground in saying that Ecclestone was a contemporary of Rice among the boys of the early King's Men.

Another promising lead comes from something written decades later in the 'Sharers' Papers' of 1635. In a petition to the Lord Chamberlain, Cuthbert Burbage described how he and his brother Richard had initially leased the Blackfriars playhouse to a company of boy actors, the Children of the Chapel. He added that 'In processe of time the boyes growing vp to bee men, which were Vnderwood, Field, Ostler, and were taken to strengthen the Kings service, and the more to strengthen the service, the boyes dayly wearing out, it was considered that house would bee as fitt for our selues, and soe purchased the lease remaining from Evans with our money, and placed men Players, which were Hemings, Condall Shakespeare &c.'[44] In its broad outlines, this story is supported by the documentary record: John Underwood, Nathan Field and William Ostler all acted with the Children of the Chapel at the Blackfriars in 1600 and 1601, according to the cast lists in the 1616 Ben Jonson Folio, and all three eventually joined the King's Men.[45] The main question for our purposes is when they made this move.

First of all, we know that Underwood, Field and Ostler were not all taken by the King's Men at the same time; Underwood and Ostler were with the company by 1610, when they performed in Jonson's *The Alchemist*, but Field did not join the King's Men until sometime after 1613. Burbage appears to say that the three were 'taken to strengthen the Kings service' only after 'growing vp to bee men'; this was true of Field and Ostler, who were in their early to mid-twenties when they joined the King's

Men, but it was not necessarily true of Underwood. Both Field and Ostler were still with the Children of the Queen's Revels (the successor to the Children of the Chapel) in 1609, when they performed before the King in Jonson's *Entertainment at Britain's Burse* alongside Ostler's 'Boye' Giles Gary, and Field and Gary performed in Jonson's *Epicoene* the same year.[46] Field was twenty-one or twenty-two at the time, having been baptized in St Giles Cripplegate, London, on 7 October 1587, and he did not join the King's Men until at least four years later.[47] The fact that Ostler had a 'boy' of his own in 1609, a year before he joined the King's Men, shows that he was an adult member of the company by then. He was probably twenty-two or twenty-three years old, assuming that he is the William Ostler baptized in St Andrew's parish in Plymouth, Devonshire on 18 February 1587, or the one baptized in Long Bennington, Lincolnshire on 15 August 1586.[48]

---

42 Riddell, 'Some Actors', pp. 285–98.

43 For example, Simon Halliwell was placed as a chorister and boy actor with Richard Farrant of the Queen's Chapel in 1577, two years after the death of his father, and in 1580 his younger brother George was similarly placed with Sebastian Westcott of St Paul's; see David Kathman, 'Four Choirboy-Actors in Sixteenth-Century London', *Notes & Queries*, 57 (2010), 347–9. Robert Stole of Bridgwater, Somerset, a 14-year-old whose parents had both recently died and was now a ward of the town, was apprenticed to one of a troupe of travelling players in 1597; see Herbert Berry, 'The Players' Apprentice', *Essays in Theatre*, 1 (1983), 73–80.

44 E. K. Chambers, *William Shakespeare: A Study of the Facts and Problems*, 2 vols. (Oxford, 1930), vol. 1, p. 66.

45 Nungezer, *Dictionary*, pp. 136, 261, 384. All three boys appeared in Jonson's *Poetaster* in 1601, and Field and Underwood appeared in *Cynthia's Revels* in 1600.

46 McMillin, 'Jonson's Early Entertainments', pp. 153–66. The records from the performance of the *Entertainment at Britain's Burse* do not explicitly say that Field, Ostler and Gary were with the Children of the Queen's Revels, but the cast list showing Field and Gary performing in *Epicoene* the same year does identify them as belonging to that company.

47 Nungezer, *Dictionary*, pp. 135–6. Field was the son of John Field, an antitheatrical Puritan preacher.

48 These are the only two William Ostlers whose baptisms are recorded in the International Genealogical Index (https://familysearch.org/search) in the second half of the sixteenth century. The actor did not leave a will when he died in 1614,

John Underwood, on the other hand, does not appear with any other company between 1601 and his appearance in *The Alchemist* in 1610 alongside Ostler. Thus, he might have joined the King's Men at any time during that span, and some evidence suggests that he had been an apprentice in the company after coming over from the Children of the Chapel. He is most likely the John Underwood, son of William Underwood, baptized on 21 June 1590 in St Clement Danes parish on the Strand, a short walk west of Blackfriars.[49] If so, he was roughly the same age as John Rice and William Ecclestone, the right age to be apprenticed in the King's Men in 1603–04 (or any time after), with the added bonus of having several years of experience on the commercial stage. He would have still been the age of an (older) apprentice by the time he performed in *The Alchemist*, but on the cusp of adulthood; as with Ecclestone, it is difficult to imagine what he would be doing with the King's Men at that age unless he was an apprentice. The annotated copy of the Jonson Folio shows that between 1616 and 1619 Underwood played Corbaccio's son Bonario in *Volpone* and the law clerk Dapper in *The Alchemist*; the latter role would have been an appropriate one for him to have played in the original 1610 production, at the age of about twenty.[50] He got married around that time, much as Alexander Cooke and Robert Gough had done at about the same age, and his son John was baptized in St Bartholomew the Less on 27 December 1610. He named one of his later children 'Burbage', suggesting that he may have been apprenticed to Richard Burbage; Nicholas Tooley, who as we saw above was certainly apprenticed to Burbage and was a leading boy of the previous generation, forgave the debts of Underwood and William Ecclestone in his will of 1623. Like several of the former boys we have seen, Underwood was a sharer in the King's Men by 1619 and one of the Principal Actors listed in the First Folio.[51] In addition to the Jonson roles noted above, the cast list in the 1623 Quarto of *The Duchess of Malfi* shows that Underwood played the courtier Delio, probably in the original 1613–14 production as well as the 1620–21 revival.[52]

If we accept the likely scenario in which John Rice, William Ecclestone and John Underwood were the three most important boy actors in the King's Men between roughly 1604 and 1610, with James Jones coming on board between 1608 and 1611, then it is natural to wonder what female roles they might have played during those years, especially in Shakespeare's plays. T. W. Baldwin tried to answer this question in his 1927 study of the Chamberlain's/King's Men and their personnel, but his analysis is undermined by the biographical problems noted earlier and by his questionable assumption that each actor was narrowly typecast into a 'line' of very similar roles throughout his career.[53] Baldwin recognized Rice's status as a leading boy in the company but believed that he was limited to a 'comico-villainous line' that included the bawd in *Pericles*, the queen in *Cymbeline*, Paulina in *The Winter's Tale*, Doll Common

---

so there are no clues to where he came from or who he was related to.

[49] City of Westminster Archives Centre STC/B. Another John Underwood with the same father was baptized in the same parish three years earlier on 23 April 1587, but he presumably died in infancy.

[50] Riddell, 'Some Actors', pp. 285–98.

[51] Nungezer, *Dictionary*, pp. 384–5; Honigmann and Brock, *Playhouse Wills*, pp. 124–8, esp. p. 125.

[52] David Gunby, David Carnegie and Antony Hammond, eds., *The Works of John Webster, Volume One: The White Devil, The Duchess of Malfi* (Cambridge, 1995), pp. 423–7, 468. The cast list in the Quarto lists one actor for most roles, but two for the major roles of Ferdinand (R. Burbidge and J. Taylor), the Cardinal (H. Cundaile and R. Robinson), and Antonio (W. Ostler and R. Benfield). These must refer to the original production in 1613–14, before William Ostler's death on 16 December 1614, and a revival sometime after Richard Burbage died in March 1619 and was replaced as the company's leading man by Joseph Taylor. The three boys listed as playing female roles – Richard Sharpe, John Thomson and Robert Pallant – must have performed only in the revival, since Sharpe and Pallant were apprenticed to John Heminges in 1616 and 1620 respectively. See Kathman, 'Grocers, Goldsmiths, and Drapers', pp. 9–10.

[53] While there was undoubtedly some typecasting in the early modern theatre, as there is today, Baldwin's notion of strict 'lines' for every actor is not supported by the evidence, as shown by Skiles Howard, 'A Re-examination of Baldwin's Theory of Acting Lines', *Theatre Survey*, 26 (1985), 1–20.

in Jonson's *The Alchemist* (1610) and Fulvia in Jonson's *Catiline* (1611). Baldwin believed that the company's two other leading boys during this period were John Edmonds (to whom he assigned Cleopatra) and James Sands (to whom he assigned Marina in *Pericles*), but these actors would have been too old to have originated these roles, based on what we now know about their ages.[54] David Grote made a similar attempt in his 2002 study of the company and, while he was less tied to the idea of acting 'lines' than Baldwin was, his casting ideas are similarly arbitrary, coloured by his idiosyncratic dating of some of the plays. The only really major female Shakespearian role that Grote assigns to John Rice is Cressida in *Troilus and Cressida*, which he argues was not written until 1607, plus arguably Cordelia in *King Lear*, who has far fewer lines than Goneril and Regan despite her importance to the plot.[55] Grote does recognize William Ecclestone as another important boy during this period, assigning him Cleopatra in *Antony and Cleopatra* and Imogen in *Cymbeline* (which he believes was first written in 1606), but he has unidentified apprentices ('Mature Boy', 'Noble Boy', 'Ostler's Boy') playing most of the other significant female roles between 1605 and 1611.[56]

The King's Men must have had other boys during these years who are unknown to us, and it is entirely possible that some of them played significant female roles. But the most prominent and challenging female roles must have been taken by the most skilled boys, and the evidence suggests quite strongly that John Rice was seen as the company's most skilled boy between 1607 and 1610, given that he was selected to perform in two very high-profile events before the king and Prince Henry. The descriptions of those events show that he was able to portray a very convincing woman even at the ages of seventeen and twenty, meaning he probably had a feminine-looking face and a high voice; recall that in the 1607 Merchant Taylors' entertainment he was described as 'a very proper child, well spoken, being clothed like an angel of gladness with a taper of frankincense burning in his hand', and that in the 1610 water pageant for Prince Henry he is described as 'a very fayre and beautifull

Nimphe . . . suited in her watrie habit yet riche and costly, with a Coronet of Pearles and Cockle shelles on her head'. We have no comparable descriptions of William Ecclestone or John Underwood, but the fact that both later became adult sharers in the King's Men, and that Underwood had experience with the Blackfriars boy company, suggests that they must have been quite skilled as well.

Assigning specific female roles to these boys is a hazardous business, but it is possible to make some reasonable guesses, as long as we keep in mind the speculative nature of the exercise. *King Lear*, written about 1605, has exactly three female roles, so it is easy to imagine Rice, Ecclestone and Underwood as the original Goneril, Regan and Cordelia, not necessarily in that order. Grote's suggestion that Rice played Cordelia is not unreasonable, though that is the smallest of the three roles, as noted above. The King's Men must have had a very skilled boy soon after that in 1606–8 to play Lady Macbeth, Cleopatra in *Antony and Cleopatra* and Volumnia in *Coriolanus*, by far the most prominent female roles in their respective plays. Rice is the most obvious candidate, since his high-profile royal performance for the Merchant Taylors took place right in the middle of that period. A sceptic might object that if Rice really did have a feminine-looking face and high voice, this would make him inappropriate for such older female roles as Cleopatra and Volumnia. But this assumes that acting in Rice's time was as naturalistic as it is today, and may underestimate

---

[54] Baldwin, *Organization and Personnel*, pp. 277–9, 409, 422–4, 435.

[55] *Troilus and Cressida* was first entered in the Stationer's Register on 7 February 1603 and is generally dated to 1601–02, but Grote argues that this could not have been Shakespeare's play. His reasoning is rather tortured; he believes that Richard Burbage could not have played Troilus, a character described as being in his early twenties, and that the Chamberlain's Men had no other sharer in 1601–02 who could have played the role (Grote, *The Best Actors in the World*, pp. 118–19). This is only one of many instances where Grote and Baldwin place far too much weight on their highly speculative casting assignments, and on their sometimes mistaken beliefs about company personnel.

[56] Grote, *The Best Actors in the World*, pp. 238–51.

the ability of Jacobean stage players to signal a character's age and/or social station through costume and gestures; it may also underestimate the ability of a skilled boy actor such as Rice to play women of various ages, especially when he was in his late teens.

Imogen in *Cymbeline* is another dominant female role that Rice may have played, but the Queen is also a substantial role in that play, and the other romances written around 1608–10 also include more substantial secondary women. In *Pericles*, Marina and the Bawd each have more than one hundred lines, as do Paulina, Hermione and Perdita in *The Winter's Tale*.[57] This change could mean that some of the other boys had grown and become capable of playing more complex roles, or it could reflect an influx of new boys into the company, at a time when the King's Men had just signed their lease on the Blackfriars playhouse on 9 August 1608. James Jones was apprenticed to Robert Armin on 15 July 1608, less than a month before the date of the lease, and it is possible that John Underwood joined the King's Men around this time rather than in 1603–4, though he would have been in his late teens and unable to play female roles for much longer.[58] Marina in *Pericles* and Paulina in *The Winter's Tale* are the largest female roles in those plays, thus perhaps the most likely roles for Rice, but it is possible that he ceded those roles to Ecclestone, Underwood or Jones and took a smaller role for himself. (Recall that Baldwin assigned the secondary but still substantial roles of the Bawd and the Queen in *Cymbeline* to Rice, along with Paulina.) Rice is also most likely to be the boy who played Desdemona when the King's Men performed *Othello* in Oxford in October 1610, four months after his performance as Corinea of Cornwall in the water pageant. One of the spectators, Henry Jackson, recorded that Desdemona, 'although she always acted her whole part supremely well, yet when she was killed she was even more moving, for when she fell back on the bed she implored the pity of the spectators by her very face'.[59]

By 1610, Rice and Ecclestone (and probably Underwood) were nearing the ends of their apprenticeship terms and the next generation of King's Men boys were starting to join the company. They are much better documented than Rice's generation. Walter Haynes was apprenticed to Alexander Cooke for a term of nine years on 28 March 1610, and George Birche was apprenticed to John Heminges for an eight-year term on 4 July 1610. Richard Robinson was apprenticed in the company around the same time, probably to Richard Burbage, but he was not bound in a livery company, so no record of the exact date survives. Haynes does not appear further in the theatrical record, but Birche and Robinson became important performers of female roles for the King's Men. Birche is presumably the 'Richard' Birche recorded as playing Lady Politic Would-Be in *Volpone* and Doll Common in *The Alchemist* for the King's Men between 1616 and 1619. Robinson played the substantial role of the Lady in *The Lady's Tragedy* (a.k.a. *The Second Maiden's Tragedy*) for the King's Men in 1611, and in Ben Jonson's *The Devil Is An Ass* (1616), 'Dick Robinson' is praised for his ability to impersonate a woman. Heminges bound yet another apprentice, John Wilson, on 18 February 1611 for eight years. Wilson was primarily a musician, writing numerous songs for the company and later becoming a well-known composer, but the Folio text of *Much Ado About Nothing* shows that he played Balthazar and sang a song in a revival of that play.[60]

---

57 I am using the line counts in T. J. King, *Casting Shakespeare's Plays: London Actors and Their Roles, 1590–1642* (Cambridge, 1992).

58 Kathman, 'Grocers, Goldsmiths, and Drapers', pp. 12, 18. Baldwin (*Organization and Personnel*, pp. 49–50) assumed that Underwood and William Ostler joined the King's Men as sharers in the autumn of 1608, but he was unaware that Ostler was still with the Children of the Queen's Revels in 1609, or that Underwood was likely born in 1590. Grote (*The Best Actors in the World*, pp. 186–7) also argued that Underwood and Ostler joined the company together as sharers, but in 1610 rather than 1608.

59 Gamini Salgado, ed., *Eyewitnesses of Shakespeare: Firsthand Accounts of Performances, 1590–1890* (New York, 1975), p. 30.

60 Kathman, 'Grocers, Goldsmiths, and Drapers', pp. 8–9; Kathman, 'How Old?', pp. 232–3.

RICE'S ADULT CAREER: ACTING AND CLERKING

As we saw earlier, Rice and Ecclestone left the King's Men in 1611, signing a bond as a member of Lady Elizabeth's Men on 29 August 1611. Ecclestone stayed with Lady Elizabeth's for at least a couple of years, performing for them in *The Honest Man's Fortune* in 1613 before returning to the King's Men soon afterward.[61] Rice, however, appears in no other record of Lady Elizabeth's, and the evidence indicates that he soon returned to the King's Men. He played the Marquess of Pescara in *The Duchess of Malfi* in the original production of 1613–14 (and later in the revival of 1620–21); this is a relatively minor role, suggesting that Rice came back to the company as a hired man. Although there were others of the same name living in St Saviour Southwark at various times, the timing makes it likely that he is the John 'Ryce' who appears in the token books for the first time in 1612, living in 'The Close' in the Boroughside region. He was still living there in 1613 and 1614, but then he disappears from the token books for the next four years, during which he presumably lived elsewhere.[62] This could mean that Rice remained with the King's Men but moved to a different parish, or it could mean that he tried his hand with a different company before returning to the company where he was trained.

John Rice shows up once again in the St Saviour token books in 1618, living 'near the playhouse' in the Paris Garden region of the parish. (The 'playhouse' here must be the Swan, which was in Paris Garden, rather than the Globe, which was in the Clink Liberty.) He continues to appear in the same location each year through 1624 (except 1622, when the token book for Paris Garden is missing).[63] In 1620 and 1621 he is listed along with a wife, but it is not clear who this wife was, or how long he was married; she must have died at some point before 1630, when Rice remarried, but there is no appropriate burial record in St Saviour's.[64] In any case, Rice was definitely back with the King's Men by August 1619, when he played a captain and a servant in *Sir John Van Olden Barnavelt*. He

was not yet a sharer at that point, since he is not listed in the licence of 27 March 1619 or the livery allowance of 19 May 1619, both of which include his contemporaries William Ecclestone and John Underwood. We might speculate that the same features that made Rice so successful as a boy performer of female roles – a high voice and feminine face – were a handicap for an adult actor of male roles. In any case, Rice was finally a sharer by the time of the next livery allowance on 7 April 1621, a decade after his apprenticeship ended. Rice's name appears last in the list of 'Principal Actors' in the 1623 Shakespeare First Folio, a list that apparently includes only sharers in the Chamberlain's/King's Men.[65]

The last records of John Rice with the King's Men are the list of company members attending King James's funeral on 7 May 1625, and the patent, dated 24 June 1625, by which the company was re-established under the patronage of Charles I. Soon after that, he quit acting for good. The records of St Saviour's Southwark show that Rice became parish clerk there on 7 October 1625, when he auditioned for the job (in effect) by reading a chapter of the Bible and singing a psalm openly in the church. Because 'both were well liked', he was appointed parish clerk in place of John Boston, who had recently died. By 23 February 1626, Rice had become a deacon, and he was officially granted

---

[61] Nungezer, *Dictionary*, p. 127.

[62] LMA P92/SAV/201 p. 29; /202 p. 30; /203 p. 30.

[63] LMA P92/SAV/296 p. 5; /297 p. 5; /298 p. 5; /299 p. 6; /300 p. 6; /301 p. 7. Another John Rice appears in the St Saviour token books in 1617 and 1618, living in Clark's Alley in the Liberty of the Clink, but the notation 'dead' in the margin in the latter year indicates that this is not the actor (LMA P92/SAV/265 p. 40; /266 p. 40).

[64] A John Rice married Mabell Hayward in St Saviour's on 1 May 1616 (Bentley, *The Jacobean and Caroline Stage*, 2.546), but this cannot be the wife that John Rice the actor had in 1620–21, because she was buried (as Mabel Rice) in St Saviour's on 9 September 1618 (LMA P92/SAV/3002). Her husband is most likely the John Rice who lived in Clark's Alley and also died in 1618; the only way her husband could be the actor is if he quickly remarried in another parish between September 1618 and Easter 1620.

[65] Nungezer, *Dictionary*, p. 297.

'all such duties as Mr Boston had time past before him'.[66] The St Saviour's token books show that by Easter 1626, Rice had moved from 'near the play-house' to 'the Churchyard within Chain Gate'.[67] As we saw above, Rice described himself as clerk of St Saviour's Southwark when he gave his Chancery deposition on 16 October 1626, and was described that way in John Heminges's will, dated 9 October 1630, in which Rice was named co-overseer of the will along with Cuthbert Burbage.[68]

Why did John Rice quit the stage to become a parish clerk? Answering that question requires us to look at the lawsuit in which Rice deposed, which is very interesting on its own terms. Rice's predecessor at St Saviour's, John Boston, had been parish clerk for more than twenty years, and the lawsuit stemmed from the contentious circumstances surrounding Boston's death. The story of that lawsuit begins with the terrible plague outbreak that started in early 1625 and was accelerated by the crowds who descended on London and Westminster for the funeral of James in early May and the arrival of Charles I with his new bride Henrietta Maria a month later. Despite efforts by the Privy Council to get Londoners to stay at home, many people who could leave the city did so, leaving it mostly desolate by August. The weekly Bills of Mortality show that 593 people in London died of the plague the week ending 7 July, with 57 parishes infected; plague deaths then rose steadily to a peak of 4463 the week of 18 August, with 114 parishes infected. Parishes on the outskirts of London, including St Saviour's Southwark, were especially hard hit. There were 40 burials in St Saviour's in February 1625, and 43 in March, but then the grim toll began increasing: the parish had 65 burials in April, 101 in May, 180 in June, 539 named people 'and many unknown' in July, and over 800 in August (including 'John Fletcher, a poet'), before the numbers ebbed to 570 in September, 90 in October and 58 in November.[69]

The person who had to deal with all these dead bodies was the parish clerk, John Boston. He lived with his wife Sarah and children in a house in the churchyard, next to the house of the parson, Mr Archer; an inventory taken after his death shows that the house contained books and musical instruments, among much else.[70] Though Boston's main duties were to assist Archer in saying daily services and keep the parish accounts, he was also a deacon and thus authorized to perform christenings, churchings, weddings and burials if necessary. As plague deaths increased in June, the regular business of the parish continued and the churchwardens continued to meet, though no doubt with a rising sense of fear and unease. When the plague became much worse in July, the parson, several of the churchwardens and the other richer inhabitants of the parish fled to the countryside, leaving Boston to conduct funerals and bury the dead. Boston soon sent his wife and children into the country as well, 'to his greate griefe', leaving him all alone to handle the overwhelming task. His widow later reported on having heard of the 'unspeakable wattchinges, labour, and travell, both daie and night' that Boston had to endure, and said that 'sometimes, in one day, there hath been twenty or thirty corpses left at the place of buriall, and the said John Boston knew not who brought them thither ... but after buryed them, and then took great paynes in inquiring and doing his best for knowing their names, so that he might make Certificat accordingly for discharge of his Dutie'.[71] This last clause refers to the fees that

---

66 St Saviour's Southwark Vestry Minute Book, 1581/2–1628 (LMA P92/SAV/0450), 547, 551. I am grateful to Alan H. Nelson for sending me transcripts of the relevant pages.

67 LMA P92/SAV/215 p. 42. No token books survive from 1625.

68 Honigmann and Brock, *Playhouse Wills*, pp. 164–8.

69 The figures in this paragraph are from Winifrede Caldin and Helen Raine, 'The Plague of 1625 and the Story of John Boston, Parish Clerk of St. Saviour's, Southwark', *Transactions of the London & Middlesex Archaeological Society*, 23 (1971), 90–97, esp. p. 91.

70 This inventory is LMA P92/SAV/1960.

71 The quotes are from the answer of Robert White and Sarah his wife (John Boston's widow), dated 24 May 1626, to the bill of complaint of Thomas Wycharley and the other St Saviour's churchwardens, in the Chancery case *White* v. *Wycharley*. The original bill and answer from the case do not survive, but a transcript of the answer survives in the London Metropolitan Archives as P92/SAV/799, and is discussed by Caldin and Raine, 'The Plague of 1625'. Unless otherwise

Boston was supposed to collect for each burial (and christening, churching or marriage) and record in the parish's monthly accounts before handing them over to the churchwardens.

Boston single-handedly dealt with these horrific circumstances through July, August and the first half of September, but in mid-September his wife Sarah got word that he was 'dangerously sick'. She returned to Southwark as quickly as she could but Boston died before she got there and was buried in the parish on 22 September. He had left no will, so Sarah took out letters of administration and began trying to settle his estate and organize the parish accounts, which were in terrible shape after the chaos of the previous few months. In particular, Boston had only sporadically been able to collect burial fees. Since many wealthy people had fled the city, a disproportionate number of the dead (an estimated one-third) were poor enough to be exempted from the fees; in addition, 'the Infeccion was so great and dangerous, and the ymployment of the said John Boston so full of continuall labour, that he could not have convenient tyme and leisure to gather up the said fees'. Boston had managed to collect the fees for July and hand them over to the churchwardens in early September, but he did not hand over any fees for August or September before his death.

On 7 October 1625, the St Saviour's vestry (including the churchwardens and other officers) met for the first time since 28 June. It was at this meeting that they named John Rice parish clerk in place of Boston, as noted above; they also named a new clerk of the vestry, Edward Collins; a new sexton, Lambert Daggett; and four new vestrymen to replace those who had died.[72] The Vestry Minute Book also records a decision 'that some course of lawe be taken to call Mrs. Boston to an account for the money which Mr Boston receaved this last summer for the use of the churchwardens'. At some point in October, either soon before or soon after this vestry meeting, Sarah Boston was visited at home by Richard Wright, one of the churchwardens who was also Keeper of the Great Account, meaning he was responsible for the parish's finances. He was trying to get the money

that the parish was owed for the burials in August and September, and asked Sarah what money she had in the house. She said she did not know, but later she went to a place where her late husband had kept money received for the use of the parish, and found £37 18s in two gloves. She gave this money to Wright, whereupon he asked her for her husband's notebook 'wherein he kept the names and numbers of the dead'. She gave it to him and he subsequently refused to give it back.

The churchwardens continued to demand the money from the August and September burials, and Sarah Boston (who subsequently got remarried to Robert White, an acquaintance of her late husband) insisted that she did not have it, beyond the £37 18s she had given to Wright. Finally, in the spring of 1626, the churchwardens of St Saviour's – Thomas Wycharley, John Wattes, John Crowder, Michael Nicholson, Thomas Stoakes and William Maddox – filed suit in Chancery against Robert and Sarah White. The bill of complaint does not survive, but the Whites' answer, dated 24 May 1626, along with the interrogatories from the two sides, allow us to reconstruct the case in some detail. The churchwardens claimed that John Boston's notebook recorded fees that he had received for 1318 burials in August and the first half of September (except for the burial of George Payne and his wife), that these fees totalled £100, and that Boston had confessed on his death-bed to having the £100. In their answer, Boston's widow and her new husband said that the notebook only recorded the fees 'accustomed to be paid' for each burial, not the amount collected; they explained that many indigent parishioners were exempt from the fees and that Boston had been unable to collect many of the fees amid the overwhelming number of dead bodies, as described above. They said

---

specified, quotations in the following paragraphs are also from this transcript.

[72] St Saviour's Southwark Vestry Minute Book, 1581/2–1628 (LMA P92/SAV/0450), 547. An Edward Collins was among the attendants of the King's Men listed in a ticket of privilege on 12 January 1637 (Nungezer, *Dictionary*, p. 97), and it is tempting to wonder whether this is the same man.

that the churchwardens had always paid Boston an allowance for the burial of poor people, and that they also owed him thirty shillings for a burial cloth.[73]

The legal wrangling continued for another five months, until in October 1626, more than a year after John Boston's death, the two sides began deposing witnesses. First the lawyers for the plaintiffs (Thomas Wycharley and the other churchwardens) deposed Richard Wright, the former churchwarden who had visited Sarah Boston shortly after her husband's death. Testifying on 16 October, Wright said that he had visited John Boston twice in an effort to get an accounting of the August fees, but that the second time, on 18 September, Boston was sick with the plague and not taking visitors. Boston told Wright out the window that he had received all the fees for August and the first sixteen days of September (except for the burial of a Mr Payne and his wife) and written out an account of them, and said to come back in an hour or two. When Wright came back, he was told that Boston was resting, and he never spoke to Boston again before the latter's death four days later. Wright said that Sarah Boston had subsequently given him her husband's book so that he might cast up the accounts and see what was due and, when he did so, the total was £103. He admitted that the parish had typically given Boston an allowance for the burial of the poor, but claimed that all but two or three of 'the better sort' had stayed in the parish through the plague outbreak. He also claimed that John Boston was worth £500 at his death.[74]

John Rice gave his testimony for the plaintiffs on the same day, 16 October 1626.[75] Rice said that as John Boston's successor as parish clerk, he was supposed to collect fees, make an account, and pay the churchwardens monthly, and he believed that Boston had promised to do so as well. He said that Boston, while on his death-bed, had admitted to having £100 in fees that were due to the churchwardens, but Rice didn't know whether Sarah Boston had promised to pay any such money; however, he had heard her say that her husband had an allowance from the parish for the burial of the

poor. He also said that 'some of the better sort' had stayed in the parish throughout the plague, somewhat undermining Wright's testimony that all but two or three had stayed.

Eight days later on 24 October, the lawyer for the defendants, Sarah Boston White and Robert White, deposed their first witness: Lambert Daggett, who had been reappointed sexton of St Saviour's on the same day that John Rice was appointed clerk. Daggett testified that he had helped John Boston try to collect burial fees in August and September 1625, but that Boston had 'very littal or noe tyme at all to collect duties', and that many fees went uncollected. He had been present when Sarah Boston handed over the £37 18s to the churchwardens and also when she handed over John Boston's notebook 'at the earnest intreaty of the said churchwardens'.[76] The following day, the plaintiffs' lawyer also deposed Daggett in an attempt to weaken this damaging testimony, but the attempt did not work very well. Daggett said that Boston had stopped collecting fees on 12 September, soon before he became sick, but he denied that Boston had claimed to have collected all the fees or that he had said on his death-bed that he held money owed to the churchwardens or that Sarah Boston had promised any money to the churchwardens.[77]

The day after that, on 26 October, the Whites' lawyer deposed two women who had been with John Boston in his final illness: Elizabeth Harbert and Jane Wyatt. Harbert said that she had tried to convince Boston to send for his wife, but he had

---

[73] The Whites' answer survives only in a transcript (LMA P92/SAV/799), as noted above.

[74] TNA C24/528, *Wycharley* v. *White* (deposition of Richard Wright).

[75] TNA C24/528, *Wycharley* v. *White* (deposition of John Rice).

[76] LMA P92/SAV/800, fos. 1–13. This deposition and the other three depositions for the defendants are summarized by Caldin and Raine, 'The Plague of 1625', pp. 95–6. Caldin and Raine were not aware that the depositions for the plaintiffs (TNA C24/528), including John Rice's, also survive.

[77] TNA C24/528, *Wycharley* v. *White* (deposition of Lambert Daggett).

refused, not wanting 'to endanger her or her children'. She had also tried to get Boston to make a will, but he also refused so as not to leave his wife indebted, adding that 'his wife was to accompte with the churchwardens . . . for a monthe's bill or thereabouts which was not summed up nor gathered in', and that once 'a juste and due accompte' was made, 'there would be more founde due from the said parishe to him than he was to pay the parishe'. Wyatt gave a largely identical account, adding that 'nothing troubled his mynde but his monthes bill, which was not summed up nor gathered in'.[78]

Finally, on 2 November, the Whites' lawyer brought in Richard Wright as (effectively) a hostile witness. Wright told the same story he had told in his deposition for the plaintiffs, about how he had tried to visit Boston on 18 September to get an accounting of the fees, and how Boston had told him out the window that he had collected all the burial fees but two. However, Wright also admitted that Boston had performed his duties faithfully with no help except on the Sabbath and holy days, that he had scarcely any time left to collect the fees, and that most of those who died in August and September were 'of the poorer sorte' who were exempted from fees. Wright further admitted that the parish owed Boston 'thirtye and odd shillinges' for his wages and customary stipend for burying the poor, and admitted receiving £37 18s from Sarah Boston in the presence of Thomas Wycharley and Lambert Daggett. Even so, he said there was still 'a greate summe of money due from the said Boston to the said parishe'.[79]

The ultimate dispute was over whether Boston's notebook recorded the fees owed to the parish or the fees actually collected, with a related dispute over whether Boston had claimed to have collected all the fees listed in the notebook. The court ultimately found the evidence presented by Boston's widow to be more persuasive, ruling against the churchwardens and ordering 'that the matter of the plaintiff's bill be from henceforth clerely and absolutely dismissed out of this Cort'.[80]

In the end, John Rice's testimony was not central to this lawsuit and, by ruling in favour of the defendants, the court effectively said that it did not believe his key claim that John Boston had confessed to having the £100 due to the churchwardens in his hands. Nevertheless, the detailed records of this suit paint a vivid picture of St Saviour's Southwark during the horrible plague outbreak of 1625 and the difficult circumstances under which Rice became parish clerk there. Rice had still been a member of the King's Men when the company received its royal patent on 24 June 1625, but the plague had already closed the playhouses by that time, two months before plague deaths peaked in August. The King's Men did survive this long plague closure, which stretched into 1626 and drastically reordered the London theatrical world, but such an outcome was far from certain as the disease ravaged the populace and effectively shut London down. Given this uncertainty, Rice's decision to leave the King's Men for a steady job at St Saviour's becomes a bit more understandable.

With the lawsuit over, Rice settled into his duties as parish clerk, living in 'The Churchyard within Chain Gate', as the token books specify starting in 1626. Soon after taking on the new job, he went through a protracted illness and began having money troubles. On 27 February 1627, 'Mr. John Reese' came to the churchwardens 'and made complaint that his means or profits arising by his office of parish clerk is not sufficient to maintain him, pretending that the whole profits thereof doth not arise to any more than £28 yearly, whereupon this house doth think fit (in respect of his long sickness, and his removing household being new come to the said place), that he shall have paid unto him (for this time only) as a free gift from this house the sum of £4'.[81] After this, Rice's fortunes seem to have improved, and he became very active in parish affairs, helping the priests with their ecclesiastical duties. A parish presentment from early 1634 said that 'our Clerk doth sometimes, to help our

---

[78] LMA P92/SAV/800, fos. 14–17 (Harbert), 17–20 (Wyatt).
[79] LMA P92/SAV/800, fos. 20–37.
[80] This quotation is from Caldin and Raine, 'The Plague of 1625', p. 97.
[81] LMA P92/SAV/450, 561.

ministers, read prayers, church women, christen, and bury, being a deacon and allowed to do so'.[82]

In October 1630, as we saw earlier, Rice served as co-overseer of John Heminges's will. He was a newly-wed at the time, for on 7 September 1630 he had married Frances Legat in St Saviour's. Rice was about forty years old and childless at the time of the marriage, but the couple had six children baptized in St Saviour's over the next eight years: Austin (14 July 1631), Ann (11 September 1632), Frances (3 October 1633), Anna (24 July 1635), Mary (7 June 1637) and John (13 January 1638). All appear in the parish register as the children of John Rice, 'clerk'.[83] The subsidy rolls show that Rice and his growing family continued to live in the St Saviour's churchyard through the 1630s; a February 1635 survey of the buildings of the parish, with their owners and tenants, shows that their landlord was John Board, gentleman, and that two other tenants occupied the same building.[84]

Rice's last two appearances in the St Saviour's token books, still living in the churchyard, are in 1640 and 1641.[85] He does not appear in the 1642 books, but he makes one last appearance in the record of the lay subsidy of December 1642, when he paid 5s 10d. This subsidy was levied by Charles I for the 'necessary defence and great affaires' of the kingdom, an allusion to the English Civil War, which had broken out that year.[86] Rice does not appear in the 1643 St. Saviour's token books, suggesting that he had left the parish, and the natural assumption is that he and his family were displaced by the war. Many actors took up arms on the Royalist side, as James Wright described years later in *Historia Histrionica* (1699), but it is unlikely that Rice did so; apart from the fact that he had quit acting nearly two decades before, he was more than fifty years old.[87]

However, another factor in John Rice's leaving St. Saviour's in 1642–43 may have been the death of his wife. Though there is no record of her burial in St Saviour's, Rice's second wife Frances, the mother of his children, certainly died at some point, and he then married a woman named Hanna (or Anna). A John Rice married an Anne Westebrooke on 29 July 1644 in St Olave Southwark,

the parish next to St Saviour's; it appears likely that this is 'our' John Rice, marrying again quickly both for companionship and for help raising his five small children.[88] In any case, our John Rice eventually ended up in Tarring Neville, Sussex, a village on the river Ouse in East Sussex between Lewes and Newhaven, about sixty miles south of London. When he made his will on 29 April 1654, he described himself as 'John Rice of Tarring Nevill in the County of Sussex clearke being sicke in body but of perfect memory'.[89] He asked to be buried in the church of Tarring Neville, which dates from the thirteenth century and survives today as a Grade I listed building, and discharged debts to Richard Wood of Meeching, Izack Baldy of Eastbourne, goodman Swan, Mr Bernard, and Mr Pennell, all of Lewes, and 'Mr. Legat my brother' (i.e. his brother-in-law through his second wife). The remainder of his estate was to be equally divided 'betweene Hanna my now wife and all my Children', namely his sons Austin and John, and his daughters Frances, Anne and Mary, except for a mare and a colt that were to go to his son John. He named his wife

---

[82] LMA P92/SAV/533.

[83] St Saviour Southwark Composite Register: baptisms, marriages, and burials, 1609–1653 (LMA P92/SAV/3002). I am grateful to Alan H. Nelson for searching his transcriptions of the parish register for me, and for his transcriptions of the documents cited in this and the following paragraph. The Ann born in 1632 presumably died in infancy (despite there being no record of her burial in the St Saviour's register) and the Anna born in 1635 was given a variant of the same name, a common practice at the time. Rice named a single daughter Anne in his will, cited below.

[84] LMA P92/SAV/215 p. 42; /216 p. 42; /217 p. 38; /218 p. 39; /219 p. 22; /220 p. 40; /221 p. 47; /222 p. 42; /224 p. 43; /227 p. 43; /228 p. 44; /229 p. 44; /230 p. 45; /232 p. 45. From 1627 on, Rice was given the title 'Mr' in the token books, probably because he was a deacon. Two copies of the 1635 survey are LMA P92/SAV/1325 and 1327.

[85] LMA P92/SAV/233 p. 43; /234 p. 34.

[86] TNA E179/187/470 m.6.

[87] James Wright, *Historia Histrionica* (London, 1699). Wright says (p. 7) that almost all of the players went into the king's army, 'except Lowin, Tayler and Pollard (who were superannuated)'.

[88] St Olave Southwark Composite Register: baptisms, marriages, and burials, 1639–1665 (LMA P71/OLA/010).

[89] TNA PROB 11/234/165v-166.

his executrix and two friends as overseers: Mr Jordan of Denton, clerk, and John Pierce of Tarring Neville, yeoman. There is no mention of any theatre people, which is perhaps not too surprising given that Rice had quit acting nearly thirty years before. His wife proved the will in Westminster on 14 September 1654.

John Rice led an eventful life by any standard. As a teenager, he was apprenticed in the leading acting company of England, for whom he performed before the king and originated some of the most famous female roles in the history of the English theatre. After finally becoming a sharer in that company at the age of thirty, he abruptly quit the stage a few years later to become a parish clerk in the midst of London's worst plague outbreak in years. He lost one wife, married again, had six children (five of whom survived), lost his second wife, married again and moved far away from London, eventually dying at the age of sixty-four. Rice's career as a boy actor for the King's Men is of obvious interest to theatre historians and Shakespeare scholars, given his status as the company's leading boy during an important part of Shakespeare's career. Looking at him alongside the company's other boys from around the same time provides a much clearer picture of the skilled actors, largely forgotten today, who first brought Shakespeare's women to life. On a broader level, Rice's life story demonstrates that early modern actors led full and often fascinating lives outside the theatre and that those lives can provide windows into some of the most tumultuous times in English history.

SHAKESPEARE'S IRISH LIVES: THE POLITICS OF BIOGRAPHY

ANDREW MURPHY

In 1901, a short biographical text appeared in the pages of the Dublin political journal *The United Irishman*, purporting to offer an account of 'The Life and Surprising Adventures' of a certain Professor O'Tonio. The professor, we are told, was born in Ballyvourney, a village in the Irish language speaking district of Co. Cork, and the details of his life may have a rather familiar feel to them for Shakespearians, as his biographer tells us that: 'Owing to having been concerned in stealing deer from the grounds of Sir Thomas Lucy, [O'Tonio] was compelled to fly from Ballyvourney, and making the acquaintance of Ben Jonson he commenced life by holding horses outside the old Theatre Royal' in Dublin.[1] As a result of a quarrel at cards, O'Tonio is forced to flee Ireland for London, where, we discover, 'He found great difficulty in obtaining employment and was indeed on the verge of starvation.' Fortuitously, at this point,

he met the notorious William Shakespeare, who was then running the Lyceum Theatre. An agreement was come to between O Tonio [*sic*] and Mr. Shakespeare, which resulted in the production of that justly celebrated work [–] at the small price of one shilling [–] popularly known as 'Shakespeare's Plays'. For a long time the impression was very generally entertained that William Shakespeare was indeed the author, but the discovery of [a] cryptogram running through the whole series finally proved beyond all cavil that O'Tonio was the man.

Among the plays written by O'Tonio under Shakespeare's name are, we discover, *Hamlet*, *Othello* – and *Arrah-na-Pogue*.[2] O'Tonio ultimately comes to a sticky end and he is publicly executed by William

Calcraft, the notorious nineteenth-century hangman.

'The Life and Surprising Adventures of a Certain Professor' was signed by 'Shanganagh', a regular contributor to the journal. Shanganagh was in all likelihood a pen-name of Arthur Griffith, the founding editor of the *United Irishman*, author of the book *The Resurrection of Hungary: A Parallel for Ireland* (1904), and creator of the nationalist political party Sinn Féin.[3] The piece is characteristic of Griffith's contributions to the journal, which tended to be whimsical flights of fancy with an underlying political bite. Various references in the piece make it clear that O'Tonio is intended as a figure for Anthony Traill, at the time Provost of Trinity College Dublin – a staunch anti-nationalist who, together with various other Anglocentric Trinity dons, served frequently as a target for Griffith's absurdist political satire. We learn in the piece that, during the course of his long and varied career, O'Tonio was made a professor at Trinity, on the basis of his 'efforts on behalf of the weak and oppressed and his services to humanity in extirpating the Celtic race'. In his speech from the gallows, O'Tonio gives 'his reasons for objecting to the Irish

---

[1] 'The Life and Surprising Adventures of a Certain Professor', *United Irishman*, 6.124 (13 July 1901), p. 6 (all quotations from here, unless otherwise specified).

[2] *Arrah-na-Pogue* was, of course, one of the most popular melodramas written by the Dublin-born Dion Boucicault.

[3] In Joyce's *Ulysses*, John Wyse asks of a humorous piece in the *United Irishman* 'Is that by Griffith?' to which the Citizen replies: 'It's not signed Shanganagh. It's only initialled: "P".' James Joyce, *Ulysses* (Harmondsworth, 1969), p. 333.

language . . . and [to] pro-Boerism', and Traill was a strong opponent of proposals to teach Irish at school and university level, also adopting a firmly pro-British line in relation to the Boer War.[4]

One striking aspect of Griffith's gallimaufry text is the extent to which it relies for its humorous effect on his readers' familiarity with the details of Shakespeare's biography – or, at least, with the anecdotal biography as set out, in the first instance, in Rowe's 1709 edition of the plays. Griffith's journal was not aimed at an affluent audience (it cost just a penny an issue), and its politics were on the separatist end of the nationalist spectrum; one article in the journal declared that 'the supreme salvation of Ireland can only be achieved by rooting the soldiers, the servants, and the flag of Britain out of Ireland equally with her language, laws and institutions'.[5] Yet Griffith is clearly confident that his readers will know enough about the English national poet that his whimsical melding of Shakespeare and Traill will be intelligible to them.

A glance at the literary interests of Griffith's fellow advanced nationalists indicates that his confidence was probably not misplaced. Richard English, in his overview history of Irish nationalism, registers that many Irish political activists in this period were, paradoxically, steeped in English literature, with a great number of them being, in particular, keen readers of Shakespeare.[6] Griffith himself was held at Gloucester prison for his nationalist activities from 1918 to 1919, and a fellow Sinn Féin prisoner, Robert Brennan, later recalled that they discussed opera and literature during their time together at the jail. Griffith had specifically, Brennan noted, 'a keen appreciation of Shakespeare and of Beaumont and Fletcher'.[7] Likewise, Patrick Pearse, the leader of the 1916 separatist uprising, also had a strong devotion to the playwright.[8] Pearse read and re-read the plays, performed them at home with his siblings, recited passages from them at public events, and included them in the curriculum of St Enda's, the nationalist-focused school which he founded in Dublin in 1908.[9] A former pupil of Pearse's, Desmond Ryan, describes the oddly fetishistic energy which attached itself to

Pearse's collecting of multiple editions of the playwright's works: 'He loved his . . . many editions of Shakespeare, all of which he watched in the booksellers' windows, nobly renounced, entered, fingered, steeled himself, fled whole streets away, lingered, wavered, turned back and purchased, radiant and ashamed until he saw the next.'[10]

Taking a broader historical perspective, we can say that Griffith's political satire is, in fact, representative of a repeated and enduring Irish engagement with the biographical Shakespeare, and of a strong tendency within that tradition to use the biography to create polemical political narratives, whether nationalist or, indeed, anti-nationalist. This tendency is particularly marked in Irish versions of the poet's life story which seek to derive supposed biographical 'fact' directly from an examination of Shakespeare's literary works. James Shapiro, in *Contested Will*, has specifically identified the Irish Shakespearian Edmond Malone as the point of origin of this kind of biographical imagining.[11] As Shapiro notes, Malone was the first person to attempt, systematically, to arrange the plays in their chronological order of composition, an order which he adopted in his 1790 edition of

[4] 'Life', p. 7.
[5] 'All Ireland', *United Irishman*, 4.80 (8 September 1900), p. 1.
[6] See Richard English, *Irish Freedom: The History of Nationalism in Ireland* (London, 2007), pp. 302–3.
[7] Bureau of Irish Military History, file number S. 537, Witness Statement 779 (section 2), p. 487.
[8] On the Shakespearian interests of the leaders of the 1916 Rising see Andrew Murphy, 'Shakespeare's Rising: Ireland and the Tercentenary', in *Celebrating Shakespeare: Commemoration and Cultural Memory*, ed. Clara Calvo and Coppélia Kahn (Cambridge, forthcoming 2016).
[9] See Patrick Pearse, 'My Childhood and Youth', in *The Home Life of Pádraig Pearse: As Told by Himself, His Family and Friends*, ed. Mary Brigid Pearse (Dublin and Cork, 1979; first published 1934), pp. 48, 84, 88–9 and Joost Augusteijn, *Patrick Pearse: The Making of a Revolutionary* (Basingstoke, 2010), pp. 52, 73, 98, 177. Adverts for Pearse's school ran 'St. Enda's, with an Irish inspiration, has classical and modern sides' (*The Leader*, 31.3 (28 August 1915), p. 69).
[10] Desmond Ryan, *Remembering Sion: A Chronicle of Storm and Quiet* (London, 1934), p. 159.
[11] James Shapiro, *Contested Will: Who Wrote Shakespeare?* (London, 2010), p. 39–53.

the plays and poems, breaking with the traditional First-Folio-derived ordering by genre. As Shapiro indicates, the attempt to establish compositional chronology led Malone, in the first instance, to seek topical allusions in the plays, and it was then a short step from finding possible historical references to discovering what were imagined to be biographical references (particularly, of course, in the Sonnets). Shapiro argues that 'With Malone's decision to parse the plays for evidence of what [the] author thought or felt, literary biography had crossed a Rubicon. Fictional works had become a legitimate source for biographies, and Shakespeare's plays and poems crucial to establishing this new approach.'[12] In an Irish context, as we shall see, finding the biography in the work often meant also locating imagined authorial politics in the work.

Malone was a graduate of Trinity College in Dublin. During his time there, literature was not taught as a formal subject, though oratory and rhetoric were and the Professor of Oratory in Malone's time at the College – John Lawson – repeatedly drew on Shakespeare's works in his teaching, observing in his *Lectures on Oratory* (published the year after Malone entered Trinity):

No Writer seemeth to have a better Title to [the] singular Character of original Genius, than our *Shakespear*. What Richness of Imagination! What Loftiness of Thought! What amazing Command of the Passions! Yet how totally different is he from every other Writer? There is scarcely a Line of his that doth not bear the impress of his peculiar Genius.[13]

The study of Shakespeare and of other writers was not, for Lawson, an end in itself – rather it was intended to sharpen his students' powers of rhetoric and argumentation. Such study was imagined as being particularly profitable for those students intending to enter the church, where advanced rhetorical skills would be of assistance to them in combatting what Lawson identifies as the works of the 'Church of *Rome*, whose Doctrines are the most grossly erroneous'.[14] Even at this early point, then, literature – and specifically the works of Shakespeare – are deeply entwined with politics in an Irish context.

The quality of teaching in the area of oratory at Trinity declined from the later decades of the eighteenth century onwards and, to quote from the standard history of the college, 'gradually the office seems to have become a sinecure'.[15] In 1852, the Professorship of Oratory passed to the polymath John Kells Ingram, who had been a Fellow of the college since 1846. Ingram disliked teaching the subject and so, in 1855, he expanded the remit of the chair to take in English literature as a freestanding subject in itself, and he began lecturing on various literary topics, including the works of Shakespeare.[16] The text of a lecture on the playwright delivered to a general audience in Dublin in 1863 has survived and in it we find Ingram asserting that, before any critical interpretation of Shakespeare can be undertaken, 'We must ascertain, with at least approximate correctness, the chronological order of his works', and he notes that '[t]he whole question of the chronology of the plays was first systematically handled by our countryman, Edmond Malone'.[17] Following Malone, Ingram notes that, among the kinds of evidence that can be brought to bear on the business of establishing the chronology of the plays, are 'supposed allusions . . . to contemporary circumstances or events', and he goes on to argue that recent work in his own time on shifting verse form patterns in Shakespeare's plays offers the possibility of further refining the chronological order that his fellow countryman had proposed in the previous

---

[12] Shapiro, *Contested Will*, p. 51.
[13] John Lawson, *Lectures Concerning Oratory. Delivered in Trinity College, Dublin* (Dublin, 1758), pp. 114–15.
[14] Lawson, *Lectures*, pp. 369–70.
[15] R. B. McDowell and D. A. Webb, *Trinity College Dublin 1592–1952: An Academic History* (Dublin, 2004; orig. pub. Cambridge, 1982), p. 61.
[16] See McDowell and Webb, *Trinity College Dublin*, pp. 230–1. On Ingram's dislike of teaching oratory, see 'The Late Professor Dowden. Lecture by Mr. T. W. Lister', *Irish Times* 18 November 1913, p. 7. Edward Dowden's notes on Ingram's lectures on English are preserved among the Dowden papers at Trinity College Dublin: TCD MS3063 'J. K. Ingram's Lectures on English 1861'.
[17] J. K. Ingram, 'Shakespeare', in *The Afternoon Lectures on English Literature* (London and Dublin, 1863), p. 99.

century.[18] (Ingram himself had also carried out some work on the weak-ending test as a possible technique for establishing chronological sequence.)[19]

Correcting Malone's chronology was not the end point of this work for Ingram – rather, the outcome of such research should ultimately, in his view, 'converge towards the illustration of Shakespeare's personality'.[20] And Ingram's sense of the poet's 'personality' extends to an understanding of Shakespeare's politics. He warns that 'we must not, of course, look in Shakespeare for any promulgation of party tenets . . . but only for the enunciation of what is universal and perennial'. Approaching the matter from this general perspective Ingram concludes that

it may be generally observed of [Shakespeare] that he is heartily loyal to all the fundamental institutions of society. He is a friend to all that is stable, orderly, and well-organized: a foe to all that is nomadic or anarchical. The distinction of ranks he respects and values. He is full of fine high-toned speeches about 'degree, priority, and place'. He has the constitutional Conservatism of Englishmen.[21]

Ingram's conservatist portrait of Shakespeare here may, at first blush, seem all too predictable, coming, as it does, from a member of the Trinity establishment, standing in the line of succession to the venerable Professor Lawson. But, in fact, Ingram's personal politics were rather more complex than his analysis here of Shakespeare would suggest. Twenty years prior to delivering this lecture – in the early 1840s – when the separatist Young Ireland movement launched the popular newspaper the *Nation*, Ingram was moved to submit a poem to the journal, entitled 'The Memory of the Dead'.[22] The *Nation* published the piece and it was subsequently set to music, and the poem, since then, has been better known in its ballad version, which usually takes its title from the first line of the opening stanza: 'Who fears to speak of '98?' The poem is a celebration of the French-inspired 1798 United Irishmen uprising, an event generally seen as the founding moment of Irish republicanism. 'The Memory of the Dead' quickly became – and,

in fact, remains – a staple of the Irish nationalist canon. Indeed, in 1900, Griffith's *United Irishman* positively heralded the appearance of a new volume of Ingram's selected poems (Ingram was, by then, 77 years old), observing, 'Irish Nationalists will give the book a hearty welcome, for it may safely be asserted that "The Memory of the Dead" has warmed the heart, and cheered the soul of every single man and woman of the Irish National millions at home and abroad.' The journal's reviewer even went on to suggest that Ingram's poem might serve as a national anthem until an alternative had been written.[23]

How do we explain the disjunction between the Ingram of the 1840s patriotic republicanism and the Ingram who produces, twenty years later, a portrait of Shakespeare characterized by a central conservatism? Is it just a product of age: of the shift from youthful 20s to staid 40s? It may well be, but an alternative (or perhaps a complementary) explanation is also possible. Ingram was, from a young age, an adherent of Comtean positivism – in fact he visited Comte in Paris in 1855 – and he believed strongly in the possibility of political reform; indeed, he believed in the power of *academic analysis* to influence and effect a reformist programme. In the year following his Shakespeare public lecture he addressed the Statistical and Social Inquiry Society of Ireland, of which he was a founding member (Ingram's greatest reputation was forged, ultimately, in the field of Economics). In his address he offers a positive account of the reforms that had been carried out in Ireland by the British administration since the

---

[18] Ingram, 'Shakespeare', p. 100.
[19] See letter from Edward Dowden to Elizabeth Dickinson West (later Dowden), dated 13 November 1874 in Elizabeth Dickinson Dowden, ed., *Fragments from Old Letters E.D. to E.D.W. 1869–1892*, vol. 2 (London, 1914), p. 67.
[20] Ingram, 'Shakespeare', p. 77.
[21] Ingram, 'Shakespeare', p. 125.
[22] For an account of the context and history of the poem, see C. Litton Falkiner, *Memoir of the Late John Kells Ingram* (Dublin, 1907), p. 5.
[23] *United Irishman*, 3.59 (14 April 1900), p. 1, section headed 'All Ireland'.

1820s – including Catholic Emancipation, franchise and legal reforms and the first steps towards what would ultimately prove to be quite radical land reform – and he asserts (rather extravagantly, admittedly) that these initiatives, taken together, constituted 'the largest peaceful revolution in the history of the world'.[24] Within the context of ongoing reform, the business of the Statistical Society was, in Ingram's view, 'to discover and demonstrate, by the application of scientific principles, the legislative action appropriate to each phase of society and each group of economic conditions'. Once the evidence-based arguments had been made, the politicians would, Ingram believed – optimistically, we might feel – eventually be persuaded by them and further change would be brought about through parliamentary initiative and legislative process. The older Ingram's preferred mode of 'revolution' was, therefore, administrative rather than insurrectionary – his admiration of the United Irish movement notwithstanding. It is not too surprising, then, that his vision of Shakespeare is of someone who places his faith in the fundamental institutions of the state. Ingram himself believed that these institutions, far from being static (or 'conservative' in the very narrowest sense), could actually be mobilized to serve as an engine of change and progress.

In 1866, Ingram took up the Regius Chair of Greek at Trinity, stepping down from the oratory and literature professorship as a result. He encouraged a former star student of his, Edward Dowden, to apply for the ensuing vacancy.[25] Dowden was successful in his application, taking up the chair in 1867, and serving as Professor of English at Trinity until his death in 1913. Ingram's interest in the chronology of the plays, and the work that establishing the order of composition might facilitate, clearly had an impact on his protégé. In December of 1873, in the wake of F. J. Furnivall's launching of the New Shakspere Society in London, Dowden wrote to Elizabeth Dickinson West (a former student who would later become his second wife):

I am glad this Shakespeare Society is started. It will do a great deal to illustrate his works, probably determine,

as far as can be, the order in which he wrote his plays, and provide material of one kind or another for at length getting at the man himself, who is certainly the biggest problem in modern literature.[26]

Some months prior to Dowden's writing to West, Furnivall had, in fact, himself written to Dowden, urging him, 'Why don't you write the long-wanted book on Shakspere? We've nothing to put into a student's hands about him.'[27] Dowden took up the suggestion and, as a first step, in 1874, he delivered a series of lectures on Shakespeare at Trinity to students from Dublin's Alexandra women's college.[28] He quickly then refined the lectures, publishing them under the title *Shakspere: A Critical Study of His Mind and Art* in 1875.

In *Mind and Art*, Dowden set out a working hypothesis for the order in which the plays were composed – drawing in part on the work of the Shakspere Society – and, like Malone and Ingram before him, he sought to read through this chronology to arrive at a sense of Shakespeare the man. As he observes in the Preface to *Mind and Art*, 'To approach Shakspere on the human side is the object of this book.'[29] More than any previous commentator in the English tradition Dowden laid stress on Shakespeare's business dealings and on the practical side of his nature. The professor was himself part of a newly reconstituted professional class which emerged during the course of the Victorian period, at a time when, as Stefan Collini has

---

[24] John K. Ingram, *Considerations on the State of Ireland: Being the Substance of an Address delivered before the Statistical and Social Inquiry Society of Ireland . . .* (Dublin, 1864), p. 17.

[25] Strictly speaking, it was not a single vacancy or professorship that Dowden applied for: Oratory and Literature formally became two separate chairs and he was given a joint appointment (and distinct salaries) for both posts. His duties as Professor of Oratory became, in due course, largely symbolic.

[26] Dowden, *Fragments from Old Letters*, vol. 1, p. 82.

[27] Letter from F. J. Furnivall to Edward Dowden, 17 July 1873, Dowden Papers, Trinity College Dublin, TCD MS 3147–54a/79.

[28] Dowden had taught at Alexandra for a brief spell prior to his appointment at Trinity.

[29] Edward Dowden, *Shakspere: A Critical Study of His Mind and Art* (London, 1875), p. vi. Further references included parenthetically in the text.

indicated, 'many of the social connotations of the old "status professionalism" were transferred to the new "occupational professionalism"'. In these circumstances, Collini argues, '[t]he ethic of work and the ethos of strenuousness which were making their mark on even the upper reaches of English society by the mid-nineteenth century endowed the energetic pursuit of a profession with additional respectability without forfeiting its traditional genteel status.'[30] It may not be too surprising, then, to find Dowden – the professionalized academic – making a positive virtue of Shakespeare's business sense. Thus he comments in *Mind and Art* that 'There can be no doubt that Shakspere considered it worth his while to be prudent, industrious, and economical. He would appear to have had a very sufficient sense of life, and in particular of his own life, as real, and of this earth as a possession' (31). Again, elsewhere, he comments, 'all through his life we observe [in Shakespeare] a sufficient recognition of external fact, external claims, and obligations. Hence worldly prosperity could not be a matter which would ever seem unimportant to Shakspere' (33).

Dowden's Shakespeare is pragmatic, hardworking, materially minded and, ultimately, prosperous in his Stratford retirement; he cuts, in this sense, a decidedly Victorian figure. But there are other aspects of Dowden's portrait that take us beyond this contemporizing construction, offering a more politically inflected image of the poet. And again, there are filiations here that can be drawn back to Ingram, Dowden's mentor. In his lecture on Shakespeare, Ingram touches briefly on the poet's religious beliefs, observing, 'A Protestant Shakespeare plainly appears to have been, but without any tincture of anti-Catholic fanaticism.'[31] Where we do find an anti-Romanist strain in Shakespeare, it is, Ingram asserts, 'dictated, not by religious rancour, but by the spirit of patriotism'. 'The Protestant Reformation in England', he proposes, 'cannot be adequately explained as a mere revolution in opinion; it was also, and still more, regarded by the people themselves as a vindication of their national independence'. Shakespeare is thus, for Ingram, very much a product of his time and of his society – a post-Reformation society, distinctive in its Protestantism and – as a direct consequence of its Protestantism – in its newly-affirmed English identity.

In 1869, six years after Ingram's lecture and six years before he himself published *Mind and Art*, Dowden contributed an article to the *Contemporary Review* in which, among other things, he discusses the topic of Elizabethan drama, describing the drama as 'the chief artistic fruit of the English Renaissance'. Dowden does not take up the issue of religion directly in this piece, but he does argue that 'The men of that period in our country found their highest selves not in the Past, but in the Present.' This is the key to understanding Renaissance drama for Dowden: it is, he says, 'before all else Elizabethan – English of the second half of the sixteenth century'. For this reason, he observes, Shakespeare 'is only putting in words the open secret of the whole artistic movement to which he belonged, when he calls his players "the abstract and brief chronicles of the time"'.[32]

In *Mind and Art* itself Dowden pushes this analysis further. He asserts that Jonson's claim – in his eulogy in the First Folio – that Shakespeare was 'not of an age, but for all time' 'misleads us', and he argues that 'Shakspere was for all time by virtue of certain powers and perceptions, but he also belonged especially to an age, his own age.' And this age in England was, for Dowden – as it had been for Ingram before him – precisely, as Dowden explicitly states, 'a Protestant age' (8). Ingram himself, characteristically, had been careful to avoid adopting a sectarian position in relation to the Reformation religious divide, observing in his lecture that Shakespeare 'never treats the old Church with disrespect'. Dowden, by contrast, is

[30] Stefan Collini, *Public Moralists: Political Thought and Intellectual Life in Britain* (Oxford, 1991), p. 32.

[31] Ingram, 'Shakespeare', pp. 119–20. All subsequent quotes in this paragraph from p. 120.

[32] Edward Dowden, 'True Conservatism – What It Is', *The Contemporary Review* (October 1869), p. 278 (all quotations). Dowden himself was not a Conservative. In a letter to Prof. William Knight, dated 15 December 1887, he observes 'I am not a Tory but a Liberal Unionist' – TCD MS 2259/1.

far less circumspect in his views. He sees a clear distinction emerging in the Reformation and sees Protestantism as the key positive force that makes Shakespeare's work possible. 'Catholicism', Dowden writes,

had endeavoured to sanctify things secular by virtue proceeding towards them from special ecclesiastical persons, and places and acts. The modern spirit, of which Protestantism is a part, revealed in the total life of men a deeper and truer sanctity than can be conferred by touches of any wand of ecclesiastical magic. The burden of the curse was lightened. Knowledge was good, and men set about increasing the store of knowledge by the interrogation of nature . . . (13)

Dowden would, in time, become one of the anti-Trinity targets of Griffith's *United Irishman*, being described in one piece in the journal as 'a blue-blooded Englishman, free from the slightest taint of Irish ancestry . . . honoured, some time ago, with the Sloper Award of Merit, in recognition of his eminent services as a spreader of civilisation amongst the mere Irish'.[33] This parody of Dowden was written in 1900, by which time he was strongly – and very publicly – associated with the anti-Home Rule movement in Ireland; with resistance to the cultural nationalism of Yeats's Irish literary revival project; and (like Provost Traill) with opposition to the formal recognition of the Irish language within the educational establishment. But we can already see here, in *Mind and Art*, that, a quarter of a century before the *United Irishman* mocked him, Dowden, in his Shakespeare work, was offering analysis that had, in an Irish context, clear potential to be politically and culturally divisive, if not inflammatory. From a solidly Anglo-Irish background (the descendant, in fact, of Cromwellian settlers[34]), and writing from within a college whose student body and faculty were still overwhelmingly Protestant, Dowden unapologetically styles Catholicism – the religion of the majority in Ireland – as being governed by the 'wand of ecclesiastical magic', as a 'curse', the 'burden' of which is 'lightened' by the coming of Protestantism, which brings with it liberating knowledge and the possibility of cultural and social progress.

And Dowden presents this as the key to understanding Shakespeare: his work, in Dowden's view, being the product specifically of a Protestant age, a Protestant culture, a Protestant mindset.

I have written elsewhere of W. B. Yeats's attempt to offer a counter-vision to Dowden's version of Shakespeare, in his essay 'At Stratford-on-Avon', which itself represents a further Irish re-imagining of the biographical Shakespeare.[35] Central to Yeats's approach is, I have argued, precisely an inversion of Dowden's fundamental position. Where Dowden sees Shakespeare as located on the near side of the cusp of the modern, embracing both the new reformed religion and the new developments in science, knowledge and culture that it makes possible, Yeats, by contrast, draws the playwright back in cultural-historical terms and locates him at the dying end of the medieval. In an essay on Edmund Spenser, Yeats observes of the English Renaissance that 'Thoughts and qualities sometimes come to their perfect expression when they are about to pass away, and Merry England was dying in plays, and in poems, and in strange adventurous men.' If one of those men were to return to England in Yeats's own time, then, the Irish poet predicts, 'he would find nothing there but the triumph of the Puritan and the merchant – those enemies he had feared and hated – and he would weep perhaps, in that womanish way of his, to think that so much greatness had been, not, as he had hoped, the dawn, but the sunset of his people'.[36] The Renaissance is thus, for Yeats, the end point of culture rather than

---

33 'Literary Intelligence', *United Irishman*, 4.88 (3 November 1900), p. 7. 'Sloper' is, of course, a reference to Ally Sloper, the Victorian comic book character who served in the period as a stock figure for idleness and bumbling dissipation.

34 In a letter to Elizabeth Dickinson West in January 1874, Dowden revealed that Cromwell was 'one of my earliest objects of hero-worship', *Fragments from Old Letters*, vol. 2, p. 49. A further letter sent two years later, dated 15 March 1876, offers, however, a modification of this view, indicating that 'Shakespeare saves me from Cromwell' (vol. 1, p. 151).

35 Andrew Murphy, 'An Irish Catalysis: W. B. Yeats and the Uses of Shakespeare', in *Shakespeare Survey 64* (Cambridge, 2011), pp. 208–19.

36 W. B. Yeats, 'Edmund Spenser', in *Essays and Introductions* (London, 1961), p. 364 (both quotations).

its point of origin – and it is precisely (and in direct contradiction to Dowden) radical religious innovation and nascent capitalism that brings about that culture's demise.

Yeats's 'Merry England' is a medievalist construct and his orientation towards the medieval arose partly from the close influence of William Morris on his thinking.[37] But his medievalism also aligned him directly with a central strand within Irish nationalist thinking in the period.[38] David Lloyd, in *Irish Culture and Colonial Modernity 1800–2000*, has written very perceptively about the persistence of forms of oral culture in Ireland within the context of a rapidly modernizing Victorian British state, and his analysis can be taken to apply more broadly beyond the narrow field of orality to a greater set of Irish cultural formations anchored in a pre-modern past. Such formations, Lloyd argues,

transform their non-modern practices into countermodern dissonances within the capitalist system they at once serve and challenge with infectious alternative possibilities. For what the Irish embody is not, in fact, simply a social formation lagging in the past of modernity and waiting on development, as historicism would have it. It represents, rather, a different social imaginary *in* the present and *for* the future.[39]

The value of a medievalist cultural programme in Ireland in this period was precisely that it facilitated a counter-definition of Irishness against Englishness.[40] If England was modern, utilitarian and imperialist, Ireland's (real and imagined) pastoralist economic and social structures – indicating, as Lloyd suggests, a state of 'under-development' in Victorian British imperialist terms – could be reconfigured as a mark of superior cultural and ethical value. Thus Douglas Hyde, the founder of the Gaelic League – a society dedicated to the revival of the Irish language – described Ireland in a 1905 lecture as 'an ancient nation whose half-deserted streets resound ever less and less to the roar of traffic, whose mills are silent, whose factories are fallen'. '[A]nd yet', Hyde declares, 'around that nation, morality of life, purity of sentiment, unswerving devotion to faith, and to fatherland, and to

language, have shed a halo in the eyes of Europe that is all its own'.[41] In this context, Yeats's rendering of Shakespeare as a belated medieval writer, rather than an Elizabethan child of the Reformation, can be said to have served to bring the playwright closely into alignment with a broader Irish nationalist agenda.

Beyond Yeats's medievalized Shakespeare, other Irish reversionings of the playwright also emerged in this period. One of the most striking was that constructed by Frank Harris in his 1907 volume *The Man Shakespeare and his Tragic Life Story*. Harris has been described in his *Dictionary of National Biography* entry as 'a journalist and rogue', and by Samuel Schoenbaum, in *Shakespeare's Lives*, as a

---

[37] Roy Foster has noted that 'Morris's ideas of creative brotherhood, a crusade against the mass-produced values of Victorian capitalism, and promoting the overriding claims of art upon life were compelling' to Yeats (R. F. Foster, *W. B. Yeats: A Life*, vol. 1 (Oxford, 1998), p. 64).

[38] Patrick Maume has pithily summed up this particular strand of nationalism in the observation that, within this worldview, 'Only when mediaevalism has been restored will the world be healed' (*The Rise and Fall of Irish Ireland: D. P. Moran & Daniel Corkery* (Coleraine, 1996), p. 7).

[39] David Lloyd, *Irish Culture and Colonial Modernity 1800–2000: The Transformation of Oral Space* (Cambridge, 2011), pp. 47–8.

[40] In an extended essay on British educational policy in Ireland – uncompromisingly titled 'The Murder Machine' – Patrick Pearse set out his opposition to modern ways of thinking, observing that 'It should be obvious that the more "modern" an education is the less "sound" [it is], for in education "modernism" is as much a heresy as in religion. In both[,] mediævalism were a truer standard' ('The Murder Machine', in *The Coming Revolution: The Political Writings and Speeches of Patrick Pearse* (Cork, 2012), p. 24). The medievalist trope gained such force in Ireland that some commentators ultimately set their face against it. Writing in the journal *Dana*, the socialist commentator Frederick Ryan observed: 'The truth is...that most of the leaders of the Gaelic League appear to desire a return to mediævalism, in thought, in literature, in pastimes, in music, and even in dress. And the fact that this desire is impossible of realisation does not affect those who proclaim it, and does not lessen its practical injuriousness' ('Is the Gaelic League a Progressive Force?', *Dana*, 7 (November 1904), p. 218).

[41] Douglas Hyde, *Language, Lore, and Lyrics: Essays and Lectures*, ed. Breandán Ó Conaire (Dublin, 1986), p. 187.

'Liar, libertine[,] blackmailer [and] scoundrel'.[42] Born in Galway, he worked for a spell as a lawyer in Kansas; was a cattle rustler on the Mexican border; a war correspondent during the Turko-Russian War; a highly successful newspaper editor in London; a friend and defender of Oscar Wilde; a supporter of Charles Stewart Parnell during the O'Shea divorce proceedings; and a man with what can most delicately be described as an extremely complicated love life. He was committed to Brixton prison for a spell in 1914 (for contempt of court) and, while there, his office was raided by the bailiffs. One of his mistresses, the novelist Enid Bagnold, happened to be present at the time, and she had the presence of mind to tie a rope around Harris's copy of the First Folio and lower it from an upstairs window, to save it from the bailiffs' clutches.[43]

Harris had something of an obsession with Shakespeare from boyhood, and he tells us that the more he read and re-read the plays, the more he discovered 'tantalizing hints and suggestions of a certain unity underlying the diversity of characters'.[44] This sense of unity ultimately leads Harris to believe that the canon actually offers a repeated series of portraits of the artist. As he puts it: 'Shakespeare painted himself at full-length not once, but twenty times, at as many different periods of his life' (x). If we read the work closely enough, then, the character of the playwright himself emerges, shifting over time. In adopting this view, Harris was, of course, following what was by then a well-trodden path – a path first laid down, as we have seen, by Edmond Malone. Harris can be said to have taken this approach to its logical – or perhaps its illogical – endpoint. For Harris, the biographical narrative imagined as being discoverable in Shakespeare's works is not to be checked for confirmation against the biographical materials that exist outside of the works, but, rather, quite the reverse. As he puts it: 'the facts as given in his works' enable us 'to accept or reject' the external biographical reports 'with some degree of confidence, and so arrive at a credible picture of his life's journey, and the changes which Time wrought in him' (357). So, with

Harris, finally, the biography generated from the work itself trumps all other forms of biographical information.

Though Harris was clearly located within a particular critical tradition – albeit at its extreme end – he was, nevertheless, entirely dismissive of the work of his predecessors in that tradition. Two years after his book appeared he wrote to Arnold Bennett to say 'I am sending Dowden['s book] today, to show you the best of what was known about Shakespeare before I began my work[;] you will see from that the incredible stupidity of the commentators.'[45] What Harris objected to most was precisely the Victorianizing impulse that we have registered as being so characteristic of Dowden. Shakespeare's commentators had, in Harris's view, 'turned the poet into a tradesman, and the unimaginable tragedy of his life into the commonplace record of a successful tradesman's career' (xi). He particularly resisted the notion that, as he puts it, 'in the fullness of years and honours [Shakespeare retired] to Stratford to live out the remainder of his days in the bosom of his family as "a prosperous country gentleman", to use Dowden's unhappy phrase' (403). Harris's vision of the final Stratford years was wholly different from this. Shakespeare, he proposes, 'was extravagant to lavishness even in cautious age. While in London he no doubt earned and was given large sums of money; but he was free-handed and careless, and died far poorer than one would have expected.' 'The loose-liver', Harris concludes, 'is usually a spendthrift' (383). And a 'loose-liver' Shakespeare certainly was, in Harris's view, a man of 'ungovernable sensuality', who spent twelve years of his life in passionate bondage to Mary Fitton, mistress of William Herbert, who,

---

[42] *Online Dictionary of National Biography* entry: www.oxforddnb.com/view/article/33727 (accessed 9 September 2014); S. Schoenbaum, *Shakespeare's Lives* (Oxford, 1991), p. 480.

[43] See *ODNB*.

[44] Frank Harris, *The Man Shakespeare and his Tragic Life Story* (London, 1909), p. ix. Further references included parenthetically in the body of the text.

[45] Quoted in Schoenbaum, *Lives*, p. 482.

Harris believed (following Thomas Tyler) was the 'dark lady' of the sonnets.[46] On the positive side of the equation, '[i]t was', Harris asserts, his 'absolute abandonment to passion which made Shakespeare the supreme poet' (391).

There is a kind of mad extravagance to Harris's biography, which is at times breath-taking in its wild certainties. He finds in the plays, for instance, 'proof upon proof that [Shakespeare] detested his wife and was glad to live without her' (374). His mother, we learn, he 'held ... in extraordinary esteem and affection, and mourned her after her death as "the noblest mother in the world"' (358). But beyond such unanchored speculation, we also find, again, a decided political element in Harris's account of the playwright's life. Shakespeare, he notes 'is continually spoken of as patriotic' and Harris concedes that the playwright 'started in youth with an almost lyrical love of country' (406). After these early years, however, Harris tells us that he 'find[s] no praise of England or of Englishmen in any of [Shakespeare's] works', with the single exception of *Henry V*, which he dismisses as having been 'manifestly written to catch applause on account of its jingoism' (407). What Harris finds ultimately in Shakespeare is, in fact, a loathing of 'the common Englishman' and, in a startling piece of analysis, he sees the figure of Caliban as offering us a distillation of Shakespeare's feelings about his fellow countrymen. 'The qualities [Shakespeare] lends Caliban', he writes,

are all characteristic. Whoever will give him drink is to Caliban a god. The brutish creature would violate and degrade art without a scruple, and the soul of him is given in the phrase that if he got the chance he would people the world with Calibans. Sometimes one thinks that if Shakespeare were living to-day he would be inclined to say that his prediction had come true. (407)

Harris offers an arresting piece of analysis here, turning Caliban from colonized native to aspiring colonizer – and refiguring the desire to people the island with creatures forged in his own image as an emblem for the imperial project itself. The leap that Harris makes from the colonial narrative of the play to the contemporary world of the empire

in his own time is also striking. He suggests that Shakespeare might feel that Caliban's fantasy has been enacted presumably because so much of the world map has, by the opening decade of the twentieth century, been coloured red, with vast tracts of territory being ruled by what Harris sees as imperial English Calibans.

It would be going too far, I think, on the basis of this passage, to style Harris as something like a postcolonial critic *avant la lettre*. But we might, nevertheless, see him as – like Yeats before him – enacting an Irish political appropriation of Shakespeare by reorienting the playwright's position away from the meliorative conservatism or imperialist anti-nationalism of the Trinity professoriate.

Issues of imperialism in relation to the biographical Shakespeare are further explored in *Shakespeare's End* – a play by Conal O'Riordan published three years after Harris's book first appeared. Born in Dublin in 1874, O'Riordan had been an actor in J. T. Grein's Independent Theatre Society in London before returning to Ireland, where he wrote, directed and acted for a time at the Abbey (serving, briefly, as Managing Director of the theatre). In 1909 he returned to London, ultimately settling into a career as a prolific novelist.[47] O'Riordan's play traces Shakespeare's final hours; drawing on the anecdotal biography, O'Riordan imagines this time as being spent in a drinking session with various fellow writers visiting the poet in Stratford. His opening conceit of Shakespeare runs quite contrary to Harris's: O'Riordan's Shakespeare is decidedly prosperous, and his final abiding ambition in life is to be granted a knighthood. Though it has not happened yet, Shakespeare asserts 'I know that it must come',

For I have pawned my laurels and bought land.
There's money in this room that would go far

---

[46] Harris had promoted the theory that Fitton was the 'dark lady' before portraits emerged revealing that she was, in fact, fair-haired.

[47] For details of O'Riordan's career, see his entry in the *Irish Dictionary of National Biography*, http://dib.cambridge.org/viewReadPage.do?articleId=a7015 (accessed 16 September 2014).

To pay my patent – mark ye, in this room.
I am already esquire, and must be
A knight when they forget I've been a poet.[48]

Over the course of the evening, the house is visited by two strangers seeking shelter and they each in turn offer radical challenges to Shakespeare's most deeply held beliefs. The first is a mariner who has served on Richard Grenville's *Revenge* – a heroic figure in Shakespeare's eyes. But the mariner's account of his imperial adventuring is profoundly shocking in its brutality:

> Once I remember on the Spanish Main
> We sacked a town, and in a convent there
> Me and my watch lay full a sen'night snug.
> Lost to the world, enjoying everything
> That man may hope for. There we had rich food,
> And costly wines and gaudy, gay attire . . .
> Ay, we had women too.
> I own I do not love a lass the less
> That she should come unwilling to the clip
> And think her soul lost. As for the men, the priests
> That would not fight or flee, we nailed them out
> On their own crosses. (115)

Shakespeare attempts to recuperate the imperial project in the wake of the shock afforded by this account of what that project means in practical human terms, asserting that England 'carr[ies] her incomparable good / To the receding ends of ocean's bounds, / To all the nations thirsting for one rule' and that the mariner is simply the 'clumsy tool'

> That works in darkness, learns to love the dark
> And breaks in it at last, and never knows
> To what great end he worked.

Ultimately, Shakespeare asserts, 'carnage shall have its day, / And little England over-lord the world – / Then comes the reign of Peace . . . ' (123, all quotations; ellipsis in original). Ben Jonson, who serves as a clear, unsentimental voice of realism in the play, observes simply, partly completing Shakespeare's own sentence for him: ' . . . And Englishmen / Will turn the charnel-houses into shops'. He then asks: 'How know you we shall war to peace at last?' (124;

ellipsis in original), thus puncturing Shakespeare's positive reimagining of the imperial quest.

The second stranger to visit the house reveals himself as an Irishman – a disguised Jesuit priest passing through Stratford en route from Spain to Ireland. Defending the English project in Ireland to the Jesuit, Shakespeare invokes the authority of Edmund Spenser, putting his faith in the poet's judgement of the Irish: 'Spenser said Irishmen were less than human – / And Spenser was a man to be believed' (142). At this point, the Jesuit reveals that he is himself a member of the Desmond family, banished in childhood from the very lands in Munster that were granted to Spenser as a settler:

> The first thing I recall
> From out the dread vault of my memory
> Is the red sky above my father's house,
> Kindled to flame by gentle Spenser's torch.
> My father perished 'neath the gentle swords
> Of Spenser's servitors. Gentle, I call those swords,
> For they were gentler than the men who held them.
> My mother's shrieks were ringing in my ears.

This is, the Jesuit observes, 'The note your gentle Spenser tuned for us' (146). The exile's tale has the effect of bringing Shakespeare to the realization, as it were, that 'there is no document of civilization that is not at the same time a document of barbarism'. It is, therefore, not just his easy faith in the imperial project that has been undermined by this point, but also his faith in the cultural superstructure that has been built upon such foundations. Like Yeats, O'Riordan foregrounds the cost of the religious, economic and political innovations which Dowden sees as being the engines of Renaissance culture – and of Shakespeare's work in particular.

As the play draws to a close, Shakespeare takes the ready money that he had thought 'would go far / To pay my patent' and hands it over to the Jesuit, to be disbursed as he sees fit. In a neat twist,

---

48 Conal O'Riordan (Norreys Connell), *Shakespeare's End and Other Irish Plays* (London, 1912), p. 100. Further references included parenthetically in the body of the text. My thanks to Raphaël Ingelbien for drawing my attention to this text.

after the Jesuit has left, the mariner rouses himself and indicates that he will set out to rob and kill the priest. When Shakespeare threatens to expose him, the mariner points out that he is himself much more vulnerable to exposure, it being a crime to harbour a Catholic clergyman. Shakespeare accuses him of being a murderer, but the mariner replies: 'I am an Empire-builder, by your leave' (155). So the play offers no easy conclusion, no simple conversion narrative affording Shakespeare redemption through rerouting his commercial gain to support for the displaced Irish. At the very close of the play Shakespeare looks back on his life and observes:

> God put good tools into my hand to make
> A world, and I have made a coat of arms
> And a trim house at Stratford. Ay, my friends,
> God chose me for His angel, but I chose
> Rather to be an English gentleman
> Who hopes, an he live long, to be a knight. (164)

Shakespeare's life is thus collapsed back into its empty formal ambitions at the end.

O'Riordan's Shakespeare is thus not unlike Dowden's in his close investment in worldly success and its visible trappings and honours. And, like Dowden's Shakespeare, O'Riordan's has been driven by an uncomplicated embracing of the political, social and economic culture of his times. For Harris, Shakespeare reaches a point of political epiphany at an early stage in his career, thereafter rejecting English nationalism and ultimately finding his way to an expression of anti-imperialist disgust in *The Tempest*. O'Riordan's Shakespeare, by contrast, comes to these positions virtually as death-bed realisations: the whole structure of his belief system is radically interrogated in the hours before his death, his faith shaken through being brought in contact with the realities of the imperial project in Ireland and further afield.

Just a decade after O'Riordan's play was published Irish nationalists achieved their ultimate goal – or, at least, a version of it – when independence was secured for the greater part of the island. Post-independence, in 1925, a new kind of Shakespearian appropriation was attempted in Ireland, when Cahill and Company, a Dublin

publisher, issued the volume *An brón-chluiche Macbeit* 'do scríodh William Shakespeare. Aistrighthe go Gaedhilge' – which is to say *The Tragedy of Macbeth* 'written by William Shakespeare. Translated into Irish'. The translator was J. L. O'Sullivan (S. Ladhrás ua Súilleabháin), who noted in his Preface (written in English) that the value of making classic literature available in translation had long been recognized by the 'great continental nations'.[49] The importance of doing the same in an Irish context 'cannot', he says, 'be over-estimated'. 'In a little while, it is our hope', he writes, that Ireland will be

Irish-speaking, Irish-reading. We have at the moment, in the desks of our National Schools, the boys and girls who will be the future writers of a new and vigorous school of modern Irish literature, and who will soon be the leaders of Irish thought. The avenue along which they will guide [the] literature which they will create must be determined to a great extent by the sources of information and cultural development which are available for them in the national language . . . Is it not a duty to present to them, in translations from the ancient, mediæval and modern classics, sources of inspiration which . . . cannot fail to be of value towards the attainment of that end which the whole nation has in view?[50]

O'Sullivan's is a hopeful and a culturally generous vision. He imagines the Irish language revived to the point where it will become the dominant tongue of the newly independent state. His hope is that the country will, in time, produce a revivified culture and literature in the revived language. But, for this to happen, he believes that the writers of the next generation need models to serve as inspiration and so he proposes that a programme be initiated to make it possible for them to read classic texts drawn into the Irish language from other cultures, including the English tradition and, specifically, the work of the English national poet.

In the event, O'Sullivan's open, incorporative vision was not the one that prevailed in Ireland in the wake of independence. The project to revive

---

49 S. Ladhrás Ua Súilleabháin, ed. and trans., *An brón-chluiche Macbeit* (Dublin, 1925), p. 3.
50 Súilleabháin, *Macbeit*, pp. 3–4.

Irish as the primary language of the state failed, yet successive governments persisted in making the language a compulsory element in the educational system, leading ultimately to resentment and to reconfirmed failure. O'Sullivan's model of embracing other literatures as a way of nurturing a nascent native culture was also largely rejected. By 1929 the Irish state had initiated a censorship regime which would see 1200 books and some 140 periodicals banned in its first decade of operation alone.[51]

I'd like to conclude by considering the first biographically driven text about Shakespeare produced by an Irish writer in the wake of independence, just at the point when the process of narrowing the national cultural field was taking hold. The text in question is a short play by George Moore, entitled *The Making of an Immortal*, performed and published in 1927. Moore came from landowning stock in Co. Mayo and lived for a spell in Paris, studying painting, before moving to London in 1879 and becoming a successful novelist. He returned to Ireland in 1901, inspired by the cultural nationalist programme of the literary revival. An eccentric figure, Moore often took delight in taking up positions which ran against the grain of those adopted by his contemporaries.[52]

The Making of an Immortal has an Irish context in that it is set in October 1599, just weeks after the Earl of Essex had returned from his controversial campaign in Ireland. Essex's unauthorized breaking in upon the queen in her bedchamber is remembered in the play and the Essex faction's later commissioning of the Globe company to stage a performance of *Richard II* is creatively anticipated, as it is reported that the play 'has been given in the streets within the last two months' – much to the annoyance of the queen, who sees the street performances as designed to stoke up a groundswell of political support for Essex. Elizabeth demands that *Richard II* be staged for her personally so that she can hear the text for herself, and she also requires that the author be brought before her, suspecting, in fact, that Essex has 'had a hand in [the] play, and . . . a traitor's intent in the writing of it'.[53]

Among the principal characters in Moore's play are Ben Jonson and Francis Bacon. Bacon is in a state of high anxiety about the authorship issue as, for the purpose of his play, Moore affects the anti-Stratfordian position, presenting Bacon as the author of *Richard II* and of the other plays in the Shakespeare canon. To reveal himself as the playwright would compromise Bacon's position, politically, not least because, as he explains to Jonson, the play has in fact entered into wide circulation precisely as a result of his close affiliations with Essex ('Essex', he reveals, 'knows all my writings; we were as brothers; his letters were written by me and my advice was sought on all matters' (35)). So someone must be found who will stand in as a 'front' for Bacon as the author of *Richard II*. Ideally, this person should be a simple country soul, a political *naïf* who might convincingly be presented as having written of medieval monarchical depositions in all innocence, and – specifically – with no contemporary political intent. Enter, at this point, an actor from the Globe company: 'We would have a word with thee, Master Shakespeare', says Jonson.

Shakespeare initially resists the idea that he should be put forward as the author of *Richard II* (and of other plays from the canon), fearing that he 'shall be in the stocks to-morrow' (48) if he agrees. Jonson and Bacon set to work on him, and it is specifically to his commercialist instincts that they appeal. Once the queen's political suspicions are dispelled, Jonson assures him, she 'will reward thy poetry with a purse of gold . . . with enough

---

[51] See Donal Ó Drisceoil, 'A Dark Chapter: Censorship and the Irish Writer', in *The Oxford History of the Irish Book*, ed. Clare Hutton and Patrick Walsh, vol. 5 (Oxford, 2011), esp. p. 291.

[52] Yeats, with whom Moore had a rather fraught relationship, observed of him that 'When logic is master and his personality is for the moment quiet, he has intellectual honesty and courage. These impersonal moods alternate with orgies of personal vanity during which he sees all the closed doors of the world and bangs them with his fist and shrieks at the windows' (W. B. Yeats, *Memoirs*, transcribed and ed. Denis Donoghue (London, 1972), p. 270).

[53] George Moore, *The Making of an Immortal: A Play in One Act* (New York, 1927), p. 33 (both quotes). Further references included parenthetically in the text. My thanks to Willy Maley, who first mentioned this text to me.

pieces in it to purchase many houses in Stratford, and thou hast a fair liking for house property' (49–50). Jonson knows his man in offering this line of inducement, as, in Moore's version of him, Shakespeare's primary and overriding interest is in money-making and investment. 'I left the country when I was a raw lad', he says,

and would entrust no money of mine to ploughing and harrowing. Put money in houses... They are safer far than crops; crops rot in the fields and cattle die, but your houses stand firm. And if the theatre... yields me what I look for, I will purchase some more houses and end my days peaceably, using belike the good sense for which I am reputed... down in Stratford.   (42–3)

After some persuasion, Shakespeare eventually agrees to be presented to the queen as the 'seeming simple-minded yokel from Stratford' who has written *Richard II* in all political innocence. She duly rewards him – and demands of him that he write a play showing Falstaff in love. The request initially panics Shakespeare, until Bacon and Jonson assure him that they will write the play for him.

Moore's short drama is, in truth, hardly more than an elaborated *jeu d'esprit*. But it is nevertheless useful to think of it as a further link in the chain of Irish biographical imaginings of Shakespeare being traced here. Dowden, as we have seen, produced a Victorianist Shakespeare, celebrated as a materially minded pragmatist. Yeats, as a consequence, accused Dowden of having 'turned Shakespeare into a British Benthamite'.[54] Yeats's own Shakespeare, so far from being thrustingly modern, is instead a romanticized belated medieval poet – and this medievalized positioning has the effect of aligning Shakespeare with a central strand of Irish cultural nationalism. Harris also rejects Dowden's Shakespeare, offering a poet who is a spendthrift, who despises his English fellow countrymen and disdains their imperialist ambitions. O'Riordan provides a Shakespeare initially obsessed with social status, but thrown in doubt at the last as he is faced with the consequences of the early modern British imperial project. What Moore offers, tongue-in-cheek, is, we can say, effectively a parodic return to the commercialist Shakespeare of Dowden, with

the new twist that now materialism trumps everything else and his Shakespeare has not even written the plays.

Throughout these various incarnations, the shifting narrative of Shakespeare's life maps also shifting narratives of Irish politics. James Shapiro has said of Malone's construction of Shakespeare that it 'introduced [a] centrepiece of modern Shakespearean biography: the tendency to confuse the biographical with the autobiographical, as writers projected onto a largely blank Shakespearean slate their own personalities and preoccupations'.[55] This certainly seems true of the writers considered here: Ingram's, Dowden's, Yeats's, Harris's and O'Riordan's Shakespeares look a lot like Ingram, Dowden, Yeats, Harris and O'Riordan, and the politics of these Shakespeares match the politics of their creators. Moore's Shakespeare is a rather different kind of construction. Writing in the context of a tradition which has idealized Shakespeare in one way or another, and effectively made him Irish – or Anglo-Irish, in the case of Ingram and Dowden – Moore produces a jokingly de-idealized Shakespeare who is little more than a bathetic, hollow cypher. It is striking, I would suggest, that Moore evokes this de-idealized Shakespeare at precisely the time when the expansive hopeful vision of national culture shared by writers such as Yeats and Moore – and, indeed, as we have seen, by the Irish language activist J. L. O'Sullivan – was in the process of being rejected by those tasked with shaping the cultural climate of the newly independent Irish state. Moore's Shakespeare is thus, perhaps, in an Irish context, not for all time, but very much of a particular Irish age: an age of cultural introversion and obscurantism.

A scene in Joyce's *Ulysses* set in the National Library of Ireland features, famously, an extended discussion of Shakespeare. Frank Harris is invoked, as is Dowden, who is gently mocked: 'William Shakespeare and Company, limited. The people's William. For terms apply: E. Dowden, Highfield

---

[54] W. B. Yeats, *Autobiographies* (London, 1980), p. 193.
[55] Shapiro, *Contested Will*, p. 48.

house'.[56] Coming in to the discussion late, Buck Mulligan pretends to struggle to recall the writer under discussion:

Buck Mulligan thought, puzzled:
– Shakespeare? he said. I seem to know the name.
A flying sunny smile rayed in his loose features.
– To be sure, he said, remembering brightly. The chap that writes like Synge.[57]

The humour here lies in the anachronism and in the incongruity of imagining Shakespeare as an imitator of one of the most linguistically distinctive of Irish writers (before Joyce himself, that is, of course). Mulligan re-imagines Shakespeare effectively as a product of the Irish literary revival – a member of the tribe of John Millington, we might say. But, as we have seen, Irish writers had in fact already been imagining and re-imagining Shakespeare for more than a century – ever since Malone first noticed that the reference to Essex's Irish campaign in *Henry V* could be used to date the play and, from that connection, began to work outwards, fashioning a flesh and blood Shakespeare from the words on the page.

---

[56] Joyce, *Ulysses*, p. 204. Highfield House was Dowden's address in Dublin.
[57] Joyce, *Ulysses*, p. 198.

SHAKESPEARE IN BLOCKADED BERLIN: THE 1948 'ELIZABETHAN FESTIVAL'

BETTINA BOECKER

I

In 1948, the Russians blocked land traffic between Berlin and the West German occupation zones. This act of overt hostility put a definite end to any remaining hopes of cooperation with the Soviets, and effected a number of major policy changes on the part of the Western Allies when attempting to meet the logistical and ideological challenges that resulted from the city's enforced isolation. The famous *Luftbrücke* (air bridge) kept Berlin connected to the rest of the country, while the Western Allies' cultural activities were intensified in order to strengthen its less tangible bonds with what was quickly becoming 'the West'. With the initiation of a war of ideologies that effectively ended only with the fall of the Berlin wall 51 years later, the British gave up their former reticence towards reeducation and launched 'Operation Trumpeter', a 'cultural offensive'[1] against the Russians designed to foster German enthusiasm for British art and culture. The Elizabethan Festival of 1948 marks both the beginning and the zenith of this campaign.

As latecomers to what became known as 'the battle for the German soul',[2] the British were at a distinct disadvantage. Until the blockade, British cultural politics had been marked by a certain restraint. A distaste for propaganda that dated from before the war was still relatively widespread and it was (rightly) suspected that Germans would be suspicious of anything that seemed remotely doctrinaire. Instead, the British relied on a concept that predated the Second World War, 'the

projection of Britain'[3]. This consisted of selecting and spreading the type of information which would prompt people to form a positive opinion about the United Kingdom – without any overt attempt at manipulation being made. (That the selection process itself could be seen as a form of manipulation was a fact not often acknowledged.) British efforts to engineer a new start in German cultural life were therefore much less intense than those of the Americans. A licensing system was in place, and there were more or less continuous attempts to promote British culture (including a list of especially 'apt' plays and novels[4]), but otherwise, it was assumed that the Germans would learn from the British example, and that the right people, given the necessary authority, would

---

[1] Public Record Office (PRO), FO 1012/166: F. G. A. Wint to Brigadier E. R. Benson, 21 July 1948.

[2] The phrase seems to go back to General Sir Brian Robertson, cf. Cyril Buffet, 'Ganz Berlin ist eine Bühne: die Kulturpolitischen Vorstellungen des Vereinigten Königreichs', in *Die vier Besatzungsmächte und die Kultur in Berlin 1945–1949*, ed. Hans Martin Hinz et al. (Leipzig, 1999), p. 191; and PRO, FO 371/70 587 (letter from Robertson to Bevin, 29 April 1948). However, the German equivalent of this expression ('der Kampf um die deutsche Seele') was in fact a catchphrase of the culture wars of the Weimar Republic and frequently deployed by Nazi ideologists.

[3] Cf. Philip M. Taylor, *The Projection of Britain. British Overseas Publicity and Propaganda 1919–1939* (Cambridge, 1981).

[4] A list of the novels selected can be found in Gabriele Clemens, *Britische Kulturpolitik in Deutschland 1945–1949: Literatur, Film, Musik und Theater*, Historische Mitteilungen, Beiheft 24 (Stuttgart, 1997), p. 157; a list of the plays licensed for performance in Germany is on pp. 194f.

eventually fund – and sustain – the right kinds of institution.[5]

Unlike the Americans, the British hence made virtually no attempt to reach people on all levels of the social spectrum but tended to rely on potential leaders, many of whom were brought to Wilton Park training camp to be prepared for their future tasks. Generally speaking, British respect for German culture was high and, despite the Nazi atrocities, many officials were extremely uncomfortable with the idea of 'teaching' Germans about the fine arts. Given the events of the previous twelve years, it is surprising with how little sense of superiority many British officials approached their task in the years after 1945. This, however, was entirely in line with the overall picture of British cultural politics in post-war Germany, described by the most comprehensive study to date as 'compensatory' in nature.[6] Unlike the Americans, the British had clearly passed the peak of their power, a fact of which they were painfully aware and which they attempted to de-emphasize in the projection of Britain aimed at German audiences. Britain was to be presented as a modern, progressive country, ready to face the challenges of the future.[7] This directive is reflected, amongst other things, in the recommendations of the Book Selection Committee, which focus almost exclusively on contemporary and near-contemporary writers, while Shakespeare and other classics are conspicuously absent.

Right from the end of the war though, this progressive vision of Britain had coexisted with a more backward-looking strain – witness e.g. the 'nostalgic ruralism'[8] of the Shakespeare feature broadcast by the BBC in June 1945. It is perhaps no exaggeration to say that the British had never been quite comfortable with the progressivism of their reeducation efforts; in any case, they readily abandoned it when faced with the increased political pressure brought on by the blockade. Britain entered the theatre of nations[9] with a firm focus on the past, though it has to be said that this was due to practical constraints at least as much as to ideological considerations. Initial plans to bring in the BBC Symphony Orchestra and Sadler's Wells Ballet failed,[10] which left the Elizabethan Festival the only

major event the British were actually able to bring to pass. This would have been impossible without massive support from the University of Cambridge, which (for reasons to be discussed below) took a central role in staging the biggest and most lavish event organized by the British during the entire blockade.[11] Two student societies provided the backbone of the festival: the Marlowe Society played Shakespeare's *Measure for Measure* and Webster's *The White Devil*, and the Madrigal Society gave two concerts. Lectures on Elizabethan literature were given by H. B. Charlton, Noel Annan and George 'Dadie' Rylands, the Marlowe's charismatic director. Annan and Rylands also provided essays for the special edition of the British-licensed newspaper *Die Welt* published on occasion of the festival, as did Donald Beves.[12] Annan, Rylands and Beves were all at King's College at the time. Events grouped around the offerings of this network of Cambridge friends and colleagues included poetry readings by Robert Speaight, an exhibition on Shakespeare and the English stage, a garden party

---

[5] This was the express opinion of Robert Birley, the educational advisor to the Control Commission. See Anthony Glees, 'Britische Kulturpolitik in Deutschland in der unmittelbaren Nachkriegszeit', in *Die ungleichen Partner: Deutsch-Britische Beziehungen im 19. und 20. Jahrhundert*, ed. Wolfgang J. Mommsen (Stuttgart, 1999), p. 230.

[6] Gabriele Clemens, speaks of 'Machtersatzpolitik' (literally, a policy that attempts to compensate for a lack of power). Clemens, *Britische Kulturpolitik in Deutschland*, p. 16.

[7] Clemens, *Britische Kulturpolitik in Deutschland*, p. 55.

[8] For an excellent analysis of this feature (which was broadcast as 'England – die unbekannte Insel'), see Andreas Höfele, 'Reeducating Germany: BBC Shakespeare 1945', in *Shakespeare and European Politics*, ed. Dirk Delabastita, Jozef De Vos and Paul Franssen (Newark, 2008), pp. 255–77; p. 264.

[9] I borrow the term 'theatre of nations' from Bernard Genton's 'Berlin als Theater der Nationen. Ein Versuch, die kulturpolitischen Positionen der Alliierten zu vergleichen', in *Die vier Besatzungsmächte und die Kultur in Berlin 1945–1949*, ed. Hans Martin Hinz et al. (Leipzig, 1999), p. 29.

[10] Buffet, 'Ganz Berlin ist eine Bühne', pp. 199 and 201.

[11] Buffet, 'Ganz Berlin ist eine Bühne', p. 202.

[12] H. B. Charlton was the Clark lecturer at Trinity College in 1946–47. Annan also played Monticelso in *The White Devil*, alongside his future wife Gabriele Ullstein as Zanche. Rylands played Angelo in *Measure for Measure*, while Beves played Flamineo and directed *The White Devil*.

complete with Yeomen of the Guard, and more lectures, among them one by Robert Birley, the Educational Advisor for Germany and later headmaster of Eton College, and one by a token American, E. T. Clarke.[13]

That the original idea for the festival came from Ernest Bevin,[14] the foreign secretary, certainly helped justify the event's obvious failure to conform to established guidelines about the projection of Britain. The decision to invite the Cambridge societies was taken in a meeting held in York House in Berlin in May 1948, though the relevant document also lists the Oxford University Dramatic Society as a possible invitee. There were obviously strong links between Oxbridge on the one hand and the Control Commission for Germany (CCG) on the other, not only in the person of Birley, a Balliol man, but also, and perhaps even more pertinently, in the person of Noel Annan, who had served on the Commission until his return to King's in 1946. Given these connections, it is perhaps not surprising that the two productions shown in Berlin were not special commissions for the festival but happened to be in the Marlowe repertoire at the time (*Devil* had premiered in Cambridge in 1937, *Measure* in 1941). A member of the educational division, Elizabeth Wyndham (née Betty Seymour),[15] travelled to Cambridge to see the Marlowe playing, but more in order to gauge its requirements than to exert any influence on the choice of plays, which was left to Rylands.[16] Given that the actors (as well as the singers and the lecturers) received nothing for their efforts apart from travel, accommodation and food, this was only fair in such an overtly ideological undertaking, albeit perhaps somewhat unusual.

Wyndham, who later worked for MI6, is a particularly fascinating figure in this network of old boy and establishment connections. In the run-up to the festival, the Educational Division of CCG specifically requested her from the Political Division (where she was originally stationed) as a kind of go-between between Britain and Berlin. Her task was to coordinate the logistics of the festival on the British side. The rationale for this ran as follows: 'Miss Wyndham . . . knows extremely well the organizers at Cambridge' and is 'also rather an expert on Elizabethan drama and music'.[17] Despite her (alleged?) familiarity with the organizers, Wyndham did not correspond directly with either Noel Annan, G. H. W. Rylands or Boris Ord, the conductor of the Madrigal Society.[18] Intriguingly, however, her itinerary in Britain includes a meeting with Anthony Blunt, the most senior of the Cambridge Five and then director of the Courtauld Institute of Art, 'especially for miniatures'.[19] Like him, Wyndham had worked at Bletchley Park during the war. In many respects, and with the necessary breadth of imagination, the Elizabethan Festival could profitably be turned into an – albeit somewhat eccentric – spy novel, in which the notorious connection between the Cambridge Five and the Cambridge Apostles, the fact that both Annan and Rylands were known Apostles, and *The Times'* 1977 denunciation of Donald Beves as the missing 'fifth man' (which it subsequently had to

---

[13] Initial planning for the Shakespearian lecture series envisioned the presence of experts from all four Allies. The Russians, it seems, were unable (or unwilling) to name a speaker. The existing documents make no mention of the French – the attempt at appeasement by the Bard seems to have been discarded when it became clear that the Russians wouldn't join in. On the various nations' uses of Shakespeare *during* the War, see Irena R. Makaryk and Marissa McHugh, eds., *Shakespeare and the Second World War: Memory, Culture, Identity* (Toronto, 2012). On Shakespeare in Berlin during the *First* World War, see Ton Hoenselaars' account of Ruhleben camp: 'In Exile with Shakespeare: British Civilian Internee Theatre at Ruhleben Camp, 1914–18', *Shakespeare in Southern Africa*, 23 (2011), 1–10.

[14] Buffet, 'Ganz Berlin ist eine Bühne', p. 198.

[15] Information on Elizabeth Wyndham is taken from her obituary in *The Times*, 21 June 2008 (available online at https://groups.google.com/forum/#!topic/alt.obituaries/6od7VsnmO6o, accessed 25 September 2013). See also www.specialforcesroh.com/gallery.php?do=view-image&id=7338&gal=gallery.

[16] 'Vom College zur Bühne: Interview mit Gillian Webb', in *Die Welt*, special issue (September 1948), p. 11.

[17] PRO, FO 1012/166: F. G. A. Wint to Brigadier E. R. Benson, 21 July 1948.

[18] The correspondence of Donald Beves is not in the Cambridge archives.

[19] PRO, FO 1012/166: 'People to see in London'.

retract) would somehow fall into a coherent narrative. I would certainly very much like to write that novel.

Such speculations aside, the fact that the Cambridge amateurs[20] came so much cheaper than a professional company would have done certainly was a decisive factor in their recruitment. But at the same time, they were particularly apt representatives of the conservative version of Englishness that the authorities had returned to in staging the Elizabethan festival. Not only was Oxbridge an embodiment of the traditionalism that had marked English identity ever since the mid-nineteenth century,[21] to many, it was also part of the 'country life' that the nation had long idealized. After the war, the old universities – their rather urban location notwithstanding – seemed the last bastions of a genuinely rural England, strongholds of a 'pastoral dream'[22] from which the nation was about to wake up for good.

While the festival line-up was thoroughly in keeping with traditional versions of Englishness, and with the elitist strain characteristic of English re-education efforts, it seems rather naive when viewed as a serious attempt to keep up with the Russians. Still, there is a rationale behind it. In Britain, the war had widely been perceived as a clash between the old world as embodied by England and the new world as embodied by Germany, between 'humane . . . old-fashionedness' and 'industrial[ism] . . . run amok'.[23] Obviously, the old world had won. It was therefore not entirely unreasonable to expect it to conquer yet another enemy, and the organizers definitely took their festival seriously: '[H]aving the approval of the Foreign Office, [the festival] is inaccurately described as "a Berlin affair". It is a definite cultural/propaganda move and should be treated accordingly.'[24] The event was to receive 'maximum publicity'.[25] Posters were the main medium of advertisement, with officials being particularly keen on a sufficient number going up in the Soviet sector, followed by newspaper and radio advertisements and a feature in *Welt im Film*, the British newsreel. The newspaper *Die Welt* brought out the special issue already mentioned, with a

reproduction of the Ermine Portrait of Elizabeth I as its title page.

II

Die Welt's choice is indicative of the festival's intentions. Although the Ermine portrait depicts Elizabeth approaching the height of her power, it avoids the potentially triumphal associations of, for instance, the Armada portrait, a strategy that continues into the text that opens the issue, an excerpt from Lytton Strachey's *Elizabeth and Essex*. While Strachey generally presents the Elizabethan age as colourful and exotic, his Elizabeth is a model of sobriety. And while he stresses her political achievements, he makes even more of her pacifism.[26] The contrast to the German and, perhaps even more significantly, the recent Russian aggression could not of course be greater. But

---

[20] On Shakespeare and amateur drama, see Michael Dobson, *Shakespeare and Amateur Performance: A Cultural History* (Cambridge, 2011).

[21] See e.g. Martin J. Wiener, *English Culture and the Decline of the Industrial Spirit, 1850–1980* (Cambridge, 1981), David Gervais, *Literary Englands: Versions of 'Englishness' in Modern Writing* (Cambridge, 1994) and, for more recent developments, Simon Featherstone, *Englishness: Twentieth-Century Popular Culture and the Forming of English Identity* (Edinburgh, 2009).

[22] Wiener, *English Culture*, p. 77.

[23] Wiener, p. 77.

[24] PRO, FO 1012/166: G. E. Bell to G.C.C., British Troops Berlin, 3 August 1948.

[25] PRO, FO 1012/166: T. R. M. Creighton to Secretariat of Military Government, Berlin, 17 August 1948.

[26] 'Like no other great statesman in history, she was, not only by disposition but in practice, pacific. It was not that she was much disturbed by the cruelty of war – she was far from sentimental; she hated it for the best of all reasons – its wastefulness. Her thrift was spiritual as well as material, and the harvest that she gathered in was the great Age, to which, though its supreme glories were achieved under her successor, her name has been rightly given. For without her those particular fields could never have come to ripeness; they would have been trodden down by struggling hordes of nationalists and theologians. She kept the peace for thirty years – by dint, it is true, of one long succession of disgraceful collapses and unheard-of equivocations; but she kept it, and that was enough for Elizabeth' (p. 14n).

while *Die Welt* allows the 'ironic, civilised, self-deprecating voice of Bloomsbury'[27] to make itself heard, it is also careful not to make the period seem anaemic in any way. The same page also features a passage from Virginia Woolf's *Orlando* in which, even more than in Strachey, the Elizabethan age appears as an age of extremes, boasting a vitality of which subsequent periods, particularly the present, are found to be sadly lacking.[28] The half-drunk Nick Greene, a fictional contemporary of Shakespeare's, rants that the time for great literature is definitely over, and that if any age deserves the epithet 'great', it is certainly not the one that he lives in. But although Greene would seem to play the role of detractor, his vivid descriptions of tavern scenes with 'Kit' Marlowe and 'Bill' Shakespeare add to the mystique of the Elizabethan period that Woolf projects. In the English original, several pages separate the general characterization of the period from Greene's diatribes. The latter's inclusion in *Die Welt*'s translation shows how welcome such anecdotes were to a nation that sought to project a dynamic, vibrant image of itself. Ironically, though, the opposition that Woolf's narrator sets up – a dynamic, lively, virile past as opposed to a pale, listless present – would have been all too familiar to German readers from Nazi rhetoric, which (reversing Woolf) often contrasted a strong, vital, almost necessarily aggressive Germany under Hitler with the weakness and decadence of former ages, particularly of the Weimar Republic.

In resurrecting this particularly usable part of their past, the British focused on the two most highly regarded branches of Elizabethan cultural production, drama and music. While the festival's construction of 'the Elizabethan' certainly seems eclectic, the inclusion of music was *de rigueur*, not so much because of the availability of a suitable Cambridge society (as one might suspect) but because the Russians were extremely active in this particular field. Only four days before the start of the Elizabethan Festival, on 18 August, the Red Army's Alexandrow Ensemble had played to an audience of 20,000 on the Gendarmenmarkt.[29] Some 150 singers, 75 musicians and 50 dancers had presented a programme that ranged from 'Kalinka'

and a 'Cantata to Stalin' to such German classics as 'Heideröslein' and 'Im tiefen Wiesengrunde'.[30] The temporal proximity of the two events invited comparison, and *Der Spiegel*, published in British-occupied Hamburg, remarked archly:

The difference between the Russians and the English was an object lesson in the psychology of nations. There, orgiastic fraternization, here, stiff politeness. There, 'Eja juchnem' alongside Schumann's 'Dreaming', here, a careful cultivating of culture and tradition, supported by the most discerning historical judgement. There, the appeal was to the masses, here, it is to the elites.[31]

As each individual ally's approach to music was perceived as a direct reflection of its overall policy and national character, the success or failure a given musical event had with the Germans could be construed as reflecting the nation's stance towards the Ally in question. The hint of disapproval discernible in *Der Spiegel*'s account of the Alexandrow

---

[27] Tim Cribb, *Bloomsbury and British Theatre: The Marlowe Story* (Cambridge, 2007), p. 88.

[28] 'Sunsets were redder and more intense; dawns were whiter and more auroral. Of our crepuscular half-lights and lingering twilights they knew nothing. The rain fell vehemently, or not at all. The sun blazed or there was darkness... The withered intricacies and ambiguities of our more gradual and doubtful age were unknown to them. Violence was all' (Virginia Woolf, *Orlando: A Biography*, ed. Max Bollinger (London, [1928] 2012), p. 16). Needless to say, *Die Welt* prints the passage in a German translation.

[29] FO 1580–352. The Russians had also requested the Olympic Stadium for a concert by Col. Alexandrowski's military choir on 22 August. The British declined, stating that the Stadium was already fully booked and they did not want to offend German promoters. When the Russians requested that the reservation be cancelled, the British did not comply. The relevant document notes that Alexandrowski's choir had been very successful in the Soviet zones; competition of this kind was not in the British interest.

[30] See Winfried Ranke *et al.*, eds., *Kultur, Pajoks und Care-Pakete: Eine Berliner Chronik 1945–1949* (Berlin, 1990), p. 239.

[31] 'Der Wechsel von den Russen zu den Briten war wie ein völkerpsychologischer Anschauungsunterricht. Dort rauschhafte Verbrüderung, hier steife Vornehmheit. Dort das Nebeneinander von 'Eja juchnem' bis Schumanns 'Träumerei', hier sorgsam bewahrende Kulturpflege, auf feinstes historisches Urteil gestützt. Dort Breiten-, hier Spitzenwirkung' (*Der Spiegel*, 4 September 1948, No. 36, p. 22).

Ensemble is certainly not apolitical and, in a similar manner, newspapers based in the Soviet Zone were generally rather unimpressed with the performances of the Madrigal Society. *Neues Deutschland* comments that the singing of this 'small' choir was in tune and well-rehearsed, but rather 'prudish' ('spröde') and 'sober' ('nüchtern') – all in all a rather 'modest' ('bescheiden') start for something that called itself a festival.[32] As regards sheer size, the select audience of the British could not stand up to the tens of thousands the Russians had attracted a few days earlier, a fact of which the latter were proudly aware. When the East Berlin-based *Tägliche Rundschau* points out that 'only a few hundred' ('jeweils nur wenige hundert Hörer') attended the Madrigal Society concerts, this brands the entire event as a failure.[33]

The musical part of the festival hence caused some anxiety. British respect for German achievements in the field was extremely high, and the attempt to (re-)educate Germans in the musical field was seen as bordering on the presumptuous. In addition, the British faced what they believed to be a German stereotype about Britain as a 'land without music'. When *Die Welt* titles its article on the English madrigal 'Land without Music' ('Das Land ohne Musik' – in heavily loaded quotation marks), the touchiness regarding this specific aspect of British cultural life is impossible to overlook:

During the Second World War, the cross-word puzzle in a German magazine asked its readers to name the 'land without music'. The solution was: England. This is a lapse both of taste and of judgement, rooted not only in the pathological spite instigated by war, but also in the prejudice, familiar to many, that denies the English people any deeper relationship with music.[34]

But, the author, Hans Wyneken, continues, this is entirely wrong, though it has to be said that England's relation to the musical arts was generally more 'receptive'[35] in kind. In his talk during the Elizabethan Festival, Wyneken reports, the musicologist and viola da gamba virtuoso Robert Donington explained that many German musicians (Haydn, Weber, Mendelssohn and above all Beethoven – not to mention Händel, of course),

were made unusually welcome in London, sometimes even more than they were back home, and that the British, up to that day, were full of 'dankbare Bewunderung', grateful admiration, for the musical achievements of the German people.[36] A bare three years after the end of the war, such flattery is indicative of how hard the British tried to make friends with the former aggressor.

Reviews of the Madrigal Society concerts, the living proof of the British dedication to music, treat the ensemble as an epitome of Oxbridge culture, and hence an epitome of (traditional) Englishness.

---

[32] 'Die kleine Chorgemeinde sang diese Motetten und Madrigale recht sauber und gut durchgearbeitet. Der Stimmklang ist freilich, besonders bei den Sopranen, etwas spröde und nüchtern. Für 'Festspiele' war dieser Auftakt ziemlich bescheiden' (*Neues Deutschland*, 24 August 1948, No. 196, p. 3). It is significant that the article should mention the size of the choir. On the same page, in an article entitled '300 sang, played and danced', the newspaper reports on the Berliner Volkskunsttagung, the Berlin Festival of the Popular Arts. Though it doesn't elide the – apparently numerous – faults of the festival's amateur performances, the tone is much more lenient than when it comes to the Cambridge singers: 'Let us not forget that all these men and women, girls and boys who serve the people's art are part of the working people, and that it is the working people they sing and play for. They do this for their own enjoyment, but also want to give joy to others. For this we are grateful.' ('Wir wollen nicht vergessen, daß alle diese Männer und Frauen, Mädchen und Jungen, die dem Volkskunstwerk dienen, aus dem arbeitenden Volk kommen und für das arbeitende Volk spielen, singen und musizieren. Sie tun das aus eigener Freude, wollen aber auch Freude vermitteln. Dafür sind wir ihnen dankbar' (*Neues Deutschland*, 24 August 1948, No. 196, p. 3)).

[33] 'Ein solches Unternehmen wird sich im Gegensatz zur Kunst des Alexandrow-Ensembles immer nur an einen kleineren gesuchten Kreis von Zuhörern wenden, und so fanden sich auch jeweils nur [*sic*] wenige hundert Hörer ein, die willig und fähig waren, ihr musikalisches Bewusstsein umzustellen' (*Tägliche Rundschau*, 29 August 1948, No. 202, p. 4).

[34] 'Während des zweiten Weltkrieges wurden die Leser eines deutschen illustrierten Blattes aufgefordert, das 'Land ohne Musik' zu erraten. Die Lösung hieß: England. An dieser denksportlichen Entgleisung ist außer kriegspsychogener Gehässigkeit ein in vielen Hirnen eingewurzeltes Vorurteil schuld, daß dem englischen Volk jede tiefere Beziehung zur Tonkunst absprechen will' (Hans Wyneken, 'Das Land ohne Musik', in *Die Welt*, special issue, September 1948, p. 4).

[35] 'rezeptiv', see Wyneken, 'Das Land ohne Musik', p. 4.

[36] Wyneken, 'Das Land ohne Musik', p. 4.

Much is made of the society's role in the cultural life of Cambridge, particularly of the annual May Week concert, which *Die Welt* describes as a pastoral idyll:

The main activity of the society consists in singing in boats on the river near Cambridge on one of the May Week evenings. The lawns are lined with spectators, and the boats assemble under the beautiful old bridge near King's College. At dusk, the singers drift slowly down the river, singing John Wilbye's 'Draw on, sweet night', until they are out of earshot.[37]

In keeping with the sort of Englishness which the Madrigal Society represents, or is made to represent, the supposedly unbroken tradition that links the Cambridge singers to the musical life of Shakespeare's day and age receives heavy emphasis. For a country like Germany, where a major composer like Wagner had just become more or less unmentionable in polite society, this was certainly a state to be envied. The music itself, 'in its clarity and simplicity' one reviewer opined, 'was a true expression of the essence of Anglicanism [*sic*]'[38] – of the tradition that Anthony Easthope, in a book written more then fifty years later, labels 'empiricist'.[39] This tradition, particularly its preference of simplicity and common sense over complexity and exuberance provided a stark contrast to the Nazi predilection for bombast – but also, and more pertinently, to Russian tastes, which, much to the chagrin of the British, tended to be more popular with the citizens of Berlin.

With their polite aversion to propaganda and their focus on German elites, the British clearly could not compete with the Russians on Russian terms, least of all when it came to music. They did, however, attempt to make the best of what they already had. In a deft sleight of hand, the special edition of *Die Welt* published for the Elizabethan Festival declares Shakespeare, the central figure of the event, not just a musician of sorts, but a musician first and foremost, thereby at least doubling the perceived musical capital of Britain. The Bard, *Die Welt* points out,

is, among other things, a significant figure in the history of English music, for his work is brimming, and imbued, not only with songs and enchanting verbal music, but also with a musical soul – that 'music in himself' whose presence or lack he took as indicative of a person's ethical stature.[40]

Having naturalized the dramatist as one of their own, it would seem that Germans now cannot but naturalize the musician as well, so that, in an extremely well-worn cliché, music, whether English or German in origin, turns out to be an ideal bridge not only between the two ex-enemies, but uniting 'all the peoples of the world'.[41]

III

A similar 'bridge' was provided by Shakespearian drama, if not necessarily for 'all the peoples of the world', then certainly between Britain and Germany: the Bard was the one British cultural export that Germans were virtually guaranteed to appreciate. The problem was that while they did venerate Shakespeare, they were not used to venerating him in his capacity as a Briton. Even before the Nazis had seized power, respected intellectuals like Gerhart Hauptmann had declared Shakespeare

---

[37] 'Die Haupttätigkeit der Gesellschaft besteht darin, zum Semesterschluß abends in Booten auf dem Fluß bei Cambridge zu singen. Die Rasenflächen an den Ufern des Flusses sind von den Zuschauern gesäumt, und die Boote nehmen unter der schönen alten Brücke beim King's College Aufstellung. Bei Dunkelwerden treiben die Sänger unter dem Gesang von John Wilbye's 'Komm, süße Nacht' langsam den Fluß hinunter, bis sie außer Hörweite sind' (*Die Welt*, special issue, September 1948, p. 4).

[38] '[...] war in ihrer Klarheit und Schlichtheit ein echtes Abbild anglikanischen Wesens' (*Der Sozialdemokrat*, 25 August 1948, No. 198/3, p. 3).

[39] Anthony Easthope, *Englishness and National Culture* (London and New York, 1999). See also Höfele, 'Reeducating Germany', p. 267–8.

[40] 'Shakespeare verkörpert [...] u.a. auch ein Stück englische Musikgeschichte, denn sein Werk ist bis zum Rande erfüllt und durchtränkt nicht nur von Liedern und hinreißender Wortmusik, sondern vor allem von klingender Seele – jener "music in himself", deren Besitz oder Nichtbesitz er zum ethischen Wertmesser des Menschen nahm' (Wyneken, 'Das Land ohne Musik', p. 4).

[41] 'allen Völkern der Welt' (Wyneken, 'Das Land ohne Musik', p. 4).

an honorary German.[42] After 1933 (and some-times even before that), the tone became much more aggressive, and German claims to Shake-speare even turned exclusive. Because of its inca-pacity to properly appreciate Shakespeare and the nation's sheer 'neglect' of its foremost poet, Nazi scholars argued, Britain had forfeited her 'rights' to the Bard. Shakespeare had therefore passed into German trusteeship ('Treuhändertum'), with the Third Reich as his 'foster nation' ('Pflegenation').[43]

Against this backdrop, the Elizabethan Festival necessarily pursued a double agenda, having both to cater to the great German love of Shakespeare and to disabuse Germans of what had long been one of the cornerstones of that admiration, Shake-speare's alleged Germanness. Although the existing documents say little to nothing about the reason-ing behind the idea of an *Elizabethan* festival, it is not difficult to see how such an event, rather than a mere *Shakespeare* festival, would have served this double purpose. The festival gave the Ger-mans something they already appreciated, but a Shakespeare embedded in the larger cultural con-text of his time – and particularly of his *place* – is an emphatically *English* writer. As Andreas Höfele has shown, this also holds true for the Shakespeare of the 1945 BBC radio feature mentioned above.[44] When considering the often rather impromptu nature of British cultural politics in Germany in the years after 1945, the consistency with which these two projects handle Shakespeare is remarkable.

The Marlowe Society's participation in the fes-tival was particularly conducive to the Bard's re-Anglicization. Their focus on text and elocution, paired with a tradition of playing on a bare stage, made the Marlowe an ideal travelling company, and ideally suited to playing in what was still the wreck-age of Berlin. From an ideological angle, their min-imalist approach, like the music performed by the Madrigal Society, fitted well with the simplicity and clarity which the British wished to present as typical of their nation. Most importantly, however, the Marlowe acted Shakespeare (and Webster) in the original English, which caused no small stir in 1948 Berlin. Shakespeare, for the majority of Berliners, as for the majority of Germans at the

time, spoke Schlegel-Tieck, so much so that, as one newspaper remarked, 'one almost cringed at hearing him in a "foreign" language'.[45] But, the respected critic Hilde Spiel pointed out in a review reprinted in the special edition of *Die Welt*,

To those who speak English, this production in the Giel-gud tradition transmits the entire range, greatness and glory of the English original, of which even the Tieck translation gives merely a faint glimmer.[46]

The newly acknowledged power of Shakespeare's language legitimizes the Marlowe's characteris-tically reduced acting style, which many in the audience, after years of Nazi pathos, apparently had difficulty relating to. But once one acknowledged that 'in the English language, the word is always already a gesture', one realized that 'the word actu-ally doesn't need any mimic supplement, as long

---

42 'There is no people in the world, not excluding the English, that has as much of a right to Shakespeare as the Germans have. Shakespeare's characters are a part of our world, his soul has merged with ours: and even though he was born and buried in England, it is Germany where he truly lives.' ('Es gibt kein Volk, auch das englische nicht, das sich ein Anrecht wie das deutsche auf Shakespeare erworben hätte. Shakespeares Gestalten sind ein Teil unserer Welt, seine Seele ist eins mit unserer geworden: und wenn er in England geboren und begraben ist, so ist Deutschland das Land, wo er wahrhaft lebt') (Gerhard Hauptmann, 'Deutschland und Shakespeare', in *Die Kunst des Dramas: Über Schauspiel und Theater*, ed. Martin Machatzke (Berlin, [1915] 1963), p. 56).

43 Quotations from Herbert A. Frenzel, 'Ist Shakespeare ein Problem?', in *Wille und Macht: Führerorgan der nationalsozial-istischen Jugend*, 8 (1940), pp. 2–3; p. 2.

44 'What, then, were British reeducators to do with an English author – *the* English author – who had become Germany's 'third classic' and whom Germans of all kinds and persua-sions – including Nazi ideologists – had claimed as a kindred spirit? The answer was to re-Anglicize him' (Höfele, 'Re-educating Germany', p. 260).

45 '... daß man sich fast ein wenig innerlich dagegen verwahrt, ihn in einer 'fremden' Sprache zu vernehmen' (*Berliner Zeitung* 27 August 1948, No. 199, p. 3).

46 '[Durch] diese Aufführung in der Gielgud-Tradition [wird] dem Sprachkundigen die ganze Spannweite, Größe und Herrlichkeit des englischen Originals vermittelt [...], von der selbst eine Tiecksche Übersetzung nur einen Schim-mer zu geben vermag' (Hilde Spiel, 'Die Aufführung im Renaissance-Theater', in *Die Welt*, special issue (September 1948), p. 9).

as it really carries full weight'.[47] Not only is the Marlowe hence 'right' in its approach to Shakespeare, it turns out that the English more generally have been right about Shakespeare all along. As one newspaper declares with equal amounts of surprise and political correctness, 'Shakespeare war Engländer',[48] Shakespeare was English.

Performing in English made an already elitist event even more exclusive. The plays chosen made no attempt to cater to the 'theatre-hungry'[49] masses of post-war Berlin; the appeal was clearly to an audience already versed in, and sympathetic to, British culture. Nevertheless, several newspapers point out that parts of the audience were unable to follow the language – a problem which had obviously been anticipated as the programmes included German summaries of the plots. Given that the festival was the kick-off event (as well as, it turned out, the major event) of 'Operation Trumpeter', this was not without irony, a fact which was lost neither on the national nor the international press, nor on the organizers themselves. At the opening ceremony, General Benson, 'with a measuring glance at the keynote speaker, who came in around 70 kilograms', joked that he was only too aware that each performer flown into Berlin had taken up space which could otherwise have been used for a sack of coal or flour.[50] The very idea of cultural warfare generated no small amount of sardonic comment. The *Sunday Dispatch* sneered:

The Russians attacked, using searchlights, balalaikas, trumpets, and harmonicas in close support. An audience of 2,500 Germans are believed to have been almost entirely captured. The British Cultural Forces counter-attack was opened by six British soldiers dressed as Beefeaters [photographs show twelve], who took up positions on the first-floor balcony armed with home-made halberds. The main fighting was borne by the crack troops of the Cambridge Madrigal Society, commanded by Boris Ord. Their Elizabethan songs are understood to have made some impression on 150 already cultured Germans. British casualties were two Beefeaters who fainted while on active duty outside Mr Birley's [the British Councillor's] bedroom. During the following days the British forces gained valuable ground with performances of *Measure for Measure* by the Marlowe Society.[51]

Judging from the reviews, Shakespeare's play was indeed a greater asset than *The White Devil*, which the *Dispatch*, rather surprisingly, does not mention – for accounts of German reactions to this offering would have considerably added to what the newspaper presents as the accidental comedy of the festival. Rather than moral outrage, the play's excessive violence provoked incomprehension and, probably even worse in the eyes of the organizers, laughter among the Berlin audience, surely not the reaction that they had hoped to elicit. Annan's essay in *Die Welt* dutifully stresses Webster's poetic strengths, but this was a quality not easily conveyed to spectators unfamiliar with the plot and, in many cases, with the English language as such. From a political point of view, the production was clearly a failure, a fact which the Soviets managed to exploit. The *Tägliche Rundschau*, published in the Russian sector, commented:

No guiding thought, no human truth, nay not even the merest hint of justice done... – borne by the staccato of expressionist verse, this evil grotesque may offer welcome inspiration to many a modern Western writer. But it seems a good sign to us that despite the excellent

---

[47] *Kurier*, 1 September 1948, No. 203, p. 3.

[48] *Berliner Zeitung*, 27 August 1948, No. 199, p. 3.

[49] For the theatre craze ('Bühnenhunger', literally: hunger for the stage) that swept Germany in the immediate post-war years, see Henning Rischbieter, 'Bühnenhunger', in *So viel Anfang war nie: Deutsche Städte 1945 bis 1949*, ed. Hermann Glaser, Lutz von Pufendorf and Michael Schöneich (Berlin, 1989), pp. 226–35. The repertoire of this period was dominated by (very) light entertainment, hence *Measure for Measure*, and particularly *The White Devil*, constitute something of an exception.

[50] '[...] mit einem abschätzenden Blick auf die 70 kg des ersten Festredners' (*Der Spiegel*, 4 September 1948, No. 36, p. 22). In his account of the festival in *Changing Enemies*, Noel Annan reports: 'The house managers and stage hands of the Renaissance Theater welcomed us as if we had been professionals, and made our get-in much easier than we had thought possible. Occasionally one of them would keel over from heat and hunger, for the Berliners were on minimal rations as stocks of coal and food were being built up, and no one knew at that time whether the city could hold out' (Noel Annan, *Changing Enemies: The Defeat and Regeneration of Germany* (New York and London, 1995), p. 238).

[51] Cribb, *Bloomsbury and British Theatre*, p. 88.

acting, despite the tasteful sumptuousness of the costumes and the scenery, the audience frequently expressed their lack of susceptibility to this grotesque horror in liberating laughter. We all know what ends are pursued by mobilizing the unconscious, the animal in all of us.[52]

The – albeit implicit – equation of Webster with the spirit of Nazism was not restricted to the Russian Zone. The reputed critic Peter de Mendelssohn did the same in *Die Welt*, where he diagnosed a basic familiarity between Renaissance Italy on the one hand and Renaissance England on the other: 'Vittoria [Corombona]'s breath is Webster's breath, no cultural interpreter was needed between their worlds. Astonishing, breathtakingly homogeneous cultural texture; the climates are identical, hearts and minds pulse in the same rhythm. Once upon a time, that was Europe.' From this European family Germany remained tragically excluded:

Between these synchronous worlds, however, now as then, stood Germany (where, already during the Renaissance, people produced little poetry and waged many wars). It is Germania's misfortune that the Renaissance more or less passed it by; then was the time to sweat out, from body and mind, everything Germany is now labouring away at, lagging three hundred years behind the times.[53]

As its involuntary bogeyman, Webster did much to turn the festival from an 'Elizabethan' into a predominantly Shakespearian event. Almost all of the lectures commissioned for the occasion focused on Shakespeare, and the Shakespeare play, *Measure for Measure*, was a much more unequivocal success than *The White Devil*. Newly popular on the post-war German stage for being 'so true to life' ('große Lebensnähe') and with 'the whole set of difficult problems'[54] ('tiefe Problematik') of its plot, the play spoke to the sensibilities of the Berlin audience in a way that Webster did not and could not have, mainly because his characters are so remarkably free from a feeling that was to become something of a leitmotif for German culture after the Second World War: guilt. By contrast, *Measure for Measure*'s intense preoccupation with sin, crime and appropriate forms of punishment lent the

play a timeliness which some perceived as 'almost uncanny'.[55] Whereas Nazi criticism had diligently avoided the figure of the corrupt ruler, preferring to focus on Isabella as an instance of a woman ready to die for her ideals,[56] Angelo now became newly relevant to – and newly likeable for – German audiences. His moral failures turned him into a kind of post-war Everyman, a quality which the Marlowe's Angelo, Dadie Rylands, seems to have played up:

---

52 'Kein leitender Gedanke, keine menschliche Wahrscheinlichkeit, ja, kaum eine dünne Andeutung waltender Gerechtigkeit... – getragen vom Stakkato expressionistischer Verskunst mag diese Groteske des Bösens manchem modernen Schriftsteller des Westens willkommene Anregung bieten... Es dünkt uns ein gutes Vorzeichen, daß das Publikum bei aller Vorzüglichkeit der Darstellung, bei aller gediegenen Pracht der Kostüme und Bühnenbilder seiner Unempfindlichkeit gegenüber den Grauenvoll-Grotesken öfters in befreiendem Lachen Ausdruck verlieh. Man weiß, welchen Kräften die Mobilisierung des triebhaft Unterbewußten dienen soll' (*Tägliche Rundschau*, 5 September 1948, No. 208, p. 4).

53 'Vittoria [Corombona]'s Atem war Websters Atem; es bedurfte keiner Kulturdolmetscher zwischen ihren Welten. Erstaunliches, atemberaubend einheitliches Gewebe; die Klimata sind identisch, Herz und Sinne pulsen im selben Takt. Das war einmal Europa. Zwischen den gleichatmenden Welten freilich lag damals wie heute Deutschland (wo auch zu jener Zeit wieder ein wenig Poesie gemacht ward und viel Krieg). Es ist Germaniens Unglück, daß die Renaissance gleichsam an ihm vorbeigerutscht ist; damals war die Zeit, all das herauszuschwitzen aus Körper und Geist, woran es heute, dreihundert Jahre hinter der Zeit herhumpelnd, herumlaboriert' (Peter de Mendelssohn, 'Die Aufführung der Marlowe-Gesellschaft', in *Die Welt*, special issue, September 1948, p. 11).

54 Wolfgang Stroedel, 'Theaterschau 1947–1950', in *Shakespeare-Jahrbuch*, 84/85 (1950), 229–36; p. 233.

55 Ernst Leopold Stahl, 'Shakespeare in Europa nach dem zweiten Weltkrieg', in *Shakespeare-Jahrbuch*, 82/83 (1948), 154–63; p. 156.

56 See e.g. Wolfgang Schmidt, 'Shakespeares Leben und der Sinn der Tragödien. Einige Leitgedanken', in *Die Neueren Sprachen*, 46 (1938), p. 341. See also Ernst Theodor Sehrt, *Vergebung und Gnade bei Shakespeare* (Stuttgart, 1952). The same emphasis on mercy and forgiveness runs through the BBC Shakespeare feature analysed by Andreas Höfele. The feature's speaker, Marius Goring, and Dadie Rylands knew each other, though the one letter from Goring in the Rylands archive dates from 1967. The network of personal connections behind British cultural politics in Germany after 1945 certainly deserves further investigation.

Rylands does not play an exceptional human being, as the German theatre likes to do with every single Shakespeare play, he plays Everyman: everyone behaves like that when faced with such a task, power is an eternal danger for us all.[57]

If the concept of universal human fallibility in the face of temptation was attractive to German audiences, the idea of mercy and forgiveness, however undeserved, was even more so. Echoing a trend in *Measure for Measure* criticism well-established since the 1930s,[58] the essays in *Die Welt* (by Noel Annan and Alec Macdonald) present the inadequacy of 'normal' jurisdiction as one of the play's main topics.[59] Reviews of the Marlowe production take up this thought with no small amount of enthusiasm, though its direct applicability to the German situation, in a manner typical for the immediate post-war years, is never made explicit. Nevertheless, spectators were aware of it, as some of them obviously were of the less advantageous ways in which both plays commented on the current situation of Germany. *Die Welt* remarks, rather ominously, that, 'naturally', there were people who objected to the two productions, and especially to the 'ethos of forgiveness' outlined in the lectures devoted to *Measure for Measure*, on the grounds that it was 'too political'.[60] It is not impossible that the newspaper is alluding to a Vansittartite faction among the audience; however, the subsequent remark that the objectors would certainly have benefited from 'even more politics' ('noch mehr Politisches') makes it very likely that they were in fact German. The article doesn't go into further detail but, as we have seen, both the atrocities of *The White Devil* and the figure of the corrupt ruler were read as references to the vanquished Nazi regime. The concept of forgiveness, so heavily stressed by the British, was a highly charged one in a society where few were as yet ready to acknowledge their individual guilt and where the concept of *Kollektivschuld* (collective guilt), so influential later on, was far from established. In the immediate post-war years, the German press, where it does indeed deal with the topic, vastly prefers the idea of a general derailing of the entire

Western World. Not all Germans necessarily saw themselves as being at the receiving end of British forgiveness.

IV

The Elizabethan festival of 1948, 'really a Shakespeare festival',[61] as one commentator remarks contentedly, is unthinkable without the idea of 'Shakespeare' as an essentially civic, rather than purely academic, phenomenon. In this initial and especially tense phase of the Cold War, the British expected to get considerable propagandistic mileage out of promoting the Bard and his times, the golden age of Elizabeth. Zany as this may have seemed to at least some contemporary observers, it is fully in keeping with the focus on German elites that had characterized British cultural politics ever since 1945. At the height of political crisis, however, the British turned backwards rather than moving forwards, giving up their previous dedication to modern British culture in favour of a more conservative version shaped by traditionalism, ruralism and common sense. This turn to tradition entailed a turn to Shakespeare, a kind of 'silver bullet' in the battle for the German soul. Not only did he epitomize the height of British cultural achievement, he also provided an approach to German benevolence

---

[57] 'Rylands spielt keinen Ausnahmemenschen, wie das deutsche Theater ihn in allen Shakespeareschen Dramen zu geben beliebt, sondern den Durchschnittsmenschen: so wird jeder bei solcher Aufgabe, die Macht ist unser aller ewige Gefahr' ('*Measure for Measure* im Renaissance-Theater', in *Tagesspiegel*, 26 August 1948, No. 198, p. 3).

[58] See e.g. M. C. Bradbrook, 'Authority, Truth, and Justice in Measure for Measure', in *The Review of English Studies*, 17 (1941), 385–99.

[59] Noel Annan, 'Eine humanistische Allegorie', in *Die Welt*, special issue (Sep. 1948), p. 7.
Alec Macdonald, 'Maß für Maß /Shakespeares Problemstück: Eine Kritische Betrachtung', in *Die Welt*, special issue (September 1948), p. 7.

[60] Herman Kamps, 'Shakespeare: Dichter, Dramatiker, Philosoph: Die Vortragsreihe der Elisabethanischen Festspiele', in *Die Welt*, special issue (September 1948), p. 10.

[61] 'es waren in Wirklichkeit Shakespearefestwochen' (Kamps, 'Shakespeare: Dichter, Dramatiker, Philosoph', p. 10).

and allegiance as no other British artist could. Because of the traditional claim on Shakespeare as 'the third German classic', there was no sense of foreignness to be overcome – and if there was, it was carefully engineered by the British. By presenting Shakespeare in the context of his own time and place, flanked by one of his lesser-known contemporaries, and, significantly, in his own language, the British reclaimed Shakespeare as their own – but, crucially, only to a degree. With quasi-religious fervour, the *Welt* concludes:

No-one who visited the Elizabethan festival could escape the uplifting impression that we all, speakers as well as listeners, were united in our veneration of the genius [Shakespeare] . . . The vigour and timelessness of his period through him became alive in us. For making this possible, here and now in Berlin, in the summer of our discontent 1948, we can best thank the organizers by cultivating his work untiringly, and in his spirit.[62]

Shakespeare becomes a peace-maker, the great common denominator of the German and the British people. It is inconceivable that anyone (let alone the Russians with their iconoclastic Tolstoy) could ever rend asunder two nations so united in their veneration of the Bard. If the Elizabethan Festival did indeed inspire these or similar feelings among Berlin audiences in the summer of the blockade, it was an effective propaganda move.

---

[62] 'Niemand, der an den Elisabethanischen Festwochen teilgenommen hat, konnte sich dem beglückenden Eindruck entziehen, daß wir alle, die Sprechenden wie die Hörenden, in Verehrung des Genius vereinigt waren . . . [D]ie Kraft und das Dauernde seiner Zeit wurden durch ihn in uns lebendig. – Daß dies möglich war, hier und jetzt in Berlin, im Sommer unseres Mißvergnügens 1948, können wir den Veranstaltern am besten durch unermüdliches Wirken an seinem Werk und in seinem Geiste danken' (Kamps, 'Shakespeare: Dichter, Dramatiker, Philosoph', p. 10).

CONNECTING THE GLOBE: ACTORS, AUDIENCE AND ENTRAINMENT

ROBERT SHAUGHNESSY

A GLOBE EXPERIMENT

Every year since 2007, the reconstructed Globe in Southwark has mounted a production of a Shakespeare play, in the period prior to the commencement of the main season, under the rubric Playing Shakespeare with Deutsche Bank. The show, which is augmented by practical workshops, is funded by the bank as part of their Experiencing Culture sponsorship programme, and presented free of charge to secondary schools across the London area. Targeted at pupils aged eleven to sixteen, the productions last just less than two hours (without interval) and are designed to offer their audiences, many of whom may never have entered a theatre before, a first taste of Shakespeare in performance. These are not, in any sense that the term has been understood at Shakespeare's Globe, 'original practices' productions: indeed, the Playing Shakespeare productions are among the theatre's most assertively contemporary, and determinedly populist, work, inhabiting a here and now that styles their multi-ethnic conspicuously youthful casts as their audience's exact contemporaries. They also make enthusiastic use of technologies that Globe performances otherwise eschew: neon signage that lights up whenever the action moved to Venice in the 2014 *The Merchant of Venice*, and, in the 2013 *Romeo and Juliet*, the mobile phone with which Tybalt gleefully films the first-scene street brawl, the police sirens and loudhailers that appear after the same character's death, and the amplified pop that soundtracks the Capulets' costume ball.[1]

In Spring 2013, the Playing Shakespeare production of *Romeo and Juliet* was the focus of an interdisciplinary collaboration between the research and education departments of Shakespeare's Globe and the author and colleagues from the School of Psychology at the University of Kent.[2] The aim of the project was to apply the methods of social cognitive psychology to the study of actor–audience interaction (a concern that has been central to Globe research and practice from its inception), focusing in particular on the significance of shared rhythms; the larger remit of this research, for which *Romeo and Juliet* served as a pilot study, is the production,

[1] The Playing Shakespeare with Deutsche Bank production of *Romeo and Juliet* ran for a month at Shakespeare's Globe from March to April 2013; prior to this it was taken on a short tour of the United Arab Emirates and Saudi Arabia. It was directed by Bill Buckhurst and designed by Hannah Clark, with music by Alex Silverman and choreography by Georgina Lamb. Its cast was as follows: Juliet: Jade Anouka; Capulet: Jason Baughan; Romeo: Will Featherstone; Mercutio/Friar John/Gregory: Richard James-Neale; Tybalt/Apothecary: Beruce Khan; Lady Capulet/Prince: Emma Pallant; Nurse: Lisa Stevenson; Friar Laurence/Peter: Dickon Tyrell; Paris/Sampson: Tom Whitelock; Benvolio: Josh Williams.
[2] The investigators were the author, Robert Johnston and Mario Weick, and Farah Karim-Cooper, Head of Higher Education and Research at Shakespeare's Globe. The project was supported by Fiona Banks, Creative Producer for Globe Education; access to rehearsals and performances was secured with the agreement of the producer, Chris Stafford, and director, Bill Buckhurst. Shakespeare's Globe also provided volunteer researchers to conduct audience observation. Particular thanks are due to Emma Pallant, for sharing her insights into the rehearsal and performance processes.

performance and reception of Shakespeare's works in relation to the phenomenon of *entrainment*. This concept that has long been familiar to the physical and natural sciences, and, under the aegis of the broader 'cognitive turn' in the humanities, has recently begun to be applied to performance.[3] Describing the process whereby initially independent rhythmic systems interact and synchronize, entrainment (alternatively, coupled oscillation or synchrony) has been observed everywhere from the activities of brainwaves in reaction to external rhythmic stimuli, such as light and sound, to the coordinated flashing of fireflies and the chorused chirping of crickets. As leading synchrony theorist Steven Strogatz puts it, 'nature uses every available channel to allow its oscillators to talk to each other. And the result of these conversations is often synchrony, in which all the oscillators begin to move as one.'[4] The phenomenon was first recorded in 1665 by the physicist and inventor of the pendulum clock, Christiaan Huygens; confined to bed with sickness, Huygens passed the hours by pondering the problem of accurate time-keeping in the context of transmeridian travel. To this end, he mounted two pendulums on a beam opposite the bed and observed their behaviour. To his surprise and initial bafflement, the pendulums always ended up in sync; and though he later worked out that the pendulums' tendency to coordinate arose from the interplay between action and reaction at a molecular level within the beam, his initial description of it in a letter to the Royal Society was as 'an odd kind of sympathy' – a sentiment that was also reported as 'the sympathy of clocks'.[5]

In the domain of human communication and interaction, entrainment takes place when two or more individuals lock into each other's rhythms of, for example, movement, speech and gesture. The significance of entrainment in a group situation lies not just in whether and how it takes place but, more importantly, in the role it plays in processes such as emotional contagion, the development of empathy and the cultivation of rapport, affiliation and pro-sociality: 'temporally coordinated actions', social psychologist Daniël Lakens

summarizes, 'are a fundamental feature of connectedness and mutual responsiveness in social interaction'.[6] The concept's potential for investigating the communicative and social exchanges between performers, individual spectators and collective audiences has already been developed in some cognitively influenced studies of dance and music, where the manifestly rhythmic nature of the aesthetic experience is not only instrumental to affect but also the mechanism 'wherein the self seems to merge with something larger', thus making these artforms 'the biotechnology of group formation because they are so effective in triggering a collective mental state'.[7] As William H. McNeill characterizes it in a foundational study, this collective state is individually experienced as 'a sense of pervasive well-being . . . more specifically, a strange sense of personal enlargement; a sort of swelling out, becoming larger than life, thanks to

---

[3] For accounts of recent cognitively-informed work in theatre, performance and Shakespeare studies, see Nicola Shaughnessy, ed., *Affective Performance and Cognitive Science: Body, Brain and Being* (London, 2013), and Laurence Johnson, John Sutton and Evelyn B. Tribble, eds., *Embodied Cognition and Shakespeare's Theatre: The Early Modern Body-Mind* (New York, 2014). As long ago as 1920, the performing arts prompted 'one of the earliest articulations of a concept of synchrony', when William McDougall, author of the first textbook in social psychology, 'noted the tendency of spectators to assume the postural strains of dancers or athletes they were watching' (Frank J. Bernieri, Steven Reznick and Robert Rosenthal, 'Synchrony, Pseudosynchrony, and Dissynchrony: Measuring the Entrainment Process', *Journal of Personality and Social Psychology*, 54 (1988), 243–53; p. 244). See McDougall, *An Introduction to Social Psychology*, 20th edn (London, 1926).

[4] Steven Strogatz, *Snyc: The Emerging Science of Spontaneous Order* (Harmondsworth, 2003), p. 3.

[5] Strogatz, *Sync*, pp. 104–6.

[6] Daniël Lakens, 'Movement Synchrony and Perceived Entitativity', *Journal of Experimental Social Psychology*, 46 (2010), 701–8; p. 701.

[7] Selin Kesebir, 'The Superorganism Account of Human Sociality: How and When Human Groups Are Like Beehives', *Personality and Social Psychology Review*, 16 (2012): 233–61; p. 238. For an overview of research on entrainment in music and dance, see Jessica Phillips-Silver, C. Athena Aktipis and Gregory A. Bryant, 'The Ecology of Entrainment: Foundations of Co-ordinated Rhythmic Movement', *Music Perception*, 28 (2010), 3–14.

participation in collective ritual'.[8] The potential significance of synchrony for the investigation of Shakespeare in performance in general, and for the actor–audience relationship in particular, is considerable; in this article, I explore its relevance to what happens between performers and their public at Shakespeare's Globe.

One finding to have emerged from the preliminary research is particularly suggestive. Among the various measures devised to determine whether entrainment was taking place within the acting ensemble, within the audience and between the two groups, were two sets of questionnaires (one for the performers, and one for the spectators). Numerically scored, these asked respondents to self-rate their sense of connectedness, group cohesion and synchrony, their degree of engagement with Shakespeare, the play and the production, and the extent to which they felt able to control or influence both the performance and the 'others' in the interaction (for the actors, the audience; and vice-versa). While some of the results were entirely predictable, others were not. It is probably no surprise that those audience members who felt connected with the actors and performance reported higher levels of engagement with Shakespeare's work (though it prompts the question of which of these factors is the cause, and which the effect), nor that those actors who felt that the performance was, so to speak, in time also reported a greater sense of control over the audience. Less expected was the conflict that was evident in the actors' responses between connecting with their colleagues and connecting with the audience; the more actors felt 'as one' with the audience, the more excited they were about the performance, but also the less they felt as one with the other actors. To put it another way, the more the actors synchronized with the audience, the less they entrained with their fellow performers. What this seems to suggest is a conflict between the demands of ensemble communication and cohesion, and those of audience interaction and engagement.

This finding offers a starting point for a consideration of what is widely acknowledged as the most

important, as well as the most unanticipated, of all of the discoveries to have been made at the Globe. When the Globe was conceived and built, 'none of us had any idea', Andrew Gurr confessed, 'that the novelty of groundlings round the stage would transform the experience of modern playgoing in the way it has done'.[9] The nature of this transformation, the factors that have brought it about, and the benefits it has brought, have all been extensively discussed.[10] Importantly, for the purposes of this essay, the Globe's characteristic mode of buttonholing give-and-take between actor and spectator, in the context of a visible, demonstrative and collectively-minded audience, has been generally identified as its most involving, exciting – and, more contentiously, 'authentic' – feature.[11] Thus when Mark Rylance, as Hamlet in 2000, posed 'Who calls me coward?' as a genuine question to the yard, castigated the 'groundlings' as 'capable only of dumb shows', and paused for the inevitable self-referential roar from the audience before delivering the killer rejoinder ('and noise'), he offered a masterclass in the outward-facing, in-the-moment technique which has become an indispensible component of what Worthen terms

---

[8] William H. McNeill, *Keeping Together in Time: Dance and Drill in Human History* (Cambridge, MA, 1995), p. 2.

[9] Andrew Gurr, 'Foreword', in *Shakespeare's Globe: A Theatrical Experiment*, ed. Christie Carson and Farah Karim-Cooper (Cambridge, 2008), p. xvii.

[10] See for example Pauline Kiernan, *Staging Shakespeare at the New Globe* (Basingstoke, 1999); W. B. Worthen, *Shakespeare and the Force of Modern Performance* (Cambridge, 2003); Rob Conkie, *The Globe Theatre Project: Shakespeare and Authenticity* (Lewiston, NY, 2006); Carson and Karim-Cooper, *Shakespeare's Globe*.

[11] In her early, enthusiastic account, Pauline Kiernan suggests that the experience of the Globe's 'first experiments' means that 'we will have to redefine the function of the space of Shakespeare's original audiences . . . and to reconsider the role of the playgoers in the performance of plays' (*Staging Shakespeare*, p. 36). A decade later, Gordon McMullan reports that he has 'a clear sense of how audiences respond to the Globe space', and that this has only confirmed his conviction that it 'has little to do with the experiences of those attending plays in a not dissimilar theatre just round the corner between 1599 and 1613' ('Afterword', in *Shakespeare's Globe*, ed. Carson and Karim-Cooper, p. 231).

'Globe performativity'.[12] However alien to original practices the Playing Shakespeare *Romeo and Juliet* was in other respects, it was in this sense a quintessentially Globe production, in that its hard-working ten-strong cast used every available opportunity to reach out to, and respond to, what were even by Globe standards unusually energetic and voluble audiences (typically described in the Front of House and Stage Management reports as 'lively and extremely vocal'; 'jovial and enthusiastic'; and 'a charming mixture of rowdy and attentive'[13]). What the actor questionnaires suggest, however, is that feeling 'as one' with the audience carried a cost: in this instance, albeit intermittently, the cohesion of the acting ensemble; in others, we might conjecture, the integrity of the actor's score, the security of character, the coherence of the production and even the affective power of the play. To what extent is Globe performance a mutually supportive, shared game, and to what a site of antagonism, a power struggle, a contest for control?

To begin to address this question, I turn to the testimony of those who have for more than eighteen years been charged with the task of putting original practices into practice: the Globe actors. My source is the verbal testimony of practitioners that is variously recorded and documented in the Globe's Research Bulletins (1997–2002) and in its online Adopt an Actor Archive, which from 1998 onwards has captured the reminiscences and reflections of selected creative personnel.[14] This latter resource, at the time of writing, holds multiple interviews with more than 150 participants, amounting to hundreds of hours of first-hand report, which, while addressing the entirety of the performance process from pre-rehearsal through to end of run, refers repeatedly to the actor–audience relationship.

The consensus is overwhelming. There is nothing, the actors say, that could have prepared them for that first public exposure in the hyper-real broad daylight of the Globe arena, nothing like the anxiety, even terror, that preceded it and nothing like the feeling of being supported, even adored ('like a rock star'), that takes its place, when you realize that the audience – all 1500 of them, but especially

the 500 standing, looking up from the yard – are on your side. This is a space in which one can be both at the highest pitch of arousal and alertness and feel safe, comfortable, even relaxed; a space where there is absolutely nowhere to hide and no option other than to be absolutely truthful; a place where the responsiveness of the crowd, as well as the interventions of the elements (the wind and the rain), of ornithology and twenty-first-century technology (the birds, the airplanes and helicopters) are as forceful as they are unpredictable, and often as much a part of a production's imaginative world as the plaster and timber of the playhouse itself. This is a playhouse where (unlike in a 'conventional' theatre where spectators skulk in the dark and can be ignored) the audience makes its presence felt, demands to be recognized, to be spoken to, to be played with. It is the most demanding arena that one could ever act in, and the most rewarding. And the vocabulary, throughout, is that of extremes, of superlatives: the experience is 'fantastic', 'incredible', 'amazing'; and key phrases and motifs recur and repeat in interview after interview. Clearly, there is something tangibly unique, strangely special and deeply challenging about performing in an environment in which emotions run high and in which hazards and rewards are intimately interconnected. What deserves further consideration is why the actors' accounts of the labour they perform at the Globe slip so frequently into the realms of the superlative, the hyperbolic and the fantastical, and what the language and imagery of these accounts suggest may reside unspoken, unacknowledged in them. Three threads, in particular, I wish to examine here. The groundlings are 'fantastic'; the audience, especially when first encountered, is a 'sea of faces'; and, as Paul Chahidi puts it (correctly guessing that 'probably loads of actors have

---

[12] Worthen, *Shakespeare and the Force of Modern Performance*, pp. 79–116.

[13] Playing Shakespeare 2013 *Romeo and Juliet*: Stage Manager's Show Report 13, 14 March; Show Report 14, 15 March; Show Report 15, 15 March.

[14] See www.shakespearesglobe.com/education/discovery-space/adopt-an-actor. Last accessed 27 October 2014.

said this'): 'it's like being at a rock concert, more like a rock concert than a play'.

GROUNDLINGS

If there is one word which appears to summarize the uniqueness of the Globe endeavour, it is 'groundlings', an archaism reinvented as a neologism, to account for the new categories of spectatorship (conducted standing in the yard) that the enterprise has brought into being. What concerns me is not only what the actors say about groundling behaviour but also what the epithet itself allows or encourages actors and others to think and feel about them. It has been pointed out from the Globe's earliest days that, as a synonym for the standing audience, the word has no early modern mandate whatsoever other than its derogatory usage by Hamlet and by Dekker in *The Gull's Hornbook* ('Your Groundling, and Gallery-Commoner buyes his sport by the penny'); as Gurr observes, its habitual deployment in popular (and sometimes academic) commentary ignores 'the scorn that Hamlet packed into the word when he invented it to describe the gapers at his feet'.[15] The word has nonetheless proved impossible to dislodge. In 2005, surveying critical reactions to the first five years of the Globe's work, Paul Prescott mapped the ways in which the activities of the groundlings were identified in the majority of newspaper reviews with all of the worst aspects of Globe performance: allegedly coarse, vulgar, insensitive and clap-happy, they represent the lowest common denominator to which the shows are designed to appeal. Groundlings, in these accounts, spend their time chatting, taking photos, flirting or groping, guzzling drink and stuffing their faces, fidgeting in noisy plastic rainwear and back-chatting the actors; they have short attention spans, a poor command of English, and an appetite for pantomime-style antics, and are so game for a laugh that they will find just about anything funny. For anyone intent on savouring the language or following the play, they are a massive irritant and a constant distraction, encouraging the actors to play shamelessly to the crowd,

constantly dragging everything down to 'their level'. In short, Prescott concludes, the groundling serves the reviewers as 'a damning commentary on a project that confounds cultural hierarchies, originals and copies, and brings crowd pollution to the potentially most sacred spot in Shakespearean theatre'.[16] For the reviewer, viewing the spectacle from the wallflower perspective of a gallery seat and siding with Hamlet against the unruly plebeian audience, the groundlings are at a party to which she is not invited. The relationship between critic and audience is fundamentally antagonistic.

Since Prescott's essay was published, critical attitudes towards the Globe's audience (which usually means the standing, most vociferous component of it) have softened, because some reviewers have on occasions opted to mingle with it rather than observe it, because spectators have generally calmed down and because the overall quality of the performance work itself has been seen to improve as it has become subtler and richer. But a gap remains between the reviewers' attitude and that of the actors. For the former, 'groundling' has been something of an insult, for the latter a compliment, or possibly even a term of abuse re-appropriated as a badge of communal identity. According to the Globe actors, the groundlings are 'fantastic': alert, responsive, supportive, demonstratively enthusiastic, quick-witted and fleet-footed, intelligent, stoic and heroically patient, respectfully attentive to, and emotionally invested in, the storytelling. The groundlings are thus the actors' friends, and the qualities conferred upon them are the antitheses of those attributed by their enemies; in similar fashion, the critics' characterization of yard denizens as an appetite-driven, taste-deficient and annoyingly self-indulgent underclass is inverted in

---

[15] Thomas Dekker, *The Gull's Hornbook* (London, 1609), sig. E2v; Gurr, 'Foreword', p. xix.

[16] Paul Prescott, 'Inheriting the Globe: The Reception of Shakespearean Space and Audience in Contemporary Reviewing', in *A Companion to Shakespeare and Performance*, ed. Barbara Hodgdon and W. B. Worthen (Oxford, 2005), pp. 359–75; p. 367.

the actors' accounts to produce a discriminating, participative, popular audience.

Clearly there is some fairly polarized thinking in play, though it is fair to surmise that the positive and negative versions of the groundling sketched here represent the rhetorically-charged extremes of a discursive spectrum. Groundlings and their behaviour are bad for the critics but good for the actors; the very attributes that define them as bad for the former are frequently those that make them good (better still, 'fantastic') in the eyes of the latter. For the reviewers, the groundlings' lack of sophistication and of conventional theatrical enculturation, their ignorance of Shakespeare and their low-cultural performance preferences, mark them as culturally impoverished and therefore disqualified as theatrical arbiters; for the actors, these are what render their response authentic, both valid and validating: 'the fact that they are so visceral and vocal in their responses to the play', claims Che Walker, demonstrates that they 'understand everything that happens on that stage'. Behaviour that would in most other contexts be regarded as ill-mannered, boorish or completely disruptive is accepted as inevitable and transvalued as somehow positive: 'there were a lot of kids ... who like to chat', observes Sally Bretton, 'I was starting to find it really distracting and then I just thought "This is part of the Globe experience"'; 'the crowd were ... mental', reports David Sturzaker of one performance of the 2006 *Titus Andronicus*: 'they were a really raucous lot, but that was great. That was wonderful.'

It is clear that 'groundling' is an overdetermined category in a way that 'audience' or 'spectator' are not, and that it comes freighted with both positive and negative qualities. Whereas Shakespeare may have thought, aquatically, of grubby, gaping fish, modern theatregoers might find the 'ground' in groundlings to contain different associative substrata: feet on the ground, a groundedness that reaches beneath the concrete of the Globe's yard to the soil of deep England as well as beyond to the pavements of the London Borough of Southwark; even perhaps, via ancestral cultural memory, to the Globe's archeological imaginary, Shakespeare's first and second Globes, submerged beneath the foundations of the luxury flats of Anchor Terrace, as well as those of its disinterred Marlovian alter ego, the Rose, both less than five-minutes' walk away.

Nouns suffixed 'ling' are almost always already tinged with quaintness or archaism: groundlings might equally suggest foundlings, changelings or, for those who can still remember the argot of 1950s science fiction B-movie aliens, earthlings. So in this sense the word is served as a compliment, and its repeated, reflex iteration almost invariably operates in a spirit of generous acknowledgement, affectionate camaraderie and inclusivity. As an act of labelling, however, it serves other purposes. Unlike the more anonymous, inscrutable 'audience', or the dispersed, atomized and somewhat aloof 'spectators', the groundlings enter the actors' field of vision already defined by their behavioural repertoire and communal identity. It is possible to read this as the benign corollary of the negative stereotyping of the critics, and there is a certain shared logic: the actors' groundlings are idealized rather than vilified, but it is still possible to generalize, to attribute motive and, now and then, to infantilize: 'The Groundlings want you to talk to them' (Jasper Britton); 'the audience, especially the groundlings, love physical comedy' (Peter Shorey).

I suggest that the yard inhabitants appear to invite such thinking not only because their behaviour as a theatre audience is demonstrably unique and unusual but also because that behaviour is characterized by a degree of synchrony that is both exceptional and, importantly, not readily explicable. The capacity of the groundlings to think and act *as one* is repeatedly remarked on: 'it is amazing' says Tonia Chauvet, 'to see how a large group of people take on their own personality'. Defining these 'fantastic' creatures as (the) 'groundlings' is a way of articulating the sense that they are both plural and singular: what is 'amazing' about the groundlings' group-minded synchrony is, I propose, what makes it *uncanny*. As Freud attempted to define the term, the uncanny is that which is at once both familiar (*heimlich*) and strange (*unheimlich*): the inanimate entity that comes to life, the human being that may be an automaton, the double. As a superorganism that seems to have acquired a life beyond the sum of its parts, 'the groundling' edges into these categories, in particular that of the doppelgänger, in that it can seem to embody on a mass scale 'the spontaneous transmission of mental processes from one of these persons to another . . . so that the one becomes co-owner of the other's knowledge, emotions and experience'. In a situation where boundaries between self and others are insecure, selves are 'duplicated, divided and interchanged'. Freud also touches on the uncanniness of unexplained coincidence – what we are considering here as synchrony – making the point that even when it can be scientifically rationalized, this 'would not necessarily remove the impression of the uncanny'.[17] Intimations of the uncanny have haunted the science of synchrony ever since Huygens anthropomorphized his oddly sympathetic pendulum clocks, reflecting both the wonder and the unease that are prompted by inanimate objects that seem to think and feel, or by flora and fauna that 'magically' behave in concert. Entrainment, as Strogatz puts it, remains 'beautiful and strange and profoundly moving . . . a wonderful and terrifying thing'.[18] It is in this spirit that we might consider the groundlings to be 'fantastic' in an etymologically double sense. Though the intended meaning is what the *OED* defines as the 'trivial' use of the term (excellent, good, beyond expectation), this is shadowed by its primary sense: groundlings are the stuff of fantasy, fabulous, imaginary, unreal.

SEA OF FACES

It's like when you dive into the sea the first time; you want to go swimming, but it does knock your breath away.   (Margot Leicester)

The groundlings are like the sea, they're moving all the time and the people sitting down are like some sort of coastline.   (Sophie Thomson)

Margot Leicester's and Sophie Thomson's observations contain one of the most insistently recurring images in the Adopt an Actor interviews: the 'sea of faces' that confronts the actor as she takes to the Globe stage. The manifest significance of the

metaphor is obvious enough: connoting vastness and multiplicity, as well as dynamism and volatility, this sea is at once daunting and inviting, distant and immediate, tangible and abstract, an environment that is immersive, in which identities might dissolve, a Shakespearian 'great vast', harbouring things rich and strange. The Globe auditorium is indeed C-shaped, and a place of see-ing: with its hundreds of faces and double those hundreds of eyes, it is a vision which is also a vision of vision, a vision that looks back. More than that, a sea is characterized by the rise and fall of waves, ebb and flow, and surge and swell, reflecting the cyclical, oscillatory quality of actor–audience interaction, its rhythms of arousal and inertia, of attentiveness and disengagement, and of noise and silence.[19] A sea of faces can be imagined as waves of energy (a much-used term) that an actor can ride, like a swimmer or, more appropriately, a surfer. When it works – that is, when the audience's and the actors' rhythms are in synchrony – it results in feelings of connectedness, solidarity, mutual empathy and wellbeing that can be anything from satisfying to euphoric. Repeatedly, the actors evoke what performance psychologist David Roland, following Mihaly Csikszentmihalyi, has identified as 'flow' experience, the components of which include strong indices of entrainment: as Roland puts it, 'there is a merging experience between you and the activity, so that you lose the sense of yourself as being separate from the activity'; 'even though you feel in control . . . there is a sense that something greater than yourself is making it happen'; and 'your

---

[17] Sigmund Freud, *The Uncanny*, trans. David McLintock (Harmondsworth, 2003), pp. 141–2; p. 145.

[18] Strogatz, *Sync*, p. 289.

[19] The image also strongly resonates with Darren Newtson's influential modelling of 'activity in social interactions' in terms of 'correlated behavioural waves' (R. C. Schmidt, Samantha Morr, Paula Fitzpatrick and Michael J. Richardson, 'Measuring the Dynamics of Interactional Synchrony', *Journal of Nonverbal Behaviour*, 36 (2012), 263–79; p. 275); see Darren Newtson, 'The Dynamics of Action and Interaction', in *A Dynamic Systems Approach to Development: Applications*, ed. Linda B. Smith and Esther Thelen (Cambridge, MA, 1993), pp. 241–64.

sense of time is altered so that what seems like minutes to you could be an hour in real time'.[20] 'It feels like time froze for about three hours of my life', says Jessie Buckley, 'it made me very excited to be part of something.'

In its most tangible forms, synchrony, and the rapport that it fosters, occurs when rhythms of movement, posture, gesture and speech on stage converge with or diverge from the demonstrative rhythmic actions of the audience, its waves of laughter and applause, cycles of swaying and fidgeting, and patterns of movement around and in and out of the space. Rhythmic awareness also undergirds the ways in which actors recognize and respond to the less demonstrative aspects of audience behaviour, where the signs of arousal and positive or negative valence are less visibly or audibly manifest. The capacity for concentration on the part of the audience is much remarked upon by Globe actors: 'Each audience is incredibly energized', says Meredith MacNeill, 'you can see them really paying attention, and just by looking at them, holding their gaze, you suddenly feel energized yourself.' As facets of communicative behaviour, stillness and silence have their own rhythms, and 'can be described in terms of cycles, periods, frequencies and amplitudes';[21] the actor discriminates between attentiveness and indifference by reading them relationally and durationally, knowing without thinking when and where to look, how often and for how long. MacNeill meets the sustained, focused gaze of audience with hers, an act of mirroring that is *timed*. It is such moments of entrainment that generate the affective experience of mutually reinforcing, aroused well-being.

This sense of the interrelatedness of shared rhythms and mutual pleasure occasionally surfaces in the reviews. Writing of the 2008 revival of *Merry Wives*, in a rare instance of a reviewer abandoning the us-and-them distinction between himself and the 'Globe audience', Mark Shenton observed 'the audience who become a vocal, collaborative player all of its own ... It is our nearly constant laughter that provides the motor for this escalating farce of failed cuckoldry to take hold.'[22] It is not only laughter that is infectious. Responding to Mark

Rylance's Richard II in 2003, Georgina Brown writes feelingly of her emotional immersion in a collectively-experienced event: 'I abandoned my seat and became a groundling to get nearer to him ... Later, when he is in his prison cell, he hears music and, for a second, breaks into a joyful, Elizabethan, high-kicking jig. I almost wept.' The production 'finished with another jig, danced by the whole company. And their high spirits are infectious. I left the theatre on a tide of exhilaration.'[23]

Tides of strong emotion call for confident swimmers, and an ocean of faces is also, potentially, a sea of troubles, with scope for turbulence, freak waves, and the risk of drowning. Beneath the relentless positivity of the actors' testimony (and, given the public relations function of the Adopt an Actor initiative, it is hardly surprising that this is predominant) are undercurrents of unease. It is no secret that the unique excitement of the Globe is partly rooted in the perception that it is a high-risk environment, and the actor's work is in part defined by the techniques that he or she develops to negotiate its challenges. In any theatre situation, the management of stage fright, which is a fight-or-flight response to the risk of failure, is one such technique.[24] Pre-show anxiety is a normal and necessary component of the actor's work, but in Globe performance, stage fright operates at seemingly unimaginable, almost unbearable levels. When asked about the experience of performing

---

[20] David Roland, *The Confident Performer* (London, 2001), p. 75. See Mihaly Csikszentmihalyi, *Flow: The Psychology of Optimal Experience* (New York, 1990).

[21] Bernieri *et al.*, 'Synchrony, Pseudosynchrony, and Dissynchrony', p. 244.

[22] *Sunday Express*, 22 June 2008.

[23] *Mail on Sunday*, 25 May 2003.

[24] As Roland reassures his readers, 'anxiety is helpful for the performing artist', in that it enhances her 'ability to perform simple tasks better and more quickly, up to an optimum point'. He cautions, however, that 'if the anxiety goes beyond this optimum point, then the person's performance becomes worse' (*Confident Performer*, p. 6). Richard Eyre recalls the pithy advice offered by the veteran actor and comedian Jimmy Jewel: 'You can't be any bloody good if you're not bloody nervous' (*National Service: Diary of a Decade at the National Theatre* (London, 2004), p. 222).

in the space for the first time, the majority of actors describe it as 'terrifying': it is overwhelming, intimidating, extraordinary, daunting, frightening, nerve-wracking, distracting, 'the strangest experience I have ever had on stage' (Che Walker), 'like going into a whirlwind' (Roger Lloyd Pack). The audience ('literally like fireworks' (Ellie Piercy)) and the ambience – 'mad, weird and stunning' (Kanunu Kirimi), 'naked...exposed and fragile' (Jamie Parker) – are likewise crazy, bonkers, mental, raucous, rowdy, hysterical, and even 'animalistic' (Laura Rees). The question arises as to whether the rewards of playing the Globe are sufficient pay-off for its very considerable demands, which are emotional as well as technical. As Mark Rylance reflected, one of his greatest challenges during his period as artistic director was trying to persuade 'established classical actors to come and take a risk'. To perform, let alone to lead, on the Globe stage 'was exhausting and actors felt extremely vulnerable'. 'Most of the actors I asked', Rylance reports, 'were too frightened or just not interested.'[25] Just occasionally, the actor's vulnerability becomes visible. 'It can be the best place in the world if you're confident', says Arthur Darville, 'but as soon as you feel that you're not confident it can be the most horrible place in the world because everyone's just there.' Laura Rees, as Lavinia in the 2006 hit *Titus* takes her interview into even more difficult territory. Confessing to feeling 'exposed', and reminding her interviewer that 'you are putting yourself out there for applause every night...it is like a drug', she offers an account of how it feels to play Lavinia:

Sometimes the play really gets under your skin, because it is so unforgiving, there is no hope in it... On some level, every night being taken off stage and being raped and being mutilated, and then walking forward downstage, especially in the Globe space, you get a sense of the reality of it. You can't push it away, which I try to do a lot, I have to go through those emotions every night.

The honesty, and the distress, seem very real, and what is particularly disturbing is that it is *especially in the Globe space* that the 'reality' of Lavinia's rape becomes so palpable; whereas the space is elsewhere conceived as challenging but ultimately benign, it seems here to be actively threatening, placing the actor in an all-but intolerably vulnerable position. This makes for uncomfortable reading alongside David Sturzaker's remarks, quoted earlier, about the same production's 'wonderful', 'mental' and 'raucous' audiences. Rees's report instances a predicament which admits of no easy solutions, and it is little surprise that she states that 'Lavinia has left me with more of a wound than I thought she would. It's something I don't really want to think about.'[26]

Generally, the actors recognize that the show is most at risk of unravelling not when the performance is going not badly but too well. Any entrainment situation is a site not only of convergence and integration but also of resistance and dissonance, of struggles for power and control, and the positive accounts that are offered of the audience are shadowed by worries about the possibly disproportionate power that it is licensed to exercise. Frequently, the actors frame this anxiety in terms of the dangers of being 'seduced', not least by 'the groundlings'. The idea that performance is an art of seduction as much as seduction is a – possibly duplicitous – act of performance is familiar enough (as Jean Baudrillard – who labels it a 'strategy...of deception' – has it, 'To seduce is to die as reality and reconstitute oneself as illusion. It is to be taken in by one's own illusion and move in an enchanted world'[27]). But it is conventionally understood to be the actor's task to seduce

---

[25] Quoted in Carson and Karim-Cooper, *Shakespeare's Globe*, pp. 195–6.

[26] Rees's comedown is perhaps the inevitable corollary, or indeed consequence, of Globe acting's narcotic appeal. It is relevant here that Rowland identifies flow performance as 'so enjoyable in itself' that it becomes '*intrinsically* rewarding...which can make it addictive' (*Confident Performer*, p. 75). The scope for trauma in potential in the playing of Lavinia is not, it must be said, confined to Globe performance, but has been remarked by a number of actors in the part. For a detailed account, see Pascale Aebischer, *Shakespeare's Violated Bodies: Stage and Screen Performance* (Cambridge, 2004), pp. 24–63.

[27] Jean Baudrillard, *Seduction*, trans. Brian Singer (Basingstoke, 1990), pp. 69–70.

the audience, not vice versa. The risk of seduction in its more self-obliterating form is ever-present, especially in the early performances, because the actor is exposed and vulnerable: a point made with telling directness by Dickon Tyrell:

I can understand that, especially in those early performances when you are feeling insecure, you may well leap for the nearest relationship – which might well be with a groundling. You will probably then lose about 95% of the house.

Playing Lodovico, Tyrell was ideally placed to witness what happens to those who love 'not wisely, but too well'. While an element of abandonment is intrinsic to the formation of group rapport, loss of control is a persistent worry, and there is constant concern that Globe performance can all to easily get out of hand, and that the audience can take charge: 'there's a very fine line between encouraging them', notes Jules Melville, 'and losing control of the situation'. This refers to the audience's capacity to subject the rhythms of individual and group performances to their own. 'If you're not careful when they are a particularly wild audience', Paul Hunter warns, 'they will dictate the rhythm of the play.' Fergal McElherron, who played Peter in the 2009 season's *Romeo and Juliet*, agrees: 'you always have to keep them in check...and you have to hit your beats'. Interviewed a month into the run of this production, Rawiri Paratene (Friar Laurence) registers concern that he was 'on automatic', and that the show's first half was running five or six minutes longer than it should. Guessing that 'a good three minutes of that extra time is the audience's contribution', Paratene declares: 'I've stopped worrying about it' (stage management might well have taken a different view). That 'contribution' is cued and orchestrated by his and his colleagues' 'moments' ('a look to the audience' that 'gets a delicious laugh', and adds 'about six to eight seconds'):

There are sixteen of us onstage and that is just one of my moments, so multiply that by sixteen, that's getting up there for a few minutes, if we've all got those moments and lots of us have got many of them. Fergal...has got so many of these moments, so what do we do?

On the one hand, 'We're not going to take all of those out, because we've worked hard at earning them'; on the other, apropos the six-to-eight-second laugh, 'I'm loathed [*sic*] to let it go, but I may have to for time.' What is gratifying for the actor is not necessarily in the service of the show; at such instances, the desire to accommodate audience response comes into conflict with the basic discipline of keeping to time and, potentially, the ensemble's capacity to function cohesively.[28] Paratene's laughter score (the sum of his 'moments'), and McElherron's, are just two of sixteen individual cycles of call-and-response in their shows, which in an ideal production might be expected to operate pretty much in sync, but which in the unpredictable world of the Globe are by no means certain to do so. Navigating the Globe's sea of faces is anything but plain sailing.

LIKE A ROCK STAR

On the whole, the Globe actors tend to be circumspect about the less desirable aspects of their audiences' behaviour, and, as noted earlier, the staff responsible for policing the activities of spectators on the ground – the stage management and front of house teams – also exercise lenience. Occasionally, however, raucousness reaches levels that are no longer amusing or energizing but seriously disruptive. With their almost exclusively teenaged audiences, the Playing Shakespeare productions are more prone to this than most, and the show reports for the *Romeo and Juliet* matinee on 18 March 2013 document a particularly egregious example. Stage management reported 'a positively raucous audience this afternoon with some extreme cheering', and attributed this behaviour to 'a large majority of the audience being female and taking a liking to

---

[28] Unexpected laughs, especially in its productions of the tragedies, have become a Globe trademark, and one of the factors that has fuelled critical suspicions about the enterprise. 'We tend to gauge the success of the show by the number of laughs that we receive', says Michael Gould in 2001; given that he was playing Edmund in *King Lear*, it is hard not to feel that such suspicions are at least partially justified.

certain cast members'. The Front of House report furnishes further details: 'a rowdy crowd today of mostly girls, who took the opportunity of screaming with teen and pre-teenage adoration towards Benvolio & Romeo from the start'. The consequence: audience complaints that 'it was impossible to hear what was being said because of the noise' and, stage management noted, 'some late entrances . . . company has difficulty hearing cue lines'.[29]

Two aspects of this incident are noteworthy. First, the students' synchronized performance of arousal exemplifies a cognitive phenomenon which is especially characteristic of Globe performance, which underpins many of the actor's comments cited here, and for which entrainment is a key mechanism: emotional contagion. Describing the process whereby moods are communicated and shared between members of a group, the phenomenon is generated by largely involuntary acts of mimicry, which may be facially expressive, gestural, postural, muscular and, as in this case, vocal; as the authors of the standard work on the topic emphasize, persons are most susceptible to 'catch' the emotions of others when they 'rivet their attention on others . . . construe themselves in terms of their interrelatedness to others . . . tend to mimic facial, vocal and postural expressions' and 'are emotionally reactive'.[30] In terms of its visual and acoustic environment and spatial organization, Shakespeare's Globe is an highly emotionally contagious space: the audience is visibly and audibly on display to itself, thus maximizing the opportunities for behavioural mirroring, and also making it likely that the act of mimicry can rapidly become a self-sustaining spiral of escalation. Front of House observed that the noise initiated in one section of the yard, 'then started all the others around them yelling and screaming'. In this respect emotional contagion is a function of the Globe's distinctive acoustics: as Bruce R. Smith notes, 'Performers . . . have commented on the way audience response can start in one part of the theatre and then spread laterally to the rest.'[31]

Second, the 'bad' behaviour of this audience sheds light on the third of our actors' recurring

images: that, at its best, performing at the Globe makes you feel 'like a rock star'. Although on this occasion the students' enactment of emotion was deemed inappropriate and disruptive, theirs was a legitimate and perhaps inevitable response both to a show that at times cultivated the raucous atmosphere of an open-air gig, and (it must be said) to the boy-band charms of 'certain cast members'. Romeo and Benvolio, Will Featherstone and Josh Williams, may or may not have been gratified by the attention, but the stage management's report of late entrances and missed cues indicates that the audience's demonstration of infatuated connectedness with the performers interfered with the connections between the performers. This is not what being a rock star at the Globe is usually taken to mean. It is, in some ways, an incongruous simile: as the most inauthentic, mass-produced, synthetic, technologized and commodified of all performance artforms, rock culture is demonstrably at odds with many of the Globe's core values. And yet the comparison makes sense: it invokes not just the scale and intensity of the audience's response but also the participatory, festival ambience of the Globe, the directness, rawness and immediacy of the encounter, the aura of youthfulness, transgression and the potential for anarchy. But what it also captures is rock's solipsism, its narcissism, its hedonism; its promise that while its highs are very high indeed, its lows are among the worst imaginable (as Laura Rees, as Lavinia, who described Globe acting as 'like a drug', seemed to discover). The image of the rock star pictures a performer and his (as it usually is) audience moving in time; it also, we should notice, celebrates the solo rather than the ensemble (as the University of Kent researchers found, the more the actors felt as one with the audience, the less they felt as one with their colleagues). So dominant is the focus

---

29 Playing Shakespeare *Romeo and Juliet* 2013: Stage Manager's Show Report 16. 18 March; FOH Show Report, 18 March.
30 Elaine Hatfield, John T. Cacioppo and Richard Rapson, *Emotional Contagion* (Cambridge, 1994), p. 182.
31 Bruce R. Smith, *The Acoustic World of Early Modern England: Attending to the O-Factor* (Chicago, 1999), p. 214.

on actor–audience communication in the Globe archive that the performers very rarely address the issue of the actor–actor relationship (though in fairness they are not asked about it), other than in terms of how difficult it is to sustain it.

At the end of the Playing Shakespeare's *Romeo and Juliet*, the actors engaged in that other practice common to all Globe productions, other than talking to the audience, by launching into the last of the production's three dances.[32] There was, of course, nothing particularly 'authentic' about it, but its inclusion asserted the production's connectedness with the traditions and style of the theatre but also the actors' connectedness with each other, in an energetically choreographed, contagiously joyous spectacle of coordinated movement; as such it was an exemplary enactment of what McNeill, cited at the beginning of this essay, identifies as one of humankind's most fundamental mechanisms for securing group rapport and fostering a shared sense of well being: 'keeping together in time', he concludes, 'arouses warm emotions of collective solidarity and erases personal frustrations as words, by themselves cannot do'.[33] The Globe's jigs have attracted less attention than they should, and are rarely mentioned by critics and little discussed by the actors. But both as a show's culminating rhythmic display and, sometimes, as an eloquent summation of both production and play, they deserve more.[34] In the meantime, I will simply record that

at every performance of *Romeo and Juliet* that I attended, the jig was a unifying moment of release for actors who had battled the ferocious weather of one of the coldest springs on record and the roaring of a sea of groundling faces that had at times threatened to become a deluge: it was a clapping, stomping, collective act of both celebration and defiance. That, perhaps, is how it feels to be a rock star on the Globe stage.

---

[32] The first opened the show; the second was the Capulets' costume ball. In a smart act of homage to Luhrmann's film version, the guests were costumed as their fantasy alter egos, so that Capulet, played as a nouveau riche East End loudmouth, came as Vegas-period Elvis, Tybalt as Darth Vader, and Mercutio and Benvolio as Batman and Robin. In a neat metatheatrical joke, Juliet and Romeo, elsewhere behoodied in jeans and trainers, arrived in cut-price fancy-dress farthingale and doublet and hose, unwittingly playing versions of themselves in a period-costume production of their play.

[33] McNeill, *Keeping Together in Time*, p. 152.

[34] Roger Clegg and Lucie Skeaping's recent survey of the jig in early modern performance makes no mention of the Globe's resuscitation of the form. Presenting texts, scores and suggested choreographies for nine extant playhouse jigs, they observe that 'very few people were involved in practical investigations into the genre' and hope that making these accessible will 'encourage performers to breathe the life back into these amusing musical dramas once more' (*Singing Simpkin and other Bawdy Jigs: Musical Comedy on the Shakespearean Stage: Scripts, Music and Context* (Exeter, 2014), p. x).

'FREETOWN!': SHAKESPEARE AND SOCIAL FLOURISHING

EWAN FERNIE

1. FREETOWN!

Shakespeare drops the word into *Romeo and Juliet*. When the Prince intervenes to quell the riot between the Montagues and Capulets in the first scene, he concludes his speech as follows:

> You, Capulet, shall go along with me,
> And Montague, come you this afternoon,
> To know our farther pleasure in this case,
> To old Freetown, our common judgement-place.
>
> (1.1.97–100)[1]

Freetown[2] – Shakespeare got it from Brooke, where Capulet's castle is called Freetown; Brooke Englished it from Painter, where Capulet's place is Villafranca. But, by transferring 'Freetown' to the Prince, transposing it beyond the story's scene, and making it 'our common judgement-place', Shakespeare endued it with an authority which is suggestively otherworldly and egalitarian. By making it '*old* Freetown' he lent it a further, immemorial quality, as if it were somehow always there, somehow positively shadowing the imperfections of our civic life. There is a breath of equality in the Prince saying, 'You, Capulet, shall go *along with me*'. And the use of the word 'pleasure' in conjunction with Freetown anticipates something of the sex and mutuality of Romeo and Juliet as opposed to the violence the Prince interrupts. But Freetown is not a fantasy land of libertarian license. It is FreeTOWN, placeholder for a real civil society: FREEtown, one that is defined above all by liberty and freedom. And it also is 'our common judgement place', whose freedom is sourced in and

Given as an Inaugural Lecture at the University of Birmingham on 29 January 2014; and to celebrate the 150th anniversary of the Deutsch Shakespeare Gesellschaft in Weimar on 25 April 2014.

[1] References are to the Arden edition of *Romeo and Juliet*, ed. René Weis (London, 2012).

[2] Shakespeare and freedom has been a central topic in Shakespeare criticism since Hegel's lectures on fine art in the 1820s, which were posthumously published as his *Aesthetics* in 1835. The German philosopher described Shakespeare's characters as 'free artists of their own selves' (G. W. F. Hegel, 'Dramatic Poetry', from *Aesthetics: Lectures on Fine Art*, in *Philosophers on Shakespeare*, ed. Paul A. Kottman (Stanford, 2009), p. 77). In 2010, Stephen Greenblatt reiterated that 'Shakespeare as a writer is the embodiment of human freedom' (*Shakespeare's Freedom* (Chicago, 2010), p. 1), thereby belatedly affirming what he had failed to find in Shakespeare and Renaissance literature in his seminal *Renaissance Self-Fashioning: from More to Shakespeare* (Chicago, 1980). In that work, Greenblatt admitted, 'the human subject itself began to seem remarkably unfree, the ideological product of the relations of power in a particular society' (pp. 256–7). To my mind, Peter Holbrook's *Shakespeare's Individualism* (Cambridge, 2010) makes a more powerful case for Shakespearian freedom than does Greenblatt's slighter study of the phenomenon. And where Greenblatt reads Shakespeare's freedom against the absolutism of his own day, Holbrook finds in it a resource with which to counter the crushing instrumentalization of human labour and personality in our increasingly administered world. This is the context in which Holbrook suggests '[w]e need to recognize that Shakespeare's poetic personality is deeply wedded to one particular value: individual freedom' (p. 68). Richard Wilson's *Free Will: Art and Power on Shakespeare's Stage* (Manchester, 2013) sets limits to that freedom and carries on the important wave of work initiated in *Renaissance Self-Fashioning* of determining its scope in a world where human personality is as much determined by culture as by nature. But it sees Shakespeare as modelling political resistance in seeming compliance, bowing to sovereign power in

guaranteed by totally inclusive conversation and agreement.

In this small but significant moment of literary history, then, Shakespeare turned Freetown from the mere, meaningless name of a posh villa into a real place and prospect, grounds for hope, albeit ones that remain just off stage. Verona may be fair ('In fair Verona, where we lay our scene' (Chorus, 2)) but Freetown is fairer, and this activates a significant pun where Freetown *is* fairer because it is *fairer* – more just.[3]

Freetown! It flashes on the mind's eye, and then it is gone: 'like the lightning which doth cease to be / Ere one can say "it lightens"' (2.2.119–20). But, for me at least, it appears in another fleeting epiphany in *Romeo and Juliet*. Capulet has somehow tasked an illiterate servant with inviting a list of people over to his momentous masked ball, where of course Romeo and Juliet will meet. When this nonplussed man asks for help with reading the relevant names, Romeo sympathetically obliges:

> Signor Martino and his wife and daughters;
> County Anselm and his beauteous sisters;
> The lady widow of Vitruvio;
> Signor Placentio and his lovely nieces;
> Mercutio and his brother Valentine;
> Mine uncle Capulet, his wife and daughters;
> My fair niece Rosaline, and Livia;
> Signor Valentio and his cousin Tybalt;
> Lucio and the lively Helena.   (1.2.62–71)

Now I'm interested in the way that Mercutio and Tybalt appear in this list. Later in the play Tybalt sneers, 'Mercutio, thou consortest with Romeo', to which Mercutio snorts, '"Consort"? What, dost thou make us minstrels?' (3.1.44–5). The implication seems to be that Mercutio is gay, though, if he is, he's unfulfilled – it being something of a downer to be a gay man in love with the most famous heterosexual in history. But then the list for Capulet's party actually intimates that Tybalt's gay as well. It's in verse, with each line economically, deftly, rather emblematically *placing* those to whom Capulet is extending his invitation. Some are presented in terms of the patriarchal family – Signor Martino and his wife and daughters; the lady widow of Vitruvio (a rather nice line of blank

verse); Mine Uncle Capulet, his wife and daughters. Other lines pair men with attractive women: County Anselm and his *beauteous* sisters, Lucio and the *lively* Helena. And I feel compelled to say that Signor Placentio with his trophy nieces sounds particularly disagreeably pleased with himself. Anyway, it is in this overwhelming context of patriarchal families and lovely girls that Mercutio and Tybalt are accompanied by male valentines – which in this the greatest and most famous drama of sexual love in Western culture is highly suggestive to say the least.[4] The continuing conversation between

the process of making an art which renounces all sovereignty, including its own. I agree that any new interest in Shakespearian freedom needs to contend with the challenges with which new historicism and cultural materialism struggled, and not just wishfully ignore them (for an astute critique of 'wishful theory', see Jonathan Dollimore, *Sex, Literature and Censorship* (Cambridge, 2001), pp. 37–46). Indeed, I hope that will be evident in the otherworldly, then dark account of freedom offered in my sketch of *Romeo and Juliet*. Nevertheless, I am, like Holbrook, most interested in moments when, against the odds, Shakespearian freedom actually does burst into being, seeking to change the social world, for good or for ill, and sometimes actually succeeding. Most of the materials I address have been expertly treated by theatre historians. They have been less attended to by critics with philosophical or political interests, which I hope to show is a shame.

3 Notable recent readings such as Simon Palfrey's *Romeo and Juliet* (Chippenham, 2012) and Paul A. Kottman's 'Defying the Stars: Tragic Love as the Struggle for Freedom in *Romeo and Juliet*' (*Shakespeare Quarterly*, 63 (2012), 1–38) in their different ways reinforce the notion that the play turns, with its lovers, emphatically away from the civic. That also is Wagner's reading in *Tristan und Isolde*, but Wagner had to excise the civic from Shakespeare and I would argue that a central interest of *Romeo and Juliet* remains its dialectical exploration of free love in relation to the possibilities of civic flourishing.

4 *Romeo and Juliet's* male valentines have, for the most part, been overlooked by criticism. Joseph A. Porter deserves credit for properly noticing Mercutio's Valentine, who, he observes, does not appear in Brooke. He asks, 'what is he doing in the play at all, where does he really come from, what are we to make of him? Who is Valentine really?' ('Mercutio's Brother', *South Atlantic Review*, 49.4 (1984), p. 32). Though you get the impression he knows the answers, what he actually says is somewhat coy: 'Mercutio develops a brother, however ghostly and evanescent, in *Romeo and Juliet* because of the increased brotherliness and decreased amorousness he also develops there'; 'Valentine is there to begin the characterization of Mercutio as fraternal'; 'Who is he really?

Romeo and Capulet's unlettered retainer infuses this prospect of sexual liberty with a transcendent, even heavenly aura:

Romeo. A fair assembly. Whither should they come?
Servingman. Up.
Romeo. Whither? To supper?
Servingman. To our house.
Romeo. Whose house?
Servingman. My master's. (1.2.72–7)

Of course the richest, most vivid icon of freedom in *Romeo and Juliet* is the superbly realized, transgressive conjunction of Romeo and Juliet themselves, but this exchange between Romeo and Capulet's unlettered servant fleetingly extends the privileges of their love. 'A fair assembly': the pun on 'fair' – just as well as beautiful – comes together with the political connotations of 'assembly' and 'house' to suggest that this heavenly fantasy could really be achieved by something resembling democratic struggle. After all, the pleasures proffered by the Capulet ball are very much this-worldly ones: good company, good food, romance, the possibility of sex. That the benighted Capulet of Shakespeare's play is momentarily invested with a more celestial authority sustains the possibility that sexual freedom might actually be realized here.

But then of course brother Valentine and Signor Valentio don't actually 'consort' with Mercutio and Tybalt at the Capulet ball; the play doesn't indicate that they make it to the party at all. And yet, Capulet's bash as much as any other scene in the play dramatizes the political possibility of Freetown. This is because it is masked. Given identities, privileges, prejudices and names are suspended, and the dialogue hints that the disguises worn are actually truer to the undetermined potential of human freedom than the socially recognizable, limited and corrupted faces they cover.[5] It is this which enables Romeo and Juliet to meet, converse, dance and fall in love. The ball truly is a fair assembly; and to that extent, can be thought of as really taking place in Freetown, not Verona.

But the fair assembly could be fairer still. *Romeo and Juliet* condemns Mercutio to wild, hilarious and melancholy opposition to a world which can't accommodate him. In Tybalt, Mercutio's surreal irony becomes sheer fury. The male Valentines which Shakespeare so briefly conjures for them express the tantalizing possibility that Mercutio's and Tybalt's amazing energy could be redeemed into a love which expresses the same degree of force in more positive form. Romeo and Juliet lose their bliss in the process of attaining it: that is their tragedy. But at least Romeo and Juliet attain their tragedy. We pity them but they make it that far. Mercutio and Tybalt stand for the many more who don't.

Here's something *we* can do for Shakespeare and *Romeo and Juliet*. We can make good on the hints, imagining Mercutio and Brother Valentine, Signor Valentio and Tybalt, masked or unmasked, wearing what you like – or, better still, what they like – and dancing with four hundred years of emancipated joy. Of course Romeo and Juliet are there too, their words, bodies and beings describing one shared smile, which this time isn't the least bit star-crossed, misadventured or otherwise doomed. That's what a party in Freetown looks like. Let's drink to it directly!

In a sense Valentine is a possibly subliminal double of the play's lover-hero Romeo' (p. 37). Porter develops his case for this last judgement in *Shakespeare's Mercutio* (Chapel Hill, NC, 1988), pp. 1–10, 145–63. There is something in it, given Mercutio's frustrated passionate friendship for Romeo; but I prefer to see 'brother Valentine' as a figure in his own right for the amorous fulfilment that, though it is not available in Verona to Mercutio, surely would be in Freetown. It is left to Goldberg to notice that his name 'resonates (assonates) with another name down the list, "Signor Valentio and his cousin Tybalt". 'This second Valentine', he concludes, 'participates in a cousinship that, like the brotherhood of Mercutio and Valentine, may name properly what cannot be said' (Jonathan Goldberg, 'Romeo and Juliet's Open Rs', in *Romeo and Juliet*, ed. R. S. White, New Casebook Series (London, 2001), p. 206).

5 Mercutio suggests he is always masked when he says, 'Give me a case to put my visage in: / A visor for a visor' (1.4.29–30). And Juliet expresses even more directly the point that what others think of as our faces may in fact conceal what we are. Her (as he thinks) husband-to-be, Paris, says to his intended when she remarks on her own unlovely face, 'Thy face is mine, and thou hast slandered it'. Juliet responds, 'It may be so, for it is not mine own' (4.1.35–6).

'FREETOWN!': SHAKESPEARE AND SOCIAL FLOURISHING

Freetown, the place with no bar to Romeo and Juliet's love, no bar to Mercutio and Valentine's! Bring it on!

* * *

OK, so far, so (I hope) uplifting. But we're not finished yet. Shakespeare's fearless exploration of free love suggests there is more to Freetown. The balcony scene, for instance, takes us to the next level. Here are some of Juliet's best lines:

> My bounty is as boundless as the sea,
> My love as deep; the more I give to thee,
> The more I have, for both are infinite.
>
> (2.2.133–5)

Mmm, oceanic feeling phasing softly into endlessness . . .

I've suggested the unfulfilled Mercutio relates to the unredeemed world of Verona which can't positively accommodate him by means of energetic irony, but of course such irony ultimately feeds off and so negatively preserves the status quo. Juliet's speech is actually *more* negative, going beyond all bounded forms of life as we know it. Indeed, it is worth remarking that one of the most cherishable things about Shakespeare's play is the way in which the utterly particular – a teenaged girl's amorous enthusiasm – becomes universal. But where does this leave us here below? Indeed, where does it leave Juliet? It leaves her hungering for two things with a chance of accessing the infinite: sex and marriage. Indeed, inasmuch as both aim at absolute union, these two are one. But sex and marriage are forms of this life; they communicate with the infinite only inasmuch as they become hospitable and even transparent to death. And this is where the implied vision of Freetown and civic flourishing in *Romeo and Juliet* is radically, even frighteningly changed. For it is clear that no simply positive adjustment, such as gay liberation, will enable final fulfilment in Freetown. Identity politics isn't enough. Certainly the play asks us to imagine how Mercutio's negativity might be more positively fulfilled by the negation of negative conditions that gay liberation would entail. It insists Freetown has to be able to accommodate Mercutio and Valentine as well as Romeo and Juliet. For Mercutio and Valentine are entitled to their basic liberties, to sex and (why not?) marriage, just as Romeo and Juliet require theirs. Nevertheless, it won't do to imagine a smug and sated Mercutio; it wouldn't even be Mercutio. Nor will it satisfy to imagine Romeo and Juliet in a better world where they get married, have kids and get fat.

There is no Mercutio without his restless energy; no Romeo and Juliet without their more positive negation of ordinary life for which another name is the infinite or eternal.

But wait: what form of social organization could possibly accommodate *this*?! Juliet's ecstatic speeches turn explicitly away from light, just as Romeo was said to have done in the first scene, favouring instead night, death and darkness. This is strange love grown bold indeed, and its implications are more than personal in a play which doesn't indulgently withdraw from the world but instead fearlessly explores the nature and destiny of free love in relation to civic questions (3.2.15).

Remember Juliet says, 'Come, *civil* night', and with that the precious and enigmatic idea of Freetown becomes a considerably darker thing (3.2.10).

2. FREEMAN!

In September 1769, the great Shakespearian actor David Garrick made Freetown a bit more real; and he did so in the then obscure provincial English town that happens to be Shakespeare's birthplace – and of course now houses the Shakespeare Institute, not to mention the Shakespeare Birthplace Trust and the Royal Shakespeare Company. Garrick's Stratford Jubilee wasn't just the first major Shakespeare celebration; it seeded all others. More than anything bar Shakespeare's birth itself, it put Stratford on the map: indeed, for the first time it provided decent access to the town by road. Whenever there's cause to celebrate Shakespeare, the Jubilee comes to mind, and it's no accident that the three authoritative book-length studies were published in the previous anniversary year of 1964.[6]

---

[6] Christian Deelman, *The Great Shakespeare Jubilee* (London, 1964); Martha Winburn England, *Garrick's Jubilee* (Ohio,

Now that 2014 and the four-hundred-and-fiftieth anniversary of Shakespeare's birth are upon us – and what with 2016's four-hundredth anniversary of Shakespeare's death fast approaching – the Jubilee's interest freshens again. But it's worth stressing that in 1769 it was *all freshness*. Cosy, ironic or weary familiarity with what literary festivities have become can prevent us from grasping how novel and surprising it was, perhaps even to Garrick himself. I suggest the Jubilee moved *through* Garrick. It was a *happening*, mocked and marvelled at, ideologically disorganized, susceptible to different interpretations; and yet – if only we have eyes to see it – instrumental to the association of Shakespeare with freedom that proved important to Western modernity and might still provide us with a credible, substantial and interesting reason for celebrating Shakespeare today.

Stratford Town Council precipitated the Jubilee by making Garrick its first ever Freeman, successfully flattering him into donating a statue for the gaping niche in the Sheep-Street-facing façade of the recently rebuilt Town Hall. But, practical considerations apart, transforming Garrick into the Freeman was a decisive step towards the creative conjunction of Shakespeare and freedom. The actor had already done much to link his name and fortunes with Shakespeare's, both on stage at Drury Lane, and by erecting a 'Shakespeare temple' in his garden at Hampton, whose fine statue by Roubiliac (now in the British Museum) was said to look as much like Garrick as it did the Bard. And yet, Garrick's encroachment on the great man's identity and reputation was justified inasmuch as he really did possess an actor's gift that was supremely well matched to Shakespeare's talent for characterization. With his darting glance and mobile face, he alone could live up to the chameleon poet.[7] Now Richard III, now Romeo, now Macbeth, he could seemingly become anyone: Freeman indeed! Stratford formally honoured this freedom in an exquisite box carved from the mulberry tree it maintained was 'undoubtedly planted by Shakespear's own hand'.[8] This artefact, too, is now kept in the British Museum. It is a finely carved piece, detailed with beguiling Shakespeariana, and

a frieze on its back of Garrick as Lear on the heath.

In return for this rich gift of freedom, Garrick furnished the Town Hall with its Shakespeare statue – which (have a look next time you're there) still stands proud, if somewhat blackened by age, over Sheep Street – along with a portrait of Shakespeare to hang inside, though this was lost in the same fire that did for the rather better and better-known portrait of Garrick with Shakespeare's bust that the Corporation acquired at its own expense. Most importantly, Stratford's first Freeman gave the town its Jubilee in honour of its most famous son. And with that the idea of Freetown really shimmers into life again.

Of course Garrick saw the Jubilee as a wonderful opportunity to enhance his own interests, celebrity and identification with Shakespeare – and you've got to say, why not? But it seems equally clear he was moved to extend and share the Shakespearian freedom which the Corporation had conferred on him, and with which he no doubt felt already blessed by the dramatist in the form of his vocation for the Shakespearian stage. With the Jubilee, Garrick took Shakespeare to the people; he took him out of the institutions of the theatre and scholarship and, quite literally, to the streets. A contemporary watercolour from the collection of the Shakespeare Birthplace Trust shows Garrick presiding over the Jubilee in gorgeous style, sporting his long staff, with his large mulberry-wood medallion hanging round his neck, trimmed in multicoloured ribbon: the Freeman as the rainbow man.[9]

1964); Johanne M. Stochholm, *Garrick's Folly: The Shakespeare Jubilee of 1769 at Stratford and Drury Lane* (London, 1964). I have drawn on all of these sources in what follows.

7   See Keats's letter to Richard Woodhouse, 27 October 1818, in *Letters of John Keats: A Selection*, ed. Robert Gittings (Oxford, 1970), pp. 157–8.

8   Quoted in Hugh Tait, 'Garrick, Shakespeare and Wilkes', *British Museum Journal*, 24 (1961), p. 102. Tait also features an image of the box.

9   ER1/82: Watercolour drawing of David Garrick as Steward at the Stratford-upon-Avon Jubilee, *c.*1769 in 'An Account of the Jubilee celebrated at Stratford-upon-Avon in honour of Shakspeare, 1769'. Saunders papers, *c.*1813, p. 78 (Shakespeare Centre Library and Archive).

19. A rosette made of the 'rainbow' ribbon worn at the Garrick Jubilee, *c.* 1769.

But Garrick wasn't just arrogating the Bard's many-splendoured freedom to himself. On the contrary: he really did give Shakespeare's freedom away. To the schedule of the day's entertainments he added this: 'The Steward hopes that the Admirers of Shakespeare, will, upon this Occasion, wear the Favors which are called the Shakespeare Favors.' Note the Freeman is happy to turn Steward in order to celebrate Shakespeare's freedom. The sashes, rosettes and badges he commends to the crowd were made of a rich silk ribbon, three inches wide, with a picot edge. The ribbon maker, one Mr Jackson of Coventry, explained in the flyers that were handed about:

A Ribband has been made on purpose at Coventry call'd The Shakespeare Ribband; it is in imitation of the Rainbow, which, uniting the Colours of all Parties, is likewise an emblem of the great Variety of his Genius. 'Each change of many colour'd Life he drew'.   Johnson.[10]

Thus did every lapel in Stratford gorgeously proclaim that Shakespeare's inclusive genius really was for each and all (Illustration 19).

It was a constant theme of the Jubilee. Communal feasting and singing were central. At the most ceremonious banquet the Freeman served up

[10] See Deelman, *The Great Shakespeare Jubilee*, p. 184; and Stochholm, *Garrick's Folly*, p. 21. The quotation from Johnson derives from the lines he wrote to be spoken by Garrick at the opening of Drury Lane on 15 September 1747. Stochholm reports Boswell's comment in *The Public Advertiser* that 'I dare say Mr. Samuel Johnson never imagined that this fine Verse of his would appear on a Bill to promote the Sale of Ribbands' (p. 21). As we shall see, Boswell was otherwise an enthusiastic participant in the Jubilee. Kate Rumbold is good on the curious and shifting ambiguities of the festival ('The Stratford Jubilee', in *Shakespeare in the Eighteenth Century*, ed. Fiona Ritchie and Peter Sabor (Cambridge, 2012), pp. 254–76). My view is that they were inevitable given its novelty; as I have argued, the Jubilee is a happening, one through which an inspiring, mutually enhancing and enlivening association of Shakespeare with freedom is originated.

turtle: a hell of a turtle in fact – it weighed, when living, no less than 327 pounds. Why turtle? 'Let the type and shadow of the master grace his board', Garrick's great correspondent Edmund Burke had written, explaining that it was the consummation of all meats, and therefore most fitting for a dinner in honour of one who 'can represent all the solidity of flesh, the volatility of fowl, and the oddity of fish'.[11] 'The lad of all lads was a Warwickshire lad', sang Stratford, and thus was Shakespeare's freedom at once celebrated and brought home.[12] And if the keynote was of bright festivity, this wasn't exclusive of more serious, even quasi-religious feelings, as became clear when, after Garrick had edified everyone with his Shakespeare Ode, they all passed round and eagerly drank from a mulberry goblet that was ornamented with silver. 'Garrick was a worshipper himself', as Cowper wrote in *The Task*:

> He drew the liturgy, and form'd the rites
> And solemn ceremonial of the day,
> And call'd the world to worship on the banks
> Of Avon, fam'd in song.[13]

He called *the world* to worship. 'It is scarce credible the Number of Persons of all Ranks that came to see it', marvelled *The Public Advertiser*.[14] The costs may have been prohibitive, and Garrick may have ridiculed the Stratford locals when he reprised the Jubilee for his Drury Lane audiences, but the original intention and atmosphere of his first ever Shakespeare Jubilee was unprecedentedly liberal and inviting.[15]

And if it at least symbolically involved everyone, it also extended a new spirit of tolerant inclusiveness to all aspects of human personality: 'Wenches! never was any paradise so plentifully and beautifully inhabited as here at this time', according to the excited correspondent of *Lloyds Evening Post*.[16] And if you didn't like wenches, there was a horse race.

Garrick didn't dodge the darker aspects of freedom which we have seen already in *Romeo and Juliet*. His Bard is the more god-like for his daemonic inscrutability. Consider lines such as this for instance:

> The subject passions round him wait;
> Who tho' unchained, and raging there,
> He checks, inflames, or turns their mad career.[17]

This presents Shakespeare as a sorcerer possessed of a hectic and rather frightening power in tension with the civilizing mission that the Ode otherwise invests him with. And when Garrick tries to phase away from such daemonic passions into an overwhelming joy, that joy quickly darkens into a wildly permissive sensuality which seems to remember and reprise them. 'With kindling cheeks, and sparkling eyes...the Bard in transport dies' (p. 9): this makes us very intimate with Shakespeare indeed. The Ode goes on to envision in intricate detail his ecstatic mental impregnation, the huge fruit of which is testimony, of course, to his amazing fertility, but also suggests an exceptionally painful birth. For what springs fully formed from Shakespeare's head isn't a paragon of conventional virtue – nor even some sylph-like goddess, nor even Hamlet – but rather the enormous libertine Falstaff, his superabundant largeness very explicitly expressing a vitality that exceeds all limits. Or, as Garrick, puts it: 'a world where all

---

[11] Quoted in England, *Garrick's Jubilee*, p. 58.
[12] Written by Garrick, and set by Charles Dibdin, according to Deelman this 'at once became the hit tune of the whole festival' (*The Great Shakespeare Jubilee*, p. 184).
[13] Quoted in Deelman, *The Great Shakespeare Jubilee*, p. 261; on the religious aura surrounding the communal drinking from the mulberry goblet, see Péter Dávidházi, *The Romantic Cult of Shakespeare: Literary Reception in Anthropological Perspective* (Houndmills, Basingstoke and London, 1998).
[14] *The Public Advertiser*, Sept. 16, 1769, 3, col. 1; quoted in Stochholm, *Garrick's Folly*, p. 58. 'No company, so various in character, temper, and condition, ever formed, at least in appearance, such an agreeable group of happy and congenial souls', according to Tom Davies (quoted in Deelman, *The Great Shakespeare Jubilee*, p. 183). Looking back in 1964, Martha England wrote, 'Hairdressers and earls, townspeople, runaway apprentices, lords and ladies and actors all rejoiced together' (England, *Garrick's Jubilee*, p. 46).
[15] See Dávidházi, *Romantic Cult of Shakespeare*, p. 39.
[16] See *Lloyds Evening Post*, Sept. 4–6, 1769, 25, 231, 2; quoted in Stochholm, p. 47.
[17] David Garrick, *An Ode upon Dedicating a Building, and Erecting a Statue, to Shakespeare, at Stratford upon Avon. By D. G.* (London, 1769), p. 5.

pleasures abound', for, we're told, 'the world too is wicked and round'.

> So FALSTAFF will never decline, . . .
> And his rain and his rivers are wine; . . .
> And away with all sorrow and care.   (p. 10)

Thus the rainbow man presents the fat man as the happy avatar of all the freedom and fullness of Shakespearian being. And he does so without blanding out the darker shades of the spectrum such freedom entails. That he does in public and in relation to rebuilding a town hall and, by implication, a real community is striking, and perhaps should put us on our mettle as we celebrate Shakespeare in 14/16. At its heart, Garrick's civic Shakespeare Ode offers an undiscriminating celebration of life. *Banish plump Jack, and banish all the world*;[18] but Falstaff returns from banishment to Stratford in 1769 to become the unexpected type of civic flourishing, a flourishing based not as it usually is on sacrifice and repression but on emancipating all we desire and are.

The first ever Shakespeare Jubilee has been especially mocked for not, in fact, including any Shakespeare – and it is difficult to imagine that a Shakespeare festival today could get away without including any plays or poems. But I've been trying to bring out a neglected radical stripe to what Garrick did. He celebrated Shakespeare not so much as literary heritage to be preserved against the depredations of time and change, but instead as example and inspiration. He celebrated Shakespeare as the very quintessence of freedom, as the proof and promise of *new* life.

3. WILKES AND LIBERTY!

The political muse of the Jubilee was the maverick demagogue John Wilkes. Champion of electoral reform, freedom of religion, freedom of the press and even a free America (more of which later), Wilkes was the foremost figurehead for liberty in British politics. But he was just as much a *libertine*: author of the pornographic poem, 'An Essay on Woman', and leading light of the Hellfire Club, who dressed in Franciscan robes to enact

mad, drunken debauchery with courtesans attired as nuns – and, on one infamous occasion, a baboon. The inspiring attractions of political liberalism, and the darker freedoms it might entail, come together in Wilkes. When he was imprisoned for seditious libel for his attack on George III in number 45 of his radical paper, *The North Briton*, the cry of 'Wilkes and Liberty!' rang through British politics. The protest was serious and sustained, with seven protestors dying as they chanted, 'No liberty, no King' at the St George's Field Massacre in 1768. Coverage of events in Stratford in *Lloyd's Evening Post* on the 8 September 1769 made the connection between Garrick and Wilkes, but Garrick also alluded to it himself in a cryptic announcement placed in the *Public Advertiser* of 8 July 1769:

A CARD
The Mulberry Box presents Compliments to the Standish of the same Materials, hoping they shall meet very soon at the London Tavern, and that an uninterrupted Friendship may thenceforward succeed to their late Separation, as they are appointed to Joint Shares in the same Office, viz. Grooms of the *Stool* to the Supporters of the *Bill of Rights*.[19]

Well, I say cryptic but you'll recognize the mulberry box as the exquisite artefact mentioned

---

[18] *1 Henry IV*, 2.5.438. Shakespeare references unless otherwise indicated are to *The Norton Shakespeare*, ed. Stephen Greenblatt (London and New York, 2008).

[19] Quoted in Tait, 'Garrick, Shakespeare and Wilkes', p. 106. Links between Garrick and Wilkes are suggested by Michael Dobson, *The Making of the National Poet: Shakespeare, Adaptation and Authorship, 1660–1769* (Oxford, 1992), pp. 218–19, n. 48. The following is evidence of an association between Wilkes and Shakespeare before the Jubilee: *The three conjurors: a political interlude, stolen from Shakespeare, as it was performed at sundry places in Westminster; on Saturday the 30th of April, and Sunday the 1st of May: most humbly dedicated to John Wilkes, Esq* (London: printed for E. Cabe, 1763). Pertinently to my theme, Dobson also notes that '[o]ne conservative reviewer of the *Ode*, indeed, objects anxiously to Garrick's invocation of Euphrosyne by 'a new title, not to be found in any books of celestial heraldry, either ancient or modern, I mean that of "Goddess of *Liberty*"' (quoted in *Anti-Midas: A jubilee preservative from unclassical, ignorant, false and insidious criticism* (London, 1769), p. 29).

already within which Garrick received his Freedom of Stratford. The 'standish of the same materials' was a gift given by the town to George Keate for delivering his freedom to Garrick. The Society of the Supporters of the Bill of Rights was founded in 1769 to aid Wilkes and press for parliamentary reform; it is the first major extra-parliamentary political association in Britain. Garrick therefore, in the *Evening Post*, is making a connection between the Freedom of Stratford and the serious campaign for political freedom that is getting underway in this period; indeed, he subordinates Shakespeare and Stratford to that real-world campaign by casting himself and Keate as 'Grooms of the Stool to the Supporters of the Bill of Rights'.

But of course the political vitality of the association of Shakespeare and freedom outlasts Wilkes, as we'll see. And though it's true that Wilkes influenced Garrick's Shakespeare Jubilee, it is much more the case that the Jubilee in turn influenced the cause of Wilkes and liberty. After Stratford, jubilees very much based on what Garrick had done for Shakespeare were held in Wilkes's honour. Wilkes's forty-fifth birthday on 28 October 1769 – a special one, since it resonated with and recalled that consequential number 45 of *The North Briton* – was duly celebrated in the King's Bench Prison, with songs adapted from the Jubilee song book, *Shakespeare's Garland*, and another three-hundred-pound turtle.[20] It was done all over again on the 18 April 1770: the day of Wilkes's enlargement. The published text on this occasion is dedicated to 'the spirited and noble freeholders of Middlesex', who had repeatedly voted for Wilkes each time his election was declared void by the government on questionable grounds.[21] These celebrations recognize that 'Mr. Garrick may brag / Of his Warwickshire wag' (p. 26), but they reappropriate the greatest hit of the Jubilee as follows:

No threats, no persuasions can move him,
Still true to a people who love him;
Their laws and their rights he will ever defend,
For the friend of all friends is a Middlesex friend:

Middlesex friend,
Freedom defend,
And the friend of all friends is a Middlesex friend.
(p. 3 ff.)

They also include a ninth song, 'To Liberty', to be sung 'to any tune the reader pleases' (p. 18).

And the freedom train rolls on, carrying the hope of Freetown into a post-Jubilee future. If we now look, just briefly, back at the Shakespeare Tercentary of 1864, for instance, we find this boldly printed handbill:

TIME! SHAKESPEARE THE POET
OF THE PEOPLE

People of Stratford! Where are the seats reserved for you at the forthcoming festival? What part or lot have you who originated it, in the coming celebration? None! But you will be permitted to see the Fireworks, because they cannot be let off in the Pavilion; and you are promised something for yourself *after the swells have dined.* Only wait till the next week, and see the dainty mess that shall be BREWED for you out of the cold 'wittles'. PEOPLE OF STRATFORD, who would not see your town disgraced on such an occasion, your streets empty, or blocked up by the carriages of *profitless swells,*

take counsel without delay!
Call a meeting without delay!
Form your own Committee!!
Hold your own Festival!!!
Look to your own business. Lay out your own money.
Get up your own out-door sports and in-door
     pastimes, and let your watchword be

SHAKESPEARE the POET OF THE PEOPLE
AND HURRAH FOR THE PAGEANT[22]

The people got their pageant, and some 30,000 came to enjoy it. Meanwhile, in London, the

---

[20] Deelman, *The Great Shakespeare Jubilee*, p. 264. See also *Shakespeare's Garland. Being A Collection of New Songs, Ballads, Roundelays, Catches, Glees, Comic-Serenatas, &c. Performed at the Jubilee at Stratford upon Avon. The Musick by Dr. Arne, Mr. Bartholomew, Mr. Allwood, and Mr. Dibdin* (London, 1769).

[21] *The Patriot's Jubilee, being songs proper to be sung on Wednesday, the 18th of April, 1770; the day of Mr Wilkes's enlargement from the King's-Bench* (London, 1770), p. iii.

[22] Reproduced in Richard Foulkes, *The Shakespeare Tercentenary of 1864* (London, 1984), pp. 35–6.

20. Staffordshire ceramic figures of Garibaldi and Shakespeare

Working Men's Shakespeare Committee planted a tree in Shakespeare's memory on Primrose Hill, and then went on to conduct a political protest in favour of General Garibaldi, a demonstration that had to be broken up by police. The concreteness and sheer popularity of the historical association of Shakespeare and liberty in this country is evinced by the production in 1864 of matching ceramic figures of Garibaldi and Shakespeare (Illustration 20).[23]

They really look like twins, and theirs, presumably, is the face of freedom. If you look harder at this face, perhaps you can see the ancestral resemblance to Garrick. Wilkes was uglier; but if you look hard enough, maybe you can see him too.

4. VIVA LA LIBERTÀ!

Michael Dobson has pointed to a major apparent contradiction of the Jubilee: its celebration of Shakespeare both as a universal genius *and* as specifically English.[24] *The lad of all lads is a Warwickshire lad.* But the centrality of the idea of freedom to the festival can perhaps help resolve this tension.

---

[23] For more on the theme of Shakespeare and real world political emancipation, see Peter Holbrook, 'Shakespeare, "The cause of the people", and the Chartist Circular 1839–1842', *Textual Practice*, 20 (2006), 203–29 and Andrew Murphy, *Shakespeare for the People: Working Class Readers, 1800–1990* (Cambridge, 2008).

[24] See Dobson, *The Making of the National Poet*, p. 219.

21. James Boswell Esqr from *The London Magazine*, September 1769, print made by Johann Sebastian Müller after Samuel Wale.

Shakespeare's freedom frees the English to be themselves, throwing off the yoke of more established cultures: Greece, Rome and France. Free Shakespearian England then, in turn, sets other cultures free. This romance of freedom explains why news of the first Shakespeare Jubilee was enthusiastically received even in France, despite Garrick's mocking subversion of French pretensions to cultural superiority: during the festivities Garrick saw off a planted actor (Tom King) pretending to be a French Shakespeare detractor. But it was from the *Mercure de France* (December 1769) that Goethe copied an extensive account of Garrick's 'Fête de Shakespeare' into his volume of Wieland's German translation of the Bard's works.[25] Germany is the most striking example in Western culture of how Shakespearian freedom fuelled nascent nationalism; Shakespeare comes to represent their own potential freedom to the Germans.

But the international potential of Shakespeare's freedom was in fact already evident during the Jubilee itself. 'It was not confined to the English only', reported *The Public Advertiser*, 'for the Scotch and the Irish were as eager in paying their devotion.'[26] We have seen that Garrick's subsequent account of the festival to Drury Lane mockingly excluded Stratford residents; it also excluded the Irish. Perhaps Garrick was finally overwhelmed by the relentless attacks of theatre folk such as Samuel Foote, and scholars such as George Steevens, who were horrified by the threat Garrick's great Shakespeare give-away represented to their own Shakespearian interests. But Garrick was probably also influenced by resuming his own institutional role back in the capital of discrimination in London as its leading actor-manager. In any case, he partially retreated from the radical inclusivity of what he had attempted in Stratford. Still, the part played there by the Scot, James Boswell, sufficiently demonstrates that the first Shakespeare jubilee really wasn't just English for the English.

Boswell came to Stratford resplendent in the costume of a Corsican chief (Illustration 21). As the latter-day editors of his journals suggest, he saw in Corsica's fight for independence – first from the Genoese, then from the French – his own private struggles for liberty externalized.[27] Boswell visited Corsica, went native with the rebels there, and launched himself when he returned into an elaborate newspaper campaign intended ultimately to persuade the British government to intervene and support them. He personally raised money to arm the rebels, and edited a volume of essays 'in favour of the brave Corsicans'. But his 'little monument to liberty' was his own book: *An Account of Corsica; The Journal of a Tour to That Island, and Memoirs of Pascal Paoli* (the Corsican rebel leader). It was a great success in Britain and in Europe, and had a real impact on European politics. The French government commissioned a translation and the British sent secret supplies to the Corsicans. But, in spite of Boswell's efforts, they weren't about to declare war on France on behalf of a small island of apparently little strategic interest and the rebels had been decisively routed by the time of the Stratford Jubilee.[28]

But that didn't stop Boswell from hitching his one-man international liberation movement to Garrick's Shakespeare festival. His diary entry for the 2 September 1769 tells how, in preparation for Stratford, he sought out 'an embroiderer in Bow Street, Covent Garden; gave him, cut out in paper as well as I could, the form of a Corsican cap, and ordered *Viva la Libertà* to be embroidered on the front of it in letters of gold' (p. 288). Two days later he was tramping all over London searching for other Corsican necessaries, then happily observing that he could get it all in his 'travelling-bag, except my musket and staff'. The staff he describes as 'a very handsome vine with the root uppermost, and upon it a bird, very well carved'. 'I paid six shillings for it', he records. 'I told the master of the shop, "Why, Sir, this vine is worth any money. It

---

25 See Martha Winburn England, 'Garrick's Stratford Jubilee: Reactions in France and Germany', in *Shakespeare Survey 9* (Cambridge, 1956), p. 94.

26 *The Public Advertiser*, 16 September 1769, 3, col. 1; quoted in Stochholm, *Garrick's Folly*, p. 58.

27 See James Boswell, *Boswell in Search of a Wife, 1766–69*, ed. Frank Brady and Frederick A. Pottle (Melbourne, London, Toronto, 1957), p. xvi.

28 See Boswell, *Wife*, p. xvii.

is a Jubilee staff. That bird is the bird of Avon'" (pp. 291–2). Only a deep and natural association of Shakespeare and freedom will make of Boswell's Corsican kit and a staff that might have been carved in Arden such a miraculously coherent ensemble. It suggests that the time was ripe for Garrick to turn Stratford into Freetown.

In the course of his trip there, Boswell attempts to keep his Shakespearian-cum-Corsican thirst for liberty pure, by marshalling the image of his fiancée or, as he prefers to call her, 'my valuable spouse' against any spectres of sexual temptation. He takes to the road in high excitement, travelling part of the way in the company of an agreeable and familiar female escort. 'I allowed myself no other liberty than once drawing my hand gently along her yellow locks', he insists (p. 293). When he finds himself at the Jubilee chatting up Captain Sheldon's wife, and with the image of his 'valuable spouse' fading alarmingly, he improvises: 'I rose and went near the orchestra, and looked steadfastly at that beautiful, insinuating creature, Mrs. Baddeley of Drury Lane, and in an instant Mrs. Sheldon was effaced' (p. 299). Here that same tension between liberty and libertinism we saw in Wilkes is brought into a much more explicit association with Shakespearian freedom.

But Boswell also lived it up in the sense of being seriously edified by the Jubilee. He felt for a moment he could live a better life if he lived it in Stratford; but we all grow out of that delusion. His Corsican contribution was a hit, and he wrote his 'Verses in the Character of a Corsican at Shakespeare's Jubilee' in the very midst of festivities. They tell the story of a proud and noble exile come '[t]o soothe my soul on Avon's sacred stream', offering a piteous glimpse of the Corsican river Golo '[o]'er which dejected, injured freedom bends'. They suggest that if Shakespeare had lived 'our story to relate', and Garrick had deigned to act it, then 'from his eyes had flashed the Corsic fire, / Men had less gazed to pity – than admire'! 'O happy Britons!', the peroration swells, 'on whose favoured isle, / Propitious freedom ever deigns to smile / . . . let me plead for liberty distressed, / With generous ardour make

us also free; / And give to Corsica a noble jubilee!'[29]

A word on Boswell's timing. In one sense, it was sheer vanity to have continued the campaign for Corsican liberty when that had clearly become impossible. But Walter Benjamin's 'Theses on the Philosophy of History' suggest that in order to save the future we first have to save the past, redeeming its lost potential in the interest of a better tomorrow.[30] Perhaps it was in that spirit that Boswell took it upon himself to embody and plead for Corsican liberty just as it was sliding into the dustbin of history. Though he excluded the Irish, Garrick included the Corsican Boswell in his stage play about the Jubilee, and Boswell seems to have lent Garrick his costume so that the impersonation might be more apt. That figure of the Corsican Boswell embodies the hope of the Jubilee at its best that Shakespeare's freedom might come to be the glory of a free people who felicitate in the freedom of others.

5. LAND OF THE FREE!

But if the Jubilee was associated with nationalism, it has also been associated with the inception of Empire. In support of this Dobson, for example, fished out the following anonymous but contemporary verses from the bowels of the Bodleian:

> While Britons bow at Shakespear's shrine
> Britannia's sons are sons of mine.

---

[29] Quoted from *The London Magazine*, September 1769 in Stochholm, *Garrick's Folly*, p. 95. Boswell's verses linking Shakespeare, freedom and the cause of Corsica give the lie to the following lines from Peter Barnes's 2001 RSC play, *Jubilee*:

Garrick. James Boswell will appear as a Corsican patriot. What Shakespeare play is that from?

Boswell. It's got nothing to do with Shakespeare. I'm promoting my new book, Travels in Corsica. I have a few signed copies left. Not at Jubilee prices.' (*Jubilee* (London, 2001), p. 82).

[30] Walter Benjamin, 'Theses on the Philosophy of History', in *Illuminations*, ed. Hannah Arendt, trans. Harry Zorn (London, 1999), pp. 245–55. See also Ronald Beiner, 'Walter Benjamin's Philosophy of History', *Political Theory*, 12 (1984), 423–34.

Like him shou'd Britons scorn the Art
That binds in chains the human heart
Like him shou'd still be unconfin'd
And rule the world as he the mind.[31]

But it is notable that the Shakespearian conception of Empire expressed here is explicitly imagined as freedom at its fullest extent, and freedom is also crucial to that more familiar and less Nietzschean rationalization according to which Empire actually liberates its British subjects.[32] Having said that, if Shakespearian freedom inaugurates Empire, it also inspires Americans, for instance, to resist English domination before and after the Revolution. The nascent German nation appropriated Shakespearian freedom as its own destiny; the Americans were quicker to mobilize Shakespearian freedom *against* the English.

Instructive here are the rival New York performances of *Macbeth* by the American actor Edwin Forrest, known as 'The Native Tragedian', and the great English Shakespearian of his day, Charles Macready: a head-to-head which precipitated the Astor Place Riots, one of the most lamentable episodes in the city's history before 9/11.

Forrest, who at his smouldering best looked like an 'ante-bellum Elvis', was the very incarnation of American independence.[33] 'Early in life', he said, 'I took a great deal of exercise and made myself what I am, a Hercules.'[34] But perhaps even that's too traditional and derived from civilized models since, according to one reviewer, his voice was, 'replete with a rough music befitting one who in his youth had dwelt, a free barbarian, among the mountains'.[35] His acting lent Shakespeare's great male parts an explosive physical immediacy and power. Other favourite roles included the peasant revolutionary Jack Cade, whose last, triumphant utterance is 'The bondman is avenged, my country free!'; and the Native American Metamora, whose piercing battle-cry goes, 'Our lands! Our nation's freedom! Or the grave!'[36] In nineteenth-century New York, Forrest was the hero of the gangs and theatre of the Bowery, the latter being as Walt Whitman recalled, 'no dainty kid-glove business, but electric force and muscle from perhaps 2,000 full sinew'd men'.[37]

This presented, to say the least, a very different kind of theatre from that in which Macready excelled.

In fact, on the transatlantic Shakespeare circuit Forrest at first made a friend of the Englishman, but he was increasingly offended by Macready's more academic and reflective style, which to The Native Tragedian smelt of the persistent pretensions of English imperialism. Their rivalry played out on both sides of the pond and when Macready's Edinburgh Hamlet sported distractedly with a handkerchief in a gesture Forrest would subsequently denominate a 'pas de mouchoir', the American was there to hiss him; and it wasn't long before he was referring to his rival as 'the superannuated driveller'.[38] It is actually unfair that by the time of the crisis Macready in New York had come to stand for the elite exclusivity of English culture since, unlike his friend Charles Dickens, he was a great admirer of American liberty and at one time had wanted to retire to Massachusetts.[39] But Forrest and his supporters were bent on punishing Macready and the English in the name of Shakespearian freedom, and nothing could stop them now. When Macready's Macbeth was being heckled and pelted in the upscale Astor Place theatre on the evening of the 7 May 1854, Forrest roared from one of the city's other stages, 'What rhubarb, senna

---

[31] *Ode to Shakespeare*, in Bodleian Library MS Mus d 14, quoted in Dobson, *The Making of the National Poet*, p. 227.

[32] For more on the way in which imperialism can in fact yoke together 'the classically incompatible ideas of liberty and empire', see David Armitage, *The Ideological Origins of the British Empire* (Cambridge, 2001), p. 8 and *passim*. But of course the trouble with freedom as justification for Empire is that it eventually furnishes imperial subjects with a motive for revolt.

[33] Nigel Cliff, *The Shakespeare Riots: Revenge, Drama and Death in 19th-Century America* (London, 2007), p. 131.

[34] Quoted in Cliff, *Shakespeare Riots*, p. 20.

[35] See Cliff, *Shakespeare Riots*, p. 90.

[36] See Michael Dobson, 'Let him be Caesar!', *London Review of Books* (2 August 2007).

[37] Quoted in Cliff, *Shakespeare Riots*, p. 88.

[38] *Public Ledger*, November 22, 1848; quoted in Cliff, *Shakespeare Riots*, pp. 167 ff.

[39] See Cliff, *Shakespeare Riots*, pp. 175–6.

or what purgative drug would scour these English hence?' As Nigel Cliff tells the story, 'Four thousand people rose as one, and for several minutes they cheered for America.'[40]

Macready kept his dignity throughout the crisis, but he was ready to go home, and who can blame him? That he didn't was only because what turned out to be a misguided delegation, led by Washington Irving and horrified by the fast-developing stain on New York's international reputation as a centre for civilized culture, persuaded him to perform again. In the meantime, posters were rushed up all over New York that exactly anticipate the idiom of revolt we have already encountered on the handbills distributed for the tercentenary celebrations in Stratford-upon-Avon ('Shakespeare the Poet of the People!', 'People of Stratford!' etc.), but in New York the immediate consequences would be graver.

WORKING MEN,
SHALL
AMERICANS
OR
ENGLISH RULE
IN THIS CITY?
The Crew of the British steamer have
Threatened all Americans who shall dare to express
    their
opinions this night, at the
ENGLISH ARISTOCRATIC OPERA HOUSE!
We advocate no violence, but a free expression of
    opinion
to all public men.
WORKINGMEN! FREEMEN!
STAND BY YOUR
LAWFUL RIGHTS!
American Committee.[41]

The crew of the British steamer hadn't actually threatened anything of the sort, but when Macready resumed the stage at Astor Place on the 10 May a 15,000-strong mob descended and attacked the theatre.

It all ended with soldiers firing at point-blank range on a civilian crowd, at least twenty-six of whom died; in a sense, these dead are casualties of the idea of Shakespearian freedom. Macready

had to be smuggled out of the city in disguise. It is surely one of the darkest days in the history of Shakespeare reception.

But Shakespearian freedom had another major effect on American politics, and in such a way as still further darkens the motif. We have seen that Wilkes was, via Garrick, associated with Shakespeare as a proponent of freedom, and he had a major impact on American revolutionary thought.[42] But in American history Wilkes and Shakespeare are most strikingly reunited in the career of John Wilkes Booth, who of course assassinated Abraham Lincoln. His is a story which perversely reconjoins, as Albert Furtwangler puts it, 'the English master of action and the American ideal of human freedom'.[43]

'But who was this Booth?' as Carl Sandburg asks in a famous passage. 'In what kind of green-poison pool of brain and personality had the amazing and hideous crime arisen?'[44] Booth was the son of the English Shakespearian actor Junius Brutus Booth, who was Edmund Kean's greatest rival. Junius Brutus was named after the most obvious exemplar of Shakespearian freedom, and the one who, at least in part, inspired Booth to kill the President. Kean, for his part, could be cast as an exemplar of Shakespearian freedom at its most unrestrained, and the assassin's alcoholic bigamist and not infrequently deranged dad (aka 'The Mad Tragedian') certainly gives him a run for his money, but that's another story.[45] Booth himself was named after that other

[40] See Cliff, *Shakespeare Riots*, p. xx.

[41] See Cliff, *Shakespeare Riots*, pp. 211–12.

[42] See Pauline Maier, *From Resistance to Revolution: Colonial Radicals and the Development of American Opposition to Britain 1765–7* (New York, 1992); see also, Jack Lynch, 'Wilkes, Liberty, and Number 45', *Colonial Williamsburg Journal* (Summer 2003).

[43] Albert Furtwangler, *Assassin on Stage: Brutus, Hamlet and the Death of Lincoln* (Urbana and Chicago, 1991), p. ix.

[44] Carl Sandburg, *Abraham Lincoln: The War Years* (New York, 1939), vol. 4, p. 301.

[45] Here's a choice memory of Edmund Kean: 'Kean requested the rehearsal might not be till twelve as he should get drunk that night – said he had frequently three women to stroke during performances and that two waited while the other was served . . . That night he had one woman (Smith) though

avatar of liberty we have met already: John Wilkes, a distant relative. His family home, which is still standing, was called Tudor Hall. He went to the Milton's Boarding School for Boys. He became an actor, making his stage debut at seventeen as the tyrant-killer Richmond in *Richard III*. If he acted in *Julius Caesar* (or excerpted scenes) just six times, he nevertheless knew the play by heart from childhood. He was a notable talent, Whitman (again) suggesting that he had flashes of 'real genius'.[46] In 1863 in Washington he was billed as 'The Pride of the American People'.[47]

Booth's sister recalled that as the Confederacy's defeat became more and more certain her brother started to fulminate in 'wild tirades' against Lincoln 'making himself a king'.[48] When Robert E. Lee surrendered at Appomatox Court House, Booth said he was done with the stage and that the only play he wanted to be in now was *Venice Preserv'd*, which is about assassination. Booth shot the President in his box at Ford's theatre in Washington, subsequently jumping on a stage on which he had frequently acted.

Whitman takes up the story in a transfixed present tense:

Booth, the murderer, dress'd in plain black broadcloth, bare-headed, with full, glossy, raven hair, and his eyes like some mad animal's flashing with light and resolution, yet with a certain strange calmness, holds aloft in one hand a large knife – walks along not much back from the footlights – turns fully towards the audience his face of statuesque beauty, lit by those basilisk eyes, flashing with desperation, perhaps insanity – launches out in a firm and steady voice the words *Sic semper tyrannis* – and then walks with neither slow nor very rapid pace diagonally across to the back of the stage, and disappears.[49]

'Sic semper tyrannis', 'Thus always to tyrants', is attributed to Brutus at Caesar's assassination, and is also the Virginia state motto. Whitman contends that what happened at Ford's theatre 'illustrates those climax-moments on the stage of universal Time, where the historic Muse at one entrance, and the tragic Muse at the other, suddenly ringing down the curtain, close an immense act in the

long drama of creative thought, and give it radiation, tableau, stranger than fiction'.[50]

Certainly there is something ultimate about Booth's act, though it did not quite bring the curtain down on Shakespeare and freedom. Indeed, Booth's own brother Edwin Booth's celebrated and sustained performances of Hamlet after the assassination constitute more than just a strenuous refutation of what John Wilkes had done; they equally refute the association it implied between Shakespeare and political violence, for Edwin's Hamlet presented 'political murder as a futile act, a hollow victory', 'corrosive and self-destroying'.[51] And yet, it is impossible to deny that mixed up in Booth's assassination of the President were Shakespeare, Brutus, John Wilkes, Milton and the heady modern idea of freedom to which they all contribute. According to Thomas Goodrich, 'All the elements in Booth's nature came together at once – his hatred of tyranny, his love of liberty, his passion for the stage.'[52] The diary of the hunted

---

he was much infected' (James Winston, *Drury Lane Journal: Selections from James Winston's Diaries 1819–27*, ed. Alfred L. Nelson and Gilbert B. Cross (London, 1974), p. 4).
[46] Quoted in Gene Smith, *American Gothic: The Story of America's Legendary Theatrical Family, Junius, Edwin, and John Wilkes Booth* (New York, 1992), p. 80.
[47] See Gordon Samples, *Lust for Fame: The Stage Career of John Wilkes Booth* (Jefferson, North Carolina and London, 1982), p. 105.
[48] Asia Booth Clarke, *John Wilkes Booth: A Sister's Memoir* (Jackson, Mississippi, 1996), p. 89.
[49] Walt Whitman, 'Death of Abraham Lincoln: Lecture deliver'd in New York, April 14, 1879 – in Philadelphia, '80 – in Boston, '81', in *Prose Works 1892, vol. 2: Collect and Other Prose*, ed. Floyd Stovall, *The Collected Writings of Walt Whitman* (New York, 1964), pp. 505, 508.
[50] Whitman, 'Death of Abraham Lincoln', p. 508.
[51] Furtwangler, *Assassin on Stage*, p. 141.
[52] Thomas Goodrich, *The Darkest Dawn* (Bloomington, 2005), p. 62. 'One of his theatrical friends even claimed that the actor's admiration for the classical Brutus was the "mainspring" of the assassination' ('Introduction' to John Wilkes Booth, *'Right or Wrong, God Judge Me': The Writings of John Wilkes Booth*, ed. John Rhodehamel and Louise Taper (Urbana and Chicago, 2001), p. 8). The footnote to this sentence reads: 'The remarks of John T. Ford, owner of Ford's Theatre, were quoted in a letter (signed 'A MARYLANDER') to the editor of the *Philadelphia Press*, 27 November,

assassin suggests unstable alternations between self-assertion and self-doubt that are reminiscent of James Hogg's *The Private Memoirs and Confessions of a Justified Sinner* even as they return again to Shakespeare. 'With every man's hand against me,' Booth writes, 'I am here in despair. And why; For doing what Brutus was honored for . . . And yet I for striking down a greater tyrant than they ever knew am looked upon as a common cutthroat.'[53] *The best o' th' cut-throats:*[54] as his final diary entries betray, and as Stephen Dickey recognizes, Booth ultimately havers in Shakespearian terms between 'the valiant tyrannicide Brutus' and 'the murderous tyrant Macbeth'.[55] Frederick Douglass called the assassination an 'unspeakable calamity' for African Americans, and of course a major irony of all Confederate fighting talk about American freedom is that it was premised on denying the freedom of their slaves.[56] Yet the tyrant Macbeth is also a rebel against all the forces of the universe, including monarch, morality and destiny. The last words of Booth's diary are 'but "I must fight the course" Tis all thats left me'.[57] Shakespearian freedom resonates much more hopefully with the emancipation that was Lincoln's most important moral legacy to America and to the world, and it would no doubt be most comfortable just to leave it at that, but John Wilkes Booth – son of a Shakespearian actor; himself a Shakespearian actor; namesake of that radical politician most associated with the first great Shakespeare jubilee – unavoidably expresses something of the disturbing instability of the phenomenon. Liberalism and its discontents. And yet, presumably we don't wish to give up on it, either. It could cut Mercutio free; it's the ecstasy tasted by Romeo and Juliet; it's what Stratford's first Freeman proclaimed when he called the world to worship at Freetown on the banks of the Avon.

1881' (n. 10). 'Within days of the shooting, newspapers began to report that an anonymous source had once heard Booth talk about killing the president. Asked why he would do such a thing, he had quoted a couplet from the Colley Cibber version of *Richard III*:

The daring youth that fired the Ephesian dome
Outlives in fame the pious fool that reared it.'
(Michael W. Kauffman, *American Brutus: John Wilkes Booth and the Lincoln Conspiracies* (New York, 2004), p. 245).
[53] Quoted in Smith, *American Gothic*, pp. 197–8; see also, *Writings of John Wilkes Booth*, ed. Rhodehamel and Taper, p. 155.
[54] *Macbeth*, 3.4.16.
[55] See Stephen Dickey, 'Men of Letters: Lincoln, Booth, and Shakespeare', *Folger Magazine* (Spring 2009), 4–10.
[56] See Philip B. Kunhardt III, 'Lincoln's Contested Legacy', *Smithsonian*, Smithsonian Institution, 39.11 (February 2009), 34–5.
[57] *Writings of John Wilkes Booth*, ed. Rhodehamel and Taper, p. 155.

WE'LL ALWAYS HAVE PARIS: THE THIRD HOUSEHOLD AND THE 'BED OF DEATH' IN *ROMEO AND JULIET*

NICHOLAS CRAWFORD

Miserable riddle, when the same worme must bee my mother, and my sister, and myselfe. Miserable incest, when I must bee maried to my mother and my sister, and bee both father and mother to my owne mother and sister, beget & beare that worme which is all that miserable penury[1]

Romeo and Juliet occupies a privileged, almost sacrosanct, place in the Western imagination as the iconic drama of innocent love, wherein the star-crossed pair escape through death the tyranny and incomprehension of their families. The quintessential image of *Romeo and Juliet* features the lovers together alone, tragically deceased but freed forever in their final embrace. What the play actually stages in its death tableau, however, seems not to be Romeo and Juliet in solitude, everlastingly entwined in each other's arms, but rather Paris and Romeo piled together with Juliet, and Tybalt nearby, in a claustrophobic, vermiculated and sexualized space where, as Romeo laments, 'I remain / With worms that are thy chambermaids' and 'death is amorous' (5.3.108–9; 103), and where, as Juliet puts it, 'the bones / Of all my buried ancestors are packed' (4.3.39–40).[2] While recent critics have noted the play's yoking of sex, death and romance,[3] the importance of Paris's abiding presence in Romeo and Juliet's 'bed of death' (5.3.28) has been routinely diminished or dismissed by stage and film directors and, as we shall see, almost utterly neglected in the critical literature.

I shall argue that accounting for Paris's place in the lovers' *Liebestod* (love-death) – a place granted by Romeo himself – provides a necessary

triangulation of the play's graveyard erotics and its kinship structures, just as it helps us resist the critical habit of fetishizing Romeo and Juliet's final embrace as private, transcendent and triumphant.[4] The laying of Paris with the lovers not only heightens the tomb scene's aura of necrophilic abjection and communal disaster, it highlights death's role in annihilating the social distinctions

---

I wish to thank Jill L. Levenson, A.E.B. Coldiron, and Russ McDonald.

[1] John Donne, *Deaths duell, or, A consolation to the soule...* (London: Printed by Thomas Harper, for Richard Redmer and Beniamin Fisher..., M.DC.XXXII. [1632]); pp. 20–1 ([D2v]-D3[r]).

[2] *Romeo and Juliet* Q1 and Q2 quotations are from *Romeo and Juliet: The Oxford Shakespeare*, ed. Jill L. Levenson (New York and Oxford, 2000).

[3] As Julia Kristeva describes the pair, 'the adolescents of Verona who mistook love for death'. *Tales of Love*, trans. Leon S. Roudiez (New York, 1987), p. 210. For more love and death linkage, see, e.g., Clayton G. Mackenzie, 'Love, Sex and Death in *Romeo and Juliet*', *English Studies*, 88 (2007), 22–42; Ronald Knowles, 'Carnival and Death in *Romeo and Juliet*: A Bakhtinian Reading', in *Shakespeare Survey 49* (Cambridge, 1996), pp. 69–85; François Laroque, 'Tradition and Subversion in *Romeo and Juliet*', in *Shakespeare's Romeo and Juliet: Texts, Contexts, and Interpretation*, ed. Jay L. Halio (Newark, DE, 1995), pp. 18–36; William C. Carroll, '"We Were Born to Die": *Romeo and Juliet*', *Comparative Drama*, 15 (1981), 54–71; Coppélia Kahn, 'Coming of Age in Verona', *Modern Language Studies*, 8 (1978), 171–93.

[4] Numerous critics describe the lovers' final death embrace as 'triumphant'. See, for example, Carroll, 'Born to Die', p. 54; Kahn, 'Coming of Age', p. 354; Marilyn L. Williamson, 'Romeo And Death', *Shakespeare Studies*, 14 (1981), 129–37; p. 134; D. A. Traversi, from 'An Approach to Shakespeare' in *Romeo and Juliet: Critical Essays*, ed. John F. Andrews (New York, 1993), pp. 13–40; p. 38.

that animate the play. Paris's rank as Count and his affiliation as kinsman to both the Prince and Mercutio further suggest that the play is not a story of 'Two households, both alike in dignity' (Pro.1), but of three households unalike in dignity, until they are made alike through the indignity of an eroticized and vermiculated death, where Death lies with everyone, marrying each to all in the kinship of the crypt. This third household, gathered around the Prince, represents a structural disruption to the play's easy binaries and helps us understand the drama's homosocial dimension, its kinship complexities and its surprisingly sceptical view of romantic love.[5]

In Shakespeare's primary source, Arthur Brooke's narrative poem, *Romeus and Juliet*, Paris does not even appear in the tomb scene.[6] Shakespeare added Paris to the graveyard proceedings, and it seems incumbent upon us to account for his presence there better than we have done. Additionally, Brooke removes the bodies of the lovers and gives them a private monument before the poem ends, whereas Shakespeare opts for the bodies to remain in the vault with only the promise of their eventual transmutation into statues and stories. Instead of preserving the lovers' privacy and isolation, Shakespeare crams nearly every other important character into the tomb. As Catherine Belsey observes, 'Finally, the whole community crowds in, the community which is ultimately responsible for the arbitrary and pointless ancestral quarrel.'[7] The play ends with an *exeunt omnes*, which in many productions excepts those actors playing the dead. In such cases, we should be left with the same disturbing picture as the morbidly erotic climax of the play: that of Juliet, among the dead Capulets, lying with Romeo and Paris simultaneously.[8]

The necrophilic, adulterous and incestuous eroticism implicit in the imagery of combining the lovers with Paris and the Capulet family in a space that has been relentlessly sexualized throughout the play should dispel any notion that Romeo and Juliet leave life through a private, redemptive escape hatch. Instead, the two lovers cluster with kin and sexual rivals in a violated, defiled, 'womb of death' (5.3.45), where they will remain.

Shakespeare's vision of a *ménage à tous éternel* seems to have generated not just a wilful blind spot in the popular imagination but a pronounced skittishness among directors and scholars. To Paris's dying wish, 'If thou be merciful, / Open the tomb, lay me with Juliet' (5.3.72–3), Romeo responds, 'In faith, I will' (5.3.74). We have no reason to think that Romeo will not keep his word. Romeo agrees to lay Paris with Juliet in Q1, Q2 and the First Folio. While the dead Paris's exact location on stage can never be a certainty, the play gives every indication that his corpse stays jumbled with those of the two lovers. And yet we almost never see the promised scene as it was apparently written. Even more peculiar, there is almost no critical analysis of this compelling and provocative tableau.[9] Paris has been effectively

---

[5] I am indebted to an anonymous reader at *Shakespeare Survey* for much of this sentence's phrasing.

[6] The full title is *The Tragicall Historye of Romeus and Juliet written first in Italian by Bandell, and nowe in English by Ar. Br.* (1562). Brooke's version, one in a long line, is a verse translation from the French of Pierre Boaistuau's rendering of Matteo Bandello's Italian version, itself not the earliest telling of the Romeo and Juliet story in Italy. On sources, see Geoffrey Bullough, *Narrative and Dramatic Sources of Shakespeare* (New York, 1957).

[7] Catherine Belsey, 'The Name of the Rose in *Romeo and Juliet*', *The Yearbook of English Studies*, 23 (1993): 126–42; pp. 140–1.

[8] Some authorities, such as Andrew Gurr, speculate that the trap (rather than the discovery space) may have been used as the tomb in original stagings of the play. Such stagings might necessitate Romeo's pushing Juliet up from the trap to Paris instead of carrying Paris below to Juliet. 'The Date and Expected Venue of *Romeo and Juliet*', in *Shakespeare Survey 49* (Cambridge, 1996), pp. 15–25; pp. 22–5.

[9] Sometimes the omission of commentary on Paris in the death tableau is especially striking. Jonathan Goldberg, for example, claims that 'the coupling of Romeo and Juliet is not a unique moment of heterosexual perfection and privacy but part of a series whose substitutions do not respect either the uniqueness of individuals or the boundaries of gender difference' (p. 222). For a critic who is more than eager to attack the play's heteronormative critical tradition – and I think is correct in doing so – it is puzzling that he remains silent about the two male suitors figuratively marrying and literally lying together with Juliet in the sexualized space of the womb/tomb. See '*Romeo and Juliet's* Open Rs', in *Queering the Renaissance*, ed. Jonathan Goldberg (Durham and London, 1994), pp. 218–35.

effaced by directors and critics alike from Romeo and Juliet's final consummation in death.

This article draws on performance history, the critical heritage, and some textual analysis to demonstrate the tradition of eliminating or minimizing Paris in the death tableau. It then rereads the tomb scene, explicating the play's investment in three households rather than two. The argument finally enlists a sociological approach to show how restoring Paris to his proper place with the lovers in death reshapes our understanding of the drama's engagement with kinship, eroticism and memorialization.

THE BANISHMENT OF PARIS

Looking first to the popular modern film versions of the play, we find Paris strikingly absent from the death tableau in both Franco Zeffirelli's *Romeo and Juliet* (1968) and Baz Luhrmann's *Romeo + Juliet* (1996). He is simply not there. These films each gradually isolate the lovers as the scene progresses. In the Zeffirelli film, we enter a tomb in which Juliet is clearly only one of many dead, but the camera then inexorably tightens its shot, fixing finally only on the two lovers. Paris is left out of the scene altogether. Luhrmann's version adopts a similarly revisionist retreat from the play's scripted tomb scene. For all its cinematographic swagger and bluster, *Romeo + Juliet* also deletes Paris from the scene. Exchanging gunfire with a pursuing helicopter, Romeo arrives at the Capulet tomb. Once he is inside, the camera begins increasingly restrictive concentric circles, again enthralled only with the lovers. Just as in its more sentimental, quasi-Italianate predecessor, Paris is nowhere to be found. Brooke's version would seem to hold more sway than Shakespeare's in these films. The blockbuster film, *Shakespeare in Love* (1998) shows the death scene in *Romeo and Juliet* played on stage but affords us only the occasional glimpse of dead Paris's legs, poking out from the corner of the frame. Even the dutifully faithful BBC series' version (1978) has Paris slain, lugged into the monument, but then laid on the floor well away from Juliet, who lies inert on a raised slab many feet above. Although

Paris is brought into the tomb, he is separated from Juliet in two dimensions. The camera then assiduously avoids the County's corpse for the remainder of the film. It is as if directors find themselves uncomfortable with Paris's presence. Or perhaps they view Paris's presence as superfluous, even distracting, as a figure who detracts from the heart and soul of the drama, which they imagine to be the two lovers in their final death-cum-love scene.[10]

The stage history of *Romeo and Juliet* seems to prefigure and then coincide with the screen habit of banishing Paris from the death tableau. The most authoritative histories of the play in performance, as well as recent works that attend to the details of performance, often have little or nothing to say about if and how Paris is present in the death tableau.[11] Most accounts of the play's stage history, for example, include the famous 1882 production, featuring Ellen Terry and Henry Irving, which had Romeo carrying Paris in dramatic fashion down a flight of stairs into the tomb, but these accounts then neglect to mention – or simply cannot know – where Romeo laid Paris. Perhaps Romeo's carrying Paris into the tomb seemed like a stage anomaly as early as the late nineteenth century. The habit of not laying Paris with Juliet clearly begins well

---

[10] Of course references to Rosaline are the other common casualty of modern productions, because Rosaline, like Paris, complicates the idea that this is a simple story of true love.

[11] See Jill Levenson, *Romeo and Juliet: Shakespeare in Performance* (Manchester, 1987); *Romeo and Juliet*, ed. René Weis (London, 2012), esp. notes on pp. 320–30; *Romeo and Juliet*, ed. James N. Loehlin (Cambridge, 2002), esp. notes on pp. 237–42; Jay L. Halio, Appendix 2: '*Romeo and Juliet* in Performance', in *Romeo and Juliet: Parallel Texts of Quarto 1 (1597) and Quarto 2 (1599)*, ed. Jay L. Halio (Newark, DE, 2008), 147–59; Edward L. Rocklin, *Romeo and Juliet: A Guide to the Text and the Play in Performance* (New York, 2010); Maria Macaisa and Dominique Raccah, eds., *Romeo and Juliet: The Sourcebooks Shakespeare* (Naperville, IL, 2005); Lynette Hunter and Peter Lichtenfels, *Negotiating Shakespeare's Language in Romeo and Juliet: Reading Strategies from Criticism, Editing, and the Theatre* (Farnham, 2009). This last volume contains an accompanying DVD with the death tableau staged various ways – all without Paris. The tide, however, may be shifting. The notes in the Loehlin and Weis editions (Cambridge and Arden, respectively) devote significant attention to Paris's role in the tomb scene if not in the death tableau.

before the twentieth century. At my request, Jill L. Levenson generously reviewed her collection of 170 prompt-books from the Restoration to the 1980s used in preparing her 2000 Oxford edition of the play. She observes that 'Among early prompt-books, little attention is given to Paris's death', and that, in one 1904 production, 'a note says that Romeo is so absorbed by the sight of Juliet that he forgets his promise to "lay [Paris] with Juliet"'. Levenson explains that notes in twentieth-century productions tend to concentrate on 'placing Paris and Romeo in relation to each other which has little to do with Juliet'. Most significantly, she has attested that not one instructs Romeo to lay Paris with Juliet: 'I haven't found any prompt-book directions which specify that Paris is to lie with, or right next to, Juliet.'[12]

Likewise, the record of visual artistic renderings further bears out the distinct trend to exclude or distance Paris from the lovers' death tableau. James Fowler reveals that 'The very first illustration of *Romeo and Juliet*, in Nicholas Rowe's 1709 edition of Shakespeare ... shows Juliet beside the bier between Romeo and Paris stabbing herself by torchlight as the Page and Watch arrive in the background.'[13] Fowler has no special interest in the role of Paris, but his historical sequence of images leads us to believe that this very early Rowe edition features Paris's proximity to Juliet in a way that will begin to diminish even over the subsequent fifty years. By mid-century, depictions of the death tableau often have Paris either set well aside from the couple or simply absent. Anthony Walker's 1754 illustration of *Romeo and Juliet* shows Juliet in the tomb with one arm over Romeo's dead body, the other preparing to stab herself, as the Friar looks on with his lantern. Paris is in the background, several feet behind the Friar, and well apart from the couple.[14] Fowler also shows us a painting from 1751–52 by Benjamin Wilson entitled *David Garrick as Romeo and George Anne Bellamy as Juliet in the Tomb Scene from 'Romeo and Juliet'*. In this depiction, based on a celebrated stage production, we see only Romeo and Juliet. Paris has disappeared from the tomb altogether,[15] as he so often does in modern stage and film productions.

The critical tradition mirrors cinema and stage history in neglecting Paris's significance in the death tableau. I could find only two articles in the past forty years that explicitly attempt to interpret the picture of Romeo, Juliet and Paris dying and lying together. One of these laudable essays appeared more than thirty years ago in a small-circulation journal.[16] The other, by Ramie Targoff, is quite recent; Paris's role is not its main topic, but Targoff's fine essay does engage with the County's presence in the tomb, seeing it as additional evidence that in this play 'love has no meaningful posthumous future'.[17] While a number of the critical works that I cite here do comment on Paris outside the tomb, they do not note any particular significance in Paris's scripted inclusion in the death tableau.

The tendency to neglect Paris in general comes perhaps from measuring the importance of a character by the length of its part. Although Paris's lines and appearances are limited, he not only figures prominently in the play's culminating scene, his force and presence as the parental choice – even *in absentia* – weighs heavily throughout. We need

---

[12] All Jill L. Levenson quotations in this paragraph are taken from personal correspondence, 4 July 2012. Since then I have been able to examine these prompt-books (now accessible in database form) myself, and I concur with Levenson's report. '*Romeo and Juliet*: Searchable Database for Prompt Books', *Iter: Gateway to the Middle Ages and Renaissance*, U of Toronto Libraries, accessed 19 October 2012. www.itergateway.org/romeo_juliet.

[13] James Fowler, 'Picturing *Romeo and Juliet*', in *Shakespeare Survey 49* (Cambridge, 1996), pp. 111–130; p. 113.

[14] Fowler, 'Picturing', pp. 116–17.

[15] Fowler, 'Picturing', pp. 114–15.

[16] Paula Newman and George Walton Williams, 'Paris: The Mirror of Romeo', in *Renaissance Papers 1981*, ed. A. Leigh Deneef and M. Thomas Hester (Raleigh, NC, 1982), pp. 13–19. These authors argue that Paris represents Romeo's youth, which dies alongside the 'mature' Romeo. While one might have reservations about its main thesis, the essay includes some striking insights, e.g. 'Romeo carries the body of his dead rival into Juliet's bridal chamber where all three marry in the same instant that they die in the feasting presence full of light' (p. 16).

[17] Ramie Targoff, 'Mortal Love: Shakespeare's *Romeo and Juliet* and the Practice of Joint Burial', *Representations*, 120 (2012), 17–38; pp. 33–4.

only remember Cordelia in *King Lear* to understand that a character may speak little and may disappear for much of the play, but may still be absolutely essential to the drama's conception. While Paris's centrality does not equal Cordelia's, his role is nonetheless crucial. The neglect of Paris's presence in the death tableau in particular, however, likely stems from the fact that to acknowledge it fully must radically unsettle our usual understanding of the play.

REREADING THE TOMB SCENE

Before being killed and carried into the tomb by Romeo, Paris explains that he is strewing flowers and sprinkling perfumed water on Juliet's tomb.[18] Not coincidentally, when Juliet earlier appears to be dead, Capulet tries to commiserate with Paris by invoking the play's frequent floral imagery:

> O son, the night before thy wedding day
> Hath death lain with thy wife. See, there she lies,
> Flower as she was, deflowered by him.
> Death is my son-in-law, death is my heir;
> My daughter he hath wedded. (4.4.1–5)

That flowers are now 'strewn' by her grave invites a parallel between thrown petals and youth cut down, just as it redeploys imagery that has Death, through its de-flowering, engendering more death, dispersal and decomposition. Paris's attempt to 're-flower' her grave reminds us of this earlier talk of Death's rape and its consequences.[19] Like Paris, Romeo employs the word, 'strewing', to threaten Balthasar with violence if he interferes with Romeo's doings in the tomb, promising Balthasar that he will 'strew this hungry churchyard with thy limbs' (5.3.36). Much in the same way that the idea of strewing Ophelia's grave with flowers is contrasted with flowers decking her marriage bed in *Hamlet*, floral imagery in *Romeo and Juliet* alternates between its associations with beautiful regenerating youth and deflowering, dismembering Death.[20] At the same time that Paris is both strewing flowers upon Juliet's grave and, in a sense, decking her marriage-in-death bed, he is

also sprinkling perfumed water, depositing his fluids on Juliet, his would-be bride, as she lies inside or beneath (only sleeping, as we know).

When Romeo kills Paris at the entrance to the tomb, he kills a rival suitor who has come to Juliet's grave, one who is in this sense Romeo's analogue. Romeo's exclamation, 'Let me peruse this face. / Mercutio's kinsman, noble County Paris!' (5.3.74–5), aligns Paris with Mercutio as well, in that they are both kinsmen and dead men. This moment of quasi-equivalence and exact equivalence between Paris and Mercutio – quasi-equivalent because related by blood and of the same 'household', exactly equivalent as dead men – heralds the final tableau that conveys more emphatically Death's power to create a community of equals, individuals to be rendered indistinguishable from one another.

By fatally stabbing Paris and agreeing to his dying wish to be laid with Juliet, Romeo makes Paris a companion and complement to his own endeavour. Through this gesture, Romeo now

---

[18] Flowers in this play occupy a polyvalent imagistic space and are associated not only with youth and beauty but with poetic flourishes, signification, poison and with sexuality that ranges from tender to violent and deadly. Much criticism has been devoted to the floral imagery, and attention has been paid to signification debates prompted by the lines, 'What's in a name? That which we call a rose / By any other word would smell as sweet' (2.1.85–6). See, e.g., Belsey, 'Name of the Rose', pp. 126–42. Critics have also attempted to find meaning in particular flowers. See Susanna Greer Fein, 'Verona's Summer Flower: The "Virtues" of Herb Paris in *Romeo and Juliet*', *American Notes & Queries*, 8.4 (1995), 5–8; or Jonathan Bate, 'An Herb by Any Other Name: *Romeo and Juliet*, V.iv.5–6', *Shakespeare Quarterly*, 33.3 (1982), p. 336.

[19] There are many other ways that floral imagery functions in the play as well. For example, at different points, Romeo, Juliet and Paris are all figured as flowers; and the Friar remarks on poisonous floral properties, 'Within the infant rind of this weak flower / Poison hath residence' (2.2.23–4).

[20] Michael Neill sees this moment in *Hamlet* in terms of 'the funeral as a kind of grim marriage, the "bringing home" of Ophelia as Death's bride (v.i.232–3): "I thought thy bride-bed to have decked, sweet maid, / And not have strewed thy grave" (lines 245–6)'. Neill, *Issues of Death: Mortality and Identity in English Renaissance Tragedy* (New York, 1997), p. 234.

treats Paris as an equal, even while Paris is clearly both his social superior, with regard to familial status, and his romantic inferior, with regard to Juliet. Romeo essentially brings Paris to join him in the couple's death bed and wedding-in-death feast:

> For here lies Juliet, and her beauty makes
> This vault a feasting presence full of light.
> *[He bears the body of Paris to the tomb.]*[21]
> Death, lie thou there, by a dead man interred.
>
> (5.3.85–7)

We encounter feasting imagery earlier in the play, most notably at the Capulets' feast, where Romeo and Juliet meet. The tomb scene inverts this earlier imagery, first comparing the vault itself to a great 'maw' and then metaphorically enacting its feasting through multiple deaths. The feasters will now be feasted upon, equally and indiscriminately, demonstrating once more death's power to undo individuation.

With his line, 'Death, lie thou there, by a dead man interred', Romeo may be calling himself a dead man proleptically or may instead be commanding Death (its allegorical personification) to lie down beside the dead man he is interring, i.e. Paris. This line could also signify that Death is now the freshly dead Paris whom Romeo lays down next to Tybalt (the already interred dead man).[22] Conversely, the line could indicate that Death, now in the personage of Paris, is being interred by Romeo, a self-styled dead man (and now himself Death, as well). In any and all of these readings, Death is still implicated and shared by all in the tomb. Death unites them.

In this particular tomb, however, Death is a distinctly sexual creature, whose sexuality has been developed throughout the play. As Juliet vows when she learns that Romeo is banished, and imagines she will never see him again, 'I'll to my wedding-bed, / And death, not Romeo, take my maidenhead' (3.2.136–7). When Romeo now contemplates Juliet, whom he takes to be recently deceased, he too casts Death as lover, expressing his fears that Death keeps Juliet in the tomb as his paramour:

> Death, that hath sucked the honey of thy breath,
> Hath had no power yet upon thy beauty.
> Thou art not conquered; beauty's ensign yet
> Is crimson in thy lips and in thy cheeks,
> And death's pale flag is not advancèd there.
> Tybalt, liest thou there in thy bloody sheet?
> O, what more favour can I do to thee
> Than, with that hand that cut thy youth in twain,
> To sunder his that was thine enemy?
> Forgive me, cousin. Ah, dear Juliet,
> Why art thou yet so fair? Shall I believe
> That unsubstantial death is amorous,
> And that the lean abhorrèd monster keeps
> Thee here in dark to be his paramour?
> For fear of that I still will stay with thee,
> And never from this pallet of dim night
> Depart again.   (5.3.92–108)

After remarking on Juliet's life-like and comely appearance (of course she still is in fact alive) and figuring in martial terms Death's failure to make her appear entirely dead, Romeo comments on Tybalt's bloody aspect, while offering up his own life in a plea for forgiveness. But Romeo immediately returns to Juliet's beauty, her sexual appeal in 'death'. Even though he vows to remain with her as a jealous husband might stand guard to see that his wife takes no lovers, Romeo himself brings Paris, whom he has recently figured as Death embodied, to lie with them.

The mixing of martial and sexual metaphors in this passage, so common in early modern poetry, invites us to see the recent sword combat as sexualized. The inclusion in this scene of those whom Romeo has penetrated with his blade, Paris and Tybalt, reinforces the play's figuring of death as fatal sexuality. Because the description of Juliet's necrophilic appeal is sandwiched between Romeo's talk of Paris and Tybalt, the passage weakens the focus of her morbid allure for Romeo alone, adds a homosocial dimension to the scene, and in effect eroticizes the interaction among all

---

[21] This stage direction does not appear in either Quarto. Paris has asked to be laid 'with' Juliet, not merely in the tomb.

[22] Romeo as the 'dead man' and Paris as 'Death' is a standard gloss. See, for example, Levenson, *Romeo and Juliet: The Oxford Shakespeare* (New York, 2000), p. 343n.

four.[23] Tybalt, however, has already been entombed and would seem to remain somewhat apart from the other three, who die in close succession and remain together in close proximity.

Soon after the Prince has entered, the deaths of Romeo, Paris and Juliet are mentioned by the Chief Watchman, by Capulet's Wife and by Friar Laurence, and each time all three deaths are noted together. Just before, when the Friar finds Juliet waking by Romeo's and Paris's dead bodies, he describes the scene he is witnessing, as he urges her to leave with him: 'Come, come away. / Thy husband in thy bosom there lies dead, / And Paris too' (5.3.154–6). Given that Romeo agreed to lay Paris with Juliet, these lines imply that all three remain close together, with Romeo and Paris both lying on Juliet's bosom. If Romeo dies next to Juliet, he dies next to Paris as well. When Juliet awakens and then stabs herself with a dagger, she will have to die next to Paris if she wishes to die next to Romeo. Recent critics and editors seem to have just begun to insist on this picture. As Targoff's recent article puts it, 'they [Romeo and Juliet] are left in the complicated tangle with the corpse of Paris'.[24] And René Weis writes for the 2012 Arden edition, 'Juliet wakes from her drugged sleep to find herself next to Romeo and Paris, both dead, side by side.'[25] Such a picture differs greatly from the common critical and performance one of the lovers finally isolated in a tragic but oddly triumphant embrace.

It is also perhaps worth noting that the Friar's lines do not appear in the first Quarto and so belong only to what is usually considered the pre-ferred version, Q2, which may or may not be the earliest version.[26] Whatever relative value we wish to place on Q1 and Q2 – and many would now argue that we should simply respect each text on its own terms – what is clear is that Q1, Q2 and the First Folio preserve Paris's importance in the tomb scene, and do so in slightly different ways.[27] For example, when the Chief Watchman first enters the tomb in Q1, he mentions only Juliet, 'two days buried, / New bleeding, wounded' (5.3.119–20), whereas in Q2, these lines become 'Here lies the County slain, / And Juliet bleeding, warm and newly dead, / Who here hath lain this two days buried' (5.3.174–6). There is no mention of Romeo's death in either version for many lines. We can perhaps attribute Paris's being named first in Q2 to his rank and civic importance, but the fact that he is mentioned right away and Romeo is not would seem to indicate that Q2 promotes Paris's significance in the tomb scene even further than Q1 does. That said, Q1, with its greater number of stage directions, provides a number of Paris-enhancing protocols, especially in regards to Romeo's and Paris's behaviour before entering the tomb.

It is only in Q1 that we learn explicitly that County Paris arrives at the tomb 'with flowers and sweete water' and that Romeo comes with

---

[23] Sexualizing death during this period was often not merely figurative. 'The playing of sexual games around a corpse reveals one aspect of the closeness of the living and the dead during the early modern period.' (Clare Gittings, *Death, Burial and the Individual in Early Modern England* (New York, 1984), p. 106).

[24] Targoff, 'Mortal Love', p. 34.

[25] Weis (Arden edn), p. 329n.

[26] In an essay on the methods and results of Shaxicon, his computer program for dating and authorship, Donald W. Foster wittily explains, '*The Most Excellent and Lamentable Tragedy of Romeo and Juliet* was published in two Quartos (1597, 1599). According to a long-established scholarly consensus, the second is most excellent, and the first, lamentable.' 'The Webbing of *Romeo and Juliet*', in *Critical Essays on Romeo and Juliet*, ed. Joseph Porter (New York, 1997), pp. 131–49; p. 136. Foster also remarks that 'the most controversial (but I think inescapable) conclusions to be drawn from Shaxicon's evidence are that Q1 precedes Q2 in point of date, and that both are principally or entirely Shakespeare's own work' (p. 134). As to precedence, we have on the other side, David Farley Hills, for example, joining H. R. Hoppe and others, in maintaining that 'Q1 represents an abridgment of Shakespeare's original and not a first draft.' Hills, '"Bad" Quarto of *Romeo and Juliet*', in *Shakespeare Survey 49* (Cambridge, 1996), pp. 27–44; p. 29. For dating of later Quartos, see R. Carter Hailey, 'The Dating Game: New Evidence for the Dates of Q4 *Romeo and Juliet* and Q4 *Hamlet*', *Shakespeare Quarterly*, 58.3 (2007), 367–87.

[27] For Quarto discussions that go well beyond dating, see especially Laurie Maguire, *Shakespearean Suspect Texts* (Cambridge, 1993) and Lukas Erne, *Shakespeare as Literary Dramatist* (Cambridge, 2004).

'torch, a mattocke, and a crow of yron'.[28] Paris arrives in veneration, carrying flowers and sprinkling perfumed water; Romeo in violation, toting his prying tools, a detail often left out in modern productions. For Alan Dessen, 'To cut the mattock and crow of iron today is to sustain a "romantic" view of Romeo that is undercut or qualified by signals in the Quartos.'[29] The gentle lover presents himself here as the violent intruder, whereas Paris, formerly depicted as aggressively entitled, an agent of patriarchal imposition, is here portrayed as gentle and respectful. Romeo describes himself as 'savage-wild' (5.3.37), and is armed with tools specifically designed to penetrate the womb/tomb.

Paris, fearing that Romeo 'here is come to do some villainous shame / To the dead bodies' (5.3.52–3), as Q2 has it, attempts to arrest him. These lines, which immediately evoke the seeming-dead Juliet and hint at necrophilia, are far more suggestive and sinister than Q1's simple 'Can vengeance be pursued further than death?' (5.3.41), which directs our attention to Tybalt instead. When challenged by Paris, Romeo penetrates him with his sword. As Robert N. Watson and Stephen Dickey note, 'Shakespeare's contemporaries did not need Freud to help them recognize stabbing as a version of rape.'[30] Romeo not only violates and desecrates the vault with his tools, his mattock and wrenching iron, he violates Paris's body as well. He will further defile the vaginal womb/tomb by inserting into its interior two non-Capulets – Paris and himself. Showing Paris as newly sympathetic and Romeo as the possessive and aggressive lover works towards eliding the difference between them.

Another indication of Paris's importance to the tomb scene reveals itself in Q1's rendering of Romeo's long speech after dragging Paris into the tomb. While Q1 omits many lines of this speech that appear in Q2, including the portion where Romeo talks to the dead Tybalt, Q1 not only retains the section where he addresses Paris but adds 'I will satisfy thy last request, / For thou has prized thy love above thy life' (5.3.62–3). Although we have no doubt in Q2 that Romeo intends to lay Paris with Juliet, Q1 implies something additional about Romeo's state of mind, and that is that he identifies with and perhaps now even admires Paris. Romeo gives every indication in Q1, as he does in Q2, that he intends to lay Paris *with* Juliet and not in some remote area of the tomb.

Once Romeo has kept his promise and placed Paris with Juliet, he reveals that, like Paris with his 'sweet water', he has brought his own fluid to the grave site. He consumes the liquid poison he has procured from the apothecary for gold and kisses Juliet, presumably imparting some drops from his dying lips. He then joins Paris and Juliet in a kind of second and final consummation of his marriage to Juliet, a fulfilment that resonates with the early modern slang sense of 'dying' as climax, but one that includes not only the secretly still-living Juliet but his freshly dead rival, Paris. This is perhaps not a consummation devoutly to be wished, because Paris not only triangulates the would-be romantic tableau, he and the rest of the tomb's occupants obstruct the very privacy and intimate transcendence that so many directors and critics seem determined to preserve. Moreover, his presence undermines the exclusivity of the kinship structures upon which the usual reading of play is premised. The Capulet family tomb now melds representatives from three households in its newly inclusive confines.

The intricate exchange of penetrations and fluids between Romeo, his rival Paris and Juliet that immediately precedes the final death tableau only reinforces the unsettling nature of the final resting place and its growing population. When Juliet

---

[28] See Alan C. Dessen, 'Q1 *Romeo and Juliet* and Elizabethan Theatrical Vocabulary', in *Shakespeare's 'Romeo and Juliet': Texts, Contexts, and Interpretation*, ed. Jay L. Halio (Newark, DE, 1995), pp. 107–22; p. 108.

[29] Alan C. Dessen, *Rescripting Shakespeare: The Text, the Director, and Modern Productions* (Cambridge, 2002), p. 117. Dessen also reminds us that these tools in the context of original staging probably served the purpose of indicating location and state of mind, and were not likely put to direct use on the bare stage (pp. 116–17).

[30] Robert N. Watson and Stephen Dickey, 'Wherefore Art Thou Tereu? Juliet and the Legacy of Rape', *Renaissance Quarterly*, 58 (2005), 127–56; p. 132.

awakens and finds Romeo dead, she penetrates herself with Romeo's dagger and finally dies – in both senses – as well: 'She [Juliet] reclaims pleasure by consensual death with Romeo; she brings together the phallus and the sword, welcoming Romeo's "happy dagger" into what she calls – as Shakespeare's Lucrece did in a parallel moment, 1723–24 – the "sheath" (5.3.169–70) of her body.'[31] The sexualized exchange of deaths is then not just between Romeo and Juliet, but between Romeo, Juliet and Paris, and thus between all three households. Or, as Jonathan Goldberg contends, 'the homosocial order in the play cannot simply be reduced to a compulsive and prescriptive heterosexuality . . . sexuality in the play cannot be sheltered from sociality'.[32] This exchange exceeds its triangulation of familial and amatory vectors by also including and implicating the apothecary (and thus gold), and the Friar; or medicine, commerce and the church. We are made to understand that a great many participate in the various types of social and physical intercourse that result in these deaths. The tomb scene insinuates the entire community into its morbidly theatrical and sexual enclosure.

THE KINSHIP OF THE CRYPT

Such a reading of the tomb scene reinterprets not only the play's erotic energies but its kinship dynamics and strategies of memorialization. It asks us to recognize that the play's structure is more complex than its evident binaries allow, and that Romeo and Juliet never exist in isolation. Paris's insistent presence in the lovers' death embrace reminds us that this is not a play just about the subjectivity of two lovers but about their effect on, and inseparability from, a community of enmity, discourse and desire stratified across the fault lines of kinship. In this regard, some critics have been correctly sceptical of separating the couple's private subjectivity from the logic of its ideological interpellation. As Susan Snyder has remarked, 'Shakespeare did not need Althusser's analysis in order to grasp the workings of interpellation or to feel the force of the dual meaning of *subject*, the

autonomous agent who is formed by and in a social formation to which he is subjected.'[33] The play begins, as we know, by demonstrating the social formations within which the lovers are enmeshed, the staging of a conspicuous conflict between two families, two loci of kinship, who perceive their differences to be incontrovertible and irrevocable. By including what I am calling the 'third household', which comprises the Prince and his relations (Paris and Mercutio), we can see how this apparently central conflict actually links to networks of competing allegiances and how the drama also shows us that the Montagues and Capulets are remarkably interchangeable while the third household stands apart. The play's end, the inclusion in the death tableau of Paris along with the imagery of vermiculation, suggests less the resolution of differences between two opposing households than it does the equalization in death of three households: the erasure of both clan and class distinctions.

By opening and closing in this manner, the play engages an argument about the force of perceived differences to engender tragic outcomes, and also one about the constructed and temporal nature of such dearly held distinctions. The central conflict in *Romeo and Juliet*, then, becomes not simply one between the lovers and their disapproving families, i.e. between romance and kinship or, as it has often been understood, between public and private desires, but one between *kinds* of kinships: familial, amical, civil and romantic.

---

31 Watson and Dickey, 'Wherefore', p. 154.
32 Goldberg, 'Open Rs', p. 221.
33 Susan Snyder, 'Ideology and Feud in *Romeo and Juliet*', in *Shakespeare Survey 49* (Cambridge, 1996), pp. 87–96; p. 90. See also Naomi Conn Liebler, who relies as much on Bourdieu's idea of 'habitus' as on notions of Althusserian subjectivity. Liebler, '"There is no world without Verona walls": The City in *Romeo and Juliet*', in *A Companion to Shakespeare's Works, Volume I: The Tragedies*, ed. Richard Dutton and Jean E. Howard (Malden, 2006), pp. 303–18. For historicizing early modern cultural constructions of desire, see Dympna C. Callaghan, 'The Ideology of Romantic Love: The Case of *Romeo and Juliet*', in *Romeo and Juliet: Contemporary Critical Essays*, ed. R. S. White (Basingstoke, 2001), pp. 85–115.

The term 'kinship' here should be understood in its broad senses: sociological and anthropological, as well as biological. In *Romeo and Juliet*, we find three households, each with its claim to kinship based on consanguinity, but we can also locate other allegiance structures. Family kinship becomes complicated by the kinship of amity, wherein, for example, Mercutio is ready to fight and die for his friend Romeo. Romance and marriage constitute another mode of elective kinship and allegiance, wherein members band together as a distinct group of two and pledge fealty to each other. Superimposed upon these competing and overlapping spheres of kinship lies a powerful form of civic kinship, wherein many identify and are identified as citizens of Verona and are subject to its laws. The Prince makes it explicit that the kinship of a civil community trumps all others. He chides the feuding families who 'Have thrice disturbed the quiet of our streets' (1.1.87), and forbids any further violation, on pain of death (1.1.78–100).[34] Such diverse forms of kinship, though not equivalent in force, function in similar ways. As Mark Shell observes, 'Most sociological kinships are identical to biological ones in that they, too, divide the human world into two groups of people – those who are kin and those who are not – and group kinfolk together on the basis of some common measure or something consubstantial.'[35] We have only to think of such institutions as the church, represented in the play by Friar Laurence, and such fringe-kin figures as the Nurse to understand that the previous list of kinship types is by no means exhaustive and that such structures intertwine in complex ways. The final tableau, however, both represents and cancels many of the play's most notable kinship forms.

Paris's proximity at this final cancellation not only adds the third household to the other two but implies that the kinship of death ultimately negates that of family, class and romance. By virtue of his relation to the Prince and his membership in the upper aristocracy, Paris brings to the worm feast the social station to which the feuding families aspire; additionally, as Mercutio's kinsman, Paris connects the kinship of family to the kinship of amity and romance.[36] Paris is at once related by family to Romeo's friend, just as he is related to the central romance as competing suitor. Most provocative, however, is that Paris's lying together with Romeo and Juliet undermines the eponymous characters' kinship of coupledom, effectively marrying the three together in death.

In this way, the play challenges the exclusivity of kinship, and not simply in the usual sense that this drama's tragic formulation demands that familial kinship be rejected for romance to succeed. Sophocles's *Oedipus*, as Shell observes, is the prototypical tragedy of kinship. There, class exogamy seems to manifest itself when Oedipus, thought to be of humble birth, marries the queen Jocasta; but class exogamy in that play turns out to be familial endogamy, i.e. incest. In *Romeo and Juliet* we have nearly the opposite configuration. The taboo for the Montagues and Capulets is marrying into each other's families, which are of the same class. The Capulet parents in fact encourage class exogamy, hoping to have Juliet marry into the echelons of the aristocracy via Paris. Given that the feuding families appear so alike in general, not just in 'dignity' but in attitude and affect, class endogamy, that is, the pairing of Romeo and Juliet, here looks very much like familial endogamy. This interfamilial feud closely resembles an intrafamilial feud, and the classic Freudian reading of the play sees the story of Romeo and Juliet as just that, the anxiety of incest.[37]

---

[34] See Liebler's perceptive remarks on civic culpability and the forces of kinship in the play, '"There is no world without Verona walls"', esp. pp. 310–11 and 315.

[35] Marc Shell, *The End of Kinship: 'Measure for Measure', Incest, and the Idea of Universal Siblinghood* (Stanford, 1988), p. 8.

[36] David Bevington maintains convincingly that the Montagues and Capulets are not of the aristocracy; I follow his conclusion in this article (Bevington, *How to Read a Shakespeare Play* (Oxford, 2006), p. 43). As Weis (Arden edn) points out, p. 119, the designation of 'Lady' Capulet dates from Nicholas Rowe's 1709 edition of the play. However, even if they are intended to be aristocrats, they are minor ones and certainly well outranked by Paris and the Prince.

[37] See M. D. Faber, 'The Adolescent Suicides of Romeo and Juliet', *Psychoanalytical Review*, 59 (1972–73), 169–81. By

The resultant rancorous skirmishes of these families should be confined to their own members but instead fold into their fray Mercutio, Paris and others. The romance of Romeo and Juliet, their kinship to each other, is thus imbricated in, and set against, a variety of competing forms of kinship with which the play's other characters are preoccupied. Not the least of these forms manifests as the kinship of citizenship, where the play enacts, as Glenn Clark puts it, 'the civil challenge to aristocratic prestige'.[38] The Montagues and Capulets instantiate models of blood kinship, as two households that huddle on the same social rung. The community, however, imposes its own form of social kinship. And it is this last form which finally proves most potent, as the Prince insists, and as the families recognize. The civic order and interest must override the familial. As we have seen, it does so in the tomb as well, where Paris is added to Romeo Montague and the Capulets. The tomb becomes Verona writ small, or writ representatively.

The tentative union of the Capulets, Montagues and the Prince that we see at the play's close echoes the necro-matrimony of Juliet, Romeo and Paris that precedes it. In the Capulets' tomb we find both sexes and all three families. Death has lain with everyone and has in a sense equalized everyone. The three families become alike, their bodies 'strewn' through the violated vault. In death, they are not separated by family name or by class or by gender. The corpses serve as food for the great 'maw', as 'paramours' for Death's pleasure, and as fertilizer for regeneration. The play persistently affiliates its engendering womb trope with its tropes of annihilation, not only in the tomb scene but much earlier when the Friar connects birth and death directly in a soliloquy: 'The earth that's nature's mother is her tomb; / What is her burying grave, that is her womb; / And from her womb children of divers kind' (2.3.9–11). Although the Prologue equates the end of strife with the sacrifice of Romeo and Juliet, the play's ending, which announces 'A glooming peace' brought forth with the morning, only hints at regeneration, and does so in a hedging and despairing fashion.

The final death tableau, then, delivers a paradoxical message. On the one hand, it would seem that in death Romeo and Juliet will be forever unable to escape the blocking figures of family and the unwanted suitor, Paris. The Capulets and Paris will commingle with them for eternity, imposing their cramping presence upon the lovers in death, as they did in life. On the other hand, in death, familial enmity, class and gender distinctions, sexual rivalry, all dissolve into dust. What was oppressive or objectionable in life becomes wholly irrelevant in death. Individuals are stripped of agency and sensibility. The play refrains from any talk of their souls ascending to heaven or of an afterlife of any kind. We may wish to see their suicides as defiant acts that preserve the purity of their love, but the play shows death itself as triumphant. The promise of golden statues hardly rises to the level of a corresponding recompense for the wretchedness of the death tableau, with its evocation of an ever-after of group violations by indiscriminate fatted worms.

VERMICULATION

The figure of the worm neatly links sexuality to death's power to erase difference. The bodies are imagined to be uncomfortably stuffed into a tight space, all sharing the worms that traverse their bodies indiscriminately, penetrating and exiting each and all, enjoining the pile of corpses in an orgy of decomposition. The play introduces such worm imagery early, when Montague likens Romeo's introversion, then from his infatuation with Rosaline, to 'the bud bit with an envious worm' (1.1.147). Vermicular visions continue with Mercutio's protestation at his death that they have made worms' meat of him; and they resurface in the figuration of worms as Juliet's attendants in the tomb.

Worm imagery elsewhere in Shakespeare illuminates his use of it here. In *Antony and Cleopatra*, the worm trope sexualizes Cleopatra's death in

'intrafamilial', Faber means within each family and does not extend the idea, as I do, to include both families as one.
[38] Glenn Clark, 'The Civil Mutinies of *Romeo and Juliet*', *English Literary Renaissance*, 41 (2011), 280–300; p. 290.

something like the way that amorous Death does in Juliet's. While Juliet dies, according to Romeo, 'With worms that are thy chambermaids' (5.3.109), Cleopatra, who already has plenty of real maids, is poised to take pleasure from the worm. Referring to a poisonous asp, the Clown wishes Cleopatra 'all joy of the worm' (5.2.255), prefiguring a death scene that contains many bawdy early modern puns on 'dying' as orgasm. While the tone of these two tragic scenes is quite different, and the worm imagery in Cleopatra's scene is overtly erotic in a way that it is not for Juliet's, both scenes link death, vermiculation and sexual release. The death scene for Egypt's ruler also eroticizes and exploits the paradoxical pleasure of certain pains. As Iras falls and dies, Cleopatra remarks, 'The stroke of death is as a lover's pinch, / Which hurts and is desired' (5.2.290–1). The asp, though a snake, serves as a synecdoche for a larger class of worm-like creatures, such as those in *Romeo and Juliet* and, more generally, those found commonly in the literature of the period. The worm figures, as phallic signifier and metonymy for Death, as both ravisher and ravager.[39]

In addition to conflating phallic and death imagery, the worm emblematizes the processes of decomposition, and thus death's power of indistinction. Worms' work consists of consumption and excretion: to penetrate, eat and redistribute all flesh. Where worms are concerned, as Hamlet remarks, 'Your fat king and your lean beggar is but variable service – two dishes, but to one table. That's the end' (4.3.23–5). In *Hamlet*, 'Death homogenizes everything',[40] resulting in 'the tragic and genocidal conjunction of kinspersons all in death'.[41] In much the same way, *Romeo and Juliet* sends representatives of each kinship cluster to be embedded in what was the Capulets' vault but becomes the death cavity for all three households. When Mercutio is accidentally killed by Tybalt earlier in the play, he announces proleptically the themes that haunt the final tableau: death, vermiculation and indiscrimination. 'A plague a both your houses! / They have made worms' meat of me' (3.1.106–7). Mercutio's self-description as worm food also adumbrates the inverted feasting

imagery of the tomb scene and announces the third household's undifferentiated place at Death's banquet.

In 'Death's Duel', from which this article takes its epigraph, John Donne despairs about vermiculation and the corporeal dispersion and exchange that occur after burial, the manner by which these inexorable processes physically commingle all, as though sexually. A few lines later, however, Donne adds that death also renders social classes indistinguishable: 'nor the poorest receiue any contentment in being made equall to Princes, for they shall bee equall but in dust'.[42] As Watson notes on attitudes towards death in the early modern period: 'The terror lies in its indifference, which steals away the differences by which and for which we live.'[43] Death demolishes social distinctions as well as distinctions between the feuding families, the suitors, and even distinctions between family members. It also logically effaces gender difference, making Tybalt not just like Paris and Romeo but like Juliet. As Donne so eerily describes it, vermiculation obscenely marries each to all, robbing each being of distinctiveness, transforming the privacy imagined in death into a grotesquely shared event.

MEMORIALIZING INDISTINCTION

Even the golden statues which are to commemorate the two lovers seem to be ironically conceived as tributes to indistinction and reinforce the difference-erasing function of the tomb. While

---

39 One of the most famous and recognizable examples of such ravager/ravisher worm imagery occurs in Andrew Marvell's 'To His Coy Mistress': 'then worms shall try / That long preserved virginity' (lines 27–8). In Marvell's poem, 'The grave's a fine and private place, / But none, I think, do there embrace' (31–2). In *Romeo and Juliet*, the grave is anything but private and is replete with suggestions of embracing (Andrew Marvell, *The Poems of Andrew Marvell*, ed. Nigel Smith (London, 2003)).

40 Marc Shell, *Children of the Earth: Literature, Politics, and Nationhood* (New York, 1993), p. 122.

41 Shell, *Children of the Earth*, p. 123.

42 Donne, *Deaths duell*, p. 21.

43 Robert N. Watson, *The Rest is Silence: Death as Annihilation in the English Renaissance* (Berkeley, 1994), p. 98.

they do not appear in the play, and exist only as a promise of compensatory reverence, their equality is made to be a point of honour.[44] Their genesis from the two fathers' attempts to outdo each other renders suspect this 'rebirth' in shimmering currency. Additionally, their goldenness associates them with both the gold that Romeo named as responsible for more deaths than poison and with the gold clasps of Paris-as-book that would result, as Capulet's Wife figures it, from pairing his attractive exterior with Juliet's beauty (5.1.80–1; 1.3.81–90).[45] Although the two fathers are almost compulsively identical in their vying to build a more impressive statue of the other's offspring, they will end up building explicitly equal ones: 'As rich shall Romeo's by his lady's lie' (5.3.303). In the afterlife, Romeo and Juliet will not be man and woman, husband and wife, but dust and dust in the ground, and gold and gold above it – members of two households alike in powder and precious metal. Likewise, the evident indistinction in life between the Montagues and Capulets echoes here in death through the vermicular erasure of physical difference. The materiality, integrity and durability of the golden statues to be erected *in memoriam* contrast radically with the certain prospect of the bodies' swift decomposition in the ground; and yet the suspect nature of gold in this play and the equivalence of the statues keep these monuments strangely commensurate with the permanence of the couple's ignominious dissolution into dust.

Paris's presence adds a further dimension to Death's levelling of identity. Not only does Paris join the lovers in their final decomposition but in doing so he marks the end of class distinction between the third household and the two feuding families. The statues link to Paris because they are enlisted to substitute for the play's earlier metaphor of Paris-as-book, unbound and requiring the 'gold clasps' that Juliet's beauty could complete to lock in 'the golden story' (1.3.94). After their deaths, it is Romeo and Juliet whose two golden figures mark the tragedy of their tale for posterity, reconnecting the association of golden ornaments – clasps and statues – with the completion and preservation of a story.[46] If the true *exegi monumentum* of the play

is to be understood as the text itself, then this too is undermined by the imagery of vermiculation, where the worm-eaten book and the worm-eaten body are conflated through Paris's interment.[47]

The final lines of the play, 'For never was a story of more woe / Than this of Juliet and her Romeo' (5.3.309–10), effectively convert the Prologue's conceit of a storyteller (Chorus) announcing a play, 'two-hours' traffic of our stage' (Pro. 12), into the play's calling itself a story. The Prince, now the third household's only remaining spokesperson, has affirmed that he himself has 'lost a brace of kinsmen' (5.3.295). He then ends the play by reprising the rhetoric of posterity and foregone conclusion originally introduced by the Prologue's bracketing statement that the lovers, 'With their death bury their parents' strife' (Pro. 8).[48] By leading with the burial, Shakespeare would seem to fulfil by chiastic coincidence the modern journalistic credo not to bury the lead. The play at its close has put itself between two clasps, one of drama, the other of narrative. Unlike Paris-the-book, who remains unbound and lacking the pair of imaginary gold

---

44 Some directors have chosen to represent the statues on stage anyway; a notable example is Michael Bogdanov's 1986 RSC production.

45 For gold as corruptive, see Greg Bentley, 'Poetics of Power: Money as Sign and Substance in *Romeo and Juliet*', *Explorations in Renaissance Culture*, 17 (1991), 145–66.

46 For connections between the gold clasps and the statues, as well as their relation to the play's self-characterization as a story, see also Bryan Reynolds and Janna Segal, 'Fugitive Explorations in *Romeo and Juliet*: Transversal Travels through R&J Space', *Journal for Early Modern Cultural Studies*, 5 (2005), 37–70; pp. 57–60.

47 Some might even find a French pun in this 'Parisian' imagery, wherein we discover the lexical equivalence between the play's verses (*les vers*) and the worms (also *les vers*) that will devour them.

48 For works linking the play to a concern with textuality, poetry and rhetoric, see, for example, Gayle Whittier, 'The Sonnet's Body and the Body Sonnetized in *Romeo and Juliet*', *Shakespeare Quarterly*, 40 (1989), 27–41; Robin Headlam Wells, 'Neo-Petrarchan Kitsch in *Romeo and Juliet*', *Modern Language Review*, 93 (1998), 913–33; Belsey, 'Name of the Rose', pp. 126–42; Jill L. Levenson, 'Shakespeare's *Romeo and Juliet*: The Places of Invention', in *Shakespeare and Language*, ed. Catherine M. S. Alexander (Cambridge, 2004), pp. 122–37.

clasps, the story of Paris finds itself finally book-ended between the pair of golden statues. Paris *in memoriam* discovers himself not figuratively covered and completed by Juliet, as he had hoped, but rather clasped between the gilded Romeo *and* Juliet, both of whom he has married in death; and it is their story that covers and nearly buries his own.

Sandwiched with Romeo and Juliet in the tomb, Paris remains physically unpreservable but ultimately interchangeable with the lovers in Death's deflowering and devouring embrace. Not for nothing, the three die and lie forever *together*. Paris's inclusion in the death tableau, then, disrupts the self-sealing pretence of romantic love, as well as the parenthetical nature of other forms of kinship. He serves as a crucial triadic presence not only in the Capulet crypt but in the play's overall conception and its commentary on love, mortality and kinship. The theatrical and scholarly marginalization of Paris from the central imagistic, ideational and thematic threads of the play illustrates how critical and performance traditions may illuminate canonical works but may also preserve blind spots. Whether we like it or not, Romeo and Juliet will always have Paris. And so shall we.

THE 'SERPENT OF OLD NILE': CLEOPATRA AND THE PRAGMATICS OF REPORTED SPEECH

JELENA MARELJ

For all of her 'infinite variety', which has earned her the title of 'masterpiece' as well as comparisons with Hamlet and Falstaff, Shakespeare's Cleopatra has been customarily subject to either critical condemnation or praise, which flatten her variety and diminish her transcendent greatness as a character.[1] Ever since L.T. Fitz exposed the sexist bias of male critics who espoused 'public, Roman values' to reduce Cleopatra 'from the position of co-protagonist to the position of antagonist at best, [or] nonentity at worst', critics have attempted to empower and extol the Egyptian monarch but have done so by championing Egyptian values and sidelining the Roman perspective or context that necessarily contributes to her complexity.[2] Offsetting the moralizing, patriarchal interpretations of Cleopatra as a devious Eve, a cunning serpent and a Circe-like temptress who symbolizes Antony's sexual enslavement, early feminist critics aspired to redress the Egyptian monarch's reputation by glorifying her as an archetypal female goddess or as a transcendent feminine principle.[3] Politically inclined critics in the 1990s, valorizing Cleopatra's agency and her sexual diplomacy, further re-conceptualized Cleopatra as a politically autonomous and sovereign monarch who plays a crucial role in orchestrating the power relations in the play. As Julius Caesar's, Gnaeus Pompey's and Mark Antony's seductress and concubine, Cleopatra deftly employs sexual strategies to retain her political power and her kingdom: Theodora Jankowski claimed that Cleopatra tactically unites her bodies natural and politic to maintain her power on the Egyptian throne;

Mary Ann Bushman contended that Cleopatra's role-playing allows her to renounce a limited Roman identity and to construct an idiosyncratic and politically autonomous identity predicated on performance; Linda Charnes similarly contended that Cleopatra's '*histrionic* constitution' enables her to subvert Roman voyeurism in order to safeguard her sovereignty; Heather James equally noted how Cleopatra 'exploits artistry, spectacle, and theatricality as self-representational materials in the exercise of her royal power'; and Catherine Belsey claimed that Cleopatra's strategic seduction-by-deferral endows her with power,

---

[1] William Hazlitt calls Cleopatra a 'masterpiece': *Characters of Shakespeare's Plays* [1817] (Oxford, 1955), p. 75; A. C. Bradley compares Cleopatra to Hamlet and Falstaff: 'Shakespeare's *Antony and Cleopatra*', in *Oxford Lectures on Poetry* (London, 1950), pp. 279–305, p. 299.

[2] L. T. Fitz, 'Egyptian Queens and Male Reviewers: Sexist Attitudes in Antony and Cleopatra Criticism', *Shakespeare Quarterly*, 28 (1977), 297–316; p. 306. The play's Roman political context is intertwined with, and inseparable from, its Egyptian love plot; see, for instance, Rick Bowers, '"The luck of Caesar": Winning and Losing in Antony and Cleopatra', *English Studies*, 79 (1998), 522–35; p. 535. See also James Hirsh, who deconstructs the Rome–Egypt binary in the play: 'Rome and Egypt in *Antony and Cleopatra* and in Criticism of the Play', in *Antony and Cleopatra: New Critical Essays*, ed. Sara Munson Deats (New York and London, 2005), pp. 175–91.

[3] For a survey of 'moralistic' and 'romantic' criticism on Cleopatra, see Sara Munson Deats, 'Shakespeare's Anamorphic Drama: A Survey of Antony and Cleopatra in Criticism, on Stage, and on Screen', in *Antony and Cleopatra: New Critical Essays*, ed. Deats (New York, 2005), pp. 1–93; pp. 7–8 and 15–18.

for her self-representations masquerade absence as presence while allowing her to be 'inconsistently *elsewhere*'.[4] That Cleopatra's political manoeuvring is inextricably intertwined with and dependent on her theatrical strategies of seduction is now a critical commonplace. However, in endowing Cleopatra with absolute agency, these critics do not acknowledge that Cleopatra is always and already a subject of – and hence subjected to – the Roman Empire. As Cristina León Alfar notes, the highly optimistic view of Cleopatra as 'an agent of events, as a woman in control of her body and her own representation' fails to account for Cleopatra's political subordination to patriarchal Roman rule, which not only instigates but also constrains her reactions.[5] Egypt's non-violent colonization, to quote Alfar, makes Cleopatra's 'celebrated sexuality both an effect of imperial domination – rather than an erotically motivated act on her part – and a practical mode of natural preservation'.[6]

Moreover, while critics have examined how Cleopatra uses histrionic tactics and strategies to consolidate her power, they have overlooked Cleopatra's speech and her pragmatic use of language. Aside from Russ McDonald's vague assertion that Cleopatra is 'the play's main figure ... of verbal prowess and ambiguity' and David Schalkwyk's brief exploration of how Cleopatra and Antony engage in an 'overt staging of the performative', or in other words how they theatrically perform their illocutionary acts, discussions of Cleopatra's language have tended to focus on 'linguistic typology', to borrow Robert D. Hume's term: critics have often identified general rhetorical traits or figures like paradox and hyperbole that characterize Cleopatra's speech and underwrite the thematic and poetic structure of the play.[7] Nevertheless, in a play like *Antony and Cleopatra* which infamously trades in reports and messages – more so than any other of Shakespeare's plays, as critics have noted – investigating how Cleopatra pragmatically uses or reports other characters' speech as well as her own speech vis-à-vis what is reported about her by the Romans is as crucial in accounting for her political agency and her greatness as a character as examining her theatricality, since Cleopatra's

linguistic acts not only complement but also constitute her histrionic performances.[8]

[4] Theodora A. Jankowski, *Women in Power in the Early Modern Drama* (Chicago, 1992), p. 153; Mary Ann Bushman, 'Representing Cleopatra', in *In Another Country: Feminist Perspectives on Renaissance Drama*, ed. Dorothea Kehler and Susan Baker (Metuchen, NJ, 1991), pp. 36–49; p. 43; Linda Charnes, 'Spies and Whispers: Exceeding Reputation in *Antony and Cleopatra*', in *Notorious Identity: Materializing the Subject in Shakespeare* (Cambridge, MA, 1993), pp. 103–47; p. 127; Heather James, *Shakespeare's Troy: Drama, Politics, and the Translation of Empire* (New York, 1997), p. 136; Catherine Belsey, 'Cleopatra's Seduction', in *Alternative Shakespeares*, ed. Terence Hawkes, vol. 2 (New York, 1996), pp. 38–62; p. 42.
[5] Cristina León Alfar, *Fantasies of Female Evil: The Dynamics of Gender and Power in Shakespearean Tragedy* (Newark, DE, 2003), p. 137. Alfar's analysis is centered on Cleopatra's use of her material (sexual) and metaphorical (political), but also racialized, body 'as an object of desire' (p. 139).
[6] Alfar, *Fantasies of Female Evil*, p. 151.
[7] Russ McDonald, 'Late Shakespeare: Style and the Sexes', in *Shakespeare Survey 46* (Cambridge, 1993), pp. 91–106; p. 101; David Schalkwyk, *Speech and Performance in Shakespeare's Sonnets and Plays* (Cambridge, 2002), p. 33; Robert D. Hume, 'Individuation and Development of Character through Language in *Antony and Cleopatra*', *Shakespeare Quarterly*, 24 (1973), 280–300; p. 300. Rosalie Colie notes that Cleopatra 'has a lovely imagination and considerable command of language' but, like McDonald, she does not develop her observation: *Shakespeare's Living Art* (Princeton, 1974), p. 188. Janet Adelman identifies paradox (for Cleopatra) and hyperbole (for Antony) as the protagonists' defining linguistic traits as well as the tropes which shape character and structure the play: *The Common Liar: An Essay on Antony and Cleopatra* (New Haven, 1973), pp. 111–13. Carol Cook, referring to the use of language in the play rather than to Cleopatra's speech specifically, states that this language 'locates or creates Cleopatra in linguistic and logical gaps, in puns that tease us out of sense and paradoxes that tease us out of thought': 'The Fatal Cleopatra', in *Shakespearean Tragedy and Gender*, ed. Shirley Nelson Garner and Madelon Sprengnether (Bloomington, 1996), pp. 241–67; p. 246. Cf. Katherine Eggert: 'betrayal, fecundity, and startling invention interwrap themselves inextricably both as modes of speaking and as metaphors in which to speak', in *Showing Like a Queen: Female Authority and Literary Experiment in Spenser, Shakespeare, and Milton* (Philadelphia, 2000), p. 149.
[8] Linda Charnes claims that '[t]he word "report" occurs more frequently in this play than in any other': 'Spies and Whispers', p. 106. See also Michael Goldman, *Acting and Action in Shakespearean Tragedy* (Princeton, 1985), p. 117, and Leo G. Salingar, 'Uses of Rhetoric: *Antony and Cleopatra*', *Cahiers Élisabéthains*, 55 (1999), 17–26; p. 20.

In this article, I will demonstrate that the peculiar ambivalence that marks Cleopatra's character – her capacity to produce sexual greatness within the context of her subordination – is an effect of her use of report as a particular linguistic strategy. In other words, I will show that Cleopatra's character is determined not so much by the gender and imperial relations depicted in the play as by the type of speech acts that populate the play. Approaching Cleopatra from the perspective of linguistic pragmatics, I contend that Cleopatra's instances of reportage – her reporting other characters' speech and commanding that her own responses and behaviour be reported – illustrate her powerless submission and adherence to Roman authority as a pretext for asserting her superiority and sexual dominance over the Romans. This oscillation between Cleopatra's sexual power and her revelations of political powerlessness – or rather, her ability to fulfil her powerless Roman role while simultaneously exceeding it by turning it into a source of sexual self-empowerment – produces her charisma and ultimate power as a character. An examination of Cleopatra's linguistic performances within a pragmatic framework can silence the critical debate about whether Cleopatra is the play's Roman victim or Egyptian victor by demonstrating that Cleopatra's victorious sexuality is predicated on the enactment and transformation of her victimization. I first outline the performative nature of reported speech and briefly depict Caesar's use of it in Rome before illustrating how Cleopatra deploys report to fashion and control her representation as an Egyptian queen in a Roman political context.

Although reported speech has long been approached syntactically as an object of formal analysis in linguistics, it has also been gaining increasing acceptance as 'a category of discourse analysis rather than syntax'.[9] The syntactic approach, which examines the speech units of reported speech to determine the grammatical difference in meaning between its manifestation as indirect and as direct quotation, is 'chiefly concerned with positing rules for converting one RS [reported speech] construction into another'.[10]

Criticized for being 'reductionist', the syntactic approach does not account for the context or utterance frame of the report which, to borrow Duranti and Goodwin's phrasing, 'provides resources' for 'its appropriate interpretation' such as 'cultural setting, speech situation, shared background assumptions' as well as participant perception.[11] The meaning of reported speech, according to the pragmatic perspective, is not determined exclusively by abstract grammatical and syntactical rules; rather, it is shaped by the reporter's linguistic performance within a given discourse context that involves speaker intention and hearer reception. A discourse-pragmatic approach takes into account the variability between the reported speech and

---

[9] Daniel E. Collins, *Reanimated Voices: Speech Reporting in a Historical-Pragmatic Perspective* (Amsterdam, 2001), p. 11; see also Matylda Wlodarczyk, *Pragmatic Aspects of Reported Speech: The Case of Early Modern English Courtroom Discourse*, Studies in English Medieval Language and Literature, vol. 17 (Frankfurt, 2007), pp. 39–40. Reported speech is also known as direct and indirect quotation. Although the term 'reported speech' lacks consistency in linguistics, it tends to be synonymous with indirect speech (speech that is quoted indirectly) rather than with direct speech (speech that is quoted directly); see Wlodarczyk on terminology, pp. 30–2. I use 'reported speech' to signify speech that is reported either indirectly *or* directly. I also use 'reportage' to signify not only variegated instances of reported discourse (i.e. speech that is direct, indirect or hypothetical) but also reported thought, reported occurrences and the use of reports themselves. On the inseparability of reported thoughts, feelings and perceptions from reported speech, see Anna Wierzbicka, 'The Semantics of Direct and Indirect Discourse', *Papers in Linguistics*, 7 (1974), 267–307; p. 297.

[10] Collins, *Reanimated Voices*, p. 11. As an example, linguists would examine how the meaning of the direct report in the sentence 'He said "it's raining"' is altered by its transposition to the syntactic unit of a *that*-clause which characterizes indirect speech: 'He *said that* it *was* raining' (italics mine). The syntactic transposition of direct to indirect speech would also entail an examination of 'pronoun shift, tense shift, [and] mood shift'. See Mike Baynham, 'Direct Speech: What's It Doing in Non-narrative Discourse?', *Journal of Pragmatics*, 25.1 (1996), 61–81; p. 62.

[11] Collins, *Reanimated Voices*, p. 11; Alessandro Duranti and Charles Goodwin, 'Re-Thinking Context', Introduction, in *Re-Thinking Context: Language as an Interactive Phenomenon*, ed. Duranti and Goodwin (Cambridge, 1992), pp. 1–42; p. 3.

the reporting context as well as the intentionality of the reporter who, as Daniel Collins shows, shapes and presents the reported speech 'to interpreters in a specific context, for his own communicative purposes'.[12] Reacting against the structuralist foundations of Saussurean-based linguistics, pragmatics holds that meaning is actively produced between speakers and hearers in a given discourse context.

The pragmatic approach to report and reported speech is heavily indebted to Mikhail Bakhtin's and Valentin Vološinov's dialogical and heteroglossic theory of language, in which utterances are evocative of and responsive to prior utterances. Defined by Vološinov as 'speech within speech, utterance within utterance, and at the same time also *speech about speech, utterance about utterance*', reported speech is a discursive category that emphasizes the 'dynamic interrelationship of . . . the speech being reported (the other person's speech) and the speech doing the reporting (the author's speech)', or between the reporter and the original speaker's speech.[13] Since the '"authorial" context surrounding the reported speech' is comprised of reply and commentary, the act of reporting is never neutral, nor can it transmit the original utterance verbatim.[14] Rather, reporting is an interpretive or performative act that renders the reporter an active participant in the construction of meaning rather than a passive instrument of its use. The reported speech thus conveys not only the form and content of the original utterance but also registers the reporter's stylistic, syntactic or compositional adaptation of the speech to suit his or her communicative intentions.[15] An intentional and creative act, reportage thus inscribes the reporter's commentary or response onto the utterance that the reporter purports to report within his or her reporting context.

In *Antony and Cleopatra*, reportage is a trademark of Roman discourse and a measure of its political power. If Rome, as Linda Charnes claims, is the locus of the 'narrative imperative' that 'drives imperialist historiography', then this narrative imperative is instantiated in the use of report, which is a tool for conquest and imperial domination as much as it is a reflection of them.[16] Caesar's use of report and reported speech primarily serve as a means of verbally appropriating or territorializing the foreign Other and absorbing its contours into a politically sanctioned, standardized Roman narrative. But report also serves as a means of public self-display and plays a crucial role in shaping Roman public opinion. If Caesar exercises the narrative imperative through his use of report to discursively construct a mighty Roman Empire, he also fashions himself for the Roman public as a powerful and exemplary Emperor at its helm.[17] Caesar commands and receives reports from his messengers as well as reports other characters' speeches, written words and actions to consolidate his power in an environment where not only reports but also his *grand imperial narrative* is constantly 'exceeded, overtaken by new narratives formulated by interpreting subjects across the empire'.[18] In a Rome rife with political competition, Caesar strategically uses report and reported speech to memorialize himself as a powerful ruler for the historical record – and does so by discreetly belittling his rivals, Antony and Cleopatra.

Caesar's tribute to Antony's past greatness as a stoic general at Modena (1.4.55–71) exemplifies his use of report to promulgate his desired public image. Although Caesar laments Antony's loss of his heroic Roman nature as well as his

---

[12] Collins, *Reanimated Voices*, p. 3.
[13] Valentin N. Vološinov, *Marxism and the Philosophy of Language*, trans. Ladislav Matejka and I. R. Titunik (Cambridge, MA, 1973), pp. 115 and 119.
[14] Vološinov, *Marxism*, p. 118.
[15] See Vološinov, *Marxism*, p. 116.
[16] Charnes, 'Spies and Whispers', pp. 110 and 107.
[17] See Charnes, 'Spies and Whispers', p. 108.
[18] Andrew Hiscock, '"Here is my Space": The Politics of Appropriation in Shakespeare's *Antony and Cleopatra*', *English: The Journal of the English Association*, 47 (1998), 187–212; p. 196. See also Charnes, who observes that reporters are 'not just the play's ubiquitous anonymous messengers but also major figures – such as Octavius, Enobarbus, Antony, and Cleopatra – all of whom deliver discursive re-creations of other characters' performances': 'Spies and Whispers', p. 106.

self-indulgence in Egypt where 'he fishes, drinks, and wastes / The lamps of night in revel' (1.4.4–5), Caesar's tribute to Antony's past glory is an effectively calculated rhetorical performance that merely masquerades as praise. Caesar uses report to degrade and criticize Antony under the pretext of praising him in order to reinforce his public image as a righteous ruler who displays no ill will towards his rival. Caesar's oral report of Antony, framed by the written report from Alexandria that Caesar reads out to Lepidus in order to dispel his rumoured distaste towards Antony, is orchestrated to display his admiration of Antony's Roman qualities. Just as Caesar praises Antony's temperance and stoic abstinence from proper nourishment at Modena, he undercuts this tribute by his use of degrading imagery ('Thou didst drink / The stale of horses, and the gilded puddle / Which beasts would cough at' (1.4.61–3)), which discreetly de-mythologizes Antony's heroism.[19] Moreover, instead of praising a victorious soldier at Modena, Caesar praises a defeated Antony who is 'beaten from Modena' (1.4.57); Antony's heroism is depicted in a personal war with famine for survival (58–61) rather than in a political battle for the Roman state. As Heather James points out, Caesar's description of the famished Antony in a desolate landscape is meant to critique Antony as an inept and anachronistic leader for 'the emerging bureaucracy of the Roman empire' by highlighting Antony's association with 'Rome's myths of rugged origins'.[20]

Along with images of depravity, Caesar's use of reported speech in his tribute serves to undermine his praise of Antony's heroism and turns his tribute into a critique of the Triumvir. Significantly, all of Caesar's eight instances of reportage in the play typify indirect reported speech. Indirect report – or what Vološinov calls the 'pictorial' style of speech – is structured on a reporting context that 'strives to break down the self-contained compactness of the reported speech, to resolve it, to obliterate its boundaries': by 'infiltrating [the] reported speech with authorial retort and commentary', the report is subordinated to the reporter.[21] Indirect reported speech thus suppresses the original speaker's voice

to reframe and convey only the content of the speech in the reporter's reporting context in order to make it appear objective and official; indirect report allows Caesar to control the imperial narrative over which he presides by manipulating, to quote Hiscock, 'the textual remains of the past, to re-create history and to delimit its meaning' in order to 'reinvent himself so that he too may become part of the Roman narratives of heroic lineage which are greeted with awe by the city-state'.[22] Nevertheless, the report contained in Caesar's tribute to Antony is not an indirect report of Antony's speech. Rather, the report is what Caesar has *indirectly heard reported* about Antony: 'On the Alps / It is reported thou didst eat strange flesh, / Which some did die to look on' (1.4.66–8). This unofficial word-of-mouth that Caesar hears at second-hand is made into official public record. While it may announce Caesar's wonder or incredulousness at Antony's hardiness and heroic endurance, the report nevertheless belittles Antony by underlining his uncontrolled appetite, which urges him to consume 'strange flesh' in lieu of the praiseworthy berries and bark that befit a hardy soldier. Caesar perhaps even attributes a particular savagery to Antony, something that he had just, ironically, claimed Antony's stoicism enables him to transcend (1.4.60–1). Although Caesar's report admirably illustrates that Antony's physical

---

[19] Alexander Leggatt, *Shakespeare's Political Drama* (New York, 1988), p. 166. 'Gilded', if construed as golden rather than yellow, could also be read ironically to underscore Caesar's ridicule of Antony.

[20] James, *Shakespeare's Troy*, p. 128.

[21] Vološinov, *Marxism*, p. 120. Indirect reported speech, for Vološinov, also includes mixed forms of speech reporting such as quasi indirect and quasi direct discourse (see *Marxism*, p. 122).

[22] Hiscock, '"Here is my Space"', p. 194. An example of Caesar's use of indirect report, broadly defined, occurs in his confrontation with Antony: 'you / Did pocket up my letters, and with taunts / Did gibe my missive out of audience' (2.2.76–8). Although Caesar does not report the exact words spoken by Antony, he nevertheless recounts the manner of Antony's speech ('gibe', 'taunts') to portray him antagonistically.

form does not diminish after his 'strange' feast (his 'cheek / So much as lanked not' (1.4.70–1)), his note of admiration covertly registers his implicit criticism of the Triumvir's intemperance and self-indulgence as he sexually feasts on Cleopatra's – not coincidentally – strange Egyptian flesh and loses his physical shape as a result. The comparison is subtle yet it registers Caesar's haughtiness and superiority as a virtuous leader – even as the passive voice of the report ('it is reported') distances him from owning his critique – by altering the referential context of Antony's heroism in order to ridicule it. Contained within a reporting context in which Caesar laments the loss of Antony's past heroism and urges him to return to Rome, Caesar's indirectly heard report renders Antony's past heroism questionable. Under the pretext of singing of Antony's past greatness at Modena, Caesar deflates Antony's heroism and tarnishes his reputation 'in the world's report' (2.3.5) in a discreet attempt to promote his own greatness as a ruler and 'earn[ ] a place i'th' story' (3.13.44).

Although Rome's 'narrative imperative' may distinguish it from Cleopatra's Egypt as the realm of 'mimetic improvisation', as Linda Charnes claims, Cleopatra nevertheless adopts Roman reportage to re-script her social and political power within a Roman discursive context.[23] Charnes' juxtaposition of Cleopatra's 'mimetic improvisation, or mimetic subversion' against this Roman narrative imperative with which it competes prevents her from recognizing that not only are Cleopatra's verbal acts and histrionic deeds mutually constitutive, but also that Cleopatra does not merely exemplify 'the subjection, and resistance, to the narrative imperative' – she also embraces and transcends it.[24] Whereas Caesar reports the past and present in order to control and contain them and thereby underlines his political status as a powerful Triumvir, Cleopatra's use of report marks the absence of her political power even as it conveys her desire to negotiate an identity that is, ironically, self-sufficient and self-empowering while inevitably being subjugated to Roman authority. Despite her political powerlessness, reportage allows

Cleopatra to stage herself as an independent female sovereign who both enacts and directs her self-staging.

Unlike Caesar who celebrates Antony's past stoic greatness at Modena, Cleopatra celebrates Antony's present greatness as her war-like lover. But while Cleopatra's monologue competitively counters Caesar's tribute to Antony, it nevertheless proves to be as self-serving as Caesar's tribute. As a means of combating her political and emotional vulnerability after Antony is summoned back to Rome, Cleopatra's direct report of Antony's words in her monologue marks her self-glorification and sexual dominance over Antony under the pretext of glorifying Antony as a hero and acknowledging his Mars-like power over her. The direct reported speech allows Cleopatra to turn her political powerlessness as a mere woman and sexualized Roman object into a sexual power that she can memorialize. Addressing Charmian and Iras, a seemingly melancholic Cleopatra makes Antony the subject of her ruminations:

> O, Charmian,
> Where think'st thou he is now? Stands he or sits he?
> Or does he walk? Or is he on his horse?
> O happy horse, to bear the weight of Antony!
> Do bravely, horse, for wot'st thou whom thou mov'st? –
> The demi-Atlas of this earth, the arm
> And burgonet of men. He's speaking now,
> Or murmuring 'Where's my serpent of old Nile?' –
> For so he calls me. Now I feed myself
> With most delicious poison. Think on me,
> That am with Phoebus' amorous pinches black,
> And wrinkled deep in time. Broad-fronted Caesar,
> When thou wast here above the ground I was

---

[23] Charnes, 'Spies and Whispers', p. 107.

[24] For Charnes, all of the 'power relations' in the play are figured in terms of the subjection, and resistance, to the narrative imperative. Charnes, 'Spies and Whispers', p. 108. While Charnes claims that 'mimetic subversion' is not essentially anti-discursive since 'it filches from and poaches on existing discourses', she nevertheless views mimesis and narrative as opposite ends on a spectrum rather than as complementary modes of representation (p. 107).

A morsel for a monarch, and great Pompey
Would stand and make his eyes grow in my brow.
There would he anchor his aspect, and die
With looking on his life.   (1.5.18–34)

In littering her monologue with rhetorical questions and an apostrophe that hyperbolically dramatizes her (arguably feigned) longing for Antony and her fantasizing over his quotidian motions, Cleopatra depicts herself as an enamoured woman lamenting her lover's absence and obsessively pining for his presence. Alluding to Antony as a 'demi-Atlas' and metonymically referring to him as the 'arm / And burgonet of men' (1.5.23–4), the smitten Cleopatra praises Antony's heroic magnanimity and military prowess as she pictures him mounted on a horse in preparation for battle. Extending her praise of Antony's heroism, Cleopatra imagines Antony speaking and directly reports his epithet for her: '"Where's my serpent of old Nile?" / For so he calls me' (1.5.25–6).[25] This instance of direct reported speech used by Cleopatra creates the impression of her homage to, and admiration of, Antony. Direct reported speech – or what Vološinov calls the 'linear' style of reported speech – is an imitative act underwritten by the desire to maintain the original speech's 'integrity and authenticity' by 'demarcat[ing]' and 'screen[ing] it from penetration by the author's [read: reporter's] intonations' or syntactic reformulations.[26] In thus granting authority to the original speaker of the utterance, direct reported speech underscores the reporter's concession to and acknowledgement of the utterance's encoded authority. Nevertheless, as sociolinguists Patricia Mayes and Deborah Tannen have pointed out, direct reported speech is not factual nor is it an authentic reconstruction of a previous utterance; instead, it is a form of creatively 'constructed dialogue' which is used by the reporter or speaker 'as evidence . . . to present a more believable story'.[27] In thus casting herself into a subordinate role as a longing, passive beloved by putting a chivalric Antony on a pedestal, Cleopatra underlines the social distance between her and Antony by adopting the 'deference or self-suppression' attendant on

direct report to present a seemingly more believable story of her love for Antony.[28]

In performing her role as a powerless woman in love, Cleopatra turns her apparent deference to her sexual advantage. Even though Cleopatra, as Ania Loomba claims, 'plays the Egyptian flamboyantly, thus appropriating, and flaunting, the difference that Rome assigns to her', her performances do not necessarily imply that her love for Antony is merely feigned.[29] Although the Egyptian queen loves Antony, her love for him is closely intertwined with self-interest. In hyperbolizing her love for Antony by turning it into a spectacle worthy of public admiration and report both in her monologue and in the play's opening scene, Cleopatra clearly subordinates love to her political agenda of self-promotion in order to stave off

---

[25] While Cleopatra's report of Antony's speech is not circumscribed by quotation marks in the Folio, modern editors have – more often than not – chosen to place the speech within quotes. However, quotation marks (or a lack thereof) do not necessarily signify direct or indirect reported speech. In linguistics, if the deictic centre of the speech 'is that of the original utterance' and 'gives the illusion that the incident is presently occurring' – as is the case with Cleopatra's report of Antony's speech – the reported speech is direct. See Patricia Mayes, 'Quotation in Spoken English', *Studies in Language*, 14.2 (1990), 325–63; p. 346. If the deictic centre of the speech is 'in the report situation', the reported speech would be indirect: see Florian Coulmas, 'Reported Speech: Some General Issues', in *Direct and Indirect Speech*, ed. Coulmas (New York, 1986), pp. 1–28; p. 6. An indirect report of Antony's words would read: 'Antony is speaking or murmuring, and asking where his serpent of old Nile is.' As Coulmas notes, direct reported speech is neither syntactically restricted by, nor partially absorbed into, the reporting context like indirect reported speech is (see 'Reported Speech', p. 5).

[26] Vološinov, *Marxism*, p. 119.

[27] See Patricia Mayes, 'Quotation in Spoken English', p. 330. Deborah Tannen calls reported speech 'constructed dialogue' in *Talking Voices: Repetition, Dialogue, and Imagery in Conversational Discourse* ([1989] Cambridge, 2007), p. 112; Mayes, 'Quotation in Spoken English', p. 348.

[28] Collins, *Reanimated Voices*, p. 69. Direct report can evoke a 'sense of objectivity' (p. 71).

[29] Ania Loomba, *Shakespeare, Race, and Colonialism* (Oxford, 2002), p. 133.

complete Roman colonization. As a result, her deference to Antony proves to be self-serving, for her direct report of Antony's speech ('"Where's my serpent of old Nile?"') registers not just the extent of her obsessive preoccupation with Antony but depicts an Antony longing for *her* presence. In glossing Antony's act of speaking as murmuring ('He's speaking now, / Or murmuring' (1.5.24–5)) in the very act of pronouncing it, Cleopatra portrays Antony as a man in love who privately guards his passions, is emotionally dependent on her and longs for her as much as she pines for him. Direct reported speech, as Anna Wierzbicka contends, is 'theatrical' or 'playful': it is an act of ventriloquism that temporarily allows the reporter to 'assume[ ] the role of that other person, [to] "play[ ] his part", that is to say, imagine[ ] himself as the other person [i.e. as the original speaker]...' or to dramatize another speaker's reported words in order to affectively involve the audience in the inference of meaning, for the speech in direct speech is 'shown' rather than explicitly told as it is in indirect reported speech.[30] Rather than solely convey the content of Antony's speech, direct reported speech allows Cleopatra to additionally communicate the *affective* aspects of meaning that are associated with, and conveyed through, the wording, 'modality or prosody of the utterance' in order to persuade her audience of Antony's sentiments as well as to highlight her applause-worthy impersonation of him.[31]

In showing her on-stage audience that Antony is emotionally bound to her, Cleopatra also shows that Antony's greatness is due to her. The military associations of Antony's horse quickly give way to erotic associations as the horse, symbolizing 'the unreined lust of concupiscence' according to Plutarch, doubles as a sexual self-reference to Cleopatra who literally and physically 'bear[s] the weight of Antony' (1.5.21) and makes him 'move' in bed, but also 'bears' the weight of Antony in her memory as she performs her report.[32] Antony's heroism, as Cleopatra reveals, is premised on his Egyptian sexuality which is (laboriously) brought to life and praised by Cleopatra, who urges herself to '[d]o bravely' (1.5.22) and depict him in a chivalric light: *she* is the agent or source of *his*

greatness and his greatness is not defined by abstinence or austere Roman measures. Antony is great because of Cleopatra's sexual performance; he is also great because of her theatrical performance of Antony's words, which allows her to ironically re-enact his 'greatness' as a chivalric lover. While the horse reference thus seems to undermine Cleopatra's authority by associating her with the ardent lust of Egyptian femininity that the Romans ascribe to her, she nevertheless uses it self-servingly to construct her sexual authority. Moreover, even though her allusion to Antony as a heroic 'demi-Atlas' (1.5.23) lauds him, it is also spoken ironically since it registers her belittlement of an Antony who is unable to embody a complete Atlas. As Janet Adelman claims, the allusion registers an ambivalence of praise and criticism to remind the audience 'of the degree to which Antony has dwindled from the heroic stature of his great ancestor [Hercules]' at the same time as it 'emphasizes [the] grandeur' of Antony's ventures.[33] In labelling Antony a 'demi' Atlas, Cleopatra may be implying that she is the other half-Atlas, or perhaps even a complete and self-contained Atlas, who grants Antony his greatness and acts as the standard of greatness against which she measures him. In thus 'praising' an Antony who reportedly longs for her, Cleopatra indirectly praises herself by putting words into the mouth of a heroic Antony to show that she is the cause of his greatness. But being the Roman subject she is, Cleopatra also needs Antony to gain a political foothold in Rome in order to become 'great' herself. Cleopatra's verbal sleight-of-hand allows her to re-fashion her

---

[30] Wierzbicka, 'Semantics', p. 272.
[31] Mayes, 'Quotation in Spoken English', p. 338. Mayes observes that direct speech often conveys 'affective elements' of meaning in addition to factual information (p. 358). Vološinov contends that indirect speech cannot register emotion (*Marxism*, p. 128).
[32] North's Plutarch, quoted in Adelman, *Common Liar*, p. 60. For the connection between motion and sexual copulation, see Martin Spevack, ed., *Antony and Cleopatra: A New Variorum Edition of Shakespeare* (New York, 1990), n. 141, pp. 23–4.
[33] Adelman, *Common Liar*, p. 135.

dependence on Antony as Antony's dependence on her, so that she may combat her vulnerability during his absence from Egypt. Cleopatra pleases herself by imagining that Antony imagines her as having great seductive power; the report rebounds back to flatter the reporter.[34]

Cleopatra moreover reinterprets Antony's 'serpent of old Nile' in an Egyptian context to turn her political disempowerment – suggested by the negative Roman connotations of the word 'serpent' – into a valorizing self-reference that showcases her erotic power and sexual dominance. While Cleopatra's direct report of Antony's epithet sounds her self-praise by implying that Antony's heroism is not entirely his own, it may also subtly ridicule Antony for condemning *her* as he adheres to possible Roman connotations in referring to her as a serpent. That Antony adopts Roman words and calls Cleopatra his 'serpent of old Nile' off-stage is not questionable; what is questionable is Antony's intention in pragmatically using the epithet, which renders Cleopatra's contention that Antony spoke the words in a state of amorous longing for her (as she imagines him doing) suspect. Given that 'murmuring' also connotes 'to complain in low muttered tones' or 'to give voice to an inarticulate discontent', it may suggest that Antony is complicit in Cleopatra's power games and is dissatisfied with – or bemoaning – Cleopatra's control over him; alternately, it may suggest that Antony is using flattery in a self-serving manner to disguise his one-upmanship with Cleopatra.[35] The report of Antony's 'murmur' is contextualized by a negative tissue of allusion to, and repetition of, the word 'serpent' in the play, which allows Antony's Roman (as opposed to his Egyptian) sympathies to emerge. Connoting Satanic wiliness and postlapsarian deceit in the Roman lexis, 'serpent' is used by Antony to negatively characterize Pompey's impending invasion of Rome (1.2.185–7) as the latter 'creeps apace' (1.3.50). Although Antony does not explicitly refer to Cleopatra as a devious snake, the metaphorical connection between the serpent and Cleopatra is implied by Pompey's association with the snake. Just as Pompey 'creeps' quietly and stealthily into the idle hearts of Romans to win

their favour and 'poison' their loyalties towards the state, Cleopatra 'creeps' into liking with Antony to win his love and disempower him by 'poisoning' or sexually over-indulging him. Like the Romans whose idleness is partially at fault for inviting this pestilential invasion that is Pompey, Antony's self-acknowledged idleness and his wilful complicity in his bondage to Cleopatra are similarly at fault: 'Ten thousand harms more than the ills I know / My idleness doth hatch' (1.2.122–3).[36] Antony's references to Cleopatra as 'this enchanting queen' (1.2.121), who is 'cunning past man's thought' (1.2.137) and who employs 'strong Egyptian fetters' (1.2.109) and crocodile 'tears' to ensnare him, illustrate his awareness of Cleopatra's duplicity and her manipulative strategies.[37]

Within this interpretive context, Cleopatra parenthetically draws attention to her act of reporting Antony's epithet ('For so he calls me' (1.5.26)). In a monologue saturated with mid-line prosodic switches for the actor that, as Simon Palfrey and Tiffany Stern demonstrate, indicate 'actable shifts in voice, gesture, or attitude', these mid-line switches serve to illustrate that 'power is truly at work – minds at a cusp, fates undecided, fear and anxiety afoot'.[38] The switches that occur after

---

34 Cleopatra's dream-vision report of Antony (5.2.81–91) further instantiates her indirect self-praise. In mythologizing and reconstituting a colossal Antony, Cleopatra draws her auditors' attention to her own powers of self-renewal through report. The report achieves its perlocutionary effect by moving Dolabella to sympathy and transforming him, as Michael Goldman notes, from 'a ready tool of Caesar into [her] devoted servant' (*Acting and Action*, p. 119). Affectively overpowered by Cleopatra's report, Dolabella divulges Caesar's plans to Cleopatra (5.2.106–9).

35 'Murmur', *Oxford English Dictionary*, 1a.

36 Caesar similarly compares Pompey to a snake that '[t]hrives in our idleness' (1.4.77).

37 The pun on 'queen' (quean) indicates Antony's ambivalence toward his Egyptian lover since it registers his admiration of Cleopatra at the same time as it reflects his demeaning Roman perception of her as a sexual play-thing. The pun suggests that Antony may be as wily as Cleopatra. See Loomba, who notes that Antony's performances are politically motivated (*Shakespeare, Race, and Colonialism*, p. 134).

38 Simon Palfrey and Tiffany Stern, *Shakespeare in Parts* (Oxford, 2007), pp. 329 and 364.

and also possibly before Cleopatra's parenthetical 'For so he calls me' suggest a change in tone or attitude: 'And burgonet of men. [switch] He's speaking now, / Or murmuring "Where's my serpent of old Nile?" – / [switch?] For so he calls me. [switch] Now I feed myself' (1.5.24–6). The mid-line switch between 'men' and 'He's speaking' in line 24 marks Cleopatra's movement away from acting the role of a gushing beloved for it attunes her audience to hear the words that Antony speaks and that she reports. The switch in line 26 between 'me' and 'Now' (and possibly also before 'for') marks Cleopatra's distance from glossing the report: she undercuts her praise with a pause pregnant with ironic commentary that serves to mock or condemn Antony's potentially negative use of the epithet as she addresses her female attendants. As Dan Sperber and Deirdre Wilson illustrate, irony is a case of echoic 'mention' rather than the 'use' of certain words: irony is created when the speaker expresses a 'belief ABOUT' the utterance 'rather than BY MEANS OF it'.[39] Evidenced by the parenthetical 'for so he calls me', Cleopatra's ironic mention of Antony's speech draws attention to Antony speaking or, as Sperber and Wilson would say, to 'the expression itself' rather than 'to what the expression refers to'.[40] The combination of prosodic switches and the ironic mention in Cleopatra's report of the serpent epithet may highlight her teasing contempt of Antony and detract from the praise she initially lends him. Irony allows Cleopatra to condemn an Antony who has deserted her for Caesar and to instate her self-praise comfortably.

Despite the possibility of Antony's insinuated belittlement of, and thus domineering Roman attitude towards, Cleopatra in calling her his serpent, Cleopatra re-interprets the epithet in an Egyptian context and turns it into a source of personal pride and power as she recollects her successful sexual conquests of both Julius Caesar and Gnaeus Pompey. In an Egyptian context, the serpent carries positive connotations: as Egypt's pre-eminent mythical creature, the serpent is spontaneously born of the mud of the ebbing Nile 'by

the operation of [the] sun' (2.7.27) and symbolizes fertility, renewal and resurrection. As figured in the ancient symbol of the ouroboros, the serpent additionally encompasses antitheses such as mortality and eternity and thus instantiates a cyclicality that Cleopatra's seduction of both Caesar and Pompey embodies as she renews – or re-scripts – herself as a sexually powerful sovereign.[41] Just as she performs the role of a woman in love for Antony, Cleopatra performs her scripted role as a denigrated courtesan for Caesar and Pompey only to valorize this sexual role in an Egyptian context and to assert her sexual power over the Triumvirs. Employing her feminine wiles to seduce Caesar and Pompey, Cleopatra embraces her scripted role as a subjugated female Egyptian; she is a 'morsel' (1.5.31) of food that serves to satisfy Caesar's sexual appetite, as well as a woman-mirror that subserviently reflects Pompey's image back to him (1.5.31–4). Cleopatra's mention of 'morsel' in her monologue, like her mention of 'serpent', suggests her awareness of its negative Roman connotation even as she re-structures its meaning in an Egyptian context. Whereas 'morsel' in the Roman lexis is used in a derogatory fashion to belittle Cleopatra as a worthless leftover, as an irate Antony's use of the word following the defeat at Actium demonstrates (3.13.117), in the Egyptian lexis a 'morsel' – evocative of Egyptian feasting – may refer 'to the folk tradition that if one ate the food of the supernatural realm one could never leave'.[42] Although it is not identifiable as a category of reported speech proper, Cleopatra's mention of 'morsel' is an implicit and ironic report that serves to undermine Roman power. Re-interpreted in an Egyptian context where it signifies the inescapable

[39] Dan Sperber and Deirdre Wilson, 'Irony and the Use-Mention Distinction', in *Radical Pragmatics*, ed. Peter Cole (New York, 1981), pp. 295–318; p. 302.

[40] Sperber and Wilson, 'Irony', p. 303.

[41] The Ouroboros is depicted as a black-headed snake devouring its white tail in the *Chrysopoeia of Cleopatra*. Adelman claims that the '[p]opular tradition associated the serpent with his tail in his mouth with the cosmos and with eternity' (*Common Liar*, p. 62).

[42] Adelman, *Common Liar*, p. 66.

bondage to which Cleopatra subjects her rivals through her erotic ploys, the 'morsel' suggests that Cleopatra not only feeds others' appetites but also feeds her own appetite by rendering her opponents subservient to her. Playing Caesar's sexual game, as Agrippa reports (2.2.234–6), Cleopatra wields sexual power and politically outwits Caesar by bearing him an heir.

Cleopatra's conquest of Pompey is similar to her conquest of Caesar. While her self-dramatization as Pompey's narcissistic mirror of 'self-contemplation' underlines her status as an object of consumption, Cleopatra re-interprets herself in an Egyptian context as a consuming subject. Alluding to herself as the power-wielding Gorgon Medusa whose stony gaze makes Pompey 'anchor his aspect, and die / With looking on his life' (1.5.33–4), Cleopatra overturns the desiring male gaze as she had done on Cydnus to become, as Heather James notes, 'the bearer of the desiring gaze, not its Petrarchan object'.[43] The pun on 'die', which indicates Pompey's sexual fulfilment in a Roman context, also suggests Pompey's political destruction at Cleopatra's hands in an Egyptian context following their sexual tryst; Cleopatra uses the pun to valorize herself as a powerful ruler who ironically grants Pompey 'life' in her report as *her* powerless political subject in Egypt after his Roman 'death'. In turning the Triumvirs' sexual surrender and loss into self-gain in the same manner that she turns her lack of youth and a dark complexion (1.5.28–9) into a desirable vitality to bait her men, Cleopatra embodies the renewal of the Egyptian serpent and glories in her conquests. The oxymoronic 'delicious poison' (1.5.27) with which Cleopatra 'feed[s]' herself (1.5.26) in a self-congratulatory manner underscores her ouroboric self-identity as she mythologizes herself as a self-sustained, self-sufficient and self-begetting serpent; Cleopatra's claim to superiority rests on her being her own beginning and her own end.[44] Cleopatra's poison, or the pleasurable reminiscence of her triumph over the three Triumvirs, enables her to valorize herself as a great and sexually powerful monarch while also foreshadowing her suicide with the asp

that she maternally 'feeds' with her poison. This self-generated poison grants Cleopatra immortality in report and ensures that she is memorialized for posterity. In the face of patriarchal Roman power, Cleopatra's re-contextualized Egyptian serpent comes to symbolize her phallic power which enables her to vie with Caesar in a battle 'staked out across the terrain of Antony's "identity"'.[45]

Not only does Cleopatra's direct report of Antony's epithet sound a self-congratulatory note of praise but it also urges her female attendants – along with the off-stage theatre audience – to praise and applaud her performance. Due to its inherent theatricality, as Collins notes, direct reported speech 'allows the audience to participate both in the new event (the re-creation) and, vicariously, in the prior event, real or imagined, that is being represented'.[46] In reporting Antony's epithet, Cleopatra speaks as Antony to indirectly *tell* her audience of her sexual power while impeccably performing her role as a passive beloved to directly *show* and thus affectively persuade her audience – through prosody, physical enactment or both – of this power by directly involving them in the interpretive process. Embedding her direct report of Antony's epithet in a monologue that opens with the verbal performance of a smitten beloved and closes with an account of her sexual conquests, Cleopatra directs her audience to honour not only her conquest of the Triumvirs but also her past and current improvisational performance of a powerless Roman subject that is a prerequisite to her triumph.[47] Cleopatra's

---

43 Heather James, 'The Politics of Display and the Anamorphic Subjects of *Antony and Cleopatra*', in *Shakespeare's Late Tragedies: A Collection of Critical Essays*, ed. Susanne L. Wofford (Upper Saddle River, 1996), pp. 208–34; p. 212.

44 See also Antony's tautological description of Cleopatra as a crocodile, which reinforces Cleopatra's self-identity (2.7.41–3).

45 Charnes, 'Spies and Whispers', p. 112.

46 Collins, *Reanimated Voices*, p. 74.

47 Cleopatra's apostrophe to Antony's horse (1.5.21) and to the imaginatively present Caesar (1.5.29) in her monologue clearly indicate that she stages her speech as a spectacle.

imperative injunction to her on-stage and off-stage audiences to 'Think on me, / That am with Phoebus' amorous pinches black, / And wrinkled deep in time' (1.5.27–9), accompanied by mid-line switches which both introduce and conclude the injunction, is a public request that her audiences glorify her sexuality and hold her in the same awe-inspiring esteem in which she holds herself. In desiring to hear others speak of her and in imagining others (particularly Antony) speaking, even as she ironically controls this speech, Cleopatra wishes to be ever-present in others' speech and thoughts and thus publicly memorialized as a sexually noble monarch. Like Caesar, Cleopatra uses report as a means of self-flattery to publish her magnanimity to posterity by re-styling her homage to Antony as self-homage. Nevertheless, Cleopatra's monologue highlights her sexual charisma and performative greatness which allow her to transcend her Roman script and exhibit herself as the director, actor and spectator of her own show.

If Cleopatra aspires to condition her on-stage audience's response by directly reporting Antony's epithet, she also attempts to control Antony's emotional response by directly reporting Caesar's hypothetical words to him.[48] In an attempt to turn her powerlessness into power, Cleopatra mocks Caesar through direct report. Her theatrical performance of the words she imagines Caesar uttering serves to manipulate Antony into craving Cleopatra's command over that of Caesar in order to render Antony subservient to her. In the play's opening scene, Cleopatra shames Antony and exposes Caesar's emasculation of him even as she urges him to hear the messengers from Rome:

> Nay, hear them, Antony.
> Fulvia perchance is angry; or who knows
> If the scarce-bearded Caesar have not sent
> His powerful mandate to you: 'Do this, or this,
> Take in that kingdom and enfranchise that.
> Perform't, or else we damn thee.'   (1.1.20–5)

In urging Antony to attend to the messengers ('Your dismission / Is come from Caesar, therefore hear it, Antony' (1.1. 28–9)), Cleopatra plays

her role as an obedient subject who respects and adheres to Caesar's authority. Nevertheless, this urging is quickly undercut by Cleopatra's effeminizing reference to Caesar as a 'scarce-bearded', pubescent boy while she possibly, as Marvin Rosenberg suggests, 'boys' or parodies Caesar's tone and gestures in performing her report.[49] As María Luisa Dañobeitia Fernández claims, Cleopatra hopes to stir 'a profound animosity' in Antony toward Caesar 'by making him *feel* like a foolish servant ready to jump at "[Caesar's] powerful mandate"'.[50] Manipulating Antony through the perlocutionary force of her report of Caesar's hypothetical speech is a way of persuading Antony to stay in Egypt. In addition to her mockery of Caesar, Cleopatra's unflattering description of Fulvia as 'angry' (21) and 'shrill-tongued' (34) is further meant to shame Antony by hinting at his emasculation, which also results from his submission to his wife, under the pretext of endorsing his submission. Cleopatra hopes to persuade Antony to redirect his loyalties towards her by making him desire a freedom and a reciprocal relationship that are characteristically Egyptian. However, this implied freedom and reciprocity are illusions since Cleopatra ironically exposes her adoption of Fulvia's and Caesar's modes of speaking to gain power over Antony. In reporting how 'shrill-tongued Fulvia scolds' (1.1.34), Cleopatra uses Fulvia's shrillness as a pretext for her own scolding of Antony, which she implicitly performs in the very act of ridiculing Caesar and exposing Antony's shame. Moreover, as her opening imperatives attest, Cleopatra adopts Caesar's '"Roman" language of command' in a Lear-like fashion to challenge Antony to quantify his love for her ('If it be love indeed, tell me

---

[48] Hypothetical, because Cleopatra imagines what Caesar would say.

[49] Marvin Rosenberg, *The Masks of Antony and Cleopatra*, ed. Mary Rosenberg (Newark, DE, 2006), p. 58.

[50] María Luisa Dañobeitia Fernández, 'Cleopatra's Role-Taking: A Study of *Antony and Cleopatra*', in *Spanish Studies in Shakespeare and His Contemporaries*, ed. José Manuel González (Newark, DE, 2006), pp. 171–95; p. 173 (italics mine).

how much' (1.1.14)) as she repeatedly commands Antony to hear the messengers from Rome (lines 20, 29 and 50).[51] In proclaiming that she will 'set a bourn how far to be beloved' (1.1.16), Cleopatra adopts the Roman values of calculation and order and thus directly competes with Caesar to secure Antony's faithfulness to her and to Egypt by making Antony desire exactly what she warns him against desiring: control and subservience. Performing the role of a calculating monarch, Cleopatra theatrically directs Antony to display his love for her verbally so that she can showcase, and thus boast of, his submission to her and her power over him not only to her audience but also to the voyeuristic Romans in Egypt who would report this as a challenge to Caesar. Cleopatra directly reports Caesar's hypothetical speech in an attempt to reinforce her affective control and command over Antony under the pretext of, paradoxically, showcasing her inability to command Antony *to* him, even as she attempts to stage this command for her audience. By impersonating Caesar and his imperiousness at the same time as showing how undesirable it is to be subject to Caesar, Cleopatra draws attention to her performative greatness which allows her to exceed her containment in Roman report.

In addition to reporting other characters' speech, the actions and behaviour that Cleopatra commands her messengers to report to Antony also serve to secure his political and emotional loyalty to her. While Cleopatra's commands clearly bear illocutionary force for her messengers since she orders them to speak on her behalf, this illocutionary force is transposed into perlocutionary force for Antony. Fearing that Antony's re-alliance with Caesar will spell Egypt's demise upon learning of Fulvia's death and Pompey's plot to invade Rome, Cleopatra attempts to sidetrack Antony from his 'Roman thought[s]' (1.2.77) by ordering Charmian to report her feigned emotional state to him in response to his emotional state: '*If* you find him sad, / Say I am dancing; *if* in mirth, report / That I am sudden sick' (1.3.3–5, italics mine). Cleopatra's conditional and unobtrusive command is effectively calculated to persuade Antony to

return to her. Divulging Cleopatra's strategy of reinvention through performance, the report highlights how Cleopatra embraces the stereotypical role of a fickle woman to subvert Antony's expectations and condition his response; she shows that she is, to use Belsey's term, consistently 'elsewhere'.[52] Cleopatra's contradictory actions, disguised here as potential *reactions* in report, are orchestrated to render Antony subservient to her as well as to test where his loyalties lie. By making Antony's reactions dependent on her 'reactions', Cleopatra hopes to emasculate Antony and make him incapable of acting without her supervision. Antony's eventual return to Rome similarly triggers an emotionally and politically vulnerable Cleopatra to summon Antony back to her by dispatching messages: she vows that 'He shall have every day a several greeting, / Or I'll unpeople Egypt' (1.5.76–7).[53] In line with her performance as a longing beloved, the excessive messages with which Cleopatra vows to shower Antony are intended to flatter him by proving to him how great her love for him is, at the same time as they serve to distract him from his political dealings with Caesar in order to prevent the Triumvirs from forming a league against her.

Cleopatra's final test of Antony's loyalty similarly occurs through report: she commands that her impersonation of a love-sick beloved on her death-bed be reported to Antony. Enclosing herself in her pyramid to escape Antony's rage following their defeat at Actium, a powerless Cleopatra orders Mardian to 'go tell [Antony] I have slain myself. / Say that the last I spoke was "Antony", / And word it, prithee, piteously' (4.14.7–9). Dramatizing the degree of her love for, and reliance on, Antony by having it reported that his name was the last

---

[51] Paul Yachnin, 'Shakespeare's Politics of Loyalty: Sovereignty and Subjectivity in Antony and Cleopatra', *SEL. Studies in English Literature 1500–1900*, 33 (1993), 343–63; p. 347.

[52] Belsey, 'Cleopatra's Seduction', p. 42.

[53] Since she lacks political power, Cleopatra's dispatching of messages is reactive rather than proactive. See Marion Perret, 'Shakespeare's Use of Messengers in *Antony and Cleopatra*', *Drama Survey*, 5 (1966), 67–72; p. 69.

word she spoke, Cleopatra flatters Antony by signalling to him the extent of his power over her. She attempts to move Antony to pity and guilt by making him feel partially responsible for her death – which she, reportedly, performs in grievance at the thought that he blames her for their defeat and urges Mardian to tragically ('piteously') report. Serving as a political 'test of [Antony's] love' as well as a 'testimony of her love', the report of Cleopatra's feigned suicide is deployed to incite Antony as well as her on-stage audience to commemorate her as Antony's noble and faithful beloved, to the same extent that she has just (reportedly) modelled the nobility of her love for Antony by committing suicide.[54] Like a true serpent that daily sheds its skin only to renew it, Cleopatra plays and thus maintains her scripted role as a fickle, weak, powerless and love-struck yet devoted Egyptian while discreetly shedding or exceeding these roles to wield affective power over Antony.[55] Cleopatra strives to emasculate and disempower Antony through the affective force of her reports so that she can use Antony as a pawn in her contest with Rome.

As with Antony, the words that Cleopatra commands to be reported to Caesar further illustrate her strategic manoeuvring in report to gain the upper hand. By enacting her submissive role as Rome's subject and feigning loyalty to Caesar, Cleopatra exceeds this role and asserts her superiority to challenge Caesar's power. Under the pretext of paying homage to Caesar and acknowledging his superiority, Cleopatra's reported words to Caesar instantiate instead her pride and self-glorification. In keeping with her personal philosophy that news should flatter the hearer rather than report the 'honest' truth (2.5.85), Cleopatra's encomium of Caesar is accompanied by a rhetoric of submission. Following the defeat at Actium, Cleopatra uses deference to flatter Caesar and to sue for political favour, as revealed by the Roman ambassador's report to Caesar: 'Cleopatra does confess thy greatness, / Submits her to thy might, and of thee craves / The circle of the Ptolemies for her heirs' (3.12.16–18). As 'confess', 'submit' and 'crave' suggest, Cleopatra's obedience to Caesar is underwritten by her

acknowledgement of his greatness. However, in her conference with Thidias who is sent by Caesar to 'win' (3.12.27) Cleopatra from Antony through manipulative rhetoric (3.12.26–9), Cleopatra punningly asserts her own superiority in commanding Thidias to

Say to great Caesar this in deputation:
I kiss his conqu'ring hand. Tell him I am prompt
To lay my crown at's feet, and there to kneel
Till from his all-obeying breath I hear
The doom of Egypt. (3.13.74–8)

The pun on 'crown', signifying diadem but also head, undermines Cleopatra's proclaimed submission and turns her obsequiousness into a challenge intended to obstruct Caesar's quest for absolute domination. Insinuating that she will fully obey Caesar only when she is decapitated and her 'crown' lies at his feet, the pun reveals that Cleopatra's death is a precondition for her subservience. In a characteristic move marking her implicit self-praise, Cleopatra responds to Proculeius's request that she flatter Caesar by allowing him to report her 'sweet dependency' (5.2.26) on him with a request that Proculeius 'tell [Caesar] / I am his fortune's vassal, and I send him / The greatness he has got' (5.2.28–30). Under the pretext of foregrounding her submission and accepting her fate, Cleopatra coyly hints that she is the agent of Caesar's greatness. She not only 'sends' or pays homage to Caesar's greatness as his subject, but also equivocates on 'send' to imply that *she* grants Caesar his greatness by giving him Egypt. If Antony is a heroic warrior of colossal proportions thanks to Cleopatra, then Caesar is also a great ruler thanks to the great Cleopatra who has bestowed her own greatness upon him. In 'sending' Caesar her greatness, Cleopatra glorifies herself as the origin or agent of Caesar's greatness even as she embraces her

---

[54] Jan H. Blits, *New Heaven, New Earth: Shakespeare's 'Antony and Cleopatra'* (Lanham, MD, and Plymouth, 2009), p. 175.
[55] Cleopatra boasts of her success in commanding Antony's mood to her attendants: 'I laughed him out of patience, and that night / I laughed him into patience' (2.5.19–20).

vassalage. 'Wording' Caesar who also 'words' her (5.2.187–8) in an endless game of one-upmanship, Cleopatra transforms her political powerlessness into power to challenge Caesar's power.

The final act presents a politically astute monarch whose verbal and visual self-ennoblement successfully transforms her into a praiseworthy object of report. In conjuring up a speaking Antony who beckons her and praises her imminent suicide, Cleopatra achieves the public recognition she had so passionately sought and is praised by him on whom she had conferred heroic greatness:

> – methinks I hear
> Antony call. I see him rouse himself
> To praise my noble act. I hear him mock
> The luck of Caesar, which the gods give men
> To excuse their after wrath.   (5.2.278–82)

This official tribute to the Egyptian monarch, imagined and reported by Cleopatra herself, not only validates her intended suicide and conveys her self-satisfaction at the thought that Antony is hers but also enjoins her on-stage and off-stage audiences to praise her after Antony's honourable fashion. Responding to Antony's praise with 'Husband, I come' (5.2.282), a declarative akin to Austin's matrimonial 'I do', Cleopatra's performative speech act instantly turns her into Antony's wife and grants her a new life-in-death as his spouse. In verbally completing the visual family portrait she staged in Alexandria's marketplace as a matriarchal Isis (3.6.1–11), Cleopatra underlines her authoritative sexual power which enables her to not only woo, but also win over, Antony as a husband. Her verbal self-ennoblement is complemented by, and reified in, her Roman suicide. Suicide allows Cleopatra to commemoratively fix her sexual power and self-proclaimed greatness as a political monument by showing herself 'like a queen' (5.2.223) instead of a spouse; it also enables her to affectively overpower and verbally emasculate the Romans-as-reporters by turning them into awe-filled spectators who cannot 'boy' her greatness (5.2.216) in report. Although Caesar adamantly strives to diminish Cleopatra's

glory by presenting her – through reporting her physician's words (5.2.348) – as a weak and irresolute woman whose flight from pain impels her to 'pursue[ ] conclusions infinite / Of easy ways to die' (5.2.349–50), this report is itself diminished by the spectacle of a powerful sovereignty premised on a seductive Egyptian sexuality akin to that staged by Cleopatra on Cydnus. While Caesar reports Antony's and Cleopatra's deaths to promote himself as a noble-hearted reporter who has the affective power to beget his audience's lament (5.2.350–7), Cleopatra's on-stage and off-stage audiences witness the superiority of Cleopatra's reportage which seamlessly ties her verbal performance together with a theatrical performance that allows her to transcend the reductive parameters of Roman report and make her infinitely greater than Caesar.

Cleopatra's instances of reportage in *Antony and Cleopatra* reveal a diplomatic female monarch who uses her sexual power to offset the total loss of an already politically compromised identity. In a play-world where she is labelled a 'gipsy[ ]' (1.1.10), 'strumpet[ ]' (1.1.13), 'slave' (1.4.19) and 'whore' (3.6.67) by the Romans, Cleopatra's adoption of Roman report allows her to re-script herself in an Egyptian context while 'seem[ing] the fool [she is] not' (1.1.44). In reporting Caesar's and Antony's speech and in having her own behaviour and speech reported to them, Cleopatra praises herself and glorifies her sexuality to counteract the political power she does not possess under the pretext of performing her Roman-scripted role as a submissive, weak, inconstant, Egyptian paramour. Under the guise of adhering to Roman authority as a Roman subject, the wily Egyptian turns her powerless subordination into a powerful sexual dominance over the Romans while using the affective power of report to urge her audience to memorialize her sexual greatness, even as her idiosyncratic sexuality is not freely chosen but is an effect of Rome's imperial domination. Cleopatra's pragmatic use of report allows her to straddle both Egypt and Rome as she re-scripts her Roman identity in an Egyptian context and theatrical medium that invite her audiences to (re)construct a mighty and glorious monarch on stage. If the geographical extent and political mightiness of the Roman Empire are made present through continual acts of reportage, the transcendent greatness of Cleopatra as a character is equally generated through her acts of reportage which demonstrate a female sovereign who is able to contain others in her linguistic performances instead of being contained by them.

'THIS INSUBSTANTIAL PAGEANT FADED': THE DRAMA OF SEMIOTIC ANXIETY IN *THE TEMPEST*

LYNN FOREST-HILL

The range of modern interpretative strategies that have been deployed in critical analysis of Shakespeare's last non-collaborative play over the last half-century have shown it to be intensely polysemous within the range of interpretations that are for us culturally and politically significant. Recent work on the effect of early modern semiotics in the play has focused on the Eucharist.[1] However, when approached from the perspective of drama and literature that was traditional and historical in Shakespeare's time, some of the most prominent signs that make up the richly semiotic texture of *The Tempest* can be seen to be profoundly unstable in ways that are equally specific to the cultural and political environment, not just of 1611, but of the preceding century.

It would not be surprising if a playwright at the end of his career looks back, but *The Tempest* appears to be less a personal retrospective than a meditation on a century of politico-religious change and the effect that had had on some of the most long-lasting and resonant signs in English culture. The deployment of historical perspectives had, as Donna B. Hamilton shows, long been a strategy by which polemicists on both sides of the Reformation sought to prioritize their political claims.[2] However, as Hamilton also shows, antiquarians such as the Protestant John Foxe and the Catholic Richard Verstegan could read a single topic such as the history of the Anglo-Saxons in profoundly different and politically sensitive ways. Thus a 'backward-looking' play would be in keeping with the prevailing antiquarianism, which itself participated in the destabilizing of semiotic values.

Gary Taylor observes that '[s]emiotics does not confine itself to language but studies any and all signs – aural, visual, physical . . . Renaissance drama is the site of a particularly complex and influential conjunction of literary and theatrical codes'.[3] Alessandro Serpieri has drawn attention to the way some elements of Shakespeare's vocabulary may be 'textually and macrotextually overdetermined by ritualistic-symbolic values'.[4] And Stephen Geenblatt has written that the 'mimetic economy of Jacobean England' depends on 'an institutional circulation of culturally significant narratives'.[5] While all these critical views are useful, they do not entirely address the problems that confronted later sixteenth- and early seventeenth-century society as the process of Reformation destabilized the meanings of many familiar symbols, tropes and images.

---

[1] Jay Zysk, 'Performing Corporeality: Eucharistic Semiotics in Early Modern English Drama', unpubl. thesis, Brown University, Providence, RI, May 2011. See also Sarah Beckwith, *Shakespeare and the Grammar of Forgiveness* (Ithaca and London, 2011), pp. 150–3.

[2] Donna B. Hamilton, 'Richard Verstegan and Catholic Resistance: The Encoding of Antiquarianism and Love', in *Theatre and Religion: Lancastrian Shakespeare*, ed. Richard Dutton, Alison Findlay and Richard Wilson (Manchester, 2003), pp. 87–104.

[3] Gary Taylor, *Reinventing Shakespeare* (London, 1989), p. 313.

[4] Alessandro Serpieri, 'Reading the Signs: Towards a Semiotics of Shakespearean Drama', in *Alternative Shakespeares*, trans. Keir Elam, ed. John Drakakis (London and New York, 1985), pp. 119–43; p. 120.

[5] Stephen Greenblatt, *Shakespearean Negotiations: The Circulation of Social Energy in Renaissance England* (Berkeley and Los Angeles, 1988), p. 149.

When these appear in Jacobean drama they carry with them their semiotic history of earlier stability and recent change.

Much of the drama and lasting fascination of *The Tempest* lies in the instability of its semiotic resonances. One of the most traditional of these is called into service as Act 1 opens with the familiar trope of a tempest-tossed ship, and it is upon the fluctuating significations of this imagery that this article concentrates. A ship in a storm is an obvious sign of instability, but both together and separately ship and storm imagery had a long tradition of culturally loaded meanings. The audience is immediately presented with more signs of instability onboard the tempest-tossed ship as the traditional hierarchy of authority is inverted. Alonso the King appears on deck asking for the ship's Master and urging the sailors to greater efforts. The Boatswain urgently tells him to 'keep below'. The Italian nobleman Antonio appears, but the Boatswain responds to him sharply: 'You mar our labour. Keep your cabins; you do assist the storm.' Even old Gonzalo is told 'To cabin! Silence; trouble us not' (1.1.10–17).[6]

These brusque commands disturb the expected structure of power relations. Potentially, the meteorological chaos and this blasphemous inversion of the established hierarchy mirror each other, as they do in *King Lear*, where filial subversion of patriarchal and royal authority leads to Lear's derangement; both subversion and the consequent derangement are symbolized by the storm. But blasphemous inversion in *The Tempest* is not so easily defined. In the circumstances of impending shipwreck the Boatswain may be justified, from practical considerations, in asserting authority over his divinely appointed social superiors. The storm-battered ship is the first, and simple, metadramatic image of instability, which depends upon a semiotic tradition which is apparently quite different to that connoted by the Italian ship.

William Strachey's 1609 eyewitness account of shipwreck on Bermuda has long been regarded as the source of the shipwreck in the play.[7] This essay does not argue against the relevance of this, even though Shakespeare's knowledge of this event has

only been *presumed* by scholars.[8] Rather, it suggests that Strachey's account, published after the publication of the First Folio, is unlikely to have been the only context, and probably not the first context, in which the majority of original playgoers understood the plight of the ship in *The Tempest*. Ship-and-storm imagery was culturally significant, not simply because England was at the time a dominant maritime power. Contemporary commentators had attributed the defeat of the Armada in 1588 to God's intervention in the form of storms, but for early modern audiences the symbolic traditions of Christianity potentially evoked a constellation of culturally and politically sensitive meanings. Furthermore, the year in which *The Tempest* was first produced – 1611 – also saw the publication of the Authorized Version of the Bible. The sequence is noteworthy: the Authorized Version was published in May, *The Tempest* was performed at court in November.[9] The combination of Strachey's account of his recent shipwreck with the publication of the new Bible would have been a reminder, if one were needed, that the assertion of divine wrath and power through the commanding of storms was one of the ongoing traditions of the Christian faith. Strachey himself wrote of the perilous state of the ship he was in during the Bermuda storm. Recording that it also sprang a leak, he declared, 'It pleased God to bring greater affliction yet upon us.'[10]

Biblical stories inevitably provided familiar, immediately accessible, interpretative contexts for ship-and-storm imagery and biblical references to ships in storms had been glossed to offer doctrinal meanings. In the Old Testament, both the

---

[6] William Shakespeare, *The Tempest*, in *William Shakespeare: The Complete Works*, ed. Stanley Wells, Gary Taylor, John Jowett, and William Montgomery (Oxford, 1988).

[7] Greenblatt observes that verbal echoes between Strachey's narrative and *The Tempest* were first noticed in 1808 (*Shakespearean Negotiations*, p. 147).

[8] Greenblatt, *Shakespearean Negotiations*, p. 147. My emphasis.

[9] William Shakespeare, *The Tempest*, ed. Virginia Mason Vaughan and Alden T. Vaughan (London, 2003), p. 6.

[10] Strachey cited in *The Tempest*, ed. Vaughan and Vaughan, p. 290.

Flood and the story of the prophet Jonah depict storms as God's punishment of human disobedience. In the New Testament Jesus demonstrates His benign power when the disciples see him walking towards them across the stormy Sea of Galilee.[11] St Matthew's Gospel recounts that Jesus slept through a storm until

his disciples came to him, saying, Lord save us: we perish. And he saith unto them, Why are ye fearful, O ye of little faith? Then he arose, and rebuked the winds and the sea; and there was great calm.[12]

St Augustine wrote that Noah's story 'gives a prophetic picture of the Church',[13] but glossed the calming of the storm in more detail as 'exposed to waves and tempests . . . we must needs be at least in the ship. For if there be perils in the ship, without the ship there is certain destruction.' He went on to declare that, now Christ is in heaven rather than on earth, 'the ship that carries the disciples, that is, the Church, is tossed and shaken by the tempests of temptation . . . and the devil her adversary, rests not, and strives to hinder her from arriving at rest'.[14]

The image of the Church as a ship was part of traditional Christian symbolism and was known as 'the Ship of the Church'. Most commonly depicted as a rudderless ship, having no steering mechanism it was therefore at the mercy of wind and waves and was thus understood to be guided by the will of God. V. A. Kolve discusses the pervasive influence of the Ship of the Church motif from the early Middle Ages onward in *Chaucer and the Imagery of Narrative*, with special reference to its significance to *The Man of Law's Tale*. In his chapter 'The Rudderless Ship and the Sea', Kolve describes the widespread use of the image and its representation in visual arts as well as in literature, noting its presence in English literary tradition as far back as Anglo-Saxon hagiography.[15] The ship could be depicted carrying a saint or carrying souls. It could be an image of the means by which the Christian faith was spread, which is its use in *The Man of Law's Tale*. Alternatively, the church could be seen as the ship in which the faithful weathered the storms of the world.

The Ship of the Church motif is part of a number of stories relating to religious conversions in Christian but unbiblical contexts in medieval hagiography. In *The Man of Law's Tale*, Constance, the Christian daughter of the Emperor of Rome, is married to the Sultan of Syria. His mother conspires to kill her because of her religion and she is set adrift in a rudderless leaky ship. By God's grace, she survives and lands on the coast of Northumberland. There she meets and marries the king after converting his kingdom to Christianity. While he is away his mother plots against her. When Constance gives birth to a beautiful baby boy the Queen Mother sends word telling him that Constance has borne a monstrous child because of her witchcraft. Horrified, he orders Constance and his son to be cast adrift again in the leaky ship. They survive to be reunited with her father in Rome and later reconciled with the king.[16]

The late medieval East Anglian play *Mary Magdalen* also unites ship imagery with conversion.[17] This play includes Mary's repentance for her early sins, her journey by sea to Marseilles and the miracles attributed to her. The story of her voyage shows similarities with other tales of saints who sailed across the Mediterranean and further afield. Like the story of Constance, this play includes

---

[11] The Holy Bible, Authorized Version (AV), Gospel of St John, 6:19.
[12] AV, Gospel of St Matthew, 8: 23–6.
[13] St Augustine, *The City of God*, trans. Henry Bettenson (London, 1984), pp. 643–4.
[14] St Augustine, *Sermons*, in Philip Schaff, ed., *Nicene and Post-Nicene Fathers of the Christian Church*, vol. 6 (New York, 1908), Sermon 25, p. 337.
[15] V. A. Kolve, *Chaucer and the Imagery of Narrative* (London, 1984), pp. 297–358.
[16] On this aspect of the relationship of *The Man of Law's Tale* to *The Tempest*, see Lynn Forest-Hill, 'Giants and Enemies of God: The Relationship between Caliban and Prospero from the Perspective of Insular Literary Tradition', in *Shakespeare Survey 59* (Cambridge, 2004), pp. 239–53.
[17] *Mary Magdalen*, in *The Late Medieval Religious Plays of Bodleian MSS Digby 133 and E Museo 160*, ed. Donald C. Baker, John L. Murphy and Louis B. Hall Jr., EETS 282 (Oxford, 1982). The manuscript is dated 1515–25, although the language suggests a slightly earlier date (p. xl).

the 'Ship of the Church' motif as Mary converts the King and Queen of Marseilles after the Queen miraculously conceives a child. The play tells Mary's story partly from biblical accounts and partly from substantial references to the account of her life in the *Legenda Aurea*. William Caxton's translation of this work under the title *The Golden Legend* (1483) was one of the first books to be printed in England.[18] It was then printed during the sixteenth century by a succession of publishers until it fell out of favour at times during the Reformation when veneration for saints was officially forbidden.[19]

Nevertheless, the story of Mary's repentance was well known and in 1566 the playwright Lewis Wager wrote an interlude of *The Life and Repentance of Mary Magdalene*. Described by Darryl Grantley as 'a curious work... the sole example of a type of Protestant saint's play',[20] it necessarily omits any hint of Mary's miracles and concentrates on the process of her fall into sin and conversion to repentance. However, later evidence of the ongoing popularity of the older pre-Reformation version of her story throughout the sixteenth century is provided by an incomplete copy of *The Golden Legend* dated to the last quarter of the sixteenth century.[21]

In the East Anglian play and in Caxton's translation the King of Marseilles and his pregnant Queen set out by sea to visit St Peter in the Holy Land after Mary has converted them. During their voyage a great storm assails the ship, the Queen goes into labour and, having given birth to a son, dies. Her body is then left on a rock in the sea, and the baby is abandoned with its dead mother for lack of a wet nurse. The grieving king sails on but after his pilgrimage returns that way, to find the baby miraculously alive. The play is less explicit than the book, in which the infant is left tucked under the mantle that covers its dead mother. When the ship bearing his father home again passes the rock the little child can be seen

playenge with stones on the see syde... and when the childe sawe them whiche neuer had seen people tofore [he] was aferde and ran... and hydde him under the mantell.[22]

Velma Richmond briefly notes 'other analogues of the Ship of the Church' when she refers to *The Tempest* and *The Man of Law's Tale*,[23] and the combination of a mother, child and shipwreck is one that Shakespeare uses in other plays with Mediterranean settings. In *The Comedy of Errors* Emilia and her children are tied to the masts of a storm-battered ship, in hopes of being saved.[24] In *Pericles*, Thaisa is delivered of a daughter in a storm and being supposed dead is placed in her coffin and cast overboard.[25] Neither Richmond, nor Robert S. Miola in *Shakespeare's Reading*,[26] notice that in *Pericles* Shakespeare reuses the mariners' superstition found in *Mary Magdalen* concerning the need to abandon a 'dead' Queen,[27] although Robert Grams Hunter has discerned the influence of this play in *Pericles*.[28] While the East Anglian play echoes in all these plays, the detail from Caxton's *Golden Legend* reverberates more overtly and with greater impact in *The Tempest*.

The abandoning of a mother and infant on an unidentified rock somewhere in the Mediterranean is analogous to, though not identical with, the fate

18 N. F. Blake, *William Caxton and English Literary Culture* (London, 1991), p. 108.
19 Blake, *William Caxton*, p. 115.
20 Darryl Grantley, 'Saints' plays', in *The Cambridge Companion to Medieval English Theatre*, ed. Richard Beadle and Alan J. Fletcher (Cambridge, 1994), pp. 265–89; p. 286.
21 See N. F. Blake, *English Literary Culture* (Rio Grande, OH, 1991), pp. 296–7. Also www.medievalportland.pdx.edu/q=leaf-from-wm-caxton%E2%86%90s-golden-legend (accessed 3 May 2013).
22 William Caxton, *The Golden Legend* (1483), STC 24873, reel 1760, f. clxix verso.
23 Velma Bourgeois Richmond, *Shakespeare, Catholicism and Romance* (New York and London, 2000), p. 173.
24 *William Shakespeare: The Complete Works*, ed. Wells, Taylor, Jowett, and Montgomery, 1.1.62–87.
25 *William Shakespeare: The Complete Works*, ed. Wells, Taylor, Jowett, and Montgomery. sc. 12, lines 49–90.
26 Robert S. Miola, *Shakespeare's Reading* (Oxford, 2000).
27 *Mary Magdalen*, lines 1779–80. Caxton, *The Golden Legend*, f. clxix recto.
28 Robert Grams Hunter, *Shakespeare and the Comedy of Forgiveness* (New York, 1965), p. 139. Hunter does not consider the presence of any aspect of *Mary Magdalene* in his treatment of *The Tempest*.

of Sycorax and Caliban. But the infant's response to seeing unknown humans is very closely reflected in the encounter between Caliban and Trinculo, when Caliban hides himself under the enveloping gaberdine he is wearing, mistaking Trinculo for another of Prospero's spirits (2.2.16–17). The repetition of the motif of a castaway motherless child hiding under an enveloping garment at the sight of an unknown human can hardly be coincidental. Furthermore, and more subtly, Miranda's assertion that she taught Caliban to speak implies his original state as *infans*: speechless like an infant, which he is again at the approach of Trinculo. The hiding action is later burlesqued when Trinculo himself hides under the gaberdine (2.2.37–8).

Although there are striking echoes in *The Tempest* of the discovery scene in the legend of Mary Magdalene, there are clearly glaring differences. I will go on to argue that it is around those differences that the play's engagement with semiotic anxiety develops in order to explore the effect of semiotic instability created by religious change during the preceding century.[29]

Wager's play illustrates the continuing usefulness of older traditions as a vehicle for dramatizing the shift from sinfulness to repentance as configured in accordance with Protestantism.[30] While *The Life and Repentaunce of Mary Magdalene* does not contain any of the details shared between the *Golden Legend* and *The Tempest*, it illuminates the process by which the symbols and traditions of medieval Catholicism were appropriated and reconfigured to suit the Protestant taste. This was not a new technique. Wager could look to the Protestant playwright John Bale for an example of how to turn old drama to new uses as Bale had only recently expanded his Protestant morality play *King Johan* to suit Elizabethan taste. Richard Wever's slightly earlier morality play *Lusty Juventus* also shows 'a sharp Protestant bias'.[31] Shakespeare's reuse of ship and storm motifs that also occur in the East Anglian play and *The Golden Legend* does not preclude the possibility that he was influenced by other sources for such imagery. But these specifically insular contexts, whose earlier semiotic value had shifted within his lifetime under the pressure

of religious change, appear to be parodied in his last play.

The Tempest has elements in common with Chaucer's hagiographic tale, with the East Anglian *Mary Magdalen*, and with the saint's life in *The Golden Legend* that imply the play's engagement with pre-Reformation Christianity. However, Shakespeare's treatment of these hagiographical echoes takes the form of a series of parodic inversions of saintly female conduct. Sycorax's circumstances echo those of Constance: both are accused of witchcraft, and their sons are both said by other characters to be monsters. While these are malicious lies in *The Man of Law's Tale*, they are parodically borne out in the case of Sycorax and Caliban. Sycorax, banished from Algiers, her life saved only because she was pregnant, is also a parodic inversion of the virtuous pregnant Queen of Marseilles who willingly sets out on pilgrimage. The parody is extended through the setting adrift of Sycorax and Caliban, which is a skewed echo of the fate of mother and infant in *The Golden Legend*, where the abandoned Queen is later found to be alive. Sycorax dies on the Island, leaving her child to be found, not by its own father, but by another father. The sequence of parodic inversions is capped off by Caliban's behaviour as he hides during his first encounter with Trinculo, burlesquing that of the frightened infant in the hagiographic story.

If Sycorax is a parody of virtuous women like the Queen of Marseilles and Constance, and Caliban is a burlesque version of the sons in their

---

[29] Greenblatt details many causes of anxiety in Elizabethan and Jacobean England in his analysis of anxiety on the early modern stage, but he does not consider the destablizing effect of religious change (*Shakespearean Negotiations*, pp. 137–8).

[30] The Reformation elided the steps of the Catholic sacrament of penance into the concept of repentance. See Beckwith, *Shakespeare and the Grammar of Forgiveness*, pp. 2–3.

[31] Bale's final version dates from 1560–63. See John Bale, *King Johan*, ed. Peter Happé, vol. 1 (Cambridge, 1985), p. 101. Bernard Spivack dates Wever's play to 1547–53, in *Shakespeare and the Allegory of Evil* (New York, 1958), p. 209.

tales, Prospero is a gendered inversion of their well-known stories. While Constance's voyage in a leaky ship leads to the conversion of Northumberland, and that of Mary Magdalene to the conversion of the King and Queen of Marseilles, Prospero also travels in a leaky rudderless ship, but with his infant daughter. And far from bringing Christianity where he lands, although he too is a victim of conspiracy and expulsion, he has brought his perilous exile upon himself by ignoring his ducal responsibilities in favour of the study of occult magic, an interest he shares with Sycorax. The gender inversions and difference in hierarchical power between Constance the obedient daughter and wife, Mary the repentant sinner, Sycorax the witch and Prospero the Duke/magician, configure all comparisons as condemnatory parody.

Indeed, the inverted reflections of the stories of Constance and the Queen of Marseilles in *The Tempest* create a pattern of parody that becomes more obvious as further traditional Christian contexts shed light on the Italian ship caught in the tempest Prospero conjures. This ship carries those who conspired against him, and his justification for his action – revenge against them – parodies the wrath of God that punishes biblical sinners like Noah's community and the disobedient Jonah with storms.

Stephen Orgel has remarked that 'modern critics are made exceedingly uncomfortable by the idea of Prospero as God',[32] and troubling comparisons are explicitly set up when Miranda introduces the Ship of the Church image, exclaiming,

> *Poor souls*, they perished.
> Had I been *any god of power*, I would
> Have sunk the sea within the earth, or ere
> It should the *good ship* so have swallowed and
> The fraughting *souls within her*.
>
> (1.2.9–13, my emphases)

The 'good ship' carrying 'souls' clearly recalls the Ship of the Church. Although by implication the Italian ship is seaworthy until the crew shout 'We split, we split!' (1.1.59), it is controlled by Prospero's action, which, as Miranda innocently observes, merely pretends to god-like power, leaving his

perverse display to be read as the blasphemous use of occult power in imitation of God's power.

Storms themselves had been regarded as having both Christian and superstitious significance long before the sixteenth century. From a Christian perspective, the storm motif gains significance from St Paul's wish that disunited Christians should not be 'tossed to and fro, and carried about with every wind of doctrine, by the sleight of men, and cunning craftiness, whereby they lie in wait to deceive' (Ephesians 4: 14). In this case the power of the wind is not under God's command but besets the Church because it arises from conflict within it. Maurice Hunt provides an additional insight into the range of interpretation of storms when he writes that in the 1580s:

For the Puritan George Gifford the instruments of God's Providence, when they are mentioned at all, are not natural agents such as sea tempests but almost always wicked men and women who are likened to God's ax or rod, mortifying his elect.[33]

The implications of passivity or impotence in the face of fluctuations of doctrine created by deceivers could have had no more resonant contemporary context for early modern theatregoers than their own experiences of the doctrinal conflicts of the Reformation. Under the influence of the Reformation the Ship of the Church became an unstable sign of faith and security. John Foxe's *Actes and Monuments* (1583) contains a woodcut depicting 'The Ship of the Romysh Church' in which figures carry various goods, including a censer, towards a vessel at the water's edge. Small captions declare 'Ship ouer your trinkets & be packing you Papistes', and 'The Papistes packing away their paltry'.[34] '[T]rinkets' and 'paltry' were disparaging Protestant terms for the ritual objects and vestments of the

---

[32] Stephen Orgel, *The Illusion of Power: Political Theatre in the English Renaissance* (Berkeley, 1975), p. 48.

[33] Maurice Hunt, *Shakespeare's Religious Allusiveness* (Aldershot, 2004), p. 83.

[34] Reproduced in Velma Bourgeois Richmond, *Shakespeare, Catholicism, and Romance* (London and New York, 2000), p. 51 verso.

Roman Catholic Church.[35] The fluctuating image of the Ship of the Church, seen in the context of such polemic, implies that schismatic conflict had the potential to wreck it.

Nevertheless, in the latter half of the sixteenth- and the early seventeenth-centuries hegemonic use of symbolic maritime imagery was based upon and exploited popular understanding of existing traditional symbolism. Interpretation of ship and storm imagery, and of actual storms, was disseminated through written accounts and by word of mouth. The reinterpretation of such imagery can be seen in process in some of the London records from the mid-sixteenth century when Londoners had witnessed the use of symbolic ship imagery.

A record from 1562 reports Edward Underhill's impression of Mary I's coronation in 1553, giving his comments on the spectacle when the tall, slender steeple of St Paul's cathedral was rigged like a ship in celebration of the new monarch:

The first day of October was Queen Mary crowned ... I went forth ... to the West end of Paul's; and there placed myself ... to see the queen pass by.

Before her coming, I beheld Paul's steeple bearing top and top-gallant [yards] like a royal ship, with many flags and banners ... I said unto one that sat on horseback by me, who had not seen a coronation, 'At the coronation of King Edward, I saw Paul's steeple lie at anchor, and now she weareth top and top gallants. Surely the next will be shipwreck, ere it be long!' Which chanceth sometimes by tempestuous winds, sometimes by lightnings and fire from heaven.

But I thought it should rather perish by some horrible wind, than with lightning or thunderbolt ... but such are the wonderful works of GOD, whose gunners will not miss the mark that He doth appoint.[36]

Underhill's outspoken anti-Catholic comments interpret the difference between the steeple of St Paul's at the coronation of the Protestant King Edward VI, which lay 'at anchor', symbolizing peace, and the steeple dressed for Queen Mary's coronation which, in Underhill's opinion, carried so much sail that it was likely to be wrecked by high winds.[37] This Protestant comment recalls St Paul's 'winds of doctrine' in the local context of

the Ship of the Church, situating both within the influence of religious factionalism, while demonstrating the relevance of ship and storm imagery for mid-sixteenth-century Londoners.

While the maritime decoration reiterates the image of the Ship of the Church, and recalls the Roman Catholic past, its use on this occasion demonstrates its accessibility as a symbol to the wider population, and how its political potential was perceived. Its interpretation by a Protestant illuminates the continuation of a shared cultural background upon which the religious factions imposed their own partial readings. In one respect at least, however, the people regardless of doctrinal allegiance shared a common anxiety that God intervened in human affairs through storms.

Of no less significance than the dressing of St Paul's steeple, was a natural event that beset it. In 1561 a great storm struck London. The steeple of St Paul's was hit by lightning and the cathedral set on fire. It was interpreted as a sign of God's displeasure. More radical Protestants interpreted the storm as specifically a sign of God's wrath at the accession of a new Catholic monarch after the apparent triumph of Protestantism during the reign of Edward VI. *The True Report of the burning of the Steeple and Church of Paul's in London* sets out the account and response as follows:

The true cause, as it seemeth, was the Tempest, by GOD's sufferance. For it cannot otherwise be gathered, but that, at the said great and terrible thunderclap, when St Michael's Steeple was torn, the lightning (which by

---

[35] Such insults were not isolated. In the early version (1538) of John Bale's *King Johan* the King similarly tells the Cardinal 'Take to ye yowre trash, yowre ryngyng, syngynge and pypyng', l. 1392.

[36] *Tudor Tracts 1532–1588*, intro. A. F. Pollard, *An English Garner*, 8 vols. (New York, 1964), Harl. MS 425; *Narratives of the Days of the Reformation* (Camden Society, 1859), pp. 162–3.

[37] Other symbolic measures were also taken to allay the controversy surrounding the accession and coronation of Mary. See Alice Hunt, 'Legitimacy, Ceremony and Drama: Mary Tudor's Coronation and Respublica', in *Interludes and Early Modern Society: Studies in Gender, Power and Theatricality*, ed. Peter Happé and Wim Hüsken (Amsterdam and New York, 2007), pp. 331–51.

natural order smiteth the highest) did first smite the top of Paul's steeple.

On Sunday following... [James Pilkington] Bishop of Durham, at St. Paul's Cross, made a learned and fruitful sermon.... [He] answered by the way to the objections of such evil-tongued persons which do impute this token of GOD's deserved ire to alteration, or rather, Reformation of Religion; declaring out of ancient records and histories the like, yea, and greater matters had befallen in the time of superstition and ignorance.[38]

Eamon Duffy refers to the sermon as 'a sign of the seriousness of the early Elizabethan regime's anxiety about the capital which conservative critics of the religious settlement had made of the fire'.[39] That anxiety confirms the problem of interpreting traditional signs such as storms as indications of God's wrath when the semiotic system within which they belong has become so destabilized as a result of religious change that they can be interpreted with an eye to factional advantage.

Although this Elizabethan record looks back to the age of Catholicism referred to here as 'the time of superstition and ignorance', in an attempt to refute religious factionalism, the storms that wrecked the Armada were believed to be God's intervention on behalf of Protestant England against Catholic Spain. By the early Jacobean period, storms were still interpreted as evidence of God's wrath at apostasy. On 20 January 1607, four years before the first performance of *The Tempest*, counties around the Bristol Channel suffered a great inundation of water and many people perished. Modern science suggests it was a tsunami caused by tectonic activity under the Atlantic. Lacking such knowledge, seventeenth-century pamphleteers such as the anonymous author of *God's Warning to his people of England* (1607) defined it as a storm and urged England to recall the Gunpowder conspiracy in 1605, implying that the flood was God's punishment for England's religious complacency:

Many are the dombe warnings of Distruction, which the Almighty God hath lately scourged this our Kingdome with... All which in bleeding hearts, may inforce vs to put on the true garment of Repentance... let us

also call to remembraunce the most wicked and pretended malice, of the late Papistcall Conspiracie of Traytors, that with powder practised the subversion of this beautiful Kingdome: And lastly let vs fix our eyes vpon theise late swellinges of the outragious Waters, which of late now hapned in divers partes of the Realme, together with the ouerflowing of the Seas in diuers and sundry places thereof.[40]

It is likely, given the remarkable scale of the event, that Shakespeare would have known of the inundation and its interpretation as a warning from God intended, like the Gunpowder Plot, to encourage repentance. While much Catholic imagery and symbolism were swept away by the Reformation, some was capable of being reused, even if its old meanings were inverted. What was once evocative of Catholic doctrine became a sign of its reconfiguration as 'superstition'; what once symbolized an encompassing state of human sin, now only referred to one section of the community. When the old ship and storm imagery is reused in *The Tempest* it is in such a way as to show that such patterns of inversion result in parody and burlesque. However, that is by no means all that the play offers by way of illuminating the consequences of semiotic instability.

In his essay 'Bare Ruined Choirs' Eamon Duffy argues that Catholicism remained a nostalgic and constant presence in Reformation England.[41] Neil MacGregor writes that 'In his plays Shakespeare captures this painful transition, the moment when the Catholicism that his parents practised became something to be spoken of only in the past tense.'[42]

---

[38] *The True Report of the burning of the Steeple and Church of Paul's in London*, in *Tudor Tracts 1532–1588*, ed. A. F. Pollard, pp. 406–7, originally printed by William Seres, 1561.

[39] Eamon Duffy, 'Bare Ruined Choirs: Remembering Catholicism in Shakespeare's England', in *Theatre and Religion: Lancastrian Shakespeare*, ed. Richard Dutton, Alison Findlay and Richard Wilson (Manchester, 2003), pp. 40–57; p. 44.

[40] *God's Warning to his People of England* (London: printed for W. Barley and Io. Bayly, 1607), BL ms. 1103 e62, STC 10011 reel 1379.

[41] Duffy, 'Bare Ruined Choirs', pp. 40–57.

[42] Neil MacGregor, *Shakespeare's Restless World* (London, 2012), p. 26.

The Ship of the Church was only one of the potential traditional interpretations of ship imagery in *The Tempest*. At least as well known to early modern audiences would have been the Ship of Fools. Sebastian Brandt's original version that he called *Narrenschiff* (1494), written in the Swabian dialect, was much translated and adapted during the next two centuries. It was originally intended to correct the folly and vices of pre-Reformation society, and especially the laxness of Catholic clergy. The concept of a ship full of vices could be traced back to 1288, but early Tudor versions included one by John Skelton, tutor to Henry VIII. In 'The Bowge of Court' (1498) Skelton restricted the fools in the ship to a selection of knavish courtiers.

In 1509 Alexander Barclay published an English adaptation of the *Narrenschiff*. The vessel, though not necessarily unseaworthy, carried very different characters from those traditionally depicted in the Ship of the Church. Like the *Narrenschiff* it was crammed with representatives of perverse and foolish humanity. Barclay called his English version *The Ship of Fools*. In this ship the passengers' deviation from social, political and spiritual virtue constitutes their foolishness. They and their ship are specifically associated with England. Barclay wrote,

> To Shyp galantes the se is at the ful.
> The wynde vs calleth our sayles ar displayed.
> Where may we best aryue? at Lyn or els at Hulle?
> To vs may no hauen in Englonde be denayd.[43]

Barclay follows Brandt's original and sets his adaptation in the ancient tradition of the satire intended to reform the vices of society,[44] stating that his intention was 'reprehension of foulysshnes'.[45] His work, like Brandt's, belongs to the period when Catholic critics were trying to encourage reform of their Church from within. As T. H. Jamieson, who edited Barclay's work in 1873 declared, *The Ship of Fools* was 'motivated by ... the discontent with "abusions" and "folys" which resulted in the Reformation'.[46] Its usefulness outlasted the original intention.

A woodcut accompanying Barclay's 1509 text shows St Peter placing his symbolic key into a ship at anchor – the Ship of the Church. Above,

seated on a broken rainbow, in a parody of Christ in Judgement, a figure named 'Antichrist' is accompanied by others in eared fools' caps and bells, some in another ship and some wallowing in a stormy sea. The storm is associated visually with the Antichrist, the ultimate symbol of inversion, and its consequence is the potential drowning of the fools who have fallen out of the ship.

As Prospero's storm-raising parodies divine righteous anger, the depiction of the Italians is initially equally parodic, although its full significance does not emerge until Ariel confronts them as 'men of sin' and then exclaims: 'You fools!' (3.3.53, 60). In their high-handed, interfering behaviour the Italian nobles cannot be compared to the trusting saintly travellers in the Ship of the Church, but may be seen as analogous to the travellers in the Ship of Fools. Stephen Greenblatt notes that in the Strachey account the 'unmerciful tempest' that almost sank the ship off Bermuda 'provoked an immediate collapse of the distinction between those who labour and those who rule'. In such extreme danger all ranks of society worked together, 'the better sort, even our Governour, and Admiral themselves, not refusing their turn ... And it is most true, such as in all their life times had never done hours work before ... were able ... to toil with the best.' As Greenblatt points out the terminology expresses an inversion of the hierarchy reminiscent of that aboard the Italian ship as 'the better sort' – those who are social superiors – assist the 'best', the common sailors.[47] However, the willingness of Strachey's 'better sort' to work for the common good in the face of danger illuminates the foolishness of the Italian nobles who, far from assisting their sailors, 'do assist the storm' (1.1.13).

The theme of a ship containing fools inevitably parodied the Christian virtue implicit in the image of saints or souls of the Ship of the Church,

---

[43] *The Ship of Fools*, trans. Alexander Barclay, ed. T. H. Jamieson, 2 vols. (Edinburgh and London, 1873), p. 3.

[44] Barclay, *Ship of Fools*, pp. 5–10.

[45] Barclay, *Ship of Fools*, p. 17.

[46] Barclay, *Ship of Fools*, p. 11.

[47] Greenblatt, *Shakespearean Negotiations*, p. 149.

whether the forms of folly were secular or doctrinal. By the time John Cawood published his edition of *The Ship of Fooles* in London in 1570, ship imagery had shifted to serve religious factionalism. Nevertheless, the motif could still be used with the intention to satirize, correct and condemn because folly may be so diversely constructed according to specific bias or perception. The English destination of Barclay's Ship adds significance to the maritime imagery in *The Tempest*. Any perceived allusion to the Ship of Fools then transforms the Italian ship as the instability of all the relationships in the play manifests itself through instances of betrayal. Hierarchical allegiances, as much as servant/master relationships, are shown to be unstable through devotion to self-interest thus exposing the particularly English folly of factionalism as the reinterpretation of traditional signs foolishly motivated by self-interest. John Bale had already flirted with similar imagery in 1538 when his character King Johan demands 'Were yt so possyble to hold thes enmyes backe, / That my swete Ynglond perysh not in this sheppwracke?'[48]

By 1611 the storm-tossed ship in *The Tempest* configures instability in a widening sense because as a simple 'sign' it denotes instability while at the same time tapping into the potential semiotic resonances of both the Ship of the Church and the Ship of Fools without quite coalescing into either. Stephen Greenblatt asserts that 'the transfer of cultural practices and power depends... upon networks of resemblance'.[49] It is through the slippage that defines resemblance, rather than perfect identity, that the play sheds light on the relationship between semiotic anxiety and power. In so far as the Ship of Fools can be discerned as a context for understanding the characterization of the Italians, there emerges in *The Tempest* an elaborate satire on the effects of English factionalism. This has not only rendered the traditional (Catholic) semiotic system unstable and therefore uncertain, but has consequences for the individual which result in the subversion of identity.

The drama of cultural change that had been played out in sixteenth-century England and had

rendered so many traditional signs unstable results, by extension, in the instability of many of the signs that connote individual identity. Neil MacGregor has surveyed the importance of changing identities in Elizabethan society no less than in Shakespeare's plays through the wilful use of disguise.[50] However, after the storm in *The Tempest*, although the identities of all the characters are unstable, this is not generally a matter of choice. The opening scene depicts the process of hierarchical instability that calls into question the absoluteness of a link between social status and authority, but throughout, the play suggests that unstable signs result in unstable individual identities.

Caliban, whose (at times) childlike behaviour sits uneasily alongside his propensity to violence, is the most obvious source of semiotic instability in the play. He does not contest his demonic parentage – born of Sycorax the witch and the devil Setebos. He has had a mutually nurturing relationship with Prospero and Miranda, which has broken down because of his desire to regain control of the Island. He is a necessary servant, but is named in many reductive terms as a 'freckled whelp' (1.2.284) and 'slave' (on many occasions) by Prospero; as 'monster' by Stephano (throughout 2.2.) and 'mooncalf' by Trinculo (2.2.105, 108); but he speaks, like Prospero, in blank verse. This was a sign of cultural and social status in previous Shakespearian drama. His unstable identity is summed up by Trinculo's puzzled 'What have we here, a man or a fish? Dead or alive?' (2.2.24–5). At a more subtle level with reference to *The Golden Legend* he takes the role of the dead Queen, as Trinculo shelters under his gabardine to avoid the storm. Caliban is in effect a parody interrogating all the signs that might make an early modern man. The underlying implication is that manhood depends on conforming to the customary signs, and having these recognized. Lack of conformity and recognition creates something monstrous. But if Caliban

---

[48] Bale, *King Johan*, l. 1658–9. Sheppwracke = shipwreck.

[49] Greenblatt, *Shakespearan Negotiations*, p. 148.

[50] MacGregor, *Shakespeare's Restless World*, p. 194.

is monstrous because he is composed of unstable signs so too is Prospero, who claims this would-be rapist for his own in a feeble attempt to assert some shadow of his former lordly status before his social equals (5.1.278–9). But as Caliban has already told him bluntly, 'I am all the subjects that you have' (1.2.343).

It is hardly surprising that Prospero appears to make and remake his identity at will, having initially altered it from Duke to magus, a change that unexpectedly led to his exile and loss of status. His presence on the Island alters and redefines Caliban's identity; it defines that of Miranda, and changes that of all the Italian nobles and servants who have been shipwrecked; Ferdinand's identity is altered when Prospero physically enslaves him, turning a prince into a 'log-man', like Caliban. Ariel (whose shape-shifting gives him the most obviously unstable identity in the play) tells Ferdinand of the change to his father's identity: 'Nothing of him that doth fade / But doth suffer a sea-change / Into something rich and strange' (1.2.402–4). Caliban, however, exerts his own status-changing influence, when he persuades Stephano he can inherit the Island by killing Prospero. This is an Island where all identities are subject to change, and the destabilizing of personal identities circulates self-reflexively around the fate of the ship wrecked in the tempest Prospero has created so that his identity is again not secure. He wants revenge and the restoration of his power by non-occult means, through the marriage of his daughter to the heir to the kingdom of Naples. But his means of effecting the changes he imposes are both occult and brutal. Stephen Greenblatt has drawn attention to the exertion of 'salutary anxiety' in early modern society as a means of socio-political control[51] and links the social and the theatrical when he declares that 'Prospero's chief magical activity throughout *The Tempest* is to harrow the other characters with fear and wonder and then to reveal that their anxiety is his to create and allay.'[52] After the vanishing banquet, itself heavily infused with the shifting semiotics of the Eucharist, Prospero's spirits who come '*with mocks and mows*' (3.3.82, s.d.) recall the devils of earlier medieval drama. Unseen, he expresses satisfaction that

> My high charms work,
> And these, mine enemies, are all knit up
> In their distractions.   (3.3.88–90)

Alonso, in his next speech, reveals his suicidal feelings prompted by Prospero's cruel trickery. The combination of vengeful satisfaction and suicidal despair recalls the pattern of medieval morality plays, in which devils and Vices attempted to drive 'Everyman' characters to suicide and damnation.

Prospero becomes, then, the focus of a profoundly problematic sequence of parodic inversions. His vengeance, intended to punish the Italian noblemen, is played out with a pretence of God-like omnipotence based on occult power, until Ariel introduces the concept of pity. Prospero responds with a renunciation of his power in a speech that defines the extent to which his power itself is an inversion, shown most clearly in the images of uprooting the 'pine and cedar', and opening graves (5.1.47–9). From the perspective of traditional medieval iconography the upsetting of trees and raising of the dead (no more than a deceptive trick) were signs of the Antichrist.[53] Protestant polemicists had reconfigured this metaphysical demonic parody, applying the name to the Pope and the papacy.

However, the Antichrist 'sign' does not function as propaganda for either faction in the play but links the old concept of inversion with the process of cultural change because Prospero's renunciation of occult power also echoes Medea's renunciation of her sorcery in Ovid's *Metamorphoses*. How then is the audience to understand the signs from which Prospero's is created? Is the Antichrist image deployed to continue the dissection of the effects of the Reformation on traditional semiotic systems?[54]

---

[51] Greenblatt, *Shakespearean Negotiations*, p. 135.

[52] Greenblatt, *Shakespearean Negotiations*, p. 142.

[53] Forest-Hill, 'Giants and Enemies of God', p. 247.

[54] Peter Milward has drawn attention to the 'Controversy over Antichrist' and the 'mutual accusations' that 'appeared from

Or is Medea now the 'sign' by which superstitious inversions are to be understood, as fashionable secular and humanist learning ousts the older interpretative framework, even though the figure of the Antichrist remained a potent symbol of blasphemous subversion? Rainer Pineas has written in the context of Tudor and early Stuart drama that 'parody was another weapon in the arsenal of the polemicist by which his opponents were made to condemn themselves'.[55] But in the case of *The Tempest*, the answer, of course, is not that either context is correct, but that the renunciation sets up these choices as a provocative flourish on the way to introducing a new vision which moves beyond the parodic and destabilizing effects of semiotic change.

Prospero's renunciation speech initiates a change in the focus of the play from one of hermeneutic perplexity towards a view of change as beneficial. His description of the nature and effects of his subversive power offers a fast-moving series of signs of instability whose confusing semiotic potential is mimetic of a wider hermeneutic perplexity created by the changes that had overtaken familiar and traditional imagery (5.1.34–51). The play does not critique these changes, but exposes their effects. Stephen Greenblatt has argued that Renaissance England was 'institutionally committed to the arousal of anxiety'.[56] He comments that 'Prospero's chief magical device is to harrow characters with anxiety, to create in them a state of "managed insecurity"'.[57] Thus the treatment of anxiety in the play is mimetic of a more serious sense of anxiety. The Antichrist and his traditional attributes – or the Medea echo – become the sign of inverted and misapplied power. But now this is willingly renounced, on reciprocal terms: if the Italians are penitent, Prospero will be forgiving. In this instance a willed change takes place which is not in the end destabilizing, even though it briefly evokes a physical sense of instability in the Italians and causes anxiety. This transitory effect enables the anxiety caused by instability to be reconsidered in the light of signs that remain unchanged. Just as the clothes of the Italians are not stained by their occult drenching, so, the play reveals, some signs remain unchanging. The most significant of these

unchanging signs are repentance and forgiveness, but these require Prospero's readiness to change.

Sarah Beckwith has written that '*The Tempest* examines the hold of the past over the one who has been harmed, and the means by which the present can make its peace with the past.'[58] However, she goes on to define the presence of mutuality in the text, drawing attention to Ariel's description of the spell-bound Italians. He tells his master, 'They cannot budge till your release' (5.1.11). Beckwith notes that 'your release' may be read as both 'an objective and subjective genitive'.[59] The medieval Catholic story of Mary Magdalene survived into the Protestant period with its theme of repentance untouched and, although religious change meant that penance was no longer a sacrament,[60] the Reformation continued to promote the concepts of repentance and forgiveness. Although *The Tempest* shifts these concepts into a fantasy secular context as Prospero repents his savage vengeance and prepares to forgive his enemies, the introduction of the twin themes of repentance and forgiveness becomes an assurance that not all change is bad or destabilizing. Indeed, without change there is no repentance, and therefore no forgiveness. Anxieties caused by signs that cannot be relied upon, including the effects of change on individual identity, are resolved by the concepts that remain unchanged.

Hamilton has described the effect of religious changes on individuals, society and Shakespeare's plays, in terms of the need for alternative discourses by which political and religious controversy could be addressed.[61] It is not necessarily a matter of artistic choice, then, on Shakespeare's part when

the beginning of James' reign', in *Religious Controversies of the Jacobean Age* (London: Scholar Press, 1978), p. 131.

55 Rainer Pineas, *Tudor and Early Stuart Anti-Catholic Drama* (Nieuwkoop, 1972), p. 37.

56 Greenblatt, *Shakespearean Negotiations*, p. 137.

57 Greenblatt, *Shakespearean Negotiations*, p. 137.

58 Beckwith, *Shakespeare and the Grammar of Forgiveness*, pp. 147–9.

59 Beckwith, *Shakespeare and the Grammar of Forgiveness*, p. 149.

60 Beckwith, *Shakespeare and the Grammar of Forgiveness*, p. 40.

61 Donna B. Hamilton, *Shakespeare and the Politics of Protestant England* (Hemel Hempstead, 1992), p. 126.

Prospero refers to the masque of the goddesses as an 'insubstantial pageant' (4.1.155) as he dismisses the spirits: 'pageant' had formerly referred to medieval religious drama created to stage Catholic doctrine. Protestant playwrights like John Bale and Lewis Wager had rewritten the form for their own purposes. It is not surprising, then, that Shakespeare in his last non-collaborative play examines the instability of culturally significant signs within a consciously metatheatrical context in order to address the effect of semiotic anxiety created by religious change. But he exposes the limits of that anxiety.

In early modern London, just as in medieval cities, staged performance was inherently created from unstable signs as actors took on the identities of the characters they performed and even gender roles were altered as men performed the roles of women. Exploiting the fictional status of performance, theatrical semiotic instability becomes mimetic of social and cultural semiotic instability. This is represented initially in the play through the image of the storm-tossed ship which pulls together two culturally significant motifs – the Ship of the Church and the Ship of Fools – and, because the ship in *The Tempest* does not entirely reflect either, it functions as a sign of the instability caused by change. The deployment of well-known iconography exposes the fundamental instability of traditional signs that had their origins in the Catholic past. The consequences of rewriting those signs in a Protestant context is seen, through the instability of their echoes in *The Tempest*, to create a series of parodies in which all identities, even that of the Island, are called into question. The implication is that the signs that once were considered stable and constant under the validation of Catholicism have been shown to be unstable by the continual acts of rewriting them, culminating in a play whose own theatrical identity is far from certain.

' . . . this insubstantial pageant faded' defines the passing of the masque, comments ironically on the older certainties based on traditional imagery, and maybe even on Shakespeare's own career. The playwright leaves now that the old iconography has been rewritten. The play's inherently unstable theatrical representation serves as an extended metaphor for the mutability of socially and culturally accepted signs,[62] opposing it against the publication in the same year of the Authorized Version of the Bible and the presumed semiotic stability of the Word of God.

In his book *God's Secretaries: The Making of the King James Bible*, Adam Nicolson surveys the tensions surrounding the project and writes that 'Integration is both the purpose and method of the King James Bible', and that 'the words of the Bible were the ultimate and encompassing truth itself'.[63] The problem was that the succession of revisions and translations of the Bible throughout the sixteenth and early seventeenth centuries, including those of the Counter-Reformation, had required the interpretation of words, which created anxiety concerning even that divine semiotic system. Eamon Duffy has compared the English translation of the Bible to the effect of the church service in English:

Some people were thrilled by it, like the arrival of the English Bible. For many people that was literally a revelation and an empowerment; for others it was tiresome gobbledegook.[64]

In the face of such variation in response, the most basic question asked of the play – is Prospero a black magician or a white magus? – seems trivial but in fact sums up the problem it sets out to address. Such specifics are not the issue. The issue is how hard it is to judge the nature or identity of things, concepts and people in the Jacobean world where so many signs are now unstable. Reassurance comes in the form of those things that do not change and

---

[62] Hunter declares that Shakespeare's contemporaries delighted in visual or theatrical 'metaphors . . . They were meant . . . to invite interpretation and they needed to be puzzled over' (Hunter, *Shakespeare and the Comedy of Forgiveness*, p. 233). Eamon Duffy asserts that 'It is well recognised that the Henrician dissolution of the monasteries was crucial for the emergence in Tudor England of an acute sense of the *mutability* of even the most apparently permanent institutions.' Duffy, 'Bare Ruined Choirs', p. 41.

[63] Adam Nicolson, *God's Secretaries: The Making of the King James Bible* (London, 2003), pp. 220, 182.

[64] Eamon Duffy, cited in Neil MacGregor, *Shakespeare's Restless World*, p. 26.

the play's emphasis on repentance and forgiveness offers the consolation that some changes are both good and necessary.

The play draws to its conclusion with a barrage of unstable identities as Prospero's change rewrites his own identity and those of all the other characters. Antonio is stripped of his usurped status and he and Sebastian are revealed as traitors by Prospero. Alonso changes from bereaved father to rejoicing father as Ferdinand is revealed alive and betrothed to Miranda. The changes to Trinculo and Stephano are comedic, while Caliban changes allegiance from their subversive servant to Prospero's. The final change for Caliban, as for Ariel, is from enslavement to freedom. The last scene demonstrates that having passed through acts of repentance and forgiveness the characters reach points of reconciliation so that the unequivocally human characters can sail away, leaving behind what are effectively the signs of their dichotomous (hence unstable) human identities – spirit (Ariel) and appetite (Caliban) in the fantasy space of the Island.

Prospero's Epilogue lends one last twist to the theme of unstable semiotics, when he speaks in apparently religious language to invoke the audience's intervention before he can leave the Island. Sarah Beckwith's observation of the unclear grammatical function of the phrase which includes 'release' earlier in the scene (5.1.11) should be set alongside Prospero's later use of the word in his Epilogue where it is unequivocal: 'But release *me* from *my* bands / With the help of your good hands' (Epi.9–10 my emphases). As he seeks the audience's aid Prospero collapses the theatrical fiction. The sense now becomes not of actions distanced by their theatricality but that everyone present is involved with the resolution of this drama. Some uncertainty still continues: are their hands applauding or to be closed in prayer? Equally, when Prospero says 'Gentle breath of yours my sails / Must fill, or else my project fails' (Epi.11–12), prayer may be indicated. A moment later he openly declares that without his occult powers 'my ending is despair, / Unless I be relieved by prayer' (Epi.15–16). However, the play comes to an end

with another hermeneutic challenge to playgoers that illuminates with blinding clarity its thematic concern with semiotic instability caused by religious change. Prospero famously pleads:

> As you from crimes would pardoned be,
> Let your indulgence set me free. (Epi.19–20)

The term 'indulgence' had shifted through many meanings throughout history, from kindness and fondness, to its later ecclesiastical meanings of forgiveness and the much-condemned abuses of the remission of sin. However, its most tantalizing meaning, which might be added to more familiar ones, is an original Latin form found in Pliny: *indulgentia caeli*, mild weather.[65] Though this particular meaning would have been unfamiliar to many playgoers, they are still unmistakably confronted at a more obvious level with the challenge to participate in a reciprocal act of repentance and forgiveness.

Velma Richmond, arguing from a perspective of her interest in links between medieval (Catholic) romance and Shakespeare's work, observes that *The Tempest*, like other late Shakespearian 'romances' has for many people 'remained illogical, full of strange actions and inconsistencies, most notably concluding in forgiveness, resolution, and reconciliation'.[66] Robert Grams Hunter has declared that 'the ultimate source of the tempest in the play is the hatred and evil of the older generation'.[67] This assertion may be taken in a wider context to refer to the view of the Reformation from the vantage point of 1611. Arthur F. Marotti, in his essay 'Shakespeare and Catholicism' surveys the double critical dichotomy which has not only sought to read Shakespeare in terms

---

[65] Charleton T. Lewis and Charles Short, eds., *A Latin Dictionary* (Oxford, 1993) Indulgentia, II. I am most grateful to my colleague Dr David Freemantle for directing my attention to the several meanings of 'indulgentia' and for reading and commenting on an earlier version of this essay. Robert S. Miola notes that Shakespeare used 'Holland's Pliny', in *Shakespeare's Reading*, p. 168. This refers to Pliny's *The Historie of the World*, trans. Philemon Holland (London, 1601).
[66] Richmond, *Shakespeare, Catholicism, and Romance*, p. 15.
[67] Hunter, *Shakespeare and the Comedy of Forgiveness*, p. 227.

of Protestantism *or* Catholicism, but has done so through later historical bias. Richard Wheeler notes that when Prospero relates the circumstances of their exile to Miranda it is 'history in the making – a rendering of the past by one who has a compelling interest in telling it as he does, as if recounting its only possible truth'.[68] The play's own historical dimension, its backward-looking engagement with changes to older semiotic systems, challenges such partiality.

In *The Stripping of the Altars*, Eamon Duffy provides a balanced view of popular support for, and resistance to, religious change throughout the sixteenth century.[69] The later historian's empirical analysis is necessarily different from contemporary Jacobean theatrical representations of the continuation of earlier tensions. John D. Cox has seen in *Twelfth Night* – notably another shipwreck play – 'a strategic satire aimed at both religious extremes'.[70] By looking back to medieval religious iconography and sketching its dissolution into instability it is possible to see that in *The Tempest* the process and consequences of factionalism symbolized by the storm-tossed ship are logically resolved through those things that remain stable: repentance and forgiveness lead to reconciliation and the ability to move forward. But these require changes in order to take place. James Shapiro has stated that by 1600 'Shakespeare could count on an unusually discriminating audience, one sensitive to subtle transformations of popular genres'.[71] The instability of ship-and-storm imagery and the patterns of identity confusion finally resolved lead in *The Tempest* to a desire to move on which can only be achieved, so the audience is told, by its own involvement. It is a fitting end to a playwright's career to summarize the most important cultural chaos of the previous seventy years, without partiality, as a shipwreck that has taken place. It is equally fitting to end this play with a speech that encourages the audience to recognize their own part in that drama in hopes of the 'pardon' that will enable the ship to set sail again, this time in mild weather.

---

[68] Richard P. Wheeler, 'Fantasy and History in The Tempest', in *The Tempest: Critical Essays*, ed. Patrick M. Murphy (New York and London, 2001), pp. 293–324; p. 293.

[69] Eamon Duffy, *The Stripping of the Altars: Traditional Religion in England 1400–1580* (New Haven and London, 1992).

[70] John D. Cox, *The Devil and the Sacred in English Drama* (Cambridge, 2000), p. 155.

[71] James Shapiro, *1599: A Year in the Life of William Shakespeare* (London, 2005), p. 10.

SHAKESPEARE PERFORMANCES IN ENGLAND 2014

CAROL CHILLINGTON RUTTER

1 January 2014. A day for totting things up, drawing lines in ledgers, balancing accounts. A day, invited by the two-faced god, to look backwards and forwards. In my case, a day to look back over six years writing this annual survey as I prepare to hand it over, at the end of year seven, to my (as yet) unidentified successor. I'm looking at my review diary, counting the nights (and days) I've spent in the theatre: to date, 127 productions; 32 plays; lacking only *Pericles*, *Cymbeline* and the three parts of *Henry VI* to make up the full canon. I've seen nine *Dream*s, eight *Hamlet*s, eight *Tempest*s. These numbers were perhaps to be expected, not least because 2012 was reckoned to be *The Tempest*'s anniversary year. More interesting to me, statistically, are the five *Winter's Tale*s I've seen: clearly, this once-popular play, fallen for a couple of decades out of the regular repertoire, is firmly back in the theatre. Equally suggestive, I'd say, are the three *All's Well That Ends Well*s and three *Troilus and Cressida*s I've reviewed: plays that used to be neglected but now look to be performed as often as *Romeo and Juliet* (marking an interesting post-modern shift, perhaps, in the love stories our appetites turn to). Then there are the one-offs, the deeply under-performed plays any spectator is lucky to cross off her hit list: *King John*, *Henry VIII* and *The Two Gentlemen of Verona*. (Though I can see, looking ahead at my 'What's On in 2014' that the RSC, for the first time since 1998, is staging *Two Gents*, and on the main stage, where it hasn't appeared since 1981 when it was staged as half of a bizarre double bill with *Titus Andronicus*, both plays radically chopped to fit on either side of an interval. Not one of John Barton's better ideas.)

Doing the sums is one thing. What, of this six-year-long marathon, will stay with me? The acting. That is, what actors do, making Shakespeare. Penny Downie's Gertrude (RSC), ignoring husband and wittering adviser, silently reading her son's love letters to Ophelia, discovering a boy she never knew. Simon Russell Beale's Leontes (Bridge Project), instinctively rocking the newborn he's hugged to his chest – moments before sending the baby to death. Lenny Henry's Othello (Northern Broadsides), bearing his huge bulk down upon the thrashing body of his tiny wife. Jon Trenchard's Puck (Propeller), in ruby-red twinkly slippers, emerging feet first out of a magic box to referee a *Dream* (Richard Clothier's Oberon going hammer and tongs with Richard Dempsey's Titania, while the lovers at war made fairy tiffs looks like an ice cream social) that was ensemble work at its best: I won't forget fairies asleep, snoring. Des Barritt's geriatric seducer Falstaff (RSC) measuring his long-retired 'get the girl' boxer shorts against his girth. Richard Harrington's Aufidius, at the wheel, staring stonily out through the windscreen of his clapped-out Mondeo as Richard Lynch's Coriolanus, in the passenger seat beside him, his window half rolled down, deafly heard messages from Rome (National Theatre Wales): this, undoubtedly the most audacious, ballsy and literally sensational production of my time reviewing. Judi Dench's Titania (Peter Hall Company), fairy queen-turned-giggling schoolgirl, cradling Bottom-turned-Ass.

Richard Cant's cross-dressed Corporal Klinger-esque Thersites (Cheek by Jowl), the Greek army's medical expert on communicable disease, spraying every wipeable surface with antiseptic – that he then reinfected spewing out toxic speech. Derek Jacobi's Lear (Donmar) *whispering* his defiance to the storm. Roger Allam's greasy Falstaff (Globe) working his audience like wax between finger and thumb. Kelly Hotten's slatternly, bubblegum-popping Porter in Cheek by Jowl's *Macbeth* ignoring the intercom buzzer between bored flicks through a celebrity mag. Rory Kinnear's Hamlet (NT), just wanting out of Elsinore, making his school footlocker his hidey-hole retreat for mad antics, a 'nut shell' to be 'bounded in'. Sandy Grierson's impassive, moon-faced Ariel (RSC), shadowing the castaways, mimicking their movements, trying on the 'if' of being human. Adrian Lester's Othello (NT), his service revolver pointed at Emilia's temple, turning to the corpse of his wife on the bed with a shrug as if to ask her advice on how to handle yet *another* lippy female.

Then, of course, there were the brilliant performances put in by inanimate actors: the Little Angel chickens in *Macbeth*; Pyramus and Thisbe in the Russian remake of *A Midsummer Night's Dream*; Propeller's dummy kids in *Richard III*; Caliban in the Little Angel/RSC *Tempest*, a monster who just needed a bit of love (and scratching behind the ears).

Actors are the reason I go to the theatre. But during my tour of duty, I've also been thrilled by the visual worlds designers have made for actors to play in, functional gymnasia: Vicki Mortiner's weirdly wonderful post-apocalyptic *Dream* woods populated by recyclables (Bristol Old Vic); Jon Bausor's post-industrial wastelands, post-modern cabinets of curiosities working as memory banks (RSC); Nick Ormerod's elemental abstractions (Cheek by Jowl), a narrow runway, the only 'set' in *Troilus and Cressida*, stretching the length of the traverse playing space and curling up one end, lit by turns gold or dead skin grey, and by turns the Grecian tents, a catwalk for preening narcissists (Achilles, Helen) or the frontline in the killing fields (Hector); Michael Pavelka's endlessly reconfigurable structures, built

for touring double-bills (*Richard III* in an asylum-cum-abattoir; *Comedy of Errors* on the Costa-del-Grunge) and for foregrounding Propeller's signature chorus-as-story-tellers, his sets literally 'hang-outs'; Jonathan Fensom's 3-D snakes-and-ladders scaffolding holding up Henry Bolingbroke's (and John Falstaff's) rickety kingdoms (Globe); the significant minimalism of Christopher Oram's ancient Britain, clad floor-to-ceiling in distressed wood planks that let in *Lear's* storm as lightning flashes through the joins (Donmar) or of Jessica Worrell's 'little academe' (Northern Broadsides), a single wooden library ladder Berowne's 'hide'.

As for directors, I've reviewed work by the legendary (work that makes you know, even in residual traces, why they're legends): Peter Hall, Trevor Nunn, Jonathan Miller, Terry Hands (the latter, after all these years, still on top form at Theatr Clwyd); and by the directors I guess the next generation will think of, one way or another, as legendary (Declan Donnellan, Nicholas Hytner, Barrie Rutter, Edward Hall). The four directors of whom I'm most interested to ask 'what next with Shakespeare?' are Marianne Elliot (whose quirky *All's Well That Ends Well*, NT, starring, unforgettably, Michelle Terry, caught the fairy tale oddity of this play – memorably, the shadow-play seduction of Bertram – along with its deep humiliations and final wonder); Lucy Bailey (a risk-taker with, to my mind, about a 50% success rate: acceptable odds, in the theatre); Greg Doran (who'll be setting the agenda at the RSC now and wrestling with the problems his new theatre is posing for actors, designers and audiences); and Phillip Breen (whose partnership with the superb designer Max Jones looks to be the stuff of future legends, like Donnellan/Ormerod and Hall/Pavelka).

So much for looking back. Turning my Janus head around to look forward and think about what's coming, I think my successor is going to need to keep a watching brief on this new-fangled business of watching 'Shakespeare down the lens': watching, that is, not movies of Shakespeare, but theatre Shakespeare turned into movies. Will the theatre industry rue the day it invited the film cameras in to capture 'Live' Shakespeare that it streams

'Live' to 'a Cinema near You'? The NT started the ball rolling in 2009, unashamedly admitting to filching the idea from the Metropolitan Opera, New York ('Live from the Met') who'd launched live video streaming in 2006, and who, in any case, had been radio broadcasting opera live for decades. The National Theatre put together its own in-house production company (NTLive) to do this business, and the RSC just last year jumped on the bandwagon, streaming the 2013 season's *Richard II* (with David Tennant) 'Live from Stratford'. The profits for theatre companies (and the tidy bonuses to, I'd guess, grateful actors) of worldwide ticket sales and royalties are pretty staggering, even after paying the costs – some £200,000 – of the 'Live' event. The RSC reckons cinema box office receipts for *Richard II* were over a million dollars.

So who could grouse about this innovation? The companies get income. The public, not just in the UK but worldwide, get access to productions they could never see in the theatre, not just because they can't afford train fare from Wigan but because top price seats at the RSC are now £62. (You can get a ticket for £14; but it's in the top gallery, way around the side, with 'restricted view'.) By contrast, NTLive, as the strapline has it, gives punters, for the price of a cinema ticket, 'the best seats in the house'. And there's the rub. What about the audience *not* in 'the best seats in the house'? Since these live streams are shot from the front of the stalls (with six or seven cameras, fixed and mobile giving different perspectives and close-ups, but all front-on), and since there is core collaboration between the screen director and the stage director from the beginning of rehearsals (so that the stage director can, from the first, focus his production for the camera), and since the RSC (for one) can meet, in one 'Live from' event, the entire audience it reaches during the whole run of a production in the theatre, what incentive will directors have to look beyond what the camera sees – that is, to look from every seat in the house, to understand what the *real* audience is seeing and to direct productions for the whole house, not just the 'best seats'? (Last year cinema audiences watching Doran's *Richard II* had full view of the set design – denied to

some 30% of the theatre audience who couldn't see the CGI projections that set the opening acts in Westminster Abbey.) If live streaming can take 'the Best of British Theatre' anywhere there's projection equipment and a link, what incentive will Arts Council England have to fund touring and the provision of live theatre in the provinces? Will the NT and, more particularly, the RSC simply extend their monopolies over what constitutes 'best' Shakespeare? What incentive will provincial audiences have to buy theatre tickets for productions recast for touring out of London or Stratford when they can see the 'real thing' in the cinema? (A recent NT tour bombed for this very reason, when the tour put on stage the equivalent of the second eleven.) And most importantly, how is filming – sending Shakespeare down the lens; putting him on a flat screen; handing his authority over to the over-determining visual medium – going to change what actors do with Shakespeare and how audiences look and hear Shakespeare? To say nothing about how reviewers review him . . . Watch this space.

HISTORIES

Big anniversaries this year remembered various histories: 450 years since Shakespeare's birth; 100 years since Dylan Thomas's; a century since the outbreak of the First World War. Some of Shakespeare's best producers whose work I most anticipate reviewing were involved with projects that did this remembering. Terry Hands (Theatr Clwyd) toured a production of *Under Milk Wood* and Northern Broadsides, *An August Bank Holiday Lark*; Declan Donnellan and Nick Ormerod staged *Shakespeare in Love* in London. Ironically, because Propeller were gearing up for their big history cycle, 'Total Rose Rage', a couple seasons hence, they were touring revivals of comedies I've already recently reviewed. So: history, but no Shakespeare histories to report from any of them – a disappointment in my 'exit pursued' year.

The histories that were staged this year were handsome enough. They were well directed, staged and performed. But unlike the plays themselves, which contain plenty of grit to stick in the craw, grit that's produced as the constant time shifts between immediate presents knock up against each other – Shakespeare's own contemporary London featuring in scenes he's sequencing with events he's dramatizing from history he's found in Holinshed, putting 'right now' in constant interrogative or subversive parallel play with 'back then' – these productions (except for gestures, and with one spectacular exception) located history firmly in the past where it stayed put, behaved itself and looked good in period dress.

Jude Law's Henry V, directed by Michael Grandage at the Noel Coward Theatre, wore his battered padded medieval surcoat and studded gauntlets with the easiness of a biker in broken-down motorcycle leathers, like a second skin. His crown was familiar, not so much an object, symbolic of royal person or power, as an extension of self and thought that served symbolic business, thoughtfully removed when he hunkered down to listen to the prelates chunter on about inheritance rights in France, firmly tugged onto his temples to meet the French ambassadors. This was a Harry who, unlike the scamps who flanked him, his younger brothers (visibly thrilled by the prospect of war), appeared to keep deep counsels with himself while silently watching, evaluating all around him, as if the policy of his younger self ('I know you all, and will awhile uphold / . . . Yet . . . will I') had become a way of life. When was Harry acting? When playing for real? At Southampton, exposing the traitors, was his grim-lipped rage, grappling eyeball to eyeball with Scroop, wondering at the enormity of Scroop's treachery, truly felt – or was it carefully managed histrionics, staged to the surrounding gaze to put fire in the bellies of the men he was leading to war, to prove he was no 'skipping king'? At Harfleur, warning the city that he could not be responsible for the 'liberty of bloody hand' the 'fleshed soldier' would take, spoiling Harfleur if it refused to parley, 'mowing like grass / Your fresh fair virgins and your flowering infants', that, 'naked' would be 'spitted upon pikes': was this a rhetorical tactic, policy 'roted' in his 'tongue' (as Volumnia might advise) but 'Of no allowance to

[his] bosom's truth'? Or did he really mean it when he shrugged of the threatened slaughter 'What is't to me . . . ?'

And what about his encounter with Katherine? Was the stumbling and bumbling (and wild inappropriateness of his address) the sign of a besotted but clueless novice in love? Or was it a calculated cover for a 'jolly thriving wooer' who 'will you, nill you' will, 'Kate', 'marry you'?

The ambiguity was hard to decipher partly because Jude Law as an actor here was literally histrionic, almost hyper-actively signing verbal images with physical gestures, so that his long speeches – and there are a lot of them in this play – became a series of mimes that made it impossible for me to see Law's Henry as anything but a player king.

In interesting ways it progressively became clear how this performance was suited to, even mimicked, the world in which it was located. England was a stockade, solid, but distressed, constructed of scarred wood planking: of walls set to curve upstage towards a back wall designed against invasion; of raked floorboards, paint-peeled. This was a world (designer: Christopher Orman) that had been left out in the rain, that gave the grim sense from the first of an army in retreat. But like the play between surface and depth in the king's countenance, this space could shift façades: could open to reveal spaces behind that gave insight into other ways of being. So, once 'O for a muse of fire!' ended with its instruction to the audience, and the spin-doctoring prelates came on with their foxy debates that ran in busy circles on the forestage, doors in the seemingly solid back wall slid open to discover behind a sumptuous golden tableau of medieval monarchy, lit with candles, hazy with incense, Henry enthroned, his court massed. The foxes in the foreground, then, were literally superimposed upon the iconic lion behind.

This trope of mixed verbal/visual messages would be repeated. On the eve of Agincourt, as Chorus detailed the 'dreadful note of preparation' of an out-numbered English army, who, in bedraggled twos and threes huddled in the foreground around low-burning campfires in 'war-torn coats' and mud-caked hoods, 'condemned' 'like sacrifices' and so 'low-rated' by the 'over-lusty French' that they could 'play at dice' for their lives, the back wall slid open. Against a deep blue night sky, bright with starlight (almost a Christmas card) stood in profile the chisel-jawed king, gazing into the middle distance (at an angelic host? annihilation?) as musical underscoring swelled to a climax. Here, one felt, 'the little touch of Harry in the night' would be not so much a manly clap on the back as a laying on of hands.

That this production didn't harden into sentimental toffee was down to the likes of Noma Dumezweni's long-memoried Mrs Quickly (whose remembering of times – 'O times!' – spent with Falstaff hauntingly informed her report of his death), Ron Cook's small-man-bigged-up Pistol (whose hyperbolics – 'rouse thy vaunting veins . . . bristle / Thy courage up' – made him the king's uncanny double while operating as implicit critique) and Christopher Heyward's hang-dog Nim ('I cannot kiss' was as bleak as a kiss of death). There were some odd (to my mind) directorly choices here, as if Grandage were deliberately ignoring Shakespeare's theatre craft in favour of his own. There were no tennis balls; only three Captains; no 'Non Nobis'. The one bid for topicality was Chorus (Ashley Zhangazha) who, conspicuously a time traveller from 'now', came on in a Union Jack T-shirt then reappeared (a school kid's pack on his back over the T-shirt) to double the Boy.

While Grandage, with *Henry V*, was finishing a one-off five-play season in the West End that had occupied him since standing down as Artistic Director of the Donmar, Gregory Doran was just getting his feet under the table in the top office at the RSC, this the first full season he'd scheduled as the company's new Artistic Director. Traditionally, directors have set their marks on the RSC (or indeed, made a bid for the company's top job) by staging history cycles: Peter Hall, Terry Hands, Adrian Noble, Michael Boyd. Doran is following example, but at a leisurely pace. Last year he directed *Richard II*, this year the sequels, the two parts of *Henry IV*. That Doran is aiming at

a future cycle seems clear from the links between plays that he's now establishing. In *I Henry IV*, King Henry, making his first exit after postponing his 'holy purpose to Jerusalem', a 'voyage' to 'wash' his cousin-king's 'blood from off my guilty hand', his gaze was distracted by something no one else saw. Above, in the shadows, stood the spectre of murdered Richard (instantly recognizable from the near waist-length hair David Tennant wore in the part last year). The cousins' eyes met for a long second before the dead vanished and the haunted living passed on.

Another bid for connection came earlier, in this production's opening sequence. Last year, in a long tableau that operated as a silent prologue, the Duchess of Gloucester, prostrate over the coffin of her husband, embraced the dead, a ritual of mourning. This year, in a near-dark chapel, beneath a life-sized crucifix suspended above his head, the king, arms extended like the side-pierced Christ's, prostrated himself full length beneath the shadow of the cross, a ritual of penance interrupted by news from Wales – which gave place, in the second scene, to an altogether different ritual that travestied remorse and suggested just what order of snook the son would be cocking at the dad. In the early modern version of a super-king-sized bed 'thrust out' Hal was discovered vigorously being serviced by not one but two doxies. Then the tangle of covers was thrown back and a grunting John Falstaff surfaced – also in bed with the heir apparent.

You got the feeling they spent a lot of nights like that. Because in Part 1, Antony Sher's Falstaff, for all his barely belted-in paunch and filthy dowlas shirt and sagging boots and bird nest beard and greasy grey hair shoved back in tangles from a far-receded hairline, was one of the lads, a geriatric Peter Pan. Alex Hassell's Hal clearly adored the old rogue, loved his performances, gave in with hardly a fight to his outrageous table-turnings – as when Falstaff, outed over the Gadshill caper, paused for only a split second before beaming, 'I KNEW *YOU*!' Was it out of deference that this Hal was willing to play Michael to Falstaff's 'lost boys' Peter? He, after all, had been named

22. *Henry IV Part 1*, 1.3. Royal Shakespeare Theatre, directed by Gregory Doran. Simon Thorp as Sir Walter Blunt, Elliot
Barnes-Worrell as Prince John, Jasper Britton as King Henry IV, Nicholas Gerard-Martin as Sir Michael,
Youssef Kerkour as Westmoreland.

Prince of Wales (when his father became King) only about twenty minutes ago while 'Sir' John was knighted three lifetimes back and, even long-tarnished, continued (as Sher played him) to display through the cracks of debauchery his lustrous pedigree. Or was it just that this Hal was as utterly amiable and as inclined to laughter as he was handsome and upright, the image of clean living? (I didn't for a moment believe that opening, the dirty sex sequence.) Without edginess or edge, Hassel's Hal revealed nothing of any secret other self in the soliloquy that declared 'I know you all . . . ' His knowing, here, was untroubled.

That said, trouble did come later, for while the elders in Part 1 struck one character note and held it (Jasper Britton's King, guilty and turbulent-souled; Sher's Falstaff, jolly comic chancer) Hassell's Hal moved up and down the scale. The little scene with Francis ('anon, anon, sir!') discovered an ugly side to him, the aristo baiting the pleb; an elaborated 2.5, a dangerously impulsive side. The knock at the door that broke up the parallel performances ('Do thou stand for my father . . . ') brought on the sheriff whose men began ransacking the house, frogmarching away the low-lifers Hal had just motioned into hiding. But not just the sheriff. As an enraged Hal began to protest the arrest of his servants he took a swing at the sheriff, who stepped aside. The punch met the jaw of the man stood behind him, the Lord Chief Justice (an interpolation what would make sense in Part 2).

Hal's double in the play is, of course, Hotspur (played here by Trevor White as *Game-of-Thrones*-meets-*Trainspotting* by a period-dressed but punk-haired Percy evidently on meths, resolutely performing post-modern behaviours, like duck-walking and punching the air). An early performance moment made you wonder where this nemesis, this *other* Harry, the lad whom his dad wished could be proved 'fairy... exchanged' in his 'cradle clothes' and Bolingbroke's *real* son, sat in Hal's unconscious. Having robbed the robbers and sent Falstaff roaring from Gadshill, 'sweat[ing] to death, / And lard[ing] the lean earth' as he went, a self-satisfied Hal turned to exit, and crossed the entrance of Hotspur, reading a letter. Hal felt Hotspur the way King Henry felt Richard. A haunting. A shiver down the spine that put a morose spin on his drunken 'I'll play Percy!' in the next scene.

Given the perfect materials Shakespeare hands any subsequent director of *Henry IV* (a text that insistently twins Hal and Hotspur throughout while stagecraft keeps them just as insistently apart until the final one-on-one show-down in 5.4, an early modern shoot-out at the OK Corral), it's almost unbelievable that Doran blew the ending. Perhaps because he wanted to show how nearly Hotspur came to winning, or how little Hal had come into his heroic entitlement ('I saw young Harry with his beaver on'), Doran directed the fight (while the Douglas was otherwise engaged with 'killing' Falstaff) to disarm Hal. But then of course he had to *rearm* him, so had to invent 'alarums and excursions' and a sudden burst of soldiers across the stage, one of whom tossed Hal a sword. (Why didn't he simply rescue the beleaguered Prince?)

The narrative logic of this was incomprehensible. Theatrically, it was muddle, and it made the young bloods' martial climax fizzle out like a damp squib. (In any case, isn't adjusting our take on heroism Falstaff's job: 'Em*bowelled*?'?)

It was all the odder for being so unusual. Doran usually has such a fine sense of Shakespeare's stagecraft and shows it to advantage to build memorable stage pictures, like Falstaff, enthroned on one of Quickly's sturdier armchairs, surrounded by a 'court' of drunks, punks and cheats, playing King with a red velvet cushion for a crown, its corners drooping like donkey' ears. Doran's single set for both parts (designed by Stephen Brimson-Lewis)

felt like a homage to Shakespeare's Globe. Balconies that wrapped around the up-stage area gave a sense of a wooden-O. Shutters looked to be made of wattle and daub. A back wall of lath split apart to reveal behind a tangle of trees or a full moon, or in one poignant (or maudlin) sequence, a seeming endless parade of the lame, the crippled, the hunchbacked on the march, Falstaff's recruits, surveyed by him with bland indifference ('good enough to toss; food for powder') while Hal, suddenly adjusting his views on 'witty' Falstaff, looked on appalled. This design was built for furniture 'thrust out' on mobile platforms. The Boar's Head, then, was set on one such platform, a stage upon a stage, neatly real-izing the meta-theatricality of what went on there (but at the same time cramping a world that needed much more room for blusters to swell and swaggers to strut).

There were also some telling objects that bound the two parts together. The ox-hide sized map was one, first brought on by Joshua Richards' Glendower, a tribal chieftain who wore it like a cloak of rough leather and threw it down with a heavy thud in answer to Hotspur's fretting that he'd 'forgot' it; then, after Shrewsbury, folded, handed by the reluctant rebel Vernon in sign of obedience to the King (who, anyway, had him, wild-eyed with surprise, sent to execution). Meanwhile the victors ended rebellion (and Part 1) by shaking it out, reclaiming England by planting their boots on it. In Part 2, the kingdom again under threat, it was the King who wore the map, in his sleeplessness, like some sort of comfort blanket – or maybe hair shirt. Or shroud.

Part 2 was very much a play of old men. In the theatre, you're aware how long it is before youth, in the form of Hal and Poins, show up, and when they do, they've aged. They're 'exceeding weary', prematurely geriatric. This was a world that had visibly greyed, as though everything in it were covered in ash. The insomniac King staggered through a seemingly deserted palace, dragging the map – hankering after his son. Falstaff (for all his new apparel, his 'gong' won 'killing' Hotspur at Shrewsbury and the ostentatious feather sprouting from his hat) was sickening, shuffling, his speech slowing, his

23. *Henry IV Part 2*, 2.4. Royal Shakespeare Theatre, directed by Gregory Doran. Nia Gwynne as Doll Tearsheet, Paola Dionisotti as Mistress Quickly, Antony Sher as Falstaff.

way with women growing more wheedlingly nasty. (Paola Dionisotti's excellent Mistress Quickly, a fox terrier crossed with a bottle brush and with a voice like tin cans scraped down a washboard, first put up a spirited defence against more fobbing off from the ruinous 'infinitive thing upon [her] score', but finally collapsed into exhausted complicity.) Jokes at the Boar's Head were running out of steam. Martial enterprise was reduced to the tedious swaggering of Pistol (Antony Byrne) and Bardolph (Joshua Richards). It was as if they'd all 'look[ed] into the book of fate', shut it, and decided 'to sit [them] down and die'.

Shakespeare's antidote to terminal illness in Westminster and Eastcheap is to remove Part 2 to the country, to Gloucestershire, to the teeming orchards and groaning barns of Justice Shallow and his aphasic cousin Slender. Of course, men are dying in autumnal arcadia, too (set by Doran at harvest time, the season of gathering in, amongst the paraphernalia or rural life: barrels and buckets, wheat sheaves and handcart, a board table laden with produce). But as told by Oliver Ford-Davies's Shallow and Jim Hooper's Slender, the deaths ('And is old Double dead?') become maunderingly celebratory, part of a human comedy mixed up with the price of bullocks at Stamford fair and memories of 'bona robas' groped behind Clements Inn in their youth. Their double act was priceless: Hooper's Slender wandering vaguely from word to word, losing the beginnings of sentences before he reached endings; Ford Davies's schoolmasterly Shallow ('"Accommodated" – it comes of "*accommodo*"'), his saucer eyes gazing vacantly at the empty past ('Jesu! Jesu! the mad days I have spent'), turning his mouth into a mournful slump

375

24. *Henry IV Part 2*, 3.2. Royal Shakespeare Theatre, directed by Gregory Doran. Jim Hooper as Justice Silence, Oliver Ford Davies as Justice Shallow.

(the labial equivalent of an erection deflating) when reminded that he was 'called lusty Shallow then'.

Like Grandage's *Henry V*, Doran's *Henry IV*s made one bid to mark the present relevance of his richly upholstered costume dramas. Part 2 opened with someone coming on whom we'd first take for a stage manager, until we saw that the black regulation crew T-shirt he was wearing was emblazoned with the famous Mick Jagger red tongue logo on its front. He gave the now-standard theatre instruction to 'turn off your phones'. Then continued: 'Open your ears'. He was Rumour. And when his own phone went off, he cheekily extracted it from his pocket and took a 'selfie', which projected on the back wall 'RUMOUR' –

and fragments of Shakespeare as text messages. It was a gimmick, but plugged us instantly into the broadcaster's message. 'Which of [us]' indeed in an age of tweeting, texting, instagramming, 'will stop / The vent of hearing when loud Rumour speaks?'

You got the feeling in Doran's production that the rejection of Falstaff represented the momentary pause of a well-oiled machine, the presidential motorcade slowing to avoid mowing down the overenthusiastic spectator who's breached the barricade. While security bundles off the 'risk', power moves smoothly on. A blip. So Hassell's King Henry, transformed in his coronation gear, flanked by his new-adopted father, the Lord Chief Justice, dealt impassively with a Falstaff who misrecognized him as 'King Hal'.

This moment worked very differently in Phyllida Lloyd's production at the Donmar. Indeed, every moment worked differently in an interpretation of *Henry IV* that exploded the idea of 'history' as 'his story'; of the past as finished; of 'ago' as well behaved and safe. Lloyd cut the two parts into a single play, performed without interval at a cracking pace in just over two hours with scenes landing like punches thrown at the work-out bag that hung as a permanent fixture in a corner of the set. She redeployed the conceit that operated in last year's *Julius Caesar* (*Survey 67*): we were observing inmates in an all-female prison under the watchful gaze of Her Majesty's prison officers, minders and enforcers, rehearse Shakespeare's play. All the lags had parts. The Dublin-voiced lass (Clare Dunne), sent down no doubt for drugs-related crime (and still dealing inside), was Hal. The bad-ass 'souf' London girls were Hotspur and Poins (Jade Anouka, with hammer-head shark afro, and Cynthia Erivo, squat, with wrestler's shoulders), nobody's 'hood rats', 'wifeys' or 'side chicks' but gang leaders tougher than any male street toughs (their crime clearly GBH). A Cockney blowze (Ashley McGuire) played Falstaff as some distant East End relative of the Krays, a kind of androgynous bloat of breast sagged into belly, her brutish face hardened by fags, booze and sleeping rough (or drunken brawls outside low-down pubs in Bethnal Green). A Glaswegian (Sharon Rooney, making her stage debut from television's *My Mad Fat Diary*) played Kate Percy, her voice a bagpipe, whining, keening; her pasty obesity confirming jokes about her city's staple diet of deep-fried Mars bars. And the white collar criminal – in for major credit card fraud or shoplifting in the diamond department at Harrods – was the posh-accented 'director', facilitator and player of the titular role: Harriet Walter, King Henry.

This conceit was no gimmick but prompted serious thought. At one level, it spoke to the ways Shakespeare and performance have been used – where the money can be found in an overcrowded prison system working to slashed budgets and reduced staffing levels – in rehabilitation. Like *Caesar*, *Henry IV* employed actors trained by Clean Break theatre company, it being 'fundamental' to Lloyd's 'mission' (as she wrote in the programme) not just to give 'women . . . a crack' at these parts, 'jewels in our dramatic crown', but to give women who've started acting with Clean Break higher visibility and a further professional leg-up. But that prompted another thought: the way Shakespeare's 'authority' operates in women's lives; the way Shakespeare's male-dominated plays can be seen paradoxically as prisons of female exclusion (six parts for women across the two *Henry IVs*, against 80+ for men), like holding pens in refugee camps where the women and children are dumped, marginalized, silenced and, while highly visible as background, kept away from the men who get on with the active politics in front of the cameras. Could Lloyd's gang be seen as busting the pens, dismantling the barriers, knocking down the walls?

The prison conceit folded such speculations into each other. We spectators, seated on three sides of a rectangle, were in a space that simultaneously brutalized and infantilized women, the inmates' rec room, painted two shades of institutional gun metal grey, the walls plastered with posters ('You are not invincible'; 'Are you close to the boil?': aimed at who, the jailed or the jailors?). Overhead were massive interrogation lamps. A metal gantry ran the length of the facing wall, with metal steps leading to a space above where an antiquated coin telephone hung. Below, child-sized plastic tables and chairs in primary colours furnished this 'play' room (depressingly gesturing at the kids who'd be visiting their banged-up moms?), along with other seeming refugees from pre-school: a toy 'kitchen' (that would morph into an Eastcheap tavern where everyone would have to sit cramped, knees against chins); a teddy bear; a miniature electric car (that would be used to stage the Gadshill caper, here, a traffic accident, set up by Falstaff operating the car and Bardolph (Karen Dunbar) dropping the bear in its path, the anguished 'toff' motorists suddenly appearing from off-stage, loudly lamenting the road kill – only to be ambushed, stripped of

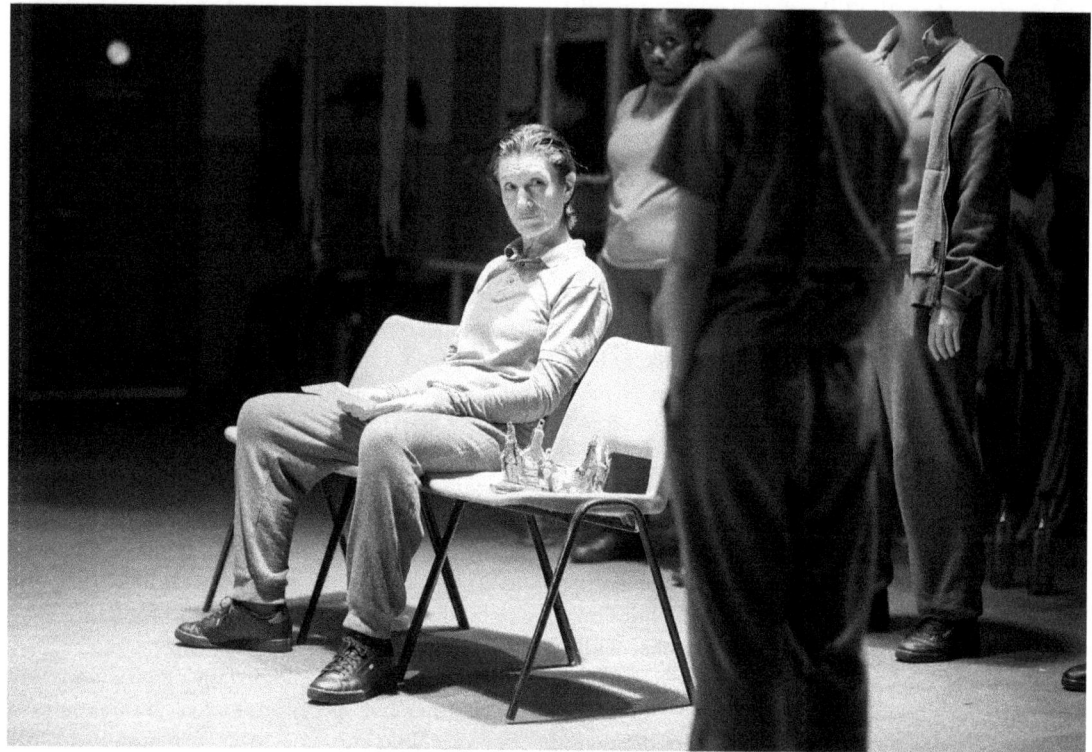

25. *Henry IV Part 1*, 1.3. Donmar Warehouse, directed by Phyllida Lloyd. Harriet Walter as King Henry IV.

their fur coat, diamond collar, wallet and keys). The bright red punching bag that hung in full view as a backdrop to the toys was both incongruous in this 'domestic' space – and right at home.

The production's opening beat established the drill: a siren; pulsing lights; a line-up of inmates in shapeless baggies; an inspection; a whistle signalling 'at ease'; the muster breaking out into rough-housing and noise as inmate Walter (lank hair scraped back, gaunt-faced) mounted the metal stairs, put on a striped bathrobe and a crown that looked like it was cut out of cardboard cereal boxes stuck with aluminium foil, leaned over the balcony and silenced the hooting cons (who were punching the air, getting the message that inmate Dunne would be out in three weeks): 'So shaken as we are, so wan with care . . . ' This was a voice dragged across splintered glass. That voice cut *Henry IV* free

from exclusive casting. And from over-stuffed costume drama.

Stripped, raw, urgent, this production in this setting understood loyalty, promise-breaking and betrayal. It understood delinquency: riot, stain, what it meant to be a 'misleader of youth'. (The first cut to Falstaff ('Now, Hal, what time of day is it?') showed him snorting a line of coke – and pushing charlie on the un-protesting Prince.) It had instant access to gang identity. It built aggro into muscle-memory: Anouka's Hotspur was not so much 'hare-brained' as jackhammer-fisted, hyperactively pounding punches into the work-out bag, dancing around the king who'd demanded his prisoners (and who, splay-legged, remained seated and visible though 'off' during this sequence) like a boxer positioning the killer blow. Listening to his wife, this Hotspur (who'd argued in 2.4 – 'The purpose you undertake is dangerous' – with some

26. *Henry IV Part 1*, 5.3. The Battle of Shrewsbury. Donmar Warehouse, directed by Phyllida Lloyd. Full company.

pusillanimous hood on the outside down the telephone, slamming down the receiver as though battering the yellow-belly's head) was calmly tapping his hands. As the conspirators prepared for Shrewsbury, they were doing reps in the gym, sit-ups, bench presses, squats, building bodies fit for combat displayed in naked animal power. Hotspur, Worcester (Ann Ogbomo, muscled like a panther) and Worcester froze, mid-chin-up, biceps strained, mid-jokes about the 'nimble-footed madcap' and 'his comrades' who 'daffed the world aside', listening to Vernon report ('All furnished, all in arms'). On 'I saw young Harry with his beaver on', they dropped liked stones.

Later, facing a ranked army of King Henrys (all wearing paper Harriet Walter face masks, a bizarre mass of the incognito), Worcester was a whirling dervish, a ninja, legs, arms, feet, hands, head moving faster than the eye could follow, single-handedly taking down every comer. Still later, the show-down between Hotspur and Hal began in a make-shift ring, a boxing match, until the gloves came off, bare knuckles turning this into an ugly brawl before a flick knife came out and Hotspur was suddenly dead.

In this setting where loyalties and rivalries inside set up stakes that felt like a weird simulation of 'official' politics in the outside world, McGuire's Falstaff (in stained singlet, flat cap, bovver boots) was conscienceless, a dangerous buffoon, the entertainments – and McGuire made the prison roar with laughter – he supplied offering artificial highs. This old lag didn't give a damn for anyone. Would use and discard anyone. Covered predation with a verbal smokescreen. We saw Iago in the making.

All kinds of performance details made spectators sit up and take notice: the way the argument over the map was conducted by scrawling chalk lines on the floor, representing England as graffiti (and its boundaries, as permanent as dust); the way Hal's 'I know you all' speech, which concludes with a promise about 'redeeming time', actually ended, after a beat, with Dunne's Hal snatching up what had lain there ignored throughout, a plastic envelope of coke supplied by Nym along with a home-delivery pizza, pocketing it, and exiting at a run, reformation not at all guaranteed in a place where habits – and habit – clung on hard to inmates' lives, hard to kick.

But this company of women also owned Shakespeare's writing with glorious confidence. Henry's rebuke of Hal (3.2) and Worcester's rebuke of the king (5.1) were master classes in story-telling, speech as act, rhetorical structure embodied; in short, writing turned into performance, Walter and Ogbomo showing their pedigrees and how Shakespeare offers greatness to actors. And in both scenes, the ones who had to take the speech on the chin (Hal, Henry) were as much constitutive of its power as its speaker. A whole history passed across Walter's Henry's face as Worcester remembered Gaunt, Lancaster, Richard, remembered when his family 'were the first and dearest of your friends', when 'you swore to us', when 'you took occasion . . . to be wooed', 'forgot your oath', violated 'all faith and troth': pain, irritation, winces as barbs struck home, discovering even as he sat there, like Monty, in that wide-legged posture of male imperturbability, that these were thoughts festering in his own conscience.

After the death of Hotspur, all of Shakespeare's *Part II* was condensed into three high-definition snap-shots. Kate rocked the body of her dead husband and persuaded Northumberland (Elizabeth Chan) to further ignominy, already guilty beyond any restitution of betraying his son: 'For God's sake, go not to these wars!' King Henry, pushed out on a prison bed, died as his son Hal sat watching, then as Hal weeping exited wearing the crown he'd called 'care', 'polished perturbation', his father's assassin, a voice from the grave stopped him in his tracks. Walter's post mortem growl ('Are you so hasty . . . ') here had the stunning effect that productions so

seldom get from Falstaff's '*Embowelled*?!' The audience jumped. Finally, his peace made with his dad, his dad giving him final instructions, breath running out, a crown handed on, Dunne's Hal fixed it to his brows, climbed the metal stairs, put on his father's dressing-gown, and leaned over the balcony. It was about to start all over again. But first, Falstaff had to go. And here the rejection was real and meaningful – and personal, breaking through the play-making conceit. 'I know you not, old man' was a flat statement of inmate Dunne's UDI (as he started up the stairs to put on his father's mantel) from inmate McGuire – who suddenly lunged forward, shrieking, limbs flailing. Whistles and sirens blared; wardens instantly appeared; they locked McGuire in a disabling restraint, and locked the prison down. Above, the new king announced 'So shaken as we are . . . new broils . . . strands far remote.' Blackout.

As the Tweet had it after press night: 'Move over boys, the girls have arrived!' Too true!

COMEDIES

There may be excellent reasons why *The Two Gentlemen of Verona* hasn't been produced on the main RST stage in nearly 35 years. (Though the sheer delight of hearing daft lines by Shakespeare rarely spoken can't be one of them: 'She hath more qualities than a water-spaniel'; 'Sir, there is a proclamation that you are vanished'.) It's essentially a series of double acts (Valentine/ Proteus, Julia/Lucetta, Pantino/Antonio, Valentine/Speed) whose actions consist in spinning out post-adolescent debates on pupil themes plucked from schooldays in the 'grammar' ('Home-keeping youth have ever homely wits'; 'maids in modesty say "No" to that / Which they would have the profferer construe "Ay"'; 'Why, how know you that I am in love?', 'Marry, by these special marks: first . . . ') intercut with solo turns like the 'prodigious son' Lance's farewell to his family ('This shoe is my father'; 'No, no, . . . my mother'). Even where the playwright brings on four players (in 2.4, for the first time: a 'crowd'!) he gives them only one-liners, chat that operates as low-level male banter and aggro. It's hard to find in this theatre writing, which perhaps marks the playwright as a novice just learning his craft (or an actor-turned-playwright mimicking his efforts at line-learning from cue scripts), the kind of scenic magnitude to fill the big thrust of the RSC's main stage. Simon Godwin didn't duck the challenge. Making his RSC debut from the Royal Court where he has directed mainly new writing, Godwin was happy to treat the Shakespeare of *Two Gentlemen* as a 'new writer', not yet capable of Capulet's ball or even the Temple Garden scene in *Henry VI*, but clearly ambitious. (This play has rope tricks, a gender swap, cross-dressing, extended business around a letter, a 'speaking' portrait, as problematic a 'comic' ending as Isabella's in *Measure for Measure*, and a part for a dog.) Helpfully, then, the director gave the 'new writer' a bit of scenic boost.

The opening, a good fifteen minutes of pre-show activity, set Verona (designed by Paul Wills) in small-town 'dolce vita' territory, where life, dressed à la 1950s, was lived al fresco on a bustling piazza among cafe tables covered in red and white gingham-checked cloths under heart-shaped balloons (Valentine's day?) in front of the frosted glass-fronted doors of 'Padrone' Pantino's pasticceria, 'Antonio's'. A local combo (clarinet, cornet, tympani) played street music in one corner of the piazza; a vendor sold gelati from a trolley; local 'types' wandered through (the priest; the tramp; the gawky boyfriend waiting anxiously at a table for his girl to show up, managing, as he righted the vase he'd knocked over, to clear the table of cutlery; the waitress (later Lucetta) with blonde Shirley Temple corkscrew curls and hips that rolled in time to the ogles, her eyes rolling as she chatted up 'customers' in the stalls). All of this got whisked away as a crack of thunder ended 1.3, rain clearing the piazza of people and furniture, stacked, collapsed and taken indoors, the wings of café 'da Antonio' swinging out and around to reveal curved iron stairs leading up to a balcony where, under a strobe light and to the deafening sound of a big, up-tempo night-club beat, a professional dancer strutted her stuff. The scene change (that seemed

to fast-forward time, the big city clearly twenty years ahead of the provinces) established high-life Milan: modern, stylish, expensive; its chic girls thin as vermicelli in heels so high their country cousins would have needed ladders to climb into them.

So there were loads of establishing 'shots', plenty of scenic cross-traffic, plenty of background business. But what about the business in the *foreground*? What about the two lads at the downstage corner table, when they pushed back their chairs, leaned into each other, and the play started talking?

New writing or not, this play, as soon as it opens its mouth, is rhetorically urgent, alert, muscles tensed, and densely crafted. There's a clue in the opening line: 'Cease to persuade . . .' The two gentlemen of Verona volley lines like top seeds on centre court at Wimbledon. Here, though, it felt like the ball boys were in the game. Michael Marcus (Valentine) and Mark Arends (Proteus), both making their RSC debuts (and credited with only two 'previous' Shakespeares between them), were simply o'er parted (or, which I rather suspect, under-rehearsed textually). They didn't know what to make of this writing – or with it – I suspect because they (or their director) didn't recognize the rhetorical games young Shakespeare was so consciously riffing on, the actors constantly failing to find the rhythm and pace of the banter between themselves and with others. The wonderfully contrived 'woman's wit' scene (2.1) that has Sylvia (Sarah Macrae) arranging for Valentine in clerkly mode to address a love letter to himself (a scene that is written, thanks to Speed's (Martin Bassindale) interjections and interpretations, to play like 'The Dating Game' as performed by the Keystone Cops) was as flat-footed as Valentine's dim-witted incomprehension. Nor did they find the play's wondrous lyricism – those gorgeous lines about poetry, about 'Orpheus's lute' being 'strung with poets' sinews', about song able to 'Make tigers tame, and huge leviathans / Forsake unsounded deeps to dance on sands.' This last, though, was also down to the kind of directorly miscalculation that gave 'Who is Sylvia?' not to Proteus but Turio who played

27. *The Two Gentlemen of Verona*, 1.1. Royal Shakespeare Theatre, directed by Simon Godwin. Full company.

the aubade as a rock star wannabe's gusset-busting audition for 'Britain's Got Talent'.

Equally inexperienced, all of them in their RSC debut seasons, and two of them without any Shakespeare to their professional credit, the women principals managed to produce much more serious work than the men here. But perhaps that's down to Shakespeare giving them scenes that parallel the lads' but show the choices women make to be much more painfully complex than the straight adolescent either/ors ('home-keeping'/court keeping; honour/love) that appear to direct youth's lives. Julia (Pearl Chandra) and Lucetta (Leigh Quinn) conspired on a beach towel how to get the guy. Silvia scrubbed of cosmetic flush and glitz now that Valentine was banished,

her clubbing days far behind her, cinched into a shapeless raincoat, on her way to somewhere, like confession, dealt with the jerk who stopped her way to chat of love and demand her portrait. Julia-as-Sebastian doing a message for her perjured lover to collect that portrait had to stand being quizzed by its original, then sat forlornly quizzing the rival she saw not in life but in paint, 'shadow' interrogating 'shadow'.

Most importantly for the women, and to his credit, Godwin refused to 'fix' the ending of this play (*pace* Andrew Hilton interpolating lines for Sylvia in last year's Tobacco Factory production, *Survey 67*). 5.4 was a generic whirligig. Melodrama. Farce. Romantic comedy. Revenge tragedy. The attempted rape was shocking – not least in its statement of classic misogynistic domination ('Nay, if the gentle spirit of moving words / Can no way change you to a milder form/ I'll...force thee'). But so was the brutal assault that Valentine committed upon his perfidious friend, first water-boarding him, then pulling a pistol that he aimed at his head. The rigmarole around 'Sebastian's' faint and the rowdy entrance of the outlaws with yet more human booty raised raucous laughter that died in the throat when 'Sebastian' removed his shirt – to expose Julia's bound breasts. And the final sequence of exits left the two couples (damaged? reconciled?) warily confronting each other before Valentine put an arm around Sylvia (as much a gesture of exhaustion as protection) and led her off. Proteus and Julia stood rooted. He put out a hand. She took a step forward. Before they touched: blackout.

Later in the season the RSC twinned *Love's Labour's Lost* with *Much Ado About Nothing* (styled, for publicity purposes, *Love's Labour's Won*), recruiting them to the year's memorial project in Britain of commemorating the Great War: *Lost* would end with the sounds of distant artillery and the boys from Navarre kitted out in uniforms marching off to the trenches; *Won* would open with them (all of them) miraculously returning, whole of skin and sound in mind. But I couldn't help thinking that *Love's Labour's Lost* actually makes a better double bill with *The Two Gentlemen of Verona*. It pursues the same core debates that preoccupy Verona's adolescents (fame v. friendship, homosocial bonding v. heterosexual love) but reverses the conceit about home-keeping by establishing the exclusive 'little academe' at home while doubling the trouble: four lads instead of two. My sense is that Shakespeare in both plays is more interested in interrogating tropes of masculinity than valorizing them. So for me, probably the most enduring image from Godwin's *Gentleman* came not from the production but from the row of mug shots on the programme cover. They aligned Valentine and Proteus – lanky, scruffy, uncombed, unshaved – with Crab (played with superb indifference by the lurcher, Mossup: lanky, scruffy, uncombed, unshaved), showing more than a passing resemblance between man and dog, presenting them –

all of them 'servants' – as types of each other and implicitly prompting questions about love's risks, commitments, endurance and sacrifice, questions that take centre stage in *Love's Labour's Lost*. Crab, we remember, is the 'cur' who 'takes upon him to be a dog indeed', committing stinking outrages under gentlemen's tables and cocking his leg on Lady Sylvia's farthingale. Nevertheless Crab is so beloved of Launce that the 'master' sacrifices himself to his 'servant' dog. Who else does this sound like? Question: are all the young pups of these plays hounds, mongrels, 'dog[s] indeed' lurching into knowledge? And what does Crab's yawning impenetrability suggest about the educability of men?

As it happened, Christopher Luscombe's *Love's Labour's Lost* did a bunk on those questions. The first thing to observe about his production was that it was scenically lush, almost a return to nineteenth-century pictorial realism, its soundtrack borrowed from the West End, so marrying *Downton Abbey* to Andrew Lloyd Webber with nods at Gilbert and Sullivan. The opening scene set 'Navarre' in rural Warwickshire, re-creating on the RSC's thrust stage a facsimile of the library at Charlecote Park (location of Shakespeare's apocryphal deer poaching), a move that preserved the early modern in the late Edwardian. Portraits of Elizabethans, Stuarts and Georgians looked down; leather-bound volumes stocked the shelves. There was a globe, a pair of astrolabes, a telescope, a desk with one of those new fangled things called the (nearly) 'noiseless typewriter' (used for banging out the academicians' contract), chaises longues (available for male flopping and posturing); and four more-Wodehouse-than-Waugh male specimens, in white flannels, wing collars, silk waistcoats (Navarre: Sam Alexander; Berowne: Edward Bennett; Longaville: William Belchambers; Dumaine: Tunji Kasim). Later, in the four-deep eavesdropping scene, this quartet would appear in their dressing-gowns, Dumaine in a hairnet and clutching his teddy bear, one after the other climbing out of a dome-shaped skylight onto the rooftop leads where they'd have to take refuge from each other by hugging the backsides of the

28. *Love's Labour's Lost*, 1.1. Royal Shakespeare Theatre, directed by Christopher Luscombe. Tunji Kasim as Dumaine, Edward Bennett as Berowne, William Belchambers as Longaville, and Sam Alexander as the King of Navarre.

chimneys or perching on the outside ledge of the parapet.

Technically, this roof-top re-creation was delivered (and returned) from below stage on a lift that showed off more of the theatre's capabilities, others of which had been displayed earlier when the library (of the opening scene) receded on a truck, the whole thrust-out set disappearing from view in the theatrical version of a crash pan that revealed in its wake a green sward covering the forestage in front of thick oak doors that now blocked the proscenium aperture. They carried a printed notice: NO WOMEN. And it was in front of this notice that the Princess of France (Leah Whitaker), Rosaline (Michelle Terry), Katherine (Flora Spencer-Longhurst) and Maria (Frances McNamee) arrived, every bit as pictorially 'finished' as the set. They were dressed

authentically for a time when women wore 'costumes' not clothes – and when women must have spent most of the day getting into and out of them while men ran the empire: costumes for travelling, costumes for hunting, for receiving billets doux, for entertaining Muscovites; hats, gloves, parasols, striped silk, cutaway sleeves, lace jackets, tweed coats, leather boots, satin slippers. I could feel fashion envy radiating through the auditorium.

So we got the picture. This was a world that took its elegant superficiality very seriously indeed. Jamie Newall's splendid Boyet was its epitome: plums in his mouth, and marbles – you felt – held tight between his buttocks, patent shoes that gave off enough light to read a newspaper by, archness capable of holding up Waterloo Bridge. When he silkily sneered of Costard's entrance 'Here comes a member of the commonwealth', you understood the war England needed to fight was not against the Hun but the Edwardian class system.

But the second thing to say about Luscombe's production was that he showed how this was also a world addicted to the sound of its own voice. None of the young men used a dozen words when two would do. Dozen, that is. Like their post-adolescent fellows in *The Two Gentlemen of Verona* they talked as if quoting their commonplace books, riddlingly, conceitedly, wittily, sententiously, and utterly artificially: 'Light seeking light doth light of light beguile'; 'How well he's read, to reason against reading'. The women mocked their discourse, viz. Rosaline rebuffing Berowne's daft chat-up line with repetition ('Did not I dance with you in Brabant once?' 'Did not I dance with you in Brabant once?') or the Princess archly batting back Navarre's oath-saving device, his intention to lodge his guests 'in the field': 'I hear your grace hath sworn out housekeeping. / 'Tis deadly sin to keep that oath, my lord, / And sin to break it'. Nor did this addiction end with the toffs. Every man was infected. They'd all 'fed on the dainties' in books, 'eaten paper', 'drunk ink' (and were wonderfully comic because so utterly unselfconscious of personal affectation): Don Armado (John Hodgkinson, a lugubrious cross between Salvador Dalí and the man of woeful countenance, frequently horizontal, felled by love); Mote (Peter McGovern, his humoural opposite, bright as the buttons on his 'hall boy's' uniform – his billing in the cast list – and light on his feet with quips, and with the sofa cushion he wooed in song and dance to demonstrate to Armado how it was done); Holofernes (a definitive performance by David Horovitch, definitively pedantic, who'd clearly never been out of his academic gown since coming down from Oxford forty years back and who made the tension between releasing his bowl (4.2 set on a bowling green) and releasing his next observation a master class in comic interruption). It was entirely to Luscombe's credit as a director of actors, one who'd clearly spent a lot of rehearsal time on rehearsing the writing, that the audience wasn't simply sucked into the slipstream of this verbiage. Actors lifted images from lines so we could follow

their conceited elaboration in subsequent lines. They marked the writing's rhetorical turns. How often we heard that word 'but'. And they did this without overt signposting or signalling. They lived the language the way they lived their costumes.

Of course, Shakespeare has a deep purpose in serving up this 'great feast of languages'. And, despite all that Luscombe's production achieved, it was this seriousness that it ultimately missed. *Love's Labour's Lost* is Shakespeare's public inquiry into education, whether conducted in an exclusive 'little academe' or a parochial 'charge-house on the top of the mountain'. Should study be theoretical or practical? 'Still and contemplative' or active? Learned from books or bodies – specifically, from 'women's eyes'? The screws are tightened on this investigation when the lads' course enrolment is made a matter of sworn subscription. They swear an oath to books. And start breaking it the moment it's sworn, the play turning into a comedy of substitute oath-making as the men transfer their vows to books to vows to women. But as Berowne writes (in the sonnet addressed to Rosaline that not insignificantly gets misdelivered to illiterate Jacquenetta and so read out viva voce by Holofernes), 'If love make me forsworn, how shall I swear to love?' It's a good question, that's not satisfactorily answered by the assurance that follows: 'Though to myself forsworn, to thee I'll faithful prove.'

Really? Luscombe's musical director set these lines to what had been established from the first moment of this *Love's Labour's Lost* as its theme tune, the production opening on a music cue (that we'd recognize retrospectively) captioned '1914 Imperialist'. This tune returned as underscoring in keys major and minor (swelling up under 4.2) then came into its own in Act 5, now orchestrated as the full-blown song setting. Finally, after a swingeingly truncated 'Nine Worthies', played as jolly Gilbert and Sullivan and shorn of all the ugly, smug laddishness that the audience of toffs exhibits in Shakespeare's original as they bait the plebs' performances, it returned, overwhelming the simple solo *a capella* soprano voice that had started 'When daisies pied and violets blue, / And lady-smocks, all silver white'. In this vocal take-over, Berowne's uneasy question metamorphosed into an exclamation that was given a rousing West End musical finale treatment with full orchestra and full cast, the 'plebs' joined by the 'aristos', mustered *Les Mis* style facing front and belting out what began to feel like a national anthem: 'To thee I'll faithful prove!' The boys of Navarre, who'd exited when the soprano solo began, now reappeared in a single line. Transformed. They faced the massed household; and the women they were leaving behind. Dressed in military uniform. Headed for the trenches. As the lights faded we heard in the distance heavy gun fire. Then the echoing return of the theme tune. Played on a lonely harmonica.

It wasn't the sentimentalism of this ending that I objected to – the end of an era; the death of innocence; the passing of England's golden lads and lasses; the premonition contained in the shower of red poppies that rained down on Hector's head as he played 'Worthy'. You could just about excuse that as reproducing the naiveté of 'It'll all be over by Christmas'. Besides that, we'd seen it before, this ending. Ian Judge directed it in a production in 1993 when a twenty years younger Christopher Luscombe played Moth.

What I objected to was the hi-jacking of one of Shakespeare's most challengingly feminist endings for default position male heroics. As Shakespeare scripted the dying moments of *Love's Labour's Lost*, the women are asked by Berowne and Co. (in terms tangled up in conceited sententiousness to the point of incomprehensibility) to pledge love to men who have shown themselves not only perjurers, traitors to themselves incapable of keeping oaths, but students perversely capable of applying their learning to reframing faithlessness as faith, perjury as fidelity. 'Good Berowne,' cries Navarre when all four guilty lovers have been outed in 4.3, 'now prove / Our loving lawful and our faith not torn'. 'Some authority how to proceed,' begs Longaville, 'to cheat the devil'. And Dumaine, 'Some salve for perjury'. No other play of Shakespeare's uses the word 'perjury' so often. No other play offers such a case study of male faithlessness – or of the way studious ingenuity can 'nickname

virtue', turning the broken 'oath' to 'troth'. Or hands to women at the end the authority to test men. Whittaker's Princess of France and Terry's Rosaline were stolid testers. If Navarre wanted her troth, he'd have to do more than swear. 'Perjured much', 'full of dear guiltiness', he'd have to 'bear' a 'trial'. She set the assignment and made it clear there'd be no compromise. 'Go with speed' to a 'hermitage/Remote from all the pleasures of the world.' Stay there a year, in 'frosts and fasts'. Then if the heat of love's protestations survived, she'd have him. Terry's Rosaline was even tougher. The man 'replete with mocks' needed curing of his 'gibing spirit'. She assigned him, grim faced, a year in a hospital, visiting the 'speechless sick', tasked to make the 'painèd impotent to smile'. 'To move wild laughter in the throat of death?' That's impossible, says Berowne, – yes, about as impossible as proving he could be 'faithful' to her 'though to [himself] forsworn.'

During the exchanges when they heard and accepted their trials, the men from Navarre were dressed as Edwardian gents. When they returned, in uniform, they were off to war, not to the hermitage, not to the hospital; not to face women's challenges but to reroute penance into male adventure. Perjury and corrupt study were dismissed by nostalgia into the pity of male sacrifice.

Playing *Love's Labour's Won* (as it was styled for this season, a.k.a. *Much Ado About Nothing*) as a companion play to *Lost* must have looked like a nifty idea in planning meetings, not least since the two productions would be playing back-to-back over the weeks in November when the 100-year commemorations of the Great War would be at their height. But *Won* sat uneasily as a post-war play, set notionally at Christmas 1918 – uneasily, understatedly, because *Much Ado About Nothing* is simply not equipped as a script to carry the trace memories of a trauma like the 1914–18 conflict.

The library at Charlecote/'Messina', now the country house of Leonato (David Horovitch), had been converted to a military hospital (think: Downton Abbey Series 2), now recommissioned for soldiers in transit, crowded with metal beds, patient charts, medicine bottles and women (Hero: Flora Spencer-Longhurst; Beatrice: Michelle Terry) in nurses' uniforms. When the men who'd left four years back arrived home, their entrance to *Won* replayed their exit from *Lost*, a military line-up that relaxed 'at ease' when they stepped into Leonato's house. Miraculously, their outfit had suffered no casualities (though there was, of necessity, strategic re-casting, with only Benedick (Edward Bennett) returning here as his *Lost* doppelgänger, Berowne). Nor, as things developed, had these lads suffered any mental damage inflicted by the war. (The script to *Much Ado* hardly allows for it, though one had to wonder, given the scenario of the Great War, what treachery Don John (Sam Alexander) had committed against his brother (Don Pedro: John Hodgkinson) – collaborating with Germans? Surely he'd have been shot. As it was, he'd been wounded in the leg; needed a crutch.) Only Dogberry, played here by Nick Haverson with tedious self-indulgence that killed comedy deader than dead, in his local policeman's uniform, with nervous twitches and winks, his side-parted hair jerkily smoothed, his Hitler moustache stretched in grimaces, might have been recovering from shell shock. (That we were meant to laugh at?)

Just as disconcerting, there seem to have been no material consequences of the war. Leonato had a full hall of servants (Butler: Peter Basham, Footman: Chris Nayak; Housemaid: Sophie Khan Levy; Lady's Maid: Frances McNamee). Beatrice had ten changes of costume (uniform, mourning, bride's maid, pyjamas, two trouser outfits – very 'modern' – day dresses, party dresses). Demobbed, the men appeared in white tie or dress military as every-day 'mufti'. The furnishings were unfrayed, unworn. The billiard table that arose through a trap was in perfect condition. The ceiling-high Christmas tree that stood splendidly in the drawing room (where much of the action took place) spoke of parklands still unfelled.

Most dispiriting was Beatrice and Benedick as Rosaline and Berowne *redux*, because four years at the front had done nothing to cure his 'gibing spirit' and infected wit, here elaborated in strung-out gags that should never have made it out of the rehearsal room, not least because of their laziness, going for cheap laughs instead of committing to the highly specific world in which these lives were notionally living. Is it possible to wreck 2.3? This production did, first having Benedick announce he would 'Hide behind the arras' [sic], then allowing him to indulge in a series of footling jokes involving the curtains, a levitating head, a hand shooting out of the Christmas tree to be poured (by Don Pedro) a glass of whisky, and an explosion of the fairy lights that had Benedick answering Beatrice's summons to supper from behind a blackened face that made him look like he'd spent the afternoon sweeping the house's chimneys.

Whenever the production gave itself a respite from this nonsense and forgot the impossible terms of its historical context, it rollicked along, particularly in the evenly matched 'war' between 'Lady Tongue' and 'the Prince's jester'. There was enough acid in Terry's performance to eat through Bennett's self-satisfaction; enough outrageousness in his sententiousness to grapple with her fleering. They finally struck serious silence in 4.1, the end of the wrecked wedding scene. Thinking the church had emptied and herself alone, Terry's Beatrice broke into heaving sobs – that she choked back when she heard 'Lady Beatrice, have you wept all this while?' 'Kill Claudio' hit Benedick like a joke; and 'I would eat his heart in the market place' like female extravagance; but Beatrice's sheer relentlessness ('Talk with a man . . . she is slandered . . . manhood is melted into courtesies . . . '), bearing down on the grief she felt at injustice, insult, misprision and female impotence to do anything about it, finally backed Benedick's jesting spirit into a corner where his backbone finally stiffened. 'Think you in your soul . . . ?' was drained of mock. 'Enough, I am engaged' was the first genuinely serious sentence the man had ever spoken in his life. Beatrice instantly understood what it meant. A challenge might leave the man she'd just declared love to dead. Now the sobs she broke into when he'd exited were not for her cousin's love, but her own. Details like this – and the way, at the end, she hung back from embracing Claudio even when Hero had forgiven and forgotten – made

29. *Love's Labour's Won* (*Much Ado About Nothing*), 1.1. Royal Shakespeare Theatre, directed by Christopher Luscombe. Michelle Terry as Beatrice, Edward Bennett as Benedick.

Terry's performance alone worth the price of a ticket.

Would there had been more that measured up to it – or that the production's concept had allowed for. But Horovitch was miscast (or misdirected). Nothing in his teddy bear dad anticipated his metamorphosis into patriarchal monster ordering an honour killer ('These hands shall tear her'). Tunji Kasim didn't have the emotional range (and performance equipment) required for Claudio, who moves from sullen to mortification via heart-pierced humiliation matched with incensed pride finally to arrive at heart-stopping miracle: Hero alive! The one-liners traded between Claudio and Don Pedro, hearing Borachio's confession, ought to be show-stoppers: 'Runs not this speech like iron through your blood?' 'I have drunk poison while he uttered it'. Here, blood-stopping iron

was missing. Along with recognition that freezes to the bone marrow.

That men (at Christmas, 1918) could perform such ugly, gratuitous treachery upon men – the story at the heart of Shakespeare's play – and loop it through slander upon women: this simply dissolved amnesiac-ly at the end as the whole household (below *and* above stairs) gathered around the Christmas tree and launched into a Charleston.

Still, there *was* the acting of Michelle Terry to 'make wonder familiar'.

At the Globe, a season of Shakespeare's Roman tragedies was capped with Shakespeare's Roman comedy, *The Comedy of Errors*, set in the marketplace (boxes, merchandise, baskets spilling contents) of an Ephesus that looked like a Greek colony (its architecture faux-Athenian temple) and whose citizens dressed like exuberant, full-flushed Turks.

30. *The Comedy of Errors*, 1.2. Globe Theatre, directed by Blanche McIntyre. Simon Harrison as Antipholus of Syracuse, Brodie Ross as Dromio of Syracuse.

(Costumes, designed by James Cotterill, seem to have been inspired by Bernardo Buontalenti's 1589 costume drawings of dancing girls and Delphic revellers. Think: Inigo Jones in technicolour.) Trailing a string of directing awards (including 'Most Promising Newcomer'), Blanche McIntyre made her Globe debut with this *Comedy* which was also (it appears from her credits) her debut directing Shakespeare.

So she can be forgiven for making some beginner's mistakes. The first was to make the identical twins identical – an objection that seems illogical in a play that's about a double set of identical twins. But the comedy arises from the characters' confusion, not the audience's, and an audience (like the Globe's) that's largely made up of tourists who are understanding more from what they're seeing than what they're hearing (like me watching Goldoni in

Venice) needs clear markers of Dromio Ephesus v. Dromio Syracuse, Antipholus Ephesus v. Antipholus Syracuse if they're not to be totally bamboozled and if the hilarity and poignancy of the identity failures are to work. Different coloured socks. Or hats. Something that clearly signals the mistaken identity to us each time the doppelgängers step on stage, even if the wife and neighbours (wonderfully, desperately) fail to see it. (Twenty minutes in a Canadian couple sitting next to me asked as one Dromio exited and another entered, 'So are there *two* of them?' I understood why they were mystified.)

McIntyre's second mistake was not to kill off some of her (or her actors') darlings. Every gag was milked. Every chase scene ran – and re-ran, then ran again. The slap-stick was lumbering. To begin with there was extended business involving

389

a ladder, a pole, a *longer* pole and one of the Dromios (Jamie Wilkes; Brodie Ross: I couldn't tell you which) attempting to take down a line of laundry strung across the stage and being defeated by a pair of bloomers snagged in the heavens. (When they finally fell, *hours* later, they got the biggest laugh of the night.) Fish were thrown. An octopus wrestled. A turkey jammed down on one of the Dromios' head to shut him up. (It didn't. He kept talking through the beak.) The lock-out of Needham's Antipholus/Ephesus, conducted in front of his many-panelled front door where the panels opened up like doors on a cuckoo clock (discovering Dromio/Syracuse's head sticking out: a bit of a spoiler), escalated from bun fight (everything from bread rolls to cabbages issuing from behind the door) to grievous bodily harm, Grecian urns (Ephesus's answer to the plant pot as domestic weapon) hurled down from the balcony. Clearly, actors in rehearsal had had a lot of fun devising this mayhem. And then elaborating the jokes. A more experienced director would have cut half of them, brought this *Comedy* in under two hours (instead of letting it sprawl to nearly 2 hours 45 minutes by which time the gags had run out of steam and the audience, of attention), and delivered comic gold.

Bright stuff did shine through the leadenness. Becci Gemmel (last seen as Lucentio in the Globe's all-women *Shrew*) played the usually sugar-wouldn't-melt Luciana as a shrewish spinster whose expertise on marital relations lasted only until it was tested by the bewildering come-on of the man she thought was her brother-in-law (who'd clearly always treated her like furniture), prompting hilarious moves between weak-kneed lust recovering into stiff-spined indignation. The cross-stage traffic that brought on bustling crowds of hawkers and shoppers, and twins that just managed not to bump into each other was beautifully choreographed. Ross's Dromio's hapless anti-blazon of Luce the greasy kitchen wench was a triumph of spoken comic timing (rare in this 'frantic assembly' production and therefore all the more delightful): 'She is spherical.' Beat, beat, beat. 'Like [rapidly

searching a catalogue of monstrous mental images and an analogy dawning] a *globe*' sent up a shout from the Globe audience. That 'wonder' became 'familiar' in the final ten minutes was down to the delicacy and restraint of Linda Broughton's wrinkled Abbess recognizing her 'husband', 'old Egeon' (James Laurenson) and the breath-taking magic of his response: 'If I dream not, thou art Aemilia'. Broughton and Laurenson are veterans of the stage, with about a century of acting experience between them. It showed. (As they took their curtain call, the Canadians nudged me. With an instant review. 'They were best.' I agreed.)

If McIntyre made beginner's mistakes at the Globe, Andrew Hilton, the veteran in-house Shakespeare director at the Tobacco Factory, directing a vaguely 1930s *As You Like It*, made the mistake veterans make of falling back on habit, casting over-used Factory regulars, most problematically Dorothea Myer-Bennett as Rosalind and Paul Currier as Jacques. Both of these actors gave stirling service in the Factory's *Two Gentlemen of Verona* last year; here, their performances were clichéd, repetitive and predictable, perhaps because their director asked for nothing new out of them. Currier played the melancholic Jacques as an alcoholic depressive failed schoolmaster intent on drilling things into his captive audience(s) sententiously between swigs on the bottle. Every time he opened his mouth, the energy level on stage plummeted. Myer-Bennett as Ganymede in Arden (in 1930s tweeds, flat cap, boots and braces) was permitted to get away with 'Hullo. I'm a guy' acting: clearing her throat, ostentatiously dropping her voice – but only momentarily – an octave, thrusting hips out, shoulders back and hands into pockets, swaggering forward. At home in the black-and-white Court of Duke Frederick (Chris Bianchi, a well-judged performance matched to his eupeptic double, exiled in Arden), Rosalind and Celia were dressed after Mrs Simpson. In Arden, given the period cut of Ganymede's trousers, no one could have been fooled for an instant that the derrière they were looking at was anything *but* female.

But then, the costumes and period frequently made little coherent sense of the story in this *As You Like It*. Who was Touchstone in Hilton's 1930s set-up – appearing in burgundy plus fours, plaid golf socks, correspondent brogues, a jacket of floral patterned linen like something you'd use for upholstering a chesterfield, and a pork pie hat? Vic Llewellyn clearly didn't have much of a clue, so in place of characterization he fell back on tired gags. (There was the one about the city-boy courtier's first encounter with a sheep's turd: yawn. But why if he were disgusted by something on his shoe would he also pull off his sock? To raise laughs about improbable feats of balance devised out of artifical scenarios?) Silvius and Phebe (Ben Tolley, Sophie Whittaker) were dressed out of *Heidi* and like Corin (Alan Coveney) had Birmingham (city) accents. (Why? When Bristol has a perfectly brilliant local rural accent they might have used for the rustics. Or was the point just to mock them as 'stupid plebs' who always have 'foreign' accents?)

The best things in this production were brought to it by Factory newcomers. Jack Wharrier's open, free, naturally handsome Orlando was an unassuming belt-and-braces sort of lad whose complaint to Adam of his brother's misuse ('He lets me feed with his hinds, bars me the place of a brother, . . . mines my gentility with my education') was spoken in sorrow, not rage, until his sleek brother (Oliver: Matthew Thomas) in his 3-piece suit and slicked-back hair first goaded then pushed him over the edge, calling him 'villain'. Wharrier's Orlando erupted into violence, slammed his brother's head against the floor, held him in a choke that turned him purple. He deserved better direction in Arden. Myer-Bennett made the wooing all about herself and about her acting rather than about Orlando and the appalled radical tuition he is taking from an in-the-know Ganymede. ('But will my Rosalind do so?' was a stunned rush of anguish from Wharrier's Orlando that gave a lot more substance and seriousness than it merited to the display of trite mimickry Myer-Bennett ran through in both 3.2 and 4.1 ('like him . . . loathe him . . .

entertain . . . forswear . . . weep . . . spit': each pose 'acted').

Equally good (and equally deserving of better direction) was Daisy May's Celia, first seen tunelessly scraping her bow across her violin, practising, making the same mistake over and over at the same place, until her clearly tetchy cousin slammed shut the book she wasn't reading, which prompted Celia's apologetic 'sweet my coz be merry'. After the boys' wrestling match, these cousins did a bit of imitative play back in their private apartment, themselves wrestling, rolling around on a carpet under an art deco standing lamp, in short nightgowns and silk kimonos, conducting girl-talk, full of laughter, and misery, until a sudden light change marked the entrance of the Duke's courtiers, then the Duke, a male invasion felt as a shocking intrusion, a kind of violation. The cousins tried to cover themselves; some of the men turned away. But May's Celia shed shame when her father responded to Rosalind's bold 'MY FATHER WAS NO TRAITOR!' by felling her with a backhand across the face. She was fearless standing up against the father she made a tyrant. Her statement of fact was both a threat and ultimatum: 'I cannot live without her.' In scenes where Celia is the on-looker (and the actor's job is to be present, immediate, reactive and telling a story in reaction without pulling focus) May was delightful: bamboozled by what was happening between Orlando and her cousin after the wrestling and gobsmacked by Ganymede's posturing, playing 'jolly thriving wooer' in Arden. When this Celia crossed her own threshold (4.3 set in the sheep-cote the exiles had bought) and saw Jacques sitting there, she froze like a deer picking up the stink of human blood.

Individual performances, then, were intermittently very good indeed. But what was most curious about this production was Hilton's seeming determination to ignore the Tobacco Factory's best attribute as a space: its intimacy, which allows actors always to be 'on' and scenes to move continuously. Here, Hilton invented time lapse scene/location changes that slowed the pace and sometimes ground things to a halt. An example: having invited Celia and Rosalind to see the 'excellent sport' of the wrestling, Le Beau exited with them (Hilton having cut Shakespeare's smart scene-covering instruction about how, perforce, they must see it if they 'stay[ed] here, for here is the place appointed'). They then did a noisy circuit around the back of the auditorium's seating, to arrive back where they'd started, which was now transformed by the unrolling of a wrestling mat. Daft. Equally daft: ignoring the four structural pillars that are a permanent feature of this space. Why not turn them into trees? Why not use them as arboreal hoardings for love poetry?

TRAGEDIES

Last year I moaned about the fact that the late opening of *Coriolanus* at the Donmar meant that I'd have to hold the review of that production over to this year's survey, which also meant that I'd be deprived of a chance to review all four of Shakespeare's Roman plays in one season. I needn't have fretted. The Globe this year produced a season of Roman plays, three of them tragedies strap-lined 'Arms and the Man', kicking off with a revival of Lucy Bailey's *Titus Andronicus* from 2006 (*Survey 60*) that advertised 'Brutality of the highest order'. Much of Bailey's original production concept survived. The *frons scenae* and stage pillars were covered in black. A black canopy was stretched at roof-level across the empty space of the yard two storeys below, this velarium figuring not so much a sun shade as a death trap, and the place feeling like a sports arena multi-tasking as a temple of doom. (There were enormous shallow bowls of smoking incense on-stage and a smoke hole in the pit belching black billows as if direct from Pluto's kitchens.)

Again, scaffolding towers, like monstrous black metal chariots on castors, were used to mount the competitive electioneering of the opening scene, Saturninus (Matthew Needham) wheeled on from one direction to hector the crowds, Bassianus (Steffan Donnelly) from another. Later, they served to stage the triumphant entry of Titus (William

Houston) into Rome, a procession that worked its way slowly through the packed crowds, hauled by captive Goths, their queen (Tamora: Indira Varma) literally bound to the 'victorious car'. Still later, these gantries were used like dodgems by Aaron (Obi Abili) and his riotous thugs (called 'Bestiari' in the programme), careering through Rome, shoving groundlings out of the way, shouting (extra-textually) 'More death! More death!'

As in 2006, William Dudley's costume designs set the 'primitive' against the 'civilised' and against the contemporary (lest we imagine violence a thing of the past) – at least to begin with: before Tamora's barbaric boys appropriated the signs of civilization and spoiled distinction. The Romans wore sashed tunics, but also laced up basketball boots. The Goths, mostly stripped to the waist, were covered in tribal body painting, not unlike several in the audience who were displaying the new (retro) fashion in full-body tattooing. Bailey's Rome was both distant and proximate, 'ago' and 'now', its sound-scape a medley of vibrations off a thunder sheet, dull horns moaning between two notes, weird rattles like snakes and rusty bird calls, and the rasp of a saw across bones. As in 2006, her direction produced atrocity full-on and full frontal: Mutius (Jamie Wilkes) died smearing his blood along the edge of the stage he clutched, crawling towards his brothers; Titus's hand was chopped off before spectators' eyes; the caterwauling Nurse (Bryonie Pritchard) was thrust onto all-fours and spitted like a pig with a sword up her anus.

But perhaps advised by the management (or the St John's Ambulance Corps parked outside the theatre who regularly had to deal with spectators passing out: Michael Dobson counted 'four or five just immediately around me in the yard' the night he reviewed *Titus* in '06), Bailey this time around introduced slapstick 'comic relief' to counter the sights spectators couldn't stomach. At least, I think she did. I can't imagine Dobson failing to notice the joke geriatric Bacchus character (David Shaw-Parker) Bailey introduced to Shakespeare's play, who bumbled and leered his drunken way through the crowds, a kind of toga-ed MC/greeter, crowned with grapes, ad-libbing

31. *Titus Andronicus*, 5.2. Globe Theatre, directed by Lucy Bailey. William Houston as Titus Andronicus, Brian Martin as Chiron, Flora Spencer-Longhurst as Lavinia, Samuel Edward-Cook as Demetrius.

lines like 'Is it someone's birthday?' and who, as the sounds of an orgy (off) crescendo-ed to cover the last of Mutius drowning in his own blood, stumbled into view attempting to grope a shrieking servant: the night's original 'rape' moment, played for laughs. And not the kind of laughs Shakespeare scripts for Titus, that 'Ha, ha, ha' in 3.1 that we hear as the left-over sound of humanity echoing hollowly from an empty chest once the screws that have turned on his life have squeezed every tear out of him along with any words to make sense of them. Not those kinds of laughs. Rather, cheap laughs.

Indeed, unlike Dobson in 2006 who was struck by the 'terrible' in that production (Lavinia's 'terrible involuntary recall' of the rape; Titus's 'terrible vulnerability') I was baffled by direction that turned

this revival into '*Titus*: the Comedy' or even 'the Farce'. Tamora played her disingenuous 'reconciliation' ('pardon what is past'; 'Lose not so noble a friend') as fake laugh lines, smirking and ogling the audience. Her over-heated tête-à-tête with Aaron in the woods left her swooning with a groan of orgasmic disappointment. The hunt was reduced to a lark by a panting Bacchus who couldn't keep up with the chase. 'Revenge', flanked by 'Rapine' and 'Murder', came on like Japanese geishas re-imagined by Seneca writing for the Goon Show, clomping, teetering, shuffling in high-rise enamel red cothurni, grotesque Roman comedy masks with gaping red mouths covering their faces, a ritual of ridiculous posturing. Titus literally fell backwards into the arms of the audience after his last arrow, aimed at Justice in the skies, throwing him off balance, brought down a flurry of white feathers.

I had to wonder how any of this addressed the profound ideas Bailey talked about in her programme note, the 'disastrous suffering' she saw in Shakespeare's play; the way the audience's sharing in Titus's grief made them complicit in his violence, eager for revenge even as Shakespeare refused to 'promote revenge as a way of forwarding a culture'; instead, 'depict[ing]' in revenge 'the end of civilization'. Certainly, the silly business and interpolated jokes kept the groundlings on their feet. I saw no one fainting. And just occasionally I saw another *Titus*, Bailey's 'suffering' *Titus*, a play that searched and probed the meaning of violence, that asked whether savagery is aberrant or constitutive of human life, only humans capable of institutionalizing acts like the 'cruel, irreligious piety' of the human sacrifice of Tamora's son, 'religiously' offered 'T'appease' the 'groaning shadows' of Titus's sons slain in battle. The oxymorons this play offers shouldn't be lost on a culture whose newspapers regularly headline 'Holy War' and 'Senseless Violence'.

The entrance of Lavinia (Flora Spencer-Longhurst) mutilated killed laughter. Bailey's *Titus* was no longer a comedy, nor rape a joke. Earlier Tamora had guffawed in her face as she appealed for a woman's mercy while her lads (Chiron: Brian Martin; Demetrius: Samuel Edward-Cook) – now dressed like Bassianus, like Romans – circled the girl, feinting, taunting, hunting nets loosely draping in their arms before being heaved over her head to catch her like animal prey. Raped, she entered at a stumbling run, tangled in the net now also tangled with white petals, like the flowers she had strewn on her brothers' funeral. But these petals were blood-boltered. As her uncle Marcus (Ian Gelder) needed the entire stretch of the long speech the playwright scripts for him to wrap acknowledgment around the appalling spectacle his nerve-stunned words groped towards, so her father needed the weight of her body in his arms to admit the heaviness of his pain. Moments before, begging for the lives of the sons accused of Bassianus's murder, Houston's Titus was nearly

hysterical, choking on language, his voice jumping octaves from bass growl to shrill wail, the vocal equivalent of an erratic heart monitor spiking and diving. Saucer-eyed seeing Lavinia, his 'When will this fearful slumber have an end?' as he looked at the heads of his sons was toneless; his laughter, when it came, nearly inaudible. The man who headed for revenge's cave was mad, mind-blasted, querulous, a monstrous adult infantilized by grief whose mouth gaped, eyes bulged as though his crisis of sensibility was exploding his traumatized interiority outwards.

Did we, as audience, become complicit in Titus's revenge as Bailey proposed we would? Mostly the grinning and gurning of Bacchus kept me emotionally remote from this production. But just once my unreconstructed primitivism was fully engaged. The boy-rapists, surprised by Titus, were strung up by their feet (now the more or less de rigueur method of staging this moment), hanging upside down, gagged, their eyes and writhing bodies doing their pleading. Placid, a clinically curious Lavinia, her body and head wrapped in white gauze like swaddling clothes or a winding sheet, gazed impassively at the proleptic carcases. Her mad father stood between them, staring at his daughter, wrist-flicking his knife, right, left, right, left. Whose throat first to cut? Eh? Lavinia's choosing felt deeply satisfying.

On the other hand, deep edits Bailey made to the final scene of mayhem – that had Tamora stabbed and thrust face down into the plate of pie she was eating, triggering serial murder so frenzied the eye couldn't follow it – cut too quickly from Marcus's lines on knitting Rome's broken bones and Lucius's on the end of 'pity' to – yee! ha! – the whole company up on their feet doing a line dance, jigging away. Shakespeare at the end writes us speeches that give us time to register, reel, recoil, re-balance. This 'cut, cut, cut' editing of the ending felt designed for a computer games generation. It is, I'd say, irresponsible to serve up the spectacle of atrocity without, as Shakespeare requires, making us look at it. Long and hard. For the violence this play stages is not of the past. In the newspaper that day was the report of two girls, 14 and 15, in rural India who'd been gang-raped then hanged by their throats in a tree for their village to find. Policemen were arrested and charged with the crime.

Like Bailey's *Titus*, Dominic Dromgoole's *Julius Caesar* started outside the auditorium, in the foyer, with hawkers street-vending food and drink and a couple of carnival clowns got up as cod-Romans performing their take on the Lupercal festivities. On stage, Romans in faux-Elizabethan dress (for this was, residually, an 'original practices' production), under the direction of a be-ruffed, be-hatted, and be-doubleted 'architect' who consulted a set of drawings, busily constructed the false front of 'Rome' (designer: Jon Fensom). They faced the *frons scenae* with imitation marble pillars brought on like giant early modern Lego; fixed an imperial capital, blazoned 'SPQR', onto the balcony; lowered flying decoration into view (the pines of Rome, swaying aloft). So: this was to be a place of superficial sophistication? Façades? The stage itself was enlarged with a blunt-nosed triangular extension that gave stairs down into the yard where three raised wooden boxes gave Romans – usually plebs – platforms for their own pronouncements. So: an oppositional place? A place where different points of view could hold forth and harangue each other?

To begin with, my anticipation was answered in the most clichéd way, the action kicking off with crowds of Elizabethan Roman plebs pushing through the yard shouting in the style of today's football chants, 'Cae-*sar*! Cae-*sar*!' then sing-songing 'We love you Cae-e-e-sar! Oh yes we dooooo!' Caesar's entrance (George Irving) among his retinue dressed out of 1599 (doublet, hose, ruff, farthingales; with Romanesque toga-like sashes) was accompanied by a trio of deep bass horns ('navelurs' according to the programme) that sounded like a herd of Hannibal's elephants struck simultaneously with flatulence. The 'fertility race' had half-naked competitors led by Mark Antony (Luke Thompson) cut a circuit through the groundlings.

But when this production settled down and started talking it had terrific things to offer, starting with the tentative political manoeuvring between Cassius (Anthony Howell) and Brutus (Tom McKay), launched by an underplayed question, Cassius almost as sycophantic as Osric, 'Will you go see the order of the course?'

Listening to this verbal push and shove, tease and tickle, come-on and back-off (first draft for Othello and Iago?), part of my brain had leisure to reflect. Was this the play that opened the Globe in 1599? (If so, Shakespeare's company must have been delighted at what a fantastic talking shop this play demonstrated they'd built on the bankside.) Did Shakespeare call it *Julius Caesar* to pull in the punters, knowing, or discovering in the writing, that his real interest wasn't the big man but the Antony/Brutus/Cassius triangle; the acts of political persuasion, some of them monologic self persuasion; the orations, the public speaking? Here, Howell's Cassius, after that ingratiating opening gambit, used rhetoric on Brutus like a cattle-prod, the two of them (as actors) making the exchanges electric, intently listening to each other, cuing each other but not knowing where the next line was coming from, the effect quick, blunt, metallic, rude, unrehearsed.

There was equally good work from Thompson's Antony in 3.2, smiling and affable temporizing with the conspirators; grief-stricken, pleading for a hearing addressing the plebs ('Friends, Romans, countrymen...'), winning that hearing through self-deprecation ('I am no orator as Brutus is.../...a plain blunt man...'). It was his act of memory ('You all do know this mantle; I remember / The first time ever Caesar put it on'), an act of personal, intimate remembering so very different from the conspirators' idea of public, even civic memory, the way they imagined how the bloody scene they were performing would be remembered ('How many ages hence / Shall this our lofty scene be acted over...'), that finally turned the crowd from hearing the assassination as an act of liberation, 'Free Rome!', to an act of human betrayal ('Et tu, Brute?'). And when they turned, Antony flipped. His roar let slip the dogs of war, a mutiny sponsored with a comment ('Now let it work. Mischief, thou art afoot / Take thou what course thou wilt!') spoken with such dead-toned nihilism as to prophesy the end of civilization.

It wasn't just the big bow-wow, high-rhetorical parts that made a mark in this production. Paul Rider's Cicero in 1.3, the storm, was superb, a stumpy sceptic in huge hat stoically unperturbed by meteorological mayhem. Katy Stephens in 2.2 was a Calpurnia I'd never seen before, a wife silenced by a man who patronizingly mocked her prophetic fears to her husband who then sided with him, excluding her from male bonding, exposing her to patriarchal ridicule, further isolating her as more and more noble Romans – Brutus, Cassius, Casca – arrived to escort her husband to the Capitol. As the men yammered on with their morning chat she walked among them, almost a ghost, silent, staring into each man's eyes. 4.1 was grimly, terrifyingly comic, the triumvirate slumped in chairs, pricking down names of those to die, tallying scores, trading brothers and nephews to even things up, Octavius (Joe Jameson) a callow boy, but sleek and dangerous, his hair oiled, his eyes glittering, Antony clinically and cynically calculating, the dazzling rhetorician reduced by the boy opposite to a state machine, an emotionally dead bureaucrat mechanically crunching numbers. (You had to long for this Antony, like Lepidus, to be sent on some footling message, to get him out of Octavius's new-model Rome, a trip to Alexandria perhaps.)

But the recurrent problem for me with a Dromgoole production is the way he, as a director, constantly lets down his actors, betraying their evident quality with stupidly disastrous directorial miscalculations: the opening football chants were a case in point; permitting Jameson's Octavius to enter 4.1 braying 'Oh, shut up, Antony' another (not least because Shakespeare's scripting of the coalition coming apart at the seams is so much more intelligent); or staging the political assassination against a female choral backing-group chanting (in tongues), which meant that the knives had to work to the rhythm and timing of the song, the conspirators having to hold off their final thrusts to wait for the divas to finish; or bringing on a geriatric goof-ball at the end of the Cassius/Brutus argument scene in a silly hat like some early modern hippy preaching 'LOVE!' who then jigged and strutted through a ridiculous sequence in a

completely modern dance idiom. Dromgoole lacks, to my mind, that essential director's skill, the ability to edit. Now, having seen several years' worth of his work, I think that inability is linked to a kind of theatrical dimness. He can't actually tell his good ideas from his naff ones. The enduring image from this *Caesar*, which somehow captured and unintentionally framed my difficulties with a production that aimed at deep seriousness while exposing such silliness, came from the onstage activity during the interval. A Roman female household servant in Elizabethan dress (one of the spick and span 'rent-a-mob' who'd shortly take Cinna the Poet's eyes out, and then, at a leisurely pace that made a nonsense of mob frenzy, savage the body) busily pushed a modern plastic wheelie bucket across the stage as she mopped up Caesar's blood.

Having idly fantasized that Luke Thompson's Antony deserved an escape from his future in Joe Jameson's emotionally anaemic Rome, I would not have condemned him to even a short Roman holiday in the Alexandria of Jonathan Munby's conceptually limited (production strapline: 'Roman virtue and Eastern vice' [sic!]), visually dull (designer: Colin Richmond) and (in terms of casting) politically objectionable Globe *Antony and Cleopatra*. The set gave us two views: a red-washed wood-plank stockade for Egypt, a white gauze map of the Mediterranean, torn through the middle, for Rome. A golden winged throne was pushed out for the death scene. Eve Best (a quirkily sassy Beatrice in 2011) was miscast as Cleopatra. Her default-position quizzical smirk rarely left her lips while she appeared (frequently arms akimbo, hips thrust out in 'model' poise) in a bizarre sequence of get-ups: a Kate Middleton/Duchess of Cambridge wig; black biker's leathers (I think they were meant to be 'early modern' hose, worn for the fake, gender-reversed sword fight with an Antony (Clive Wood) in Carmen Miranda headdress); and versions of Greek holiday white gauze (sometimes accessoried with Elizabethan add-ons, since every once in awhile – as when the scene shifted to Rome where strait laces and starched ruffs were the standard issue uniform – this production remembered it was meant to be an 'original practices' show: I'll come back to this). Best can hold her own triumphantly in the kind of limited action 'merry war' Beatrice offers her; but the scale of Cleopatra's wars – merry, bloody, carnal, presentational, international, metaphysical, earthy, earth-dissolving – are just too vast for Best's talents (at least under this director), not least in Cleopatra's ability to move in a milli-second from the macro to the micro, approving the 'common liar' (since every truth about the Queen of Egypt is also a lie). She *is* both 'tawny front' and 'lass unparallel'd'. Best played (was directed to play?) Cleopatra in soap-opera mode, good on the one-liners ('O happy horse!'), unequal to the epic arias ('I dreamed there was an Emperor Antony...'). She appeared to enjoy talking to the audience, flirting (even leaning into the yard to kiss a groundling; Cleopatra? I don't think so!). But she rarely connected with those on stage, who seemed to be in quite different productions. Except for two excellent moments. When Octavius (Jolyon Coy, prissy and priggish) entered in 5.2 she knelt. He took her hand and raised her. Eyes never leaving his, she imperceptibly slid the touched hand behind her back, held it at a broken angle, and flexed it as though it had been poisoned. Earlier, needing to get hard information out of Dolabella (Philip Correia) about Octavius's plans for her, she plonked herself down on her throne's step, patting the place beside her and inviting the soldier to join her, budging up a bit when he did, the two shoulder to shoulder and thigh to thigh, the Queen 'No more but e'en a woman' or 'the maid that milks'. But I realize that what actually made this sequence magic was Correia's reactions. Earlier he'd played Pompey. Now he returned as a pleb-speaking Dolabella, who entered shyly as a nobody from the ranks into the presence of a Queen. His face showed him seeing her as a shining phoenix, dazzling, holding his attention rapt. Once he gingerly lowered his body next to hers, he was captured for whatever work Cleopatra might assign him: betray his master, cut his father's throat in the church.

Getting at least some of the 'lass', what Best couldn't do was to move in the opposite direction, to get the full measured stature of 'Egypt'.

Between this Cleopatra and Clive Wood's Antony there was hardly any electricity, he a man evidently happier swigging bottled ale with the lads on Pompey's galley than tangling with her in the sheets on Ptolemy's bed. Wood has a face that looks like it's lived Antony's military cv, but while the body has gone appropriately to seed, it doesn't convey even a memory of the sensual swagger and carnal appetite Shakespeare writes for Antony. He wasn't helped by costumes that flapped open exposing old man's sagging pectorals, or by the particularly ridiculous image he was required to present just before the interval, a set-piece walk-down in a shower of gold sparkles accompanied in voice-over by Octavius railing about how Antony and Cleopatra were displaying themselves in the marketplace in Alexandria. While Best's feather-headdressed Cleopatra-as-Isis looked like something out of burlesque, à la Wilson, Keppel and Betty, Wood's unfortunate Antony, dressed as Bacchus, was out of Aristophanes. He had on his head a turkey-platter-sized crown of ivy intertwined with vines and grapes the size of bulls' gonads. Still, he too achieved a moment of magic. Hearing of the death of Cleopatra, his instruction to Eros, 'Off, pluck off, / The seven-fold shield of Ajax cannot keep / The battery from my heart', produced the authentic sound of a heart breaking.

But to return briefly to the question of 'original practices'. The Folio *Antony and Cleopatra* contains, near the top, one of the most challenging stage directions Shakespeare ever laid upon his actors (if it was he who included it; or the book holder): 'Enter Antony, Cleopatra, her ladies, the train, with eunuchs fanning her'. How do you 'do' eunuchs on the early modern stage? What does Shakespeare, in 'eunuchs', signify in theatrical shorthand for London *c*.1606? Ideas of the exotic, the 'other', the erotic male body captured by a queen who can literally toy with (his) sex? How does the Globe in 2014, responding to 'original practices', translate the challenge of the 'eunuchs'? This is where I found Mumby's production distasteful, his casting politically objectionable. He coded 'exotic' with tourist brochure cliché, opening his show with a *show*, a big carnivalesque production number set in an 'eastern' bazaar with lots of 'Alexandrians' jiving in the streets, the main markers of their ethnic identity being their dangly ear-rings, arm-fuls of Primark gold bangles, harem trousers, incense and non-specific music producing non-specific 'exotic' dancing (that turned into a Haka on Pompey's galley, which returned in lieu of the standard Globe jig at the end). This was just lazy direction and design. What was insulting was the casting. Among some seventeen actors, Mumby cast five who might describe themselves as 'British Black, Asian or Eastern'. But cast them in parts they could have been playing in 1972 when Trevor Nunn staged *Antony and Cleopatra* at the RSC (a production, back then, that demonstrated progressiveness by casting black actors in *any* parts). Today, this casting feels reactionary: Peter Bankolé was Messenger/Eros; Jonathan Bonnici, Soothsayer/Thidias; Kammy Darweish, Alexas; Sirine Saba, Charmian (who predictably performed the sensuality that eluded Best's Cleopatra); Obioma Ugoala, Mardian. Frequently stripped to the waist, mostly shoved to the peripheries of the scene, these actors were employed in scene after scene to stand as human air conditioners, pulling on ropes that wafted carpets that created drafts to cool (unnecessarily) a whiter-than-white gypsy's lust which, ironically, never rose to a simmer, never mind a boil. After Tarell McCraney's *Antony and Cleopatra* last year (*Survey 67*) with Joaquina Kalukango's 'unparall'd' royal gypsy Queen of Egypt this sort of thing simply won't do.

If Munby had problems scaling up concept, design, and actors' performances to meet the requirements of a play whose scale is 'past the size of dreaming' at the Globe (capacity audience: 2080), Josie Rourke had equivalent problems scaling down Shakespeare's strapping final Roman play, *Coriolanus*, to cram into the 250-seater Donmar Warehouse. She defended her decision to direct *Coriolanus* as a chamber play by supposing (in a programme note) that it had its Jacobean premiere at the Blackfriars. But to make that defence good, to see what it meant to set Triton swimming in a gold fish bowl, she would have needed to play the whole play Shakespeare wrote for the space, to

see how its big-boned, rebarbative writing 'acted', contained in a room so narrow that, were the figurative hammers and tongs people constantly throw at each other in Martius's Rome real, they'd have been bouncing off the walls and smashing audience skulls. As it was, Rourke cut the play down to (her) studio size. What she produced was undoubtedly intense, fast-paced, slick, lucid, and undoubtedly aimed at the 'NTLive' cameras (and won for Tom Hiddleston's Coriolanus the Evening Standard's 'Best Actor' award – after Rory Kinnear and Iago pipped him for the 2014 top Olivier prize). But it was also diminished.

What this production was up to was announced in the opening moments. A child (Joe Willis, later, young Martius) ran into the black-box space and, led by directional lighting, painted a red square onto the floor. Lines, we observed, were drawn in this Rome, drawn on collision courses, at right angles, the colour of blood. That square (which later would be even further limited to another painted square, soap-box sized, black, where the Tribunes would stand Coriolanus to answer their indictment) limited the space of performance, making Rome claustrophobic, its 'plebs' and 'aristos' hostile neighbours living cheek-by-jowl. That a child was in charge here continued to haunt my viewing. As I would reflect later, his busy body inducted me into a world where the uses boy-children are put to would be interrogated along with the masculinity they're intended to grow into. This boy (who returned later, swinging a toy sword) retrospectively troped another 'boy' (and another, deadlier sword), boyed first by his adoring, controlling mother then by his envious, treacherous comrade. And that suggestive exchange of 'boy' for 'boy' anticipated the final tragedy of this *Coriolanus*: only when Hiddleston's Coriolanus showed himself a boy did he prove himself a man.

The child's work done, the rest of the ensemble (minus Martius) swarmed onto the stage and formed lines facing the audience, their backs to a grungy wall (designer: Lucy Osborne) that looked industrial, like a tunnel in the London tube, thick with layers of red and black paint that later would be written over with graffiti, slogans, plebeian

32. *Coriolanus*, 1.4. Donmar Theatre, directed by Josie Rourke. Tom Hiddleston as Coriolanus.

protests ('Grain at our price'; 'He mocked us'). This Rome was entirely sunless. As one of my students spotted for me, Osborne's costume designs (hoodies, cotton jerseys, military-esque trousers, boots; this designer street-style supplemented with leather wrist bands and military-issue body armour; a colour palette that ran from black to grey with brown to relieve the dreariness) appeared to riff on that season's 'All Saints' atelier collection ('elements of the garments are physically pulled away to reveal partial or complete views of the layers that lie beneath': sounds like Coriolanus in the market place).

As the First Citizen (Rochenda Sandall, radiating class anger and bolshie swagger) stepped forward to launch into a speech about speaking that was actually a strident prompt to violent action ('Before we proceed...speak'), the others sat in chairs, lined up, facing outward. Thus, Rourke established a performance conceit that would be adopted throughout, making some or all of the company spectators on most of the scenes. Physically, this meant that Tribunes sat next to Senators, citizens next to nobles, Volsces, Romans. Everyone, that is, could rub along with their political differences, have a place. Except Caius Martius. Thematically, it highlighted two ideas: playmaking and speechmaking. It was baldly Brechtian (or more recently, Cheek by Jowlian). But it intensified the sense of Caius Martius needing, at least when he grudgingly moved at his mother's behest from 'the casque to the cushion', to act what he wasn't, failing to star in his own play, *scripted for him* by master dramaturgs who couldn't drum into his head the lines or the moves. What the conceit offered speechmaking was even more compelling. Sitting outside the red-outlined square, spectators were watching action taking place in a boxing ring, or in an *agora*, or maybe the House of Commons. When on-stage watchers had a point to make – Second Citizen, Menenius, Brutus – they stepped up, entered the argument; speech finished, they sat. What this produced was a sense not of simple polemics (them, us; right, wrong) but of complex political debate where no one had the right of it. Rourke's staging, then, staged dilemma.

The biggest dilemma was what to make of Caius Martius. Hiddleston managed to suggest he was an oxymoron. Lithe, muscular, utterly at ease with his weapon and lethal in the simply staged but nerve-shredding battle sequences where, amid scaling ladders crashing and smoke bombs detonating, he terminated his foes in seconds, Hiddleston

(who's physically built to look down his nose at most people on the planet, and certainly in this Rome and Corioli) didn't even have to break sweat cursing the plebs or mocking them in wheedling tones that mimicked their infra-dig accents. His vituperation ('curs', 'geese', 'hares') was effortless, the natural opinion of the class supremacist, represented naturally in the political rhetoric of class division, class exclusion: 'By mingling them' – 'the mutable, rank-scented many' – 'with us, the honour'd number' we 'nourish 'gainst our senate / The cockle of rebellion, insolence, sedition'. So much evident fact. (And fact that spoke directly into the political debates 'austerity' Britain was conducting with itself over welfare ('the undeserving poor'; the 'politics of envy'), immigration ('johnny foreigner taking our jobs'), Scottish independence (challenging the political class in England, the Westminster village, a privileged elite ignorant of 'real' lives); the rise of UKIP (and a politics the tribunes in Coriolanus could sign up to).

Aloof with both wife (*Borgen* star Birgitte Hjort Sørenson, a kind of snow princess whose access to her husband was constantly barred by his mother) and son, he barely thawed with Menenius (Mark Gatiss), played here not a generation older than Martius, a surrogate father, but his age, a genial-seeming acolyte, perhaps his 'fag' at public school where Martius would have been the prefect in charge of early morning cross-country and cold showers and where Gatiss's little Menenius would have learned the craft to manage his arrogant boy-master. Now he'd grown into a kind of Peter Mandelson. Still a 'fag', still adoring, but groaning at each disastrous gaffe politically uneducable Martius committed. Martius, after all, was his mother's son. A creation fashioned by a monster. As Deborah Findlay played her, bulky, bullish, square-jawed, a study in vicarious living through a child, Volumnia could show passion (enumerating with sickening glee that forced incredulous laughter from the audience the wounds her son would have to display to the people to buy their votes in the Consular elections). But never to her son. Not even in her final browbeating that achieved salvation for Rome. Her blackmail was calculated, emotionally a ruse. And ultimately all about herself. This was a mother who could have written the advanced military textbook on emotional deprivation, where tough love graduates to total desensitization, man into machine.

But if Hiddleston's Coriolanus was his mother's machine, he was also, ultimately, the boy she couldn't drum out of him while failing to drum the politician into him. He gave early signs of vulnerablity. A thing of blood after Corioli, he stood stripped to the waist under a power shower that, as it washed him, exposed his open wounds and, pounding into them, made him flinch. Only in the arms of Aufidius, in 4.3, in Antium, a welcome that began as a stranglehold, knife pressed against throat, and ended in an embrace, did Coriolanus seem fully alive. These were bodies that understood each other.

Then came the capitulation, the 'betrayal' of Aufidius's Coriolanus to Volumnia's Coriolanus, or a stunning new version of him. For capitulating, Hiddleston's Coriolanus wept – boy, man – while his mother, hand held, stood implacable, job done. Moments later Aufidius and his crew fell upon him with animal ferocity, spearing, hacking, thrusting swords and knives into his reeling body, and Aufidius smearing himself in Martius's blood. Martius finally died strung up by his heels (the image perhaps a homage to another Coriolanus, Laurence Olivier in 1955, or a memory of Mussolini that aimed at satirizing the narcissistic hero-turned-tyrant or, perhaps, as a series of *Titus Andronicus*es have now made it, just a cliché of brutal revenge). Of the female embassy returned to Rome, only his mother stood watching, red petals (this was the year of red petals) raining down on her as earlier they had on her son victorious after Corioli. This final stage picture was spectacular, but paradoxically anti-dramatic: a lot of faffing around at close range had to be done to get the actor into a safety harness, the days of Olivier throwing himself backwards off a platform to be caught by the ankles every night by a couple of spear-carriers being long gone.

To achieve this ending, Rourke did a lot of cutting, finally diminishing the political play she'd announced at the beginning. All of 4.4 was axed ('See you yond coign of the Capitol?') along with anything more from Menenius, the Tribunes or the plebs. So was 4.5, cutting Virgilia, Valeria and Young Martius. 4.6 was cut to focus on martial bodies and dangerous, hyper-militarized seconds, shorn of 'Lords' and any voice that widened the angle on this ending. Gone was that most challengingly limp of 'political' statements, the one that so anti-climactically gathers up the past in *Coriolanus* and spells the future: 'Let's make the best of it.' The lights went down on a bleeding corpse. Off, came the sound of a child's voice singing.

This last flourish made no sense at all, was merely decoration, the initial idea of the child long-dropped from this production. Still, I was ultimately glad that Hiddleston's Coriolanus wouldn't survive in a Rome that didn't need real heroes – didn't need them because the Tribunes, matrons, Senators, citizens would all be spin-doctoring fake 'heroes' in their own image.

It wasn't until I got to *Hamlet* in Manchester that I detected a sub-theme running through this year's productions. Seriously dysfunctional mothers. Volumnia and Tamora are undoubtedly in a league of their own. The mothers of history and comedy are 'guilty' by their absence, leaving the mothering to the disreputable likes of Mistress Quickly (God help the child!), 'Mistress' Falstaff and screwball 'aunty' Beatrice. Cross-casting Polonius as Polonia, mother to Laertes and Ophelia, Sarah Frankcom's *Hamlet* at the Royal Exchange Manchester created a new category of maternal dysfunction, Polonius no longer a Machiavellian elder statesman or wittering maunderer, but, as Gillian Bevan played her, a ruthless, savvy, sartorially sharp career civil servant, Elsinore's answer to C.J. in *The West Wing*, a woman I suspected sang 'The Jackal' to her kids in their cradles instead of nursery rhymes. This mother would hustle her son shipboard by extending to him her credit card – then whipping it away while she dumped on him just a bit more life coaching. This mother, business-like, would force her cringingly humiliated daughter to read out to the King and Queen their son's puerile love letter, then would collude with her boss to use that daughter as 'bait' to out Prince Hamlet. It was Gertrude who instinctively put a protective arm around the girl and reacted to the plan with appalled incredulity that registered it as child abuse. (Gertrude here was magnificently played by Barbara Marten, making the most of silences to show how her husband's attentions were focused on another woman who contemptuously dismissed her.)

This production's most anticipated (and touted) casting decision was Maxine Peake as Hamlet. Now, as my colleague Tony Howard has brilliantly documented in *Women as Hamlet* (2009), cross-casting the Prince of Denmark – whom the Victorians picked out as 'feminine' for his 'unmanly' 'sensitivity' – has a long and star-studded history (Sarah Siddons, Sarah Cushman, Sarah Bernhardt, Asta Neilsen, Zinaida Raikh, Margarita Xirgu). But in England, it's not casting that's been explored for nearly forty years, since Frances de la Tour in 1979, playing a 'harsh, heartbroken' Hamlet (as Howard wrote in this year's programme note) delivered 'one of British theatre's first powerful responses to Thatcherism's claim that there is no such thing as society'.

The politics of Frankcom's production were nothing like as inflected. Initially, it looked like this modern-dress *Hamlet* designed by Amanda Stoodley was going to be all about acting. The centre of the octagonal Exchange space was occupied with tables piled with the materials of performance: boxes marked 'this way up', foils protruding; crowns, bags, nursery-school-sized chairs, signals that disappeared (along with the stylization they perhaps suggested) when these tables were slid out to be replaced in the first court scene (naturalism settling in) with a long dinner table whose guests emptied it, leaving Peake's Hamlet miserably alone. (Briefly, and too late to be anything but perplexing, stylization did return late in the play, when the graveyard was constructed of jumble sale clothing – the cast-offs of the dead? – dumped from above, pushed into coffin-sized shapes that one of the gravediggers laid himself inside, to measure the fit. The skulls, including Yorick's, were fashioned from knotted jumpers.)

Did it matter that Peake was cross-cast? For the most part, no. Hamlet knows he is an actor who's having trouble acting. Peake was simply the latest actor to think through Hamlet's struggles of conscience, consciousness and actorly method. Her Hamlet could have passed for the Winslow boy: hair boyishly cropped and lightened to childish fairness; an adolescent, pre-sexual frame; given to mischief (reading *The Prince* when Polonia interrupted him); but also to the kind of cruel rage that comes from a kid whose adult-derived opinions haven't yet been tested, bashed around, and forced by experience into the kindness of compromise. This Hamlet's savaging of Ophelia left the girl's lacerated mind in tatters. (A heart-breaking performance by Katie West, an actor definitely to keep an eye on. She made Ophelia, achingly, as much a child teetering on adulthood as Hamlet and as much an object of adult manipulation. During her big brother's embarrassing homily about keeping 'chaste treasures' locked up from princely pilfering, her 'big' act of defiance was to pour herself an adult glass of wine, tilt her chair back from the dinner table, and swig it.) Her 'rose of fashion' speech came from a mind in shards, the words merely distraction for her tongue while she gathered up the pieces of her shredded love letter, hiding them behind her back, hands working spasmodically, when the Toms who'd been peeping on that scene emerged to dismiss her to invisibility.

For the most part, no again – given Frankcom's further cross-casting throughout: the Player King was a Queen (and it was deeply satisfying to hear the story of Hecuba in Troy told by the powerful Claire Benedict); the Queen, played by Ben Stott. Rosencrantz was a female youth (Jodie McNee) who doubled, alongside Michelle Butterly, the Gravediggers. As in a Propeller production, actors played parts, not gender positions.

But occasionally the cross-casting did matter – mattered by releasing something new to spectators' eyes. As in 3.4. Hamlet was in mid-tirade, haranguing his mother in graphic, not to say hysterical, terms about her love life, stewing in 'the rank sweat of an enseamed bed', reviling her replacement husband as 'A slave', 'A king of shreds and patches',

33. Hamlet, 4.4. Royal Exchange Theatre, directed by Sarah Frankcom. Maxine Peake as Hamlet.

when he was interrupted by another king of shreds and patches, the ghost of his father, played by John Shrapnel who also doubled Claudius. Hamlet's reaction was shocking. He shrank, suddenly infantilized by terror like a child into the protection of his mother's lap, cowering from this ghost, in desperate need of the prophylactic of a prayer jibberingly choked out: 'Save me, and hover o'er me with your wings, / You heavenly guards!' It was as though Peake's Hamlet saw both father-figures collapsed into one, both contemptuous of 'unmanly'-ness, both bullish and bullet-headed, both demanding, both menacing, punishing. Terror made this Hamlet not just childish but womanish. And that was the irony. Had he been able to admit the woman in him, a thought that came naturally, seeing Peake as Hamlet, he might have been able to reject the assignment both fathers laid on their sons (natural or adopted): revenge.

He and Laertes might have gotten out of this play alive.

But if cross-casting Hamlet made little difference here, casting Maxine Peake in the part in Manchester certainly did. She's a Mancuian lass-made-good, stage and TV star who started her climb to the top in the Royal Exchange Youth Group and this year returned for a two-year stint as Associate Artist. Her commitment, and Frankcom's, to building up the youth company and youth audience were visibly articulated in this Hamlet. They cast a total of 21 youngsters, children and members of the Royal Exchange's Young Company, to work on stage beside her, Shrapnel, Marten and Benedict, making up the numbers in a cry of players along the lines of Molière's family outfit, under the watchful eye of Benedict-as-matriarch. They earned their keep. As kids (able to collapse in spectacular fashion and *bounce*) they performed a much more alarmingly athletic Dumbshow than normally is on offer. Highlighting locality, Peake in the programme declared she felt 'no need to compete with London'; 'local people', she wrote, needed 'a voice and a creative outlet' locally. So this *Hamlet*, as the strapline had it, was 'a *Hamlet* for now, a *Hamlet* for Manchester'.

But if so, why did Peake (whose radio interviews were all spoken in her 'native' accent) play Hamlet in a non-Manchester voice? A fake London voice? Why (beyond the obvious, local rivalry) were the gravediggers the only regionally voiced parts, 'comic' Scousers? What was she telling the children about Shakespeare, Hamlet and Manchester?

Initially, Sam Mendes's *King Lear* at the National Theatre, like Frankcom's *Hamlet* in Manchester, looked to be all about acting. A functional runway connected the Olivier theatre stalls to the stage. On it was set a low chair, facing, on stage, another chair, that also faced upstage towards a blank wall, a microphone on a stand set next to it. The chairs looked like they were expecting a performance; the microphone, like it was going to have something to say about that performance. The chairs' two locations suggested multiple points of view: long shot, close up.

But this set-up, scaled to human bodies – of course we recognized the meta-theatrical conceit; we were sitting one row back, spectators waiting for a performance – was framed by something much larger, stranger, metaphysical, cosmic: the projection on a blue-black screen overhead of a pulsating sun, volcanically erupting at the edges with outbursts of what looked like gigantic coronal loops giving off orange aureoles. Anthony Ward's design suggested that Mendes's *Lear* would be having it both ways: micro, macro; a play about family dysfunction; a play about the 'frame of nature' 'wrench'd' 'From the fix'd place', the universe collapsing in a black hole, time ended. His design would take spectators past a number of false fronts, receding sets of blank walls that would fly out to reveal, ultimately, vast vistas, then a wasteland that reified the wilderness of Lear's 'child-chang'd' mind.

The opening exchanges ('I thought the king...') established Stephen Boxer's goateed Gloucester as the kind of court flunky who survives despotic regimes by always standing just outside the limelight (so, later, groping about in the most earth-shattering storm known since Noah, he carried a pencil torch); Stanley Townsend's Kent as a bearish bruiser in military uniform primed to throw his weight around; and Sam Troughton's Uriah Heepish Edmund, peering through horn-rims, as a fully signed-up meritocrat determined to wipe out bastardy with sycophancy, in Whitehall-issue suit, waistcoat and striped tie, his dad's lackey, hugging the papers Gloucester couldn't be bothered any longer to shuffle, standing to attention like somebody's doorman so far stage left as to be in the wings, waiting to be noticed but demonstrating in every tensed muscle that he was listening to every word passed.

When a sound cue announced Lear's entrance the wall behind this trio flew out, discovering a table stretching the width of the stage, set up as though for a press conference in some vast, dark, industrial warehouse, the table set with three microphones. Simon Russell Beale's Lear rolled in, leading with his chin, barrel-chested, a geriatric skin-head with a white beard, his uniform not service-able, but the kind you see on military dictators. He settled himself into the chair facing the table where the family had filed in, the daughters taking seats, the husbands beside them, an empty chair flanking Cordelia, while behind them mustered, in the deep shadows, a platoon of black berets. On the runway, a figure squatted: Fool (Adrian Scarborough), watching Lear as he swung the arm of his microphone and growled down it, dividing his kingdom, then pushed it away to pause, to address his family direct. 'Tell me, my *daughters*...' made whatever he was up to something dreamed up on the spot. Goneril (Kate Fleetwood) and Regan (Anna Maxwell Martin) checked their husbands; Cordelia (Olivia Vinall) stared straight ahead. When Goneril, like a cat negotiating barbed wire, a mass of tensed repression that registered her the responsible daughter who always aimed to please (and failed), finished,

34. *King Lear*, 1.1. National Theatre, directed by Sam Mendes. Simon Russell Beale as King Lear, Stanley Townsend as Kent.

put down her microphone (for these were girls expected to address dad down the apparatus), her father rose, circled behind her, fronted her, peered into her eyes, searched her face, and began a slow handclap that mocked her speech by turning it into 'merely' a performance. It was terrifying. Humiliating. Mental cruelty in action. Next came Regan, the hatchet-faced sister who made up for her plainness with studied sexual allure and little girl flirtatiousness. She crooned down the microphone, circled *to* daddy, sat on his lap, gave him a big kiss, giggled when he slapped her bottom. Then came Cordelia. She pushed the microphone away. Her 'Nothing' needed no amplification. Her 'Nothing' puzzled Lear. He stood, silent, polishing his fingertips across the table surface. Then lifted his grizzled head. And exploded.

'Let it be so! Thy truth then be thy dower!' caught everyone unaware, released a ferocious

flash-flood that swept away everything in its reasonless current. Cordelia reeled. Kent wedged his body between hers and Lear's. Fool ran down the gangway and tried to intervene. No time for reaction. The multi-vehicle pile-up raced towards head-on collision. 'Better thou / Hadst not been born than not t'have pleased me better!' was bellowed down Lear's microphone. When the scene finally emptied of its human wreckage, a spotlight picked out Edmund. Left over. Motionless. Watching.

This opening set the terms of all that followed. The fine detail of these actors' performances made the stories *Lear* tells utterly lucid – and taking sides impossible. (As things turned out, the multiple point of view of the opening set up was the only way to see things clearly in Lear's Britain.) The whole family (and their extras) had a mean streak. Meanness whose apotheosis was exquisite cruelty. At home at Goneril's Russell Beale's cardiganed

Lear had to pad around in his sock feet because his daughter had Oswald 'lose' his slippers. To reach his audience, Fool walked over Goneril's dining table where Lear's rowdies had dumped their bleeding kill, a stag, then launched into a patter routine, wheeling a little shopping cart, out of which he pulled props and gags, getting the lads to belt out a round that he suddenly cut, leaving Lear the only one singing, pitilessly exposed as the fool, stranded in his 'nothing'-ness. Regan mashed a high-heel into disguised Kent's face as he sat manacled in Gloucester's courtyard to a massive, fascist-design statue of King Lear in his hey-day. Attending her husband's funeral under black umbrellas in a fetchingly stylish widow's fascinator, she propositioned Edmund with sexual threats. Cornwall took Gloucester to his wine cellar to put out his eyes – but at the last moment substituted for a broken bottle his bare hands. Cordelia talked of 'love, pure love' – holding an assault rifle, and wearing combat gear. Goneril, twitchily chain-smoking, tried patience with her wayward dad, coaxing him like a slightly dim three-year-old, but when he turned vicious, cursed her womb, she suddenly slapped him hard across the face, a slap she instantly moved to recall. And couldn't. Lear's incredulous 'Yea, is it come to this?' met with Goneril slowly nodding her head.

These domestic close-ups were devastating; Mendes's pull-backs into long shot nothing like as effective. He wanted *Lear* somehow to be about the 'matter' of (greater) Britain. Besides, he had thirty extras to keep occupied, fine when Lear has troops of knights in tow, harder when his 'need' is cut to less than 'one'. After they'd lost their jobs as soldiers, Mendes redeployed the extras as homeless wanderers across Edgar's heath (or David Cameron's London). But they were in hoodies and carrying sleeping bags, living rough; he, stripped naked, rattling a tin cup. By any measure of contemporary urban destitution, Edgar was improbably underdressed (and surely would have been arrested as a flasher). Other effects grated: a hydraulic lift that raised Lear and Fool vertiginously upwards in the storm (why?); a silly wedge

that literalized the edge of Dover Cliff (why again? the *edge isn't there!*); the Medical Corps running the mad old king to ground, strait-jacketing and injecting him, then bringing him back round to consciousness in a military field hospital not with music but a hypodermic. It was as though Mendes was thinking of the Olivier stage as a film set, striving for big effects to make good that opening bid for cosmic scale.

But little of that mattered against the stature of Russell Beale's performance – a performance that mapped the progress of dementia with awful precision, from the common or garden variety madness of the totalitarian (who goes crazy for real when he discovers he's not 'ague proof') and the 'normal' insanity of the authoritarian patriarch (who goes berserk for real when he can't recognize his 'changed' daughters: 'Your name, fair gentlewoman'; 'Degenerate bastard!') to the kind of dementia that comes with senility, when the world's sense no longer makes sense, when old age, knowledge coming into and out of focus, intermittently recognizes its loss of power, as when this old man, sitting on an up-turned suitcase, realized, 'I did her wrong', or quietly confided to Fool, a moment of terrible discovery, 'O let me not be mad, not mad, sweet heaven.' Russell Beale's Lear was never more farcically pitiful than when taken to asylum, out of the storm and hovel, into some back room at Gloucester's where packing crates and spare parts for future plumbing emergencies were stored. There, with, as justices, Fool perched on a bathtub and Bedlam Beggar on an up-turned loo, Lear conducted his mad assizes, arraigning his 'pelican' daughters and, when Goneril attempted an escape, falling on her – or what he took to be her – and battering Fool to death.

Nor was he more tragically pitiable than when he stumbled upon blind Gloucester on Dover beach. He'd escaped from therapy, still had an IV line taped to the back of his hand, wore a hospital gown tied up the back – and Fool's hat. When he claimed he knew Gloucester's 'eyes well enough', he raised the mutilated man's bloody bandages and gazed into his empty eye sockets. The pain of these two old men cradling each other, talking about office, authority, the way of the world, but then mortality, and patience was that they were both momentarily completely sane men, Lear a kind of Tiresias, seeing into a different dimension.

This was a *Lear* that, finally, didn't let Lear off the hook. Or his daughters. Waking, roaring, protesting 'You do me *wrong*', he was still the old codger; Cordelia, still steely. Her father's lapse into bewilderment ('Do not mock me . . . ') and miraculous supplication ('Pray you now, forget and forgive. I am old and foolish') was surrounded with dead silence. For all his asking, this Lear was never redeemed. His tragedy, finally, was that he never *knew love*, or himself loved. Taken with Cordelia to prison his hands were tied behind his back, so there was no embrace on 'Have I caught you now?' In the last moments, he was heard before seen, howling like an animal or a soul caught in a man trap, carrying on the body of Cordelia, dumping her like so much dead meat on a table, bellowing at Albany and the rest to 'LOOK ON HER!' Kent turned away. And Albany. Looking wasn't possible. They were looking away when Lear had a heart attack in front of us – that is, we watched an old man's heart break, his breath run out. Edgar, who'd moments earlier simply stepped up to his brother, no heroics, no trial by combat, and stabbed him,

was the last man standing. He was the future. And he was wrecked.

* * *

December 2014. Going off duty, writing my last *Survey* review, I have to hand *Reviewing Shakespeare: Journalism and Performance from the Eighteenth Century to the Present*, the fine book by my colleague, Paul Prescott, published at the end of last year. I could have done with it earlier. I've been asking myself, every year for seven years, what I'm doing, as a reviewer; what the academic review of Shakespeare *is*. Prescott gives some answers. Answers, had I had them seven years back, that would have stopped me cold, not a word written, for the reviewer 'is still popularly perceived to be . . . a fault-finder, a traffic warden of the emotions, a fly in the soup at life's feast'. S/he is a 'eunuch in a harem', a 'domineering pedant' (as Berowne makes the 'critic' in *Love's Labour's Lost*: a 'night-watch constable'. Stern criticism of critics! Still, as I go off duty, I take some comfort that it's the night-watch constables, on duty in the dark, witnessing something, trying to get a version of what they saw down on paper, who do good service in Messina. Dogberry the patron saint of academic Shakespeare reviewers? One could do worse!

PROFESSIONAL SHAKESPEARE PRODUCTIONS IN THE BRITISH ISLES JANUARY-DECEMBER 2013

JAMES SHAW

Most of the productions listed are by professional companies, but some amateur productions are included. The information is taken from *Touchstone* (www.touchstone.bham.ac.uk), a Shakespeare resource maintained by the Shakespeare Institute Library. Touchstone includes a monthly list of current and forthcoming UK Shakespeare productions from listings information. The websites provided for theatre companies were accurate at the time of going to press.

ALL'S WELL THAT ENDS WELL

Royal Shakespeare Company. Royal Shakespeare Theatre, Stratford-upon-Avon, 19 July–26 September; Theatre Royal, Newcastle-upon-Tyne, 5–9 November.
www.rsc.org.uk
Countess: Charlotte Cornwall
Parolles: Jonathan Slinger
Helena: Joanna Horton
Director: Nancy Meckler

ANTONY AND CLEOPATRA

Another Way Theatre Company. Minack Theatre, Cornwall, 3–7 June and tour.
www.anotherwaytheatre.co.uk
Director: Chris Chambers

Royal Shakespeare Company and GableStage (Miami). Swan Theatre, Stratford-upon-Avon, 13–30 November; and USA tour January-March 2014.

www.rsc.org.uk
Cleopatra: Joaquina Kalukango
Antony: Jonathan Cake
Adaptor and Director: Tarell Alvin McCraney
Set in Napoleonic Haiti.

AS YOU LIKE IT

Royal Shakespeare Company. Royal Shakespeare Theatre, Stratford-upon-Avon, 24 April–28 September; Theatre Royal, Newcastle-upon-Tyne, 29 October–13 November.
www.rsc.org.uk
Rosalind: Pippa Nixon
Director: Maria Aberg
Music: Laura Marling

Marjanishvili Theatre, Tbilisi, Georgia. Shakespeare's Globe, London, 6–11 May.
www.shakespearesglobe.com
Director: Levan Tsuladze
Performed in Georgian with scene synopses in English.

Cut to the Chase Company. Queen's Theatre, Hornchurch, 4–14 June.
www.queens-theatre.co.uk
Director: Bob Carlton

Illyria Theatre Company. Greys Court, Henley, 22 June and tour to 18 August.
www.illyria.uk.com

The Lord Chamberlain's Men. The Tobacco Factory, Bristol, 10 July and tour to 8 September.

www.tlcm.co.uk
Director: Andrew Normington

Rose Theatre, London, 1–26 October.
www.rosetheatre.org.uk
Director: Jessica Ruano
Comic sub-plot completely cut, including Touchstone.

Transport Theatre with Les Theatres de la Ville
de Luxembourg. New Wolsey Theatre, Ipswich,
9–12 October and tour to 22 November.
www.transport-theatre.eu
Director: Douglas Rintoul
Opens in a Calais detention centre and explores
issues of banishment.

THE COMEDY OF ERRORS

Rain or Shine Theatre Company. Bishops
Waltham School, Bishops Waltham, 23 May and
tour to 1 September.
www.rainorshine.co.uk

Stamford Shakespeare. Rutland Open Air Theatre,
Tolethorpe Hall, 4 June–20 July.
www.stamfordshakespeare.co.uk

Principal Theatre Company. Capel Manor,
Enfield, 13–22 June and tour to 2 August.
www.principaltheatrecompany.com
Directed: Paul Gladwell

Oddsocks Productions. The Lights, Andover,
3 July and tour to 8 September.
www.oddsocks.co.uk

CORIOLANUS

Donmar Warehouse, London, 17 December–13
February 2014. Broadcast live in cinemas around
the world as part of National Theatre Live,
beginning 30 January 2014.
www.donmarwarehouse.com
Coriolanus: Tom Hiddleston
Volumnia: Deborah Findlay
Menenius: Mark Gatiss
Director: Josie Rourke

Adaptation
Beijing People's Art Theatre. Edinburgh Playhouse, 20–21 August.
www.eif.co.uk
Directed: Lin Zhaohua
Including live music from Chinese heavy metals
bands. Performed in Mandarin with English surtitles.

CYMBELINE

Pistachio Choice Productions. The Drayton Theatre, Upstairs at the Drayton Arms, London,
5–30 March.
www.pistachiochoice.com
Director: Antonio Ferrara

Les Foules Theatre Company. The Space Arts Centre, London, 28 May–15 June.
http://lesfoulestheatre.com
Director: Nathalie Adlam

Adaptation
Cymbeline: Love's Reason's Without Reason
Phizzical Theatre. Tacchi Morris, Taunton,
2 October and tour to 5 December.
www.phizzical.com
Director: Samir Bhamra
Cymbeline played as a Bollywood mogul.

HAMLET

Rose Theatre, London. 5 February–3 March.
www.rosetheatre.org.uk
Hamlet: Jonathan Broadbent
Voice of Ghost: Simon Russell Beale
Director: Martin Parr
Performed on the site of the original Rose Theatre.
A cast of four with only Hamlet undoubled.

Everyman Theatre. Cardiff Arts Centre, Cardiff,
12–16 March.
www.everymantheatre.co.uk
Set as a play-within-a-play in the sixteenth-century
village of Canton.

Royal Shakespeare Company. Royal Shakespeare Theatre, Stratford-upon-Avon, 26 March–28 September; Theatre Royal, Newcastle-upon-Tyne, 18–26 October.
www.rsc.org.uk
Hamlet: Jonathan Slinger
Director: David Farr

Ouroboros Players. Drayton Arms Theatre, South Kensington, 2–27 April.
www.thedraytonarmsnorthkensington.co.uk
Directors: B. E. Johnston and Richard Crawford

Principal Theatre Company. Southgate Old Ashmolean Rugby Club, London, 3–5 July and tour to 2 August.
www.principaltheatrecompany.com
Director: Paul Gladwell

Bedouin Shakespeare Company. Network Theatre, London, 17 December 2012–12 January.
www.networktheatre.org
Director: Jimmy Walters

Ballet
Bloomsbury Theatre, London, 15–24 May.
Composer: Rued Langgaard
Choreographer: Peter Schaufuss
Using monologues recorded by John Gielgud.

Adaptation
The Purple Hibiscus Theatre Company. The Space Arts Centre, 12–16 February.
www.purplehibiscus.org.uk
Adaptor and Director: Marco Rossi
All-female cast.

Something is Rotten at The Rose!
The Rose Theatre, London, 16–18 April.
www.rosetheatre.org.uk
Director: Kitter Krebs
Selection of sonnets and passages from *Hamlet*.

Hamlet's Fool
Cockpit Theatre, London, 10–11 May.
www.thecockpit.org.uk
Playwright: Peter Cutts
Director: Mandy Fox
One man show focusing on the life of Yorick.

Hamlet de los Andes
Teatro de los Andes (Bolivia). The Pit, London, 2–3 October.
Director: Diego Aramburo
Set in modern Bolivia with a cast of three. Performed in Spanish with English surtitles.

KDC Theatre. Lion and Unicorn Theatre, London, 26–30 November.
www.lionandunicorntheatre.com
Director: Kat Wootton
Hamlet as teenage girl.

HENRY V

Michael Grandage Company. Noël Coward Theatre, London, 3 December–15 February 2014.
www.michaelgrandagecompany.com
Henry V: Jude Law
Director: Michael Grandage

Adaptation
Henry the Fifth
Unicorn Theatre Company. Weston Theatre, London, 11 October-16 November.
www.unicorntheatre.com
Adaptor: Ignace Cornelissen
Director: Ellen McDougall
Staged as an escalating playground fight over a sandcastle.

HENRY VI, PART I

Henry VI: Harry the Sixth
Shakespeare's Globe. Globe Theatre, London, 23 July and on tour.
www.shakespearesglobe.com
Director: Nick Bagnall

HENRY VI, PART 2

Henry VI: The Houses of York and Lancaster
Shakespeare's Globe. Globe Theatre, London, 23 July and on tour.
www.shakespearesglobe.com
Director: Nick Bagnall

HENRY VI, PART 3

Henry VI: The True Tragedy of the Duke of York
Shakespeare's Globe. Globe Theatre, London, 23 July and on tour.
www.shakespearesglobe.com
Director: Nick Bagnall

JULIUS CAESAR

Iris Theatre. St. Paul's Church, London, 26 June–26 July.
Director: Daniel Winder
Cast of four.

Bard in the Botanics. Kibble Palace Glasshouse, Glasgow, 12–27 July.
http://bardinthebotanics.co.uk
Director: Jennifer Dick
Cast of four.

Venture Wolf Productions. London Theatre, New Cross, London, 19–24 November.
www.venturewolf.yolasite.com

Donmar Theatre Company, 4 December 2012–9 February.
www.donmarwarehouse.com
Caesar: Frances Barber
Brutus: Harriet Walter
Director: Phyllida Lloyd
All-female cast. Set in a women's prison with the inmates staging the play.

KING LEAR

Shakespeare's Globe. Globe Theatre, London, 13 May and UK and international tour to 3 August.
www.shakespearesglobe.com
Lear: Joseph Marcell
Director: Bill Buckhurst

Lazarus Theatre Company. Greenwich Theatre, London, 16 May–1 June.
lazarustheatrecompany.webs.com
Lear: Jennifer Shakesby
Director: Ricky Dukes
Female Lear.

Theatre Royal, Bath, 31 July-10 August.
http://theatreroyal.org.uk
Lear: David Haig
Director: Lucy Bailey
Set in 1960's gangland London.

Belarus Free Theatre, Minsk, Belarus. Globe Theatre, London, 23–28 September.
www.shakespearesglobe.com
Performed in Belarusian with scene synopses in English.

Chichester Festival Theatre. Minerva Theatre, Chichester, 31 October-30 November; at the BAM Harvey Theater, Brooklyn, NY, 7 January–9 February 2014; and on tour.
www.cft.org.uk
Lear: Frank Langella
Director: Angus Jackson

LOVE'S LABOUR'S LOST

Grassroots Shakespeare London. Old Red Lion, London, 19 June–27 July.
www.grassrootsshakespearelondon.com
Director: Siobhan Daly

MACBETH

Titan Repertory Theatre Company. Camden People's Theatre, London, 5–24 February.
titantheatrecompany.com
Director: Amber Elliot

Trafalgar Studios, London, 9 February-27 April.
www.trafalgar-studios.co.uk
Macbeth: James McAvoy
Lady Macbeth: Claire Foy
Director: Jamie Lloyd
Set in a future dystopia.

Shakespeare's Globe. Globe Theatre, London, 22 June-13 October. Broadcast as part of Shakespeare's Globe on Screen in cinemas throughout the UK, beginning 25 June 2014.
www.shakespearesglobe.com
Director: Eve Best

The director played Lady Macbeth at the Globe in 2001.

WOH Productions. Rose Theatre, London, 3–28 July.
www.wohproductions.com
Macbeth: Clive Moore
Lady Macbeth/Banquo: Francesca De Sica
Director: Manuela Ruggerio

Manchester International Festival, St Peter's Church, Manchester, 5–21 July 2013; at Park Avenue Armory, New York, 31 May-22 June 2014; and tour. Broadcast by National Theatre Live to cinemas worldwide, beginning July 2013.
www.mif.co.uk
Macbeth: Kenneth Branagh
Lady Macbeth: Alex Kingston
Directors: Rob Ashford and Kenneth Branagh

Cordial Theatre. The Duke New End Theatre, Hampstead, London, 10 September–5 October.
www.cordialproductions.co.uk

Horsecross Arts. Perth Theatre Company, and Tron at Perth Theatre, Perth, 20 September–5 October, and tour.
www.horsecross.co.uk
Director: Rachel O'Riordan

Little Angel Theatre, London, 10 October–10 November.
www.littleangeltheatre.com
Director: Peter Glanville
Well-received puppet version, with the characters represented by birds.

Infinite Space Theatre Company. Cockpit Theatre, London, 10–26 October.
http://cockpittheatre.org.uk
Director: Nick Hastings
Set in a world of corporate finance, featuring the Royal Bank of Dunsinane led by Duncan.

Ballet
Mac//Beth
De Oscuro. Wales Millenium Centre, Cardiff, 1–6 November; Royal Opera House, Linbury Studio, London, 12–13 November and tour.

www.de-oscuro.com
Director and choreography: Judith Roberts
Predominantly Welsh language translation combining dance and text.

Adaptation
Ubu Roi
Cheek By Jowl. Warwick Arts Centre, University of Warwick, Coventry, 30 January–2 February and tour to 20 April.
www.cheekbyjowl.com
Playwright: Alfred Jarry
Director: Declan Donnellan
In French.

Macbeth in Pitch Black
London Contemporary Theatre Company. Brentwood Theatre, Brentwood, 23–24 May; Swindon Arts Centre, 11 November.
www.londoncontemporarytheatre.com
Director: Kevin Williams
Performed in the dark.

Dunsinane
National Theatre of Scotland and The Royal Shakespeare Company. His Majesty's Theatre, Aberdeen, 3–7 September and tour to 12 October. Revival of 2010 production.
www.nationaltheatrescotland.com
Playwright: David Grieg
Director: Roxana Silbert
Explores events after Shakespeare's play.

MacBheatha
Citizens Theatre, Glasgow. 25–28 September.
http://citz.co.uk
Gaelic version for two actors.

Macbeth of Fire and Ice
Double Act Ltd. Arcola Theatre, Studio 1, London, 4–16 November.
Director: Jon Gun Thor
Influenced by Norse mythology, including a prologue involving Nordic creation myth.

The Scottish Play
Tap the Table Theatre, London Theatre, New Cross, London, 12–17 November.

www.tapthetable.com
Playwright: Tom Loveridge
Focusing on mental health issues through the use of devised material, Shakespeare's text and physical humour.

MEASURE FOR MEASURE

The Cockpit. Cockpit Theatre, London, 14–23 March.
www.thecockpit.org.uk

Immersion Theatre Company. Jack Studio Theatre, London, 2–20 July.
www.immersiontheatre.co.uk
Director: James Tobias

The Steam Industry. Union Theatre, London, 2–27 July.
www.steamindustryfreetheatre.org.uk
Isabella: Daisy Ward
Vincentio: Nicholas Osmond
Director: Phil Willmott

THE MERCHANT OF VENICE

Worcester Repertory Company. Lady Chapel, Worcester Cathedral, Worcester, 15–18 October; Malvern Priory, Malvern, 25–26 October.
www.worcester-rep-co.uk
Director: Chris Jaeger

Lazarus Theatre Company. Jack Studio Theatre, London, 19 November–7 December.
http://lazarustheatrecompany.webs.com

Adaptation
Shylock
Theatre Tours International. Assembly George Square, Edinburgh, 12 August.
www.theatretoursinternational.com
Playwright: Gareth Armstrong

Pocket Merchant
Propeller Theatre Company. Gorvy Lecture Theatre, Victoria & Albert Museum, London, 30 September and tour to 9 November.

www.propeller.org.uk
Director: Edward Hall
Immediately following the show the audience were invited to express their response.

THE MERRY WIVES OF WINDSOR

Oxford Shakespeare Company. Moser Theatre, Wadham College, Oxford, 8 July–16 August.
www.oxfordshakespearecompany.co.uk
Composer: Nick Lloyd Webber
Director: Gemma Fairlie

Creative Cow. The Rosemary Branch, London, 15 October and tour to 3 November.
www.creativecow.co.uk

Opera
Falstaff
Glyndebourne Opera House, 19 May–14 July.
www.glyndebourne.com
Composer: Giuseppe Verdi
Director: Richard Jones

A MIDSUMMER NIGHT'S DREAM

Grassroots Shakespeare Company. The Lion and Unicorn Theatre. The Giant Olive Theatre, London, 11 December 2012–5 January.
www.grassrootsshakespearelondon.com
A company without a director.

Custom/Practice. Hall of Cornwall, Truro, 14 January and UK tour to 17 March.
www.custompractice.co.uk
Director: Rae McKen

Sell a Door Theatre Company. Town Hall, Falkirk, 21–22 February, and tour.
www.selladoor.com
Director: Bryn Holding

Bristol Old Vic and Handspring Puppet Company. Old Vic, Bristol, 7 March–4 May; Barbican, London, 10–15 February 2014 and tour.
www.bristololdvic.org.uk
Director: Tom Morris

Featuring puppets from the company that designed the puppets for *War Horse*.

Norwich Players. Maddermarket Theatre, Norwich, 21–30 March.
Director: Chris Bealey

Royal & Derngate. Royal & Derngate Theatre, Northampton, 19 April–11 May.
www.royalandderngate.co.uk
Director: Gary Sefton

Shakespeare's Globe. Globe Theatre, London, 30 May–12 October. Broadcast as part of Shakespeare's Globe on Screen in cinemas throughout the United Kingdom, beginning 15 July 2014.
www.shakespearesglobe.com
Titania/Hippolyta: Michelle Terry
Bottom: Pearce Quigley
Director: Dominic Dromgoole

The Festival Players. Whittington Castle, Whittington, 1 June and tour to 18 August.
www.thefestivalplayers.co.uk

Taking Flight Theatre Company. Brighton Festival, 1–2 June and tour to 18 August.
www.takingflighttheatre.co.uk

Stamford Shakespeare. Rutland Open Air Theatre, Tolethorpe Hall, 11 June–17 August.
www.stamfordshakespeare.co.uk

Chapterhouse Theatre Company. Nottingham Castle, Nottingham, 20–21 June and tour until August.
www.chapterhouse.org

Butterfly Theatre Productions. St James Studio, London, 4–13 July.
http://wearebutterfly.com
Director: Aileen Gonsalves
45-minute version billed as lunchtime theatre.

Chester Performs. Grosvenor Park Open Air Theatre, Chester, 5 July–25 August.
Director: Alex Clifton
Puck played by identical twins.

Whistlestop Theatre. Baron's Court Theatre, London, 31 July–11 August.
www.whistlestoptheatre.co.uk

Rose Theatre, London, 1–24 August.
www.rosetheatre.org.uk
Director: David Pearce

Tooting Arts Club. Broadway Studios, Tooting, London, 13 August–7 September.
www.tootingartsclub.co.uk
Director: Bill Buckhurst

Michael Grandage Company. Noël Coward Theatre, London, 17 September–16 November.
www.michaelgrandagecompany.com
Bottom: David Walliams
Titania/Hippolyta: Sheridan Smith
Director: Michael Grandage

Ballet
Ballet Cymru. Theatre by the Lake, Keswick, 13–14 May and tour to 27 October.
www.welshballet.co.uk
Composer: Felix Mendelssohn

Northern Ballet. West Yorkshire Playhouse, Leeds, 6–14 September and tour to 31 May 2014.
www.northernballet.com
Composer: Felix Mendelssohn

Opera
Royal Conservatoire of Scotland & Scottish Opera. Theatre Royal, Glasgow, 25–26 January; King's Theatre, Edinburgh, 31 January–1 February.
www.scottishopera.org.uk
Composer: Benjamin Britten
Director: Olivia Fuchs

Opera North. Grand Theatre & Opera House, Leeds, 28 September–24 October and tour to 15 November.
www.operanorth.co.uk
Composer: Benjamin Britten

Adaptation
Titania
Moon Fool. Drill Hall, Lincoln, 8 May and tour to 13 July.

www.moonfool.com
Adaptor and Performer: Anna-Helena McLean
Solo musical cabaret.

MUCH ADO ABOUT NOTHING

Bard in the Botanics. Botanic Gardens, Glasgow, 12–27 July.
http://bardinthebotanics.co.uk
Director: Gordon Barr

Old Vic, London, 16 September–30 November.
www.oldvictheatre.com
Benedick: James Earl Jones
Beatrice: Vanessa Redgrave
Director: Mark Rylance

Traffic of the Stage. Upstairs at the Gatehouse, London, 1–12 October and tour to 27 November.
www.trafficofthestage.com

ACS Random. Park Theatre, London, 3–15 December.
Director: Andrew Shepherd

OTHELLO

Peckham Theatre Company. Bussey Building, 25 January–22 February.
Director: Anthony Green

The Black Box Theatre Company. Theatr Colwyn, Colwyn Bay, 13 March and tour to 27 April.
www.blackboxmerseyside.co.uk

Grassroots Shakespeare London. Lion and Unicorn Theatre, London, 16 April–11 May.
www.grassrootsshakespearelondon.com

National Theatre Company. Olivier Theatre, London, 23 April–5 October. Broadcast by National Theatre Live to cinemas worldwide, beginning 12 October.
www.nationaltheatre.org.uk
Iago: Rory Kinnear
Othello: Adrian Lester
Director: Nicholas Hytner

The Evening Standard award for best actor was shared between the two leads.

Bard in the Botanics. Botanical Gardens, Glasgow, 21 June–6 July.
Director: Gordon Barr
http://bardinthebotanics.co.uk

The Icarus Theatre Collective and Original Theatre Company. Kings Theatre, Southsea, 12–13 September and tour to 7 April 2014.
www.icarustheatre.org
Director: Max Lewendel

Suba Das Company. Broadway Theatre, London, 24–26 October.
www.thebroadwaybarking.com

East London Shakespeare Company. Etcetera Theatre, London, 12–17 November.
http://eastlondonshakespearecompany.org

Actors from the London Stage. The Cockpit, London, 25 November and tour.

Opera
Otello
Opera North. Leeds Grand Theatre, Leeds, 16 January–16 February and tour to 23 March.
www.operanorth.co.uk
Composer: Giuseppe Verdi

Adaptation
Come Heavy Sleep
Kindle Theatre. Studio, Birmingham Rep, Birmingham, 13–14 December.
www.kindletheatre.org.uk
A murder story inspired by *Othello*.

Othello Syndrome
Sky Or The Bird Theatre Company. The Drayton Theatre, Outer London, 3–28 September.
www.skyorthebird.com
Adaptor and Director: Hannah Kaye
A narrator inserts contemporary historical information relating to violence against women.

Othello the Remix
The Q Brothers, Chicago Shakespeare Theater, Unicorn Theatre, London, 12–29 September.

www.qbrothers.com
Hip-hop version.

PERICLES

Pistachio Choice Theatre Company. 5 February–2
   March, Drayton Arms, London.
www.pistachiochoice.com
Director: Drew Mulligan
Cast of four.

RICHARD II

Royal Shakespeare Company. Royal Shakespeare
   Theatre, Stratford-upon-Avon, 17 October–
   16 November; Barbican Theatre, London,
   9 December–25 January 2014. Broadcast live to
   cinemas worldwide, beginning 13 November.
www.rsc.org.uk
Richard II: David Tennant
Duchess of Gloucester: Jane Lapotaire
Director: Gregory Doran

Adaptation
Hip Hop Shakespeare Company. Richard II Live
   Tour. The Drum, Birmingham, 5 June and tour
   to 6 October.
www.hiphopshakespeare.com
Director: Akala
Hip-hop version. A medley of songs adapted from
   the text and themes of *Richard II*.

RICHARD III

Shakespeare at the Tobacco Factory. Tobacco Factory, Bristol, 20 February–30 March.
http://sattf.org.uk
Richard: John Mackay
Director: Andrew Hilton
The opening speech delivered with the house lights
   up.

Nottingham Playhouse/York Theatre Royal, 29
   October–16 November.
www.nottinghamplayhouse.co.uk
Richard: Ian Bartholomew
Director: Loveday Ingram

Shakespeare's Globe Company. Apollo Theatre,
   West End, 2 November 2012–10 February.
www.shakespeares-globe.org
Richard: Mark Rylance
Director: Tim Carroll

Adaptation
Crookback
Etcetera Theatre, London, 9–21 July.
www.etceteratheatre.com
Playwright: Tim Welham
Director: Megan Watson
One man play.

The Resistible Rise of Arturo Ui
Chichester Theatre Company. Minerva Theatre,
   Chichester, 15 August–14 September; Duchess
   Theatre, London, 18 September–7 December.
www.cft.org.uk
Playwright: Bertolt Brecht
Director: Jonathan Church
Arturo: Henry Goodman

ROMEO AND JULIET

Icarus Theatre Collective & Kings Theatre Southsea. Hawthorne Theatre, Welwyn Garden City,
   21 January and tour to 13 May.
www.icarustheatre.org
Director: Max Lewendel

Hiraeth Artistic Productions. Upstairs at the Gatehouse, London, 6 February–2 March.
www.hiraeth-theatre.co.uk
Director: Zoe Ford

Theatre Sotto Voce. Holy Trinity Church, Sloane
   Street, London, 21 February–9 March.
www.theatresottovoce.co.uk
Director: Emma Butler

Theatre Royal Bury St Edmunds. Theatre Royal
   Bury St Edmunds, 21 February–9 March.
Director: Lynn Whitehead

Shakespeare's Globe. Globe Theatre, London, 13–
   26 March and international tour.

www.shakespearesglobe.com
Director: Bill Buckhurst

Geboo Productions. Leicester Square Theatre, London, 29 April.
Director: Bryn Williams

Heartbreak Productions. Jephson Gardens, Leamington Spa, 5–6 June and tour to 31 August.
www.heartbreakproductions.co.uk

Festival Players. Summer Tour. Kington & Dormston Village Hall, 8 June and tour to 18 August.
www.thefestivalplayers.co.uk

Grassroots Shakespeare. Old Red Lion, London, 18 June–27 July.
www.grassrootsshakespeare.com

National Theatre. The Shed, London, 24 July–2 August.
www.nationaltheatre.org.uk
Director: Bijan Sheibani
A version for younger audiences.

Cut String Theatre. The Rag Factory, London, 7–17 August.
www.cutstringtheatre.co.uk
Director: Max Packman-Walder

Reading Between The Lines Theatre. Greenwich Theatre, London, 4–5 October.
www.readingbetweenthelines.co.uk
Director: Hal Chambers

Ballet
Moscow City Ballet. Theatre Royal, Bath, 11–12 March.
Composer: Sergei Prokofiev

National Ballet of Canada. Sadler's Wells Theatre, London, 17–21 April.
http://national.ballet.ca
Composer: Sergei Prokofiev

Ballet Cymru. The Riverfront Theatre, Newport, 3–4 May.
www.welshballet.co.uk
Composer: Sergei Prokofiev

Peter Schaufuss Ballet. Royal & Derngate, Northampton, 9–11 September; Grand Opera House, Belfast, 16–21 September.
www.schaufuss.com
Composer: Sergei Prokofiev

Royal Ballet Theatre. Royal Opera House, London, 19 October–7 December.
www.roh.org.uk
Composer: Sergei Prokofiev

Russian State Ballet and Opera House. Lighthouse Theatre, Kettering, 26 October and tour to 4 December.
Composer: Sergei Prokofiev

Adaptation
Box Clever Theatre Company. Unicorn Theatre, London, 29 April–9 May; Contact Theatre, Manchester, 19–20 November.
www.boxclevertheatre.co.uk
Director: Iqbal Khan
Aimed at primary school audiences.

Killing Romeo
The Lion and Unicorn Theatre, London, 21 May–8 June.
www.giantolive.com
Playwright and Director: Jazz Martinez-Gamboa
Two actors begin a relationship during rehearsals for *Romeo and Juliet*.

Romeo + Juliet
The Watermill Theatre, Newbury, 17–21 September and touring schools.
Director: Clive Judd
Cast of two.

West Side Story
Lyceum Theatre, Sheffield, 1–12 July.
Director: Joey McKneely
Composer: Leonard Bernstein

THE TAMING OF THE SHREW

Propeller Acting Company. Wurtele Thrust Stage, Guthrie Theater, Minneapolis, MN,

28 February–6 April; the Rose Theatre, Kingston, 23–27 April and tour.
http://propeller.org.uk
Director: Edward Hall
All-male company.

Shakespeare's Globe. Globe Theatre, London, 19–21 June and UK and international tour to 13 October.
www.shakespearesglobe.com
Director: Joe Murphy
All-female company of eight.

MadCap Theatre Productions. Old Fire Station, Oxford, 21–22 June and tour to 3 August.
http://madcaptheatreproductions.co.uk

Red Rose Chain. Theatre in the Forest 2013 at Jimmy's Farm, Suffolk, 23 July–25 August.
www.redrosechain.com
Director: Joanna Carrick

Time Zone Theatre Company. Rose Theatre, London, 3–28 September.
www.timezonetheatre.com
Director: Pamela Schermann

Adaptation
Kiss Me, Kate
The Old Vic Theatre, London, 30 November 2012–3 March.
www.oldvictheatre.com
Composer: Cole Porter
Director: Trevor Nunn

Classic Cuts: The Taming of the Shrew.
A Play, a Pie, and a Pint. Oran Mor, Glasgow, 24–29 June.
Director: Rosie Kellegher
50-minute version based on 1950s rock'n'roll.

THE TEMPEST

Giant Olive Theatre Company. The Lion & Unicorn Theatre, London, 11 December 2012–5 January.
http://giantolive.com

Shakespeare 4 Kidz. Ashcroft Theatre, Croydon, 14 January and tour to 21 March.
www.shakespeare4kidz.com
Director: Julian Chenery

Shakespeare's Globe. Globe Theatre, London, 2 May–18 August. Broadcast as part of Shakespeare's Globe on Screen in cinemas beginning 28 May 2014
www.shakespearesglobe.com
Prospero: Roger Allam
Director: Jeremy Herrin

Such Stuff. The Old Court Room, Brighton, 25 May–2 June.

Cut String Theatre. Rag Factory, London, 31 July–17 August.
http://cutstring.com
Director: Noah Carvajal

Adaptation
Indian Tempest
Footsbarn in collaboration with Abhinaya Theatre at Globe to Globe, the Globe Theatre, London, July-August.
www.footsbarn.com
Director: Paddy Hayter
An adaptation involving circus skills, mime, street theatre, and puppetry.

Tiny Tempest
Mini Mall Theatre, Pleasance, London, 20–26 May and schools tour.
Adaptor and Director: Alex Packer

TITUS ANDRONICUS

PurpleCoat Productions. Unity Theatre, Liverpool, 5–6 February.
www.purplecoatproductions.com
Director: Karl Falconer

Royal Shakespeare Company. Swan Theatre, Stratford-upon-Avon, 23 May–26 October.
www.rsc.org.uk
Titus: Stephen Boxer
Director: Michael Fentiman

Malachite Theatre. St Leonard's Church, Shoreditch, 31 July–31 August.
www.themalachites.co.uk
Director: Benjamin Blyth
Inaugural production from a company that promises to present works by Shakespeare written when he was a resident in Shoreditch between 1592 and 1599.

Smooth Faced Gentlemen. Bedlam Theatre, Edinburgh, 2–24 August; Theatre Royal, York, 17 October.
http://smoothfacedgentlemen.com
All-female Shakespeare company.

The Playhouse. The Playhouse Theatre and Arts Centre, Derry, 23–28 September.
www.derryplayhouse.co.uk
Director: Kenny Glenaan

Hiraeth Productions. Arcola Theatre, London, 11–26 October.
Titus: David Vaughan Knight
Director: Zoe Ford
Set in 1980s skinhead culture.

Adaptation
Titus
Sheep Theatre. The Old Court Room, Brighton, 4–5 May and Edinburgh Fringe.
Comic version.

TWELFTH NIGHT

Shakespeare's Globe. Apollo Theatre, London, 2 November 2012–9 February.
www.shakespeares-globe.org
Olivia: Mark Rylance
Director: Tim Carroll

Blue Orange Arts. Blue Orange Theatre, Birmingham, 27 January–9 February.
www.blueorangetheatre.co.uk

Custom/Practice. The Lion and Unicorn Theatre, London, 29 January–23 February.
www.custompractice.co.uk
Director: Rae McKen

Propeller Acting Company. Wurtele Thrust Stage, Guthrie Theater, Minneapolis, MN, 28 February-6 April; the Rose Theatre, Kingston, 23–27 April and tour.
http://propeller.org.uk
Director: Edward Hall
All-male company.

Chapterhouse Theatre Company. Langley Priory, Diseworth, Derbyshire, 27 June and tour to 25 August.
www.chapterhouse.org
Open air theatre.

Filter (in association with the RSC). Tobacco Factory, Bristol, 9–14 September and tour to 1 February 2014. First performed at the RSC Complete Works Festival 2006.
www.filtertheatre.com
Director: Sean Holmes
Loose adaptation concentrating on knockabout comedy.

Rose Theatre, Bankside, London, 5–30 November.
www.rosetheatre.org.uk
Director: Sean Turner

Adaptation
I, Malvolio
Nuffield Theatre, Lancaster, 18–19 October. Revival from 2010.
www.timcrouchtheatre.co.uk
Playwright and Malvolio: Tim Crouch
Director: Karl James

THE TWO GENTLEMEN OF VERONA

Shakespeare at the Tobacco Factory. Tobacco Factory, Bristol, 10 April–4 May and tour.
http://sattf.org.uk
Director: Andrew Hilton

THE WINTER'S TALE

Royal Shakespeare Company. Royal Shakespeare Theatre, 30 January–23 February.

www.rsc.org.uk
Hermione: Tara Fitzgerald
Leontes: Jo Stone-Fewings
Director: Lucy Bailey

White Fox Theatre. Bierkeller Bristol, Bristol, 8–18 April.
www.bristolbierkeller.co.uk
Director: Natasha Harper-Smith and Callum Buckler

Sheffield Theatres. Crucible, Sheffield, 7 October-2 November.
www.sheffieldtheatres.co.uk
Director: Paul Miller

Adaptation
In a Pickle
Oily Cart and Royal Shakespeare Company. Unicorn Theatre, 6 December 2012–6 January and tour.
www.oilycart.org.uk
Director: Tim Webb
An adaptation for pre-school children.

The Winter's Tale Re-Imagined
New Shakespeare Company. Regent Park's Open Air Theatre, London, 20 June–20 July.
http://openairtheatre.com
Director: Ria Parry
Included a prologue providing a plot summary.

POEMS AND APOCRYPHA

Fair Em
Steam Industry. Union Theatre, London, 10 January–9 February.
www.steamindustryfreetheatre.org.uk
Director and Adaptor: Phil Willmott
Billed as a revival of the play sometimes attributed to William Shakespeare.

Sonneteers Come to The Rose!
Rose Theatre, London, 19–28 April.
www.rosetheatre.org.uk
A range of actors reading *The Phoenix and The Turtle* and *The Lover's Complaint* plus work from Shakespeare's contemporaries.

Venus and Adonis
Isango Ensemble, Cape Town, South Africa. Shakespeare's Globe, London, 29 April–4 May.
www.shakespearesglobe.com
Originally performed at 2012 Cultural Olympiad. Performed in English, IsiZulu. IxiXhosa. SeSotha, Setwsana, and Afrikaans.

MISCELLANEOUS

The Complete Works of William Shakespeare – Abridged
Chelmsford Theatre Workshop. The Old Court Theatre, Chelmsford, 16–20; 23–27 April.

The Complete Works of William Shakespeare – Abridged
Reduced Shakespeare Company. Theatre Royal, York, 5–6 April and tour to 8 December.
www.reducedshakespeare.com

Dark Lady of the Sonnets / Overruled (Double Bill)
Pentameters Theatre. Pentameters Theatre, London, 1–19 October.
www.pentameters.co.uk
Playwright: George Bernard Shaw
Director: Michael Friend

Looking for William: A Theatrical Play
Theatro Technis, London, 4–5 October.
www.theatrotechnis.com
Director: Konstantina Ritsou
Touring players learn of Shakespeare's death in April 1616. Performance in Greek with English surtitles.

Machamlear
Live Wire Theatre. The Rondo Theatre, Bath, 12–15 June. Revival from 2011 Shakespeare Unplugged Festival.
Playwright: Dougie Blaxland
An East End soap opera using characters from *Macbeth*, *Hamlet*, and *King Lear*.

A Star Danced
Guerilla Shakespeare Company. Mercury Theatre, Colchester, 1–2 May.

www.guerillashakespeare.org
Selections from the plays.

Waiting on Shakespeare
English Theatre Company. Courtyard Theatre, Hoxton, 2–28 July.

www.englishtheatrecompany.uk
Playwright: Michael Harry
Director: Christopher Jeffries
Beckett-inspired drama about two Elizabethan actors waiting for Shakespeare. Previously called *Halcyon Days*

THE YEAR'S CONTRIBUTION TO
SHAKESPEARE STUDIES

---

1. CRITICAL STUDIES
reviewed by CHARLOTTE SCOTT

DEATH BECOMES HIM

One of the challenges of reading so many books in succession is that – much like reading a slew of undergraduate essays – you start off with high hopes and expectations but by the end of the pile you're just grateful that somebody has written on something other than *Richard II*. Many of this year's books are very good, but when you read them alongside each other the standards and expectations inevitably change. For other authors this year, Brian Cummings has a lot to answer for since his book – *Mortal Thoughts* – is very good: erudite, scholarly and enlightening. In *Mortal Thoughts, Religion, Secularity and Identity in Shakespeare and Early Modern Culture*, Cummings begins by confronting one of the most profound assumptions in western theory, namely that the idea of self begins in secularization. This foundational principle of modernity ascribes individualization to rationalization, or what Burckhardt would famously describe as the lifting of the veil – the awakening of the self from its long and dark sleep in medieval collectivism. Such a position is inevitably provocative but it is also the pivot upon which the idea of the 'early modern' rests. Summarizing this position Cummings rehearses the argument in which scientific knowledge usurps religious belief and gives way to a new understanding of the self. Understood as a process of secularization, Cummings sets out to test the now commonplace thesis that the

Reformation (and the Renaissance) gave birth to the modern as well as the individual. In the process he takes on the task of anatomizing what we have come to mean by secular as well as religion and the complex positions that both art and literature have come to occupy in the debate between them. His book is organized around some of the central concepts in this debate – the self-portrait, 'conscience', the private, freedom and embodiment, are some examples – and each chapter aims to engage with how these concepts have come to define as well as inaugurate notions of inwardness. Key figures of the sixteenth and seventeenth centuries are crucial to the book's conceptual narratives and Cummings links his themes to their early modern ambassadors. To this end we meet the usual suspects – More, Montaigne, Foxe, Milton, Donne, Dürer, Lucretius – as Cummings examines the impact that these intellectuals had on inventions of the self. Perhaps unsurprisingly we see much of this narrative emerge in the nineteenth and twentieth centuries and part of Cummings' project is to scrutinize the legacies of Burkhardt, Taylor and Blumenberg and to see what happens when we 'abandon the framework of secularization'. It is an erudite and complex book which takes on some of the most defining and fundamental aspects of western history and culture. Sometimes, the sheer scope of the narrative and the conceptual ambition makes it cumbersome to read but it is always rewarding, and when Cummings focuses on individual authors or characters he is at his best. The section on *Othello* is persuasive in its attention to the utterance. Here Cummings is less concerned with post-structuralist accounts of language and more invested in the modulations of the voice on stage and how utterances can 'render interior meaning in an exterior action'. Examining the oath as a public convention as well as a personal transgression, Cummings identifies the terrifying way in which the play collapses the binaries we have come to rely on:

Exterior and interior explanation, and public and private valuation, fold in on each other: interior virtue requires exterior verification, while external crimes are revealed only by internal interpretation.

Part of the project here is to explore the ways in which the histories of selfhood and secularization have become erroneously simplified into categories of identification. In one of his finest chapters Cummings tackles a dearly loved theory of the birth of the self – the soliloquy. Apparently both revelatory and artful '[t]he soliloquy is thus we might say the *locus classicus* of the problem of the self'. Pursuing the problem of the self in Shakespeare's most famous soliloquizers, Cummings announces 'If it is clear who is speaking, it is not at all clear who is listening.' Attending to the various ways in which the soliloquy can work on stage, Cummings analyses the extent to which the solitary speech is 'always *performative* rather than *cognitive*', and whether there is a decisive moment in the history of its dramaturgy. What is most engaging about Cummings' account of the soliloquy is his subtle attention to the multiple ways it can function in a single play as well as a single speech and the different ways in which we are asked to listen to a character. But Cummings' point is that it is never entirely clear – are we eavesdropping or actively listening, being talked to or presumed absent? The same of course might be asked of prayer or meditation: is it necessary that God is listening or can the words be spoken anyway? These are some of the questions that drive the book's analysis of selfhood and the secular focus of Cummings' wider

narrative which asks: how necessary is the Reformation to the Renaissance? Challenging the critical commonplace that modernity emerges from the ruins of the Reformation Cummings notices that in spiritual terms a soliloquy 'is a synonym for a prayer of any kind' and 'in 1620 the word is used as an alternative to "psalm", a song in which the soul meditates to itself'. The conceptual and etymological links between the soliloquy and meditation are convincing and reveal a very different narrative to the prevailing associations between secularism and individualism. *Mortal Thoughts* is not, however, straightforward revisionism: Cummings is less interested in redrawing the lines between the development of the secular and the self and more invested in demonstrating that those lines are porous, flexible and indistinct. To this end, Cummings understands the soliloquy as a literary and philosophical form which can present us 'with a fragmentary repository of alternative selves'. *Mortal Thoughts* pursues some of the most complex and profound concepts in literary history – 'to be or not to be' is at the centre of this dialogue – but it moves far beyond Hamlet's musings and into the very corners of the body, the mind, the self, the spirit and the soul. Cummings produces some wonderful close readings: his section on Richard II's prison speech is excellent; he is the only critic who has made sense of the camel, the needle and the antagonistic 'word'. But he is equally good on Montaigne, Donne and Milton. It is an erudite and important book that addresses the intellectually and aesthetically symbiotic relationships between faith and personhood and the profound ways in which they have shaped our 'secular' subjectivities.

Moving from the spiritual secularity of our mortal selves to the inscrutability of the self in action we encounter David Scott Kastan's captivating book, *A Will to Believe: Shakespeare and Religion*. But where Cummings is concerned with the affective landscape of the human journey into self-knowledge, Kastan understands that 'Inner lives are inner lives'; in other words they are by their very nature supressed, hidden or obscure. Kastan sets out to examine how 'Religion provides Shakespeare with the fundamental language of value and understanding in the plays, from the beginning of his career through its end.' Kastan is not, thankfully, on the hunt for Shakespeare's soul (in fact he demonstrates very adroitly that it is almost impossible to clarify anyone's personal faith in this period since most Elizabethans are living on a smorgasbord of Christianity); instead the book explores the terms and debates through which religion manifests in Shakespeare's work. Giving a nuanced account of the divergent ways in which many of the plays articulate religious debate *A Will to Believe* explores residual sympathy (as well as antipathy) towards Catholicism and the often humorous and spiteful ways in which Shakespeare's characters record this debate. Attending to a variety of plays – *King John, All's Well, Measure, The Merchant* and *Hamlet* – Kastan demonstrates the capacity of Shakespeare's art, which is 'at once too sceptical and too sympathetic to be zealously committed to any confession'. His terrific chapter on *Hamlet* offers a very subtle reading of Old Hamlet's apparition and a revealing relationship between metaphor and metonym through the 'mind's eye'. Writing about Hamlet's most famous question, Kastan observes 'Some editions . . . should put the line inside quotation marks, marking it as what he is reading rather than what he is thinking.' Kastan's point is that the play engages, often vigorously, in *debate* and that much of that debate is precipitated by religious texts, but the presence of religious ideas and texts 'neither exhausts nor explains the play's mysteries, and they function neither as an index of Shakespeare's faith nor as a prompt or challenge to our own'. His close-reading of this speech is very rewarding and would be a gift to students of *Hamlet*; a play, Kastan writes, predicated on uncertainty which 'transforms theology into tragedy'. Exploring the confessionally complex role of purgatory in the play, Kastan cites Donne's observation that 'the general disposition in the nature of every man, [is] to wish well to the dead': but Hamlet forgets his father even as he tries to satisfy him, and 'ultimately Hamlet neither remembers nor revenges'. There are equally subtle and penetrating readings of other plays, including *The*

Merchant of Venice, Othello and *Measure for Measure* but it is the sections on *Hamlet* that really stand out.

Had Hamlet eaten more and thought less, however, he might have been more successful at both remembering and revenging, or so we might think having read *Eating and Ethics in Shakespeare's England*. Here David B. Goldstein is interested in eating, and what he calls the ethics of eating; in other words how the act of sharing food produces certain relational codes which affect networks of identity. Like Kastan and Cummings, Goldstein is writing about identities and how Shakespeare's drama constructs versions of selfhood. For Goldstein, however, we are not so much what we eat but how we eat and who we eat with. Understanding the impulses of both hunger and hospitality reveals the many ways in which repast is fundamental to our social and spiritual selves. In Shakespeare, however, Goldstein observes an unhappy relationship to food where almost all mealtimes are antagonistic at best and homicidal at worst. Despite the title only two Shakespeare plays are given in-depth consideration – *Titus* and *The Merchant* – and the rest of the book focuses on a range of early modern texts associated with consumption, from communion to recipe books and finally *Paradise Lost*. The sections on Shakespeare are mixed: there are some wonderful moments when the author focuses on specific characters – especially Lavinia who is often neglected by critics of the play. Here Goldstein explores some of the most gripping visual spectacles of the play in the context of cannibalism and sacrifice. His readings of the play amplify the grisly relish with which we observe the trafficking of various body parts across the stage. Suggesting that we reposition our humanist focus on this play to the colonial texts of New World conquests, Goldstein argues that 'New World cannibalism forces a consideration of the value of a person by converting that person into a leftover of violence, removing that person from personhood (an act which is always violent)'. Drawing on narratives and images of human sacrifice and cannibalism, Goldstein emphasizes the ways in which the plays divests characters of their identities and makes them fodder – quite literally – for tragedy. What remains of the bodies and their parts has reduced the human and the self to scraggy leftovers; surplus to requirements. In *The Merchant*, however, he is more interested in the social acts of eating and the ways in which commensality performs networks of inclusion. As Goldstein argues, this play is replete with references to food, eating and consuming and yet we never actually witness a meal time. His point is that forms and ideas of consumption establish a network of allegiances as well as ethics within the play and it is through the exploitation of these terms that the drama produces some of its most worrying and enthralling instances. Some of Goldstein's readings are terrific and some are a little tendentious: he can sometimes become so embedded in his own terms of reference that he seems to forget where we started. There is a superb section on Shylock, for example, and his famous speech of putative empathy but this is followed by a less convincing section on Jessica who – by virtue of some linguistic circus acts – becomes a 'trifle' (frivolous and a pudding of boiled cream). Only when Goldstein makes these moves does he lose me; otherwise it's a clever and bold book which reveals that 'meals . . . are not opportunities for the development of community, but for the exercise in hegemony'. Understanding the insidious power of hospitality in these plays reveals the extent to which we rely on codes of communality, even as we destroy them.

'POWER'S ODE'?

Richard Wilson continues the exploration of 'the artist's paradoxical desire for powerful powerlessness' in his compendious new book, *Free Will, Art and Power on Shakespeare's Stage*. This is a veritable cornucopia of insights, quotations, oxymorons, tautologies, paradoxes and epithets that even Erasmus himself might have struggled to assemble on the relationship between art and politics. Wilson stuffs his prose to the brim with quotations from the plays, so that almost every thought is a reflective reconstruction of the playwright, dissected, reproduced and reiterated in a series of philosophical

excavations. Wilson seems to tacitly identify himself with the archaeologist as he variously describes his project as 'deducing' or 'excavating'. In his attempt to uncover the artistic relationship between autonomy and authority, Wilson offers a series of intense close readings, through which he engages with both historicism and theory. *Free Will* is about the relationship between autonomy and the self – how the subject defines itself in relation to external forms of power, how it may be internalised and therefore deconstructed and how, ultimately, Shakespeare is more interested in dismantling the subject than defining it. Central to Wilson's thesis is the notion that free will and sovereignty are not dependent on either success or authority. On the contrary, he argues that Shakespeare pushes questions of power to their limits and in doing so reveals the illusory fabrics upon which they stand. There follows a series of case studies in which Wilson analyses various plays (*Hamlet, Julius Caesar, Henry IV, King Lear, Macbeth, Coriolanus, Antony and Cleopatra* and *Othello*). Attending to questions of power and art in these plays, and their various manifestations, Wilson produces some very fine readings through a blend of psychoanalysis, deconstruction, historicism and queer theory. At the centre of many of them is the question of theatre itself and the extent, if any, to which it celebrates its own miasma: 'Thus, valorising "disinterestedness against interest", "largesse against prudence", as Bordieu wrote, Shakespearean theatre prefigured the later mystification of art as "a world elsewhere", through its pretence of being the pretty plaything of some despot like Theseus or Hal.' Thinking through the representations of the mind in *Othello*, however, and the vertiginous moments of ironic self-awareness ('As if there were some monster in my thought') Wilson explains:

In such reflections on his own cultural poetics we can hear the writer meditating, I therefore propose, not only on his utopian dream of separating art from mimesis, representation from presence, language from power, but on their tragic indivisibility, in that 'double or enfolded act of (re)cognition that makes art possible' on the liminal terrain 'occupied by aesthetics before aesthetics emerge', or rather, when the aesthetic and political have yet to be divorced.

As this excerpt suggests, Wilson is deeply wedded to his own post-structuralist aesthetics and sometimes such verbosity detracts from the argument, as I found myself wading through endless rehearsals of 'powerful powerlessness'. But Wilson is also very poetic and his habit of continually mediating his argument through quotations from Shakespeare's plays is often illuminating. In fact, the experience of reading this book is not unlike watching the Reduced Shakespeare Company perform the *Complete Works* in 90 minutes. Reading *Free Will* takes a good deal longer but if you can pick your way through the prolixity it is very rewarding.

Adjusting the philosophical focus to a more precise engagement with certain strands of renaissance humanism, however, is *Shakespeare and Renaissance Ethics*, edited by Patrick Gray and John D. Cox. Here the idea of ethics is both broader and more specifically historicist. The collection argues that the moral dialogues in Shakespeare's plays take part in the collective, as well as individual, experiences of religion, philosophy, politics and culture that define what we understand as the Renaissance. Here, of course, the term 'Renaissance' is revealing since it marks a subtle but consistent pattern in the current shape of literary criticism. For the editors of this collection (unlike its intellectual predecessor, *Shakespeare and Early Modern Political Thought* (2010)) the Renaissance defines a period which can be characterized by a self-reflective – self-conscious, even – involvement with certain intellectual positions, rather than a pre-emptively 'modern' engagement with specific political philosophies. Central to this concept of the Renaissance is the understanding of ethics and what shapes (rather than defines) moral categories, as well as the agency of the individual. In their introduction the editors chart this debate in phlegmatic terms:

The scope of human agency can be found somewhere in between Augustinian debasement and Pelagian exaltation; there is no need to push the question so far to one side or the other.

This even-handed attitude characterizes many of the essays in this excellent volume, which tend to observe the debate that surrounds questions of human agency, rather than attempt to resolve it. Whether the human is a product or an agent of its socio-political world is central to the exploration of ethics in this period and to that end the range of subjects covered is intriguing as it centres on two fundamental 'concepts or systems for ethical reflection [which] were classical philosophy and Christianity'. The essays that follow cover a range of plays and subjects, including shame and self-knowledge in *Love's Labour's Lost*; suicide and autonomy in some of Shakespeare's Roman plays; the social effects of laughter (as well as humiliation) in *Twelfth Night* and *The Merchant*; and the affective dynamic between breast-feeding and morality through the interrelations of maternity and wet-nursing in *Romeo and Juliet*. While these essays tend to focus quite specifically on an action or idea, some of the other essays engage with a concept – in the latter half of the book we encounter explorations of empathy, prayer, contrition, reason and conscience. The more subtle readings of the first half of the collection are balanced through the grander intellectual and ethical narratives of these often troubling, but profoundly human, structures of thought. It's a very good collection which offers a range of thoughtful and intelligent essays on the interrelations between social thought, collective emotional and individual agency and how social worlds produce, rather than reproduce, ethics through their interrelations with each other as well as 'hypothetical variations or alternatives'. Although the literary emphasis is on Shakespeare (here, neither anecdotal nor exemplary), Montaigne and Aristotle feature widely and seminally in the discussions of moral thinking. Robert S. Miola provides a compelling essay on *Cymbeline* wherein he explores some 'searching questions about marriage, the moral obligations of spouses, and the imperatives to punish and forgive'. The focus on adultery is fascinating, if a little grisly, as Miola recounts the various ethical traditions through which attitudes to infidelity crystallized. Central to the ethical debate was the perspectives of punishment or forgiveness, wherein certain biblical traditions made way for a justification of both, depending on how you read your Paul or Matthew. Miola, however, focuses on forgiveness, and Posthumus's exceptional decision to forgive Imogen *before* she has been proved innocent:

Posthumus's singular act of forgiveness contradicts the standard valuation of female chastity, redefines male–female relations, and overturns the ethical foundations to support marriage and society.

Turning from outward forms of punishment to inward forms of moral audit, Miola observes how two of Shakespeare's 'perennially puzzling' characters (Old Hamlet and Mariana) forgive their errant spouses by referring them to their conscience. The celebration of conscience leads onto a further section of essays, wherein the focus is largely on Montaigne and the intellectual traditions of a spiritual mind. William Hamlin's essay on Montaigne and *Measure for Measure* is better on the play than it is on Montaigne, where the essay, 'On Conscience' tends to flank rather than develop the argument. Montaigne is given a more fulsome treatment in the chapters by Peter Holbrook and Peter Mack. Holbrook focuses on literary character and the extent to which the attribution of human capabilities, especially free will, determines both narrative action and audience identification. Within this scope, Montaigne emerges as the sceptic who 'rejects a central strand of that tradition, denying that reason is of much – even any – use to human beings'. And here, Holbrook suggests, Shakespeare is like Montaigne in demonstrating a fascination with *characters*, 'people who are what they are, and who could not (by, e.g., any great effort of conscious intention, will or reason) be any different'. Attending to the idea of choice, and the act of choosing, the essay goes on to explore the humanist legacies of political freedom. Holbrook ranges across a number of plays but focuses most effectively on *A Lover's Complaint* in which he observes the compelling, and perhaps all too 'human', response of the maid who would, she declares, make the same mistakes again: 'so

much for philosophic counsel'! Where Holbrook dispenses with the usefulness of reason, however, Peter Mack focuses on the value of madness and the ways in which 'Shakespeare uses the extraordinary logical leaps of Lear's madness to extend the reach of possible ethical thinking'. He provides a wonderful exploration of some of the key moments in the play and how Shakespeare synthesizes language and image to 'invite thinking that provokes a moral response'. Mack frequently uses the word 'astonishing', which reveals, I think, not only his own infectious passion for the play but also the extent to which we are being invited to think beyond the boundaries of our own instincts and into the very corners of the ethical questions that the play provokes. What he uncovers are the powerful effects of fragmentary reason, emotional identification and piercing insight: 'As readers and audience we are compelled to work hard to make meanings on which it seems our own understanding of the world may depend. This is a jarringly new method of teaching ethics.' One of the most original essays in the collection, however, focuses on breast-milk and the often inscrutable dynamic between the physical and social bodies. In her essay Beatrice Groves maintains that the intense association of milk and morality 'makes the breast into a locus of female power'. Tracing the ethical relationship between the baby and its milk supply, Groves observes the profound anxiety that wet-nursing could produce in a patriarchal culture in which children were being characterized through a 'lower-class breast'. Attending to how and why such anxieties took root, Groves refers back to the proverbial lore that enshrined such prejudices and how the 'early modern period changed a proverb about mankind's tendency towards sin into one about the effect of nursing on a child's ethical outlook'. Groves demonstrates how attitudes to nursing changed during this period to celebrate maternal breast-feeding (in line with an increasingly Protestant emphasis on the family unit) and thereby redefined cultural attitudes to breast milk. Shakespeare's plays, however, reveal an intriguing line-up of attitudes to nursing (including some very morally dubious breast-feeding mothers and some morally robust children who were wet-nursed). By nuancing these fears, Groves writes, Shakespeare's representations of nursing 'can be read as an ethical position celebrating the non-blood ties that bind communities together and a redemption of the female, lower-class "other". Shakespeare's plays question the stereotype encoded in his society's misogynist proverb ("he sucked evil from the dug") and also invert the proverb itself.'

'YOUTH IS WASTED ON THE YOUNG'

Keeping the focus on women but more precisely on young women, is Deanne Williams' *Shakespeare and the Performance of Girlhood*. Here the idea of girlhood is a porous and flexible concept which includes many factors beyond the biological or social. Williams' book is dedicated to what it means to be a girl on Shakespeare's stage, how we recognize such categories and what these forms of recognition produce in terms of representation. What she reveals in the process is riveting – and, at times, bitter-sweet. For to be a girl is to take part in an act of being that is at once liberating and risky. Beginning with a summary of the idea of the girl in Shakespeare's plays, Williams demonstrates how the term can signify a feeling, a state, a condition and social status. Most intriguing here is how the sign can function as a relational metaphor or analogy as when Macbeth, unhinged by the ghost of Banquo, 'compares himself to a frightened, babbling "baby of a girl"'. Compellingly, of course, Macbeth is not the girl, but the baby, and, as Williams observes, 'Macbeth's words remind us of the reality of childhood on Shakespeare's stage' as well as the relational forms of both 'baby' and 'girl'. Unique to Williams' project is the extent to which she analyses the girl as distinct from woman and daughter, and by disentangling some of these associations she is able to scrutinize the myriad and compelling ways in which the idea of the girl is constantly under construction – often by men but also by women. The first half of the book focuses on girl

characters, as fictional people but also disguised boy actors, attending to various 'girls', including Julia, Silvia, Bianca, Joan La Pucelle and, finally, Juliet who, she observes, is a character 'whose mutability and movement, flexibility, resistance and transformative creative imagination, dramatize the limitless possibilities of girlhood itself'. Williams then moves from the girl Juliet, self-possessed and a teenager to the ten-year-old Isabelle de France, second wife of Richard II. Here she demonstrates that history has tended to edit out the youthfulness of this character and by thinking about Queen Isabelle as a 'girl' (child) we can observe 'how Shakespeare's dramatization of medieval child marriage both challenges our expectations about girlhood and broadens our understanding of medieval and early modern girls as dramatic characters, as well as historical individuals'. Extending her focus to historical individuals, including Elizabeth I, Princess Elizabeth Stuart and Alice Egerton, Williams examines education and performance (theatrical, musical and social) and the dangers and pleasures of both. Moving through Shakespeare to his reception and afterlives, Williams demonstrates how the masque's, and specifically Comus's, 'dramatization of virginity engages Shakespearean models of girlhood, mobilizes an extremely current musical taste or fashion to communicate a kind of unassailable virginal integrity'. Moving well into the seventeenth century Williams focuses on the court masque as the 'genre par excellence for girls' theatrical patronage and artistic creativity' and here she seems to observe a turn of fortune for 'girls' wherein they can claim some authority, autonomy even, as the 'centre of power at the country house' as well as discerning in Shakespeare's work 'a story in which girls are different from women, even as they aspire and prepare to be adults'. Although for Williams, the representation of the girl is central to the ways in which we should read many of Shakespeare's characters, never has it been more important or more relevant to think about the values that any given culture assigns to its girls and the shaping of their histories.

Palgrave's publication of *Shakespeare's Boys: A Cultural History* by Katie Knowles appears on first inspection to be a companion to Williams' focus on girls, but the perspectives and ranges of the books are very different. Like Williams, Knowles sets out to historicize the concept and argue that 'Shakespeare's plays reflect the ambiguous, fluid and transitional status of boyhood in early modern England, and [that] the portrayal of these on-stage boys has been a crucial, and sometimes defining, factor in the performance history of these plays'. Whereas Williams' focus is on identity and status, Knowles is more specifically engaged by the concept of youth: her dismissal of Shakespeare's girls as 'often babies' or teenagers, and thus 'entering the adult phase of life', defines her focus by the observation that 'most of Shakespeare's child characters are boys'. This may be true, but Williams' book demonstrates a fascination with girlhood that extends beyond the categories of age and into the fundamental structures of social behaviour. While Williams' book is engaged in the conceptual, as well as performative aspects of Shakespeare's young women, Knowles is more specifically wedded to questions of gender and youth. Knowles's book is divided into two sections, the first is largely historicist in its exploration of some of the boy characters in Shakespeare's plays, as well as the institutions that define them; the second deals with their afterlives and the various ways in which these characters have been performed or appropriated in the last four hundred years. One of the most interesting things about this study is how Knowles chooses to group the characters. Rather than confine her study to genre, for example, she focuses on status: the first chapter deals with male heirs which leads her to examine a range of young men from all genres. Here she is especially interested in the fated predicament of male children who are destined for responsibility but notable for their vulnerability. The second chapter attends to notions of masculinity through an anatomization of violence in the *bildungsroman* of the Roman warriors, Young Lucius and Young Martius, while the third focuses on representations of teaching and the idea of the schoolboy. Although most of this material is predictable Knowles offers subtle readings of some of the plays, especially *Love's Labour's Lost* where she observes the play's satire of immaturity

through the juxtaposition of Moth and the Lords. One of the best sections of the book is her attention to Falstaff's Boy, who as a 'silent witness' to adult life offers an acute, and often touching, image of the anguish of growing up; 'The Boy does not react to, or comment on, any of what he witnesses, and as the play closes we are left in the dark as to what the result of his "education" will be.' This is a poignant statement and one that resonates through a play in which 'the massacre in the English camp denies Falstaff's Boy the opportunity to put the lessons he has learned from his worldly education into action'. The latter half of the book addresses Shakespeare's afterlives and offers some interesting insights into the performance history of boy characters as well as changing historical emphases (the Victorian period is perhaps the most resonant here). Although Knowles's treatment of boys here is not, perhaps, as sophisticated as Williams' exploration of girlhood, and the methodological range is narrower, it nevertheless provides a thoughtful focus on some frequently overlooked characters.

Keeping the focus on character but moving more specifically onto the relationship between mind and body is an invigorating collection of essays, *Embodied Cognition and Shakespeare's Theatre*, edited by Laurie Johnson, John Sutton and Evelyn Tribble. One of the central tenets of this collection is to dismantle the conventional dualism associated with the body/mind dynamic and to explore not only what those terms mean in themselves but the fluid, reactionary or symbiotic relations between them. Similarly, although Shakespeare's work features extensively across the essays, the emphasis is on his plays as part of a wider 'early modern' culture, rather than discrete examples of an autonomous thinker. Thus the body becomes more than the sum of its parts, including the mind, and a site of exploration in which it can affect and be affected. In divergent ways James A. Knapp and Tiffany Hoffman both attend to the 'blush': the body's apparently involuntary response to shame or guilt. Knapp's focus in *Much Ado*, however, is on forms of recognition that involve judgement, or perhaps interpretation, and the ways in which the body may produce signs which are simultaneously meaningful and immaterial:

These mental bodies, being dependent on rather than free from matter, are subject to its distortions, to the vagaries of sense experience, to suggestion, and to time.

All of which, of course, has intriguing implications for a medium dependent on the body as its centre of action. Focusing on Coriolanus's blush Hoffman offers a revisionist reading of the hero's bodily response. Rather than evince shame or personal anxiety, she argues, the blush is a markedly social response to a fear of disclosure. The essays in this collection are largely historicist in method and Hoffman focuses her interrogation on Aristotle and 'its translation into early modernity as a religious affect linked to conscience and prominently involved in theological attempts to address the bodily determinism inherent in Galenic theories of temperament'. Crucially, Hoffman argues, Coriolanus's blush supports a physically transitional moment where the imperatives of social duty over-rule the solipsistic self.

In general, *Embodied Cognition and Shakespeare's Theatre* is a very good collection but one essay really stands out: David Hawkes' 'Proteus Agonistes, Shakespeare, Bacon and the "Torture" of Nature'. Hawkes's essay begins with an analysis of Bacon's famous observation that science is nature under torture in order to explore what 'torture' might reveal about the relationship between art and nature. In these terms, Hawkes asks, is science 'aggressive and exploitative' towards nature or 'harmonious and complementary'? Most absorbing in this respect is what this debate exposes about our cultural understanding of torture. Pursuing this debate Hawkes touches on *Othello*, *The Merchant* and *The Winter's Tale* to expose the extent to which Shakespeare perceives torture as both revelatory and destructive: something that can turn the body inside out; and something that can reveal the body as empty. *The Winter's Tale* dominates the discussion in most of the essays here and especially in the second half which focuses more precisely on the senses. Some of these essays draw more distinctly on cognitive theories than others and

some are more concerned with what we might call the affective layers of interpretation produced through cognition – allegory or fantasy for example. Mary Floyd-Wilson also provides a stimulating essay on the relationship between cognition and conscience. Attending to the demonology in Heywood's *A Woman Killed with Kindness*, Floyd-Wilson asks 'can you call your thoughts your own or were they planted by the Devil?' Central to her thesis is the role of temptation in the formation of both thought and action. She provides a fascinating insight into the points at which individual agency apparently breaks down through the domestic and patriarchal structures that endorse diabolic interference: 'Far from a safe haven, the home is the frontline for struggles with an insidious and invasive Devil, and the domestic tragedy proves the apt genre for representing this spiritual warfare.'

Turning from one domestic tragedy to another we discover Laurie Maguire's contribution on *Othello* to the new Arden series, *Language and Writing* (*Macbeth* and *The Tempest* reviewed last year). Each contributor is obviously chosen for their particular gifts and Maguire demonstrates her exceptional ability to combine learned scholarship with lucidity and flair. The book is divided into sections, each of which takes 'language' as its central tenet but explores the multiple ways in which language behaves in the drama: concentrating on narratives (including 'stories'), genre and word-play Maguire provides a wonderfully comprehensive account of the play. Each chapter works through the intricacies of how its semantics perform meaning, and how linguistic detail creates conceptual frameworks within the drama; how certain characters exploit form and structure; 'what happens when language crosses boundaries (as when Othello starts to speak with Iago's vocabulary)'; and what 'types' of language emerge and at what points. This aspect of Maguire's approach leads her to multiple questions that centre on our responses to gender, performance, morality, identity, rhetoric, legality and meta-theatre. She is a very self-aware critic and the book is full of questions and reflections on the process of writing itself, how and why certain choices are made and what governs our expectations of formal analyses. As I read this book, I found myself marking something on almost every page, whether it was an insight into the art of literary criticism or an observation of the play itself; Maguire writes with such verve that she reinvents the art of language even as she describes it. One of the defining aspects of this series, as well as *Othello* in particular, is that it is very up-to-date in terms of criticism. To that end, Maguire has digested a range of critical approaches to the play (including performance, race, psychoanalysis and materialism) to provide a thorough and accessible survey of the multiple angles students can take. There is a wonderful section on the handkerchief (including recent work suggesting that it was dyed black, rather than white), as well as focal sections on 'lexical tics'. Here Maguire draws on unpublished research on the phrase 'no remedy' and the question 'Is't possible?'. Later sections focus on adaptation and performance where Maguire examines various ways in which *Othello* has been modernized, transformed, gutted or streamlined; in each case she observes what effects such differences produce and how they can amplify our understanding of Shakespeare's play as well as the cultural milieu in which such adaptations take shape. There is a strong emphasis, too, on Iago and how Shakespeare defines him through his lexicon. Each chapter pursues its argument through similitude and context and to that end produces convincing and comprehensive readings of the play. It is a very thoughtful and well-devised book which will be invaluable to both teachers and students of the play.

ALL THE WORLD'S A STAGE

In *Shakespeare's Stage Traffic: Imitation, Borrowing and Competition in Renaissance Theatre*, Janet Clare offers a reappraisal of the imitative and foundational relationships between plays on the early modern stage. Arguing that almost all drama defined itself not through overarching claims to originality but through 'the lively cross-currents of Renaissance theatre', Clare presents some very compelling evidence on the development of 'textual networks'

and the circulation and adaptation of intertexts in Renaissance drama. One of her central and perhaps most provocative claims is that we rethink the valorization of originality and the almost obsessive need in Shakespeare studies to present the playwright as the creative originator of all that is good on the early modern stage. To this end, Clare re-examines the relationships between certain Shakespeare plays and their apparent derivatives and reveals that the need to keep Shakespeare on top has often skewed not only the dating of certain plays but also their authority. In analysing *King John* and *Richard II*, for example, she reveals that Shakespeare's history owes a great deal to the repertory of the Queen's Men as well as to Marlowe and that we need to rethink the chronology of certain texts in order to fully understand how Shakespeare adapted drama rather than invented it. Her detailed analysis of the relationships between the history plays, chronicle history, Protestant polemics and tragedy offers engaging insights into the ways in which Shakespeare developed, manipulated or excised contemporary interests and the ways in which 'one play provides a cue for another'. In her section on *Richard III*, for example, she reveals Shakespeare's innovation in terms of metatheatre and his fusing of performance and revelation. In an analysis of *Richard II* Clare not only shows that the play owes its greatest moments to Marlowe but that Shakespeare was also building on contemporary interests in citizen and chronicle history. By attending to the generic movements of the drama Clare's book reveals the ways in which plays were always building on the structures and successes of each other – developing innovations, augmenting themes or borrowing events – and thus how the various plays of the period were perhaps more invested in harnessing elements that worked theatrically than constantly innovating. On the much debated relationship between *The Shrew* and *A Shrew*, for example, Clare suggests that instead of thinking that the former is a better version of the latter we treat the plays independently and 'jettison these vexed questions of derivation and listen, instead, to the dialogue between texts'. Being attentive and receptive to this dialogue is Clare's argument throughout her book and to that end she offers detailed, informed and engaging accounts of the varied and wonderful 'stage traffic' of early modern drama. Perhaps most absorbing here is her approach to genre and the ways in which she breaks down notions of history, tragedy and comedy to observe how Shakespeare's dramaturgy belonged to a climate in which plays were, for the most part, in perpetual motion. Such a concept is at its most resonant in *Hamlet*, which, she argues, 'evolved in the face of other productions and publications'. Looking at the three texts of *Hamlet* (although focusing most specifically on Q1 and Q2), Clare observes their evolutions in relation to Marston and, to a lesser extent, Jonson. Examining the texts alongside revenge motifs in Kyd, Seneca and Marston, Clare provides a very thoughtful and detailed account of the play's genesis, suggesting that 'the publication of Q2 could have been something of a riposte to the generic inventiveness of *Antonio's Revenge*: a literary makeover of a popular play in response to the former's de-construction of the genre'. This is a very thorough and engaging book which takes in a great many plays. Clare's tone is always discursive rather than dictatorial, preferring to open up discussions on chronology, source texts, originality, intention and status. Her focus extends beyond individual plays to repertory companies, theatres, and patronage and she offers wonderful insights into the cornucopia of Renaissance drama.

Taking a more specific view of the company rather than the plays, however, is Eva Griffith's *A Jacobean Company and Its Playhouse: The Queen's Servants at the Red Bull Theatre (c. 1605–1619)*. This book focuses on the role, company and history of Queen Ann's Servants at the Red Bull theatre in Clerkenwell. Griffith's project is partly revisionist in terms of providing a more nuanced and thoughtful account of the playing company – beyond its more mainstream reputation for ribaldry and jocularity, a reputation she suggests which has led to the company being neglected by scholarship and, to some extent, misunderstood. Her detailed and thorough account provides an analysis of the contexts for the theatre – 'location, environment and proportion of the site' – as well as focusing on the

company itself, its pre-history, actors, and investment in pleasing the Queen. Arguing for the significance of the 'multivenued' playing companies, Griffith demonstrates that the Queen's Servants were a wide-ranging company, who played at both the Red Bull and the Curtain, and had an investment in both. Her book celebrates the impact and significance of this company, which, she says, has too long been side-lined by a Shakespeare-centric attitude to repertory. What she demonstrates is how rich a resource our study of this company can yield not only in terms of how share-owning systems operate in the period but also how women (usually as wives) functioned in the development and maintenance of the company. Most interesting here is the story of Susan Greene, married to two men in the business; she ended up after her second husband's death as 'sole owner of their Red Bull playhouse shares'. Attending to such beguiling figures, Griffith reveals the way in which money was invested in both playhouse and company and the different profits and business opportunities they produced. Arguing for a better understanding of the Queen's Servants, Griffith goes on to explore their repertoire and the types of drama they became associated with. Here she observes their apparent interest in martial plays, their penchant for 'the bang and clash of battle' and the resonance of military prowess:

A European flavour was associated in many minds with readiness for Protestant military action, and early Red Bull/Queen's Servant's auditors, many of them practising their skills with the trained bands, must have relished the 'Sword and Target' practice practised on stage with the many large-scale battle and sword-fight scenes.

Griffith's great skill in *A Jacobean Company and its Playhouse*, is not only to shed new light on the Queen's Servants but also to excavate and demonstrate the compelling and revealing ways in which the playhouse and players engage in the very history they were in the process of making.

Moving from the specific analysis of a Jacobean company to a more general survey of the subject is *Acting Companies and their Plays in Shakespeare's London*, by Siobhan Keenan. It is a very good introduction to the subject of playing companies which manages to blend the broader climate of repertory with a detailed focus on the formative relationship between playwrights and acting troupes. Developing her argument in a similar vein to those of Clare and Griffith, Keenan presents a very clear, well-structured and focused account of the various and dynamic ways in which the interrelationships between writing, performance and acting shaped early modern theatre. The book is divided according to key aspects of that dynamic, and the various stages of its development. Central to these are the acting companies (children and adult) themselves, for which Keenan provides various 'case studies', focusing on specific performance practice, repertoire and spaces; she also examines how traces of practice and innovation can be read through Henslowe's *Diary* and manuscript playbooks. Keenan attends to the physical spaces of early modern theatres and the ways in which design reflects use, as well as the role of audiences and patrons in the shaping of the Renaissance stage. This is a valuable book for students as it is well pitched, even-handed and digests a lot of often unruly material into a comprehensive analysis. Departing, however, from the conventional narrative of displacing individual authorial autonomy Keenan suggests that the 'playwrights were the chief artistic force in the creation of plays' and to that end she offers a thoughtful reassessment of playwrights as well as the conditions in which they developed.

WHO'S THERE?

Moving from the material to the mnemonic we discover *Shakespeare and Memory*, in which Hester Lees-Jeffries considers the idea of memory, and the act of remembering, through a variety of different, both modern and early modern, perspectives. As Lees-Jeffries shows, memory inflects every moment of our existence, from who we are to how we operate in the world, the multiple ways in which we record or absorb mnemonics being only a part of the larger experience of remembering. Her point is that the Elizabethans had very

different, if not necessarily less sophisticated, mnemonic aids but also that the idea of memory was undergoing something of a 'crisis', something which we can in our contemporary culture identify with. Although, as Lees-Jeffries points out, memory is precisely what joins every moment of our material and metaphysical lives this can make it a rather unruly concept within the book and one that tends to relate so expansively that it sometimes becomes hard to harness the concepts to the literature with any degree of percision. Memory inheres in performance records, audiences, actors, stage properties, material objects, words and print, images and gestures. At the centre of the project, however, is a claim that Shakespeare was instrumental in the ways in which the early modern period changed its memory: 'that is, Shakespeare both engaged with and changed the ways in which people remembered'. *Hamlet* is, of course, the play which becomes the focus for the larger claims for the impact of memory on Shakespeare's work but the book is at its best when it focuses on the detail. Lees-Jeffries pursues her narrative through various different perspectives: the skill and practice of remembering; education and intertexts and the ways in which stories are reproduced; history, perception and nostalgia; mourning, fantasy and mementos. Throughout the chapters the book moves between the play-worlds and their audiences and the cognitive networks produced by certain signs, characters or stories. Although she writes beautifully and often movingly on memory I don't always agree with the readings, especially on *The Winter's Tale* where Lees-Jeffries observes Hermione's statue: 'Art revives the dead, and makes memories live; recovers and preserves the things that have been lost.' The play is surely more cynical than this; but that does not detract from a comprehensive, thoughtful and largely persuasive book in which the idea of human nature, as well as its capability, is at the forefront of what it means to remember as well as forget.

In Karen Raber's *Animal Bodies, Renaissance Culture*, nature becomes an altogether less abstract idea. Here in this provocative and thought-provoking book Raber confronts the human–animal divide with a piercing gaze. Her argument centres on the relationship between the human and animal body: unlike most anthropocentric criticism, however, Raber is less interested in what makes us human and more interested in what makes us animal. In looking at the often porous boundaries between the animal and human body, Raber uncovers a much more fluid, reciprocal relationship. In pursuit of this relationship she examines medical treatises, books on anatomy, and husbandry and horse-training manuals to reveal an almost symbiotic dynamic between human and animal bodies. Some of what she uncovers is fascinating, especially medicinal remedies which require mutual ingestion of animal and human by-products. Less convincing, however, is her argument for revising attitudes to bestiality, whereby we see the animal in a reciprocal relationship with the human, rather than in a position of subjection or passivity. Although I would agree that humans and animals have developed a shared language and 'gestural repertoire' this is only true in the case of domesticated or trained animals; animals, in other words, that have been conditioned to respond in certain ways. Raber is particularly fascinated by the horse and some of the most intriguing aspects of the book focus on the various ways in which the horse manifests in Shakespeare, both figuratively and physically. As is widely known, the period is replete with references to horses and Raber's interpretations are often intriguing as she offers some provocative re-readings of the *Faerie Queene* as well as *Venus and Adonis*. The book explores the multiple activities that involve intense relationships between animal and human bodies, including eating, riding, managing, petting, dissecting, healing, mutilating and observing. On *Hamlet*, for example, she argues that the play is 'fundamentally about parasitism, the kind practiced by animals, and the kind experienced and practiced by humans – a parasitism that is based on the confusion of human and animal embodiment, realized in the play mainly through images of their shared bodily processes'. Most of *Animal Bodies* is about such 'shared bodily processes' from the parasitic and reciprocal to the cognitive and behavioural.

Moving squarely from the animal body to the human body, however, we encounter Lisa S. Starks-Estes' *Violence, Trauma and Virtus in Shakespeare's Roman Poems and Plays: Transforming Ovid*. Specifically focusing on appropriations of Ovid – especially the story of Philomela – Starks-Estes suggests that 'Shakespeare's entire artistic trajectory hinges on this particular tale'. Focusing on 'Ovid's mythological and poetical world' the book examines the many and wonderful ways in which Shakespeare appropriates *Metamorphoses*, including gender, sexuality, transgression, violence, ritual, and 'vulnerability, culminating in his treatment of the traumatic anxiety generated by the newly bounded self'. Similarly attuned to 'Ovid's most radical poetic move – his assault on the Virgilian epic and the ideal of Augustan virtus that it endorses' Starks-Estes considers the rich and complex effects of the epic tradition and its values. Focusing on the dizzying and mutable worlds of *Metamorphoses* Starks-Estes pursues the various narratives of desire through which gender is both explored and defined. Stark-Estes' argument is at its most engaging on the narrative poems where she observes Shakespeare's use of Ovid as a platform for the development of an explosive relationship between violence and eroticism. Here the book employs elements of psychoanalysis as well as 'contemporary trauma theory', although, as she observes, trauma theory, as such, is still developing; what constitutes 'trauma' is often under negotiation by competing cultural discourses. *Lucrece* is probably most persuasive in this respect, as this book shows, since the representation and identification of trauma are one of the preoccupations of the poem. Starks-Estes' particular interest here is the relationship between myth and the unconscious and the ways in which the effects of violence (in oneself as well as others) manifest through appropriations of Ovid. As the lengthy introduction discusses, trauma is not only a modern concept but even our contemporary understanding of trauma is diffuse, contested and subjective. Drawing on both *Metamorphoses* and *Fasti* for *The Rape of Lucrece*, she argues, Shakespeare 'fully explores the traumatic effects that erupt from the collision of these models of selfhood'. The idea of the self is manifestly tied to the various narratives of trauma that the book discusses as it moves through various different forms of experience, including fantasy, violence and sadomasochism. Although many of the readings are engaging, sometimes the idea of trauma becomes so capacious and diffuse that it is difficult to retain its sense of significance within the wider interpretations of violence and distress. The book's focus, however, is persuasive and the attention to forms of ritual particularly insightful within the context of both psychoanalysis and humanism.

Agnes Lafont's edited collection, *Shakespeare's Erotic Mythology and Ovidian Renaissance Culture*, continues the focus on Ovid. Here, however, the essays range from an emphasis on the visual arts, emotion, eroticism, to allusion and translation. Both books share an interest in sexual fantasy and the development of certain erotic narratives in Shakespeare's Ovid. Although there are some engaging essays, particularly those on *A Midsummer Night's Dream* and *Romeo and Juliet*, for example, Lafont's introduction is clotted, as when she refers to the ways in which Ovid is read as an intertext in Shakespeare: 'This interpretation plays on the possible irony and discrepancies between what is alluded to and its multiple gloss thus revealed.'

Moving from trauma to curse, however, we encounter some of the same conceptual knots in Björn Quiring's *Shakespeare's Curse: The Aporias of Ritual Exclusion in Early Modern Drama*. Quiring is tenacious and insightful in his explorations of precisely the kinds of aporias that such concepts precipitate: 'Curses thus mark the point where absolute power and complete impotence blend and become indistinguishable: the curse is a sovereign speech act that demonstrates the impossibility of sovereign speech acts.' Quiring's study focuses on what he calls 'royal dramas', but primarily *Richard III*, *King John* and *King Lear*, in which he observes that 'the structures of the curse stand out with an extraordinary, almost dazzling clarity'. Quiring focuses on the interrelations, similitudes and effects that support the early modern theatre, law, market and church: here he invokes Foucault and the crisis of representation that occurred when signs moved

from the essential to the suggestive. Within this matrix the curse becomes a fascinating and historically valuable gesture through which both power and performance are defined: 'In the early modern speech situation, this theatrical curse is ideally suited to unfolding the aporetic, crypto-theatrical structures of christologically legitimated kingship and of a jurisdiction supported by theology.' Perhaps unsurprisingly, *Richard III* provides an absorbing case study within the context of his thesis and the focus on Anne is riveting: 'By blaming all his acts of violence on Anne's beauty, Richard outlines a new image of society in the immobile center of which the Lady herself stands as an angel of destruction.' However, the density of the material and the conceptual complexities of the argument make the prose often difficult to read. The chapters on *King Lear* and *King John* are informative and offer some insightful readings of the plays but the emphasis on the opaque and self-referential rituals of forms of epistemology are sometimes clotted and unresolved.

Moving from the curse to the sublime, however, we find *Shakespeare and the Culture of Romanticism*, edited by Joseph M. Ortiz, which offers a range of essays dedicated to one of the most formative periods in the defining of Shakespeare criticism. The perspective here, however, is essentially revisionist in its de-centring of some of the most dominant voices in Romantic literature as well as rewriting certain prevailing assumptions about Shakespeare's genius and imagination. Most of the essays explore lesser known writers of the late eighteenth and early nineteenth century and some offer a new focus on lesser known texts, including Coleridge's *Zapolya*. Some of the most interesting essays here reorientate our understanding of particular dynamics, including Emily Dickinson and *Hamlet* and Ophelia and the idea of genius. The second half of the book turns its gaze first to the theatre and the ways in which romantic attitudes to and appropriations of Shakespeare's plays redefined contemporary drama; and the last section looks at how perspectives on Shakespeare – exhibitions, editions and novels – reveal a culture in which 'nearly all Renaissance poets and dramatists were available for conscription by individuals of all literary, religious, national or political persuasions'.

THE GREAT FEAST OF LANGUAGE

One of the great pleasures of this year's work has been an emphasis on Shakespeare's language through both formal linguistics and the arts of versification. Marina Tarlinskaja's *Shakespeare and the Versification of English Drama, 1561–1642* is an almost forensic study of meter and verse form in this period, and it is very compelling. One of the many strengths of this study is that it makes no attempt to homogenize or standardize our understanding of iambic pentameter. Instead, Tarlinskaja explores the variant and often complex ways in which meter behaves, from weak and strong stresses, deviations in regular patterns of verse and inversions of stress. Although the emphasis is on Shakespeare, Tarlinskaja analyses many other playwrights of the period covered and is attentive to the various ways in which writers developed their own syntactical style as well as imitated each other. Intriguingly, however, she observes that 'to mimic a poet's verse rhythm is much harder than to imitate his lexicon and phraseology'. To that end, the book explores the development and behaviour of versification in (predominantly) dramatic texts. She is also concerned with verse form as 'evidence' – of a moment, author, play, period or character – and the way in which this develops across the period as well as the careers of individual authors. Tarlinskaja's approach is largely formalist so she is mostly concerned with the statistical analysis of language, rather than any of its incumbent conceptual complexities. As a literary critic I sometimes found the profoundly rational approach frustrating but there is no doubt that Tarlinskaja makes a few more concessions here to the literary than she has in previous work. It is a very dense and very accomplished book which consistently demonstrates the performative and multifaceted potential of language to produce and reproduce meaning across a range of styles, semantics, stresses, suffixes, prefixes and syllables. Beginning with Wyatt and Surrey, the book moves through some of the major writers of the period to reveal the extent to which versification was always in development: 'verse rules are not only about "yes/no" but about "how many, how often". But every period had its range of "do's" and "don'ts"; "don'ts" in one period may become "do's" in another.' She takes in a wide range of instances as examples from a vast range of plays but they are almost always treated anatomically rather than conceptually and as a result the book has little interest in the plays themselves, only in the linguistic compositions that define them. Having said that, there are the odd moments of insight into the period which helps to contextualize the significance of statistical analysis:

It was important for an early Elizabethan poet to keep a clear contrast between everyday colloquial speech and the literary iambic poetry of a tragedy. Jacobean poets...had an opposite aim in mind: to make the language of their plays sound more like everyday speech. Fletcher's numerous enclitic phrases within the lines and his heavy feminine endings performed the same role as Shakespeare's unstressed grammatical monosyllables...that effaced syntactic boundaries between his lines. The different strategies had the same aim: to make the style of plays closer to everyday non-poetic speech.

From a literary perspective, the book is at its most absorbing when it discusses the relationship between form and content – lexical verbs and epic poetry, rhythmical italics and emotion, and the ways in which certain disyllabic suffixes (*ion*) were used to amplify declamation. Each chapter ends with a helpful summation of the most salient points and the book is structured clearly and comprehensively. The sections on Shakespeare offer more convincing evidence for certain questions on authorship (the 1602 additions to *The Spanish Tragedy* probably are by Shakespeare, and *A Lover's Complaint* probably isn't) and provide riveting insights into the development (albeit non-linear) of his 'style'.[1] It's not an easy read – and as a novice in linguistics I would have appreciated a glossary – but it is an important and rewarding study.

---

[1] Peter Kirwan continues discussion of the volume's implications for authorship below (pp. 456–7).

The final book of this year's round-up is not strictly a work of criticism but it is certainly a pleasurable read; Keith Johnson's *Shakespeare's English: A Practical Linguistic Guide* is a linguistics text, but I mention it here because I think it is a valuable text that may be of great interest to pedagogy. This is not a work of literary analysis; Johnson makes no promises to explain, explore or interpret the plays. Instead, what he offers is a fascinating and practical guide to the uses and development of the English language in Shakespeare's work. Focusing on how language can behave; its endless and mercurial possibilities; the effects of structure, word-order, grammar, syntax and diction; declensions, pronouns, compounds, implicature, speech acts, negatives, and the use of Middle English (to name only a few), Johnson unpacks the cornucopian world of Shakespeare's English. He attends to word clusters, compounds, pronouns, forms of address, curses, archaisms, verbal patterns and word order to explore the ways in which Shakespeare's vocabulary can be understood as part of the 'creative chaos' (to quote Russ McDonald) of this period. As he unpicks some of the plays' speeches Johnson observes Shakespeare's use of Latinate words and the dynamics between Anglo-Saxon and French words in the development of an 'English' language; how word order creates effect and the ways in which that effect can build up over several lines by virtue of structure as well as emphasis. Johnson is very good on context, too, and attends to certain key humanist texts and their role in the development of Shakespeare's art. The book is presented very clearly and helpfully for students and includes specific sections on rhyme, meter, pronunciation and grammar. Johnson is excellent at establishing a general picture and then moving in to focus on the detail. The structure of the book is very well thought through in the ways in which it allows the reader to grasp conceptual approaches to language and then witness the language in action. There are some subtle and clever readings of how Shakespeare uses word-order to build up and develop character as well as demonstrating the effects of compound or complex sentences, for example. What makes this an invaluable book for students is that it reveals the architecture behind much of what we take for granted. In other words, they may recognize and feel the effects of Shakespeare's language, but this book helps to explain how words produce effects and how by manipulating syntax, grammar, or even pronunciation the landscape of language can change from character to character or moment to moment. Throughout his book, Johnson keeps a keen eye on the relationship between modern English and early modern English, recognizing moments of alienation or misunderstanding as meaning has changed or morphed over the centuries. He is never patronizing but always informative and this book would be a valuable companion to any student or teacher of Shakespeare's work, irrespective of their interest in or knowledge of linguistics. It is a detailed, light-hearted, informative and wholly comprehensive guide to the pleasures and vicissitudes of Shakespeare's – and our – English.

BOOKS REVIEWED

Clare, Janet, *Shakespeare's Stage Traffic: Imitation, Borrowing and Competition in Renaissance Theatre* (Cambridge, 2014)

Cummings, Brian, *Mortal Thoughts, Religion, Secularity and Identity in Shakespeare and Early Modern Culture* (Oxford, 2013)

Goldstein, David, *Eating and Ethics in Shakespeare's England* (Cambridge, 2013)

Gray, Patrick and John D. Cox, eds., *Shakespeare and Renaissance Ethics* (Cambridge, 2014)

Griffith, Eva, *A Jacobean Company and its Playhouse: The Queen's Servants and the Red Bull Theatre, 1605–1619* (Cambridge, 2014)

Johnson, Keith, *Shakespeare's English: A Practical Linguistic Guide* (Harlow, 2013)

Johnson, Laurie, John Sutton and Evelyn Tribble, eds., *Embodied Cognition and Shakespeare's Theatre* (New York and Abingdon, 2014)

Kastan, David Scott, *A Will to Believe, Shakespeare and Religion* (Oxford, 2013)

Keenan, Siobhan, *Acting Companies and their Plays in Shakespeare's London* (London, 2014)

Knowles, Katie, *Shakespeare's Boys* (Basingstoke, 2014)

Lafont, Agnes, ed., *Shakespeare's Erotic Mythology and Ovidian Renaissance Culture* (Farnham, 2014)

Lees-Jeffries, Hester, *Shakespeare and Memory* (Oxford, 2013)

Maguire, Laurie, *Othello, Language and Writing* (London, 2014)

Ortiz, M. Joseph, ed., *Shakespeare and the Culture of Romanticism* (Farnham, 2013)

Quiring, Björn, *Shakespeare's Curse: The Aporias of Ritual Exclusion in Early Modern Royal Drama* (Abingdon, 2014)

Raber, Karen, *Animal Bodies, Renaissance Culture* (Philadelphia, 2013)

Tarlinskaja, Marina, *Shakespeare and the Versification of English Drama, 1561–1642* (Farnham, 2014)

Williams, Deanne, *Shakespeare and the Performance of Girlhood* (Basingstoke, 2014)

Wilson, Richard, *Free Will, Art and Power on Shakespeare's Stage* (Manchester, 2014)

2. SHAKESPEARE IN PERFORMANCE
reviewed by RUSSELL JACKSON

In *Shakespeare Performance Studies*, W. B. Worthen addresses issues important not only to Shakespeare studies but also to the specific field of *performance* – hence the title, with no 'in' or 'and' to conjoin the three words. The choice of 'performance' is significant because it 'implies something more unstable than theatre, at least in the context of contemporary scholarly and disciplinary debate, leveraging a sense of the stage resistant to notions of authorial, literary, textual determination'(1). Worthen examines the claims made, notably by Lukas Erne, for Shakespeare as a literary dramatist, while at the same time questioning the notion of the play-texts as in some sense blueprints or scores to be rendered, with varying degrees of fidelity, by the theatre. The arguments of Hans-Thies Lehmann's *Postdramatic Theatre* and recent responses to it also feature in the first chapter's persuasive discussion of the status of the written script.[1] The project is 'to model a way of engaging with performance that attends to its practices, to the use it makes of Shakespeare in fashioning the precise differential between the theatrical and the worldly where the meanings of performance are born.' (12) The written text is displaced from a position of control, but recognized for the 'affordances' it offers: 'writing has a dialectical relation to performance, serving at once as one of the materials the performance works on and as one of instruments it works with' (13). At a number of points the reader is invited to engage with theoretical debates about the audience as an active participant in the performance event – Jacques Rancière's *The Emancipated Spectator* (2009) is an important text here – and to question the claims of cognitive theatre studies, which are characterized as promoting 'a regulatory blend of philosophical and theatrical realism' (112).[2] Worthen does not so much discount the notion that an audience might be 'moved' by performance as question the ways in which that experience might be characterized beyond an appeal to the limiting notion of emotional identification with 'characters' established by corresponding acts of emotional imagination and recall on the part of the actors.

Worthen's lucid and wide-ranging account of the theoretical significance of this approach and its nature as a critical practice is followed by detailed examination of three examples: Nature Theatre of Oklahoma's *Romeo and Juliet*, Punchdrunk's *Sleep No More*, and Michael Almereyda's film *Hamlet*. Although all these might be considered in common critical parlance as *deconstructive*, Worthen effectively treats them as *constructive*: as complex and effective works that respond to and rechannel images and ideas from the texts that are their starting point. Indeed, the immersive *Sleep No More*, with its audience being masked witnesses of events

---

[1] Lukas Erne, *Shakespeare as Literary Dramatist* (Cambridge, 2003); Hans-Thies Lehmann, *Postdramatic Theatre*, trans. Karen Jürs-Munby (London, 2006).

[2] Jacques Rancière, *The Emancipated Spectator*, trans. Gregory Elliott (London, 2009).

and tableaux in a 'hotel' inhabited by *Macbeth*, complicates the distinction between 'text-based theatre' and 'performance'. In effect 'few conventional theatrical *Macbeth*s so richly concretize the play's language, the rich imagery of death, darkness, guilt and infanticide', and 'each spectator's progress [through the rooms] creates an associative narrative' (84). Each member of the audience wears a mask and, in accord with a defining characteristic of immersive performance, 'enters the space rather than observing it'. As many reviews and reports have testified, the experiences of individual audience members, although broadly comparable within a range constituted by what is presented, will differ according to the paths they take, and the 'associative narrative' each constructs for her- or himself will be their own.

This do-it-yourself element, albeit one carefully controlled by 'minders' who keep the audience out of areas not available to them, makes *Sleep No More* an especially powerful example for Worthen's critical project. The *Romeo and Juliet* and *Hamlet* (especially the latter, by its very nature as a filmic 'finished product') engage their audience less directly in the making process. Worthen is not the first critic to identify the sophisticated relationship between the different media employed within Almereyda's film, which is lent a particular extra-diegetic edge by its very nature as images captured on coated celluloid, seen *via* the digital media by most viewers since its initial release. But he is the first to explore this so fully in relation to the play's own equivalent of the digital media's transformational effects. The play *Hamlet* gives its own account of dramatic writing: 'it's hypertextual, capable of being reordered, inseparable from a gestural archive, unable to determine performance, always lost and recreated by intermedial transformation' (195).

Worthen's discussion of *Sleep No More* can be compared to that in Stephen Purcell's *Shakespeare and Audience in Practice*. Purcell cites a number of accounts that effectively question Punchdrunk's claim that their chosen format for this and other performances 'rejects the passive obedience usually expected of audiences' (114, quoting the Punchdrunk website), and he examines the equivocal effect of masking spectators. It is intriguing that the 'unashamedly escapist ends' (135) are contrasted with the more active role given to audiences by some other immersive productions considered by Purcell, such as Mike Pearson and Mike Brooks's *Coriolan/us* (National Theatre Wales, 2012) and the Toneelgroep Amsterdam's *Roman Tragedies* (2010). Involvement of the audience in immersive (or any kind of) theatre can take many forms, from absorption by Punchdrunk into a dream-like experience of *Macbeth*, with no specific political dimensions, to a stimulus to activism, or at least to the critical positions that might lead to it. Purcell lays the ground for his analysis of recent performances with a necessarily brisk account of concepts of the audience in the work of major twentieth-century practitioners and theorists.

Although 'audience' may well be a role that we ourselves prepare 'well before we step into the theatre', it remains 'an identity which individual spectators might never fully subscribe to at all' (153). Recognition of this brings us close to the truism that (as every actor will confirm) no two audiences are the same. Tim Crouch's *I, Malvolio*, a one-man performance in which the audience are confronted with their responses to the aggressive but pitiful steward, 'much abused' but not blameless, furnishes Purcell with detailed information (from the actor/author as well as from the critic) of the variability of these reactions in different venues and with a range of audiences. *I, Malvolio* also figures in Bridget Escolme's *Emotional Excess on the Shakespearean Stage*. Escolme's valuable examination of the nature and scope of affect in early modern performances, combined with examples from recent productions, reminds the reader of the distance between the two. Thus, although '*Twelfth Night* may be read as a comedy of social othering that is certainly unkind to the social climber', it also 'suggests that ostracization and contempt are exactly what he deserves', and the play 'un-kinds Malvolio, makes it clear that he is not one of us' (103). By the same token, the appeal by Caius Martius (Jonathan Cake) for their 'voices' to the theatre's 'groundlings' as citizens of Rome in Dominic

Dromgoole's 2006 production at Shakespeare's Globe elicited a response that effectively enlisted their support for his 'appropriate anger at the perceived inauthenticity of politicians in the world of the audience' (32). Escolme's book is a reminder that we should be wary of assumptions about early modern predecessors in their – and our – reactions to spectacles of madness or humiliation or appeals to political sympathies in the plays. The example of *Coriolanus* points to the troublesome political as well as social dimensions of the topic. General statements by performers and scholars regarding audiences and reception are thus questioned and qualified by such evidence as Purcell's accounts of audience behaviour at performances in 'shared-light spaces' like Shakespeare's Globe, and at schools during Propeller's *Pocket Henry V.* Propeller's production is examined through a dialogue between Purcell and Dr. Penelope Wood, and their divergent reactions to both the show and its reception make for an effective conclusion to a thought-provoking book.

Worthen and Purcell both take their discussion of the theory and practice of audiences far beyond the simplistic construction of theatre history in which narcotized, submissive acceptance of what is shown beyond the proscenium arch of a 'conventional' theatre is contrasted with the Brechtian ideal of distanced, thoughtful spectatorship, ideally leading to political activism. The complexities of the real situation, and the considerable (if not quite infinite) nature of the ways in which audiences respond to performance, are evident from three recent volumes in the Manchester University Press 'Shakespeare in Performance' series – on *Coriolanus*, *Titus Andronicus* and *Julius Caesar* – and in Andrew James Hartley's *Shakespeare and Political Theatre in Practice*.

Hartley provides a succinct description of the cornerstone of Brechtian thinking and practice, the 'distancing' or (in a misleading but well-established translation) 'alienating' *Verfremdungseffekt*: 'This vexed term does not imply that the characters experience only a limited range of emotions, rather that their full emotional range is held up for scrutiny by an audience that has been encouraged to maintain a critical distance from the characters rather than associating with them as in conventional realist theatre' (13). By revealing them as 'constructs on two levels, both inside and outside the play's internal logic', the performance of the characters becomes 'a device to reflect upon the social, political and economic forces which shape both the character and the conditions from which the audience beholds that character' (14). It would be difficult to devise a clearer brief account of Brecht's intentions, but two reservations have to be made – implicit, I would argue, in Hartley's accounts of the productions he discusses. Firstly, that not every duly 'distanced' performance effectively achieves the desired response; and secondly, that characters created in quite different modes and in a different theatrical context do not necessarily fail to have such an effect.

Hartley is refreshingly realistic about the factors that qualify the political effectiveness (however we define that) of Shakespearean performance: 'Theatre – Shakespearean or otherwise – does not, or cannot, create utopia by itself, but then neither does anything else' (35). Among other productions that made explicit reference to historical or contemporary events, Hartley cites a *Julius Caesar* in Atlanta, Georgia, on which he worked as a dramaturg. It illustrates the part played by contingencies on the reception of any given interpretation, political or otherwise. The production was set in 1930s Louisiana and specific reference was made to the career of Huey Long, the demagogic and charismatic governor assassinated on the steps of the state capitol in Baton Rouge in 1935. The lynching of Cinna the Poet, a young black man attacked by a white mob, a risky choice in itself, potentially 'opened up wounds from Georgia's not-too-recent past'. Because its first performance came two weeks after the September 11 attacks it was interpreted in the light of 'revenge' attacks on Muslim Americans (98). 'Productions', as Hartley points out, 'are not always in control of their own political messages.'

The same awareness of the distance between directorial intentions and audience response informs Hartley's *Shakespeare in Performance: 'Julius*

Caesar', where a survey of productions that have connected in various ways and to varying degrees with the politics of their time leads to the suggestion that 'The trick, it seems, is to find ways for the production to speak its full range of meaning if not in a contemporary voice, then at least in a recognizable political register' (135). Orson Welles's 1937 New York production and Joseph L. Mankiewicz's MGM film (1953) made significantly different connections with the political circumstances, and Hartley makes clear the latter's balancing act between implicit commentary on dictatorship and the troubling reflection of McCarthyite anxieties about 'Red' subversion. In particular, he points out the significance of the director's standoff with the forces of reaction in Hollywood, personified by Cecil B. DeMille. The productions discussed in detail are placed in the context of theatrical institutions and political issues, with a keen eye for the quality of their theatrical or cinematic failings and achievements. The problematic nature of 'colour-blind' casting; the advantages and disadvantages of a 'promenade' performance; and the paradox of an anti-heroic ethos when a star actor such as Welles is in charge and on stage, are duly weighed. This is excellent historical writing: even-handed, scrupulous in documentation and suggestive in its arguments.

The series' standards are maintained in the other two recent volumes: Robert Ormsby's *Coriolanus* and the second edition of Alan Dessen's *Titus Andronicus* (1989), extended beyond the first's terminal date (and almost doubled in length) by Michael D. Friedman. Ormsby is especially interesting on the Berliner Ensemble production of Brecht's adaptation – unfinished at his death – and its impact beyond as well as within Germany. He also analyses the RSC's 1970 production of Günter Grass's *The Plebeians Rehearse the Uprising*, in which a thinly disguised Brecht has to cope with the obligation to respond to the 1953 East German workers' uprising, a situation the 'Boss' (as he is called) deals with in a characteristically equivocal manner. This extends the topic of *Coriolanus* into what might be called 'the matter of Brecht', and Ormsby points to the London reception of both the

Ensemble's staging of the Brecht/Shakespeare version and a National Theatre production of Shakespeare's play by two directors from the German company as exemplifying a broader rejection of political theatre: 'The Ensemble's combined profession of fidelity to Shakespeare and to vaguely articulated Marxist principles was met by an ostensibly depoliticizing understanding of performance that both incorporated Brecht's politically motivated theatrical theory and served as an exclusionary reactionary force' (65). It seems from this account that the productions existed in a swirl of equivocation and misunderstanding, if not actual bad faith. There is no disputing Ormsby's claim that British reviewers 'frequently coded Brechtian theatre as an ideologically hostile and distinctly foreign threat to Shakespeare' (48). The 1971 National Theatre production, in which Anthony Hopkins took over as Caius Martius after Christopher Plummer left early in rehearsals, illustrated the tension between the desire for heroic acting in the mould of Olivier's 1959 Stratford performance and the disciplines of an approach less dominated by the exploration of the individual personality in and for itself.[3]

Engagement in this debate gives Ormsby's book an effective through line, although at times it does seem as though access to the play is inevitably stymied by appeals to the mostly unattainable goal of a fully realized Brechtian exploration of its contradictions. The story ends with Ralph Fiennes's 2012 film, and 'most reviewers . . . simply pleased with the meshing of cinema and Shakespeare'. It is claimed that 'this bland response reflects the longevity of relevance, character, narrative and language as critical categories of assessing Shakespeare,

---

[3] The NT production's background and reception are also discussed by Peter Holland in the introduction to his 2013 Arden edition of the play (120–9). A vivid eyewitness account is given by Michael Blakemore, *Stage Blood: Five Tempestuous years in the Early Life of the National Theatre* (London, 2013), pp. 24–9. Blakemore recounts that Olivier, watching the final dress rehearsal, murmured 'What a marvellous text.' When Blakemore responded with 'Yes, it's a great play', Olivier 'gently corrected [him]. "No, not a great play. A great text"' (29).

the same categories that animate the director's convictions about the film' (242). In his final paragraph Ormsby reflects ruefully on the 'resilience of Hollywood Shakespeare' exemplified by Fiennes's film, which 'strengthens the playwright's brand – based on star power, a cut script, "respectfully" interventionist direction and spectacle – that has prevailed . . . for most of the postwar era' (243). By way of contrast, Bridget Escolme's discussion of the film in *Emotional Excess* is less dismissive of its political resonances: 'Fiennes's performance of anger in political space foregrounds the political uses of emotion and the subjectivity of emotion as I would argue the play does' (44). Despite his apparent pessimism, the evidence provided by Ormsby's own chapters also suggests that the stage history of the play has not been quite an unmitigated story of unchallenged false consciousness. It is arguable that the changes made by Brecht and his successors at the Berliner Ensemble made the play's uncomfortable study of heroism, its failure to reconcile taints and honours, and its political contradictions more palatable and less challenging. Kenneth Tynan's response to the production, which he first saw in Berlin in 1965, is significant: up to Caius Martius's banishment it was 'a masterpiece: politics and theatre exquisitely wedded'. Unfortunately, 'in the later acts Shakespeare lets Brecht down by stressing personal relationships in a way that goes against the Brechtian grain'. The 'anti-hero' is 'historically convincing', but from this point on 'stripped as he is of emotional complexities, he becomes theatrically uninteresting, if not redundant'.[4]

Michael Freedman's account of *Titus Andronicus* in performance since 1988 is attached to – and simultaneously distanced from – Alan Dessen's text by a 'Segue' in which the author distinguishes between his approach and that of his predecessor. Broadly speaking, where Dessen evaluates productions according to the extent to which they realize the play, Freedman stresses 'the contingent, rather than the universal quality of the play in performance.' That said, he accepts that he follows Dessen's precedent 'in examining recent productions by way of their solutions to the various "problems" presented by *Titus*' (130). The productions range from New York Shakespeare Festival's 'weirdly moderate' 1988 staging (147, quoting the reviewer Michael Feingold) to the 'grand and ruthless stage images' of Yukio Ninagawa (235, quoting Michael Dobson's *Shakespeare Survey* review.) From the point of view of political engagement, pride of place goes to Gregory Doran's 1995 production for the Market Theatre of Johannesburg and Silviu Purcarete's for the National Theatre of Craiova, Romania (1992). In the image-making category, a *Titus Andronicus* Academy Awards contest would have to weigh the nominations of Ninagawa, Daniel Mesguich (Paris, 1989) and Julie Taymor – who enters the field with both theatre and film versions (New York, 1994 and 20th Century Fox, 1999).

Taymor's film shared many ideas and images, now more fully realized, with her 'black box' production for Theatre for a New Audience, including the prologue with the boy playing destructive games at a kitchen table, the bathing of Titus and his sons after their return from war, and the 'penny arcade' images that reinforce the on-stage (or in the film, diegetic) action. Mesguich, whose Shakespeare productions have evinced a profound respect not only for the text of the play in question but for all sorts of other texts that have found their way into them, placed his *Titus* (Paris, 1989) in an upended library, with books falling in flames to the stage in a librarian's dystopian nightmare. (In his 1999 *Tempest* at the Comédie-française Caliban and, in his turn, Ferdinand, were set to work moving books from the – vertical – stacks: as one tome was hefted out, another dropped down the pile and took its place.) Although Friedman's approach pays due respect to these extraordinary works that take the play's text as a starting point rather than seeking to 'realize' the script as it stands, the pattern emerges of a series of litmus tests. These include the characterization of Aaron and its racial implications; the treatment of young Lucius and his status as witness as well as promise (or threat) for the

---

[4] Kenneth Tynan, *Tynan Right and Left* (London, 1967), pp. 161, 162.

future, especially in the final moments; and the depiction of the politics of Rome.

Brecht haunts these volumes in the series, often as a reproach to productions that allegedly undercut or failed to bring out the the plays' political potential by succumbing to the audiences' desire for psychologically convincing individual characters or, alas, heroes and heroines. Can Brecht himself be claimed as a 'great Shakespearean'? David Barnett admits at the outset in his essay in Volume 14 of the *Great Shakespeareans* collection that this may seem 'overblown' (112). But the pervasive influence of Brecht on twentieth-century Shakespearean performance supports the claim as much as, if not more than, the specifics of his work on and with Shakespeare. For his own theory and practice, 'Shakespeare offered Brecht an exemplary type of theatre, alive with complexity, contradiction, and historical realism, against which he could contrast the shortcomings of the institution of bourgeois theatre' (127). On the other hand, as the history of the Brecht/Shakespeare *Coriolanus* and its reception testifies, 'The major problems that Brecht encountered when re-reading Shakespeare concerned the central subject matter of so many of the plays – their great individuals' (119). Barnett's conclusion carries conviction: the relationship between the playwrights was dialectical: 'Shakespeare, the thesis, met Brecht, his antithesis, and this led to a wealth of syntheses, which, just as in any dialectical process, were non-deterministic' (154).

Like most of the other essays in this series, Barnett's achieves an appropriate balance between exposition (we want to know what these Shakespeareans have done) and evaluation (we want to know what it signifies and what it's worth). Ruth Morse, the editor of Volume 14, has the difficult task in her own essay of explaining Victor Hugo's credentials to readers who may be unaware of the Shakespearean dimension of his work, or, indeed, may know little of the immense Hugolian corpus beyond the novels *Notre Dame de Paris* (aka *The Hunchback of Notre Dame*) and *Les Misérables* (aka *Les Mis*, the musical). *William Shakespeare* (1864) the voluminous work that, in translation, represents

this aspect of Hugo to the Anglophone world, begins with what his biographer Graham Robb has described as 'one of the most inaccurate lives of Shakespeare ever published' and goes on to chapter after chapter in which 'vastly extended metaphors move over the subject like weather systems'.[5] The title of her essay is 'Les Hugo', and, as Morse points out, it took two Hugos, *père et fils*, to make up the one Great Shakespearean: Victor, the force to be reckoned with and master of afflatus, and his son François-Victor, the able and meticulous scholar and translator of the edition published in 1859–65. The father had absorbed Shakespeare, not always (or usually) through direct study, as a weapon in his fight as a dramatist against 'the dead hand of national greatness-in-correctness' (29). Shakespeare 'gave him what he needed', and his needs were prodigious. Morse gives a detailed account of the translations and their legacy, and of Hugo's dealings in and with the Bard (a title he welcomed for himself, so no harm is done in adopting it in this context). Hugo *père* was a cultural omnivore – although he did not always read the books on which he expounded his opinions – and a multitude of other authors and artists figure in the story, not least Walter Scott and Verdi. Hugo's political career and his status as France's most prominent exile during the years of the Shakespeare translation are inextricably bound up with all his poetic, dramatic and novelistic productions. Notoriously, in politics he could turn and turn again, and still ended up with spectacular obsequies and burial in the Panthéon, the funerary destination of choice for the nation's officially recognised Great Men. (Although admission is not now restricted to male luminaries, the inscription on the pediment remains: 'Aux grands hommes, la Patrie reconnaissante'.) In *Shakespeare* Hugo effectively welcomed the senior dramatist into his own personal pantheon. As Robb points out, the book was 'a vast development of the 1824 obituary of Byron in which Hugo had imagined the great names of literature forming a new family about him'.[6] Morse's

---

[5] Graham Robb, *Victor Hugo* (London, 1997), pp. 399, 400.
[6] Robb, p. 400.

subtle and thorough study, with a conciseness the expansive Great Man would have found insulting, gives a persuasive picture of Shakespeare's place in the grandly egocentric art of the father as well as the great services done to French Shakespeare by the respective prestige and industry of father and son.

The unifying theme of this volume is the translation and repurposing of Shakespeare's works into cultures as well as tongues other than his own. In an essay that is both informative and moving, Anne Pasternak Slater discusses the place of Shakespeare in the poetry and translations of Boris Pasternak and their significance in the culture of the Soviet Union. Slater's work complements that of Courtney Lehmann on Grigori Kozintsev in Volume 17 (reviewed in *Shakespeare Survey 67*, pp. 480–1), especially in its reminder that the use of the translation in the films of *Hamlet* and *King Lear* is in itself significant: it is intriguing to learn that in Innokenti Smoktunovski's performance 'Hamlet himself, young and blonde, in this black-and-white film looks uncannily like the white-haired Pasternak in his last years' (111).

In the theatres of Soviet Russia the translation of *Hamlet*, 'the play [Pasternak] worked hardest over, lost three directors in turn' and the text was 'extremely fluid'. When his son came to edit the version for publication in 1968 he 'found he had twelve different versions to work from, as well as manuscript corrections...in a late edition of the text' (107). Slater, who is the daughter of Boris Pasternak's youngest sister, Lydia, has had access to an unpublished photocopy in the family archive of the 1940 prompt copy from Nemirovich-Danchenko's production, which records every alteration made in the course of rehearsals. Rehearsal was as far as that production had gone: in one of many hazardous intersections between art and political reality, the production's progress was halted in June 1941 by the Nazi invasion. When the director died in 1943 the work was taken up by his co-director Sakhnovsky. Pasternak and the actor who was to play the prince, Boris Livanov, continued to refine the text. In 1945, at the end of the war, it seemed that *Hamlet* was

about to reach its audience. Livanov was waiting to go on for the final dress rehearsal when the production was 'terminated without explanation'. The translation had originally been commissioned by Vsevolod Meyerhold, who was arrested, tortured and shot in 1940, and Slater comments that 'it now seems probable that the deaths of not one but two of the three directors connected with the production were deliberate' (69). Stalin's distaste for 'Hamletism' together with the repressive cultural policies that sought to enforce 'socialist realism' made any kind of public performance a risky, if not potentially deadly, business. 'Hamlet' is the first of the cycle of Yuri's poems at the end of the novel *Doctor Zhivago*, and one of the two that were read over Pasternak's open grave. Slater quotes the translation by his sister Lydia. The final lines are especially poignant: 'I am alone; all round me drowns in falsehood; / Life is not a walk across a field' (78). These essays on Brecht, Hugo and Pasternak and Timothy Mathews' 'Aimé Césaire, *Une Tempête*: On Poetry, Legacy and Work', an illuminating reading of a major postcolonial text, make this volume a notable contribution to the study of the politics, local and general, of adaptation and translation.

Volume 18, edited by Peter Holland, offers essays on Peter Brook, Peter Hall, Yukio Ninagawa and Robert LePage. Holland traces Brook's journey from radicalism 'within the core of the theatrical establishment' to a world (or worlds) elsewhere, but does so without shaping his essay in strict chronological order: he begins with the 1970 *Dream* and then takes three *Hamlet* productions, from the Phoenix Theatre, London in 1955–56, via *Qui est là?* at the Bouffes du Nord in 1995, to *The Tragedy of Hamlet* in 2000. Like the comparison of Brook's stage and film versions of *King Lear* (1962 and 1971), Holland's tracing of the history of Brook's dealings with *Hamlet* encompasses the director's innovations in terms of different theoretical and practical approaches, configurations of the audience/performance relationship, and developing ideas about the texts. They amount to a dialogue between Brook and Artaud, Grotowski, Brecht and Shakespeare. Shakespearean productions at the

Bouffes du Nord (*Timon of Athens*, *The Tempest*, *Measure for Measure*, *The Tragedy of Hamlet*) have complemented such undertakings as *Orghast at Persepolis* and *Maharabata*, *The Ik* and *Conference of Birds* to build Brook's range and that of the actors he has worked with. It is tempting to see a return to the source in the austerely staged two-hander, *Love is My Sin* (2009), which shapes a number of the sonnets into a narrative that is not the familiar triangle of poet, dark lady and rival. But this would provide too neat a narrative: Holland is surely right to order his essay by ideas, influences and the sense of an ongoing dialogue. In his final section, 'Dreaming Again', drawing here as elsewhere on his experience as a member of the audience, he recalls his response to Puck's invitation to 'give me your hands' at the play's conclusion: 'For the one and only time in my playgoing, I did reach out my hands, not threatened by the breaking of the barriers between actors and audience, but instead thrilled to be able to join with them physically, as we had all joined together throughout the performance' (46). (So did I, and for the same reasons.)

In Peter Hall, Stuart Hampton-Reeves takes on another pivotal figure in the modern history of British Shakespearean performance (47), whose career has intersected at important points with Brook's but diverged from it significantly after the 1960s. Hampton-Reeves explores 'the interrelatedness of his artistic and political lives, and the dissonances between them' (48). 'In [Hall's] best work', he suggests, 'Shakespeare became a dialogic language through which the ensemble and the audience were engaged in a broader debate about the present' (49). Who – even Brecht – could ask for anything more? Nevertheless, Hall's troubled tenure as artistic director of the National Theatre, with instances of managerial ruthlessness and accusations of self-seeking planning decisions, was marked by some notable artistic failures (*The Tempest* with Gielgud in 1974) as well as triumphal successes (*Coriolanus* with McKellen in 1984, *Antony and Cleopatra* with Dench and Hopkins in 1987). The ruthlessness led to accusations of self-interest in artistic and programming

decisions, chronicled fully in Daniel Rosenthal's *The National Theatre Story* (London, 2014) and driven home with vigour (and a spirit of settling scores) in Michael Blakemore's *Stage Blood*. Hall's approach to the texts of the plays, particularly in matters of verse speaking, became less open and flexible from the 1990s on. The 'radical centre' he sought to achieve at Stratford in the 1960s is described as 'a careful balance between furthering his ambitions for the RSC as an established public institution and the anti-authoritarian impulse driving innovation in performance practice' (62). At times this perceptive study takes on a sombre, reflective and almost elegiac tone, but its conclusion rightly credits Hall with having 'transformed Shakespeare performance from a traditionalized pageant into a medium through which the contemporary world could be politicized and resisted' (78). *The Wars of the Roses*, in which Hall collaborated as director with John Barton and Clifford Williams, and the 1965 *Hamlet* made a lasting mark on the attitudes of a generation, as well as establishing an approach that for at least two decades characterized the RSC as a source of innovation and excitement.

The other essays in the volume are by Alexander C. Y. Huang on Yukio Ninagawa and by Margaret Jane Kidnie and Jane Freeman on Robert Lepage. Huang sees Ninagawa's Shakespeare work as 'nurtured by Japan's rebirth and consolidation of its national identity after the [Second World] war', and as thriving 'in the contentious space between two cultures' (81). The beauty and strangeness of the productions has been responded to differently by audiences within and beyond Japan, and Huang makes the all-important point that in them the Japanese theatrical traditions they draw on have a different valency within their own culture: 'Ninagawa's signature metatheatrical framing and use of the exoticized and stylized Kabuki, Noh and Bunraku techniques may seem radical, but his works shed light on an often-overlooked aspect of English Shakespeares: the naturalized filtration through realism and naturalism' (110). As well as raising familiar questions about the nature of international (if not strictly intercultural) performance and its reception, Huang's essay touches on themes that have recurred in many of the other books reviewed here. Techniques for 'making strange', defamiliarizing performance and questioning audience assumptions depend on a sense of what is familiar or assumed: productions that travel the world, as Ninagawa's have done, encounter different realities and illusions from those on which their effects have been predicated.

The significance of Lepage's work and that of his Montréal-based production company Ex Machina in his native Québec is not apparent when it is presented beyond its borders: there is no appeal to a specific 'national' or local performance tradition in the radically innovative staging and acting, and when the text is in English rather than 'standard' French or Québecois, the national or regional identity is not apparent. (Even when the performance is in 'standard' French, as with *Coriolan*, most members of an Anglophone audience are unlikely to distinguish between one variety of French and another.) But, as Kidnie and Marshall point out, 'Lepage treats Shakespeare's scripts, whether in English, French or Québecois, as a theatrical resource, not as a means to articulate national identity' (133). The most striking example of a production profiting from issues of language politics, though, would seem to be the *Romeo and Juliette* (sic) directed with Gordon McCall in 1989. The Montagues and Capulets were played in their own language by Anglophone and Francophone Canadians respectively. In the balcony scene, when Juliette began to speak, it was in a mix of English and French, even though the character thought she was alone: 'This tactic of code-switching within a single speech extended the perception of Juliette's immersion in an exploratory daydream' (135).

'Manipulation of audience perspective is something of a trademark in Lepage's theatre' (137), from the use in *Coriolan* of a variable 'proscenium' aperture that at times allowed only parts of the actors' bodies to be seen, or revealed them manipulating marionettes while they voiced the characters, to the complex construction that made his *Elsinore* into one of the most technically elaborate one-man shows in theatre history. Lepage has an international reputation for productions that bring together technology, acrobatics and dramatic texts, but does not figure significantly in the overall picture of Québecois Shakespeare given by Jennifer Drouin's *Shakespeare in Québec: Nation, Gender and Adaptation*. From her perspective, the 'tradaptations' (his term) of *Macbeth*, *The Tempest* and *Coriolanus* by Michel Garneau are far more important. Garneau's scripts do not change the plot or characters, but translate the text into 'an approximation of an eighteenth-century dialect spoken in New France prior to the [British] Conquest'. Locations and historical details are changed to 'conflate the action within the world of Shakespeare's plays with the Conquest and contemporary neocolonialism' (89). Although the versions in which gender is addressed have more resonance outside Québec (and English Canada), Drouin's main focus is on productions, translations and 'tradaptations' that are by and for a community (or nation) that needs them 'in the service of the nation's decolonization'. English Canadian adaptations, she claims, struggle to wrest authority from an undead author and lack the paradoxical advantage of being made within a theatrical culture that has Québec's 'complex colonial, postcolonial, and neocolonial relationships with France, Britain and English Canada' (191). As Kidnie and Marshall point out, Lepage has used both the 'standard' translations by François-Victor Hugo and Garneau's 'tradaptations' which 'present different challenges for performance', the former carrying a freight of Romanticism the director feels bound to resist, the latter limited to the specifics of their cultural-political situation. At least in the English theatre, says Lepage, 'you aren't fighting against the text: you're using it' (Kidnie and Marshall, 129).

William Poel, Harley Granville Barker, Tyrone Guthrie and Sam Wanamaker are the Great Shakespeareans treated in Volume 15, edited by Cary M. Mazer. The intersection between innovations in twentieth-century theatre and the rediscovery of the thrust stage features in each essay. As the editor points out in his introduction, 'the four artist-advocate-polemicists' were 'enmeshed in the dynamics of their respective (if overlapping) historical moments' (6). Marion O'Connor places Poel in the context of the societies and groups he worked with, and their concepts of historical and cultural identity, and examines his historicist vision of a national theatre, which did not altogether correspond to that of Matthew Arnold: Poel conceived it as 'a dramatic museum', Arnold as 'dramatic nursery' (12). In his own essay Mazer provides insightful commentary on the relationship between Barker's personal and artistic life, his ambitions for a national theatre, and the move away from direct participation in the theatre that marked a notable change in his career, as he became 'an experimental scientist who no longer went into the laboratory' (96). Countering the interpetations of J. L. Styan and others, Mazer shows convincingly that Barker was a 'non-Shakespearean-Shakespearean', whose productions, rather than having 'rediscovered the Elizabethan Shakespeare in the modern theatre', accommodated what he learned from Poel 'while remaining a modernist'. In his criticism he was 'an uncredentialed independent scholar' who, while trying to move as a writer into the 'stuffy community of academy-based Shakespeare scholarship . . . retained his sensibilities as a theatrical modernist' (66).

With Guthrie and Wanamaker the cultural politics of Shakespearian performance play an especially prominent role. Guthrie's Stratford, Ontario theatre, Robert Shaughnessy suggests, is 'a space for Shakespeare (or, for that matter, anything else) [that] is everywhere and nowhere, neither past nor present, and yet somehow pertaining to both', a situation that 'strangely mirrored the contradictory Canadian-ness of the Stratford festival itself', and its ambiguous situation between Old and New Worlds, high art and popular, commercial culture, aligned with an Anglophone cultural identity 'uneasily shadowed by its Francophone other' (137). The complementary elements of rigour and playfulness in Guthrie's directing, and his 'gift for large-scale orchestration and potent image-making' (106) are documented and analysed with an appropriate combination of detail and appreciation for the broader interpretative vision.

Paul Prescott argues that 'the impetus for much of what Wanamaker did was psychologically determined by the need to belong' (154). His essay gives a valuable account of Wanamaker's acting career, as well as the route taken to the South Bank by this possessor of 'a dynamic stage presence that was quintessentially modern, edgy and American' (165). Rather than give a blow-by-blow account of how the theatre was built – already fully documented elsewhere – Prescott focuses on Wanamaker's 'contribution to the idea of the Globe as a cultural and artistic institution' (155). Political convictions and the price to be paid for them pursued him, from his exile as a victim of McCarthyism, through the attempt to establish a people's theatre in Liverpool, to the struggle to make Shakespeare's Globe an artistic asset for the communities of South London as well as for the public in general. There was considerable irony in this alleged 'Red' having to deal with criticism of the project from the academic left and the obstructive tactics of the Labour-led local council. Wanamaker's pursuit of his vision in Liverpool and London and his qualities of *chutzpah*, charm (as necessary) and determination (invariable) would bear comparison with Joe Papp's personal and artistic saga in New York.

As with the confluence of politics and translations in Volume 14, this makes for a strikingly coherent collection, in which fresh evaluations and effective research are brought to bear on familiar figures, seen in the context of the institutions they inhabited and sought to change. In the series' overall selection of the truly 'great', readers may be disappointed to find worthy candidates excluded from the virtual Pantheon. The list could be augmented almost indefinitely, as a parlour game for winter nights. The series editors, Peter Holland and Adrian Poole, would be the first to admit as much – as indeed they do in their prefaces: 'Deciding who to include has been less difficult than deciding who to exclude' (vi). As the editor of Volume 16, on Gielgud, Ashcroft, Olivier and Dench, which cannot of course be reviewed here, I must declare an interest, but it seems appropriate to conclude that the series has produced some excellent long essays and that Holland and Poole are to be both envied their opportunity and also commiserated with on account of the difficulties of the task.

In *Shakespeare and YouTube: New Media Forms of the Bard*, Stephen O'Neill suggests that the content available through the site 'is of value to the field of Shakespeare studies because it provides a point of connection between new media forms and Shakespeare, a connection that renders Shakespearean texts more accessible and relevant to so-called "Generation M"' (81). The range as well as quantity of content available at any one time is considerable, and O'Neill provides a discerning guide to the different varieties of commentary, parody and appropriation that have been posted. The exploration can be entertaining in itself, a new and dangerously seductive replacement for the 'parlour games' I invoked above. Because it employs the kind of algorithms that can allow Amazon.com and other Internet merchants to prompt if not altogether direct our purchasing habits, the finding process is not as untrammelled as it may seem. Time spent on YouTube partakes of the 'lessening of temporal consciousness' ('Is it that time already?') as we career or sometimes plod through the 'busy attention economy' (31, 32). Fiennes's *Coriolanus*, present in more than one of the books reviewed here, receives enjoyable paratextual commentary on YouTube, and O'Neill cites an example that qualifies its emphasis on 'the tragic pathos of the warrior', by mashing the film's battle scene between Caius Martius and Aufidius with the track 'Mutter' by the German band Rammstein (53–4).

In *Hamlet* postings, Ophelia 'emerges as a catalyst for various forms of online production, participation and expression' (114), while, perhaps unsurprisingly, the prince 'offers an especially apposite figure to explore a scenario where self-expression occurs in a heavily mediated, secondary and even belated form' (93). The downside of this plenitude of content and opportunity has to be considered, and in his chapter on 'Race in YouTube Shakespeare' O'Neill welcomes its capacity for the promotion of 'greater diversity and multiculturalism' while warning that 'the openness of online culture does not necessarily equate with an openness of

attitude' (159). A final chapter, 'The Teaching and Learning Tube: Challenges and Affordance', takes stock of the potentials and pitfalls of YouTube in education and offers 'Suggested Assignments' that will sharpen the focus of its application in the work of students and teachers, taking it beyond its common role as a supplier of sometimes vital but occasionally nugatory self-publishing and self-promotion and a source of none-too-reliable (and often illegal and temporary) copies of performance product. This savvy, informative and accessible book is an asset to teachers and learners in general as well as to researchers. A copy by every Shakespearian's laptop?

Intermediality in stage performances and the attendant radical alterations in the nature of the spectators' relationship with what is set live on stage before them feature in Worthen's *Shakespeare Performance Studies* and Purcell's *Shakespeare and Audience in Practice*. These fresh affordances extend and qualify those coming from the texts themselves. In her richly documented study, *Intermedial Shakespeares on European Stages*, Aneta Mancewicz examines a remarkable range of such performances. These include Stefan Pucher's *Sturm*, whose intermedial 'live' existence as a variation on *The Tempest* has been enhanced (or rendered more complex) by its being recorded for television and subsequently released as a DVD. The layering of technologies in this manner complicates the picture in a thought-provoking manner. With its own intermediality viewed through another medium, by her account *Sturm* becomes a work of a subtly different order. One might cite the response of many viewers of live HD broadcasts of opera productions, who claim that the greater intimacy of access afforded by skilful camerawork and editing enhances the experience, even as they inevitably lose out on the 'liveness' that goes with being present in the theatre. Mancewicz observes that, with its 'book-like set that incorporate[d] song performances and video projections', the production 'simultaneously transformed into a page and a screen, the production raises questions about originality, authority and fidelity in appropriations of Shakespeare in a digital context' (40). Mancewicz describes the subtlety with which this application of intermediality enriches the work done by *Sturm*, not only in its rendering of the play itself but in addressing broader questions of perception and understanding that then loop back into the text. Prospero (Hildegard Schmahl) and Ariel (Wolfgang Pegler) are portrayed as 'artists manipulating the action and commenting on the art of illusion', collaborators rather than master and servant. 'Seated majestically on a throne made of two stuffed tigers' Schmahl appears as a colonial ruler, who invites the audience to take on the role of Miranda (present on stage) in what became a soliloquy recounting the events that brought him and his daughter to the island (42,43). The sexual politics of the production are enhanced by Prospero's being played as a 'trouser role', rather than being gender-shifted like Helen Mirren's Prospera in Julie Taymor's film, and Ariel cross-dresses 'in white as a female fairy with white lilies' as he watches Ferdinand mourning his father. As the action unfolds, the set's 'moving white walls . . . turn with the change of scene', a reminder of Prospero's learning as the source of his magic and the cause of his exile: 'the unavoidable legacy of the Shakespearean script, as well as the role of the book in *The Tempest*' (45).

A Midsummer Night's Dream, directed by Sean Holmes for Filter Theatre (London, 2012), is at the opposite extreme in terms of resources employed, with the digital media evoked but not present on stage. The actors 'parody the behaviour of superheroes from computer games . . . through establishing a connection between a prop or sound and an action that it triggers, creating the effect of a digital medium in the imagination of the spectators' (158). In an already metatheatrical play 'intermediality becomes part of the performance's dramaturgy', with Puck controlling the lovers as if he were playing a video game. This is both 'an act of perception which leads to the reconceptualization of a medium on the part of an audience', and a great deal of fun, not always or often a priority in the world of intermedial performance, which tends to be grimmer, ironizing and alienating in both the Brechtian and the common senses of the word.

As Worthen observes in his chapter on Michael Almereyda's *Hamlet*, with its multiple digital media (in technologies rapidly changing as the film was being made), the film situates perception, recording and memory, Hamlet's not-so-fond records, alongside its own exploration of cinematic ways and means. Old regimes, even in technology, are fading and being replaced. A number of contributions to the study of screen versions of Shakespeare reflect the shift, either directly or by implication, as the topic 'Shakespeare on Film', with its reference to the fast-disappearing medium of photography onto celluloid, is replaced by 'Shakespeare on Screen'. Shakespeares made for television are now increasingly viewed on disc or streamed to a variety of new devices; time-shifted from their initial viewing time; and no longer strictly speaking 'broadcast'. Even those originated since the 1940s, as we access them now, have changed as cultural and aesthetic phenomena. The essays in *Shakespeare on Screen: Macbeth*, edited by Sarah Hatchuel, Nathalie Vienne-Guérin and Victoria Bladen, include an account of a remarkable television version – Claude Brama's 1959 *Macbeth* for what was then France's single channel – and collectively the contributors address a range of other screen performances, from a *Macbeth*-inflected episode in the crime series *Columbo* (1972) to Rupert Goold's film of his 2007 stage production, as well as most of the more familiar feature films made for the cinema (Polanski, Kurosawa, Welles) and one unrealized project (Olivier's). Goold's film is especially interesting in the context of the digital media, created as it was for television and DVD viewing rather than being shown in cinemas. From this perspective it makes for stimulating comparison with other stage-to-television versions, such as Greg Doran's *Hamlet*, and stage-to-cinema adaptations like Adrian Noble's *A Midsummer Night's Dream*. The essayists' focus is mainly on the interpretive strategies adopted with regard to *Macbeth*, but this collection also reflects the richness and variety of the opportunities offered by the media the versions use.

Taken together, the works under review convey a strong impression of this plurality, in both the performance media employed and the early modern scripts themselves. Although its theoretical approach may not carry absolute conviction for every reader, Simon Ryle's *Shakespeare, Cinema and Desire* is persuasive in its presentation of this dimension, notably in the case of the perhaps unavoidably psychoanalytical aspect of all post-Freudian *Hamlet*s. Olivier's film, with its maker's professedly Oedipal approach and its dream-like quality, lends itself readily to a post-Lacanian as well as post-Freudian enquiry. Ryle concludes his chapter on *Hamlet* with the reflection that the cinema is attracted to the play because 'in Hamlet's ghosts, mirror reflections, mimetic unfoldings and rhetorical doubles . . . the cinema finds an image of its own ghostly projections' (173). In the 'Screen Adaptations' series, Samuel Crowl, writing in plainer terms and using a different critical method, comes to a complementary if less theoretically inflected conclusion: Olivier may not show us the man failing to make up his mind, as the prologue had claimed, 'in the sense of being unable to make a decision', but his film 'does constitute, at least partially, the tragedy of a man who could not make up, in the sense of being able to invent and sustain a single and stable identity, his mind' (59).

There are times when Ryle's writing abounds in too many senses for its own good, and the lucidity of his analysis of representations of the role of Cleopatra (including DeMille's and Mankiewicz's non-Shakespearian films) is perhaps impaired rather than served by the reflection that 'Circling the wound of *das Ding*, Cleopatra's absent transcendence renews the dignity of the present by intimating a future encounter with truth' (128). This comes after George Steiner has led him to St Jerome as a confirmation that 'not everything can be translated now' – itself a very concise translation of the Latin text Ryle quotes, and one of a number of moments when the pudding of his discourse may be over-egged. Nevertheless, this is an insightful and provocative study.

From the heady and at times vertiginous heights of digital filmic Shakespeare it seems appropriate to end this review by coming down to earth, literally, with performances out of doors and on the ground. But that ground being Australian, the history of outdoor Shakespeare acquires a significance specific to the landscape as well as the colonial and postcolonial situations. As with Canadian/Québecois Shakespeare, though without the same kind of linguistic issues, Australian Shakespeare inhabits more than one situation in relation to colonialism. Rosemary Gaby's *Open-air Shakespeare under Australian Skies* describes the progress from decorous charity shows on the lawns of colonial mansions to populist 'picnic Shakespeare' and site-responsive interpretations. Indecorous playing in comedies has been embraced with gusto. For example, Glenn Elston's 2014 Sydney *A Midsummer Night's Dream* for the Australian Shakespeare Company and his other open-air productions are described by Gaby as 'characteristically Australian: they were irreverent, fun, improvisatorial, laid-back, and they featured Australian accents and popular Australian actors' (74). Nevertheless, other definitions of 'Australian' are available. Performances in landscapes that have a solemn significance for the indigenous people have to take account of ground that is sometimes sacred. Gaby's final paragraph qualifies Peter Brook's statement, 'I can take any empty space and call it a bare stage' with the reflection that the settlers' mistaken perception of a land empty and available for any use conflicted with the indigenous view of 'a complex and spiritually populated environment'. Gaby is reassured by the acknowledgement of this by directors and companies: 'More and more today . . . players and spectators alike take pleasure in the ephemeral nature of the open-air event; in the serendipity of finding a space that, far from being empty, is filled with a life of its own which will resonate with Shakespeare's vision and still endure long after the performance itself has melted into air' (111). This is site-responsive, rather than site-specific, performance, immersive in a different sense from that of Punchdrunk's *Macbeth*-haunted 'hotel'. Gaby's work reminds the reader of the multiplicity of places, each with their own significance, where Shakespeare can be found and, perhaps, rediscovered.

WORKS REVIEWED

Crowl, Samuel, *Screen Adaptations: Shakespeare's 'Hamlet': The Relationship between Text and Film* (London and New York, 2014)

Drouin, Jennifer, *Shakespeare in Québec: Nation, Gender, and Adaptation* (Toronto, 2014)

Escolme, Bridget, *Emotional Excess on the Shakespearean Stage: Passion's Slaves* (London and New York, 2014)

Friedman, Michael D. and Alan Dessen, *Shakespeare in Performance: 'Titus Andronicus'*, 2nd edn (Manchester, 2103)

Gaby, Rosemary, *Open-air Shakespeare: Under Australian Skies* (Basingstoke and New York, 2014)

Hartley, Andrew James, *Shakespeare and Political Theatre in Practice* (Basingstoke, 2013)

Shakespeare in Performance: 'Julius Caesar' (Manchester, 2014)

Holland, Peter, ed., *Great Shakespeareans Volume xviii: Brook, Hall, Ninagawa, Lepage* (London and New York, 2013)

Mancewicz, Aneta, *Intermedial Shakespeares on European Stages* (Basingstoke and New York, 2014)

Mazer, Cary M., ed., *Great Shakespeareans Volume xv: Poel, Barker, Guthrie, Wanamaker* (London and New York, 2013)

Morse, Ruth, ed., *Great Shakespeareans Volume xiv: Hugo, Pasternak, Brecht, Césaire* (London and New York, 2013)

O'Neill, Stephen, *Shakespeare and YouTube: New Media Forms of the Bard* (London and New York, 2014)

Ormsby, Robert, *Shakespeare in Performance: 'Coriolanus'* (Manchester, 2014)

Purcell, Stephen, *Shakespeare and Audience in Practice* (Basingstoke and New York, 2013)

Ryle, Simon, *Shakespeare, Cinema and Desire: Adaptation and Other Futures of Shakespeare's Language* (Basingstoke and New York, 2014)

Worthen, W. B., *Shakespeare Performance Studies* (Cambridge, 2014)

3. EDITIONS AND TEXTUAL STUDIES
reviewed by PETER KIRWAN

RESITUATING SHAKESPEARE

Opening last year's review, my predecessor Sonia Massai spoke of 'Copernican Revolutions' in the field of textual editing as she confronted some of the after-effects of the 'materialist turn' on the work of 2013 (484). In succeeding her in these pages, I would like to return to what seems to be an increasingly apt metaphor for recent interventions in Shakespeare editing and textual theory. This year has seen no major new scholarly Shakespeare-centred editions or anthologies. Rather, representing a shift away from a Ptolemaic model revolving around Shakespeare, the works reviewed in this volume – many of which are aimed at a wider readership than scholars – accord Shakespeare a less central role in his own universe, presenting him as an orbiting body (albeit a key one) in the wider universe of early modern drama. While future years will no doubt feature more traditional scholarly editions where Shakespeare assumes the dominant

role in relation to his own plays, it is a pleasure to begin my role at *Shakespeare Survey* with a collection of books and essays insistent on foregrounding the other agents involved in the shaping and contextualising of Shakespeare's plays.

RECONTEXTUALISING SHAKESPEARE'S WORK

The premise of Jeremy Lopez's *Constructing the Canon of Early Modern Drama* is the modelling of a new form of anthology, both critiquing the history and theory of the anthology form and proposing an alternative canon of early drama. Delightfully and confusingly, the book adopts the anthology form in its own layout: one can read the book 'horizontally' from left to right, 'vertically' by skipping between chapters ending in the same digit (1, 11, 21, etc.) or elliptically in the manner of the old 'Choose Your Own Adventure' books, with each chapter containing a footnote cross-reference to another chapter that touches on shared concerns. While the self-consciousness of this design is palpable, the structure reinforces the book's theoretical standpoint by insisting on shared awareness of form and content at all times. Despite the apparent linearity of the book form, the anthology invites a more active form of reading determined by the specific purposes of the reader rather than the single-minded aims of the author.

The canon proposed by Lopez aims, for purely aesthetic reasons, 'to arrive at the magical, Shakespearian number of thirty-seven (itself a useful fiction)' (201), though quite why Lopez thinks of thirty-*seven* as the 'Shakespearian' number is unclear, given that *The Two Noble Kinsmen* has sat alongside *Pericles* and the thirty-six plays of the First Folio for half a century now. Only *Macbeth* is included of Shakespeare's plays, alongside three plays that may well contain Shakespearian contributions (*Thomas More*, *The Spanish Tragedy*, *Arden of Faversham*). The book's opening gambit discusses E. H. C. Oliphant's 1929 *Shakespeare and His Fellow Dramatists*, noting that no anthology before or since has similarly combined works by both Shakespeare and his contemporaries (3). The fact that Emma Smith and Greg Walker's projects have emerged between the writing of this chapter and its publication suggests the timeliness of Lopez's call for a reorganization of the early modern drama that neither segregates nor prioritizes Shakespeare. The selections here are explicitly idiosyncratic, serving essentially whatever purpose Lopez needs them to serve in order to build particular arguments and connections. *Macbeth*, for example, is chosen 'because of its surprising, and perhaps entirely coincidental, resonances with a non-Shakespearean play (*Northward Ho*), which allow me to dramatize both the inevitability and the rewards of arriving at a formal and historical identity for "non-Shakespeare" by reading through Shakespeare' (202). It is refreshing to see so explicit and honest a statement of the author's own aesthetic and needs governing the organization of drama, and Lopez's clarity on this invites immediately the contestation of his choices. To be representative

for representation's sake, to focus deliberately on plays with little critical history, or to reorganize around authors are all inherently loaded choices, none more so than another. The point here is less to write a manifesto for a particular edited anthology, which Lopez admits would not resolve the problems raised in this book, and more to argue that our anthologies should emerge from our criticism rather than the other way round. Juxtaposing *Macbeth* and *Northward Ho*, for instance, allows the only two extant early modern plays featuring sleepwalking scenes to be read alongside one another, yet this is a juxtaposition that has never been enabled by editorial labours.

As Lopez argues, 'The contemporary anthology's construction of the category "non-Shakespeare" suggests, falsely, that a literary field *can be* divided into its component historical and aesthetic parts' (122–3). The separation of Shakespeare from not-Shakespeare is the most enduring of these divisions in the editing of early modern drama, and the relative exclusion of Shakespeare from Lopez's imagined anthology is, of course, deliberately provocative. In the case of Emma Smith's *Five Revenge Tragedies*, the inclusion of the 1603 text of *Hamlet* is similarly provocative in its insistence on transcending this division, aiming both to give attention to the most neglected early text of Shakespeare's tragedy and also to situate that play with its generic cousins. While Smith's edition is explicitly 'a reader's, rather than a scholar's, edition' (xxix), the work deserves attention for its innovation in editing *The Spanish Tragedy*, *Hamlet*, *Antonio's Revenge*, *The Tragedy of Hoffman* and *The Revenger's Tragedy* in chronological sequence with focus on the development of the genre rather than on authorial biography, as well as in making Q1 *Hamlet* available to a non-specialist audience. While Smith's edition inevitably operates within a conventional generic division that can rely on clear lines of influence and continuity between its constituent components, the choice of texts has the dual advantage of breaking down the Shakespeare/not-Shakespeare dichotomy and also insisting on the independent value of the 1603 text in discussion of revenge tragedy.

The nature of the Penguin edition precludes extensive discussion of the textual question, though a two-page appendix introduces the core terms of debate. Smith refuses to take a position on the text's provenance, rather arguing that 'in printing Q1 alongside the revenge plays with which it is clearly akin, this edition tries to break out of [a] Shakespeare-centric comparative model' and that the play's perceived textual problems only seem to be so when compared with the alternative Shakespearian texts; compared instead with *Hoffman*, for example, the play has its own integrity, an integrity implicitly undermined by the 'boastful self-presentation' of Q2 as the 'true and perfect' text (418). Smith's canonical disruption follows Lopez in refusing to allow the material and authorial assertions of early texts to predetermine value, and Q1 emerges in her brief introduction to the volume as just one exemplary instance of the genre's recurring features: the off-stage murder that precipitates action, the enactment and compromise of ethical and legal systems, the negotiation of culpability, and 'the unknowable mystery of death itself' (xxi).

The text is treated pragmatically, creating an interesting alternative to Ann Thompson and Neil Taylor's 2007 Arden edition of Q1. Smith modernizes punctuation lightly (especially in relation to commas) but eclectically, particularly in the addition of question marks such as those which turn Marcellus's lengthy speech in 1.64–73 into three separate questions and imply that Hamlet asks both Horatio and Marcellus what brings them from Wittenberg at 2.81. The text is rendered user-friendly throughout, with glosses for the general reader and notes on significant changes to the copytext, though a little more intervention would have been helpful at certain points, such as substituting an 'Exeunt' for Q's 'Exit' at the end of scene 4. Smith also adheres to Q's lineation throughout rather than 'correcting' verse lineation, preserving something of the visual distinctiveness of the text. There are sporadic errors throughout, however: 1.1.74 reads 'Marry that I can' in place of the Quarto's 'Marry that can I'; words are omitted such as in 2.11 'In this and all things [will] we

show our duty' and 2.50 'Spoke like a kind and [a] most loving son'; 2.44 expands 'gainst' to 'against' twice unmetrically whereas 2.45 retains 'gainst'; Ofelia's line 'Something touching the prince Hamlet' (3.48) substitutes the word 'concerning' for 'touching'; and Smith falls prey to eye-skip twice in converting 'This will hee say, let mee see what hee will say' to 'This will he say – let me say, what he will say' (6.19) and 'He being set ashore, they went for England' to 'He being set ashore, they set for England' (14.28). While examples such as these indicate that the Arden remains the more reliable text, however, the value of this edition remains in its arrangement of texts and prioritization of Q1 in conjunction with other tragedies, offering a useful destabilization of perceived hierarchies surrounding this canonical text.

Greg Walker's *Oxford Anthology of Tudor Drama* is explicitly concerned with disrupting canons following the work of his important co-edited collection *The Oxford Handbook of Tudor Drama* (2012). While Lopez notes the conventionality of organising anthologies chronologically, Walker depends on this convention to demonstrate the continuities in his sixteen selections from the *York Cycle* to *The Comedy of Errors*, while at the same time taking care to note that his edition 'rejects the notion of a steady evolutionary process whereby drama in the period became increasingly more secular, sophisticated, experimental, and psychologically insightful to the point where it reached its apotheosis in the works of Shakespeare' (v). The edition's point that Shakespeare should not be the prism through which all early modern drama is refracted is reiterated constantly; however, Walker repeatedly makes decisions that seem designed to do exactly this by framing the volume entirely within a Shakespearian lens. The introduction's sustained use of *Hamlet* to explain the purpose of drama as the holding up of a mirror yields immediately to the reader's assumed familiarity with Shakespeare, and of the sixteen plays two are Shakespearian, forming the volume's conclusion. Further, while the introduction repeatedly states that the volume resists myths of progression, the individual play introductions slowly grow in length from a page and a half for the *Fall of the Angels* and *Everyman* to a full six pages for *Titus Andronicus*. It is difficult to avoid the sense that Walker, far from destabilizing normative narratives, is in fact reinforcing them. This is not necessarily a problem, of course. Walker's explicit rationale for his choice of plays is to present a cross-section that will allow the reader to infer their own histories of continuity or change, but the chronological ordering and emphasis on the plays as Tudor drama means they are inevitably representative, and one wishes that Walker had been more explicit in his contention that the book's value is in offering a different teleology that looks backwards. The York *Fall of the Angels*, Walker argues, may be more sophisticated within its own genre and time than *The Comedy of Errors*, and a fuller commitment to this oppositional narrative might have extended further these retrospective reorientations of history.

Walker's text of *The Spanish Tragedy* makes no mention of recent arguments for the authorship of the 1602 additions by Shakespeare, going only so far as to dismiss the possibility that they are by Jonson as they are of 'mixed quality'. In an unusual display of subjective aesthetic judgement, he argues that only the 'Painter' scene and an extended distracted speech for Hieronimo are of good quality, and he only incorporates these ones, creating an odd hybrid text. These two additions are dropped in among the 1592 text, a heading in square brackets indicating their different provenance. Given the emphasis in recent years on attending to the specificities of variant early texts, Walker's eclectic decisions seem old-fashioned. Aesthetic concerns such as these play an important role throughout Walker's project. *Titus Andronicus* 'is also not a play for the purist, or for anyone dedicated to the idea of Shakespeare as a naturalistic playwright' (633). Yet it is unclear either what Walker means by a 'purist' or exactly whose views he is challenging. The introduction to *Titus* notes that Shakespeare's life is probably too well known to require extensive rehearsal, before going on to spend longer on biography than the medieval plays were accorded for their entire introductions. Here, Walker's scholarship is badly dated. He suggests that Shakespeare drafted the play and pays the scantest of attention to

arguments for Peele's authorship, referring only to the older author's 'draft' of the first act. A side note suggests that Shakespeare wrote in collaboration with Middleton and Webster among others, where presumably Wilkins or Fletcher was intended by the latter. Careless mistakes such as these occur throughout the volume, including a misspelling of John Jowett's name in the general introduction and editorial inconsistencies throughout. Walker claims in his introduction to *Titus* that he will use the 1594 Quarto as a base text but include the added Folio material in round brackets; yet when he reaches 4.1, the fly-killing scene, the fact that this is a Folio addition is indicated through a footnote, not brackets. The project to ensure *Titus* is not seen as superior to the earlier plays in the anthology leads to Walker adopting some rather outdated generalizations about the play. It is described as Shakespeare's 'most visceral and flamboyant, pressing hard on the borders of absurdity and artificiality' (633), and he sums up critical disdain for the play as being due to its lack of 'the prosodic and narrative control, the depth of characterization, and the seemingly effortless portrayal of the complexities of what it is to be human' as well as it being 'a very ragged, and a very savagely inhumane play' (635). Such Bloomian judgements, leading to his praise of the play as spectacle rather than poetry, seem unfortunate in light of the edition's project to revive attention to neglected plays.

The Comedy of Errors is treated more diplomatically, with Walker claiming an unusual adherence to the 1623 Folio. He states that the rarer retentions are highlighted in footnotes, but I can only find one instance: 'I buy a thousand pound a year, I buy a rope' (5.1.21), where Walker's resistance to emending 'pound' is shared by the vast majority of recent editors. Speech prefixes are standardized throughout, though Walker is a little unusual in his choice of 'Emilia' rather than 'Abbess', which arguably spoils the surprise of her identity for the reader. Walker's introduction defends the play for its unusual complexity and argues that the Folio speech prefixes of 'Sereptus' ('snatched') for Antipholus of Ephesus and 'Erotes/Erratis' ('wandering') for Antipholus of Syracuse imply a deliberate nostalgia for the quest romance and knight errantry, an allusive framework heightened by the addition of the Egeon narrative.

While Walker's edition is somewhat sloppy in execution, the spirit and purpose of the anthology is laudable. As well as making freshly available to readers important earlier plays such as Henry Medwall's *Fulgens and Lucrece* and the Croxton *Play of the Sacrament*, its resituating of Shakespeare within the continuous traditions of Tudor drama is an important intervention. That the anthology inadvertently presents Shakespeare as the culmination of this tradition is an issue but, as Lopez makes clear, no one anthology can perform all necessary critical work. Viewed in combination, however, Lopez's monograph and the editions of Smith and Walker offer a tantalizing glimpse of the possibilities, when Shakespeare is edited alongside his contemporaries, to highlight dramaturgical development, thematic parallel or genre affiliation. While none of these volumes offer a comprehensive programme for the reorganization of early modern drama, the plurality of possible canons generated in the process of exploration is more richly rewarding.

AUTHORSHIP AND CANON

If the anthologies above have aimed to situate Shakespeare more closely within the work of his contemporaries, it is perhaps fitting that the most significant new work in authorship studies also continues to insist on Shakespeare as a collaborative author. It is also something of a backhanded compliment to Brian Vickers' influence on the field that the works discussed here respond to work by him that has yet to be published in a peer-reviewed form. MacDonald P. Jackson's book *Determining the Shakespeare Canon* (Oxford, 2014) responds to work published by Vickers on the website for the London Forum for Authorship Studies suggesting Thomas Kyd was the sole author of *Arden of Faversham* and, in *Shakespeare, 'A Lover's Complaint', and John Davies of Hereford* (Cambridge, 2007), arguing that John Davies wrote the poem printed at the end of the 1609 Quarto of *Shakespeare's Sonnets*, while Gary Taylor offers a short essay responding

to Vickers' arguments in the *Times Literary Supplement* that Thomas Middleton had no hand in the revision of *Macbeth* despite the inclusion of songs from the latter author's *The Witch*. Marina Tarlinskaja is less opposed to Vickers, but in her new study qualifies her previous support for his work on the canon of Thomas Kyd, supporting some claims while reneging on others, particularly those pertaining to Shakespeare.

The headline of Jackson's study is that Shakespeare wrote the middle section of *Arden of Faversham* (scenes 4–9 in most modern editions) and was solely responsible for *A Lover's Complaint*. The bulk of the book has appeared previously in journals and book collections, but the cumulative effect as presented here makes a compelling case for both attributions. Jackson's methodological strategy is to use the texts of Literature Online (LION) to catalogue and then scrutinize unique collocations of words between the text under examination and the drama of the rest of the period. Crucially, and unlike many studies, Jackson's approach does not simply search for collocations with Shakespeare's works and then show which of those are unique, but instead searches the entire early modern dramatic corpus for a given period so that the results for Shakespeare can be contextualized against those for other authors. The results are bracing: the twenty-six lines of Arden's description of his dream in scene 6, for example, share twenty-six unique collocations with plays by Shakespeare, only three with a play by Marlowe, while no play by Kyd has any more than two connections to the speech. Similar tests are conducted for the scene depicting Alice and Mosby's quarrel, similarly showing a predominance of Shakespearian connections.

The difficulties with this research are, of course, legion. Few critics working within authorship studies dispute the utility of shared collocations as an indicator of shared authorship of texts; however, this is only one measure and is not immune to counter-charges of imitation, commonplace or coincidence. While Jackson addresses these concerns explicitly, it is less clear that his close analysis of two extracts is sufficient to prove a case for the entire section. The value of the approach, however, is its transparency: anyone with time and access to LION can replicate the results here and apply them to further sections. While it is important to recognize the problems of comparing results based on an author with several undisputed works (Shakespeare) to one with very few (Kyd), the strength of Jackson's argument comes from the precision of his choices of extract, allowing him to subject them to sustained qualitative analysis. The much heavier use of compound adjectives and the reflective conceit in the central scenes of the play are strongly reminiscent of Shakespeare's idiosyncrasies, and Jackson argues at length that the collocations shared between Kyd's plays and *Arden of Faversham* are much simpler and more mundane than the more sustained connections between Shakespeare's canon and the play. It is here that another caveat emerges: however objectively numbers may be generated (and Jackson is clear that absolute objectivity is impossible), subjective and qualitative evaluation of the results is inevitable. Jackson's skill as a literary critic is impressive, however, and the qualitative judgements are used to supplement and support both his own quantitative evidence and that of Hugh Craig and Arthur Kinney, re-evaluated and vindicated here.

This book, to my eye, appears to settle the case for Shakespeare's at least partial authorship of *Arden of Faversham*, especially when added to the weight of critical work on the play in recent years. Jackson's arguments for *A Lover's Complaint*, made on similar grounds, appear to me to leave more questions, although still mount a formidable counter-argument to recent work removing the play from the canon. Jackson's LION searches unambiguously favour Shakespeare over John Davies, Vickers' preferred candidate, and the second half of his book deploys counts of rare spellings, neologisms and rare words. The superiority of Jackson's critical eye to the more clinical computer-based tests of Ward Elliott and Robert Valenza is immediately apparent. Elliott and Valenza have previously argued that the poem has far more new or rare words than is normal for Shakespeare but, as Jackson points out, they rely for their analysis

on precise graphical units regardless of context, declension or usage. Jackson, using a finer literary toothcomb, shows how their tests are skewed by plays which have high proportions of proper nouns such as *1 Tamburlaine*, or whose content features more foreign languages such as *The Spanish Tragedy*, and argues that the statistics for this poem are far closer to Shakespeare's normal range. Yet the counter-arguments are not always on display: I would like to see Jackson show a comparative check for rare words between the poem and the works of John Davies, for example; and comparisons with *Cymbeline* ultimately hinge on a mere fifteen shared rare words. The precision of Jackson's tests on the poem, concentrating only on the first and final five stanzas, seems to demand further exploration rather than resolve the question beyond doubt.

I find Jackson's method persuasive, statistically rigorous and critically attentive, and his results appear to offer a very strong case for accepting Shakespeare's authorship of at least parts of these two texts. Also rigorous, though less rhetorically persuasive, is Marina Tarlinskaja's new volume *Shakespeare and the Versification of English Drama, 1561–1642* (discussed above by Charlotte Scott, p. 436). Tarlinskaja, a longtime collaborator of Vickers, similarly uses his work as a touchstone for much of hers. The approach here, based on the work of Russian versification schools, is to measure the stress patterns of blank verse and to note fluctuations and patterns in the level of adherence to the strict beat of the line. Tarlinskaja's painstaking work, necessarily conducted manually, covers the breadth of the period. In relation to Shakespeare, Tarlinskaja furthers the argument that he wrote the central sections of *Arden* and that Kyd was certainly not the author of the remainder of the play. Shakespeare's authorship of Hand D of *Thomas More* is akin to Shakespeare's patterns of 1603–4, and Tarlinskaja also supports recent attributions of the 1602 additions to *A Spanish Tragedy* to Shakespeare. She agrees with Vickers that Kyd wrote *King Leir* and *Fair Em* and was Shakespeare's collaborator on *Henry VI Part 1* and *Edward III*, though not beyond all doubt, and argues against Craig and Kinney's arguments that Marlowe collaborated on *Henry VI Part 2* and *Part 3*.

The main frustration with Tarlinskaja's book is its presentation. While the labyrinthine subdividing of chapters is appropriate to a book utilizing linguistic methodologies, the visual strategies of bold face, underlining, italics and upper case to introduce different kinds of emphasis, stress and subject heading is unwieldy and confusing. The line graphs used throughout the book have such thick lines that, particularly when six plays are being compared simultaneously, it is extremely difficult to distinguish between the texts under discussion. The prose also offers an odd mix of informality and Bardolatry: 'In the 1590s the looming figure of Shakespeare made the period shine' (2); 'He was also much more talented than his playwright colleagues' (123); and, in relation to a methodology that requires her to manually assess the strength of each individual stressed syllable, 'Stressing is such a headache!' (12). Teachers approaching this book may be even more frustrated by phrases which would usually be scored through in student essays, such as discussion of which text of *Faustus* is 'more true to the original' (81), or comments that Edward II is 'more believable [than Tamburlaine], and his homosexuality may incur understanding in the modern audience' (123). The reductiveness of literary analysis, the recourse to uncritical comments about Shakespeare's superiority and the distracting and unclear visual presentation all do the book severe disservice.

Where Tarlinskaja's study succeeds is in arguing for the significance of stress patterns for both dating and authorship. The overarching pattern she sees is from rigid adherence to iambic pentameter in *Gorboduc* and other early verse drama to a looser, more varied usage in later Jacobean and Caroline drama. This much is perhaps obvious, but Tarlinskaja's attention to detail demonstrates this systematically. The argument becomes more tenuous when applied more microcosmically. Tarlinskaja argues that different authors had specific propensities for iambic variation – for example, a preference for a seventh syllable stress or for feminine endings. Within authors, thereafter, she argues that chronology can be ascertained from an author's relative stress variations throughout their career. At so specific a level, the data becomes less telling: while a general trend in the entire corpus of drama over almost a century is demonstrable, a linear progression in the work of every author, resistant to local variation, stretches credibility. Furthermore, while Tarlinskaja justifies her processes for determining stresses at great length, the level of subjectivity necessary in gathering the raw data is more than that desirable for application to a statistical inquiry. It is a shame, given the volume of work undertaken here, that the presentation and prose do not inspire more confidence in the results: for a work so dependent on absolute precision and understanding of the musicality of language to be so poorly proofed must ring alarm bells.

Taylor's essay on *Macbeth* is hidden at the back of Robert Miola's revised Norton Critical Edition of the play, a strategic location designed to ensure it is encountered by students and teachers over a longer lifespan than the relatively ephemeral *TLS* article that occasioned it (though the London Forum for Authorship Studies website archives that article). It is somewhat strange that an article written so specifically and polemically as a rebuttal, with no substantial introduction to the authorship debate, should appear in a critical edition, and indeed Miola is compelled to offer an introductory statement summarizing the original article and noting that the debate will necessarily continue. Taylor's article is in sore need of editorial work: sections responding to work by John Dover Wilson and Jonathan Hope are bewildering, and there is no introduction to what Hope is meant to have said or how he has been used for support.

Despite the inappropriateness for the volume's audience, the essay is compelling, most so in its acceptance that all that can be done here is establish the grounds of possibility rather than an absolute certainty. The most damning parts of Taylor's argument are that (1) current scholarship dates *The Witch* to the final months of Shakespeare's life, making it near-impossible that he could have been responsible for inserting Middleton's song into *Macbeth*; (2) the overview of Roger Holdsworth's account of a uniquely Middletonian stage direction formula 'Enter A, meeting B', which cannot be found in any non-Middletonian works other than *Macbeth*; and (3) the clarification of Marina Tarlinskaja's (spelled 'Tarlinskaya' by Taylor) analysis of pause patterns in blank verse lines, a key part of Vickers' argument but here withdrawn by Tarlinskaja owing to a misunderstanding of the Oxford Middleton's typography for which Taylor takes responsibility. It must be noted, however, that the first and third of these are not positive arguments *in favour* of Middleton's authorship, but make clear the *possibility* of his authorship against claims that it is *impossible*. Taylor goes too far in arguing that Vickers' evidence does not stand up to the 'statistical weight' of Holdsworth, which after all only applies to a very limited sampling of text, and MacDonald Jackson warns in relation to *Arden of Faversham* in his book that arguments based on stage directions are potentially weak if they cannot be traced to the author. However, Taylor's important call is for a much more systematic and rigorous analysis of every line to be undertaken before any critic can claim either Middleton's or Shakespeare's authorship beyond reasonable doubt.

I have argued elsewhere that attribution studies might more usefully aim to articulate 'areas of ambiguity' than certainties over authorship, and both Jackson and Taylor act to do this. The cumulative weight of Jackson's different methodological strategies applied to *Arden of Faversham* suggests no compelling reason why Shakespeare *could not* have written at least part of this anonymous play, for which no other persuasive candidates have been advanced. On the other hand, Taylor's redress of major complaints about *Macbeth* leaves us with a play that undeniably contains Middletonian material and for which Middleton cannot be shown *not* to have been responsible. Quite how this will manifest in future editions remains to be seen, but the extended studies of Jackson and Tarlinskaja here go much further than other volumes in making

available the principles and tools with which other investigators can pursue their own inquiries.

REVISED EDITIONS

While Taylor's essay is the only section original to the new Norton *Macbeth*, Miola's update to his 2004 edition offers an extraordinary expansion of the resources and contexts therein contained. The unspoken aim of the series is to provide volumes offering a one-stop shop for undergraduate-level study of the plays, their reception and their afterlives, and this edition achieves this through some 300 pages of appendices and supplements (almost half of which are new to the second edition) to only 80 pages of text and notes. It is disappointing to note that there remains no substantive discussion of the text beyond a single page of notes; while the text is pleasingly free of extensive tabulation of variant editorial readings (prioritizing instead glosses of unfamiliar words), there is pedagogic value in giving more prominence than a single footnote to, for example, the implications of the handling of weird/weyard/wayward throughout, or the unusual choice to retain the Folio's speech prefix '*All*' for 1.1.10: 'Paddock calls anon!'

Instead, the major additions are sections entitled 'The Actors' Gallery' and 'Afterlives'. The former includes an impressive survey of commentary from players of Macbeth and Lady Macbeth as well as from directors and observers of key performances, all keyed usefully to line references in Miola's edition. The effect of this is to offer a form of performance-based 'Longer Notes': Thomas Davies offers a lengthy analysis of how Garrick interpreted 'Is this a dagger which I see before me!' (88), while Sarah Siddons and Adelaide Ristori's recollections offer scene-by-scene walk-throughs of their performance choices. The prime pedagogic value here will be the ability to draw the attention of malingering students to Siddons' reflections on the mood of terror and horror in which she finally attempted to learn her lines the night before her first appearance as Lady Macbeth, noting that her 'shame and confusion cured me of procrastinating my business for the remainder of my life' (91). Perhaps more usefully, Miola's selections are wherever possible tied in with productions readily available on DVD: Orson Welles, Ian McKellen, Antony Sher, Harriet Walter, Patrick Stewart and Kate Fleetwood all speak at length and with productive insight about their work on the play. The 'Afterlives' section is frustrated somewhat by the necessity of only providing excerpts of adaptations of the play, but these are often freshly edited and annotated, as with the invaluable inclusion of the new scenes by William Davenant for his 1674 adaptation. Even more fascinatingly, Miola has stitched together excerpts from four nineteenth-century 'travesties' of the play to make up a brand new patchwork parody of the play, beginning with Banquo and Macbeth congratulating themselves on sheltering from rain ('Macbeth, my fine feller / Confess 'twas well I brought the umberella [sic]') from Francis Talfourd's 1850 skit (321) and moving to rhyming doggerel mocking Macbeth's distraction ('Life's but a walking shadow – or a poor player at most – / Who murders Hamlet once, and then is cast the ghost') from W. K. Northall's 1847 version (330). To find this kind of material in a major edition is, of course, highly unusual, but Miola shows in this an expert sense of what may be of interest to students and teachers. Further selections follow from Verdi's *Macbeth*, Eugène Ionesco's *Macbett*, Welcome Msomi's *uMabatha* and Bill Cain's 2009 play *Equivocation*, the last of which features Shakespeare (Shag) commissioned by Robert Cecil to write a play celebrating the defeat of the Gunpowder Plot, but which thanks to Shakespeare's sympathies for the heroic Garnet turns out to feature Cecil as the bloodthirsty tyrant. Fittingly, the new piece added to the 'Contexts' section for this edition is an extract from Sir Edward Coke's arraignment of Garnet, bringing the frameworks for the volume full circle. The wealth of material here, and the relative paucity of attention to the text itself, means that *Macbeth* is something of an afterthought in the book predicated on it, a relatively unloaded text framed by a plurality of potential interpretations and adaptations. In work such as this, the edition reveals its potential to act as archive, fixing a version

of a text while making that version disappear within an overwhelming range of alternatives.

The main achievement of the reissuing of the entire New Cambridge Shakespeare series has been the replacement of David Hockney's feeble sketch of Shakespeare with Andrew Ward's wonderful new jacket design featuring a single, evocative image for each play. As with Miola's *Macbeth*, the emphasis of the revised editions is the updating of performance history and the extension of resources relating to performance. The basic approach has been exemplified in recent years by Bridget Escolme's and Lucy Munro's additions to, respectively, Lee Bliss's *Coriolanus* and Kurt Schlueter's *The Two Gentlemen of Verona*. While these reissues have largely escaped reviewers' attention for the brevity of the new material, Escolme does important work in extending Bliss's work on the play's politics into recent performance history, particularly pointing to productions that have utilized archetypes of masculine mythology (the samurai, the cowboy) and negotiated the balance between Martius's charisma and his posturing. For Escolme, the play's theatricality emerges from its exploitation of Martius's own antitheatricality. Munro's revisiting of *Two Gentlemen* picks up on the resurgence of interest in the play since John Madden's *Shakespeare in Love*, showing how the play's stage history has been enriched by productions exploring its identity politics and resonances, especially in the outstanding work of Two Gents Productions (a production which has received a great deal of interest in recent years and is rightly canonized here). Munro's note that only one of the fifty recent productions surveyed has used Elizabethan dress is indicative of the play's renewed fortunes, and she argues that the last decade has finally shifted discussion of the play from treatment of its 'weaknesses' to an appreciation of the play as a testing ground for experimentation.

While Escolme's and Munro's work importantly updates the older editions, the editions remain of their time. Much more important is David Lindley's revision of his own *The Tempest* a decade on. Rather than tag an update to the performance and critical history onto the end, Lindley completely reorganizes and rewrites his work, integrating new productions throughout, with particular attention to international work including the RSC/Baxter Theatre South African collaboration and Cheek by Jowl's Russian-language adaptation. Lindley's argument is that to read *The Tempest* is to engage in dialogue with it, a practice of citational exploration exploited at the opening of the 2012 London Olympics and embedded within the play's own experimentations. Lindley's expertise in masques and music allows him to move fluidly back and forth between the education in virtue offered by Prospero as part of betrothal politics and the 'proletarian', perhaps even sing-a-long, songs of Caliban (33–4). In an exhilarating discussion, the power politics of the masque give way to the machinations of the plot. Lindley traces the critical switch of sympathies from Prospero to Caliban, but shows how the play structurally mirrors its own conspiracies at different levels. With historicist application, some sympathy is returned to Prospero as Lindley argues that it is not Miranda's sexuality but Ferdinand's on which Prospero's schemes operate (86). At every stage *The Tempest* raises more problems than it answers, and Lindley offers a particularly timely (and somewhat sceptical) engagement with colour-blind and cross-gender casting, noting particularly in the case of the former that the play's own ambiguity over whether or not it codes characters by race or ethnicity makes it nearly impossible for a production to sidestep interpretation according to casting. In relation to cross-gender casting Lindley is sympathetic towards the impact of productions turning Prospero into a mother, but resists readings that turn Ferdinand, who is cowed by Miranda's chastity, into a potential rapist. Lindley's introduction is a model of revisionist editing, resituating his own work within an ever-changing critical and performative culture, defending his own readings while opening up the continuing trends and explorations. This is important work, and demands more notice than it has hitherto received.

Finally, 2014 saw two new editions of *Coriolanus* and *Richard III* published to coincide with major new London productions, and their strategies deserve some consideration, particularly given that the former was reprinted four times in 2014 alone. It is perhaps not irrelevant to note that the cover image – a topless and bloodied Tom Hiddleston – may have something to do with the book's popularity. Yet the value of these books lies also in reversing the usual logic of a performance text; rather than offer a text as blueprint for future productions, these serve as a record of a specific moment in the plays' performative history. Bloomsbury's edition of *Coriolanus* edited by Rob Hastie and Josie Rourke follows the same press's Arden edition by Peter Holland, reviewed in last year's *Shakespeare Survey*. Holland acted as textual advisor for this edition and is credited by Rourke for having helped rescue several lines while also encouraging the deletion of more, though understandably these are not demarcated within the text. The text is more adaptation than edition, turning Sicinius into the female Sicinia and cutting whole scenes as well as rewriting the end substantially. The overall strategy is to cut long speeches down to their essentials and accelerate action: thus, in 1.2, Aufidius receives a letter during the course of the scene rather than entering having already read it. At the same time, the scenes featuring the female characters are retained almost entirely intact, while Aufidius is given one extra line in 1.2 ('recall my power and fortify your city') designed to position him as a sensible alternative to Volscian expansion. The adaptation's interest in immediate drama is finally realized in a dramatic revision of the conclusion, in which Martius is immediately attacked and killed by the Volscians as soon as Volumnia has left. Lines that in Shakespeare indicate the treatment of Martius's body, including 'take him up', are here instructions to murder, turning the play's ending into a sudden and emotional display of retribution rather than a considered plot.

The Nick Hern Books edition of the far less critically successful *Richard III* starring Martin Freeman is edited by that production's director, Jamie Lloyd. In a printed interview, he explicates his process, the first part of which 'is to paraphrase every line into modern English in order to find the clearest, most interesting and most useful understanding of the text' (vi–vii). As worrying a statement as this might be when approaching a newly edited text, Lloyd's version is thankfully not a modern simplification in the manner of Julian Fellowes' 2013 screenplay for *Romeo and Juliet*, but rather an edited version of the folio text. Aiming at a young audience, Lloyd's main adjustments clarify potentially confusing terms and plot situations: early modern 'cousin' is translated to 'grandson' or 'nephew' as appropriate, while Anne enters with the corpse of her husband rather than King Henry. The most significant structural change is the conflation of several characters (including Brackenbury and Ratcliffe) into Catesby and Tyrrel, leading particularly in the case of the former to a much more substantive role. The line 'Go, tread the path that thou shall ne'er return' spoken after the departing Clarence in the opening scene is here addressed to the lingering Catesby, an instruction to him to prepare the Duke for murder. Meanwhile it is Tyrrel who feels guilt following the murder of Clarence. Richmond is introduced earlier, accompanying Lord Stanley in summoning Hastings, before being sent across the seas after Richard's coronation, and several long scenes (including Clarence's children, the cries of the women to be allowed into the Tower and the scene of the citizens) are cut. Margaret is retained and, bizarrely, delivers lines from the Scriveners' speech during the gulling of the Lord Mayor, despite there being no indication of her entrance in this scene. Finally, and as with *Coriolanus*, there is a drive to emphasize visual action and pace. Rivers is killed on stage, and Anne is murdered at the end of the coronation scene, while Tyrrel's long description of the death of the princes is axed. Most significantly, the play's ending is accelerated extraordinarily: following the departure of Buckingham's Ghost, the scene cuts instantly to the middle of battle and Richard's calls for a horse, with all of the ramifications of the dream and preparations for battle cut.

The involvement of directors in preparing print editions of their own production texts is laudable, and these souvenir texts are useful resources for performance scholars and students working on the productions in question. Yet their value is primarily commercial, serving to canonize and make money from a text necessarily generated by the production, and the value in discovering the idiosyncratic choices of a production is offset by the entire and unacknowledged loss of the omitted material. One hopes that, of Holland's two editions for Bloomsbury, the discerning teacher will continue to choose the Arden over the Hiddleston.

REVOLUTIONS

Lastly, one of the most significant sets of implications for Shakespeare in textual studies this year, as with the revised and new editions above, is rooted in a question over performance. The identification of a second manuscript of the anonymous play *The Humorous Magistrate* discovered at the University of Calgary has instigated two paired edited collections on site-specific performance and dramatic editing in the medieval and early modern periods, and the essay most relevant to Shakespeare is also that most directly connected to the implications of the manuscript discovery. James Purkis analyses the 'Arbury' and 'Osborne' manuscripts of *The Humorous Magistrate* with a view to overturning longstanding ideas that a scribal 'fair copy' would be an almost exact copy of the author's final draft or 'foul papers'. The 'Osborne' text – which might be considered a 'fair copy' – incorporates the changes and additions of the 'Arbury' text, yet the two plays contain substantial differences in structure and content that make any simple textual genealogies impossible to determine. Purkis uses this to argue that 'foul papers' were more of a fragmentary draft than a finished play, and suggests that the patterns of repetition and substitution seen in these two manuscripts are similar to those preserved in the *Thomas More* papers, a play that Purkis argues is similarly preserved in a state somewhere between 'foul papers' and a finished book.

Purkis's observations appeal to common sense, allowing for more stages of transmission between initial drafts and fair copy. *Thomas More*, in its reshapings and additions, has long demonstrated this but, in light of Purkis's arguments, seems to be far more representative than is often admitted. The idea that this unusual document – with its five or six authorial contributors and its piecemeal constitution – might demonstrate common practice is an important one. Given the ongoing work chronicled in this review of recent editions and textual studies to establish patterns of collaboration and revision, to resituate Shakespeare within the work of his contemporaries, and to reconstruct canons that attend to multiple interpretative possibilities and performative trends, we might do worse than return to documents such as *Sir Thomas More* for a fuller understanding of how Shakespeare manifests as just one figure within 'his' own texts.

WORKS REVIEWED

Bliss, Lee, ed., *Coriolanus*, 2nd edn with updated introduction by Bridget Escolme (Cambridge, 2010)

Hastie, Rob, and Josie Rourke, eds., *Coriolanus* (London, 2014)

Jackson, MacDonald P., *Determining the Shakespeare Canon: 'Arden of Faversham' and 'A Lover's Complaint'* (Oxford, 2014)

Jenkins, Jacqueline, and Julie Sanders, eds., *Editing, Performance, Texts: New Practices in Medieval and Early Modern English Drama* (Basingstoke, 2014)

Lindley, David, ed., *The Tempest*, 2nd edn (Cambridge, 2013)

Lloyd, Jamie, ed., *William Shakespeare's Richard III* (London, 2014)

Lopez, Jeremy, *Constructing the Canon of Early Modern Drama* (Cambridge, 2014)

Miola, Robert S., ed., *Macbeth*, Norton Critical Editions (New York, 2014)

Purkis, James, 'The Revision of Manuscript Drama', in Jenkins and Sanders (2014), pp. 107–25

Schlueter, Kurt, ed., *The Two Gentlemen of Verona*, 2nd edn with updated introduction by Lucy Munro (Cambridge, 2012)

Smith, Emma, ed., *Five Revenge Tragedies* (London, 2012)

Tarlinskaja, Marina, *Shakespeare and the Versification of English Drama, 1561–1642* (Farnham, 2014)

Taylor, Gary, '*Macbeth* and Middleton', in Miola (2014), pp. 296–305

Walker, Greg, ed., *The Oxford Anthology of Tudor Drama* (Oxford, 2014)

INDEX

INDEX

INDEX

INDEX

INDEX

For EU product safety concerns, contact us at Calle de José Abascal, 56–1°,
28003 Madrid, Spain or eugpsr@cambridge.org.